CAMBRIDGE LIBRARY COLLECTION

*Books of enduring scholarly value*


## Religion

For centuries, scripture and theology were the focus of prodigious amounts of scholarship and publishing, dominated in the English-speaking world by the work of Protestant Christians. Enlightenment philosophy and science, anthropology, ethnology and the colonial experience all brought new perspectives, lively debates and heated controversies to the study of religion and its role in the world, many of which continue to this day. This series explores the editing and interpretation of religious texts, the history of religious ideas and institutions, and not least the encounter between religion and science.

## Apocrypha Syriaca

The twin sisters Agnes Lewis (1843–1926) and Margaret Gibson (1843–1920) were pioneering biblical scholars who became experts in a number of ancient languages. Travelling widely in the Middle East, they made several significant discoveries, including one of the earliest manuscripts of the Four Gospels in Syriac, a dialect of Aramaic, the language probably spoken by Jesus himself. First published in 1902 as part of the Studia Sinaitica, this text is transcribed and translated by Lewis from a Syriac manuscript she acquired in Suez in 1895. As well as featuring pages of the Septaguint and the Peshitta Gospels, the palimpsest includes some Arabic pages including a very early version of the Qur'an (estimated by Lewis as seventh-century). Illustrated with reproductions of the leaves of the various texts, this is a valuable resource for scholars of Syriac, but also of interest for historians of Christianity and Early Islam.

Cambridge University Press has long been a pioneer in the reissuing of out-of-print titles from its own backlist, producing digital reprints of books that are still sought after by scholars and students but could not be reprinted economically using traditional technology. The Cambridge Library Collection extends this activity to a wider range of books which are still of importance to researchers and professionals, either for the source material they contain, or as landmarks in the history of their academic discipline.

Drawing from the world-renowned collections in the Cambridge University Library and other partner libraries, and guided by the advice of experts in each subject area, Cambridge University Press is using state-of-the-art scanning machines in its own Printing House to capture the content of each book selected for inclusion. The files are processed to give a consistently clear, crisp image, and the books finished to the high quality standard for which the Press is recognised around the world. The latest print-on-demand technology ensures that the books will remain available indefinitely, and that orders for single or multiple copies can quickly be supplied.

The Cambridge Library Collection brings back to life books of enduring scholarly value (including out-of-copyright works originally issued by other publishers) across a wide range of disciplines in the humanities and social sciences and in science and technology.

# Apocrypha Syriaca

*The Protevangelium Jacobi and Transitus Mariae*

Edited and translated by
Agnes Smith Lewis

CAMBRIDGE UNIVERSITY PRESS

Cambridge, New York, Melbourne, Madrid, Cape Town,
Singapore, São Paolo, Delhi, Mexico City

Published in the United States of America by Cambridge University Press, New York

www.cambridge.org
Information on this title: www.cambridge.org/9781108043489



This edition first published 1902
This digitally printed version 2012

ISBN 978-1-108-04348-9 Paperback

# APOCRYPHA SYRIACA

London: C. J. CLAY AND SONS,
CAMBRIDGE UNIVERSITY PRESS WAREHOUSE,
AVE MARIA LANE.
Glasgow: 50, WELLINGTON STREET.

Leipzig: F. A. BROCKHAUS.
New York: THE MACMILLAN COMPANY.
Bombay and Calcutta: MACMILLAN AND CO., Ltd.

# STUDIA SINAITICA No. XI

# APOCRYPHA SYRIACA

## THE PROTEVANGELIUM JACOBI AND TRANSITUS MARIAE

WITH TEXTS FROM THE SEPTUAGINT, THE CORÂN, THE PESHIṬTA, AND FROM A SYRIAC HYMN IN A SYRO-ARABIC PALIMPSEST OF THE FIFTH AND OTHER CENTURIES

EDITED AND TRANSLATED BY

AGNES SMITH LEWIS M.R.A.S.

HON. PHIL. DR. HALLE-WITTENBERG
LL.D. (ST ANDREWS)

WITH AN APPENDIX OF PALESTINIAN SYRIAC TEXTS FROM THE TAYLOR-SCHECHTER COLLECTION

LONDON
C. J. CLAY AND SONS
CAMBRIDGE UNIVERSITY PRESS WAREHOUSE
AVE MARIA LANE

1902

Cambridge:
PRINTED BY J. AND C. F. CLAY,
AT THE UNIVERSITY PRESS.

# PREFACE.

SINCE this book was ready for publication, I have spent a month at Mount Sinai; and have copied the eight pages of the *Transitus Mariae*[1] which form part of the under script in the Sinaitic Palimpsest, No. 30. Their text is probably of the fifth century. Two of them, those on f. 151, coincide with the more ancient of the two texts used in this volume; the other six coincide with part of Codex Harris. A comparison of these latter leads to the satisfactory conclusion that Codex Harris is substantially the same narrative, and that its immediate ancestor differed very slightly from the Sinai text.

Mrs Gibson kindly copied for me several portions of the *Transitus Mariae* from the Syro-Arabic Palimpsest No. 588, and from a newly-discovered Syro-Arabic Palimpsest No. 514, which surprised her by its re-appearance in the Convent Library[2]. These portions all coincide with some part of the older texts in this volume, but the variants are too slight to be worth recording. A closer examination has, however, upset one of our theories. Codex Sin. Syr. No. 30, and Cod. Sin. Arab. No. 588 do not contain portions of the same *Transitus* manuscript[3], for the stories of Salome and of Abgar are found on ff. 138, 32, of the one, and on ff. 69, 53 of the other.

I take this opportunity of saying that the word ܡܨܪܝܢ instead of ܡܨܪ ⌈ܕ⌉ܡ is the only one of Mr Burkitt's emendations to my transcript of the final colophon in the upper script of the Sinaitic Palimpsest of the Gospels (No. 30) as given in *Studia Sinaitica* No. IX. Appendix VIII. p. xxiv. which I can now accept. I copied the first nine lines of that colophon on Good Friday 1900, by placing two very dim photographs together. This colophon being much rubbed in the manuscript, had evidently been overlooked by all the transcribing party who visited Mount Sinai in 1893; and it alone contains the remarkable words, "Stylite" and "Antioch." Mr Burkitt, on receiving a presentation copy from me, supplied the important word ܡܨܪܝܢ from the late Professor Bensly's transcript of the shorter colophon on f. 165[b] which I had omitted; having judged, too hastily, that it was only a repetition of the Prologue on f. 2[b]. Mr Burkitt's other suggestions were made only from a study of the two photographs of f. 181[a] which I had already transcribed; and an examination of the manuscript, both with the reagent and without it, has resulted in the disappearance of his ܟܘܪ and of my ܟܘܟܒ.

[1] Cf. *The Four Gospels in Syriac.* Transcribed from the Sinaitic Palimpsest. Introd. pp. xvi, xxix.

[2] See *Studia Sinaitica*, No. III. p. 102.

[3] *The Four Gospels in Syriac.* Introd. p. xvii.

The final colophon reads as follows:

ܐܢܐ : ܒܝܢܪܐ : ܘܚܛܝܐ : ܘܡܣܟܢ : ܐܘܣܛܘܢܝܐ : ܕܒܝܬ : f. 181 a l. 18
ܡܢܝ : ܡܘܫܐ : ܕ * * * ܐ : ܕܡܕܒܪܬ : ܡܨܪܝܢ : ܡܕܝܢܬܐ : ܒܘ̈ܪܒ
ܕܐܢܛܘܟܝܐ : ܡܕܝܢܬ : ܐܠܗܐ : ܟܬܒܬ : ܟܬܒܐ : ܗܢܐ :
ܐܡܝ : ܕܠܝܛܘܪܓܝܐ : ܕܢܦܫܝ : ܘܕܐܒ̈ܝ : ܘܕܐܚܝ : ܕܢܬܪܚܡ :
ܠܗ : ܐܠܗܐ : ܡܠܠ : ܫܘܒܚܗ : ܕܡܫܝܚܐ : ܡܦܩܘܣ : ܐܢܐ :
ܠܟܠܗܘܢ : ܐܚܝܢ : ܕܩܪܝܢ : ܒܗ : ܕܢܬܠܘܢ : ܥܠ : ܫܠܝܛܘܬܝ :
ܐܬܪܐܬ : ܠ * * * * ܡܦܫܩ : ܐܢܐ : ܕܠܐ : ܫܦ * * ܐ
ܐܠܐ : ܡܢܐ ܕܦܠܓ : ܡ : ܗܢܐ : ܟܬܒܐ :
⁘ ܐܬܐ ܡܢ * * : ܠܫܠܝܐ : ܒܝܠܘܬܗܘܢ ⁘
ܐܫܬܠܡ : ܕܝܢ ܟܬܒܐ : ܒܫܢܬ : ܐܠܦ : ܘܬܫܥ * * f. 181 b
ܕܐܠܟܣܢܕܪܘܣ : ܡܩܕܘܢܝܐ : ܒܪ : ܦܝܠܝܦܘܣ : ܒܝܪܚܐ
ܬܡܘܙ : ܒܝܘܡ : ܬܠܬܐ : ܒܫܒܬܐ : ܒܫܒ * * * * *
ܕܘܟܪܢܐ : ܕܒܪܬܗ : ܕܡܪܝܡ : ܫܘܒܐ : ܡܫܝܚܐ : * * *
ܢܗܘܘܢ : ܥܠ : ܫܠܝܐ : ܕܟܬܒ : ܟܬܒܐ : ܗܢܐ : ܐ * * * *
ܠܥܠܡܐ : ܕܥܠ ܕܡܫܝܚܐ : ܐܡܝܢ : ܘܐܡܝܢ : ܘܐܡܝܢ.

I read the last six lines of this colophon originally in 1892, and during my four subsequent visits I have been able to amend them as the page has become cleaner.

My transcript of the first nine lines will be found on page ܪܦ of No. IX. *Studia Sinaitica*, and Mr Burkitt's suggested emendations to it on p. xxiv of the same book.

The word after ܡܘܫܐ in the second line ends with either ܢܐ or ܒܐ, but it is blurred by a streak of dirt. The dots which separate the words from each other are in red: and this greatly facilitates the task of decipherment from the manuscript. The text which I now print offers an interesting illustration of how much may be accurately read from the dim photograph of a faded page. And it is worthy of note that my chief difficulties have been at the end of the lines, perhaps owing to these having been a little out of focus.

AGNES SMITH LEWIS.

CASTLE-BRAE,
CAMBRIDGE.
*April 18th*, 1902.

# CONTENTS.

## LIST OF ILLUSTRATIONS.

# INTRODUCTION.

THE manuscript from which the contents of this volume are taken was purchased by me at Suez in 1895. With the exception of one paper leaf, f. 12, it is vellum, and is a palimpsest throughout. Each leaf measures 20 centimetres by 12¾, and contains from 16 to 19 lines of the later script. This is closely written Arabic of the 9th or 10th century; it represents selections from the Fathers, St Athanasius, St Chrysostom, Anba Theodosius, Mar Ephraim, Mar Jacob, Mar Isaac and the Martyrdoms of St Eleutherius and St Theodorus. These may be dealt with in a subsequent volume, but it is the under script with which we are at present concerned, and with regard to the upper one I content myself with quoting the opinion of Mr A. Cowley, of Wadham College, and the Bodleian Library, Oxford, to whom some photographs of ff. 13 a, 20 b, 150, 151 have been submitted.

"The upper writing is itself early. I remember seeing many specimens of it at Sinai, and puzzling out the probable date of it then. Plate XX., in the Palæographical Society's facsimiles, is very like it; and is dated A.D. 885. Curiously enough, it was written from Sinai. Your MS. may have been written about the same date, but I think the writing is not quite so careful as that in the Palæographical Society's book, and is probably somewhat later. As the Palæographical Society's MS. was written near the end of the 9th century, I think we cannot be far wrong in putting your MS. in the 10th century. On the other hand, it has some early characteristics, e.g. ش for ش. Also the Palæographical Society's MS. lacks some early characteristics, which one would expect in this hand in the 9th century, e.g. it does not write ة for ة.

"I spent some time at Sinai over these hands. At first, I was inclined to put them all down as 9th century. Afterwards, judging chiefly from bilingual Psalters, etc., I came to the conclusion that nearly all were of the 10th century, though some were undoubtedly of the 9th. At this distance of time one's memory is not quite fresh[1], but I have little hesitation in assigning your upper writing to the "early" 10th century. That being so, we shall not be far wrong in dating your lower writing[2] about 750 A.D. or at any rate in the 8th century."

[1] Mr Cowley visited Sinai in 1894. [2] The Corân script.

Dr Aldis Wright, of Trinity College, Cambridge, had already pointed out the resemblance between the upper writing of this palimpsest and that of Plate XX. The latter is described by Dr Ignatius Guidi as "Kufi, inclining to Nashi." I should say "inclining very strongly." It is perhaps a good specimen of the transition period. Mr Ellis, of the British Museum, tells me that the writing of the facsimile on Plate XX.=Vatican Cod. Arab. 71, dated A.D. 885, is a distinctly Christian one and that he would be inclined to assign mine to precisely the same period. It will be observed that his view differs very slightly from Mr Cowley's.

There is also some resemblance between this script and that of No. 457 in Mrs Gibson's Catalogue of Arabic MSS. in the Sinai Convent. See *Studia Sinaitica*, No. III. p. 89.

The under script is for the most part Syriac. The portion which first attracted my attention is the apocryphal *Protevangelium Jacobi* followed by the *Transitus Mariae*, both being from the same manuscript, in a hand which leads me to assign it possibly to the latter half of the 5th century; or at the latest to the beginning of the 6th. Plates VI. and VII. of this volume will enable the reader to form an independent opinion. A tedious illness prevented my beginning to copy this till 1897; and I was of course aware that the story had already been perfectly well edited by the late Dr William Wright, both in the small volume entitled: *Contributions to the Apocryphal Literature of the New Testament*, and in the *Journal of Sacred Literature* for January and April 1865. But these books have been long out of print, and the MSS. which have been used by that greatest of Arabic scholars are all half a century at least later than my own, with the exception of ff. 1—5 of Add. 14,484, and f. 39 of Add. 14,669, assigned to the latter half of the 5th century; whilst three are some five centuries later. My manuscript offers the equivalent of 39½ really ancient leaves of what is practically the same text.

I had spent many months in copying this; and some of it had already passed through the press, when I became aware that Messrs Luzac & Co. were publishing an interesting collection of Syriac texts on the same theme, edited by Dr Budge. At first it seemed as if his work would make mine superfluous, but when I realized that they were founded on a copy made by a modern Syrian, of 13th century MSS., I thought that I would not suppress my own; and my decision has already been partly justified by the appearance of a variant on fol. 132 a (page ܒ col. b, ll. 16, 17 of this volume) which will have to be taken into account in future by any one who quotes the phrase in Matt. i. 21, "she shall bear to thee a son," as evidence for the supposed heresy of the Gospel-text in the Syriac Gospels of Mount Sinai.

As I desire that the distinguishing features of the texts in this book should be their antiquity, I have given a collation only of that portion of Dr Wright's text which is founded on MSS. not later than my own; and have left Dr Budge's text entirely alone. To have included them all might have made the work more complete, but it would have greatly increased both the size of the volume, and my own labour. Those who wish to know how the story developed in the fertile soil of pious minds, as it passed down the ages, must still consult Dr Budge's book.

### *Relation of the later script to the earlier one.*

The 9th (or 10th) century Arabic translator (or editor) of these Selections from the Christian Fathers which form the upper script of this palimpsest, folded each leaf of the ancient Transitus MS. double, and then turned it half round, and wrote his Arabic text across the Syriac one (as our grandmothers used to cross their letters); thus making one Syriac leaf into two Arabic ones. This will be readily understood by reference to Plates VI. and VII. The numbering of the folios follows, of necessity, the Arabic text. To have followed the more ancient Syriac one would have resulted in confusion; for whilst the Arabic text forms a consecutive bound volume, the Syriac leaves are mingled at random, and are interspersed with leaves from manuscripts of a wholly different character.

The quires of this book are quaternions, i.e. each consists of four pairs of conjugate leaves, except the 11th which is a quinion, the 14th which is a ternion, and the 15th which has only two pairs of leaves. A single leaf, f. 103, is inserted between quire 13 and quire 14 whilst two leaves f. 114 and f. 115 come between quire 15 and quire 16. Strangely enough, the ancient text of the *Transitus Mariae* which these contain, falls into sequence with that on ff. 1, 2, the compiler of the 10th century book having evidently torn two ancient leaves in twain, and used up the four halves independently of each other.

ff. 11, 12, of which one contains an ancient text from the LXX., and the other, being paper, has not been palimpsested, have been inserted between quires II. and III. I have detected no quire marks. It is impossible to say how many leaves the book originally contained, as the beginning and the end are both lost, 162 leaves being now extant. The arrangement of the leaves will be best understood from the table on pp. xxx—xxxiv.

*Some remarks on the text of the Protevangelium and the Transitus.*

In my transcription I have not always been able to see whether the *seyyame* points which indicate the plural have been written over a letter. It is frequently impossible to detect these in a palimpsest, owing to the place where they would naturally occur being covered by the later writing. In no case have I printed *seyyame* points where I did not actually see them; but that is no reason for assuming that they are not there in other cases; and I have therefore frequently translated a noun as plural because it is so in Dr Wright's text; or for the still better reason that it is furnished with a verb or a pronoun in the plural.

Where the text of my palimpsest failed, through the loss of a few leaves, I have supplied the deficiency from a manuscript lately brought from Tûr Abdîn in Mesopotamia by my friend Dr Rendel Harris. This bears, as will be seen, a very late date, A.D. 1857. Its copyist is probably still alive; but the manuscript which is its immediate parent must be a very excellent one; seeing that it follows both my own ancient text and that of Dr Wright so closely that I need offer no apology for fitting together two texts which have a decided affinity with each other. I have not tried to give the variants from Dr Harris' MS., because they are certainly later than my own text; but I have indicated throughout where its pages begin. Dr Nestle has called my attention to an extract from the *Protevangelium Jacobi* in Dr Sachau's *Verzeichniss der Syrischen Handschriften in Berlin*, Vol. II. p. 676, which is evidently the same version as mine, although at the end of Chap. XII. it makes Mary 12 years of age instead of 16.

Page ܠ l. 6. In Cod. Harris f. 95 a we have ܐܘܠܠܬܐ for ܝܠܠܬܐ from ܐܠܠ Aphel of ܝܠܠ.

line 8. ܝܘܕܐܝܬ is Ἰουδίθ in the Greek text of Tischendorf.

f. 95 b. I am indebted to the text edited by Dr Sachau for the true place of the words ܠܗ ܐܠܐ ܠܟ which are misplaced in Codex Harris.

Dr Nestle has pointed out to me that ܕܗܐ ܐܚܕ ܐܠܗܐ ܪ̈ܚܡܘܗܝ ܒܥܠܝ might by a very slight change be made to agree with Tischendorf's *καθότι κύριος ἀπέκλεισε τὴν μήτραν σου.*

Page ܕ l. 1 we have ܠܐܡܝ ܣܪܐ *τὴν μητέρα μου Σάρραν* instead of Tischendorf's *τὴν μήτραν Σάρρας.*

On page ܗ col. b, l. 13 some light is thrown on Tischendorf's Greek text by the occurrence of the word ܟܪܒܠܐ. The scribe of the MS. which he edited has evidently misread *κόκκινον*, "scarlet" for *κόσκινον*, the sieve which Elizabeth held in her hand. Sachau's text has also ܟܪܒܠܐ.

Page ܝܒ col. b, l. 2, for ܪܘܚܐ ܕܐܠܗܘܬܐ Dr Harris' MS. has ܪܘܚܐ ܩܕܝܫܐ.

In ll. 16, 17 the angel of the Lord says to Joseph ܘܬܐܠܕ ܠܟ ܒܪܐ "And she shall bear to thee a son." This must surely either be a loose mode of expression, or more probably it may be explained by the ancient Semitic custom of reckoning the children of a woman by her first husband to her second one[1]. The phrase, as it occurs in the Old Syriac version of the canonical Gospels, does not therefore possess the importance which some have attached to it.

On page ܝܚ col. a, l. 15 it is gratifying to find the corroboration of one of Dr Wright's emendations ܦܘܠܛ instead of ܒܪܝܡ. On col. b, ll. 8, 9 my text says that there was a tumult in *Bethlehem* of Judaea, where Dr Wright's has in *Jerusalem* of Judaea; both MSS. being ancient ones.

On page ܟܐ col. b, ll. 4, 5 we find the expression ܠܘ ܓܢܒ ܦܣܛܘܪܡܐ ܕܗܝܟܠܐ "beside the porch of the temple," as the place where Zacharia was slain. Other Syriac texts have ܠܘ ܦܣܛܘܪܡܐ ܕܡܕܒܚܐ "beside the porch of the altar," and ܒܝܢ ܦܣܛܘܪ̈ܡܐ ܠܡܕܒܚܐ "between the porch and the altar." Tischendorf's text has *παρὰ τὸ θυσιαστήριον.*

In one of the Greek MSS. used by Tischendorf, it is the *φατνώματα*,

[1] See Dr Robertson Smith's *Kinship and Marriage in Early Arabia*, pp. 109—115.

the panels of the ceiling above the columns, and not the garments of the priests, which are rent from the top to the bottom.

Page ܟܓ col. a, ll. 21, 22, the words which I have transcribed as ܢܓܪܐ "carpenter," may possibly be ܢܓܕܐ "scourging." But I think I see the dot over the ܪ of the second word.

On page ܟܗ col. b, we seem to hear the echo of fierce controversies which did not arise till the fourth century.

On page ܟܘ col. b, ll. 7, 8, we are interested to learn that the number of monasteries under the jurisdiction of the convent on Mount Sinai was 320.

On page ܟܚ col. a, l. 20, Dr Nestle has suggested that something like the First "Kanūn" might be filled in. But the letters which are visible on a greasy page do not correspond to this. Some of the missing words on this page are so completely scraped away that it is impossible to recover them.

Page ܠܕ l. 17, Cod. Harris has here a contraction ܕܗܝܡ̄ which I have amplified to ܕܗܝܡܢܘܬܐ.

Page ܠܚ col. a, l. 2, Cod. Harris has always ܐܠܦܘܢܐ for ܗܠܦܘܢܐ.

Page ܡܚ col. b, ll. 8, 9, there are probably two dots over the second ܪ in ܘܒܪ ܠܐܬܪܐ but they cannot be seen.

On page ܢܒ col. a, l. 25 we have a divergence from the text of Dr Wright in the *Journal of Sacred Literature*, for it was the sister, not the nephew of King Lydan whom the Apostle Thomas was about to baptize when the message of the Holy Spirit reached him.

On page ܢܘ col. a, l. 4 we have rendered the phrase ܒܪ ܐܢܫܡ by "Son of Man" and ܒܪ ܐܢܫܐ on page ܠܛ col. a, l. 15, and page ܣܗ col. b, l. 19 by "a man."

On page ܟܐ col. a, ll. 18—20 the text is much more intelligible than that of Dr Wright's MS.[1] from which the word ܠܐܠܗܐ had probably been dropped. On col. a, l. 19 the word ܡܬܠܚܡ seems better than the ܘܚܡ of Dr Wright's text, l. 23.

[1] In the "Contributions."

On col. b, l. 19 of the same page, we have the words ܐܠܐ ܐܒܘܗܝ "except His Father," instead of the ܘܐܒܘܗܝ of Dr Wright's text.

On page ܠܒ. col. a, ll. 20, 21, we are told that in the midst of the dispute between the Christians and the unbelievers, the latter were scourged by order of the Governor in parties of six each; instead of only four being treated to that method of argument.

The story about the three crosses on pages ܠܗ and ܠܘ would be in flagrant contradiction to the tradition of the "Invention of the Cross" by the Empress Helena, were it not that the suggestion of the Christians about burning the crosses of the two thieves does not appear to have been carried out.

On page ܠܛ col. a, l. 26, we have the word ܫܪ very distinct in the palimpsest, instead of ܫܪܝ; and this alters the sense to "And everything that He said to me, *is true and perfect*," instead of "He began and He finished."

On page ܡܗ l. 24, we should have expected ܘܐܠܟܘܪ instead of ܘܐܬܦܩܪ

On page ܣܐ we may trace a purely Semitic tradition in the statement that Adam, Seth, Noah and Shem came to adore the Virgin, no mention being made of Japhet.

Page ܣܚ represents the text of both sides of a half leaf with a portion of the other half attached. The compiler of the Selections had fitted to it, as conjugate, a portion of a manuscript written in a late Estrangelo hand (f. 45) containing the text of a Syriac Hymn. This he had trimmed in order to make it fit into his *Transitus* leaves (f. 146 is from the same manuscript.) Some lines are therefore missing, on both sides of the leaf. f. 52 b on col. a fits very well into f. 52 a so far as the sense is concerned; and I have made the rest into a consecutive narrative by interpolating a few words from Codex Harris at the foot of col. a, and at the junction of f. 52 a col. b, and f. 52 b col. b; also between f. 52 b col. b and f. 62 a on the following page.

On page ܦܐ we may remark that the obligation of abstaining from meat until the ninth hour of the day (about 3 p.m.) is still enforced in many Christian families of the Coptic nation. (See *The Story of the Church of Egypt*, by E. L. Butcher, Vol. I. p. 25.)

On page ܩܝܐ the idea of guilty souls contemplating the sufferings of others who are enduring precisely what their own punishment will be in the day of judgment, is more than Dantesque in its awfulness.

It is hardly necessary to say that I endorse the opinion of Dr Ewald (as quoted by Dr Wright), in the *Gött. gel. Anzeigen* for 1865[1].

"We can certainly affirm that this book has become from the first the firm foundation for all the unhappy adoration of Mary, and for a hundred superstitious things, which have intruded with less and less resistance into the Churches, since the 5th century, and have contributed so much to the degeneration and to the crippling of all better Christianity. The little book is therefore of the greatest importance for the history of every century in the Middle Ages, and yet to-day we ought to notice far more seriously than we usually do the great amount of what we have to learn from it. The whole cultus of Mary in the Papal Church rests upon this book; we might search in vain for any other foundation to it: notwithstanding the fact that it was excluded once again in early times from the list of canonical books by the *Decretum Gelasii*[2]. The three yearly feasts in honour of Mary which the Greek Church maintains to this day, and whose number has been exceeded only by the Papal Church in the long course of centuries are ordained for the first time in this book, and are even defined by the day of the year (on which they are to be held). The delusion about the Immaculate Conception of Mary, which has in our day been elevated into a dogma, finds its foundation and its certain consequences only in this book. The similarly quite unhistorical delusion about an original adoration and consecration of the Sepulchre of Christ in Jerusalem is spoken of for the first time in the beginning of the second of the six little books of this text, that is, in the beginning of the narrative about the last days of Mary, and in such a way that we can easily understand what a deep impression such a narrative was bound to make on the world of that period; even if the well-known example of Constantine's mother had not preceded it."

The unhistorical nature of this narrative is only too apparent. It is difficult to believe that any Roman Governor who was a convert to Christianity held sway in Jerusalem at any time during the thirty-seven years which elapsed between the Crucifixion and the destruction of the city; still less during the life-time of Tiberius Cæsar, who died in A.D. 37 A.D. 44 has been fixed by competent critics[3] as the date of the execution of James, son of Zebedee, and of the imprisonment of Peter by Herod Agrippa, as recorded in Acts xii. 1—3. It is therefore passing strange that

[1] Stück 26, p. 1018 foll.

[2] Supposed to be a forgery. See *Encyclopædia Britannica*, Vol. X. p. 130.

[3] See Prof. J. B. Mayor in Hastings' *Dictionary of the Bible*, Vol. II. p. 541.

this wonderful controversy in Jerusalem, and indeed this account of the Virgin's death, which must have taken place before St Paul had well begun his ministry[1], is not included in the Acts of the Apostles. In the story of our Lord's birth no mention is made of the inn at Bethlehem, and the event happened in a desert place, in an uninhabited cave on the road side, and not in the actual town of David, there being no mention whatever of the inn (page ܡܒ). Mary's habit of weeping at the grave and at Golgotha (pp. 19, 27) would lead us to infer that she had never shared in the joy of the disciples who had been eye-witnesses of the Ascension; and is altogether out of harmony with the triumphant notes of her own Magnificat. Probably the author never intended the story to be considered anything more than a pious romance; and he would be intensely amazed if he could know the part which it has played in the great drama of human belief and conduct.

In the translation I have followed that of Professor Wright in his *Contributions to the Apocryphal Literature of the New Testament*, and his *Departure of My Lady Mary* in the Journal of Sacred Literature for January and April 1865, so far as his Syriac text agrees with mine. The portions taken from Cod. Harris are printed in smaller type.

### *Leaves from two ancient MSS. of the Corân.*

From the time that I obtained possession of this palimpsest, I was perfectly aware that at least four of its quires contained an Arabic under script. Several times I tried to identify this without success. I had a natural reluctance to take an old manuscript to pieces by cutting out the cord which held its several quires together; but without doing so I could not even see the inner margins, and there alone were lines of the ancient Arabic script to be found, perfectly free from the upper writing. Add to this the fact that the script was in Kufic, without diacritical points, and that I was trying to find a Christian text, and the reasons of my want of success are at once apparent.

I was just about to place these leaves in hands more skilful than my own; and for this purpose, on June 21st of this year[2], I was taking a second

[1] See Gal. i. 18. [2] 1901.

quire to pieces, and painting up its margins with the reagent, when two lines of writing appeared which had been hitherto invisible. This encouraged me to make another attempt; and on comparing it with the facsimiles in the Semitic Series of the Palæographical Society's publications, I found that the script was exactly similar to that in Plate LIX. assigned to the 8th century. As that represented a portion of the Corân (Sura 44) it seemed possible that mine might do so likewise, and a few minutes later I had identified the first line on f. 150 b with part of *v.* 57 in Sura 44 فَضْلًا مِنْ رَبِّكَ ذَلِكَ and on June 27th I found that the لَوْ شَآءَ ٱللَّهُ on line 11 of f. 20 b is from Sura 16 *v.* 37.

It was then evident that I had got seven leaves of a very ancient manuscript of the Corân, belonging to the first part of the 8th century, or perhaps even to the latter half of the 7th; also 15½ leaves (forming 31 leaves of the palimpsest) from a manuscript only a little later. Corân I., as I have named it, is in a flowing Kufic script, without the slightest sign of a diacritical point or of a vowel point. Each of the seven leaves has unfortunately been clipped on the one side in order to reduce its size to that of the Transitus manuscript, so that a whole word is missing at the end of some of its lines. In December I had the pleasure of placing f. 150 side by side with O. R. 2165, the MS. figured in Plate LIX. The resemblance in the handwriting, the size of the page, and the general appearance was so great that we at first suspected my leaves to be a portion of the same MS. But a closer inspection revealed the fact that there is a difference in the length of the final *ya*. Mr Ellis thinks, however, that they were both produced at the same time and place, if not by the same hand. Similar portions of Suras 24, 28, 29, 40 exist in both MSS.

Corân II. is quite legible (on the margins) without the reagent, as its script has hardly faded. The great difficulty in reading it was the closely written Arabic which lies across the top of it. It has no vowel points; and the only diacritical points which I have detected (partly by the reagent) are:

In f. 13 b the *ta* in واتيهم is written ڗ.

In the last line of f. 15 b there are either two dots or a horizontal stroke above the *waw* of يشركون, which have no connection with the line above it.

In f. 16 a there is a dot over the *nun* of امنوا.

In f. 17 b there is a dot under the *ba* of به *bis* and two dots over the *ta* of الموتى.

f. 55 b. In كنتم there is a dot on ـنـ and two dots on ـتـ.

f. 57 b. The ت of فكفرت has two dots over it: thus ث.

The following word is not بانعم, for it has a long letter like ا or ل just before the ع, and the ن is in a hole.

f. 58 a. There is a dot on the ن and two on ـتـ or ـتـ in انكثا.

f. 95 a. In افمنتم the *nun* and the *ta* have dots, the latter being written ـتـ. Also the *ta* in تخويفا of f. 102 b.

f. 98 a. The first *ba* in بعبده and that in بصيرا have each a dot. Also in f. 97 a the *ba*'s in بنفسك and حسيبا.

f. 101 a. The *ta* in متع is written ـتـ.

It has been suggested to me that other diacritical points may have once existed, in red or green paint, and that these may have been erased when the pages were palimpsested. But in the case of Corân II. this is an impossibility. The vellum is there so thin that every stroke of the stylus has left an indelible mark.

I have contented myself with printing the first and last lines of every page or half-page; although in the case of Corân II. these are by no means all that can be deciphered. The whole text might have been edited with a liberal use of the reagent, but this would have been too great an infliction on the very fine vellum of Corân II.; and would have produced only a transient effect on the more solid one of Corân I. It would also have been a severe trial to my eyes, and I cannot see that it would have served any useful purpose. I have added extra lines only in those cases where the terminal ones on a page were imperfect; and in those which show the end of one Sura and the beginning of another. Nothing occurs betwixt these except the words بِسْمِ ٱللَّهِ ٱلرَّحْمَٰنِ ٱلرَّحِيمِ.

At the beginning of Sura 45, as it may be seen in Plate IV., we perceive, after these introductory words, a row of six small circles, each of which shows the remains of some red ornament filling up its interior, as it came up under the reagent. It has been impossible to reproduce this in the facsimile, but this is the less to be regretted as we cannot form the slightest idea as to what its pattern was.

I have printed these texts in the usual Corân script with full points.

Some of my readers might have preferred an unpointed text, but this would have given no true idea of the script. To do it justice would have required the employment of purely Kufic type; which would have appealed to the understanding of only a few. And I hope that these few may be satisfied with the Plates which have been executed by Messrs Annan and Son of Glasgow, from the photographs of Mr Edwin Wilson, Cambridge.

Whatever opinion may be formed as to the exact age of these fragments, there can be no doubt that they carry us back to a very early period in the history of Islām.

Mohammed died in A.D. 632, and we are told that as he received the revelations, he wrote them down on any scrap of material that was available, on bones, white stones, ribs of palm leaves, or in the heart of men. Abu Bekr was the first who caused these scattered fragments to be collected, after the battle of Jemama in the 12th year of the Hegira = A.D. 632, by Zaid Ben Thabît. Disputes arose as to the genuineness of some portions, and Khaliph Othman in 24—35 of the Hegira = A.D. 644—655 caused four copies of a normal edition, to be made out of the several copies and their variants. The dialect of the Koraites, which Mohammed spoke, was its basis; and all MSS. which differed from it were destroyed. But the uncertainty of the writing, and the lack of diacritical and vowel points, caused fresh disputes. So it was decided, not without opposition, to add the long vowels, coloured, so as not to spoil the original form. The short vowels were next added, coloured, then other orthographical signs like the *hamza* invented by Khalid ben Ahmed 175 A.H. = A.D. 795.

These statements, which I have taken from the valuable book of Dr J. H. Möller, have an important bearing on the date of my palimpsest leaves. They narrow down the period at which these could have been written to a period between A.D. 655, when the chapters of the Corân fell into their present sequence, and that remarkable year (whichever it was) of the 8th century when diacritical points came into use. The seven lines of Corân I. (as we have already seen), show absolutely no trace of these. If we had not a printed text before us whilst deciphering it, we could not tell whether the sign ـ is a *ta*, a *tha* a *ba*, a *nun*, or a *ya*; and of its other signs, there is hardly one which may not have two values. The absence of an occasional *alif* (though required by grammar) shows that it was written when the controversy about the use of long vowels was not quite closed; and was designed rather as an aid to memory than as a "first reading book."

Several other questions arise. Were these two MSS. to which our leaves belong, amongst those whose destruction was ordered by Khaliph Othman, and do they owe their preservation to the cupidity of some faithful Moslem, who saw that they had a little value as writing material? I have been told by Dr Hirschfeld that this supposition is negatived, in the case of Corân II., by the existence of the letters الٓر at the beginning of Sura 14. Or are they parts of an authorized copy, which fell into the hands of Christian soldiers after the capture of some town, and were by them handed over to the monks, who were almost the only "clergy" of the period? We suspect that the cases are very rare indeed where a Christian writing exists on the top of a Mohammedan one.

## *The Septuagint Fragment.*

I had just completed my copy of lines from the Corân, when I observed one little leaf, f. 11, which was not only smaller than the rest, but was very thin and much crinkled, and had no appearance of being a palimpsest. It was in a sense isolated, for its conjugate f. 12 is the only paper leaf in the whole volume. With the view of ascertaining whether it might not also contain a Corân text, I passed my medicated brush lightly over the outer margin, and to my intense amazement, instead of the Arabic script for which I was seeking, a line of beautifully clear Greek uncials passed before my eyes, as if conveying a message from the unseen Past. Not one line only, but six appeared on that page, and six on the reverse side. They proved to be the text printed on p. xlviii of this volume, from Gen. xl. 3, 4, and 7.

The form of the letters, as they may be seen in Plate I. has, I thought, some resemblance to that of the Codex Bezæ. But Dr Blass, who has seen a photograph, and Dr Rendel Harris, who has seen the original, both assign it to a date not earlier than the 7th century. An examination of the facsimile on Plate I. will show that the letter C is narrower in shape than it would be in a manuscript of the earliest period.

I believe that the text on each page of this little leaf is the lower part of a column in a page which contained several columns, and which had the deep margin at its foot, usual in early Greek MSS., for by no other hypothesis can I account for the script ceasing at a point half way down each page, where there is no natural stop in its meaning.

One variant alone (from Dr Swete's text) will be observed: *παρὰ τῷ ἀρχιμαγείρῳ* instead of *παρὰ τῷ ἀρχιδεσμοφύλακι*, in Gen. xl. 3. It is not noticed in the Concordance of Redpath-Hatch; but from Field's Hexapla we learn that it exists in two other MSS. (not used by Dr Swete), in six MSS. according to Holmes; and it agrees also with the received Hebrew text בֵּית שַׂר הַטַּבָּחִים.

Before my usual summer holiday, I showed this leaf to several eminent Cambridge scholars, for the purpose of ascertaining from them, if possible, the meaning of the four small uncial letters ϲ ο μ ε, which I had detected on the margin of the Septuagint text. Their eyes were probably bewildered by the many loops of the 10th century Arabic script under which the whole ancient text lay hidden, and thus it was not until I had caused both sides of the leaf to be photographed, and had sent the photographs in September to my friend Dr Nestle of Maulbronn, that I was made aware of the full significance of my newly-revealed treasure. Dr Nestle not only found that ϲ ο μ ε was part of a Hexapla variant from Aquila's *ἐμβρασσόμενοι* but he also detected a column of other Hexapla readings on one margin of both pages. These were not difficult for me to verify, after my attention had been called to them. Dr Nestle says:

"The manuscript, from which the photographs of two pages have been placed in my hands, is important for three reasons:—

"1. Because uncial MSS. of Genesis are few; Sinaiticus and Vaticanus being defective for the greater part of this book.

"2. Because its texts appear particularly good, confirming Gen. xl. 3, the reading of Philo, *ἀρχιμαγείρῳ*, which had been changed by the latest editors of his works (Cohn Wendland, II. 211) into the reading of the Codex Alexandrinus, *ἀρχιδεσμοφύλακι*. The true reading was known till now only from the Coptic and Syro-Hexaplaric Version and from six cursives of Holmes.

"3. Because it contains marginal readings from the Hexapla of Origen, adding to those collected by Field some which were hitherto unknown, as xl. 7 *κακα* and *πονηρα* for *σκυθρωπα*."

I published an account of this leaf and of the whole manuscript, so far as I then knew it, in the *Expository Times* for November, 1901. I have since had the opportunity of submitting the leaf to my friend Dr Rendel Harris, with the result, that he has detected several breathings and accents; also the letter ϵ above the last word in f. 11 a.

After the photograph had been taken, a small fold in the margin was smoothed out. This revealed the beginning of the word ϵΜΒΡΑϹϹΟΜϵΝΟΙ, and also the existence of another word immediately following it—a word which the reagent would not bring up, so that only the indentations made by the stylus are visible. I at first thought that this word might be ἔπεισε, but Dr Harris suggests ἠρώτησε, as a variant to ἠρώτα, and thinks that it is in the larger script of the LXX text, rather than in the smaller one of the Hexapla variants.

## *Leaves from MSS. of the Peshiṭta Gospels.*

I. ff. 135, 136 represent one leaf of a very ancient MS. of Syriac Gospels in the Peshitta version, probably of the 5th century. It was easily read, without any help from the reagent, the script being of a reddish colour, which contrasted well with the black of the Arabic script over-lying it. It is in two columns, of 17 lines each; and contains a text from John vi. 49.

The only variants from Mr Gwilliam's edition which it shows, are:

*v.* 54 om. ܡܢ before ܦܓܪܝ; *v.* 55 ܝܬܘܗܝ for ܐܝܬܘܗܝ *bis*, and ܡܟܘܠܬܐ for ܡܐܟܘܠܬܐ; *v.* 57 ܡܛܠܘܠ for ܡܛܠ.

A facsimile is given on Plate II., but, owing to the imperfect resources of photography, the faint yellow of the under script has been reproduced as if it were dark.

II. ff. 77, 79, 81, 82, 84, 86 represent three leaves of a MS. of Peshitta Gospels, of the 5th or 6th century. There was very little appearance of these being palimpsests, until I tried them with the reagent (hydro-sulphuret of ammonia) in August 1901. The script is in two columns, of 25 lines each. They contain texts from Matt. ix. 5 b—24; x. 9—28 a; xv. 37 b—xvi. 17 a.

The only variants from Mr Gwilliam's edition are:

Matt. x. *v.* 12 ܕܥܠܝܢ for ܕܥܐܠܝܢ; *v.* 14 ܡܢܐ ܕܢܩܒܠܘܢ for ܡܢ ܢܩܒܠܘܢ; *v.* 19 om. ܒܗܝ ܫܥܬܐ; *v.* 22 ܟܠ ܐܢܫ for ܟܠܢܫ; xv. 38 ܠܒܪ̈ܝܡ for

ܠܥܒܪܐ; xvi. 4 ܐܬܐ for ܐܬܗ; *v.* 13 ܡܢ ܗܘ for ܡܢܘ; *v.* 14 ܕܐܘܫܠܡ for ܐܘܫܠܡ.

The following portions are illegible: Matt. ix. 10 ܘܐܬܐ—ܘܟܢܫ, *vv.* 15, 16 ܟܕ—ܠܐ.

The text is broken by a rubric between *v.* 15 and *v.* 16 of Matt. x. ܟܪܘܒܢܝܐ ܕܗܡܫܐ and between *v.* 12 and *v.* 13 of Matt. xv. ܡܪܢܝܐ ܕܐܪܒܥܐ ܒܫܒܐ ܒܫܒܬܐ ܕ . . . ܘܕܫܠܝܚܐ A row of red points occurs after Matt. ix. 17, x. 23, xv. 38, and xvi. 4.

In the inter-columnar space several sentences in red occur; they are difficult to decipher, and belong to a much later period than the gospel text. So far as I have been able to read them, they are:

On the fragment of Matt. ix. ܟܠܐ ܕܬܫܢܝܐ ⁘ ܟܠܐ ܡܕܘܫܐ; ܘܬܫܡܫܬܐ ܟܠܐ ܕܝܫܢܐ.

On the fragment of Matt. x. none.

On the fragment of Matt. xv. f. 84 ܘܬܫܡܫܬܐ ܕܟܠܐ ܕܫܒܬܐ; ܡܢܐ ܕܡܘܕܫ ܡܙܘܡܪܬܐ; ܟܠܐ ⁎ ܗܡ ܕܗܡ̈ܫܐ.

## *Arabic Document.*

For ff. 78, 83, 85, the compiler has used three small leaves of what appears to be a private Arabic document, written in the cursive hand common to these deeds. The script appeared only after an application of the reagent to the surface of the very fine vellum; it is most distinct, though difficult to read, owing to its entanglement with the lines of the upper writing.

I deciphered half a line and a few other words, but as I made no further progress, I was glad to invoke the aid of my friend Professor D. S. Margoliouth, of Oxford, to whose kindness I owe the transcription and translation on pp. lxix—lxxi.

The document is written on one side of the leaves only.

### *Double Palimpsest.*

Three leaves of this book have been twice palimpsested, viz. ff. 80, 134, 137. The two latter yielded half their secret only to the reagent. The upper text is that 9th or 10th cent. Arabic script which over-lies everything else in the manuscript, in this case a text from Chrysostom. The lowest script is Estrangelo-Syriac, that text from Isaiah which I have given on pages ܩܘܐ—ܩܘܠ. It runs the same way as the Arabic. The middle script runs at right angles to the other two; it is Jacobite and in two columns of 17 lines each. I have been unable to identify it with anything, and the only words which I have deciphered are:

f. 134 a, col. a (script med.) ܒܬܪ ܘܗܟܢ. ܠܒܢܘܗ ܢܒܝܒܐ * * * Baruch iii. 37, 38

ܗܠܝܢ ܥܠ ܐܪܥܐ ܐܬܚܙܝ. ܘܥܡ ܒܢܝܢܫܐ ܐܬܗܦܟ

ܡܒܪܟ ܗܘ

* * * * * * * * * *

„ col. b ܠܐܠܗܐ ܕܦܪܥܐ ܦܘܪܥܢ

* * * * * * ܒܗܐ

* * * * * *

f. 134 b, col. a * * * ܩܝܡܬܐ ܘܢܘܚܡܐ ܘܚ̈ܝܐ John xi. 25

* * * ܕܢܗܝܡܢ * * * * *

* * * * * * *

„ col. b * ܥܒܕܐ ܘܫ̈ܒܩ ܕ[ܐܪ]ܒܥܐ

ܬܫܒܘܚܬ. ܘܠܗ ܒܪܢ

f. 134 b, col, b, l. 14 ܐܦ * * * * * *

ܘܗܟܢ ܠܬ * * * * ܥܒܫ ܐܘܪܫܐ

* * * ܘܝܗܒܗ ܠܝܥܩܘܒ ܥܒܕܗ Baruch iii. 37.

f. 137 a, l. 17 ܥܠܡ ܢܘܗܪ * * * ܠܥܡܪܝܐ (script med.)

„ col. b, l. 1 ܐܠܗܐ ܗܘ ܕܐܬܐ ܒܬܠܝܢܐ

ܒܬ * * * ܐܬ * * * *

* * * * * * *

f. 137 b, col. a, l. 1 ܗܘ ܕ * * ܗ ܠܥܠܡ ܒܪ ܒ *

Dr Nestle identified the first line of f. 134 a (middle script) before he observed that I had identified the last line of 134 b with the same passage. The later Arabic scribe had of course turned the leaf round, and the pages being numbered according to his text, *v.* 37 does not really precede *v.* 36. If the sequence is really from John xi. 25, as seems likely, this middle script may be part of a Christian Lectionary—or more probably a Homily containing Biblical quotations. It is not easy to imagine why it should have been written on the top of a text of Isaiah in the same language.

f. 134 b has actually a fourth writing above the Arabic text, a single line scrawled transversely across the page in red ink. It appears to be Jacobite Syriac, but it is now too much blurred to be deciphered.

f. 80 presents a different problem. Here, whilst the 10th century Arabic text (from Mar Jacob) keeps the upper hand, the Syriac text of Exodus and Isaiah is the middle one. This I have deciphered almost without the reagent. But a touch of my brush on the margin has shown that beneath it and at right angles to it is an older Syriac text, which I have not yet tried to bring up for fear of blurring the two scripts which lie above it (see Plate VIII.).

### *The Syriac Hymn.*

ff. 45 and 146 contain beneath the Arabic text from Mar Isaac and Mar Jacob the Syriac hymn which I have printed on pages ܡܚܕ—ܡܕܒ. It is in a late Estrangelo hand which is probably not earlier than the 9th century, and cannot well be later, if I am correct in assigning the Arabic text to the same century, or to the beginning of the 10th. Both scripts run the same way, and the Syriac MS. has been clipped both at top, bottom, and at one side to suit the convenience of the Arabic editor. This has necessitated a column of brackets in every page. It has only one column, of which 17 lines are extant, and only on 8 lines of f. 45 a have I applied the reagent. The hymn is almost wholly composed of Biblical texts, canonical and uncanonical. The word ܠܚܠܝܪܕܐ on f. 146 a l. 1 was observed by Dr Nestle to contain a correspondence with the text of the Sinai Palimpsest; it had puzzled me not a little, because of the strange punctuation which makes the ܪ look like a ܕ. Nevertheless the dot of the ܪ is clearly on the very edge of the leaf (see Plate VIII.).

*Miscellaneous.*

ff. 116—123, 140—146 contain beneath the Arabic, Mar Jacob and Chrysostom, a very troublesome Syriac text. Both scripts run the same way, and the latter was quite invisible without the reagent. Even after the application of that powerful awakener the words remained visible for a few minutes only, in some cases only whilst the page was wet. It has therefore been necessary to copy them very rapidly as they appeared.

f. 119, part of 116 b and f. 141 are from Mar Ephraim, and I have identified the text of the two former with that of a hymn in vol. IV. of Dr de Lamy's new edition.

f. 140 b is from Mar Jacob. This we know from its rubric.

ff. 145, 122 and 117 are probably part of the same text. I have printed only those pages of it where my transcription is tolerably full; in the hope that some future identification may help me to complete the remainder: ff. 116 a, 117 b, 118, 119 a, 120, 121, 122 a, 141, 142, 143, 144.

ff. 155, 162 were originally two leaves of an Arabic MS. containing a small Arabic script, of which even with the help of the reagent I have been able to decipher very little, and to identify nothing. The only words which I see clearly are the last line of f. 155 b,

.....لان له المجد ... الى الدهر امين

and on f. 162 a .......على الطوبة وعلى عمل الحو ..........

and at the foot of f. 155 a داود and الشيطان.

These words point to a Christian text.

The text which lies above it is from Chrysostom. It will be seen that one closely written Arabic script on the top of another presents peculiar difficulties.

### *Origin of the Palimpsest.*

We are of course quite in the dark as regards the early history of a manuscript which has lost both its beginning and its end. But I have a more valid reason for including it in this series of Sinaitic Studies than I had in the case of the little Palestinian Syriac Lectionary whose text forms the basis of No. VI. It is not only that I acquired it on my homeward journey from Sinai in 1895; but that I have since traced it through several hands into those of one who spent many months at Sinai, and proved himself more of an expert than I have been in acquiring manuscripts. The late Professor Palmer also in his very interesting work on the Desert of the Exodus reported as follows:

"Amongst a pile of patristic and other works, of no great age or interest, are some curious old Syriac books *and one or two palimpsests.* My hurried visit prevented me from examining these with any great care; but they would no doubt well repay investigation."—Vol. I. p. 70.

The expression "one or two palimpsests," must surely refer to more than that of the Old Syriac Gospels. But I will not dwell on this subject, which is, after all, a mere presumption.

### *Appendix of Taylor-Schechter Fragments.*

I have, according to my promise, reprinted the text of Nos. XIV., XVIII. and XXIII. of the Palestinian Syriac Fragments in the Taylor-Schechter collection. Several emendations have resulted from Professor Ryssel's identifications of Fragments XIV. and XXV. with the life of St Philemon in the *Acta Sanctorum* of the Bollandists (first vol. for March, page 899); of Fragment XXIII. with the life of St Antony, see *S. Athanasii Opera*, 691 B, or the *Acta Martyrum*, edited by Bedjan, vol. V. p. 118, lines 7—12, the agreement in neither of these being very close.

Professor Ryssel has also identified Fragment XVIII. with the text of *Ecclesiasticus*, chap. xviii. vv. 18—33. This leaf was placed under glass before I received it, I could not therefore use the reagent: and the identification has enabled me to fill several gaps. It is the only scrap of Sirach extant in Palestinian Syriac; and it differs considerably from Walton's Syriac text.

Mrs Gibson finds that Fragment XXVI. is, as Professor Ryssel has pointed out, the Edessene Syriac text of Sirach xiii. 1—14. It agrees closely with the text of Walton, so far as it is visible, and the script is very like that of Fragment XXX. (see *Deutsche Litteraturzeitung*, for Aug. 18th, 1900). To Professor Nöldeke I owe the following suggestions. That on page 110, Numbers xxii. 17—22, should be Numbers xxii. 41—xxiii. 9; that in col. a, l. 10 ܕܘܡ̈ܣܣܝܡ should be ܒܘܡ̈ܣܣܝܡ and on line 12 ܓܢܠܡ should be ܓܠܠܡ. This is borne out by an examination of the fragment, ܠ being in it as short as ܢ.

A list of emendanda to the other Fragments will be found on p. xlvii. These have been suggested by Dr Schulthess and Dr Jacob in the *Z. D. M. G.* vol. LIII pp. 709, 713; vol. LV. pp. 142, 144 and the *Gött. gel. Anzeigen*, pp. 204, 206, and also by Mr Burkitt.

My reasons for not accepting other *emendanda* will be found in the *Zeitschrift der Deutschen Morgenländischen Gesellschaft* for 1901, Heft III. pp. 515—517. To these reprints I have added the text of three palimpsest fragments lately found by Dr Schechter. They are from John xiv, xv, 1 Kings xiv, xv, and John xi, xii, respectively, being arranged according to the order of their discovery. These fragments have suffered far more from ill-usage than my heterogeneous Palimpsest, and were therefore much more difficult to decipher. That I at first read ܦܘܗܪܐ instead of ⌜ܕܐܬܦܣܩܘܢ⌝ on f. 63, col. a, l. 1, p. ܩܢ is owing to the fact that the word has been almost rubbed away.

In conclusion, I have to thank Dr Nestle, of Maulbronn, for his kind revision of my Syriac proofs, and of the translation; my sister, Mrs Margaret Dunlop Gibson, for similar services, and for the decipherment of twelve pages; and Professor D. S. Margoliouth, of Oxford, for his decipherment of the Arabic Document; also the Reader and Printers of the University Press, for the efficient way in which they have accomplished their share of the work.

AGNES SMITH LEWIS.

CASTLE-BRAE,
CAMBRIDGE.

# TABLE OF QUIRES.

| Quire | Leaf | Contents | Arabic later script |
|---|---|---|---|
| I. | 1 | Transitus | Martyrium S. Eleutherii |
| | 2 | Transitus | do. |
| II. | 3 | Transitus | do. |
| | 4 | Transitus | do. |
| | 5 | Transitus | do. |
| | 6 | Transitus | do. |
| | 7 | Transitus | do. |
| | 8 | Transitus | Mart. S. Eleuth., Athanasius, Historia |
| | 9 | Transitus | Athanasius [in Melchisedech |
| | 10 | Transitus | do. |
| | 11 | Septuagint | do. |
| | 12 | Paper, not palimpsest | |
| III. | 13 | Corân II | Theodosius |
| | 14 | Corân II | do. |
| | 15 | Corân II | do. |
| | 16 | Corân II | do. |
| | 17 | Corân II | do. |
| | 18 | Corân II | do. |
| | 19 | Corân II | do. |
| | 20 | Corân II | do. |
| IV. | 21 | Transitus | do. |
| | 22 | Transitus | Theodosius, Chrysostom, not extant |
| | 23 | Transitus | Chrysostom |
| | 24 | Transitus | do. |
| | 25 | Transitus | do. |
| | 26 | Transitus | do. |
| | 27 | Transitus | do. |
| | 28 | Transitus | do. |

| Quire | Leaf | Contents | Arabic later script |
|---|---|---|---|
| V. | 29 | Protevangelium | Chrysostom |
| | 30 | Protevangelium | do. |
| | 31 | Transitus | do. |
| | 32 | Transitus | Chrysostom, Mar Ephraim |
| | 33 | Transitus | Mar Ephraim |
| | 34 | Transitus | do. |
| | 35 | Protevangelium | do. |
| | 36 | Protevangelium | do. |
| VI. | 37 | Transitus | do. |
| | 38 | Transitus | do. |
| | 39 | Transitus | do. |
| | 40 | Transitus | do. |
| | 41 | Transitus | do. |
| | 42 | Transitus | do. |
| | 43 | Transitus | do. |
| | 44 | Transitus | Mar Ephraim, Mar Isaac |
| VII. | 45 | Syriac Hymn | Mar Isaac |
| | 46 | Transitus | do. |
| | 47 | Transitus | do. |
| | 48 | Transitus | do. |
| | 49 | Transitus | do. |
| | 50 | Transitus | Mar Isaac, Chrysostom, not extant |
| | 51 | Transitus | Chrysostom |
| | 52 | Transitus | do. |
| VIII. | 53 | Corân II | do. |
| | 54 | Corân II | do. |
| | 55 | Corân II | do. |
| | 56 | Corân II | do. |
| | 57 | Corân II | do. |
| | 58 | Corân II | do. |
| | 59 | Corân II | do. |
| | 60 | Corân II | do. |
| IX. | 61 | Transitus | do. |
| | 62 | Transitus | do. |
| | 63 | Transitus | Chrysostom, Theodorus |
| | 64 | Transitus | Theodorus |
| | 65 | Transitus | do. |
| | 66 | Transitus | do. |
| | 67 | Transitus | do. |
| | 68 | Transitus | do. |

| Quire | Leaf | Contents | Arabic later script |
|---|---|---|---|
| X. | 69 | Transitus | Theodorus |
| | 70 | Transitus | do. |
| | 71 | Transitus | Chrysostom, Prodigal Son |
| | 72 | Transitus | do. |
| | 73 | Transitus | do. |
| | 74 | Transitus | do. |
| | 75 | Transitus | do. |
| | 76 | Transitus | do. |
| XI. | 77 | Peshiṭta Gospel (Mt. ix.) | do. |
| | 78 | Arabic Document | Chrysostom, Mar Jacob |
| | 79 | Peshiṭta Gospel (Mt. xvi.) | Mar Jacob |
| | 80 | Double Palimpsest (Exod.) | do. |
| | 81 | Peshiṭta Gospel (Mt. x.) | do. |
| | 82 | Peshiṭta Gospel (Mt. x.) | do. |
| | 83 | Arabic Document | do. |
| | 84 | Peshiṭta Gospel (Mt. xv. xvi.) | do. |
| | 85 | Arabic Document | do. |
| | 86 | Peshiṭta Gospel (Mt. ix.) | do. |
| XII. | 87 | Transitus | do. |
| | 88 | Protevangelium | do. |
| | 89 | Protevangelium and Transitus | do. |
| | 90 | Protevangelium | do. |
| | 91 | Protevangelium | do. |
| | 92 | Protevangelium | do. |
| | 93 | Protevangelium and Transitus | do. |
| | 94 | Transitus | do. |
| XIII. | 95 | Corân II | do. |
| | 96 | Corân II | do. |
| | 97 | Corân II | do. |
| | 98 | Corân II | do. |
| | 99 | Corân II | do. |
| | 100 | Corân II | do. |
| | 101 | Corân II | do. |
| | 102 | Corân II | do. |
| | 103 | Corân II | do. |

| Quire | Leaf | Contents | Arabic later script |
|---|---|---|---|
| XIV. | 104 | Corân II | Mar Jacob |
| | 105 | Corân II | do. |
| | 106 | Corân II | do. |
| | 107 | Corân II | do. |
| | 108 | Corân II | do. |
| | 109 | Corân II | do. |
| XV. | 110 | Transitus | do. |
| | 111 | Transitus | do. |
| | 112 | Transitus | do. |
| | 113 | Transitus | do. |
| | 114 | Transitus | do. |
| | 115 | Transitus | do. |
| XVI. | 116 | Mar Jacob | do. |
| | 117 | Mar Jacob | do. |
| | 118 | Mar Jacob | do. |
| | 119 | Mar Jacob | do. |
| | 120 | Mar Jacob | do. |
| | 121 | Mar Jacob | do. |
| | 122 | Mar Jacob | do. |
| | 123 | Mar Jacob | Mar Jacob, Chrysostom |
| XVII. | 124 | Transitus | Chrysostom |
| | 125 | Transitus | do. |
| | 126 | Transitus | do. |
| | 127 | Transitus | do. |
| | 128 | Transitus | do. |
| | 129 | Transitus | do. |
| | 130 | Transitus | do. |
| | 131 | Transitus | do. |
| XVIII. | 132 | Protevangelium | do. |
| | 133 | Protevangelium | do. |
| | 134 | Double Palimpsest | do. |
| | 135 | Peshiṭta Gospels (John vi.) | do. |
| | 136 | Peshiṭta Gospels (John vi.) | do. |
| | 137 | Double Palimpsest | do. |
| | 138 | Protevangelium | do. |
| | 139 | Protevangelium | do. |

| Quire | Leaf | Contents | Arabic later script |
|---|---|---|---|
| XIX. | 140 | Mar Jacob | Chrysostom |
| | 141 | Mar Jacob | do. |
| | 142 | Mar Jacob | do. |
| | 143 | Mar Jacob | Chrysostom, Mar Jacob |
| | 144 | Mar Jacob | Mar Jacob |
| | 145 | Mar Jacob | do. |
| | 146 | Syriac Hymn | do. |
| XX. | 147 | Corân I | do. |
| | 148 | Corân I | do. |
| | 149 | Corân I | do. |
| | 150 | Corân I | do. |
| | 151 | Corân I | do. |
| | 152 | Corân I | do. |
| | 153 | Corân I | do. |
| | 154 | Corân I | do. |
| XXI. | 155 | Small Arabic | do. |
| | 156 | Corân I | do. |
| | 157 | Corân I | do. |
| | 158 | Corân I | do. |
| | 159 | Corân I | do. |
| | 160 | Corân I | do. |
| | 161 | Corân I | do. |
| | 162 | Small Arabic | do. |

I have not been able to identify the extracts from Chrysostom, Theodosius, Mar Ephraim, Mar Isaac and Mar Jacob in the later script with anything extant in the works of these authors. They are possibly translations of something genuine, but if not, they are a very good imitation of the style of the writers whose names they bear.

# INDEX OF PROPER NAMES.

Names which occur frequently, such as Jesus and Mary, are not included, neither are those in the Arabic Document, pp. lxix—lxxi.

## A

## F



## G

## J

## P



## R

## S

## T



## U



## V



## W

# EMENDANDA

## TO THE XXX PALESTINIAN SYRIAC TEXTS IN THE TAYLOR-SCHECHTER COLLECTION.

(In a former book.)

| | | | | | | |
|---|---|---|---|---|---|---|
| Page 12, | col. b, | line 17 | *for* | ܕܪܐܟܘܕܡ | *read probably* | ܕܪܐܟܘܢܐ |
| ,, 20, | ,, a, | ,, 3 | ,, | ܫܠܛܗܘܢ | *read* | ܫܠܛ ܒܗܘܢ |
| ,, 20, | ,, b, | ,, 4 | ,, | ܒܚ̈ܝܠܐ | ,, | ܪܚ̈ܝܠܐ |
| ,, 20, | ,, b, | ,, 8 | ,, | ܗܒܕܢ | ,, | ܗܕܢ |
| ,, 30, | ,, a, | ,, 2 | ,, | ܫܐܘܬܐ | ,, | ܫܐܒܘܬܐ |
| ,, 56, | ,, b, | ,, 18 | ,, | ܚܠܝ | ,, | ܚܢܝ |
| ,, 58, | ,, a, | ,, 17 | ,, | ܒܒܪܢ | ,, | ܒܒܪܢ ܕܝ |
| ,, 58, | ,, b, | ,, 11 | ,, | ܘܢܝܐ | ,, | ܘܚܝܐ |
| ,, 58, | ,, b, | ,, 13 | ,, | ܒܗ...ܬܐ | ,, | ܒܒ...ܕܐ |
| ,, 60, | ,, a, | ,, 1 | ,, | ܕܢܝܐ | ,, | ܕܚܝܐ |
| ,, 60, | ,, a, | ,, 3 | ,, | ܢܝܐ | ,, | ܚܝܐ |
| ,, 60, | ,, a, | ,, 5 | ,, | ܕܐ...ܝܗܒ | ,, | ܕܐܘܦ ܝܗܒ |
| ,, 60, | ,, b, | ,, 11 | ,, | ܐܢܐ ܝܒܥܐ | ,, | ܐܢܐ ܠܢ ܝܒܥܐ |
| ,, 64, | ,, a, | ,, 13 | ,, | ܕܡܫܘܬܐ | ,, | ܕܡܫܛܘܬܐ |
| ,, 70, | ,, b, | ,, 12 | ,, | ܬܡܡ ܡ | ,, | ܬܡܡܡ |
| ,, 77, | ,, a, | ,, 12 | ,, | ܣܠ̈ܗ | ,, | ܣܠ̈ܒܗ |
| ,, 79, | ,, a, | ,, 13 | ,, | ܕܡܒ̈ܗܘܢ | ,, | ܕܡܒ̈ܗܠܘܢ |
| ,, 79, | ,, a, | ,, 14 | ,, | ܘܡܬܚܒ̈ܫܝܢ | ,, | ܘܡܬܚܫ̈ܒܝܢ |

f. 11[b] Gen. xl. 3, 4

ΚΗΠΑΡΑΤΩΑΡΧΙΜΑΓΕΙΡΩ
ΕΙΣΤΟΔΕΣΜΩΤΗΡΙΟΝ.ΕΙΣΤΟΝ
ΤΟΠΟΝΟΥΙΩΣΗΦΑΠΗΚΤΟ — α δεδεμενος
ΕΚΕΙ ΚΑΙΣΥΝΕΣΤΗΣΕ — σ παρεθετο
ΟΑΡΧΙΔΕΣΜΩΤΗΣΤΩΙΩ
ΣΗΦΑΥΤΟΥΣΚΑΙΠΑΡΕΣΤΗ — σ ελιτουργει

f. 11[a] *v.* 7

α εμβρασσομενοι — ΤΕΤΑΡΑΓΜΕΝΟΙ ΚΑΙΗΡΩΤΑ
σ σκυθρωποι — ΤΟΥΣΕΥΝΟΥΧΟΥΣΦΑΡΑΩ
ΟΙΗΣΑΝΜΕΤΑΥΤΟΥΕΝΤΗ
ασ εν τω οικω του — ΦΥΛΑΚΗΠΑΡΑΤΩΚΩΑΥ
ΤΟΥΛΕΓΩΝ.ΤΙΟΤΙΤΑΠΡΟΣΩ
α κακα
σ πονηρα — ΠΑΥΜΩΝΣΚΥΘΡΩΠΑΣΗΜΕΡΟ

SEPTUAGINT *WITH*
Gen. xl. 3,
*f. 11a, 11b*

HEXAPLA VARIANTS
4, 7.

# CORÂN I.

Folia I. II. scripti inferioris = ff. 147 + 154, 148 + 153 scripti superioris legi non possunt.

## FOLIUM III.

Scripti superioris ff. 158, 159
Scripti inferioris Sura 24, *vv.* 2—29.

### f. 158 a

| | | |
|---|---|---|
| Incipit | . . . . . . . . . . . كُمْ . . . . . . | Sura 24, *v.* 2 |
| | . . . . . . . . . . . . . . . . . . | |
| | . . . . . . . . . . . . ٱلْمُؤْمِنِينَ | |
| Explicit | . . . . . . . . . . ٱ[1]لْكَذِبِينَ وَيَدْرَؤُ عَنْهَا | *vv.* 7, 8 |

### f. 159 b

| | | |
|---|---|---|
| Incipit | أَرْبَعَ شَهَادَٰتٍ | *v.* 8 |
| | ٱللَّهِ عَلَيْهَا إِنْ كَانَ مِنَ ٱلصَّٰدِقِينَ | |
| Explicit | . . . . . . . . . . . فَضْلُ ٱللَّهِ عَلَيْكُمْ | *v.* 14 |

### f. 158 b

| | | |
|---|---|---|
| Incipit | . . . . . . . . . . . . وَيُبَيِّنُ ٱللَّهُ لَكُمُ | *v.* 17 |
| Explicit | . . . . . . . . إِن ٱلَّذِينَ يَرْمُونَ ٱلْمُحْصَنَا | *v.* 23 |

### f. 159 a

| | | |
|---|---|---|
| | . . . . . . . . . . . . . . . . . . | |
| Incipit | . . . . . . . . عَلَيْهِمْ أَلْسِنَتُهُمْ وَأَيْدِيهِمْ | *v.* 24 |
| Explicit | . . . . . . . . كُمْ وَٱللَّهُ يَعْلَمُ مَا تُبْدُونَ | *v.* 29 |

[1] sic

## FOLIUM IV.

Scripti superioris ff. 161, 156.
Scripti inferioris Sura 28, *vv.* 41—51.

Scripti superioris ff. 161 a et 156 b legi non possunt.

f. 161 b

Incipit . . . . وَجَعَلْنَاهُمْ أَئِمَّةً . . . . . . . . . Sura 28, *v.* 41

Explicit . . . . مِنْ قَبْلِكَ لَعَلَّهُمْ . . . . . . . . *v.* 46

f. 156 a

Incipit . . . بَهُمْ مُصِيبَةٌ بِمَا قَدَّمَتْ *v.* 47

Explicit . . . . . . . ٱلظَّالِمِينَ . . . . . . . . . . *vv.* 50, 51

. . . . يَتَذَكَّرُونَ . . . . . . . . . .

## FOLIUM V.

Scripti superioris ff. 160, 157.
Scripti inferioris Sura 29, *vv.* 17—30.

f. 160 a

Incipit سُولِ إِلَّا [1]ٱلْبَلَغُ . . . . . . . . . . Sura 29, *v.* 17

Explicit وَقَالَ إِنَّمَا ٱتَّخَذتُّمْ مِنْ دُونِ ٱللَّهِ *[أَوْثَانًا] *v.* 24

. . فى الحيوة . . . . . . . . .

f. 157 b

Incipit بَعْضُكُمْ بِبَعْضٍ وَيَلْعَنُ بَعْضُكُمْ بَعْضًا *[وَمَأْوَاكُمُ] *v.* 24

ٱلنَّارُ

Explicit لْمُفْسِدِينَ وَلَمَّا جَآءَ . . . . . . . . . *vv.* 29, 30

ff. 160 b et 157 a legi non possunt.

---

[1] sic * abscissum

## FOLIUM VI.

Scripti superioris ff. 152, 149.
Scripti inferioris Sura 40, *v.* 79--Sura 41, *v.* 19.

f. 152 a

| | | |
|---|---|---|
| Incipit | نَ ٱللَّهُ ٱلَّذِى جَعَلَ لَكُمُ . . . . . . . . . | Sura 40, *v.* 79 |
| Explicit | . . . . . . . . . . . . . آمَنَّا بِٱللَّهِ وَحْدَهُ | *v.* 84 |
| | . . . . . . . . . . . . . . . . . . . . | |

f. 149 b

| | | |
|---|---|---|
| Incipit | . . . . . . . . . . . . فِى عِبَادِهِ وَخَسِرَ هُ | *v.* 85 |
| Explicit | وَوَيْلٌ لِّلْمُشْرِكِينَ ٱلَّذِينَ . . . . . . . . . | Sura 41, *vv.* 5, 6 |

f. 152 b

| | | |
|---|---|---|
| Incipit | . . . . . . . . . . . . . مِنْ فَوْقِهَا وَ | *v.* 9 |
| | . . . . . . . هَا فِى أَرْبَعَةِ أَ . . . سَوَآءً | |
| Explicit | بِهِ كَافِرُونَ فَأَمَّا عَادٌ فَٱسْتَكْبَرُوا فِى | *vv.* 13, 14 |

f. 149 a

| | | |
|---|---|---|
| | . . . . . . . . . . . . . . . . . . . . | |
| Incipit | للَّهَ ٱلَّذِى خَلَقَهُمْ هُوَ أَشَدُّ مِنْهُمْ | *v.* 14 |
| Explicit | مَا جَآؤُهَا شَهِدَ عَلَيْهِمْ سَمْعُهُمْ [1] وَأَبْصَرُهُمْ | *v.* 19 |

---

[1] sic

## FOLIUM VII.

Scripti superioris ff. 151, 150.
Scripti inferioris Sura 44, *v.* 38—Sura 45, *v.* 20.

f. 151 a

Incipit ﺗِ وَٱلْأَرْضَ وَمَا بَيْنَهُمَا لَاعِبِينَ مَا خَلَقْنَاهُمَا إ[*لَّا بِٱلْحَقِّ] Sura 44, *v.* 38
وَلَكِنَّ . . . . . . . . . . . . . . .

Explicit ٱلْمَوْتَ إِلَّا ٱلْمَوْتَةَ ٱلْأُولَى . . . . . . . . *v.* 56

f. 150 b

Incipit فَضْلًا مِـنْ رَبِّـكَ ذَلِكَ هُـوَ ٱلْفَوْزُ ٱلْعَظِيمُ فَإِنَّمَا [*يَسَّرْنَاهُ] *vv.* 57, 58
بِلِسَانِكَ لَعَلَّهُمْ يَتَذَكَّرُونَ فَٱرْتَقِبْ إِنَّهُمْ مُ[*رْتَقِبُونَ] *vv.* 58, 59
بِسْمِ ٱللَّهِ ٱلرَّحْمَنِ ٱلرَّحِيمِ ○○○○○○ Sura 45.

Explicit فَبِأَيِّ حَدِيثٍ بَعْدَ ٱللَّهِ وَآ . . . . . . . . . *v.* 5

f. 151 b

Incipit وا مِنْ دُونِ ٱللَّهِ أَوْلِيَآءَ وَلَهُمْ عَذَابٌ *v.* 9
Explicit بِهِ وَمَنْ أَسَآءَ فَعَلَيْهَا . . . . . . . . . . *v.* 14
. . . . . . . . . . . . . . . . .

f. 150 a

Incipit هُمْ مِنَ ٱلطَّيِّبَاتِ وَفَضَّلْنَاهُمْ عَلَى [1]ٱلْعَلَمِينَ ∵ *v.* 15
Explicit . . . . . . . . . [1]ٱلصَّلِحَتِ سَوَآءً [1]مَحْيَهُمْ *v.* 20

---

* abscissum [1] sic

# CORÂN II.

## FOLIUM I.

Scripti superioris ff. 54, 59.
Scripti inferioris Sura 7, *vv.* 139—158.

f. 59 a.

| | | |
|---|---|---|
| Incipit | ٱلْجَبَلِ فَإِنِ ٱسْتَقَرَّ مَكَانَهُ فَسَوْفَ تَرَانِى فَلَمَّا تَجَلَّى رَبُّهُ | Sura 7, *v.* 139 |
| Explicit | يَتَّخِذُوهُ سَبِيلًا ذَلِكَ بِأَنَّهُمْ كَذَّبُوا بِآيَاتِنَا وَكَا | *vv.* 143, 144 |

f. 54 b.

| | | |
|---|---|---|
| Incipit | نُوا عَنْهَا غَافِلِينَ وَٱلَّذِينَ كَذَّبُوا [1]بِآيَتِنَا وَلِقَآءِ | *vv.* 144, 145 |
| Explicit | ٱلْقَوْمِ ٱلظَّالِمِينَ قَالَ رَبِّ ٱغْفِرْ . . . . . . . . . . . | *vv.* 149, 150 |

f. 59 b.

| | | |
|---|---|---|
| Incipit | خِلْنَا فِى رَحْمَتِكَ وَأَنْتَ أَرْحَمُ [1]ٱلرَّحِمِينَ إِنَّ ٱلَّذِينَ ٱتَّ | *vv.* 150, 151 |
| Explicit | وَلِيُّنَا فَٱغْفِرْ لَنَا وَٱرْحَمْنَا وَأَنْتَ خَيْرُ [1]ٱلْغَفِرِينَ وَٱ | *v.* 154 |
| | . . . . . . . . . . . . . . . . . . . . | |

f. 54 a.

| | | |
|---|---|---|
| Incipit | إِلَيْكَ قَالَ عَذَابِى أُصِيبُ بِهِ مَنْ أَشَآءُ وَرَحْمَتِى | *v.* 155 |
| Explicit | . . . . . . . . . اتِ وَٱلْأَرْضِ لَا إِلَهَ إِلَّا هُوَ يُحْيِى | *v.* 158 |

[1] sic

## FOLIUM II.

Scripti superioris f. 103.

Scripti inferioris Sura 7, *vv.* 158—168.

f. 103 a.

| | | |
|---|---|---|
| Incipit | . . . . . . . . . . ٱلنَّبِيَّ ٱلْأُمِّيَّ ٱلَّذِى | Sura 7, *vv.* 158, 159 |
| | يُؤْمِنُ بِٱللَّهِ [1]وَكَلِمَتِهِ وَٱتَّبِعُوهُ لَعَلَّكُمْ تَهْتَدُونَ وَمِنْ | |
| Explicit | وَمَا ظَلَمُونَا وَلَكِنْ كَانُوا أَنْفُسَهُمْ يَظْلِمُونَ | *v.* 160 |
| | . . . . . . . . . . . . . . . . . . | |
| | . . . . . . . . . . . . . . . . . . | |

f. 103 b.

| | | |
|---|---|---|
| Incipit | كَانُوا يَفْسُقُونَ . . . . . . . . . . . | *v.* 165 |
| Explicit | . . . . . . . . . يُغْفَرُ لَنَا وَإِنْ يَأْتِهِمْ عَرَضٌ | *v.* 168 |
| | . . . . . . . . . . . . . . . . . . | |

---

[1] sic

# FOLIUM III.

Scripti superioris ff. 104, 109.

Scripti inferioris Sura 9, *vv.* 18—35.

f. 104 a.

| | | |
|---|---|---|
| Incipit | [1]أُولَـٰئِكَ أَنْ يَكُونُوا مِنَ ٱلْمُهْتَدِينَ أَجَعَلْتُمْ سِقَ . . . | Sura 9, *vv.* 18, 19 |
| Explicit | . . . . . . . آؤُكُمْ [1]وَإِخْوَنُكُمْ وَأَ . . . . . . . . . | *v.* 24 |

f. 109 b.

| | | |
|---|---|---|
| Incipit | وَأَمْوَالٌ ٱقْتَرَفْتُمُوهَا وَتِجَـ . . . . . . . . . . . . . | *v.* 24 |
| Explicit | عَلَى مَنْ يَشَآءُ وَٱللَّهُ غَفُورٌ رَحِيمٌ يَا أَيُّهَا ٱلَّذِينَ آمَنُوا | *vv.* 27, 28 |

f. 104 b.

| | | |
|---|---|---|
| Incipit | إِنَّمَا ٱلْمُشْرِكُونَ نَجَسٌ فَلَا يَقْرَبُوا ٱلْمَسْجِدَ . . . . . | *v.* 28 |
| Explicit | . . . . . . . دُونِ ٱللَّهِ وَٱلْمَسِيحَ ٱبْنَ . . . . وَمَا | *v.* 31 |

f. 109 a.

| | | |
|---|---|---|
| Incipit | . . . . . . . . . . . . . . . . . . . . . | |
| | عَمَّا يُشْرِكُونَ يُرِيدُونَ أَنْ يُطْفِئُوا نُورَ ٱللَّهِ بِأَفْوَا | *v.* 31 |
| Explicit | عَلَيْهَا فِى نَارِ جَهَنَّمَ فَتُكْوَى بِهَا [1]جِبَهُهُمْ وَجُنُو | *v.* 35 |

---

[1] sic

## FOLIUM IV.

Scripti superioris ff. 53, 60.

Scripti inferioris Sura 9, *vv.* 35—59.

f. 60 a.

| | | |
|---|---|---|
| Incipit | بُهُمْ وَظُهُورُهُمْ هَذَا مَا كَنَزْتُمْ لِأَنْفُسِكُمْ فَذُوقُوا مَا | Sura 9, *v.* 35 |
| Explicit | عَذَابًا أَلِيمًا وَيَسْتَبْدِلْ قَوْمًا غَيْرَكُمْ وَلَا تَضُرُّوهُ شَيْئًا وَٱللَّهُ عَلَى كُلِّ | *v.* 39 |

. . . . . . . . . . . . . . . . . . . . . . . . .

f. 53 b.

| | | |
|---|---|---|
| Incipit | ٱثْنَيْنِ إِذْ هُمَا فِى ٱلْغَارِ إِذْ يَقُولُ [1]لِصَحِبِهِ لَا تَحْزَنْ إِنَّ ٱللَّهَ مَعَنَا فَأَنْزَلَ ٱللَّهُ | *v.* 40 |
| Explicit | . . . ا يَسْتَأْذِنُكَ ٱلَّذِينَ لَا يُؤْمِنُونَ بِٱللَّهِ وَٱلْيَوْمِ ٱلْآخِرِ وَٱرْتَابَتْ | *v.* 45 |

. . . . . . . . . . . . . . . . . . . . . . . . .

f. 60 b.

| | | |
|---|---|---|
| Incipit | قُلُوبُهُمْ فَهُمْ فِى رَيْبِهِمْ يَتَرَدَّدُونَ وَلَوْ أَرَادُوا ٱلْخُرُوجَ لَأَعَدُّ | *vv.* 45, 46 |
| Explicit | نَ بِنَا إِلَّا إِحْدَى ٱلْحُسْنَيَيْنِ وَنَحْنُ نَتَرَبَّصُ بِكُمْ أَنْ يُصِيبَكُمُ ٱللَّهُ | *v.* 52 |

. . . . . . . . . . . . . . . . . . . . . . . . .

f. 53 a.

| | | |
|---|---|---|
| Incipit | قُلْ أَنْفِقُوا طَوْعًا أَوْ كَرْهًا لَنْ يُتَقَبَّلَ مِنْكُمْ إِنَّكُمْ | *v.* 53 |
| Explicit | آتَاهُمُ ٱللَّهُ وَرَسُولُهُ وَقَالُوا حَسْبُنَا ٱللَّهُ سَيُؤْتِينَا | *v.* 59 |

[1] sic

## FOLIUM V.

Scripti superioris ff. 105, 108.

Scripti inferioris Sura 9, *vv.* 59—79.

f. 105 a.

| | | |
|---|---|---|
| Incipit | ٱللَّهُ مِنْ فَضْلِهِ وَرَسُولُهُ إِنَّا إِلَى ٱللَّهِ [1]رَغِبُونَ إِنَّمَا ٱ | Sura 9, *vv.* 59, 60 |
| Explicit | . . . . . إِنَّ ٱللَّهَ مُخْرِجٌ مَا تَحْذَرُونَ . . . . . | *v.* 65 |

f. 108 b.

| | | |
|---|---|---|
| Incipit | لُنَّ إِنَّمَا كُنَّا نَخُوضُ وَنَلْعَبُ قُلْ أَبِٱللَّهِ [1]وَآيَتِهِ وَرَسُولِهِ | *v.* 66 |
| Explicit | ٱلَّذِينَ مِنْ قَبْلِكُمْ [1]بِخَلَقِهِمْ وَخُضْتُمْ كَٱلَّذِى خَاضُوا أُو | *v.* 70 |

f. 105 b.

| | | |
|---|---|---|
| Incipit | [1]لِئَكَ حَبِطَتْ [1]أَعْمَلُهُمْ فِى ٱلدُّنْيَا وَٱلْآخِرَةِ | *v.* 70 |
| Explicit | . . . . . . . . . . [1]جَهِدِ ٱلْكُفَّارَ وَٱلْ . . . . . | *v.* 74 |

f. 108 a.

| | | |
|---|---|---|
| Incipit | عَلَيْهِمْ [1]وَمَأْوَهُمْ جَهَنَّمُ وَبِئْسَ ٱلْمَصِيرُ يَحْلِفُونَ بِٱ | *vv.* 74, 75 |
| Explicit | وَعَدُوهُ وَبِمَا كَانُوا يَكْذِبُونَ أَلَمْ يَعْلَمُوا أَنَّ ٱللَّهَ | *vv.* 78, 79 |

---

[1] sic

## FOLIUM VI.

Scripti superioris ff. 106, 107
Scripti inferioris Sura 11, *vv.* 20—39

f. 106 a.

| | | |
|---|---|---|
| Incipit | [1]شَهِدٌ مِنْهُ وَمِنْ قَبْلِهِ كِتَابُ مُوسَى إِمَامًا | Sura 11, *v.* 20 |
| Explicit | دُونِ ٱللَّهِ مِنْ أَوْلِيَاءَ [1]يُضَعَفُ لَهُمُ ٱلْعَذَابُ | *v.* 22 |
| | . . . . . . . . . . . . . . . . | |

f. 107 b.

| | | |
|---|---|---|
| Incipit | [1]أُولَئِكَ ٱلَّذِينَ خَسِرُوا أَنْفُسَهُمْ وَضَلَّ عَنْهُمْ | *v.* 23 |
| Explicit | بَشَرًا مِثْلَنَا وَمَا نَرَاكَ ٱتَّبَعَكَ إِلَّا ٱلَّذِينَ | *v.* 29 |

f. 106 b.

| | | |
|---|---|---|
| Incipit | هُمْ [1]أَرَذِلُنَا بَادِىَ ٱلرَّأْىِ وَمَا نَرَى لَكُمْ | *v.* 29 |
| Explicit | أَقُولُ إِنِّى مَلَكٌ وَلَا أَقُولُ لِلَّذِينَ تَزْدَرِى | *v.* 33 |

f. 107 a.

| | | |
|---|---|---|
| Incipit | . . . . هُمُ ٱللَّهُ خَيْرًا أَللَّهُ . . . . . | *v.* 33 |
| Explicit | ٱصْنَعِ ٱلْفُلْكَ بِأَعْيُنِنَا وَوَحْيِنَا وَلَا [تُخَاطِبْنِ]ى | *v.* 39 |

---

[1] sic

## FOLIUM VII.

Scripti superioris ff. 16, 17.
Scripti inferioris Sura 13, *vv.* 18—34.

f. 17 a.

| | | |
|---|---|---|
| Incipit | [1]ٱسْتَجَبُوا لِرَبِّهِمُ ٱلْحُسْنَى وَٱلَّذِينَ لَمْ يَسْتَجِيبُوا لَهُ لَوْ أَنَّ | Sura 13, *v.* 18 |
| Explicit | [1]قَمُوا ٱلصَّلَوةَ وَأَنْفَقُوا مِمَّا رَزَقْنَاهُمْ سِرًّا | *v.* 22 |

f. 16 b.

| | | |
|---|---|---|
| Incipit | [1]وَعَلنِيَةً وَيَدْرَؤُنَ بِٱلْحَسَنَةِ ٱلسَّيِّئَةَ [1]أُولَئِكَ | *v.* 22 |
| Explicit | ٱلْآخِرَةِ إِلَّا [1]مَتَعٌ وَيَقُولُ ٱلَّذِينَ كَفَرُوا لَوْلَا أُنْزِلَ | *vv.* 26, 27 |

f. 17 b.

| | | |
|---|---|---|
| Incipit | عَلَيْهِ آيَةٌ مِنْ رَبِّهِ قُلْ إِنَّ ٱللَّهَ يُضِلُّ مَنْ يَشَآءُ وَيَهْدِى | *v.* 27 |
| Explicit | . . . . . . . . . . . . . . . . . . . . . بِهِ | *v.* 30 |
| | ٱلْأَرْضُ أَوْ كُلِّمَ بِهِ ٱلْمَوْتَى بَلْ لِلَّهِ ٱلْأَمْرُ جَمِيعًا | |

f. 16 a.

| | | |
|---|---|---|
| Incipit | أَفَلَمْ [1]يَيْئَسِ ٱلَّذِينَ آمَنُوا أَنْ لَوْ يَشَآءُ ٱللَّهُ لَهَدَى | *v.* 30 |
| Explicit | ٱللَّهُ فَمَا لَهُ مِنْ هَادٍ لَهُمْ عَذَابٌ فِى ٱلْحَيَوةِ | *vv.* 33, 34 |

---

[1] sic

## FOLIUM VIII.

Scripti superioris ff. 14, 19.
Scripti inferioris Sura 13, *v.* 34—Sura 14, *v.* 8.

f. 19 a.

| | | |
|---|---|---|
| Incipit | ٱلدُّنْيَا وَلَعَذَابُ ٱلْآخِرَةِ أَشَقُّ وَمَا لَهُمْ مِنَ ٱللَّهِ | Sura 13, *v.* 34 |
| Explicit | وَاقٍ وَلَقَدْ أَرْسَلْنَا رُسُلًا مِنْ قَبْلِكَ وَجَعَلْنَا | *vv.* 37, 38 |

f. 14 b.

| | | |
|---|---|---|
| Incipit | لَهُمْ أَزْوَاجًا وَذُرِّيَّةً وَمَا كَانَ لِرَسُولٍ أَنْ يَأْتِيَ بِآ | *v.* 38 |
| Explicit | شَهِيدًا بَيْنِي وَبَيْنَكُمْ وَمَنْ عِنْدَهُ عِلْمُ ٱلْكِتَابِ | *v.* 43 |

f. 19 b.

| | | |
|---|---|---|
| Incipit | بِسْمِ ٱللَّهِ ٱلرَّحْمَنِ ٱلرَّحِيمِ الرٓ كِتَابٌ أَنْزَلْنَاهُ إِ | Sura 14 |
| Explicit | بَعِيدٍ وَمَا أَرْسَلْنَا مِنْ رَسُولٍ إِلَّا بِلِسَانِ قَوْمِهِ | *vv.* 3, 4 |

f. 14 a.

| | | |
|---|---|---|
| Incipit | لِيُبَيِّنَ لَهُمْ فَيُضِلُّ ٱللَّهُ مَنْ يَشَآءُ وَيَهْدِي مَنْ يَشَآءُ وَ | *v.* 4 |
| Explicit | إِنْ تَكْفُرُوا أَنْتُمْ وَمَنْ فِي ٱلْأَرْضِ جَمِيعًا فَإِنَّ ٱللَّهَ | *v.* 8 |

## FOLIUM IX.

Scripti superioris ff. 15, 18.
Scripti inferioris Sura 15, *v.* 85—Sura 16, *v.* 18.

f. 18 a.

| | | |
|---|---|---|
| Incipit | وَمَا بَيْنَهُمَا إِلَّا بِٱلْحَقِّ وَإِنَّ ٱلسَّاعَةَ لَآتِيَةٌ فَٱ | Sura 15, *v.* 85 |
| Explicit | فَسَوْفَ يَعْلَمُونَ وَلَقَدْ نَعْلَمُ أَنَّكَ يَضِيقُ | *vv.* 96, 97 |

f. 15 b.

| | | |
|---|---|---|
| Incipit | صَدْرُكَ بِمَا يَقُولُونَ فَسَبِّحْ بِحَمْدِ رَبِّكَ | *vv.* 97, 98 |
| Explicit | عَمَّا يُشْرِكُونَ خَلَقَ [1]ٱلْإِنْسَنَ مِنْ نُطْفَةٍ فَإِذَا هُوَ | Sura 16, *vv.* 3, 4 |

f. 18 b.

| | | |
|---|---|---|
| Incipit | خَصِيمٌ مُبِينٌ [1]وَٱلْأَنْعَمَ خَلَقَهَا لَكُمْ فِيهَا دِفْءٌ<br>[1]وَمَنَفِعُ . . . . . . . . . . . . . . | *vv.* 4, 5 |
| Explicit | وَمِنْ كُلِّ [1]ٱلثَّمَرَتِ إِنَّ فِي ذَلِكَ لَآيَةً لِقَوْمٍ | *v.* 11 |

f. 15 a.

| | | |
|---|---|---|
| Incipit | يَتَفَكَّرُونَ وَسَخَّرَ لَكُمُ ٱللَّيْلَ [1]وَٱلنَّهَرَ وَٱلشَّمْسَ | *vv.* 11, 12 |
| Explicit | يَخْلُقُ كَمَنْ لَا يَخْلُقُ أَفَلَا تَذَكَّرُونَ وَإِنْ تَعُدُّوا | *vv.* 17, 18 |

---

[1] sic

## FOLIUM X.

Scripti superioris ff. 13, 20.
Scripti inferioris Sura 16, *vv.* 18—41.

f. 20 a.

| | | |
|---|---|---|
| Incipit | نِعْمَةَ ٱللَّهِ لَا تُحْصُوهَا إِنَّ ٱللَّهَ لَغَفُورٌ رَحِيمٌ | Sura 16, *v.* 18 |
| Explicit | يُضِلُّونَهُمْ بِغَيْرِ عِلْمٍ أَلَا سَآءَ مَا يَزِرُونَ قَدْ | *vv.* 27, 28 |
| | . . . . . . . . . . . . . . . . | |

f. 13 b.

| | | |
|---|---|---|
| Incipit | عِدِ فَخَرَّ عَلَيْهِمُ ٱلسَّقْفُ مِنْ فَوْقِهِمْ [1]وَأَتَيْهُمُ | *v.* 28 |
| Explicit | تَّقَوْا مَا ذَا أَنْزَلَ رَبُّكُمْ (قَالُوا خَيْرًا) لِلَّذِينَ أَحْسَنُوا | *v.* 32 |

f. 20 b.

| | | |
|---|---|---|
| Incipit | فِى هَذِهِ ٱلدُّنْيَا حَسَنَةٌ وَلَدَارُ ٱلْآخِرَةِ خَيْرٌ وَلَنِعْمَ | *v.* 32 |
| Explicit | لَوْ شَآءَ ٱللَّهُ مَا عَبَدْنَا مِنْ دُونِهِ مِنْ شَىْءٍ نَحْنُ وَلَا | *v.* 37 |

f. 13 a.

| | | |
|---|---|---|
| Incipit | . . . . . . . . . . . . . . . . | *v.* 37 |
| | ٱلَّذِينَ مِنْ قَبْلِهِمْ فَهَلْ عَلَى ٱلرُّسُلِ إِلَّا [1]ٱلْبَلَغُ ٱ | |
| | لْمُبِينُ . . . . . . . . . . . . . . | |
| Explicit | أَكْثَرَ ٱلنَّاسِ لَا (يَعْلَمُونَ لِيُبَيِّنَ) لَهُمُ ٱلَّذِى يَخْتَلِفُونَ | *vv.* 40, 41 |

---

[1] sic

## FOLIUM XI.

Scripti superioris ff. 55, 58.

Scripti inferioris Sura 16, *vv.* 80—98.

f. 58 b.

| | | |
|---|---|---|
| Incipit | وَٱلْأَفْئِدَةَ لَعَلَّكُمْ تَشْكُرُونَ أَلَمْ يَرَوْا إِلَى ٱلطَّيْرِ | Sura 16, *vv.* 80, 81 |
| Explicit | عَلَيْكُمْ لَعَلَّكُمْ تُسْلِمُونَ فَإِنْ تَوَلَّوْا فَإِنَّمَا | *vv.* 83, 84 |

f. 55 a.

| | | |
|---|---|---|
| Incipit | عَلَيْكَ [1]ٱلْبَلَغُ ٱلْمُبِينُ يَعْرِفُونَ نِعْمَةَ ٱللَّهِ | *vv.* 84, 85 |
| Explicit | بًا فَوْقَ ٱلْعَذَابِ بِمَا كَانُوا يُفْسِدُونَ | *v.* 90 |

f. 58 a.

| | | |
|---|---|---|
| Incipit | وَيَوْمَ نَبْعَثُ فِى كُلِّ أُمَّةٍ شَهِيدًا عَلَيْهِمْ مِنْ أَ | *v.* 91 |
| Explicit | غَزْلَهَا مِنْ بَعْدِ قُوَّةٍ [1]أَنْكَثًا تَتَّخِذُونَ [1]أَيْمَنَكُمْ | *v.* 94 |

f. 55 b.

| | | |
|---|---|---|
| Incipit | دَخَلًا بَيْنَكُمْ أَنْ تَكُونَ أُمَّةٌ هِىَ أَرْبَى مِنْ أُ | *v.* 94 |
| Explicit | إِنْ كُنْتُمْ تَعْلَمُونَ مَا عِنْدَكُمْ يَنْفَدُ وَمَا | *vv.* 97, 98 |

---

[1] sic

## FOLIUM XII.

Scripti superioris ff. 56, 57.
Scripti inferioris Sura 16, *vv.* 98—117.

f. 56 b.

| | | |
|---|---|---|
| Incipit | عِنْدَ ٱللَّهِ بَاقٍ وَلَنَجْزِيَنَّ ٱلَّذِينَ صَبَرُوا أَجْرَهُمْ | Sura 16, *v.* 98 |
| Explicit | مُفْتَرٍ بَلْ أَكْثَرُهُمْ لَا يَعْلَمُونَ قُلْ نَزَّلَهُ رُو | *vv.* 103, 104 |

f. 57 a.

| | | |
|---|---|---|
| Incipit | حُ ٱلْقُدُسِ مِنْ رَبِّكَ بِٱلْحَقِّ لِيُثَبِّتَ ٱلَّذِ | *v.* 104 |
| Explicit | لْكُفْرِ صَدْرًا فَعَلَيْهِمْ غَضَبٌ مِنَ ٱللَّهِ | *v.* 108 |

f. 56 a.

| | | |
|---|---|---|
| Incipit | وَلَهُمْ عَذَابٌ عَظِيمٌ ذَلِكَ بِأَنَّهُمُ ٱسْتَحَبُّو | *vv.* 108, 109 |
| Explicit | كَانَتْ آمِنَةً مُطْ . . . . . . . . . | *v.* 113 |

f. 57 b.

| | | |
|---|---|---|
| Incipit | مِنْ كُلِّ مَكَانٍ فَكَفَرَتْ بِأَنْعُمِ ٱللَّهِ [1]فَأَذ<br>قَهَا . . . . . . . . . . . . . . . . . | *v.* 113 |
| Explicit | ا حَرَامٌ لِتَفْتَرُوا عَلَى ٱللَّهِ ٱلْكَذِبَ إِنَّ ٱلَّذِينَ | *v.* 117 |

---

[1] sic

## FOLIUM XIII.

Scripti superioris ff. 96, 101.
Scripti inferioris Sura 16, *v.* 117—Sura 17, *v.* 10.

f. 101 a.

| | | |
|---|---|---|
| Incipit | يَفْتَرُونَ عَلَى ٱللَّهِ ٱلْكَذِبَ لَا يُفْلِحُونَ [1]مَتَعٌ | Sura 16, *vv.* 117, 118 |
| Explicit | . . . . . . أَنِ ٱتَّبِعْ مِلَّةَ [1]إِبْرَهِمَ . . . | *v.* 124 |

f. 96 b.

| | | |
|---|---|---|
| Incipit | . . . . . . . . . . . . . . . . . | |
| | عَلَى ٱلَّذِينَ ٱخْتَلَفُوا فِيهِ وَإِنَّ رَبَّكَ لَيَحْكُمُ | *v.* 125 |
| Explicit | ٱللَّهَ مَعَ ٱلَّذِينَ ٱتَّقَوْا وَٱلَّذِينَ هُمْ مُحْسِنُونَ | *v.* 128 |

f. 101 b.

| | | |
|---|---|---|
| Incipit | بِسْمِ ٱللَّهِ ٱلرَّحْمَنِ ٱلرَّحِيمِ [1]سُبْحَنَ ٱلَّذِى أَسْرَى | Sura 17 |
| Explicit | . . . إِذَا جَآءَ وَعْدُ أُولَاهُمَا . . . . . . | *v.* 5 |

f. 96 a.

| | | |
|---|---|---|
| Incipit | . . . . . . . . . . . . . . . . . | *v.* 5 |
| | . . رِ وَكَانَ وَعْدًا مَفْ . . . . . . . . | |
| Explicit | . . . . ٱلْمُؤْمِنِينَ ٱلَّذِينَ يَعْمَلُونَ [1]ٱلصَّلِحَتِ | *vv.* 9, 10 |

---

[1] sic

## FOLIUM XIV.

Scripti superioris ff. 97, 100.
Scripti inferioris Sura 17, *vv.* 10—32.

f. 97 a.

Incipit أَنَّ لَهُمْ [1]أَجْرً كَبِيرًا وَأَنَّ ٱلَّذِينَ لَا يُؤْمِنُونَ بِٱ Sura 17, *v.* 10

Explicit كَفَى بِنَفْسِكَ ٱلْيَوْمَ عَلَيْكَ حَسِيبًا مَنِ ٱهْتَدَى *vv.* 15, 16

. . . . . . . . لِنَفْسِهِ وَمَنْ ضَلَّ فَإِ . . .

f. 100 b.

Incipit . . . . . تَزِرُ وَازِرَةٌ وِزْرَ أُخْرَى وَمَا كُ . . . *v.* 16

Explicit وَسَعَى لَهَا سَعْيَهَا وَهُوَ مُؤْمِنٌ [1]فَأُولَئِكَ *v.* 20

f. 97 b.

Incipit كَانَ سَعْيُهُمْ مَشْكُورًا كُلًّا نُمِدُّ هَؤُلَآءِ *vv.* 20, 21

Explicit وَقُلْ لَهُمَا قَوْلًا كَرِيمًا وَٱخْفِضْ لَهُمَا جَنَا *vv.* 24, 25

. . . . . . . . . . . . . .

f. 100 a.

Incipit . . . . . . . . . . . . . . . . . . .

سِكُمْ إِنْ تَكُونُوا صَالِحِينَ فَإِنَّهُ كَانَ لِلْأَوَّابِينَ *vv.* 26, 27

Explicit ا ∴ إِنَّ رَبَّكَ يَبْسُطُ ٱلرِّزْقَ لِمَنْ يَشَآءُ وَيَقْدِرُ *vv.* 31, 32

---

[1] sic

## FOLIUM XV.

Scripti superioris ff. 98, 99.
Scripti inferioris Sura 17, *vv.* 32—53.

f. 98 a.

| | | |
|---|---|---|
| Incipit | إِنَّهُ كَانَ [1]بِعِبَدِهِ خَبِيرًا بَصِيرًا وَلَا تَقْتُلُوا | Sura 17, *vv.* 32, 33 |
| Explicit | . . . لًا وَأَوْفُوا ٱلْكَيْلَ إِذَا كِلْتُمْ وَزِنُوا | *vv.* 36, 37 |
| | . . . . . . . . . . . . . . . . . . | |

f. 99 b.

| | | |
|---|---|---|
| Incipit | . . . . وَلَا . . لَيْسَ لَكَ بِهِ . . | *v.* 38 |
| Explicit | مِنَ [1]ٱلْمَلَئِكَةِ إِنَثًا إِنَّكُمْ لَتَقُولُونَ قَوْلًا | *v.* 42 |

f. 98 b.

| | | |
|---|---|---|
| Incipit | عَظِيمًا وَلَقَدْ صَرَّفْنَا فِى هَذَا ٱلْقُرْآنِ لِيَذَّ | *vv.* 42, 43 |
| Explicit | يِنَ لَا يُؤْمِنُونَ بِٱلْآخِرَةِ حِجَابًا مَسْتُورًا وَجَعَلْنَا | *vv.* 47, 48 |
| | . . . . . . . . . . . . . . . . . . | |

f. 99 a.

| | | |
|---|---|---|
| Incipit | . . . ا وَإِذَا ذَكَرْتَ رَبَّكَ فِى . . . . | *vv.* 48, 49 |
| Explicit | فَسَيَقُولُونَ مَنْ يُعِيدُنَا قُلِ ٱلَّذِى فَطَرَكُمْ | *v.* 53 |

---

[1] sic

## FOLIUM XVI.

Scripti superioris ff. 95, 102.
Scripti inferioris Sura 17, *vv.* 53—70.

f. 102 a.

| | | |
|---|---|---|
| Incipit | أَوَّلَ مَرَّةٍ فَسَيُنْغِضُونَ إِلَيْكَ رُؤُسَهُمْ وَيَقُو | Sura 17, *v.* 53 |
| Explicit | . . . . . . . . أَعْلَمُ بِمَنْ فِى ٱلسَّمَوَ | *v.* 57 |
| | . . . . . . . . . . . . . . . | |
| | . . . . . . . . . . . . . . . | |

f. 95 b.

| | | |
|---|---|---|
| Incipit | . . . . . . . . . . . . . . . | |
| | . . . . . . . . . . . . . . . | |
| | . . . . . . . . . . . . . . . | |
| | ابَهُ إِنَّ عَذَابَ رَبِّكَ كَانَ مَحْذُورًا | *v.* 59 |
| Explicit | فَظَلَمُوا . . . . . . . . . . . . . | *v.* 61 |

f. 102 b.

| | | |
|---|---|---|
| Incipit | تَخْوِيفًا وَإِذْ قُلْنَا لَكَ إِنَّ رَبَّكَ [1]احَطَ بِٱ | *vv.* 61, 62 |
| Explicit | . . آءَ مَوْفُورًا وَٱسْتَفْزِزْ مَنِ . . . . . | *vv.* 65, 66 |

f. 95 a.

| | | |
|---|---|---|
| Incipit | . . . . . . . . . . . . . . . | *v.* 66 |
| | وَمَا يَعِدُهُمُ ٱلشَّيْطَ . . . . . . . . | |
| Explicit | [1]ٱلْإِنْسَنُ كَفُوراً [1]أَفَئَمِنْتُمْ أَنْ يَخْسِفَ بِكُمْ [1]جَنِبَ | *vv.* 69, 70 |
| | ٱلْبَرِّ أَوْ يُرْسِلَ عَلَيْكُمْ . . . . . . . . . . | |
| | . . . . . . . . . . . . . . . . . . | |

---

[1] sic

# ARABIC DOCUMENT.

TRANSCRIBED BY PROFESSOR D. S. MARGOLIOUTH.

The three pieces of parchment probably contained the whole of the deed, but about a third of the breadth was cut off, when it was written over; this appears from the amount of the *Basmalah* which remains. Owing to this loss and the obliteration of many words it is probably impossible to reconstruct the document, which contained among other things a deed of sale.

Rashidiyyah (line 10) is one of the villages of Baghdad (Yāḳūt), a little above Baradan, the town about three leagues due north of Baghdad which gave its name to the city gate (Lestrange, *Baghdad during the Caliphate*, p. 174 after Ibn Serapion, J.R.A.S. 1895, p. 271). There was another place of the same name in Africa (*Bibl. Geogr. Arabb.* III. 245), but this deed clearly refers to the former.

It is vexatious that the name of the river or canal on which the irrigated land was situated (line 3) is illegible. None of the canals mentioned by Mr Lestrange seem to correspond with the remaining letters.

The name of the place after which Abdallah is called is hard to read, but must, I think, be what has been printed. A place in Syria called Sakkā is mentioned by Yāḳūt.

In the description of the dinars (line 13) there is a fragment of a word which may possibly be *Ma'mūniyyah*, i.e. dinars coined by Al-Ma'mun, who became Caliph in 198 A.H. (813 A.D.). Makrizi in his monograph on the coinage (ed. Const. 1298, p. 11) says his coins were graved like gems owing to there being no dies. This would fix the date of the contract for the early ninth century, a date which the nature of the writing renders a probable one. Of the proper names the only unusual one is Sumānah, which is probably not unparalleled. Fa'r is given as a proper name in the Ḳāmūs.

*White* land in line 3 according to Dozy means in Egypt land that requires no irrigation. Perhaps it is better to render the phrase here "corn-land."

f. 78 b

1 بسم الله الر]حيم . . . . . . . . . . . . . . . . . .

2 . . . . . . . . . . . . . . . . . . . . . . . . . . . . . . . . . . .

3 . . . . . . . . . . . . . . . . . جميعه ارض بيضا سقى على نهر لا. به حد

4 . . . . . . . . . . . . . . . . . . . . . . . مزرعة تنسب الى اهل

5 من عبد الله بن عيسى السكوى ومن اخته سمانة ابنت عيسى ومن امـ[ـه

6 الكتاب بجميع ما يصير لذلك من حق ومرفق وطريق وسرب ومسيل ماء وبكل

7 مقتضيها منهما عبد الله بن عيسى بن ابى وروان السكوى واخته سمانة

8 . . . . . . . . . . . . . . . . . . . . . الم]ذكور فى هذا الكتاب

* * * * * * * * * * * *

f. 8

9 عبد الله بن عيسى [بن ابى وردان] السكوى ومن اخته سمانة ابنت عيسى السكوى ومن امه رق[ية]

10 ..مد بحضرتهما شى وهذه القطعة من الارض تعرف بالمزرعة المتوجه الى الراشدية حدها م[ن]

11 ورحبتها ومن الغرب تنتهى الى مزرعة تنسب الى ابى سعيد بن ايوب وصالح بن فار اشترى اسط

12 ر]قية ابنت محمد بن عمرو ومن ... واسماء ابنت عبد الله هذا المذكور سابقا من جميع د...

13 ولد... الوجوه كلها باثنين وعشرين دينارا ذهبا عينا مامو.... جيادا د...

14 عي]سى وامه رقية ابنت محمد بن عمرو وحفيدتها اسماء ابنت عبد الله وافية بجوده وابراوه[م]

15 بجميع حقوقه عند عقده هذا البيع المسمى فى هذا الكتاب من قبله لم يحق عليهم شى منه

* * * * * * * * * * * *

f. 83a

16 . . . . . . . . . لا فساد فيه ولا باس ولا خسار فكل ما ارادوا . . . . . .

17 فعلى الجماعة المسمين فى هذا الكتاب ان يسلموا لهما واليهما كل حق يجب لهما علي[هم]

18 لهما عن صاحب امرهم جميع الدين . . . . . يجب عليهم ان ياخذوهم بذلك

19 حياته ووصيا عنه دون ما سواه بعد وفاتهم راض كل واحد منهم بما حكم ع..

20 . . . . . . . . . . . . . . . . . . . . . . . .

21 بدين . . يجئ بحق ثابت نحو ام واخت لا من لا حق لها بعينها فى ذلك ولا . . .

22 لهم دونهما وهولاء لهم ولكل واحد منهم المطالبة بما اوجبه الحق لهم

23 اقر عبد الله بن عيسى بن ابى رروان السكوى عن اخته سمانة ابنت عيسى وامه رقية

24 . . . . . . . . . . . . . واقروا بسماعه وفهمه ومعرفته واشهدوا بذلك كله

1 In the name of God] etc.

2 . . . . . . . . . . . . . . . . . . . . . . . . . .

3 . . . . . the whole of it irrigated corn-land on the river Lā..h bounded

4 . . . . . . . . . . . . . a farm called after the people of

5 From Abdallah Ibn ʻĪsā Al-Sakkawi and from his sister Sumānah Bint ʻĪsā and from his mother

6 the deed with all that appertains thereto of rights, and outhouses, roads, aqueducts, conduits and all

7 to be exacted of them twain by Abdallah Ibn ʻĪsā Ibn Abi Wardān (?) Al-Sakkawi and his sister Sumānah

8 . . . . . . . . . . mentioned in this deed

9 Abdallah Ibn 'Īsā Ibn Abi Wardān (?) Al-Sakkawi and from his sister Sumānah Bint 'Īsā Al-Sakkawi and from his mother Ruḳayyah.

10 ...anything in their presence. And this piece of ground is called the farm of which the boundary goes towards Al-Rashidiyyah, from

11 and its area (?). And to the west it extends to a farm called after Abu Sa'īd Ibn Ayyūb and Ṣāliḥ Ibn Fa'r bought

12 Ruḳayyah Bint Mohammed Ibn 'Amr, and from . . . and Asmā daughter of the aforementioned Abdallah of all

13 . . . all the directions for 22 good dinars of solid gold of the coinage of Mamun (?) . . .

14 'Īsā and his mother Ruḳayyah Bint Mohammed Ibn 'Amr and her grand-daughter Asmā Bint Abdallah carrying out his generosity, and the absolving of them

15 all his rights at the time when he covenanted the sale mentioned in this deed above, of them none shall be incumbent on

16 . . . . . without mischief, harm, or loss therein. And whatever they wish . . . .

17 then it is incumbent on the persons named in this deed to hand over to them twain and for them twain every right which belongs to them over the former

18 to them twain on behalf of the general manager of their affairs all the debt . . . they shall be bound to exact it from them

19 his life, and as his legatee to the exclusion of others after their death each one of them satisfied with what is adjudged

20 . . . . . . . . . . . . . . . . . . .

21 . . . . . who produces an acknowledged right, such as a mother and sister, not a woman who has no rights of her own and no

22 to him to the exclusion of them twain. And to these and each of them there shall be the right to sue for what justice gives him.

23 Abdallah Ibn 'Īsā Ibn Abi Wardān (?) Al-Sakkawi certified on behalf of his sister Sumānah Bint 'Īsā and his mother Ruḳayyah

24 . . . . . . . and they certified to having heard, understood and comprehended it and called as witnesses thereunto

## ERRATA.

| | | | | | | | |
|---|---|---|---|---|---|---|---|
| Page | ܝܐ, | col. a, | line 6 | *for* | ܪܒܐ | *read* | ܪܒܝܐ |
| ,, | ܟܒ, | ,, a, | ,, 16 | ,, | ܠܒܪܗ | ,, | ܕܒܪܗ |
| ,, | ܟܛ, | ,, a, | ,, 17 | ,, | ܣܢܐ | ,, | ܡܪ̈ܐ |
| ,, | ܠܐ, | ,, a, | ,, 2 | ,, | ܕܠܗܢܐ | ,, | ܕܠܒܐ |
| | | | ,, 19 | ,, | ܘܐܙܠ | ,, | ܘܐܙܠܘ |
| ,, | ܠܕ, | | ,, 6 | ,, | ܕܡܒܠܘ | ,, | ܕܡܒܒܘ |
| ,, | ܠܗ, | ,, a, | ,, 4 | ,, | ܛܒܘܢ | ,, | ܛܒܘ |
| ,, | ܡܒ, | ,, a, | ,, 12 | ,, | ܕܛܘܒܢܐ | ,, | ܕܛܘܒܢܐ |
| ,, | ܡܕ, | | ,, 2 | ,, | ܘܪܒܢܬ[1] | ,, | ܘܒܒܢܬ |
| ,, | ܡܗ, | ,, b, | ,, 13 | ,, | ܘܫܩܠܝ | ,, | ܘܫܩܠ̈ܝ |
| ,, | ܡܘ, | ,, a, | ,, 11 | ,, | ܕܢܩܘܡ | ,, | ܕܩܘܡ |
| ,, | ܡܙ, | ,, a, | ,, 1 | ,, | ܕܢܗܪܐ | ,, | ܕܐܬܬܚܝܘܢ |
| ,, | ܡܛ, | ,, a, | ,, 12 | ,, | ܒܗܘܢ | ,, | ܒܗܝ |
| ,, | ܢܚ, | ,, a, | ,, 10 | ,, | ܓ̈ܠܝܢܐ | ,, | ܠܓ̈ܠܝܢܐ |
| ,, | ܢܒ, | ,, b, | ,, 14 | ,, | ܒܝ ܠܢܐ | ,, | ܒܝ ܠܝܢܐ |
| ,, | ܢܘ, | ,, a, | ,, 17 | ,, | ܕܒܡܫܬܪܪ | ,, | ܕܒܡܫܬܒܪ |
| | | ,, b, | ,, 22 | ,, | ܪ̈ܚܡܐ | ,, | ܪ̈ܚܡܬܐ |
| ,, | ܣܐ, | ,, a, | ,, 9 | ,, | ܐܠܐ ܐܠܐ | ,, | ܐܢܐ ܠܐ |
| ,, | ܣܓ, | ,, a, | ,, 3 | ,, | ܕܐܫܒܚܬܘܢ | ,, | ܕܡܫܒܚܬܘܢ |
| ,, | ܥܒ, | ,, b, | ,, 11 | ,, | ܐܡܟܐ | ,, | ܐܢܐ |
| ,, | ܥܛ, | ,, a, | ,, 5 | ,, | ܘܡܒܪܝܢ | ,, | ܕܡܒܪܝܢ |
| ,, | ܦܐ, | ,, b, | ,, 25 | ,, | ܘܐܫܬܝܢ | ,, | ܘܐܫܬܟܢ |
| ,, | ܦܛ, | ,, b, | ,, 24 | ,, | ܡ̈ܚܝܢ | ,, | ܫܒܝܢ |
| ,, | ܩܒ, | | ,, 23 | ,, | ܐܒܒܪ | ,, | ܐܒܒܕ |
| ,, | ܩܚ, | | ,, 16 | ,, | ܕܠܗܬܢ | ,, | ܕܠܗܬܟ |
| ,, | ܩܝܒ, | | ,, 2 | ,, | ܘܢܫܬܪܪܢ | ,, | ܘܢܫܬܪܕܢ |
| ,, | 17, | | ,, 1 | ,, | captain | ,, | fuller |

[1] sic in Cod.

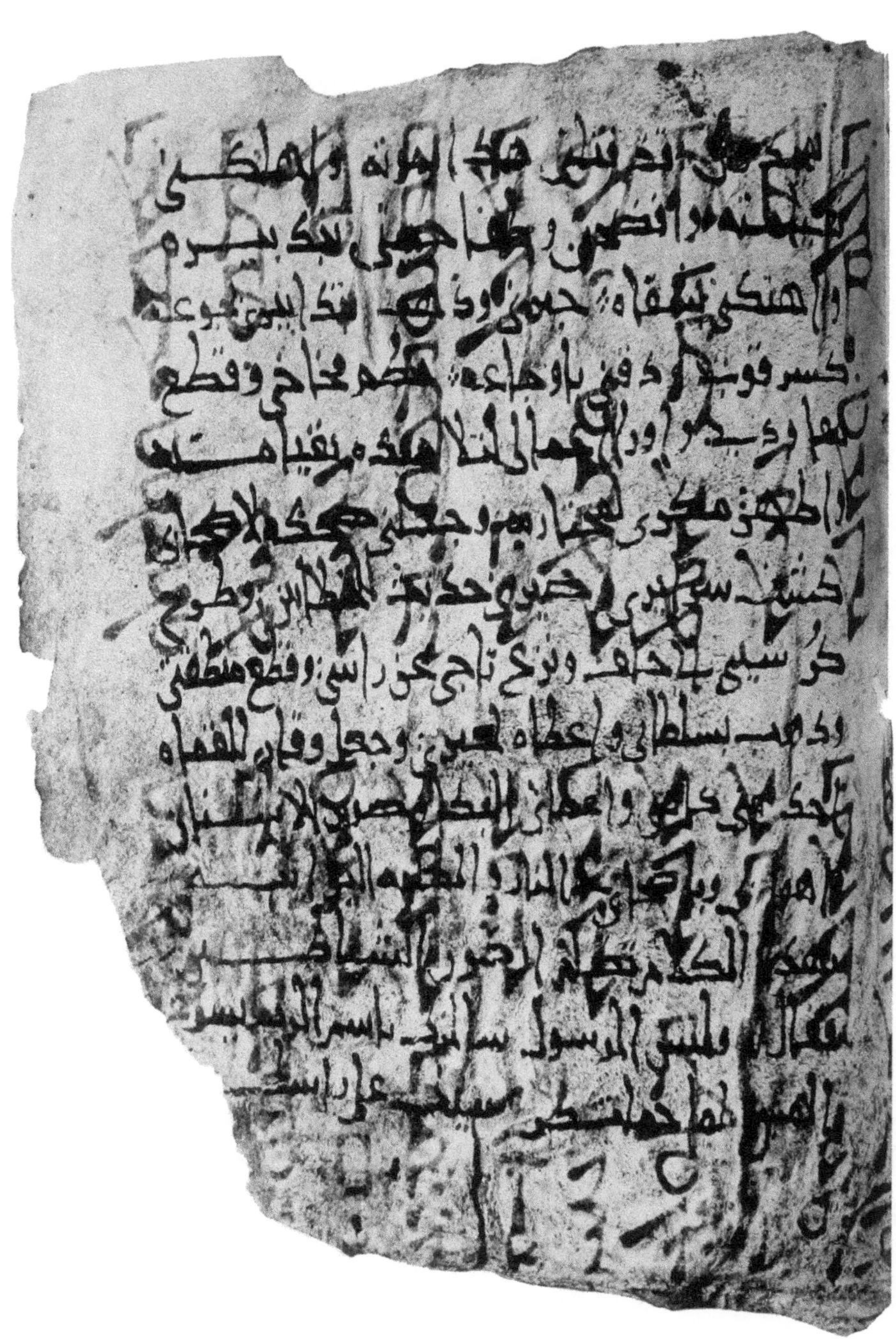

PESHITTA
John VI. 5
ff. 135a

GOSPELS
3—58
136$^{b}$

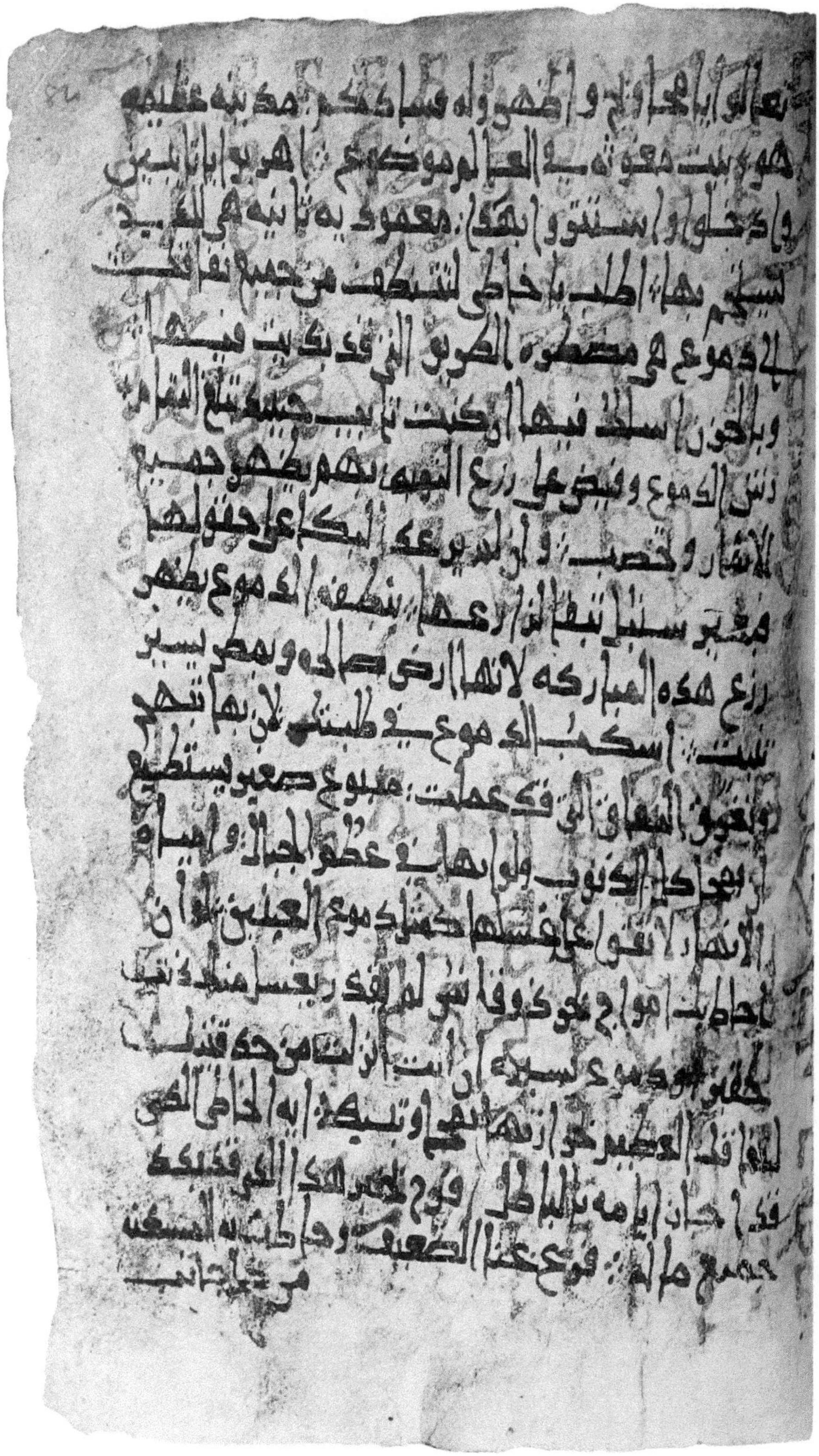

PESHITTA
Matt. x. 19.
ff. 82a

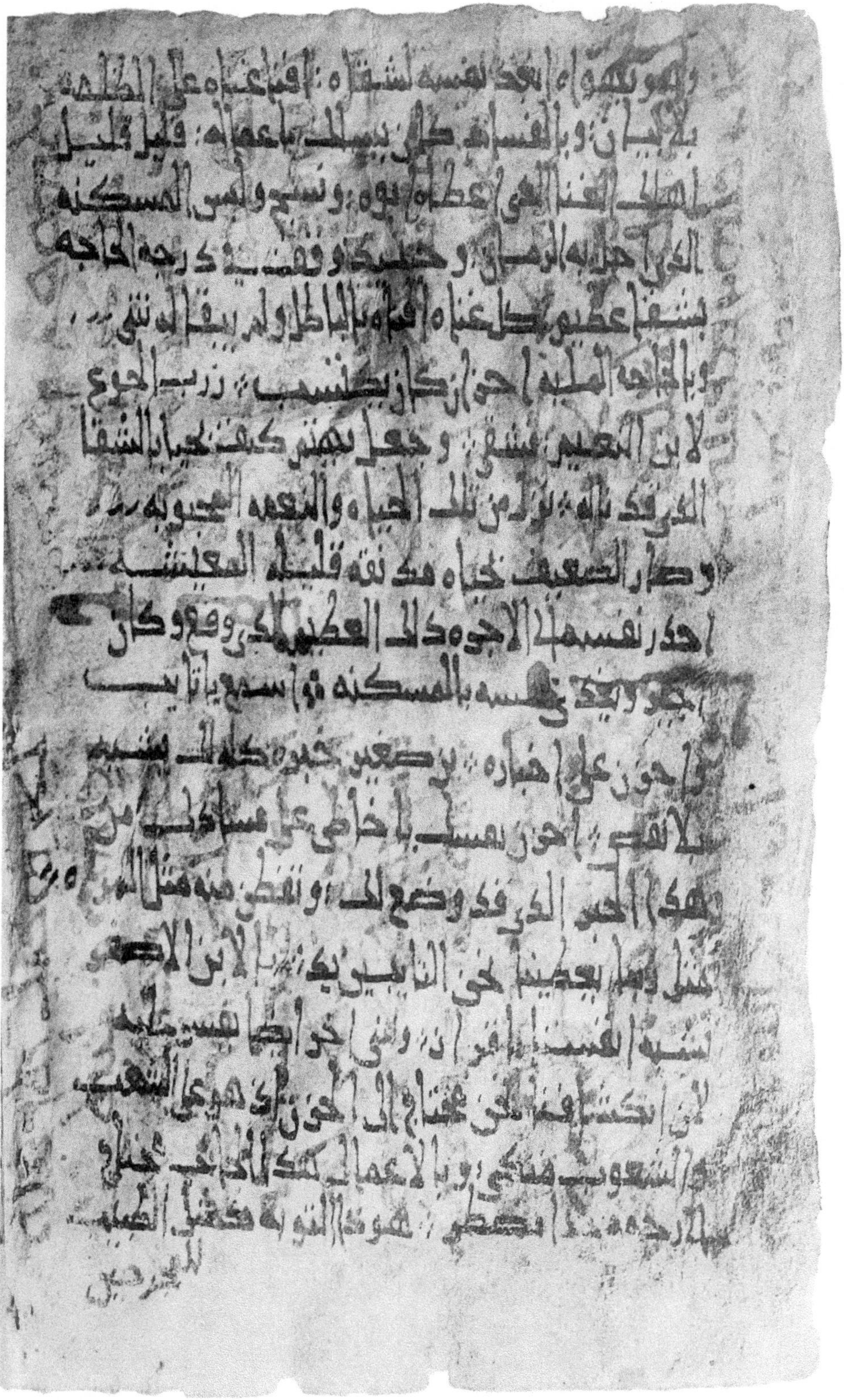

GOSPELS

—28[a]

81[b]

CORÂN I.
ff. 151,[a]
Sura 44,

150.

*v.*3 — Sura 45, *v.* 5

CORÂN
ff. 20[b]
Sura 16,

II.

13ª

*vv.* 32—41

PROTEVANGELIUM

ff. 139,[b]

JACOBI.

= page ܡܒ

TRANSITUS

ff. 39[a], 42[b]

MARIAE.

= page حد

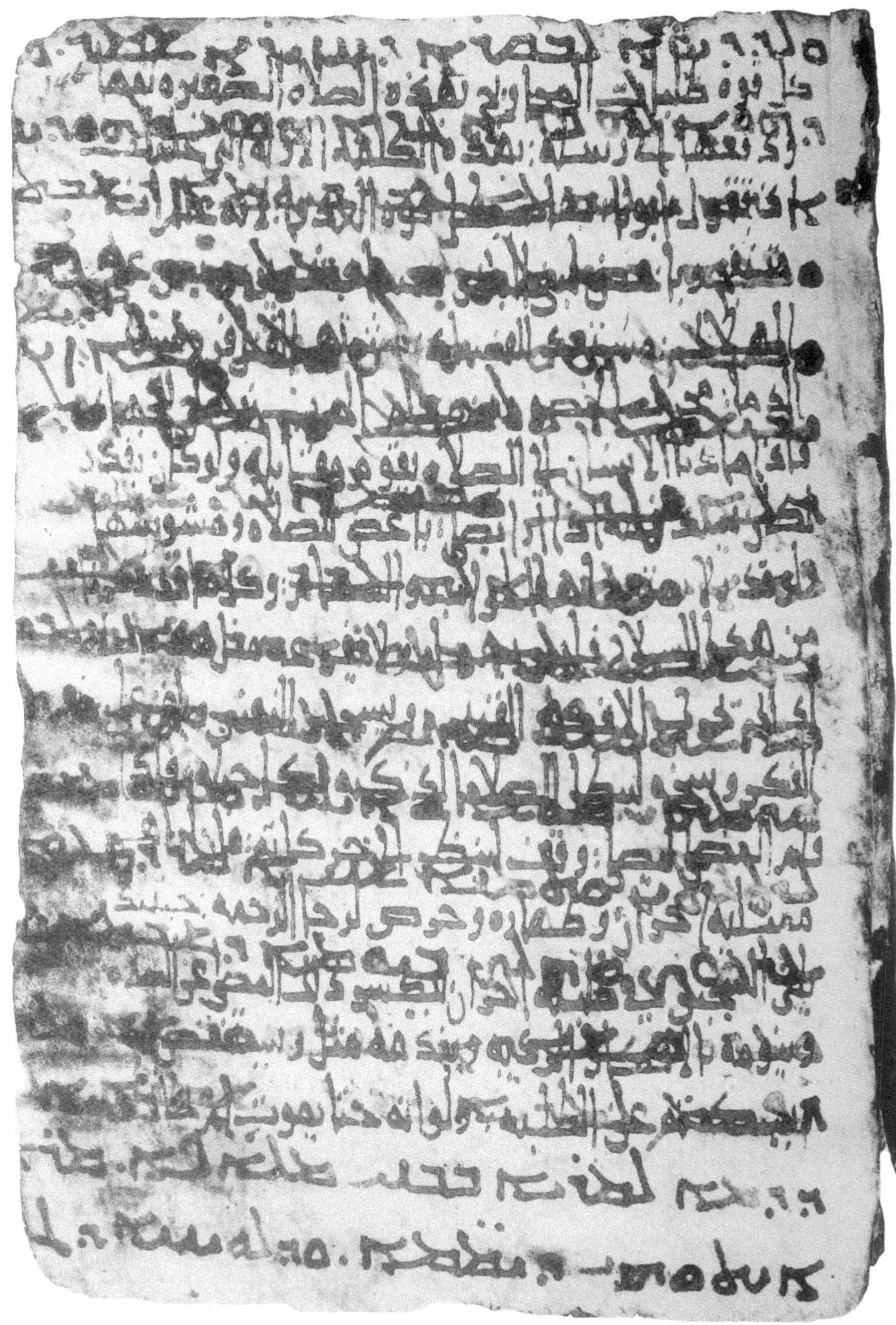

Syriac Hymn
f. 146a

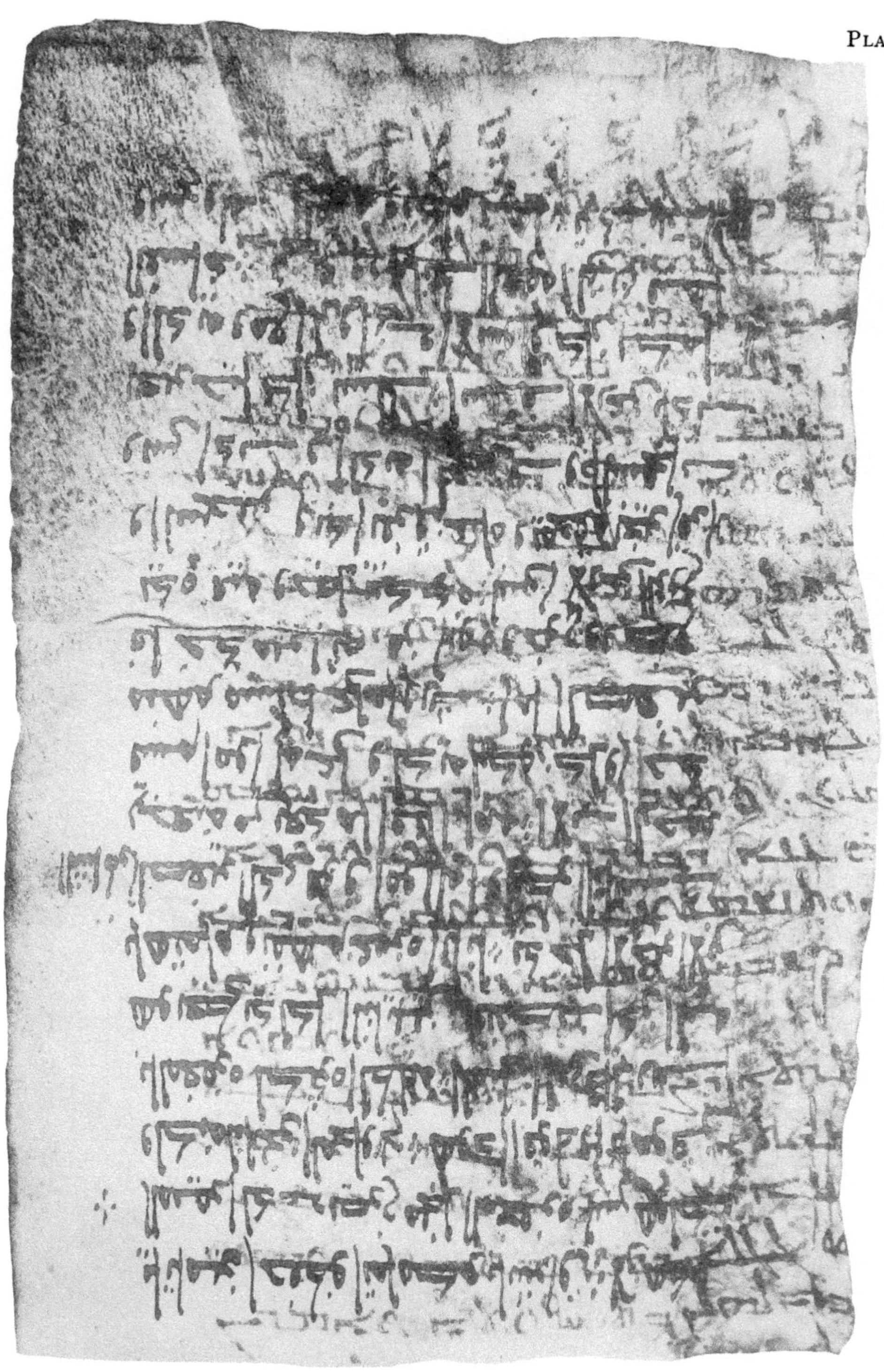

DOUBLE PALIMPSEST

f. 80[b]

Isaiah lx. 2[b]—7 Exod. xiv. 24, 25[a]

# PROTEVANGELIUM JACOBI.

## TRANSLATION.

IN the hope of the Holy Trinity, one in essence, we begin to write p. 2
the book of the History of the Mother of God, Mary, from the day of
her birth until the day of her exit from this world. May her prayer be with
us! Amen, amen.

Book the First about her parents, and also about her Annunciation by the
Angel.

There was a certain man whose name was Yônakîr who was very rich in Cf. Tisch. I
the fear of God. And he presented his offerings to the Lord in double
measure, saying to himself, "Let this superabundance which I offer be on
behalf of all the people. And that portion which I owe by the law I offer
it to the Lord that it may be to me for expiation." And when the great
day of the Lord drew near, in which the children of Israel offered their gifts,
Rûbîl arose before Yônakîr and said unto him, "It is not lawful for thee to
make an offering before me; because thou hast not produced seed unto Israel."
And Yônakîr was grieved exceedingly; and he went to his house in sadness.
And he said to the twelve tribes of Israel, "Have I alone not produced
seed in Israel?" And he looked, and sought, and investigated. And he found
that in the generations that are past, all righteous men have established seed
in Israel. And he remembered the patriarchs Abraham and Sara his wife, that
in their latest days they had a son, Isaac. And Yônakîr was grieved exceedingly. And he was neither seen by his wife, nor did he go to his house; but p. 3
he betook himself to a desert place and pitched his tent there. And he
fasted there for forty days and forty nights. And he said to himself, "I will
neither eat nor drink until the Lord God visit me. But prayer shall be to me
in the place of food and drink." But Hanna his wife sat mourning. And she Tisch. II
lamented with two lamentations saying, "I lament first because of my widow-
hood; and secondly, because I am debarred from bearing." When the day
of the Lord drew near Yônâthîm her handmaiden said to her, "How long
wilt thou humble thy soul? Behold, the great day of the Lord draweth nigh
when it is not lawful to mourn. But take to thyself this head-band, which my
mistress gave me as my wages, and bind thou it on. It is not lawful for me
to bind it on, because I am a maid-servant, and the sign of the kingdom is

upon it." She said unto her, "Get thee hence, whilst I have not committed these sins; behold, the Lord hath humbled me greatly. And mayhap this hath been given to thee with guile, and thou hast brought it to me that thou mightest make me share in thy sins."

Yônâthîm said to her, "What shall I say? would that it were good! Behold, God hath withheld His mercy from thee, that thou mayest not yield fruit in Israel." And when Hanna heard these things, she was grieved exceedingly. And she took off her garments of mourning, and washed her head, and put on royal raiment. And at the ninth hour she went down to walk in the garden. And she sat beneath the shade of a laurel tree. And she prayed, and besought, and blessed the Lord, saying, "O God of our
p. 4 fathers, bless me! and hear my prayer and my entreaty, as Thou didst bless my mother Sara, and didst give her a son, Isaac."

Tisch. III And while she said these things, she raised her eyes towards heaven, and she saw a sparrow's nest in the laurel tree. And she sighed to herself and said, "Why am I not unborn? Or how and why was the womb prepared for me? for behold I alone am a curse to the children of Israel. They deride and mock me; and they thrust me forth from the house of the Lord God. Or why am I not at least like the dumb beasts, for even they bear [children] before Thee, O Lord! Or why am I not like this earth, for it also yieldeth the fruits in their seasons, and it blesseth Thee, the Lord." And when Hanna
Tisch. IV had said these things, the angel of the Lord stood before her and said unto her, "Hanna, the Lord hath heard thy supplication. Thou shalt conceive, and shalt give birth, and thy seed shall be spoken of in all the world." And Hanna said, "As the Lord my God liveth, if there be a child, whether it be a male or a female, I will give it to the Lord God. And it shall serve before Him all the days of its life." And immediately two messengers came saying to her, "Behold Yônakîr cometh with his flock, because the angel of the Lord hath said unto him, 'Yônakîr, the Lord hath heard thy supplication, get thee down hence. For behold! Hanna thy wife is with child.'" And Yônakîr went down, and called all his shepherds, and said unto them, "Bring me hither ten ewe-lambs of the flock in which is no blemish; and let these ten fat lambs be for the Lord God. And bring me ten fat bull-calves without blemish, and let them be for the priests and for the elders of the people, and a hundred kids of the goats, and let them be for all the people."

p. 5 And when Yônakîr came with his flock, Hanna was standing by the wayside. And she saw Yônakîr; and she hung on his neck saying to him, "Now I know that the Lord my God hath blessed me exceedingly. For behold! I was a widow, henceforth I am not a widow; I was barren, and I had no children, behold I am with child." And when Yônakîr had rested the first
Tisch. V day in his house, he made offerings for himself, saying, "If the Lord my God is reconciled to me, it will be known in the insignia that is betwixt the eyes of the priest; until he goeth up to the altar of the Lord, and He seeth no sins in him." And Yônakîr said, "Now I know that the Lord my God is reconciled

to me, and He hath forgiven me all my sins." And Yônakîr went down from
the house of the Lord justified; and went to his house.

And when Hanna's days were fulfilled, in the ninth month she brought
forth. And Hanna said: "My soul doth magnify the Lord on this day," and
she lay down on the bed. And when the days were fulfilled, Hanna washed
herself as for a purification and gave the breast to her daughter. And day Tisch. VI
after day the girl grew strong; and when she was six months old her mother
set her on the ground to see if she could stand. And she lifted her foot
seven times and came to her mother. And then her mother caught her up,
saying, "As the Lord my God liveth, thou shalt not walk on this until I
shall carry thee to the house of the Lord." And her parents made her chamber
a sanctuary. And they did not allow anything dirty or impure to come near
it. And her mother said, "Let no one approach it who is not clean, but
rather let those virgins, daughters of the Hebrews come, who are undefiled.
And let them be with her." And they came and rejoiced with her.

Now when the maiden was a year old, Yônakîr made a great reception, and p. 6
he bade the priests, and the chief priests, and the elders and scribes of the
people. And they blessed her and said, "The God of our fathers bless this
maiden and give her a name glorious in all generations and amongst all
peoples." And all the people said "Amen."

And when they presented her again to the high priests they blessed her,
saying, "The God of our fathers who is on high bless this maiden with a
new blessing, which shall not pass away and shall not fail." And her mother
caught her, and took her up to the sanctuary which they had prepared for her
in her chamber. And she sung a holy hymn saying, "The Lord hath visited
me, and hath made the reproach of mine enemies to pass away from me. And
the Lord my God hath given me the fruit of righteousness. And who will
announce to the sons of Rûbîl that Hanna is giving suck? Let the twelve
tribes of the sons of Israel hear that Hanna is giving suck." And she left the
girl in her chamber and went out and served the guests. And when the feast
was ended, they went down rejoicing and praising God. And the maiden Tisch.
grew in months. VII

And when she was two years old, Yônakîr said unto Hanna his wife, "Let
us carry this maiden to the temple of the Lord, according to what we have
promised, lest the Lord turn away His face from us, and accept not our gift." Tisch.
And Hanna said, "Let us wait till the third year lest she should long for her p. 15
father and her mother." And Yônakîr said, "Thou hast well spoken." And
when the maiden was three years old, he said, "Let us call virgins of the
daughters of the Hebrews, undefiled, and let them hold burning lamps before
her, that she may not turn back and her heart be made captive, away from
the house of the Lord." And they did thus until they went up to the temple
of the Lord.

And when she arrived at His temple, the priests received her and kissed p. 7
her, and said to her, "May the Lord magnify thy name in all generations.

Because in thee the Lord revealeth redemption unto men." And the priest
made the maiden sit on the third step of the temple, and the Lord shed
grace upon her; and she danced with her feet, and all the children of Israel
Tisch. VIII loved her. And they called her name Mary. And her parents went down
thence, praising the Lord, that she did not turn towards them.

She was in the temple of the Lord like a dove that is fed; and she took
her nourishment from the hand of an angel. And when she had grown
up, the priests took counsel saying, "Behold, Mary has become twelve years
old in the temple of the Lord. What shall we do with her, that she may
not defile the temple of the Lord God?" And the priests said unto the
Tisch. p. 17 high-priest, "Go thou into the sanctuary, and pray for her, and whatsoever
God may show thee we will do."

And [he went] into the Holy of Holies, having upon him the twelve bells.
And he prayed concerning her, and besought God. And the angel of the
Lord replied saying unto him, "Zacharia, Zacharia, assemble all the widowers
of the nation and let each of them bring thee a staff. And by which of the
staves the Lord shall show thee a sign, let its owner have Mary to wife." Then
heralds went forth through all the land of Judaea, and they blew the trumpet
of the Lord, and immediately [the people] assembled and came to the chief
priests, and they gave them their staves; and when the priest had received
Tisch. IX them he went into the temple and prayed. And when he had finished his
prayer, he took the staves and went out. And he gave them their staves,
and no sign was visible. But there was the last staff belonging to Joseph.
p. 8 He took it, and a dove went out of the staff and remained on Joseph's
head. And the priests said unto him, "Joseph, the virgin has come to thee
from the Lord, by thy lot, that thou shouldest take her and keep her."
Joseph answered and said, "I have children and they are men; and
this is a girl. Perhaps some event may happen, and I may become a
scorn in Israel." And the priests said to him, "Joseph, fear God; and
remember what He did to the sons of Korah and Dathan and Abiram;
how the earth was opened, and swallowed them because they rose in
strife. And now be afraid, and take her into thy keeping." And Joseph
fearing, said to Mary, "Behold! I have taken thee from the temple of
the Lord, and now behold! I leave thee in my house, and I will go
and build my houses, and then I will come beside thee. Henceforth
p. 9 the Lord will be thy keeper."

Tisch. X And it came to pass that there was a council of the priests, and
they said, "Let us make a curtain for the temple of the Lord."
And the Priest said: "Summon to me eight virgins of the tribe of
King David who are chaste and holy." And the officers went
seeking and found seven. And the Priest remembered the girl Mary,
that she also was of the tribe of David's house; and that she was

pure unto God. And the officers went and brought her to the temple. And the Priest said: "Let them cast lots as to which of these it shall fall to weave the gold, and to which the white and to which the linen and to which the silk and to which the violet and to which the scarlet and to which the purple." And the purple and scarlet came to Mary, and she took [them] and went to her house. Now at that time Zacharia was dumb, and Samuel was priest instead of him until Zacharia should speak.

Now Mary took the scarlet and wove it: and she took a pitcher Tisch. XI
and went to fill it with water, and lo! a voice was heard which said to her: "Hail to thee O favored one! the Lord is with thee; blessed art thou among women." And Mary looked to the right and to the left that she might see whence that voice had been heard by her. And being terrified she went into her house and put down her pitcher. And she had taken the purple and had sat down, and separated it[1]. And behold! the angel of the Lord stood before
her and said to her: "Fear not, Mary, for lo! thou hast found p. 10
favour before the Lord of all; and thou shalt conceive by His word." And when she heard [it] she considered in herself, saying, "Shall I conceive and bring forth from the Lord, as all women bring forth?" And behold, the angel of the Lord was sent; and he said unto her: "Not thus, Mary; but the power of the Lord shall overshadow thee; because He Who shall be born of thee is holy, and He shall be called the Son of the Highest. And thou shalt call His name Jesus, for He shall save His people from sins." And Mary said, "Behold I am the handmaiden of God, be it unto me from His presence according as thou hast said."

And Mary made the purple and carried it to the priest. And Tisch. XII
the priest blessed her, saying, "Mary, the Lord God hath magnified thy name, and thou shalt be blessed in all generations of the earth." And Mary was filled with joy, and went to Elizabeth her cousin. And she knocked at the door. And when Elizabeth heard [it] she threw down the sieve which she was holding, and came to the door and opened [it] to her. And Elizabeth blessed her, saying, "Who hath done this unto me, that the mother of my Lord should come to me? For lo! when thou didst speak, he who is within me leapt and blessed thee."

[1] Cod. the purple.

But Mary forgot the words which Gabriel had spoken to her and
p. 11 looked up to heaven, saying, "Lord, who am I that all generations
should call me blessed?" And she was with Elizabeth for three
months, and day by day her womb grew large. And Mary was
afraid and came to her house. And she hid herself from the children
of Israel, being then sixteen years old, when these mysteries took
place

Tisch. XIII And when it was the sixth month with her, Joseph came from the
buildings which he was rearing. And he went in and found Mary
great with child. And he beat his face with his hands and threw
himself on the ground and wept bitterly and said, "With what face
shall I look to the Lord God? What shall I pray for about this girl?
because while she was a virgin I took her from the temple of the
Lord God, and I have not guarded her. Who has practised deceit?
or who has done this wickedness in my house? who has captured
this adorable virgin from me, and has defiled her? Perhaps it has
happened to me anew as to Adam; for at the moment when
Adam was praising God, (the serpent) found Eve alone and deceived
her and defiled her. Thus has it happened also to me." And Joseph
arose from the sackcloth and he called Mary and said unto her, "O
woman on whom was the care of God! what is this that thou hast
done? thou hast forgotten the Lord God; why hast thou done thus,
p. 12 and hast forgotten the Lord? Why hast thou altogether humbled
thyself, thou who wast reared in the Holy of Holies?" But she
wept bitterly, saying, "As the Lord my God liveth, I am chaste, and
no man hath known me." Joseph said unto her, "Whence then is
this that is in thy womb?" Mary said: "As the God of Israel liveth
I know not whence this is that is within me."

Tisch. XIV And Joseph feared greatly, and it grieved him concerning her; and he asked about her, what he should do unto her. And he said to himself, "If I hide this sin concerning her, I shall be found fighting against the law of the Lord; and if I reveal it concerning her to the children of Israel, I fear lest the spirit of an angel be within her, and I shall be found having delivered up innocent blood to the doom of death. What therefore shall I do to her? I shall dismiss her secretly." Then night overtook him, and behold! the angel of the Lord appeared unto him in a dream, and said unto him, "Joseph, fear not for the girl; for that which is within her is of the Holy Ghost. And she shall bear to thee a son, and thou shalt call[1] his name Jesus, for he shall deliver his people from their sins." And Joseph arose from his sleep, and praised the God of Israel, Who had given His grace, and had protected her.

And Hanna[2] the scribe came to him, saying to him, "Joseph, why p. 13
didst thou not appear in the synagogue?" And Joseph said unto Tisch. XV
him: "Because I was tired from the road, and I rested the first day." And Hanna turned and saw Mary, her womb being great. And he went to the high priest, and said unto him, "Joseph, about whom thou didst bear witness, has done a great iniquity." And the high priest said: "What is this?" And Hanna the scribe said: "Joseph has defiled the virgin whom he took from the temple of the Lord, and has secretly anticipated his marriage, and has not made it known to the children of Israel." And Hanna the scribe said unto him, "Send officers and thou shalt find the virgin who is great with child."

And the officers went and found it even as Hanna had said. And they brought them to the temple, and set them before the judges. And the priest said unto Mary: "Mary, what is this that thou hast done, and why hast thou humbled thyself and hast forgotten the Lord thy God, thou who wast reared in the Holy of Holies, and hast received food from the hand of an angel and hast heard their hymns twice and hast danced before them, why didst thou do all this?" And she wept bitterly and said: "As the Lord my God liveth, I am pure before Him, and no man hath known me." And the priest said unto Joseph: "What is this that thou hast done?" Joseph said: "As the Lord my God liveth, I am pure from her." And the priest
said unto him: "Do not bear false witness, but say truly: Hast thou p. 14
secretly anticipated thy marriage? and hast not made it known to the children of Israel? and hast not bowed thy head beneath the mighty hands of the Lord, that so thy seed might be blessed?" But
Joseph held his peace. And the priest said unto him: "Return the Tisch.
virgin whom thou didst take from the temple of the Lord." And XVI
Joseph was standing and weeping. And the priest continued, saying to him: "I will make you drink the (spiced) waters of trial of the Lord and they will reveal your sins before your eyes." And the priest

[1] or "she shall call."  [2] or "Ananias."

took Joseph and made him drink, and sent him to the mountain. And he climbed up, and came down quite well. Then he made the girl drink also, and sent her to the mountain, and she also came down quite well. And all the people were astonished that sin was not found in them. And the priest said unto them: "If the Lord God has not revealed your sin, neither will I judge you." And he let them go away, and Joseph took Mary off and led her to his house rejoicing and praising the God of Israel.

Tisch. XVII And it came to pass that there was a decree of the king that the people who were in Bethlehem of Judaea should be inscribed. And Joseph said: "I shall inscribe my sons; but as for this girl, what shall I do to her? I am ashamed to inscribe her as my wife.
p. 15 Wright's Translation p. 1 And to inscribe her as my daughter I would be false, and behold, also all the children of Israel know that she is not my daughter. But nevertheless the day of the Lord will do as it pleases."

And he saddled his ass, and made her sit (upon it), and his son led (it). Joseph came and his sons; and when they had reached the third mile, Joseph saw that she was sad; and Joseph said: "Perhaps that which is in her grieves and pains her." Then again Joseph turned and saw her laughing; and he said to her: "Mary! what is this? that at one time I see thy face laughing, and at another time sad?" And she said to Joseph, "I see two nations with my eyes, the one nation weeping and mourning, and the other nation rejoicing and exulting." And when they had got half-way, Mary says to Joseph: "Take me down from the ass, for that which is within me is hastening to come forth." And Joseph took her down, and said to her: "Whither shall I carry thee? or where shall I hide thy modesty? for behold! we are in a desert place."

Tisch. XVIII And he found a cave there, and made her go in thither, and made his sons stand by her side, and went out to look for a Hebrew midwife in the district of Bethlehem. But I Joseph was walking about, and I saw the zenith of heaven standing; and I saw the air, and I saw it astonied, and the birds quiet. And I looked at the earth, and I saw a tub standing and the labourers resting, and their
p. 16 hands were in the tub; and they were eating but not eating, and drinking but not drinking; and they were putting their hands to their mouths and not bringing them near; but their faces were all looking

upwards; and I saw they were calling to their sheep, and their sheep were standing, and a shepherd raised his hand to strike them, and his hand stopped and remained up; and I saw the goats standing on the bank of a river, and I saw them[1] putting their mouths to the water to drink, and they did not drink. And suddenly everything was loosened and ran into its place[2].

Then I saw a woman coming down from the mountain, and she Tisch.
says to me: "Man, whither art thou going?" And I said to her: "I XIX
am seeking a Hebrew midwife." And she said to me: "Art thou of
Israel?" and I said to her: "Yea." And she said to me: "Who is
this, who is in labour in this cave?" And I said to her: "She is my
betrothed." And she said to me: "Is she not thy wife?" And I
said to her: "It is Mary, who was brought up in the temple of the
Lord, and it fell to her by lot to be my wife, and she has not become
my wife, but is with child by the Holy Spirit." And the midwife
said: "Is this true?" Joseph said to the midwife: "Come, and thou
shalt see." And she went with him, and stood in that place which
was in the cave. And a cloud of light was overshadowing the cave.
And the woman said, "My soul thanks the Lord this day, for mine p. 17
eyes have seen wonderful things this day, great and glorious. For
a Redeemer is born to Israel." The cloud rose up immediately from
the cave, and a great light such as eyes could not bear, was seen
in the cave. And little by little the light withdrew until the baby
appeared, and he came and took the breast of Mary his mother.
And the midwife cried out and said: "This day is a great day for
me, for I have seen this great sight to-day." And when the midwife
had gone forth from the cave, Salome met her, and she says to her:
"Salome! God be with thee! I have a new sight to relate to thee.
A virgin has brought forth—a thing of which this nature is not
capable." And Salome said: "As the Lord my God liveth, unless I
see with my eyes, I will not believe that a virgin has indeed brought
forth."

And the midwife went into the cave and says to Mary, "Mary! Tisch. XX
Mary! show thyself; for the dispute about thee is not small; but show thyself, whether thou art a virgin." And Salome entered and drew near and saw that she was a virgin; and Salome

[1] Cod. "the goats." [2] literally, "order."

wailed and said: "Woe unto my wickedness and my unbelief! for
I have tempted the living God, and lo! my hand is burning and
dropping from me." And Salome knelt before the Lord saying, "O
Lord God of my fathers! remember me, because I am the seed of
p. 18 Abraham, and Isaac and of Jacob, and do not expose me before the
children of Israel. But send to those who gave me birth. O Lord!
thou knowest that in Thy name I practised healing, and from Thee I
took the reward." And lo! an angel answered, saying to Salome:
"Salome, the Lord hath heard thine entreaty. Go, bring thy hands
near to the boy, and lift him up, and thou shalt have healing and
deliverance." And Salome was filled with joy, and she drew near to
the boy, and approached him saying, "I draw nigh, because I have
sinned in my heart, that I may worship the boy." And she said,
"This one is born a king unto Israel." And Salome was healed and
went forth from the cave justified. And behold, a voice was heard
by her, saying to her: "Hail! do not reveal these great miracles which
thou hast seen, until the boy enters Jerusalem."

Tisch. XXI And lo! Joseph prepared to go forth into Judaea. And there
was a tumult in Bethlehem of Judaea, for the Magi came saying:
"Where is the king of Judaea who is born? For we have seen his
star in the East, and we are come to worship him." And when
Herod heard (this) he was greatly troubled, and sent apparitors after
the Magi, and sent also to call the chief priests, and asked them in the
Pretorium, saying to them: "Where is it written for you that the
Messiah shall be born? and what has been heard by you concerning
p. 19 him?" They say to him: "He will be born in Bethlehem of Judaea;
for thus it is written." And he asked the Magi, saying to them:
"What sign have ye seen in heaven concerning this king who is
born?" The Magi say unto him, "We have seen a star which is
greater in its size shining amongst these stars, so much so that by its
light they are not seen at all; and we know that a king is born to
Israel, and we are come to worship him." And Herod the king said
to them: "Go, search for him, and if ye have found him, come tell
me, that I also may come and worship him." And the Magi went
forth, and lo! the star which they had seen in the East appeared
to them [and] went before them until they came to the cave, and
it stood above the head of the boy. And when the Magi saw the

boy with Mary his mother, they fell down and worshipped him;
and they answered and said: "Glory be to God in the highest, and
peace upon earth, and good will to men." And they opened their
caskets, and presented offerings to him, gold, and frankincense and
myrrh. And the angels appeared to them and said that they should
not go into Judaea. And they came by another road. And when
Herod knew that the Magi had mocked him, he was wroth, and he Tisch.
sent murderers, and ordered them to murder all the infants, from the XXII
child of two years old and downwards, according to the time which
the Magi had told him. And when Mary heard that the infants were
being slain, she was afraid, and she took the boy, and wrapped him p. 20
in swaddling clothes, and laid him in the manger of the oxen.
Elizabeth too, when she heard that John was sought for, took him
and went up with him to the mountain, and was looking where she
might hide him. Then Elizabeth sighed, and said to the mountain:
"O Mountain of God! receive the mother with her son." And
Elizabeth was not able to climb up. And suddenly the mountain
opened and received her. And a great light lightened them in the
mountain; because the angel of the Lord was with them, and was
guarding them.

But Herod was seeking John; and he sent apparitors to Zacharia Tisch.
to the temple, and said to him: "Where hast thou hidden thy son?" XXIII
And Zacharia answered and said unto them: "I am a minister of
God, and am constantly in the temple of the Lord; I do not know
where my son is." And the apparitors went and told him all these
things. And Herod was wroth and said: "His son is going to reign
over Israel." And he sent the apparitors, and they said to him: "Tell
us truly, where is thy son? Or dost thou not know that thy blood
is under my hand?" And the apparitors went and told him all these
things. And he said: "The Lord is witness that thou hast shed my
blood; but my spirit the Lord will receive because thou hast shed
innocent blood without crime in front of the door of the temple of the
Lord." Nor did any one know how Zacharia was slain, and the p. 21
children of Israel did not know how he was slain; but at the time of
salutation the priests went; and the blessing of Zacharia did not meet Tisch.
them according to custom; and the priests were standing and awaiting XXIV
Zacharia that they might greet him in prayer and might praise the

Most High. And when he tarried, they were all afraid, and one of them dared to enter the sanctuary, and he saw beside the altar of the Lord, the blood that had been shed and was congealed. And a voice was heard, saying, "Zacharia is slain, and his blood shall not be washed away until the avenger shall come." And when he heard these words, he was afraid and he went out and made known to the priests what he had seen and heard. And they ventured to see what had happened beside the porch of the temple. And they all wailed and rent their garments from the top to the bottom. And they did not find his body but they found his blood congealed like a stone; and they were afraid. And they went out and made [it] known that Zacharia was slain. And when all the tribes of the people heard it, they mourned and wept for three days and three nights. And after three days and three nights, the priests deliberated whom they should appoint a priest in the place of Zacharia; and the lot of Simeon came up. This is he to whom it was revealed by the Holy Spirit,
p. 22 that he should not taste death until he saw the Lord the Messiah in a body.

Tisch. XXV And I, James wrote this book, when there was a tumult in Jerusalem, when Herod died a bitter death; and I withdrew to a desert place, until the tumult subsided from Jerusalem.

But I praise the Lord Who has given me wisdom to write this book.

# [TRANSITUS MARIAE.]

## [BOOK I.]

cf. J. S. L. vol. 6 p. 129. The peace of God, who sent His Son, and He came into the world; and the peace of the Son, who migrated from heaven and dwelt in Mary; and the peace of the Holy Spirit, the τραγῳδὸς who sings and the Paraclete who is praised; the peace of the Lord of created beings; the glory of whose Godhead created beings are not able to comprehend, who left the chariot that is adorned in the supernal heights, and came and dwelt in the bosom of Mary the virgin; be with us and with all our congregation to bless the crowns of the priests our fathers, who sit at the head of their flocks, for ever. Amen.

Open, Lord, the gate of heaven to our prayer at this time; and let a sweet perfume ascend from our congregation to the supernal ranks; and let the trumpets of the archangels sound in heaven, and the bands of the supernals stand rank on rank; and let there be
praise in heaven before the king, the Messiah, and from all the p. 23
mansions of the Father's house let the voices of the guardian angels sing; and let troops stand facing troops, and ranks with ranks, and armies opposite armies; and let there be praise and a sweet perfume before God, and thanksgiving and worship to the Messiah, and laudations with hallelujahs to the Holy Spirit.

The exit of the blessed Lady Mary from this world, our brethren, we call to mind before you. Command, Lord, a blessing on all our congregation who hope for thy mercies to arise upon us. Appoint the priests who are holy, with the crown of the glorious King who has chosen them for His honour. Command, Lord, a blessing and a good reward on the ministers, that they may glorify; on the rich that they may laud; and upon the poor, that they may become rich; upon the old men, that they may praise; upon the youths that they may bless; and on the boys, that they may glorify; and on the women, the daughters of Eve, answer them, Lord, in prayer, when they cry to thee; for from them was chosen the woman, the Virgin and Holy one, whom God chose before all worlds, and of her was born the Lord of glory the glorious Son of God. Therefore at this time let the righteous come with their censers, and the prophets with their trumpets, and the apostles with their proclamations, and the martyrs with their crowns, and let them stand while the earthly beings gaze on the heavenly beings; and let the psalms of those
above be hushed with those from below, and thus let them say, p. 24
"Blessed be God who sent His Son, and He dwelt in Mary, and
blessed be the Messiah who magnified His mother in the day of cf. J. S. L. vol. 7
her exit from this world. To Him be the glory, and to her a good p. 130 l. 2
memorial for ever. And may there be......and peace upon all the world for ever and ever. Amen.

Blessed be Thy grace O God, Who didst die, that Thou mightest give life. King's Son Who wast debased, Undying that didst will and

die, who didst move from the Father to Mary, and from Mary to the manger, and from the manger to the circumcision, and from the circumcision to the bringing up, and from the bringing up to the carpenter, and from the carpenter to the smiting, and from the smiting to the Cross, and from the Cross to death, and from death to the grave, and from the grave to the resurrection, and from the resurrection to heaven, and lo! thou sittest at the right hand of power. Stretch forth, Lord, Thy right hand from the glorious throne of Thine honour at this time, and bless our congregation, that glorifies the commemoration of Thy Mother, the most blessed among women, and her exit from this world. Bless, O Lord Jesus the Christ all...... Brethren, hearers, and all believers to the requital of the new world. Bend your ears and prepare your minds and listen to the book of the blessed Lady Mary the Mother of God, how she went out of this world. And come ye created things from above and from beneath,
p. 25 ranks and heavenly powers, with the prophets, and the twelve Apostles, and the seventy-two Apostles, and the righteous men, and the martyrs, and the just men, and the confessors, and the saints, and the fasting men, and Enoch and Moses and Elijah, with the rows of angels; and all the companies of the fathers, and Abraham, and Isaac, and Jacob, and David the Psalmist of the church. Let all these created beings who are buried with those who are alive come to greet her and to adore her. And our Lord Jesus the Christ came with a band of the seraphim before Him holding trumpets and singing, and a row of angels bearing horns and blowing, and choirs of cherubs came holding lamps of glory, and crowds of guardian angels came with her and spread out their wings; and the clouds of heaven were covered. And our Lord Jesus the Christ came and saw the Blessed one, and so she died.

And ye also, believing hearers, listen earnestly and intelligently to the coronation of the Blessed one; that whoso believeth in the Father Who is undivided may assert and confess that God sent His Son, and He was born of a woman; and whoso loveth Jesus the Christ may believe that the Son of God was born of Mary without marriage, and whosoever seeketh to obtain a good recompense, let him confess and adore the Holy Spirit; three persons and three names, one Mystery, God glorious for ever and ever, He whom

heaven and earth adore. He, the True God, who was born of Mary p. 26
the Virgin, neither (to the body) of angels, nor of men did He unite
the sacred body which the Holy Virgin bore.

For she was a vine of rejoicing, she who was chosen by God before
all created beings, and God sent His Son, and He dwelt in her, and
He was born of her without the intercourse of man, as said Isaia the
most glorious of the prophets. "He grew up before him as a sprout, Is. liii. 2
and as a root out of a dry ground." And again the same prophet
says: "Behold a virgin shall conceive and bear a son, and his name Is. vii. 14
shall be called Emmanuel, which is interpreted, our God is with us."
She also, the Lady Mary, was holy and elect of God before she was
born; and she purified herself from all hateful thoughts, that she
might receive the Christ who came beside her. When therefore the
time arrived that what was lost should be found, and what had strayed
should be turned back, and what was scattered should be gathered,
and what was captive should be ransomed, the mercy of God was
moved towards the wandering sheep, that is to say towards the race
of the house of Adam. And He sent His Son and His Beloved
from heaven; and He came and dwelt in the Holy Virgin; that by
His birth from her He might give life to the world which had grown
old in its sins. She is the holy woman, whose commemoration it
befits us to make, is the most blessed among women; from whom
the Redeemer of the world was born; she is the land of blessings, of
which was born the husbandman of joy, that by His going forth into p. 27
creation He might uproot the thorns, and burn the tares, and might
destroy error, and might frustrate and drive away Satan, and make
concord reign, and sow peace over all the created things of the world.

Brethren and Fathers all, believing hearers, like men who love
the Christ, remembering about this book of the Lady Mary, how
it was revealed at this time. Therefore there was much concern to J. S. L.
the blessed men at Mount Sinai, Mar David the presbyter, and Mar vol. 7 p. 131
John the presbyter, and Mar Philip the deacon, because these three
blessed men were at the altar which is placed at the top of the
mountain of Mount Sinai, where there is the thorn bush (out of) which
the Lord spake with Moses. These blessed men were there in that
temple; and they had been made directors of that shrine which is
built on the top of the mountain of Mount Sinai. And these blessed

men had authority over three hundred and twenty monasteries which were in Mount Sinai, because all Mount Sinai was adorned with the temples of the Lord. And these blessed ones wrote letters from Mount Sinai to Jerusalem, to Cyrus the bishop of Jerusalem. "That there may be solicitude to thy Holiness." And they asked concerning the book of the exit of the Lady Mary, how she went out of this world, "because we have a great desire to know with what glory she was crowned. For we have inquired about this book and nothing
p. 28 has come to our hands. And we desire that it may be shown concerning Mar John the Apostle, the young, whom his Lord loved greatly, and the matter was revealed to him, because the Lord loved Mar John more than his fellows. And according as the Christ loved him, so the Lady Mary loved him also; and this Mar John... the earth......while alive; and he gave it to that guilty one of the robbers[1] with his own hands; and he departed from the earth; and help came from him to the children of men."

In the year 809......on the birth-day of the Christ while the high beings were standing with the lower beings, and celebrating the birth-day of the Christ, the Lady Mary appeared to Mar John, at Ephesus, and said to him: "Give the book which thou hast about my exit from this world to the men who are coming to thee from Mount Sinai, because the day has arrived in which thy Lord is coming from heaven. The book shall go out, which will command that there be a commemoration and an offering to her: For thou, John, and the Apostles, thy companions, have come to her to Bethlehem; and behold! I have told thee that the hour has arrived when He will come from (heaven to judge) all created beings; and it shall be revealed concerning my glory how I departed from the world."

cf. J. S. L. vol. 7 p. 131 l. 12 And when a letter was written from Mount Sinai; and...brethren came and brought it to Jerusalem, and it was read before all Jerusalem. And they sought for the book of the Lady Mary, how she died; and
p. 29 they did not find it. And they found a certain book in which it was written thus: "I, Danton[2] the deacon, who am a native of Jerusalem (and James the bishop of Jerusalem made me a deacon, he who was the first bishop of Jerusalem while the Apostles were alive); I write thus with my autograph in the month of Haziran, in the year 336, in

[1] Cf. Clem. Alex. *Quis Div. Salv.* (c. 42).

[2] Cod. Harris "Anton."

the third day of the week at noon-day about the Jew, who was a captain. And he struck James the Bishop and he died, because the Jews hated James greatly on account of his being called the Lord's brother. And the bishop of Jerusalem and his clergy asked concerning the book of the Exit of the Blessed Mary. And they did not find it, but they found another volume on which was written in the handwriting of James the Bishop: "I, James, write thus, that in the year 345[1] the Lady Mary died off from this world, in January on the day in which she gave birth to the Christ, on that day she departed from this world. And I James bear witness, that the Apostles came, those who were alive; and those who were buried arose, and the created beings who were above with those who were beneath came to greet the Blessed One, and thus she departed from this world. And six books were written—two apostles wrote each book—about the signs and miracles and wonders from heaven and from earth which happened in her presence. And we gave thanks to the Lord who returned to the mother who bore Him with the adoration p. 30
of earthly beings, and the blowing of the horns of the seraphim. And I James the bishop of Jerusalem, have written with my own hand writing in this volume, and these books that were written, John the young, who is very blessed, carried them. And the handwriting of all the Apostles is in these books which they wrote. And they celebrated the Lady Mary, so that there should be offerings and commemorations for the blessed one three times in the year. And Paul and Peter and John the young, who is very blessed, they know where these books are about the death of the Lady Mary, because they came along with them from Jerusalem." And we make it known to Your Holinesses, O Fathers who dwell on Mount Sinai. And they sent a letter—the bishop of Jerusalem and his clergy "From Cyrus, bishop of Jerusalem and all his holy clergy to our brethren, the priests and our fathers who dwell on Mount Sinai, much peace. The letter which came from you, we have received; and we have made inquiries in all Jerusalem concerning the departure of the Lady Mary, and we have not found it; but we have found the autograph of James the Bishop, which he has written thus: 'These six books which were written when the

[1] Probably from the era of Alexander.

Lady Mary died, John the Young carried them'; and we have [1]made
known to Your Holinesses, O fathers who dwell on Mount Sinai,
Send letters to Rome to the hands of the holy Peter and Paul when
these holy books were found there, and write also letters to Ephesus
p. 31 where there are those who are very blessed, if this book of the Lady
Mary the mother of God, is found there. And if it be that book
which your Holinesses have found, make it known to us by a
letter; that in Jerusalem also the volume may be written of the
memorial of the Blessed One, and that we may despise with it the
people of the Jews; and pray ye to the Lord for us, O ye priests of
the Christ.'"

And the letter went from Jerusalem (to Ephesus) and from
(Ephesus to).........and to Alexandria and to Egypt and to the
Thebaid. And some men went and inquired in these regions, and
they did not find it. And they came to Ephesus, and stayed there in
J. S. L. the house of Mar John[1]. And they prayed in the night, and offered
vol. 7 incense, saying, "O Lord Jesus the Christ, who didst love Mar John
p. 132 the Apostle more than his fellows, if it be pleasing to Thy Godhead
that these Thy wonders and glorious deeds which Thou didst before
the Lady Mary Thy mother should be revealed to (this) lower world,
let us see the Apostle, and may he converse with us this night."
And the brethren fell upon their faces; and while they were sleeping,
behold! Mar John the Apostle stood beside them and said to them,
"Be not grieved, ye blessed, for the Christ will give you a reward;
for ye walked on your feet through the countries. Arise, take the
Book of the Exit of the mother of our Lord, for lo! it is with me;
and go to Mount Sinai, and salute our brethren, and say to them:
p. 32 'John has sent you this book in order that there may be a commemoration of the Lady Mary, the mother of God, three times in the
year; and say to the brethren: 'Do not think that I am left,
but I am standing within the earth and looking for my Lord,
who will come from heaven and say to me: Behold,'".........we saw
this sign, and we shook and trembled, and we were in great fear.
And the blessed one departed from beside us, and we were bowing
J. S. L. down. And the verger opened the door, and entered, to where the
vol. 7
p. 133

[1–1] This is probably what was on the leaf which was lost from Dr Wright's codex A. See J. S. L. vol. VII. p. 131 foot-note *p*.

grace of Mar John flows; and there he found a written volume, placed upon the mouth of the cave, whence the grace flows. He took it up before all the people, and opened it, and found that it was written in Hebrew, and in Greek, and in Latin. And there was upon it the sign manual of the seventy-two apostles and there was written in it thus: "This Jesus the Christ, Who was born of Mary the Virgin, He is God in heaven and on earth, and whosoever believeth in Him shall be saved; and the Lady Mary who bore Him departed from this world in great glory. And the twelve Apostles bear witness; and the seventy and two Apostles, concerning the miracles which the Christ did in the presence of His mother as she departed from this world. The Apostles took up the book and gave it to Mar John that he might bear witness to it; because the Christ loved him more than his fellows."

And this volume was made before the whole of Ephesus; and in the hour when this volume was opened in Ephesus, the heaven

distilled sweet dew from above, for no man can tell about the great glory p. 33
with which the mother of God, Mary, departed from this world, nor can ears hear, nor even eye see, when the chariots of the heights and the depths went into her presence in the spiritual paradise of Eden. And this volume was translated[1] from the Greek tongue to the Syriac; and it was written, and it went to Mount Sinai; and came to Jerusalem. And we all at this time thank God, that in His love He sent His Son, and He came to the world to deliver us from Gehenna; that by the prayers of the mother of God, Mary, and also of all the saints, God may make to pass away from the earth and from this place where this book is, the sword, and captivity and famine and pestilence, and all the plagues and rods of anger. Amen.

## [BOOK II.]

In the year 344, in the month of the latter Teshrîn[2] on its third day, the third day of the week, at the third hour, Mary came forth from her house, and went to the tomb of the Christ; (while she was weeping) because every day she used to go to the door of the tomb. But the Jews, immediately after the Christ was dead, closed the tomb, and heaped huge stones against it, and set watchmen over the grave and Golgotha, and gave them orders that if any one should come and pray beside the tomb and beside Golgotha, he should p. 34

[1] literally "went forth."

[2] i.e. September.

straightway die. And immediately the Jews took away the cross of our Lord, and the other crosses, and the spear with which our Redeemer had been pierced, and the sponge with which they had offered Him vinegar, and the robes of mockery with which they had clothed Him, and the crown of thorns which they had placed on His head, and the nails which they had fixed both in His hands and His feet. And they took them up and hid them; because they were shaking and afraid lest one of the kings or princes should come
cf. J. S. L. and ask concerning the slaughter of our Lord. And every day they saw Mary
vol. 7 coming to the tomb, carrying sweet spices and myrrh, and fire, and when she
p. 134 had come (there) she bent down with her face to the earth, and she prayed, saying in her prayer; weeping, "My Lord, send and lead me from this earth." And she was in great fear from the people of the Jews, for many times they sought to slay her; but the power of God who was born of her protected her, that she should not be killed by the Jews. And when the children of Israel sought to slay her, the odour of the faith that proceeded from the Blessed one smote them, and their minds were troubled,

p. 35 and they know not what they said. For immediately after they had made her drink the water of trial, they forgot themselves about her; and when they saw her continually coming and praying beside Golgotha and the grave, they stirred up a quarrel with her, so as to contend with her. And the guardians answered and said unto the priests, "We have seen no one beside the tomb, except Mary, who comes morning and evening and prays there." The priests said unto them: "And why do you allow her to go and pray there?" The guardians say, "And do you wish to forbid her?" The priests say unto them, "If she comes there, stone ye her with stones, the despiser of Israel." The guardians say, "We say nothing to her, only when she comes and prays there, we will come and make it known to you. And whatever ye will, do ye it to her." And on the Friday Mary had prepared herself to go to the tomb of the Lord, and she was carrying sweet spices and fire. And while she was praying and had lifted up her eyes and gazed at heaven, suddenly the doors of heaven were opened and a scent of myrrh went up, which the Lady Mary had thrown on the censer, and its odour went about all the regions of heaven. And in that hour came Gabriel the angel to her from heaven, and knelt to worship her; and he said to her: "Hail to thee, mother of God! thy prayer hath been accepted in heaven before thy Son, our Lord Jesus the Christ. And therefore thou shalt depart from this world unto life everlasting. For thus I have been sent to

tell thee and to cause thee to know that at the time when thou didst pray on the earth, at once thou wast answered in heaven; and whatsoever thou dost seek from the Christ, thy Son who is in heaven
on the right hand of God, thou shalt have both in earth and in heaven, p. 36
and thy will is done. These words did Gabriel speak to her. And again the Lady Mary knelt and prayed, as she saw that an angel came to her, and made known everything to her.

Then the guardians said to the priests, "Behold Mary has come
and is praying at the tomb." And she stood and worshipped and cf. J. S. L.
came to her house, to Jerusalem. And there was a commotion in vol. 7 p. 134
Jerusalem concerning the Lady Mary. And the priests say to the l. 3
governor, "Send and command Mary not to go and pray at the grave and Golgotha."

And whilst they were deliberating, letters came from Abgar, the black[1] king of the city of Urhai[2] to Sabinus the Procurator, who had been appointed by Tiberius Caesar, and the jurisdiction of Sabinus the Procurator extended as far as the river Euphrates. Because Addai the Apostle, one of the seventy-two, went down and built the church at Urhai, and had healed the disease of king Abgar; for Abgar king of Urhai loved Jesus the Christ, and asked at all times concerning Him; and when the Christ walked in Galilee, before the Jews had crucified Him, Abgar sent to Him (and said) "Hie thee to me, for I have heard that the Jews are seeking to slay Thee." And when the Christ was dead, and king Abgar had heard that the Jews had slain Him on the cross, Abgar was grieved the more because the Lord had sent Addai, (one) of the seventy-two, to him, and he had healed him of his disease. And Abgar arose, and rode, with all his army and came as far as the river Euphrates, and he wished to go up against Jerusalem and to lay her waste, because she had slain the Christ, his Lord.

And when Abgar the king came to the river Euphrates he p. 37
reflected in his mind, "If I cross it, there will be enmity between me and Tiberius Caesar." And Abgar wrote letters and sent them to the Procurator Sabinus, and Sabinus sent them to the Emperor Tiberius. For he wrote thus: "From Abgar the king son of Ma'anu of Urhai the city in Mesopotamia. Much greeting to thy royalty Lord Tiberius.

[1] or "the leper." [2] Edessa.

That thy sovereignty might not be injured with me, I have not crossed the river Euphrates; for I was wishing to go up to Jerusalem and lay her waste, because she slew the Messiah, the wise Physician. But do thou, as a great king, as thou bearest sway over me, send and do me justice on the people of Jerusalem, because she has killed the Messiah, who had done no wrong to them. For if he had wished it while he was alive, I would have sent and persuaded him to come to me to Urhai. The people of Jerusalem have slain him who had done no wrong by a harsh judgment. And let thy Majesty know, that I wish thee to do me justice on the crucifiers."

This letter was sent from king Abgar to Sabinus the Procurator, and from Sabinus the Procurator it went to the Emperor Tiberius. And when it was read in his presence the Emperor Tiberius was greatly agitated; and wished to burn and to kill all the Jews.

And when the people of Jerusalem heard (this) they were alarmed. The Jews say to the Governor, "As for the Lady Mary, let it be enough for her, that all Jerusalem has been upset by the child which she has borne, and because he called himself the son of God, we crucified him and killed him. And now command her, that she go not to pray at the grave and at Golgotha."

p. 38 The Governor said to the priests, "Go ye, and command her what ye wish." And the priests came to the Lady Mary and said to her: "The Governor commands thee not to go and pray at the grave and Golgotha; and now, Mary, we say unto thee, Remember the sins
J. S. L. vol. 7 p. 135 which thou hast committed before God, and do not lead created beings astray, and say that he who was born of thee is the Messiah. Heaven and earth witness that he is the son of Joseph the carpenter. If then thou wishest to pray, enter into the synagogue[1] and hear the laws of Moses; and if thou hast committed sins, we will take pity on thee and will call upon God, and He will have mercy on thee. Go forth to the house of prayer with thy companions. We will set up the Torah over thee; and we will have compassion on thy faults as well as on thine obstinate mind, Mary; our hands will not be slack with thee; and because we see thee sick, we call in thine ears with a trumpet, and immediately thou shalt be healed. And if thou dost not accept these words, get thee out of Jerusalem, and go into thy

[1] literally the "Sabbath house."

house at Bethlehem, for we do not permit thee to pray at the grave
and at Golgotha. What dost thou say, Mary?" The Blessed one
answered and said: "It does not befit you to come to me with these
words; for I will not do your bidding; and I will not listen to
your words; and I will not do your will. And if ye sought to
keep abstinence, from (the time) when ye made me drink the
waters of trial, I was victorious over all your devices, ye have p. 39
not come near me. And now that ye have come, Mary will not do
your will." Then the Jews turned away in anger from the Blessed
one. And in the morning they[1] again came to her and they say to
her, "Mary! in the evening we tried to persuade thee, and thou didst
not accept our persuasion; because of that son of the carpenter who
was born of thee; whom thou hast called the Son of God. And we
call him a man; knowing whose son he is, and how he was born, and
was brought up amongst us. And we laid hold of him, and scourged
him, and we put a crown of thorns on his head; and we pierced him
with a spear; and he died, and was buried. Also that without [our]
kindness thou wouldest not have found a shroud to put on his body
when he had died. And except Joseph the senator had done him a
favour and had bought him a linen girdle, and had buried him. And
we stood beside thee, and if he had not done thus, he (Jesus) would
have gone down to Sheol."

These things the Jews said to the Lady Mary, and she did not
agree to them. Then the house, where the Blessed one dwelt in
Jerusalem, had been bought by Joseph the carpenter from the house-
hold of Caleb the Sadducee, and it was near to the house of
Nicodemus. And afterwards the Lady Mary fell sick; and she
sent and called all the women of the neighbourhood in which she
dwelt, and said to them: "Go in peace, I am going to Bethlehem,
to the house which I have there, since the Jews will not allow me to
go and pray at the Golgotha of the Christ. But whoso seeketh to
go with me will receive a blessing from God. For I am trusting in p. 40
my Master whom I have in heaven, that He will fulfil my wish,
whatsoever I seek from Him." And when the Lady Mary had said to
the daughters of Jerusalem that whoso wished should go with her to
Bethlehem, these virgins who ministered to her drew near to her and

[1] MS. "the Jews."

said to her, "Whoso wishes to go with thee, Lady Mary, shall receive a blessing from God. For we will not leave thee, though we should die, because for thy sake we have left our parents, and our brothers, and all that we have, and have gone with thee to minister unto thee; and with thee we wish to die, and with thee we wish to live."

Now these virgins were with the Lady Mary night and day, that they might minister unto her, and bring to her the censer of sweet spices. And every day they tried to persuade her: "Tell us, Lady Mary, mistress of the world, and teach us how our Lord Jesus Christ was born from thee without intercourse with man." And the Lady Mary told them everything; and they spread her couch and washed her feet, and folded her garments, and arranged sweet spices. And everything in which the Lady Mary was served for herself was done by these virgins. And not one of them dared to take anything with which the Lady Mary was served, or to taste anything of it. For they were very much afraid of the Blessed one on account of the
p. 41 awful signs which they had seen by day and by night beside the Blessed one. And they used to spread (carpets) before her bed for themselves and lie down. And these virgins served the holy Virgin with great reverence. And at morningtide came men and women and they worshipped the Blessed one, and were blessed by her. And the Lady Mary stretched out her hands, and blessed these virgins, and said to them: "May your prayers be accepted in heaven, before the Master whom I have there. And no man of all the tribes of Israel has cleaved to me except you." And as the day declined the Lady Mary remained in Jerusalem. And in the night came Gabriel the archangel and appeared to her, saying to the Blessed one, "Rise, go out to Bethlehem, and stay there until thou shalt have seen crowds of angels and of apostles, and all created beings coming to greet thee." And those virgins saw the angel of God coming to her, and (heard) what he said to her. And they feared with a great fear. And the angel departed from her; and it was the morning. And the Lady Mary called the virgins and told them everything. And she opened a chest and they took out her garments and the censer, and put everything in
cf. J. S. L. vol. 7 p. 135 l. 5 order to go with her to Bethlehem. And these virgins were the daughters of rich men and rulers of Jerusalem. Their names were

these: Callĕthā[1], and Neshrā[2], and Tābĕthā[3]. Callĕthā was the daughter of Nicodemus, the friend of the Christ; and by the name of Callĕthā is designated the glorious Church, the betrothed bride of the Son of God. And the second, whose name was Neshrā, was the daughter of p. 42
Gamaliel, the chief of the synagogue of the Jews; and by the likeness of Neshrā (the eagle) is symbolized Christ the King, who on His wings, which being interpreted are His hands, carries and bears aloft the holy Church, which was betrothed to Him before the foundations of the world. And she, whose name was Tābĕthā, was the daughter of Tobia, a man of comitian rank. This man was of the gens of the house of King Archelaus. And Archelaus was of the family of the Emperor Nero, he who crucified Simon the chief of the disciples. cf. J. S. L. vol. 7 p. 136
And the interpretation of these names is thus: Callĕthā is the Catholic Church, which is Jerusalem in heaven; and this church which we have upon earth is the image of the one which we have in heaven; and on it is established the throne of the glorious God. And Neshrā is the Christ, who sits on the right hand of His Father, on the chariot of the Seraphim. And Tābĕthā is the Holy Spirit, by whom life is given to all men. These were the names of the virgins who ministered unto the Lady Mary. And these virgins arose along with the Blessed one, and went forth to Bethlehem on Thursday, and dwelt there.

And on the Friday the Blessed one was distressed, and said to them: "Bring nigh unto me the censers of incense, for I wish to pray to my Master the Christ whom I have in heaven." And these virgins brought nigh unto her the censers; and she prayed thus and said: "My Master, the Christ, listen to the voice of Thy mother. p. 43
And send me Mar John, that I may see him. And I thank Thee for Thy goodness. I know that Thou hearest me in what I ask from Thee." And thus the Blessed one prayed

And John the Apostle was in the city of Ephesus, and was alive. And the Holy Spirit informed him, saying, "The time is near for the mother of thy Lord[4] to go out of the world; arise, and go to her to Bethlehem." And at the ninth hour on Friday, John went out to pray in the church of Ephesus. When he reached the door of the temple, the Holy Spirit informed him, while lightning played around him like a flash of fire and it said to him, "Go into the temple." And he went in and bowed and prayed before the altar. The

[1] or "the Bride." [2] or "the Eagle."
[3] or "the Good One." [4] Literally "Master" *passim*.

Holy Ghost said to him: "The time is near for the mother of thy Lord to go out of the world. Arise, go to her to Bethlehem for she desires much to see thee. And lo! I will inform the Apostles thy fellows, that they may all assemble at Bethlehem from the places in which they are, those who are alive and those who are dead."

These things said the Holy Spirit to John, and departed from him. And John was amazed and sore grieved. And the day after, he arose to go. And he commanded his disciples concerning the service of the church that
p. 44 is in Ephesus; that it should offer prayer to the Lord in due time. "I am sent by the Lord that I may go, and I have knelt and have prayed: 'Lord Jesus the Christ, Son of the Living God! grant to me that I may go quickly on my feet to Bethlehem, because of what the Holy Spirit has commanded me, before the altar. I am going to see Thy mother while she is departing from the world, before she dies.'"

Thus spake John, not knowing that the Holy Spirit was catching him up in a cloud of light; but he intended to go on his feet to Bethlehem. And when he had not yet finished his prayer, the Holy Spirit hovered above him. And at the time of his rising it made him reach the door of the upper chamber in which the Blessed one was lying. "And John opened the door of the chamber, and he went in and found the Blessed one lying on the bed. And he drew near and kissed her on her breast and her knees. And he said to her: "Hail to thee, Mother of God, and hail to the Christ who was born of thee! Be not grieved, lady, for thou art departing from this world with great glory."

And then the Mother of God rejoiced greatly that Mar John had come to her. And these virgins drew near and adored her, and did not question her. Then Mary said to John: "Set the censer of incense." And he set it; and he spoke thus, "Lord Jesus the Christ, do a miracle before Thy mother, as she is going out of this world that
p. 45 the infidels who have not believed that Thou art the Son of God may be ashamed. For heaven and earth bear witness that this is the holy virgin who gave Thee birth, and that Thou art the Son of the glorious God. And every one who confesses Thee shall live for ever." And when he had finished his prayer, the Lady Mary said to Mar John: "Come near me that I may speak to thee." And John came near to her. And she whispered to him, saying: "Everything that thy Lord has said to me is true. And all the signs and wonders of which He told me have happened. And He spoke thus to me before He ascended to heaven, beside His Father. 'When I am going out of this world, a host of angels will come beside me.'" John said to her: "The Lord Jesus has come, and thou hast seen

Him ascending as He said unto thee." She said to him: "The Jews have sworn oaths and have made vows, that when I die, they will burn my corpse with fire." John says to her: "The Lord Jesus, the Christ, stands for us." The Lady Mary says: "And if I die, where shall I have a grave?" He said to her: "Where my Lord shall command me." And the tears of the Blessed one overflowed. And John wiped them with...and John wept and his tears overflowed with those of the virgins (who were) with her, for they were much grieved about the Lady Mary. And John drew near and said to the Lady Mary, "If thou, who art the mother of God, art so grieved because thou art going out of this world, what shall the upright and p. 46
the righteous do when they go out of this transient (world) to the world that passeth not away? And thy Son will place crowns upon their heads.

"For thus hath the Holy Spirit informed me by the altar at Ephesus, saying to me: 'Depart and go to her, until the Apostles thy companions shall come to adore her.'" She said to him, "Pray and set the censer." Then the Blessed one knelt on his knees, and prayed thus, saying, "Lord Jesus the Christ! hearken to the voice of Thy mother's prayer, and come to her that she may see Thee, when she is going out of this world, as Thy holy mouth said to her that Thou wouldst come to her; and let there be Thine own peace and that of Thy Father and of Thy Holy Spirit; and come to Thy mother that she may see Thee with Thy glorious hosts. And heaven and earth will give Thee glory." And while John prayed, and before he had finished his prayer, a voice was heard from heaven, which said to him, "Amen. Assemble yourselves all and come." And John listened and heard this voice. And the Holy Spirit came to John and said to him, "Hast thou heard this voice which cries from heaven?" John said: "I have heard [it."] The Holy Spirit said to him: "This voice is the herald before the Apostles thy fellows, who are coming to greet the mother of thy Lord." And while John was praying, the Holy Spirit informed the Apostles wherever they were that they should go to the blessed Mary at Bethlehem. p. 47

To Simon Cephas It made this known in Rome; when he was entering the church to offer a sacrifice on the fourth day of the week, because the offering for strangers was there. And he was bowing and praying before the altar. And the Holy Spirit whispered to him: immediately after the sacrifice was offered, "Go to Bethlehem to the mother of your Lord, because the time draws nigh for her to depart from this world."

And to Paul also It made this known in the midst of Rome, in a certain town whose name was Tiberias, which was distant fifty parasangs from Rome. And It found Paul where he had a dispute with the Jews, who were arguing with him and insulting him. And they said to him, "We do not accept the announcement which thou makest about the Christ, because thou art from Tarsus; and thou art the son of a harness-maker, and because thou art the son of a poor man, thou hast taken the name of the Messiah, and thou art a freeman by it." And the Holy Spirit drew near and informed (him): "The time draws nigh for the mother of your Lord to leave this world." And Paul was amazed. And immediately he set up the censer of incense, and knelt and prayed.

And the Holy Spirit also informed Thomas in India; who had
p. 48 gone in to visit the sister of Lydan the king of the Indians. And he sat beside her bed and talked with her. And the Holy Spirit dawned upon him like the light. And It whispered to him, saying to him, "The time draws nigh for the mother of your Lord to leave this world. But go to Bethlehem to greet her." And when Thomas heard it, he trembled. And he went immediately to the church, and set up a censer of incense, and knelt and prayed.

And the Holy Spirit informed Matthew, saying to him: "The time draws nigh for the mother of your Lord to leave this world."

And the Spirit informed James who was in Jerusalem, saying to him: "The time draws nigh for the mother of your Lord to leave this world; but go out to greet her at Bethlehem."

And the Holy Spirit informed Tholomew, saying to him: "The time draws nigh for the mother of your Lord to leave this world; but go to greet her at Bethlehem."

Now none of the Apostles had died, except Andrew, the brother of Simon Cephas, and Philip, and Luke, and Simon the Zealot. These were dead. And in that day the Holy Spirit informed them in their graves, and they arose from out of Sheol. And the Holy Spirit said to them, "Do not ye imagine that the resurrection is come.

But all this is that ye have been awakened out of your graves to-day, in order that ye may go to greet the mother of your Lord, for the time draws nigh for her to leave this world."

And the Holy Spirit informed Mark, saying to him: "The time p. 49
draws nigh for the mother of your Lord to leave this world; go to
greet her at Bethlehem."

These things the Holy Spirit made known to the holy Apostles. And while the Apostles were wondering in the places where they were, how they should go to the Blessed Mary at Bethlehem, and each of them was saying to himself, How can I have a swift car to go to Bethlehem? And while each of the Apostles was in meditation and in deliberation, their Lord sent them a car from heaven, and chariots and clouds of light to carry them. And a cloud of light came down, and snatched away Peter; and he was standing between the heaven and the earth, and waiting for the Apostles his fellows to come to him. And straightway the Holy Spirit snatched away all the Apostles on chariots of light; and they came to Peter. And terrible winds blew, and the heaven and the earth shone from the lightnings that flashed.

Now in the morning, on the fourth day of the week, the Apostles
were approached by the Holy Spirit, and by noon on the fourth day
of the week they were assembled beside the blessed Mary at Bethlehem.
And there was great fear at that time. And David the son of Jesse p. 50
came before them, and sang, saying thus, "Glory to the Father, and
the Son, and the Holy Spirit, Hallelujah." And when the Apostles
had arrived at Bethlehem, Gabriel and Michael, the angels of peace[1],
stood in the presence of the Apostles, and they entered and said to the
Apostles, "Hail to you, O disciples of Christ the King!" The Apostles
answered and said unto the angels, "Hail to you, ye angels of the
Lord!"

And the Holy Spirit informed John in Bethlehem (saying), "Go out and receive the Apostles thy fellows." And he went out and received them and did obeisance to them and led them and they went in to the Blessed one. And the Apostles and the angels entered together to the upper chamber of the Blessed one, and the Apostles kissed her on her breast and on her knees; and they adored her.

[1] or "greeting."

And the angels from afar offered her adoration. And the Apostles waited and stood before the Blessed one. And they answered and said unto her, "Fear not, O thou blessed among women! and let it not grieve thee; the Lord God who was born of thee, He will bring thee out of this world with glory, and will make thee to dwell in the glorious mansions of the blessed God; those over which thy Son hath authority and in which He makes the holy ones of His love happy."

And the Lady Mary raised herself and sat upon the bed. And she said to the Apostles, "Now I am assured that my Master will come from Heaven, and that I shall see Him, and thus I shall die;
p. 51 as you have come, and I have seen you. And now I entreat you to tell me who showed you that I am dying, and from what places ye have come to me, and on what cars ye have ridden, that now ye have arrived so quickly. Reveal it and show it to me, so that I may know of a truth that He who was born of me is the Son of God. I glorify Him and I thank Him and I worship Him, that He hath thus visited the lowliness of His handmaiden in me."

Peter said to all the Apostles, "Let each one of us tell the Blessed Mary how the Holy Spirit spoke to him; and whence we came."

The Apostles said: "Let John, who is very blessed, come first. Let him tell her how he came."

John answered and said: "The Holy Spirit announced to me in Ephesus, when I had gone in by the door of the temple, and had come near to the altar. And It whispered to me, 'The time draws nigh for the mother of your Lord to leave this world. Go to her to Bethlehem.' And the Holy Spirit snatched me up in a cloud of light and set me down and brought me to the door of the upper chamber."

Peter answered and said: "The Holy Spirit announced to me also in Rome, on the morning of the fourth day of the week, and It said to me: 'Immediately when thou hast made the offering, go to Bethlehem, to the mother of your Lord, for the time is near for her
p. 52 to leave this world.' And straightway when I had made the offering, the Holy Spirit snatched me up in a cloud of light and I stood between the heaven and the earth, and I saw the chariots of all the Apostles, which were flying and coming to me."

Paul answered and said: "And I also was in a town called Tiberias, far from Rome, and the Jews were disputing with me there. And the Holy Spirit informed me and said to me, 'The time draws nigh for the mother of your Lord to leave this world; go to her to Bethlehem.' And straightway the cloud of the Lord snatched me away and brought me to you."

Thomas answered and said: "The Holy Spirit informed me in India when I had gone in to put the seal on the sister of Lydan the king of the Indians. And the Spirit said to me, 'Go to Bethlehem, because the time draws nigh for the mother of your Lord to leave this world.' And while I was wondering at what had been said to me, the Holy Spirit snatched me away and brought me to you."

Mark said: "I was performing the service of the third hour; and as I was praying, the Holy Spirit said to me, whilst It was standing before me, 'The time draws nigh for the mother of your Lord to leave this world, but rise, go to Bethlehem.' And while I was amazed, the Holy Spirit snatched me away in a cloud of light and brought me to you."

James said: "I was in Jerusalem, and was sitting in the church p. 53
of Sion, and we were covering up the vessels of the Lord's service. And a little before, I had gone out from Jerusalem to Bethlehem, and had visited the Blessed Mary when she was sick; because the Jews withstood her, and did not allow her to go and pray beside the grave and the Golgotha of the Christ. And I went thence and came to Bethlehem, and I knew not that she would go out of this world with all this glory. And the Holy Spirit came in beside me and said to me: 'The time draws nigh for the mother of your Lord to leave this world.' And while I was going out to her, the Holy Spirit snatched me away and brought me to you."

Matthew said: "I have given and am giving glory to God, for when I was sitting in a ship, storms arose to cover it, and while the tempests were chasing it[1], behold the Holy Spirit flashed lightning around me, and snatched me away on a cloud of light, and brought me to you."

And Philip answered and said: "I was dead and I heard a voice which called me, 'Philip, rise.' And the Holy Spirit brought me

[1] MS. "the ship."

forth out of the grave, and set me on a cloud of light and brought me to you."

Simon the Zealot said: "I, too, am risen from the grave and I saw
p. 54 a right hand which laid hold of me, and it raised me up from the abode of the dead, where I was lying among them; and I arose from the tomb, and the Holy Spirit set me on a cloud of light, and brought me to you."

Luke answered and said: "I am risen from the grave; and there struck on my ears as it were the sound of the trumpet of the seraphim, and a light dawned on the grave in which I was lying, and I imagined that the day of the resurrection had arrived. The Holy Spirit set me on a cloud of light, and brought me to you."

Andrew answered and said: "I too am risen from the grave; and the voice of the Son of God struck on my ears and said to me: 'Andrew, arise, go with thy fellows to Bethlehem, and I will come to you with a host of the angels; because the time is come for the Blessed Mary to be crowned, and to go out of this world. And straightway the Holy Spirit set me on a cloud of light and brought me to you."

Bartholomew answered and said: "I too was in Thebais, and was preaching about the grace and peace of our Lord Jesus the Christ, and I saw the Holy Spirit coming like lightning from heaven, and straightway It carried me and set me on a cloud of light, and brought me to you."

These things spake the Apostles before the Lady Mary, and each
p. 55 of them showed how he had come to her. And when the Lady Mary heard these things from the Apostles she stretched out her hands to heaven and prayed, saying, "I worship and praise and sing and laud, that I am not a mockery to the nations of the Gentiles: and that the words of the Jews have not turned out true; who said that they would burn me with fire when I was dead. But I believe and am sure that He Who was born of me is the Governor of the heaven and of the earth; and I will praise His gracious name for ever and ever. And I cannot glorify His grace sufficiently, that He hath sent His holy disciples to me."

And after Mary had prayed, the Apostles set forth the censer of incense, and knelt with their faces down and prayed. And in that

hour it thundered in the heaven, and a voice was heard like the sound
of hurrying wheels striking over the surface of the air, and a sweet
scent from heaven struck on the Apostles. And the angels came
down, and guardian spirits in troops and bands without number, and
they covered with their wings the upper chamber where the Lady Mary
was lying. And another voice which had never been heard before,
except that voice saying .....the Lord God ; for heaven and earth
worship Him. And great fear was in all Bethlehem ; and there were
fearful signs, and the armies of the Lord never ceased from ascending p. 56
and descending from heaven. And there was a great tumult amongst
the heights, and a voice like that of a man spake from within the
chariots of cherubim who were standing above the upper chamber
where the blessed Mary was lying. And the people of Bethlehem
went in and told the Governor and the priests of Jerusalem what they
had seen and heard.

Here endeth the Second Book.

## BOOK III.

And men went from Bethlehem, and when they saw there the
signs which were done before the Lady Mary while she was lying in
the upper chamber at Bethlehem, when the disciples had come and
were ministering to her in the upper chamber, and they saw when
the heavens were opened, and the armies of the angels of the Lord
were coming down and singing above that upper chamber. And they
saw the lightning and heard the sound of the thunder, and they saw
the clouds coming towards the abode[1] of the Blessed one, (even) these
signs and miracles. And that the people of Bethlehem had seen more
things and mightier than these. And they gave glory to God without
wishing it. And because they offered unwilling adoration to the
Holy Child who was born of the holy Virgin ; and were rejoicing in
the miracles which were done; women came from the towns, and from
distant regions; and from Rome, and from Alexandria, and from
Egypt, and from Athens; daughters of kings, and daughters of the p. 57

[1] MS. "upper chamber."

magnates of the nations. And daughters of Procurators and of rulers; and they brought honours and offerings, and they came and adored the Lady Mary; and they believed in the Christ Who was born of her. And they asked her, and persuaded her: "Tell us, O Lady, mistress of the world, how our Lord Jesus the Christ was born of thee without intercourse with man?" And the Lady Mary told them everything that they sought from her. And whosoever had any affliction, she healed it; and when they returned to their (own) countries and to their homes, she blessed them, and prayed for them, and gave them writings that they should go with these to the house of their parents, so that they might believe. And year by year the daughters of kings came to her, and the daughters of chiefs, and made the commemoration of our Lord Jesus the Christ[1].

And a certain woman came to the Lady Mary from Berytus (Beyrout) who had a demon that at all times was strangling her. And Yuchabar came also to her from Alexandria, the daughter of Nonnus the Hyparch, who was quite filled with leprosy. And they came and did obeisance before the Lady Mary. And she straightway took water, and sealed them, in the name of the Father, and of the Son, and of the Holy Spirit. And she sprinkled (it) upon their bodies; and straightway they were healed.

And Abigail came to her, the Egyptian, the daughter of the rich Gershōn, who was sister to the king of Egypt, and she had the affliction of strangury; and she entreated the Lady Mary, and immediately when she had prayed over her she was healed.

p. 58 And Flavia came to her from Thessalonica, whose right eye Satan had destroyed; and when Mary had stretched out her hand and touched it, immediately it was healed. And Malchū came also to her, the daughter of Sabinus, the Procurator, in whom were two demons; one that tormented her by night; and the other that came upon her by day, and buffeted her; and she entreated the Lady Mary; and immediately when she had prayed over her, and had placed her hand upon her, and had spoken thus: "In the name of my Master Who is in heaven, I adjure thee at this time concerning this soul, that she may be healed." And straightway these demons came out of her, and they wailed, and cried out, saying, "What is there

[1] i.e. Christmas.

between us and thee, O Mother of God?" And these demons stood in the midst of the market place, near the door of the Lady Mary's upper chamber. And they said in the presence[1] of everybody, "Thou and the Son who was born of thee have disturbed Legion and his armies." Then the Lady Mary rebuked them in the name of our Lord Jesus the Christ. And straightway they departed towards the sea, and fell into it and were choked.

And there came also to the Lady Mary a certain boy from Egypt, sister's son to Sophrōn king of Egypt, who had elephantiasis in his head. And he wept before her, and straightway when she had stretched out her hand, and laid hold of his head, he was healed from his trouble.

And those also who were sick, who came with him and were afflicted,
in the hour that they went in to her, and took refuge with the pure p. 59
and holy Lady Mary in that hour they were healed from their afflictions.

And there was a festival in Jerusalem, and many people were assembled for it, and the sick and the afflicted who came to Jerusalem, asked: "Where is the Lady Mary the mother of our Lord?" And they said to them: "She is at Bethlehem." And persons[2] without number went forth and went to Bethlehem; and they knocked at the door of the Blessed one's upper chamber. And the Apostles did not open the door to them. And when they did not open the door to them, they implored, saying, "O Lady Mary, mother of God, have mercy upon us!" And the Lady Mary heard the voice of the persons who were crying to her, and she prayed and said: "My Master the Christ, Whom I have in heaven, hearken to the voice of these afflicted souls." And straightway great strength and help went forth from the Blessed one to all these sick people, and they were cured. And those that were cured were two thousand eight hundred souls, men, and women, and children. And there was a thanksgiving to God on that day. And those who were healed went immediately to the Praetorium, and told before the Governor and the priests everything that the Lady Mary had done to them by her prayers. And two thousand eight hundred souls were struck, and the eyes of the

[1] literally, "eye."  [2] literally "creatures."

Jews were darkened; and those of all the priests; and the Sadducees hastened and said that there was a dispute in Jerusalem.

p. 60 And the priests called the men who had come from Bethlehem and said to them: "Go put her out from there." And when the people of Bethlehem came and conspired with them that they should go and contend with the Apostles; on that night, as the third day of the week dawned[1], in Tishrin the second[2] on the 21st day of the month, as the day was declining, and all the world was asleep, there was a thanksgiving to God before the Lady Mary. And as she was lying in the upper chamber, the people of Bethlehem arose in the night and sought to go in against the Apostles. And immediately the doors of heaven were opened, and many lights without number appeared, and sweet odours were wafted over all Bethlehem. And angels of fire descended from heaven clad in raiment of flame. And John opened the door of the upper room and went out and looked at the sky, and he saw the troops of cherubim and of guardian angels and of spiritual beings who were descending in ordered ranks from heaven. And John went in and told Peter: "Behold the heavenly hosts are coming to us." And straightway the doors of the upper chamber were opened, and the angels and the Apostles who were in it[3] went out; and they received those who had come from Jerusalem, and were knocking; and they spake thus: "Blessed be Thou, O Most Holy, O Son of God!" And they went in and showed all the signs and the wonders which had been done beside the Lady Mary.

p. 61 Then the priests disturbed the Governor, saying to him: "Most noble Governor, command concerning this woman that she stay not in Bethlehem nor in the whole jurisdiction of Jerusalem." The Governor said to them, "I am not ready to send and drive a woman out of her house." They say to him: "Otherwise we will do it." They said to him: "And if not, send men with rods, and let them bring the disciples of that deceiver and her (also) with great contumely." And after they had made a great tumult, they said to him: "By the life of Tiberius, if thou dost not do our pleasure, we will make it known to him." And when the Governor perceived that

[1] The day began at sunset. [2] i.e. November.

[3] MS. "in the upper chamber."

they had set themselves all together against him: he commanded the chiliarch to go, and thirty men with him to Bethlehem; and to bring Mary and the disciples with her. And they set out and went. And the Holy Spirit said to the Apostles, "Lo! men are coming against you from Jerusalem. Arise, go out to them from here and fear not; I will carry you and make you pass through the air of heaven and above the men who are coming against you. You will pass and they shall not see you; for the power of the adored Son will accompany you."

And the Apostles arose, and went out of the upper chamber, and Paul and Peter and Thomas and John carried the bed of the Blessed one. And the rest of the Apostles and of the angels were singing praises and going before her. And while the Apostles were carrying
the bed of the Blessed one, the Holy Spirit carried the Apostles and p. 62
the Blessed one, and made them pass over the men who were coming against them, and they did not see them. And when these men came with the chiliarch to Bethlehem, they heard the sound of a tumult that passed above them; and they stood looking and saying to each other: "What is that sound?" For they heard the sound of the seraphs' wings striking, and (felt) the sweet odour that was wafted through all that place, and the voice of the hosts of angels.

And the Apostles went into the house of the Lady Mary, which she had at Jerusalem, and the angels and the Holy Spirit were comforting her. And the service for her lasted for five days and five nights. And when the men who had been sent to Bethlehem arrived, they meditated quietly how they might open the door of the upper chamber so that not one of our Lord's Apostles might escape from [their] hands. And when they had opened the door of the upper chamber, they went in and found nothing in it, neither the disciples nor the blessed Mary. Then the people of Bethlehem went into Jerusalem, and these men along with them and said before the Governor and before the priests: "We have found nothing in Mary's upper room." The priests answered, saying to them, "These disciples of the seducer have made some incantations on you, and blinded your eyes and ye have not seen them."

The Governor said to the people of Bethlehem: "If ye find news p. 63
of them anywhere, lay hold of them and bring them to us."

And after five days, the angels of the Lord were seen by them

going in and going out of the Lady Mary's house in Jerusalem. And seraphim were seen standing above her house and magnifying (her). And many people were assembled from every place, and they stood in companies, and sang praises, crying and saying, "Blessed art thou, Mary, with God." And the people of Jerusalem feared with a great fear; and the priests sent in the morning, saying, "Go, inquire who lives in that neighbourhood." And men came and inquired. And the people of that neighbourhood said to them: "The Lady Mary, the Mother of God, has come to her house, and these songs of praise have preceded her. And the armies of heaven are descending and doing obeisance before her." And those who were sent came and told the priests everything that they had heard. And the priests and Sadducees arose and cried out in the Praetorium, and they say to the Governor, "There will be a great slaughter in this city Jerusalem, because of this woman." The Governor said to them, "And what shall I do for you?" The people of Jerusalem say to him: "Let us take fire and wood, and let us go and burn the court in which she dwells." The Governor said to them, "Go, and do what you please." Then the people of Jerusalem assembled, and took fire and wood, and
p. 64 they went to the court in which the Blessed one dwelt; and the Governor was standing at a distance looking on. And when they came to the court, they found the doors shut. And they lifted their hands to pull them up, (and) straightway the angel of the Lord struck on their faces with his wings, and fire was kindled from the door and the flame blazed forth, which no man had kindled, and the faces and hair of the heads of those people who had arrived at the door of the Blessed one's court were burnt, and many of them died. And there was great fear in all Jerusalem. Now when the Governor saw this sight, that fire blazed forth from the door of the court which no one had kindled; and the many people who were burnt; he stretched out his hands towards heaven, and spoke thus: "Of a truth this deed which I have seen is that of the Son of the Living God; He who was born of the Holy Virgin and is worshipped and glorified." And the Governor commanded next day and sent to bring the people of Jerusalem, the priests, and the elders, and the Sadducees. And he said to them, "O stubborn nation, nation which has crucified the God who came to it, ye are people bitter of soul and stiff of neck, doers of

the wish of your heart. And I thank God that I am not of your country, but Tiberius the Emperor made me Governor, and sent me (to be) over you. And because ye are a fickle nation, therefore there
was a decree from the Emperor, that no Governor of your own country p. 65
should be over you. Because ye are bad and a crucifying nation. And ye have written to Herod about the Christ Who was born of this holy Virgin. And ye sent to him (to say) that He was bad. And now ye seek to burn the mother of the Christ in your error. Why do you come near this woman? Are you not ashamed? How many signs and miracles God has done by her hands! I certainly will have nothing to do with this sin."

Then Caleb the Sadducee, who was a believer in the Christ, and in the Blessed Mary, and who was afraid to make himself known to his countrymen, whispered to the Governor, saying, "Thus do thou adjure them with this oath which I tell thee, 'By the God of Israel, who brought Him up out of Egypt, and by the holy books of the Law, which were written by the hands of God, and it was given to Moses that he might give it to Israel; but tell me what ye think about the son of Mary. Do ye call Him a prophet? Do ye account Him a righteous man? (Is He) the Messiah, the Son of God? (Is He) a man? Tell me, that I may know it, for ye are readers of the law." Thus Caleb the Sadducee instructed him.

Then the judge commanded that all Jerusalem should be assembled. And when it was assembled according to the commandment p. 66
of the Governor, he came and sat on his judgment seat, and adjured them as Caleb had instructed him, by the God of Israel, and by the holy books and the Law. "Let every one who believes in the Lady Mary and in the child who was born of her, that He is the Christ, the Son of God, separate himself, and stand by himself; and let him who does not believe, show himself an unbeliever." Then the people were divided into two parties; and those who believed separated themselves on one side. The Governor said to those who believed in the Messiah, "What say ye? Do ye believe in Him, in this child, who was born of Mary?" They say, "We believe that He is the Messiah." The Governor said to them: "And do ye believe that the Messiah is the Son of the Living God?" Then they all cried out, saying, "Of a truth we believe that this Child Who was born of the blessed

Mary, is the Son of God, Who by His command rules the heaven and the earth."

The Governor answered and said unto them: "I believe in you more than in the people outside. For ye who were born and brought up in Jerusalem, lo! some of you are found to be worshippers, and some of you infidels. It is not necessary that one of the Emperors should come against you, and force you, and that you should confess
p. 67 the Messiah against your will. But ye cried out and said that He is the Son of God? Ye have seen that ye are speaking the truth."

The unbelievers say to the Governor: "My lord, according to our books, the Messiah has not yet come."

The Governor said to them, "And what do ye consider the man who has come?"

They say to him: "We consider that he is a seducer, who is not even good, like one of the righteous."

Now the Governor was praying to God in his own mind, that those who confessed the Messiah might gain the victory; because the Governor also believed in the blessed Mary, and in the child who was born of her. And the Governor said to those who confessed the Christ:

"What say ye? I desire that the secrets which are amongst you may be revealed. For until now I have thought of you with the crucifiers who have crucified the Son of God. But from this day and henceforth it is just that ye should approach (me) like men who confess the Son of God. And with Him may a portion be allotted to me and to you in the last day, when He shall come on the clouds of heaven in His glory with His holy angels. But as people who confess Him, reveal to me the signs and wonders which He did in Jerusalem."

The unbelievers say, "We will speak first."

The Governor said to them: "Speak."

The unbelievers say: "It is written for us in the books that the Messiah shall come, and till now He has not come; and this is the
p. 68 son of Mary, and He calls Himself the Messiah!"

The lovers of the Messiah say to the unbelievers: "Do ye show the signs which the first, and the middle, and the latter (prophets) have done; and we will show the signs which the Messiah did, that they are more than all created beings."

The unbelievers say to the lovers of the Messiah: "Whence show ye to us that the Son of Mary is the Messiah?"

The lovers of the Messiah say: "We are showing it."

The Governor said to them: "Not with clamour nor with uproar are ye to utter your words against each other; but speak to one another in a low voice, out of your books. I wish to see and to know where your wisdom is."

The lovers of the Messiah say[1]: "Our father Adam when dying commanded his son Seth, and said to him, 'My son Seth, lo, offerings are laid up by me in the cave of treasures; gold, and myrrh, and frankincense; because God is about to come into the world, and to be seized by wicked men, and to die, and make by His death a resurrection for all nations; and on the third day He will rise, and will take the body of Adam with Him to heaven, and will make it sit on the right hand. And lo! the Magi are coming from Persia, and will bring these offerings, which I have deposited, and will go to Bethlehem of Judah and worship the Messiah, who is born there of the holy Virgin. And p. 69
so it was. And the Magi came and brought the offerings, and they brought the testament of Adam with them. And from the testament of Adam all mankind have learned to make testaments; and from the Messiah, who was born of Mary, all mankind who were in darkness, have been enlightened. And thus from Adam to Seth writing was used; and from Seth letters were written, to the fathers and to all mankind; and the fathers gave [them] to the sons; and the sons gave [them] to the sons' sons; and they said that 'The Messiah shall come, and shall be born of Mary the Virgin in Bethlehem.' And we are not ashamed of what we say. As for you, what do ye say?"

The unbelievers say: "Is the Son of Mary better than Abraham, who called on God, and He opened the heavens and spake with him as we speak one with another?"

The lovers of the Messiah say to the unbelievers: "Ye see that ye know nothing! For we who are lovers of the Messiah, know that the Son of Mary created Abraham in the womb of his mother. He was the Messiah before all creatures. And in that ye say, 'God spake with Abraham from heaven; it was the Messiah who spake with Abraham.'" p. 70

[1] See *Studia Sinaitica*, No. VIII, p. 11.

The unbelievers say: "Is the Messiah, of whom ye are proud, better than Isaac, who became an offering, and the savour of his offering went up, and heaven and earth were gladdened by it?"

The lovers of the Messiah say to the unbelievers: "Isaac's not being slain on the altar when Abraham presented him, was entirely because the Messiah was going to be born of Mary the Virgin; and He was to die instead of all mankind; and by His death he was to deliver all the world from error. For if Isaac had died, one offering would have been offered; but when the Messiah died, the offering of all creatures were offered to God in Him."

The unbelievers say: "Is the Messiah better than Jacob, the like of whose vision men have never seen? who went up and slept on Mount Gilead, and God opened the heavens and spoke with him, and stretched a ladder of fire from earth to heaven, and even the angels came down to greet him?."

The lovers of the Messiah say: "Jacob, and the angels, and the ladder which he saw, were concerning the coming of the Messiah, and concerning the mystery of His death."

The unbelievers say: "Let Moses come, and the signs with which he smote Egypt, and delivered Israel. And when Pharaoh sought to prevent us from reaching the sea, Moses lifted up the dry rod, which was in his hand, and gathered up the waves of the sea in heaps."

p. 71 The lovers of the Messiah say: "Jesus also who was born of Mary rebuked the demons, and they were scattered before Him; and to Simon, when the sea sought to swallow him, He stretched out His hand and lifted him up, that he did not sink; and if the Messiah had not had power over the sea and the dry land, and all the creatures, whence would these creatures have obeyed Him when He commanded them?"

The unbelievers say to the lovers of the Christ: "We are not able to dispute with you, because ye have tasted of the doctrine of the Son of Mary, and ye have learned deception, and if ye were to dispute with Satan, ye would lead him astray."

The lovers of the Messiah say: "You do not say a single word in which there is peace with God, nor do ye carry off the victory."

The unbelievers say to the friends of the Messiah: "Neither

David the singer of the Holy Spirit, nor Elisha the son of Shaphat, who brought the dead to life, nor Enoch whom God took away, and no creature knew whereunto he attained—there is none amongst them more excellent before God than this Messiah who was born of Mary, who was called the son of the carpenter."

The lovers of the Messiah say: "Neither in heaven nor in earth is there any more excellent than the Son of God, Who was born of the Holy Virgin, except His Father who sent Him to us; and thus we cry out and confess, and the dead from the grave bear witness at this time, that this Christ who was born of Mary the Virgin, He is
the Messiah who was about to come, and came. And He came, p. 72
because all creatures were expecting Him, in whom light arose for them. And immediately when He was born of Mary, He frustrated the power of darkness; and the like of the miracles, and the like of the mighty deeds and the like of the wonders and the like of the cures, and the like of the healings and the like of the signs, no mouth can speak and no tongue can utter, neither the things above nor those below, what the Messiah, the Son of God, did in the world."

Then the Governor commanded, and some of the unbelievers were scourged, in parties of six, with severe stripes. And after they had been scourged, the friends of the Messiah say to the unbelievers, "Since ye imagine that ye have conquered us, if ye wish, we will show you what we shall do with you; and we will reveal all the frauds which have taken place in Jerusalem, before this just Governor, whom God hath sent to avenge by your hands the ignominy of the Messiah whom ye slew."

The Governor said to the lovers of the Messiah: "Say everything that ye wish, and be not afraid."

They say at once, "Where is the wood concealed, on which the Messiah was crucified? and where are the nails which were fixed in His hands and in His feet? and where was the sponge put, with which we offered Him vinegar, and where is the spear with which He was pierced? and where is the crown of thorns which we placed on His head? and where are the robes of infamy with which we
clothed Him? say, where are they hidden?" p. 73

The Governor said to the unbelievers, "Speak and reveal everything that they say to you."

The unbelievers say: "They too know what we know."

But when the Governor saw (this), he stood up on his tribunal, and adjured those who confessed the Christ, saying to them, "By the Messiah who was born of the holy Virgin, whom ye confess (and in whom I also believe), reveal and tell everything that ye know concerning the Messiah."

Then the lovers of the Messiah called out with one voice, and said: "O wise judge! woe to us from the judgment of the Messiah at the last day! Woe to us from Thy judgment, O Son of Mary, for we slew thee! Woe to us, how we have wronged Thee! and not Thee only have we wronged, but also the Father who hath sent Thee into the world."

The Governor said to them: "Disclose to me where the wood is on which He was crucified, and the crown of thorns, and the spear with which He was pierced, and the robes of infamy with which ye clothed Him." They say, "When we cast lots they fell to one amongst us. And we took them, and they were laid up beside His cross; and we dug deep into the ground about thirty cubits, and we wrote upon the cross of the Messiah and placed it at a little distance from the two crosses of the thieves. And we put little stones upon the crosses; and they were well hid. And over against the head of the
p. 74 cross of the Messiah we made an aperture hollowed out through the midst of the earth, so that a man's hand might reach our Lord's cross; so that when an affliction comes upon any one of us, he goes and stretches out his hand to the head of the wood of our Lord's cross, and immediately he receives help, and he that is sick is cured. And we swear by thy life, O illustrious lord Governor! and we do not lie, that the cross of Jesus has cured 5500 souls more or less, whose names are written down, men, women and children, and has delivered them from destruction; and they are of Jerusalem, and of its district. And when we see a man who is sick, we lead him and go; he stretches out his hand through that opening and is healed of his sickness. And not only is he healed, but if there be a sick person in his house, he takes some of the clay of that opening on his finger, and goes and rubs it on the limbs of the sick man, and immediately he is healed. And every one who is healed, we have taken a fee from him, and it has been decreed amongst us, that the man

who should reveal this secret should be slain, he and his wife, and whoso is left over from his family will be chased away from the whole nation. And we said among ourselves, If a man question us, what there is in that opening, whence the world is cured, we will say to him, 'The pot of manna is there, and the water of trial, and the staff of Aaron; and these things give healing to all those who go p. 75
thither.' And now, O illustrious Governor, fetch Jonadab and scourge him, because there is one of the nails in his house that were fastened in the hands of the Messiah. He has delivered 500 souls from death, and he has become rich and he does not know what he owns. Or which of the prophets or of the fathers did miracles, and healed the sick, and delivered people from death like the cross of the Son of Mary, and like one of the nails which were fastened in His hands? See how great is the power of the Messiah who was crucified upon it, who hath given help to the creatures who confess Him! And let us raise up His cross from the dust in which it is hidden; and from end to end of the earth let peoples and tongues come and adore the cross of the Son of God, who gives life to all mankind."

The Governor said: "Great is the thing that was concealed among you; and now that ye are angry with one another ye have revealed it. If the Emperor hear it, he will take off all your heads. Come away and show me where these crosses are hidden, and where ye have made that hole over the head of the Messiah's cross, from which ye have received help."

And they went and showed him. He said to them: "What shall I do for you now?" They say to him: "Command, my lord, that these crosses[1] be taken up; that on which our Lord was crucified and those two crosses of the two thieves, let them be burnt with fire. p. 76
And let the cross of Jesus be placed in the temple of Jerusalem; and let it be worshipped by all mankind."

The Governor said to them: "I have not been commanded by the Emperor to do this; but I will put you to great shame before all mankind; for I will not go near the cross of the Messiah; for the Christ who was crucified upon it, He it is who will lift it up from the earth in which it is hidden."

For the Governor gave orders immediately, and they brought

[1] Literally "woods."

clay and huge stones, and they heaped (them) upon the place in which these crosses[1] were hidden, ten times the height of a man.

The Governor said to them: "To this place ye came and received help from it. I have heaped upon it clay and stones so that help shall not go forth from the cross of the Christ to the children of Israel."

Then those who believed in the Christ said to the Governor, "Send thou thirty men of the chiefs of Jerusalem, and scourge them, because of the ignominy of the Messiah, and because they have wickedly insulted the Lady Mary." And the day declined, and the Governor abode wrathfully in his Praetorium. And when the cock crew the Governor went forth, he and his two young men and his son along with him; and his son had a disease of the bowels and the disease of gravel. And he knocked at the door of the Blessed one, and her maid came out and answered him.

p. 77 The Governor said to her: "Go in, tell the Lady Mary that the Governor of the city of Jerusalem desires to worship thee." Now the Lady Mary had commanded that the door should be opened to him; and he went in and knelt and worshipped her, and kissed her feet, and cried out, saying to her: "Hail to thee, Mother of God! and hail to the fruit which is born of thee! Hail to the heavens, which bear the divine throne[2] of thy Son, the Lord Christ who arose from thee! Mouth and tongue are too feeble to recount thy praises, and those of thy Son, the Holy Child.

"The earth on which thou walkest becomes heaven. The heaven that beholds thee gives a blessing to the creatures who believe in thee. The healthy who behold thee, receive gladness. To the sick who come unto thee thou givest health. I worship thee, Lady Mary. Stretch out thy right hand and bless me, and this my only child; and pray for the souls whom I have in the city of Rome, that I may go and see them in peace; and I will bring honours and offerings; and I will come to worship thee."

Now the Lady Mary was standing and praying, the censer of incense being placed in her hand; and when she had heard the words of the Governor, she turned and prayed, and stretched out her

[1] Literally, "woods."

[2] Literally, "the throne of the Deity."

hands, and blessed him and his son, and said to him, "Sit down.' Now the Apostles of our Lord were there beside the Blessed one in the house. And when she said to the Governor "Sit down," he did
not wish to sit down, but ran and fell suddenly at the feet of the p. 78
Apostles, and said to them: "Peace be with you, who were chosen by God before the world, and hail to the Christ, who chose you to be His heralds in the world."

The Apostles say to him: "We have heard what thou hast done to the crucifiers, and we have prayed much for thee."

The Governor said to them: "Enough for them is the shame which they are become before God and before men."

The Apostles say to him: "And what have they done that is not to their shame?"

These things the Apostles said to the Governor when he went to worship them and the Lady Mary. And he said to her: "I desire to learn from thee, Lady, mistress of the world, about thine election and thy virginity, and how God dwelt in thee."

Mary said to the Governor: "Hearken and receive my words, and give praise to Him Who sent His only Son from the heaven of His honour; and I did not know whence He entered the palace of my members; but when I was sitting in my house, and making the curtain of the door of the temple of God—on the first day of the week, at the ninth hour, the angel of the Lord flew and came beside me; and a light shone in all the house where I was sitting; and he spoke thus to me: 'Hail to thee, thou blessed among women! the Lord is with thee; and shines from thee.' And a sweet odour was diffused through all the house in which I sat; and the foundations
of the house sent forth waves of odours through the whole house in p. 79
which I sat. And after the salutation with which he announced (this) to me, the angel departed from me. And I arose, and set forth the censer of incense to God, and fell on my face, and glorified the name of the grace of the Lord, that I had seen this wonder; and since the time that I have existed, no man hath known me. And He was born of me as He willed, like a man; and was reared up like the children of Adam, and like an infant in the street, and like a child among children, so was He reared; and He showed signs, and did wonders, and worked miracles; and walked in the world

like God, and everything that He said to me was true and perfect. And I saw that men were not able to do the wonders that He did. And the Jews seized Him and slew Him, and He was laid in the grave for three days, and He rose of His own accord, and arose and appeared to all His disciples, working the wonders and miracles of His glorious Father; and He ascended with glory to His Father, who had sent Him to me. And if the Jews do not believe in Him, I and Joseph the carpenter and His disciples believe that He was Jesus, our Lord the Christ, the Son of God; and I assert and believe that He it is who shall come and require His blood of His crucifiers. And He said to me and decreed," says the Blessed one, "When I
p. 80 should leave this world, He would come to me, and hosts of angels. As He has assembled His disciples, and they have come to me from their countries, from the four quarters of the world, I accordingly am looking for Him to come to me from heaven; that I may see Him, and to place His hands on my eyes, and to take me out of this wicked world, and hide my body, and carry my spirit safely away according as He pleases."

These sweet words said the Lady Mary in the presence of the Apostles and of the Governor who came to her house. And the Governor worshipped the Lady Mary and believed much in her. And his son drew near and cast himself down on his face on the ground before her, for he had severe pains, and he adjured her by the right hand and said to her: "I beg of thee, mother of God, heal this only son for me, whom God hath given me." And the Blessed one stretched out her hand and made the sign of the cross on the boy[1] and spake thus to him: "In the name of my Master the Christ, whom I have in heaven, be cured." And straightway the boy was healed by the prayers of the Lady Mary. And the Governor went to his house, and wrote everything down; the wonders and miracles, and cures which the Blessed one did in the world. Because she asked nothing from the Christ which He did not give her; for she is His
p. 81 mother as He lived in the world; and He bears up the created things. .........in thy name, O Lady Mary, and everything adores thee as thy son."

And the Governor was dismissed, and went forth from Jerusalem,

[1] Literally, "sealed the boy."

and went to his house in the city of Rome, because he was from there. And when he went to Rome he went in unto the Emperor and the nobles of Rome, and related to them all the miracles and wonders which the Lady Mary did in Jerusalem and Bethlehem. And the disciples also of Peter and of Paul whom they had in the city of Rome went and wrote these holy words which they had heard from the Governor. And their[1] disciples wrote to the Apostles about the Blessed one from the mouth of the Governor. And they wrote letters to all the Church, to Mount Sinai, and to Egypt, and to Thebais, and to Asia, and to Pontus; and they wrote thus: "Great was the glory with which the Lady Mary hath left this world." And the disciples of the Apostles wrote to them. "When ye have buried the Blessed one, bring with you the Book of her Departure, and of how she went out of the world with you, for lo! all countries are full of the glories of the Blessed one. And people without number, both men and women, believe much in her, since the Governor who was in
Jerusalem came up and narrated to us here how she helps the souls p. 82
who call on her and believe. Often here in Rome she appears to the people who confess her in prayer; for she has appeared here on the sea when it was troubled and raised itself, and was going to destroy the ship in which they were sailing. And the sailors called on the name of the Lady Mary and said: 'O Lady Mary, mother of God, have mercy on us.' And straightway she rose upon them like the sun, and delivered the ships, ninety-two of them, and rescued them from destruction; and none of them perished.

"And again she appeared by day on a mountain where robbers had fallen upon people and sought to slay them. And these people cried out, saying, 'O Lady Mary, mother of God, have mercy on us.' And she appeared before them like a flash of lightning, and blinded the eyes of the robbers, and they were not seen by them; and there was no destruction to them[2]."

And she appeared here to a widow woman whose son had gone and peeped into a well of water; and he fell into it; and there was no one near him to lift him up; and the woman wailed at the mouth

[1] *i.e.* The disciples of Peter and Paul.

[2] *i.e.* to the people who were attacked.

of the well; and she said: "O Lady Mary, mother of God, have mercy upon us!" And straightway the Lady Mary appeared to her, and snatched up the boy, who was not choked, and she gave him to his mother.

p. 83 And she appeared here in Rome to a certain man who had been sick for sixteen years; and there were no doctors who could help him in anything all these long years. Then he took a censer and cast incense into it, and remembered the Blessed one and said, "O Lady Mary, mother of God, cure me!" and immediately she came to him, and cured him; and she sent him to the church of Rome before the whole people.

And again she appeared when a ship had been wrecked, and many people who were in it had fallen into the sea. And the Lady Mary appeared running upon the waves of the sea, and she carried the souls of the people who had fallen, to the dry land, and she rescued many so that they did not perish.

And again she appeared to two women in the land of Egypt, as they were going along the road, and a great snake came out against them; and it ran after them to devour them. And they called on the name of the Blessed Lady Mary. Then the Lady Mary appeared to them, and struck the snake on its mouth, and it split in two, and these women were delivered and did not perish.

And again she appeared here to a certain merchantman, who had borrowed 1000 dinars and had gone to trade with them in another
p. 84 place. And he was going on the road, and his purse fell from him, and was lost. And after he had gone a long distance he was sitting down to eat bread. And he changed his garments, and sought for the purse, and did not find it. And he wept and wailed and went in the way praying and saying, "O Lady Mary, have mercy upon me." Then the Lady Mary had mercy upon him, and led him, and made him stand over the purse of dinars, and he took up his own, and had lost nothing from it. And while the Lady Mary was doing these miracles in Rome and in all these countries; all the Apostles were with her in Jerusalem.

And while the Apostles and the Lady Mary were in Jerusalem, and the Friday had dawned, the Holy Spirit said to them, "Take up the Lady Mary this morning, and go forth from Jerusalem on the

road that goes out to the head of the valley beyond the Mount of Olives, lo! three caves are in it, a large outer cave, and another cave within it, and a small inner cave, and a raised bench of clay on the east side. Go in, and place the Blessed one on that bench, and minister about her until I shall speak to you." And the Apostles rose very early in the morning, and they took up the Blessed one and went forth from Jerusalem; and the Jews stood mocking and saying to one another: "Behold! the disciples of that seducer are carrying Mary and are going away." The Blessed one was looking. And the Jews p. 85
made signs one to another and said: "Lo! Mary thinks that she has conquered us, and she is going from Jerusalem." And a certain man was there who was called Yūphanyā (Jephunneh), he was a strong and tall man and handsome of figure. A scribe of Israel said to him: "Come near, Yūphanyā, and blow upon Mary, and she will fall down from her bed (litter); for lo! she and the disciples of the seducer think that they have conquered Jerusalem." And Yūphanyā went near and cast both his arms upon Mary's litter; and the angel of the Lord struck him with a sword of fire; and both his arms were cut off from his armpits. And his arms remained on the litter like ropes; and he wept and wailed and followed the Apostles crying out and saying, "O Apostles of Jesus the Christ, have mercy on me!" The Apostles say to Yūphanyā, "Why callest thou on us? Call on Mary the mother of the Christ, whose litter thou didst wish to break." Yūphanyā says: "O Mother of God, have mercy on me!" Then Mary said to Peter: "Give Yūphanyā his arms from the litter, and whatsoever of them is cleaving to me." He said, "In the name of my Lord, and also of Mary the mother of God, cleave to thy place." And after these arms had cleaved to their place, Peter took up a dry rod and gave it to Yūphanyā, and said to him: "Go, shew the power of God to all the Jews; perhaps they may be ashamed." Mary says to him: "Why hast thou done this?" and passing him, Yūphanyā fell down before her litter and he also besought her, saying, "I entreat of thee, mother of God, pray for me; and I will go and preach thine excellencies among the people of the Jews. And I will deny those who deny thy Holy Child, O mother of God." And Yūphanyā went away and arrived at the gate of Jerusalem; and struck the dry rod on the p. 86
threshold of the gate of the city. And straightway it put out leaves. And Yūphanyā cried out, saying, "Blessed is the Messiah who was born of the Virgin Mary." The Jews say to him: "What hath befallen thee?" Yūphanyā said to them: "I have become a disciple of Jesus the Son of the glorious God, and of Mary His mother who bore Him; for both my arms were cut off, and they were fastened to the litter like ropes, and I besought her for them; and she gave them to me; and immediately when she had signed (the cross) on me, my arms were put right and I was healed. And she gave me

the dry rod, and lo! ye see it, that it has put forth leaves. And I believe in her, that she is the mother of God." The Jews say to him, "Thou art surely mad, O Yūphanyā." He said to them: "Whether I be mad or no, come see what the dry rod which budded has done." The Jews say to him: "What is it doing?" He said unto them: "Peter told me when he gave me this rod: 'Every sick person whom thou dost touch with this rod and lay it upon him, shall be healed.'" And he went in to the blind man who was (so) from his mother's womb; and he laid that rod on the eyes of the blind man, and immediately they were opened, and he confessed the Christ. And every sick person on whom he laid a hand was healed immediately. And he commanded those whom he had cured to cry out: "Blessed be Mary, and blessed be the Messiah who was born of her." And Yūphanyā cured him. And he went about among all the sick people; and God helped them by his hands. And when the Apostles reached these caves at the head of the valley they placed the mother of God in the eastern one. And a service
p. 87 of angels and of apostles lasted over it for three days and three nights. And when the Jews were insulting them, and could not find them, the Holy Spirit blinded their eyes, that they might not see neither the disciples nor Mary. And the Jews came and sat at the door of the cave when they did not know it, and were talking with each other. For the scent of the spices struck on them; and the door of the cave was opened before them. And they saw the litter lying, and the angels and the Apostles standing and serving. And there were many lights there. And three of them ventured and went in to the Apostles within the cave. And when they entered, a fire which was burning there flamed up and burnt them; and the earth swallowed their bodies. And the comrades of those who had been burnt said: "Let us flee from here," for they had seen what happened, and they trembled greatly. And they gazed and looked at Mary and the angels, and at the Apostles who were serving before her. And when the men had said these words many people believed in Mary and in the Son whom she had borne. And the priests gave many bribes to the men who had gone there that they should not reveal before anyone that any of them had died there. And if they were to reveal it, all the nation would go astray after Mary and her Son, and they think that Mary is great before God; but say, "We know not where these men have gone to from amongst us." These men spake thus, according as the chief priests had told them. They had a custom that every time that one of the Jews went near the mother of God, and was healed, they gave him a bribe and said to him: "Do not tell that Mary has healed thee! but say that the priests have laid the Torah on me, and I am healed." And every cure which the Blessed one wrought
p. 88 amongst the men who went to the Jews, they ran and explained to them "that if ye reveal that Mary has healed you, here ye shall die." Because the Jews hated the Lady Mary greatly.

For whosoever loveth God and the Lady Mary`who bore Him, will not be the comrade and friend of the Jews. And if he be, the love of the Christ shall be withdrawn from him.

Here endeth the Third Book.

## BOOK IV.

And when the Apostles were ministering about the Blessed one within the cave, the Holy Spirit informed them (saying), In the sixth month the angel Gabriel was sent to the mother of your Lord, the Lady Mary, and he saluted her, and announced to her concerning the Holy Child that was to be born of her for the salvation of the world. [And the sixth month is Nisan], on the first of Nisan, on the first day of the week, as the Lady Mary was sitting, and there were lying before her dyed curtains for the front of the door, which she was making for the house of the Lord. And the Holy one had taken this in her hand, and she was sitting in her house. There was a signal between the Father and His Child; and He sent Him from His bosom, that He might come and redeem mankind; and God sent Gabriel that he might precede the king's son, and cry "Hail" before his Lord in the ears of the Blessed one in whom he p. 89
dwelt. Gabriel went and saluted the Blessed one: "Behold, the Lord is with thee, for it is God who dwelleth in thee." And while he had not yet finished his salutation, his Lord anticipated him, and entered, and dwelt in the bosom of the Blessed one. And Gabriel did obeisance before Mary. And not to Mary alone did he do obeisance, but also to his Lord. Gabriel therefore made haste and came down to greet his Lord. The Lord of the angel-hosts preceded him, not delaying; but entered and dwelt in the Holy Virgin. And at that time he said to her, "Hail to thee, O blessed among women! behold! God is with thee," as if a man were to say, "Behold, He has preceded me and has entered and dwelt in the palace of thy members." For the things on high beheld when the Messiah was sent to the womb of the Virgin Mary. And they praised God who willed in His love to go down and clothe Himself in the mortal body of Adam.

These things the Holy Spirit told the Apostles that on the first
of Nisān it was announced to the Holy Virgin that she would receive
your Lord. And He was in her womb until the Second Kanūn[1], on
its sixth (day) on the first of the week, the holy day, in her virginity,
p. 90 at the time of the ninth hour, at the time that she had borne Him,
she went out of this world. The Apostles said to the Holy Spirit,
"And to-morrow at what hour will our Lord come from heaven to
us?" And the Holy Spirit said to them: "To-morrow at the ninth
hour He will come to you from heaven." And again the Holy
Spirit said to the Apostles: "Thus believe and thus confess: that
on a first day of the week He was announced and came into the
world. And on a first day of the week in the Second Kanūn,
on its sixth day, He came into the world, and was born in
Bethlehem. And on a first day of the week the people of Jerusalem
went forth unwillingly and praised Him with hosannas heavenly and
earthly. And on a first day of the week He rose from the grave,
and put to shame all His crucifiers.

Again, after the forty days of His resurrection, on the fifth day of the week, He ascended to Heaven. And on a first day of the week He will come at the last day. But set the censer, and to-morrow He will come to His mother. And Eve will come, the mother of all mankind; and the mother of the Lady Mary; and the virgins who ministered to the Lady Mary were with her, and all the officials.

And the mother of the Lady Mary drew near and placed her
mouth on her breast and kissed her. And she said to her: "Blessed
be God who hath chosen thee for Himself that thou mightest be a
p. 91 dwelling-place for His honour; for from the time that thou wast
formed in my womb, I knew that the God of heaven would come
and dwell in thee." And our father Adam came, and Seth his son,
and Shem, and Noah, who was a leaven to the world, and they
worshipped before her. And they said: "We praise thee, O God!
Who didst come from heaven, and didst dwell in my daughter,
and I heard Thy voice in Sheol, and I rejoiced that Thou didst
clothe Thyself with a body and didst raise me to heaven, according
as Thy holy mouth hath told me in Paradise. And other chariots

[1] *i.e.* The last part of December and first part of January.

appeared coming, of Abraham and of Isaac and of Jacob, and of my lord David, the Psalmist of the church with them, and they worshipped before the Blessed Mary. And there appeared coming the chariots of the prophets, with their censers in their hands, and they worshipped before the Blessed one. And there appeared coming the chariots of the witnesses[1], with lights in their hands, who worshipped before the Holy Virgin. And there were seen coming the chariots of the seventy-two Apostles, and they worshipped before the Blessed one. And after these there were seen the chariots of the angels, and of the heavenly guardians, and of the cherubim, and of the seraphim holding their trumpets and shouting praise before their Lord; who had come and descended beside His mother. Then was seen the face of Christ the King, on the chariot of the seraphim who p. 92
were carrying Him, clothing Him with glory; and He came holding the sign of the cross, and came that He might descend beside the Lady Mary. And He came down beside her. And all created things bowed down and worshipped her. And our Lord Jesus the Christ called to His mother and said to her, "Mary!" And she said to Him, "Here I am, Rabbuli[2]," which is, being interpreted, Teacher. Our Lord said to her: "Do not grieve, arise, see the glory which my Father hath given me; and I have come to show thee." And the holy Virgin went down with Him; and she saw the glory which no tongue of man can tell of. The Messiah said to His mother: "Is everything true which I told thee of, Mary?" And she said to Him: "Yea, in truth, Rabbuli, everything is true that Thou hast told me of." He said to her: "Now I will make thy body go into the Paradise of Eden, and there it will be until the Resurrection. I will also give angels for thine honour, and they shall stand before thee holding lights and lamps until I shall come and dissolve the heaven and the earth, and shall give bliss to the righteous and torment and darkness to the wicked. For that which thou hast seen now, Mary, is but a little of the glory of my Father. Come with me and thou shalt see and shalt rejoice. For in the last day when I shall come with great glory to show to the world a glory which the eye of man cannot bear, with that will I come to the created world." Mary said to Him: "O Master! stretch out Thy hands, and place p. 93

[1] Or, "Martyrs." [2] i.e. "my Master."

them on my eyes, and bless me." And the Messiah stretched out His hands, and laid them on the eyes of His mother; and the Blessed Lady Mary took His hands, and kissed them; and answered, saying "I worship these holy hands, which made heaven and earth without labour. I praise and worship and extol that hour in which Thy Father sent Thee to me from the heaven of His glory. For I knew when thou wast in my womb, for the angels of Thy Father came down and worshipped before Thee and I dwelt in a place of light; and the angels of glory escorted me." And again she gave thanks and said: "O Son of God, O Christ, Thou art the Lord of the peace of the world, and in Thee the crowns of the priests who confess Thee are blessed."

And when the Blessed one had said these things the heights and the depths gave praise on account of her to the Christ, Who had come down from heaven to see His mother, the holy Virgin who had given Him birth. And thus she went out of this world.

Then the Apostles drew near and said to the Lady Mary, "Leave a blessing to the world out of which thou art going, that those who
p. 94 make unto thee commemorations and believe in God, that He sent His Son and [that] He dwelt in thee, confessing that He who was born of thee is God, and give praise to the Holy Spirit who escorts thee, and make commemorations, may be delivered from sore afflictions."

Then the Blessed one prayed and spoke thus in her prayer: "May God, Who willed of His own will, and was reconciled in His love, and sent His Son from Heaven, and He dwelt in the palace of my members, have mercy upon the world which calls upon Him." And again she prayed and said: "O Christ, Son of the King of Heaven, Son of God who faileth not, receive the prayers of men, who call [upon] and commemorate the name of Thy mother before Thee, and make tribulations pass away from them; and make bad times cease from the earth." And again she prayed and said: "Lord Jesus the Christ, give a crown to old age, and a bringing up to youth; and help the souls that call upon Thee; and whoso maketh a commemoration of my spirit and of my body, which have quitted this world." And she took the hands of the Lord Jesus Christ, and laid them on her face and kissed them, saying, "I entreat Thee, Lord

Jesus the Christ, that what I have sought, Thou wilt do it in heaven
and on earth. This, Lord, I would persuade Thee, that wherever men
are assembled and are making a commemoration of me, and are p. 95
presenting me with offerings, and are naming the memory of the
Lady Mary, the mother of the Messiah, accept, O Lord, their offerings
from them, and accept the prayer which goeth up to Thy presence.
And receive the supplication of men, and the tears which are shed
from their eyes; and cause to pass away from the land in which
they make my offerings, the sword, and captivity, and famine and
pestilence, and grievous calamities; and all the afflictions which befal
the children of men, do thou cause to cease from the people who
make offerings before Thee."

And again she prayed, saying, "My Master, the Christ Whom
I have in heaven, the land in which my offerings are made, bless it,
Lord, in the garland of the year [with] a blessing, that it may be
given to its inhabitants to have these lands delivered, by the offerings
which they make me, from the locust that it may not destroy; and
from the heat that it may not wither; and from blight that it may
not wear them away; and from the hailstones that they may not
fall down on them from heaven; and let every one who is sick, be
cured, and whoso is afflicted, let him be relieved; and whoso is
hungry, let him be satisfied; and whoso is poor, let him become rich;
and whoso is tormented by a spirit of Satan, and calleth on my
name, let a cure be sent to him; and whoso is bound by violence
from men, let his bonds be loosed; and those who are sailing
on the sea, and storms arise against them, and they call on the
name of the Lord, let them be delivered from destruction; and
let those who are far away in [foreign] lands and call upon my name, p. 96

come to their homes in peace. And let the fields which have given offerings for my honour, be blessed, and bring forth fruit; and let the vines yield clusters of blessing; and let the men who make offerings to me be blessed, and let these be for blessings and for a leaven of righteousness. And let all diseases and afflictions, and rods of anger pass away from them. And let there be concord and peace on all created beings that call on Thy holy name. And let the garland of the year and of the months be blessed before Thee. And the priests who present offerings and tithes before Thee, accept, O Lord their offerings, and bless their tithes; and make their temples thunder with praises; and may the Holy Spirit sing along with them. And amongst kings may there be concord, and among judges peace; and blessings and joys be on the face of the earth for ever and ever. Amen."

These prayers and blessings did Mary say when the Christ came to her, and He said to her: "I will do whatsoever is thy will; and I will have mercy on those who call on me in thy name; and also those who make commemorations of thee with offerings; and who remember that thou didst leave this earth, and who in the time of affliction make offerings on thy behalf, I will have mercy on them. And those who make memorials of thee, I will save them, and will have mercy upon them, and I will give good increase in their houses; and I will also forgive their short-comings. And the blessing of my Father who is in heaven shall abide on all offerings that are offered in thy name, and because of thy death for ever and ever. Amen."

Then the created beings drew near, and worshipped the Christ. And the Christ called to Mar John, and said to him, "Be not grieved because of Mary." Then John said: "My Lord, Mary is not dead." And He called Peter also, and said to him: "Now the time is short, raise thy psalms, and let all created beings sing Halleluia." And while they were singing with the voices of praise, our Lord Jesus the Christ prayed, and the angels gave glory, and straightway Mary departed to the mansions of the Father.

p. 97 And Mary said when she was dying: "Fare thee well, Rabbuli, lo! I am looking for Thy coming, O Christ! and immediately Peter, and John, and Paul, and Thomas ran, and John laid his hands upon her eyes and closed them. And Peter and Paul stretched out her hands and her feet; and they did not take off her tunic, but they wrapped her in it; and the woollen garment became the robe of the Holy Spirit; and the Spirit wrapped her with a covering of flame and girded her loins with a belt of fire; and covered her face with the scent of perfumes. Then John placed his mouth on her breast, and wept. And Peter, and Paul, and all the Apostles overflowed with tears, and they wept for the Blessed one, in great pain and grief. And John said, "Thou art dead, O Mary, mistress of the world!" Then our Lord Jesus the Christ commanded that they should make the Blessed one repose in a chariot of light; and the twelve Apostles bore it. And twelve chariots carried the twelve Apostles, and the voice of the trumpets of the seraphim went before the Blessed one as she went to Eden with great glory; and all the created beings were singing before her. And created beings were following her: and the mother of the Lady Mary went, and Eve our mother, and Elisabeth the mother of John the Baptist, and the three virgins who ministered to her; and chariots of light went before the Blessed one. And again after these went the chariots of Abraham, and of Isaac, and of Jacob, and of all just and righteous men, and the fathers, and the holy teachers. Then after these chariots went the twelve Apostles, and their hands were spread out to heaven from the clouds on which they were standing. And they bore the chariot of the Lady Mary.

And the Holy Spirit sprinkled dew on her face. Angels and guar-

dian angels came and sang praises before her; ranks from above and from below gave praise and laud, and a sweet scent was wafted through all corners of the world. And when she entered Paradise
with the praise and the exultation of the high beings and the low p. 98
beings, they placed her on a shining cloud, and they spread her couch with a coverlet of fire, amongst the glorious trees that are in the Paradise of Eden, whose scent is far sweeter than perfume. And the guardian angels and the angels stood before her, for her honour; and they ministered to her. And the high beings praised her with songs before God in heaven, and the Apostles returned and came to the Mount of Olives; and they wrote that there should be a commemoration of the Lady Mary three times in the year; that we might know [it] and she has sent it to us; and we have seen [it] with our eyes; that as often as a commemoration of her is made, all the hosts of angels are robed in white, because the glory shall be greater before God, life to all created beings who go to salute the mother of God and all men were blessed by her and returned. And those who were dead and had risen returned to[1] their graves, and those who were alive returned safely each man to the place from which he had come.

And the twelve Apostles went out of Paradise; and while priests are making offerings, no plagues come into the world to destroy it. And when there is an offering to the Blessed one, on the sixth day[2] in the second Kanūn, on the birthday of the Christ, they wrote, because on the day that she bore Him she went out of this world, and as it was not possible to have a commemoration on her birthday, we command that after two days there shall be the commemoration
of the Blessed one, that there may be help from her to men; and p. 99
by means of her offerings and her prayers the fruits of the earth may be blessed. And the sweet scent of her offering arose and pleased the Christ, so that kingdoms might not strive with each other: and the blood of many men be shed upon the earth, because that whensoever there are wars, heaven and earth are weeping about men who slay each other, for the air is troubled, and the odour of the air is changed by the corpses of men. Because the Holy Spirit had revealed to them that when they go out to war on the earth, and

[1] MS. "from." [2] January 6th = Epiphany.

take away each other's land, their arms are set in order all the winter, and from the month of Nisān[1] until the first Teshrīn[2] is the fear of captivity, if they do not approach God with prayers and offerings. And thus the Apostles said that there should be a commemoration of the Lady Mary in the month of Iyār[3], on its fifteenth [day] on account of the seeds that were sown; and on account of the abundance of the wheat, that there should be a commemoration and offerings to the Christ, and to the Lady Mary. And the Apostles commanded that during all the month of Iyār, men should offer many supplications and prayers...before God on account of the clusters of the vines that they may not be destroyed by wrath, and on account of the flying locusts, and the black caterpillars and the creeping things, and the white things, and the great things that they should not go out to destroy the crops[4] and there should be a famine and the world come to an end. And the Holy Spirit said to the Apostles that
p. 100 they[5] are buried in the earth until the day that is appointed for them, and they shall come forth to fulfil the will of their Lord. And when they are created, in a single hour shall they be created; and whithersoever they go to destroy, in one hour shall they destroy and desolate the lands, so that there shall not be an end of the world immediately.

And the Holy Spirit made known to the Apostles, that there should be a commemoration of the Lady Mary in the month of Iyār, because the army of your Lord is the locust and the angel of wrath, which go before Him; because of the heavy rods which strike and spare not, whithersoever they are sent; and those plagues which are kept and laid up for the wicked of the land with which the Lord is wroth, and willeth that one of these rods which are prepared be sent against her.

And the Apostles commanded that on the fourth [day] of the week and on Friday and on the first day of the week [in] all the months of the year there should be supplications, and that these days should be kept; and that nothing should happen in them, but that offerings should be made in these three days,

[1] i.e. April. [2] i.e. October. [3] i.e. part of April and May.
[4] Literally "the creation." [5] i.e. the locusts.

on all the weeks of the months of the year. And the Apostles commanded that there should be commemorations of the Blessed one in the month of Ab, on its thirteenth day, on account of the vines bearing clusters, on account of the trees bearing fruit
that the clouds of hail may not come, bearing hailstones of wrath, and the p. 101
trees be broken, and their fruits, and the vines with their clusters; and those who eat of them be sick, and there be a fearful pestilence in the world; and it slay the fathers in the presence of the children, and the children in the presence of the fathers. And on account of the creeping locust, the caterpillar, that it may not climb on the trees, and eat their fruit.

And the Apostles commanded that there should be a commemoration of Mary in these three months, that men might be delivered from sore afflictions. And the Apostles commanded that the priests and the believing peoples should fast on the day of the commemoration until the ninth hour; and at the ninth hour offerings should be made to her. And like as the power of the Most High came and dwelt in her, so the power of prayer should come and bless the land in which offerings are made. And the Apostles commanded that the vows and the offerings which should be made to the Blessed one in her name should be preserved, and that in every place where such offering is made she should come and appear there; and in every place where men call upon her she should come and appear there; and should help them.

And again the Apostles commanded that on the day of her commemoration the Old and the New Testament should be read and the volume of her decease, that is, her story; and then the Gospel should be read. And every one who goes to partake of her offering should take with him a censer of incense and lights for her honour. And before the time of the festival they should be bought and also set up in the name of the Blessed one. And they should be prepared as chosen garments which are kept for God, that He may clothe the righteous with them in the day of the resurrection.

Then the Apostles set up the censers of incense, and called on our Lord
Jesus the Christ to bless the years and their garlands. And the Apostles p. 102
prayed, saying: "Our Lord Jesus the Christ, hear the voice of our prayers and bless the garlands of the twelve months. Let Nisān come, bearing flowers of blessing. Let Iyār come, bearing sheaves of gladness. Let Haziran come, bearing joys, that from it there may be offerings. Let Tammūz come, bearing thanks because of men, who sing praises in the threshing-floors which are full of gladness. Let Ab come giving clusters (of grapes) to God, let them give praise to God Who has given ripe and unripe [fruits]. Let Ilūl come, thanking and praising Him Who has heard the Christ, and worshipping Him Who blesses the years and the months. Let Teshrīn come, thanking and praising Him Who has heard the voice of the husbandman, who has sown with the plough of the cross. Let Teshrīn[1] come, its

[1] i.e. the second Teshrīn.

good things with it, for in it comes the dew from heaven, and it will fatten the earth and its inhabitants. Let Kanūn come, and its joys with it, lightnings, and thunders, and thick clouds, and they will be poured upon mankind. Let Kanūn[1] come, and with it snow and ice, which gladden the earth. Let Shebat come, bearing honour to the Lord. Let Adar come, with lambs and with ewes."

Thus the Apostles prayed and said: "Yea, Lord God, Who didst send Thy Son to us, that He might redeem the world from error. Let Thy blessing, Lord, be upon the earth and upon its inhabitants, when an offering is made to Thy mother. And let Thy grace come to us, and be manifested to us at this time."

Then the voice of the prayers of the Apostles ascended to heaven. And
our Lord Jesus the Christ came to them in a cloud of light and spake with
p. 103 them and said unto them, "Be strong and be valiant, and fear not. Because
everything that ye seek shall be given unto you. And at all times what
ye wish shall happen with your Father Which is in heaven." And the
Apostles bowed their heads, and were blessed by our Lord Jesus. And they
arose in the place where they were standing, and said, "Come, let us go
down from the Mount of Olives to the cave of the valley; and let us write
how Mary went out of this world: and [how] she was snatched away in a
cloud of light, and the Christ bore her to the Paradise of Eden."

Now when the Apostles went down from the Mount of Olives to Jerusalem, to the cave of the valley, they set up a censer of incense and prayed, speaking thus: "We will write in this book: 'All we the Apostles, bear witness before God, that our Lord Jesus the Christ did these miracles and signs before His mother, when she went out of this world. And all those who believe in the words which are written in this book shall live for ever. And whoso doth not believe shall be condemned. This is the woman who was chosen from before the foundations of the world, that God might dwell in her, and the Christ might be born of her, He who is the Son of God. And these commemorations which we make of Mary the holy Virgin (are) with fasting and prayer and with tears and vigils and services, and with melodies of the Holy Spirit, and with gifts to the poor and the needy: thus it behoves us to celebrate the feast of the Blessed one; whilst a sweet scent was wafted through all the corners of the world; and her blessings came upon all mankind.'"

This book was written in Hebrew and Greek and Latin, and the Apostles
p. 104 placed the book with John the friend of the Christ, who is called the Son
of Thunder. And he carried it to his (house). And the Apostles prayed
and called on our Lord Jesus the Christ that He should come and bless
them, and that each of them might go to the place whence he had come.
And while they were praying, the Christ came to them. And Enoch came

[1] i.e. the second Kanūn.

and Elijah and Moses. And they prayed a long time; and the tears of the Apostles fell upon the ground, until the dust on which they stood was hardened. That clay caused a scent of perfume to exude, and the Apostles were gladdened by it; because the Holy Spirit flamed about them. And the Apostles stretched out [their hands[1]] and the Christ drew near and said to them: "Blessed be ye chosen ones who are chosen by the Father and by Me, and by the Holy Spirit. Great is the glory that is kept for you. Ye have seen the glory with which Mary My mother went from this world." They said to Him: "We have seen it and we are sure that Thou art the Christ the Son of the Living God. And blessed be Thy Father Who is in heaven, Who hath sent Thee to the world. And blessed be Mary who gave Thee birth. And may the men who believe in Thee and in Thy Father and in Thy Holy Spirit, receive from Thee the remission of their sins in the last day. Then our Lord Jesus the Christ stretched out His right hand upon their heads and said to them: "Go in peace to the places whence ye have come. And I will do your pleasure in whatsoever ye wish." And He
blessed them and ascended to heaven. And the Apostles stood and gazed
at Him; and as He passed away from them, they prayed and gave glory to p. 105
God Who had so loved them.

Then the Holy Ghost brought a cloud of light, and each one of them sat on the cloud and went to the place whence he had come. And those who had died returned to their graves, and the Apostles saluted each other and prayed, saying: "Now we pray that we may see each other on the day of the resurrection." And the Apostles entreated Peter and Paul, saying: "Let twelve books be written from this book, and let a book go with each one of us." And Peter answered saying unto them, "Let each of us in the place whence he has come write and also show to the world what the Holy Spirit is preparing by his mouth. Thus let him teach the people to whom he is going that there may be a commemoration of Mary three times in the year. And whoso shall make a commemoration of her shall be excellent in heaven before the face of the Father and whosoever shall make and magnify her commemoration before all mankind, shall be blessed by God."

The book that was written, Mar John took it up, and called to Peter and Paul, and said a word to them by themselves. The Apostles say with Peter and Paul to John, "Let us divide this volume." And when they were about to make a dispute with each other, a voice came from heaven and spake with them, saying to them, "Go in her peace, ye blessed, and be looking and waiting for my coming from heaven." And then the Apostles went and preached and taught the nations who went to them about the mother of the Christ, how she went out from this world, with the prayers of the prophets and of the
Apostles; and of the martyrs, and of the confessors, and of the just men,
and of the priests, and of every one who believes in the Father and in the p. 106
Son and in the Holy Spirit, and in the Mother of God, Mary. And in the

[1] Literally "themselves."

churches and the monasteries, and in the dwellings of the saints, which are founded on the name of the Christ. May we receive blessings from God, Who was born of the Holy Virgin Mary. And every one who makes a commemoration of her, may his commemoration be above in the heaven and beneath on the earth. And every one who writes (copies?) these books and reads in them, may the Lord have mercy on his soul and on his body in both worlds, for ever and ever. Amen.

## BOOK V.

From the same. The Fifth[1] book about her Departure.

Now when the Blessed Mary was placed in the Paradise of Eden, and was crowned with this great glory, and the Apostles had departed in all directions, our Lord Jesus Christ came to His mother to Eden. And the chariot of the spiritual beings descended from heaven, and the Paradise of Eden was covered, and all the mountains that were around it.. And the sound of nothing was heard save of the cherubim crying and the angels who were shining by means of light. For the Paradise of Eden is on earth, in that outside region and above all the high mountains; and its foundations are placed on the earth, and four rivers issue from it; Gihōn, and Pisōn, and Daklath and Euphrates. And when there was a flood rising as far as the foot of the mountain, it straightway covered (it) at a signal. For it has not dared to visit that holy mountain. Because the Lord of Paradise has fixed (His) glory there, and He stands in it and looks at the flood that is chastising
p. 107 the sons of men. And when the flood had reached the foot of Paradise, it bent its head and worshipped the Lord of created beings Who was standing in the Paradise and it turned backwards. For this Paradise is a house of return to the high beings, and a dwelling-place for the heavenly beings; and it was prepared before the times of the worlds to be a dwelling place for Adam the head of the tribes and the families. To him God came down and walked amongst the delightful trees of Paradise. To this Paradise came the body of the holy Mother of God, Mary. When our Lord came to His mother and said to her, "Mary, arise in the Paradise of Eden," she was raised, and she stood and saluted our Lord Jesus the Christ. Our Lord said to her: "To show thee the glory of My Father's house, I am come to thee." And Enoch came to Paradise, and Elijah, and Moses, and Peter; and they worshipped the Christ and His mother. The Christ said to Mary His mother: "Search and see what is kept for the just ones who love Me." And Mary saw there the mansions of the just, how fair and beautiful they are; and she searched in the tents of the sons of light. And she saw the couches

[1] Cod. Harris "Sixth."

of the martyrs. And she saw the just ones who were standing there. And they went before her weaving the crowns of the priests. For the garments of the just are being prepared for the day of the resurrection. And she saw the trees of Paradise, how glorious in their appearance! And how sweet is their fragrance! These things the Blessed one saw in Paradise.

Our Lord said to her: "Come, ascend with Me to heaven, and see the splendour of My Father." And then He signalled a command. And the horns of the seraphim sounded; and the wings of the cherubim were p. 108
struck, and the earth was covered with a sweet fragrance. And our Lord Jesus the Christ came on a chariot of fire; and Enoch and Elijah, a wheel of fire carrying them and above this was the lower heaven. And she saw all the treasure-houses of God; and also the house of the snow and the ice and the frost; and the house of the rain and the dew, and the house of the winds and the lightnings, and the house of the darkness and the storms; and the clouds which are the servants of God, proclaiming about Him; and she saw there wrath and concord, which when they are ordered go forth to mankind; and she saw the place in which Elijah stood and prayed; because it is in this lower heaven. And she mounted to the heaven of heavens, and she saw the ranks of the spiritual beings, and the heavenly armies, and created beings without end. And the heavenly armies stood and praised the Virgin Mary. Who may see it and not fear? when the supernal beings stand and offer praises to the Mother of their Lord, Who mounted beside them, the supernal beings saying: "Holy, holy, holy, O Son of the living God! This is the holy and blessed one who bore Thee without marriage." And the Blessed one stretched out her hands, and gave glory to God Who had magnified her. And again she mounted above the heaven of heavens. And she saw that ranks of angels were standing above the waters. And they were spreading their wings, and their eyes were looking upward to their Lord. And they were not able to cease from the voices which were entreating and saying: "Holy, holy, holy, the Mighty Lord, and Supreme God." Then she looked above the waters, and mounted to Jerusalem which is in heaven, wherein the Father is adored by His Son, and the Spirit by both. And she p. 109
saw that it had twelve gates in the names of the twelve Apostles, and at every gate an Apostle was standing. And the angels and archangels who were standing and singing praise; and at the inner door the two sons of Zebedee; John and James his brother at another door on the right; and then the Apostles ranged at these doors. And at the outer door there were verily standing spiritual beings without end; and they were singing praises beside the city of the great King. And all the prophets were standing and singing praises with their harps; Abraham and Isaac, and Jacob, and David the Psalmist. And they worshipped before the King, the Christ, and before His mother when she went in to worship in the heavenly Jerusalem. And she entered by the first gate, and the angels worshipped her. And she entered by the second gate, and the adoration of the cherubim was offered to her. And

she entered by the third gate, and the adoration of the seraphim was offered to her. And she entered by the fourth gate, and was worshipped by the families, and the chiefs of thousands. And she entered by the fifth gate, and the lightnings and the thunders uttered praises before her. And she entered by the sixth gate, and they cried before her: "Holy, holy, holy!" And she entered by the seventh gate, and fire and flame worshipped before her. And she entered by the eighth gate, and the rain and the dew worshipped her. And she entered by the ninth gate, and Gabriel and Michael worshipped her. And she entered by the tenth gate, and all the shining beings worshipped her. And she entered by the eleventh gate, and all the Apostles worshipped her. And she entered by the twelfth gate, and the Child who was born of her, praised and blessed her.

And thus Mary entered the heavenly Jerusalem, and worshipped before
p. 110 the Father. And in that hour Mary saw the Holy Father and the Beloved Son, and the Spirit, the Paraclete, the Father being glorified by His Son, and the Son by His Father; and the Spirit by both of them. And she saw a throne and a chariot, and from beneath the chariot there issued a river of fire; and it came and abode upon the whole heaven, burning nothing. And she saw the guardian angels who bore the chariots from beneath; and the seraphim who escorted it from above; and the cherubim who spread their wings and escorted it, and cried "Holy." And she saw the glorious throne of God; the Father sitting and His Son on His right hand; and the Spirit who was standing and hovering over them. And she saw the seraphim of fire, and the curtains of flame. [1]And Mary saw what eye hath not seen, nor ear heard, nor hath it entered into the heart of man, what God giveth to the righteous on the day of the resurrection.

And Mary said, "What are these?" The Christ said to her: "These are the tabernacles of the just, for the time has not yet arrived when they shall receive their recompenses; but they see them from afar and rejoice; until the day of the resurrection shall come when they shall receive the reward of their struggles."

And again Mary saw a place which was very dark, and much smoke going up from it, and a smell of brimstone rose before it, and a strong fire was blazing in it. And the sound of that fire was going like the sound of heavy thunder, when it is listened to with fear; and the fire which was
p. 111 blazing and burning there. And its sound went through the place; (and) men were placed outside of the darkness, and they wept and were grieved whilst they stood afar off. Mary said to the Christ, "My Master, what are these?" Our Lord said unto her: "This that is roaring and fearful is Gehenna which is kindled for the doers of iniquity, and these who are looking at it are the sinners, who behold their torment from a distance and know what is reserved for them[selves] at the last day, and they grieve and

[1] Book Sixth begins here in Dr Wright's edition.

weep. For the day of judgment is not yet come, that they should receive the portion of darkness; and they also shall be tormented in this flame at the last day; all those who have not kept the commandments of My Father shall be tormented in this flame." Then the Blessed one gazed at the place of the just, wondering at its being so glorious, and at that of the wicked, at its being so dark and fearful. And she heard the voices of the just, saying: "Glory to Thee, O God, Who givest a recompense to the righteous at the last day; in the which heaven and earth shall be dissolved." And again the people cried from out the darkness: "Have mercy upon us, Son of the Living God! when Thou comest to dissolve the heaven and the earth." And when the Blessed one heard the voice of the just, she rejoiced; and when she heard the voices of the sinners, she was very sorry. And she besought the Christ on behalf of the sinners, and offered up a prayer for them, and said: "Rabbūlī, have mercy upon those sinners when Thou judgest them at the last day, because I have heard their voice, and I am grieved because of them."

And the Christ came with His mother to show her all those who were sitting on a cloud of light. And seats of glory were arranged on a throne of
flame. And on the loins of the cherubim there were placed wheels of fire. p. 112
And those which were bearing their chariots. And in the thick darkness and the lightnings was the glory of Mary and of her Son escorted. And the glory coursed along and went above heaven. And the angels and the archangels were in commotion: and a decree went forth to all creatures, that they should come forth in glory to meet the King's Son, who had come to show the hidden things of His Father's house to His mother. And Enoch came forth; and Elijah came, and John, and Peter, and they worshipped before the Christ and before His mother. And the trumpets of heaven sounded when the time had arrived for praise to be offered to the King, the Christ. Who doth not fear at that moment, when the spiritual beings speak one to another, who offer adoration to their Lord? And the holy Gabriel arose with the angels; and they all threw [themselves] down before Him. And Michael rose from amongst the angel guards, and all the guards with him. The Father was escorted with glory, and the Son was exalted with trembling, and the Spirit sang praise by the mouth of all these armies, and of Mary and of the churches which were adorned. And there was praise in heaven, before the Lord who had come down to make for Himself a mother from the race of mortals. And there was a thanksgiving on high before the Highest Lord. For the power of His Father had made Him dwell in the womb of His mother, and the praise of all the heavenly beings lasted that Mary might see the glory and the exaltation of Him Who was born of her from the second hour on the first day of the week until the ninth hour, the angel guards and the angels singing praise. And there was a commotion amongst their ranks; and praise and a sweet scent was wafted from the hosts of angels. And the bright beings raised their eyes; and they saw the
mother of their Lord standing before the throne of her Son; and they gave p. 113

glory to God Who had exalted His Mother and had shewn heaven to her, and the heaven of heavens; and all that is therein, and there end the things of the Lord's house. And our Lord Jesus the Christ led His mother and came to the Paradise of Eden. And the lights shone in heaven; and the scent of perfume arose above all the heavens, and the guardian angels and the angels descended while their lamps were burning. And the glory of our Lord dawned and the grace of God was spread abroad. And our Lord came down with Mary to the Paradise of Eden with the heavenly hosts. And there was great praise before the Blessed one, so that the bones of the just which were imprisoned within the earth, moved, and a sweet odour was wafted through all corners of the world. And Mary led John and showed him everything which the Christ had shown her. And she said to him; "Take heed to me in these words, which thy Lord hath shown to me: that at the time which I shall reveal to thee I say to thee: books and writings shall be issued about my victories, when there shall be commemorations and offerings to me until the time when thy Lord shall come from heaven, because many shall be the distresses of mankind, and the sore afflictions that shall scourge the earth; when there shall be fearful signs and wars shall multiply. And there shall be a famine, and the earth shall shake because of the sins and the iniquities of the people who shall corrupt it by deeds of wickedness. And great also at that time shall be the affliction of mankind; there shall be darkness in the air of heaven. And winds shall blow and [there shall be] thick darkness and the times shall be shortened. And in the night-seasons men
p. 114 shall see visions; for the destruction of men shall be by one another. And plagues shall be sent on the earth, and my Son the Christ shall come, and shall not find faith on the earth." These things and more than these did our Lord reveal to His mother; and she revealed them to John. And our Lord said to her; "Blessed be thou, Mary, [1]for what[1] thine eyes have seen, and what thine ears have heard, that at the time when the afflictions of men shall multiply they may call on thee, and by thy name they may be delivered from their afflictions."

And Mary said to the Christ: "Rabbuli, I beseech Thee, have mercy on the souls who call on Thee in my name." And Mary said to John: "Thou, O John, shalt die, as thy Lord hath said to me: what I say to thee hear, and write the book about my exit from this world. At the time of the end of the world let it go forth to mankind; because there shall be signs before the coming of thy Lord, severe and awful. At that time the bones of the just shall be revealed, and shall be with their souls, and their bones shall give help from their graves: and shall proclaim praise concerning the coming of their Lord which draweth nigh; when heaven and earth shall be disturbed and the seasons in the world shall be confounded before thy Lord shall come; and then there shall be a commemoration of my bones; and men shall

[1] ܕܡܢܟܐ in Dr Wright's text.

remember me with offerings and prayers. And whosoever shall call on the name of the mother of God shall be delivered from his affliction."

These things said the Blessed one to John; and John was quiet and gave praise to God concerning what Mary had said to him. And he came and placed a censer near the Blessed one in Paradise. And the hosts of angels sang praises, and the lightnings and the thunders struck against each other.

The Christ said to her: "Whatsoever is in heaven and also on the earth
I have shown thee and I have also made known to thee concerning the bad p. 115
times that are coming on the world. And whatsoever I have said to thee shall happen. Heaven and earth shall pass away, but My words shall not pass away. Now hearken to what I command thee, Mary, what is going to happen at the time when I shall come to the world from beside My Father."

Mary said: "True are Thy words, Rabbūlī, because they are in Thy Father's presence; and whatsoever Thou hast said to me whilst Thou wast upon the earth Thou hast verified; and it is fulfilled; and all the words which Thou hast said to me in heaven have happened. And whosoever shall believe in Thee shall be raised with Thee; and shall inherit the everlasting glory which the sons of light inherit; and which the just who are with Thee are waiting for. For to thee belongeth righteousness, and (to Thee) praise is due with Thy Father and Thy Holy Spirit now and always for ever and ever. Let the mercies of God the Father and of His Only Son and of His Spirit the Living and the Holy be upon the lectors and on the readers and on the hearers and on the possessors and on the miserable and sinful scribe, and on his bodily and his spiritual ancestors, and on whoso partaketh in it. Amen.

It is finished by the help of the Most High God, the Lord of the worlds. Amen, the poor lowly priest Brother Belna'al.

Here endeth the Story of the Mother of God, the Holy Mary, on the second day of the Second Kanūn by the hands of the miserable sinner, in name a brother priest, in deeds a sinner, in the year 2168 of the crafty Greeks. Amen.

Finished by the power of God

| In the Christian year | In the year of the Greeks |
|---|---|
| 1857. | 2168. |

# HYMN.

## TRANSLATION.

p. 122 . . . . He correcteth and turneth [His] face. He smiteth with
Wisdom His hand. For in His strength He is near to the weak [in] mighty
xi. 21 deeds; and the might of His arm who shall withstand? Because
as a grain in a balance, in similitude is the whole world before Thee.
Amos v. 8 Who is like the Mighty One? He calleth for the waters of the sea,
and poureth them out upon the face of all the earth: the Lord God,
Ps. cxliv. 5 the Mighty One . . . . the Almighty is His name. He Who
Ps. civ. looketh upon the earth, and it shaketh; He chideth the mountains,
2—4 and they smoke. Who weareth light as a garment; and stretcheth
out the heaven like a curtain. Who maketh the waters His mansions;
and setteth His chariot upon the clouds; and walketh upon the
Heb. i. 7 wings of the wind; Who maketh His angels spirits, and His
Job ix. 6 ministers a burning fire . . . In His wrath He shaketh the earth
7 from her foundations; and her pillars tremble before Him. He
8 speaketh to the sun, and it riseth not; and the stars exist by His
p. 123 wisdom. He Who alone spreadeth out the heavens, and walketh
9 upon the seas as upon the land. He Who maketh the east and the
10 west, the north and the south; He Who doeth great things past
Ps. cxlvii. finding out, and glorious; and wonders without number. He Who
4 created the number of the stars; He calleth all their names. He
Who causeth the clouds to ascend from the end of the earth; and
Ps. cxxxv. maketh lightnings for the rain; He bringeth the wind out of the
7 treasury; and He numbereth the clouds in His wisdom; and the
Job xxxviii. 37 drops of rain also are counted by Him. He taketh the waters as He
cf. Ecclus. i. 2 will; for to Him alone belongeth . . . . . . . . . . .

And [sent] the demons into the herd of swine. To the chiliarch who cf. Matt.
had an only son, He healed him, and made his withered hand whole viii. 5 *Sinai Pa-*
on the sabbath day. And He rebuked the fever of Peter's wife's *limpsest*
mother, and she arose. He Who walked upon the waves as upon the cf. Luke iv. 38, 39
dry land, and He stretched out His hand to the storms that they should cf. Matt.
not drown [Peter ?]. And He rebuked the sea when it was troubled, xiv. 25—31
and made it calm. And He was glorified in His glory on the holy cf. Mark iv. 39
mountain of Tabor, and was transfigured before His disciples. And cf. Matt.
Moses and Elias went before Him. And He said to the impotent xvii. 1—3
man of thirty-eight years: "Take up thy bed, and walk," on the p. 124
sabbath day. And flee, O unclean and wicked demon and . . . cf. John v. 5—10
to the Lord in the heaven of heavens. [Who] is like unto the Lord cf. Mark
among the sons of the angels? He is Lord of the seas and there is iii. 11
no life . . .

* * * * * * * *

Who commandeth the waters, that they are gathered into one cf. Ps. xxxiii. 7
heap, and calleth the seas by their names. Who clotheth Himself Ecclus.
with a cloud; and in the thick darkness is His work. And He set xxxix. 17 Job
for it keys and doors, and said to it: "Hitherto come out, and xxxviii.
thou shalt not cross, and by it shall thy waves be stayed." And He 9, 11
set the sand a bound for it, a law for ever and ever. There is a cf. Is. xl.
measure of the waters in His hand, that are above the heavens; and 12
His grasp holdeth all the earth. And He weigheth the mountains
in His balance, and the dust in a scale. Sheol is bared before Him, Job xxvi.
and there is no clothing to Destruction. By His command He slew 4
the dragon. Who hath been mighty before Him? and He is past
finding out; Who removeth the mountains, and they know it not, and
changeth . . . . . .

ܗܐ ܗܒܝܠܐ ܚܙܝܬ cf. p. ܩܘ, l. 22
ܠܟܠ ܡܢ ܥ̈ܡܡܝܐ ܘܫܠܡܬ
ܘܚܙܝܬ ܐܘܪܫܠܡ ܕܒܫܡܝܐ
ܕܒܢ̇ܗ̇ ܡܫܬܒܚ ܐܒܐ
ܡܢ ܠܒܪܗ ܘܪܘܚܗ. ܘܚܙܝܬ
ܕܐܝܬ ܠܗ̇ ܬܪܥܣܪ ܬܪ̈ܥܝܢ
ܘܬܪܥܣܪ ܬܪ̈ܥܝܢ ܒܟܠ
ܬܪܥܣܪ ܬ̈ܠܝܬܝܐ. ܘܟܠ
ܟܠ ܬܪܥܐ ܥܠܝܬܐ ܡܐܡ
* * ܒܡ ܡ̈ܠܐܟܐ ܘܪ̈ܒܘ
ܡܠܐܟܐ ܕܡܫܡܫܝܢ
ܘܡܫܒܚܝܢ ܬܪ̈ܥܐ ܕܝܢ
ܠܒܐ ܬܪ̈ܥܘܗܝ ܒܢܝ ܕܒܕܝ
ܐܝܬ ܗܘܘ ܒܗܘܢ ܡܘܣܝܢ
ܕܒܪܝܐ ܘܡܒܘܒ ܐܝܣܘܗܝ
ܒܬܪܥܐ ܐܚܪܢܐ
ܡܢ ܡܕܢܚܐ. ܘܗܕܝܢ ܬ̈ܠܝܬܝܐ
ܐܬܝܢ ܒܢܝܗܘܢ
ܬ̈ܪܥܐ ܘܒܠܗܘܢ ܕܬܪܥܐ
ܒܢܝܐ ܕܐܘܪܫܠܡ ܡܢܝܢ
ܬ̈ܘܩܢܐ ܕܠܐ ܣܟܐ ܘܕܠܐ
ܡܢܝܢܐ ܕܡܫܒܚܝܢ ܠܒܝܕ
ܡܕܝܢܬܗ ܕܡܠܐܟܐ ܪܒܐ
ܘܡܫܒܚܝܢ ܢܒ̈ܝܐ ܟܠܗܘܢ

S. P. f. 155 b
* * * * * * * * *
ܒܢ̈ܝܢܘܗܝ ܘܐܒܪܗܡ
ܘܐܝܣܚܩ ܘܝܥܩܘܒ
ܘܕܘܝܕ ܡܙܡܪܢܐ
ܘܦܘܠܘܣ ܩܕܡ ܡܠܐܟܐ
ܡܫܝܚܐ ܘܩܕܡ ܐܒܘܗ.
ܒܕ ܒܐܠܦܐ ܕܬܫܒܘܚܕ
ܒܐܘܪܫܠܡ ܕܒܫܡܝܐ
ܘܟܠܗ ܒܬܪܥܐ ܡܕܢܚܝܐ
ܘܐܫܬܒܚܬ ܡܢ ܡܠܐܟܐ
* * * * ܘܫܠܝ̈ܚܐ ܒܠܬ
ܒܬܪܥܐ ܕܬܪܝܢ ܘܐܬܦܪܥܬ
ܠܗ̇ ܦܠܓܬܐ ܕܒ̈ܢܘܢܐ
ܕܡܪܝܐ. ܒܠܬ ܬܪܥܐ
ܕܬܠܬܐ ܘܐܬܦܪܥܬ
ܠܗ̇ ܒܒܢܘܬܗ ܕܦܪ̈ܝܐ
ܡ * * ܥܒܕܐ ܒܠܬ
ܬܪܥܐ ܕܐܪܒܥܐ ܘܐܫܬܒܚܬ
ܡܢ ܦܘܡܗܐ ܕܙܕܝ̈ܩܐ
ܒܠܬ ܬܪܥܐ ܕܚܡܫܐ
ܘܩܕܫܘ ܡܩܕܫܝܢ ܪ̈ܒܝܐ
ܘܒܫܪ̈ܒܐ ܒܠܬ ܬܪܥܐ
ܕܐܫܬܐ ܘܩܕܡܘ ܡܩܕܫܝܢ
ܩܕܝܫ ܩܕܝܫ ܩܕܝܫ
ܒܠܬ ܬܪܥܐ ܕܫܒܥܐ
ܘܦܠܓܬ ܡܩܕܫܝܢ ܠܘܪܐ

ܕܒܢ̈ܘܗܝ ܕܡܪܝܐ ܡܒܪ̈ܟܝܢ cf. p. ܣܗ, l. 7
ܟܠܘܗܝ, ܒܝܬ ܡܠܦܢܐ
ܘܦܠܠܐ ܘܣܘܟܐ ܒܝܬ
ܙ̈ܘܓܐ ܘܒܢܝܐ ܒܝܬ
ܡܥܒܕܐ ܘܒܪܦܠܐ ܘܣܝܬ
ܬܡܢ ܪܘܓܙܐ ܘܥܢܝܢܐ
ܕܐܡܬܝ, ܕܡܬܦܩܕܝܢ
ܢܦܩܝܢ ܠܒܪܝܬܐ ܘܣܝܬ
ܠܕܘܟܬܐ ܕܩܐܡ ܒܗ
ܐܠܝܐ ܢܒܝܐ ܘܡܬܠܐ
ܒܗ ܡܦܩܠ ܕܒܗܕܐ
ܥܒܝܐ ܒܪܬܐ ܐܬܘܗܝ,
ܘܣܝܬ ܡܪܬܝ, ܡܪܝܡ
ܒܗܠܝܢ ܥܒܝܐ ܕܠܒܪ
ܘܐܬܦܫܬ ܘܫܠܘܬ
ܠܡܥܢܝܢܐ ܘܣܝܬ
ܒܪܬܐ ܕܪܘܚܝܐ ܕܠܝܬ
ܠܗܘܢ ܡܢܝܢܐ ܫܪܪܐ ܒܡ
ܫܠܘܬܐ ܕܫܪ̈ܦܐ ܒܡܪܝܬܐ
ܕܠܐ ܫܦ ܐܠܐ ܒ * * ܗ
ܠܐ ܝܕܥ ܡܢܝܢܘܗܝ ܗܝ,
ܕܡܢ ܡܪܟܘ ܫܓܕܘ ܡܪܡ
ܡܪܬܝ, ܡܪܝܡ ܫܠܘܬܗ
ܕܡܪܝܐ ܟܠܗܘܢ ܗܝ,
ܡܪܒܝܬܐ ܢܬܒ ܒܗ

S. P. f. 155 a ܘܦܓܥܘ ܡܫܒܚܝܢ
ܠܒܬܘܠܬܐ ܡܒܪܟܬܐ
ܡܢܘ ܕܢܫܝܐ ܘܠܐ ܕܕܚܠ
ܟܕ ܡܢܟܝܢ ܟ̈ܠܝܐ ܘܡܥܒܕܝܢ
ܘܡܘܪܒܝܢ ܠܒܪܬ ܟܦܪܐ
cf. p. ܣܗ, l. 14 ܕܥܘܠ ܗܘܐ ܐܡܗ
ܠܡܪܘܡܐ. ܘܫܠܡܬ ܒܐܕܢܗ
ܐܡܪܝܢ ܟܠܝܐ ܡܕܝܢ
ܡܪܝܢ ܡܕܝܢ ܒܪܗ ܕܐܠܗܐ
ܕܗܕܐ ܗܝ ܡܕܝܢܬܐ
ܘܡܒܪܟܬܐ ܕܐܝܠܕܬܟܝ
ܕܠܐ ܥܘܬܒܘܬܐ ܘܥܡܦܬ
ܡܪܬܝ, ܡܪܝܡ ܐܡܝܕܝܗ
ܘܝܗܒܬ ܥܘܒܝܐ ܠܡܪܝܐ
ܕܐܘܪܒܗ ܠܐܡܐ
ܡܕܝܢܬܐ ܕܐܠܕܬܗ ܘܫܠܡܬ ܠܟܠ
ܡܢ ܥܡܟ ܥܡܡܐ ܘܣܝܬ
ܬܡܢ ܕܟܠ ܡܢܝܢܘܗ̣ ܕܡ̈ܠܐܐ
ܦܬܡܝܢ ܫܪܪܐ ܕܡܠܐܟܐ
ܘܦܪܫܝܢ ܟܢܫܘܗ̣ ܘܣܝܪ̣
ܚܢܢܘܗ̣ ܠܟܠ ܕܠܐ ܡܣܝܢ
ܗܘܘ ܕܢܫܘܪ̣ ܒ * * *
ܥܒܝܢܐ ܒܒܕܘ
ܟܕ ܠܐ ܡܒܠܠܝܢ ܗܘܘ

* * ܕܢܘܗܪܐ ܕܠܐ cf. p. ܣܕ, l. 15
ܡܣܬܝܢ ܡܛܠ ܕܦܪܕܝܣܐ
ܕܥܕܢ ܒܐܪܥܐ ܐܝܬܘܗܝ
ܒܗ ܒܣܘܦܐ ܕܠܒܪܝܐ
* ܛܘܪܗ ܒܪܝܐ ܘܫܬܩܗ
ܒܐܪܥܐ ܫܡܝܢ ܗܘܘ
ܘܢܦܩܝܢ ܡܢܗ ܐܪ̈ܒܥܐ
ܢܗܪ̈ܘܬܐ ܦܝܫܘܢ
ܘܓܝܚܘܢ ·ܘܕܩܠܬ· ܘܦܪܬ
ܘܒܬܪ ܗܘܐ ܛܘܦܢܐ
ܒܕܡܐ ܠܫܘܠܡܗܝ
ܕܛܘܪܐ ܫܠܡ ܘܡܫܝܚܐ
ܐܬܟܢܫ ܒܢ̈ ܐܡܪܐ ܠܐ ܚܙܝ
ܐܡܪܝܢ ܛܘܦܢܐ ܕܠܗܘ
ܛܘܪܐ ܡܕܒܪܐ ܠܡܕܢܚ
ܡܢܗ ܠܒܪ ܕܦܪܕܝܣܐ
ܗܘ ܢܘܚ ܥܘܒܕܐ ܟܠ
ܦܪܕܝܣܐ ܕܥܕܢ ܘܒܗ
ܩܐܡ ܗܘܐ ܘܢܚܐܪ ܕܒܗ
ܛܘܦܢܐ ܡܠܝܢ ܠܗܘܢ
ܠܐܪܥܐ ܘܠܒܢܝ ܐܢܫܐ
ܕܒܐܪܥܐ ܘܛܘܦܢܐ ܡܛܠܐ
ܠܫܘܠܡܗܝ ܕܦܪܕܝܣܐ ܕܥܕܢ
ܐܪܡ ܪܫܗ ܘܫܠܛ ܡܕܡ

S. P. f. 160 b ܡܪܐ ܕܒܪ̈ܝܬܐ ܕܩܐܡ
ܗܘܐ ܒܦܪܕܝܣܐ
ܘܗܦܟܝܢ ܠܒܣܬܪܗ ܗܘ
ܚܙܝ ܗܢܐ ܦܪܕܝܣܐ ܒܝܬ
ܓܘܒܐ ܗܘ ܕܐܠ̈ܝܠܐ
ܘܒܝܬ ܡܫܪܝܐ ܗܘ
ܕܢܝܚ̈ܢܝܐ * * * * *
ܗܘ ܪܒܐ * * * * *
ܘܠ * * ܩܘܗ * * * *
ܗܘܬ ܩܕܡ ܙ̈ܒܢܝ
ܕܥܠܡܐ ܕܢܗܘܐ * *
ܗܘܐ ܒܝܬ ܡܫܪܝܐ
ܠܐܕܡ ܪܝܫ ܛܘܗܡܐ * *
ܕܒܢܝܬ * * * * * *
ܐܠܗܐ ܘܗܠܝܢ ܒܢܝܬ
ܐܢ̈ܫܐ ܙ̈ܕܝܩܐ * * *
ܟܕ ܦܪܕܝܣܐ ܘܡܢ * * *
ܘܠܗ ܠܦܪܕܝܣܐ ܐܬܐ
ܦܓܪܗ ܕܗܕܐ ܒܥܠܬܐ
ܘܡܫܬܐ ܕܠܘܬ ܠܡܪܢ
* * * * * ܘܟܕ ܡܪܢ
ܫܘܒ ܡܫܝܚܐ ܐܬܐ
ܟܕ ܡܪܬܝ ܡܪܝܡ ܩ * *
ܘܐܡܪ ܠܗ ܡܪܝܡ ܩܘܡܝ
ܘܐܬܚܫܒܬ ܘܩܡܬ
ܘܐ * * * ܡܢ ܒܢܝ̈ܢܫܐ
ܠܝܬ ܗܘܐ ܒܡܫܡܝܐ

ܐܬܝܢܢ ܕܢܓܘܦ
* * * * * * ܦܘܓܥܐ
ܕܢܘܚܡܐ ܘܢܗܒܘ
* * * ܐܬ ܒܢ̈ܝܢܐ ܘܦܪܝܫܐ
* * * * ܡܕܝܢܬܘ ܠܗܘܢ
* * * * ܐ ܘܫܒܩܘ
* * * * ܘܐܬܬܢܝܚܘ
* * * ܦܘܪܥܢܗܘܢ ܠܒܢܝ̈
* * * * ܟܠܗ ܠܒܢܘܢܐ
* * * ܕܡܪ̈ܘܡܐ ܒܠܝܐ
* * * * * ܪܘܚܬܗܘܢ
ܒܝܠܘܬܗܘܢ ܕܒ̈ܢܝܐ cf. p. ܡܘ, l. 23
ܘܕܛ̈ܠܝܢܐ ܘܕܗܫܪܐ
ܘܕܡܒܪܢܐ ܘܕܒܐܢܐ
ܘܕܒܗܠܐ ܟܠ ܕܡܗܡܝܢ
ܒܐܒܐ ܘܒܒܪܐ
ܘܒܪܘܚܐ ܕܩܘܕܫܐ
ܘܒܡܪܬܝ ܡܪܝܡ
ܝܠܕܬ ܐܠܗܐ ܘܒܥܕܬܐ
* * * ܗ ܕܡܫܝܚܐ
* * ܒܢܐ ܕܐܝ̈ܩܪܐ ܢܦܠ
ܒܘܪܟܬܐ ܡܢ ܐܠܗܐ ܘܡܢ
ܫܘܒ ܡܫܝܚܐ ܕܐܬܠܝܕ
ܡܢ ܒܬܘܠܬܐ ܩܕܝܫܬܐ
ܕܒܒܐ ܠܗ ܕܡܒܪܟܝܢܐ
ܠܡܪܬܢ ܡܪܝܡ ܐܡܗ
ܕܟܪܗ̇ ܢܗܘܐ ܕܡܒܪܟܝܢܗ̇

S. P. f. 160a ܒܫܡܝܢܐ ܘܒܐܪܥܐ
ܘܟܠܗ ܒܢܝܢ ܕܢܫܡܒ
ܩ̈ܠܐ ܗܠܝܢ ܡܕܝܢܬܐ
ܠܒܢܝ̈ ܡܪܝܐ ܪܚܡܐ
ܘ * * ܐ ܠܟܠܗ ܒܠܡܢ
ܐܡܝܢ ○ ○ ○

cf. p. ܥܡ, l. 9 ܘܟܕ ܐܬܦܢܝܬ ܗܘܬ
ܠܘܒܢܝܢܬܐ ܒܦܪܕܝܣܐ
ܕܒܢ ܘܐܬܟܠܠܬ ܒܗܘ
ܫܘܒܚܐ ܪܒܐ ܘܐܝܩܪܘ
ܫܠܝܚܐ ܠܟܠ ܦܢܝܢ
ܘܐܬܐ ܡܪܢ ܢܫܘܒ
ܡܫܝܚܐ ܥܡ ܓܕܘܗܝ ܥܡ
ܫܡܝܢܐ ܠܦܪ̈ܕܝܣܐ
ܘܡܪܒܥܬܐ ܕܪ̈ܘܚܢܐ
ܢܚܬܬ ܥܡ ܫܡܝܢܐ
ܥ * * * ܕܠܝܬ ܠܗܘܢ
ܗܒܐ. ܘܐܬܒܣܡ ܟܠܗ
ܦܪ̈ܕܝܣܐ ܕܟܕ ܘܟܠܗܘܢ
ܠܦܘܪ̈ܢ ܕܢܕܝܢ ܠܗ
ܘܡܕܡ ܠܐ ܐܫܬܟܚ
ܗܘܐ ܬܡܢ ܐܠܐ
ܒܩ̈ܘܒܠܐ ܕܡܒܥܝܢ
ܘܡܠܐܟܐ ܕܡܫܒܚܝܢ

ܒܙܒܢܐ ܗܢܐ ܗܘܕܝܢ cf. p. ܡܕ, l. 21
ܩܠܐ ܕܓܠܘܬܗܘܢ
ܕܢ̈ܒܝܐ ܠܡܫܝܚܐ
ܫܠܘ ܘܡܪܢ ܝܫܘܥ
ܡܫܝܚܐ ܐܬܐ
ܓܐܕܡܗܘܢ ܒܒܢܝܢܐ
ܢܗܝܪܬܐ ܘܡܠܠ
ܡܢܗܘܢ ܘܐܡܪ ܠܗܘܢ
ܐܬܚܝܠܘ ܘܐܬܒܝܢܘ
ܘܐܬܓܒܪܘ ܘܠܐ
ܬܕܚܠܘܢ ܘܠܐ ܬܙܘܥܘܢ
ܕܟܠ ܡܕܡ ܕܡܢܝܪܬܘܢ
ܬܫܬܒܚܘܢ ܘܒܟܠܝܡ
ܢܗܘܐ ܓܒܢܝܟܘܢ ܓܒܪ
ܐܒܘܟܘܢ ܕܒܫܡܝܐ.
ܗܝܕܝܢ ܢ̈ܒܝܐ ܐܬܚܕܝܘܢ
ܐܪܒܥܘ ܗܘܘ ܘܐܬܒܪܟܘ
ܡܢ ܡܪܢ ܘܦܩܕܘ
ܢ̈ܒܝܐ ܡܢ ܕܒܘܬܐ
ܕܡܓܠܝܢ ܗܘܘ ܒܗ̇
ܐܡܪܝܢ ܘܬ ܢܣܒܘܬ
ܡܢ ܛܘܪ ܐܝܬܐ
ܠܡܥܒܪܬܐ ܕܢܚܠܐ
ܘܬܡܢ ܢܟܬܘܒ ܕܐܒܝܢܐ
ܐܬܫܠܡܬ ܡܪܬܝ،
ܡܪܝܡ ܒܒܝܢܐ ܕܢܘܗܪܐ

S. P. f. 156b ܘܡܪܢ ܝܫܘܥ ܘܐܘܒܠܗ̇
ܠܦܪܕܝܣܐ ܕܥܕܢ. ܘܢܣܒܬܗ
ܢ̈ܒܝܐ ܡܢ ܛܘܪ
ܐܝܬܐ ܠܡܥܒܪܬܐ
ܕܢܚܠܐ ܘܓܠܘ ܗܘܘ
ܘܫܒܚܘ ܒܫܘܒܚܐ ܘܩܕܫܘ
ܕܢܟܬܘܒ ܒܟܬܒܐ
ܗܢܐ ܙܒܢܐ ܕܫܗܕܝܢ
ܟܠܗܘܢ ܢ̈ܒܝܐ ܩܕܡ
ܡܪܢ ܝܫܘܥ ܡܫܝܚܐ
ܘܩܕܡ ܦܘܪܩܢܐ ܕܩܘܕܫܐ
ܕܗܠܝܢ ܬܫ̈ܒܚܬܐ
ܘܗܠܝܢ ܬܕܡܪ̈ܬܐ
ܘܗܠܝܢ ܚܝ̈ܠܐ ܘܗܠܝܢ
ܐܬܘ̈ܬܐ ܥܒܕ ܡܪܢ
ܝܫܘܥ ܡܫܝܚܐ
ܩܕܡ ܐܠܗܘܬܗ ܡܪܬܝ،
ܡܪܝܡ ܒܕ ܢܦܩܬ ܡܢ
ܚܠܡܐ ܗܢܐ. ܘܟܠ ܡܢ
ܕܡܗܝܡܢ ܢܗܝܡܢ
ܠܗܠܝܢ ܡ̈ܠܐ ܕܟܬܝܒܢ
ܒܟܬܒܐ ܗܢܐ ܘܚܝܐ
ܘܐܢܫܐ ܕܠܐ ܡܗܝܡܢ
ܡܬܕܝܢ ܘܗܕܐ ܐܢܬܬܐ
ܕܐܬܓܒܝܬ ܒܟܠܡ ܡܢ
ܩܕܡ ܬܪܦܝܬܗ[1] ܕܚܠܡܐ

[1] Cod. ܬܕܦܪܬܗ

* * ܐ ܩܘܪܒܢܐ ܠܡܪܝܐ cf.
ܢܝܬܐ * * * * * ܒܪ̈ p. ܩܟ l. 4
ܓܘܙܠܝܢ ܚܕ * * *
ܥܘܠ ܠܐ * * * ܓܘܙܠܝܢ
* * * ܢܝܬܐ ܚܛܝܗ̇
* * * * * * * * *
ܢܝܬܐ ܬܡܘܢ ܒܪ̈ ܓܘܙܠܝܢ
ܬܘܕܝܬܐ ܡܓܠܠ ܒܢ̈ܝ
⌜ܐ⌝ܢܫܐ ܕܡܩܪܒܝܢ * * *
* * ܡܠܝܢ ܚܕܘܬܐ.
ܢܝܬܐ ܐܦ ܝܗܒ
⌜ܒܗ⌝ ⌜ܦ̮⌝ܓܕܬܐ ܕܒܪܟܬ
⌜ܘ⌝ܝܗܒܬ ܠܗ ܒܒܝܠܐ
⌜ܒ⌝ܡ̈ܫܚܐ. ܢܝܬܐ
ܐܝܠܘܠ ܒܪ ܥܒܝܚ ܠܗ
ܘܡܘܕܪܐ ܠܡܫܝܚܝܐ
⌜ܕ⌝ܓܘܙܠܝܢ ܘܝܗܒ ܟܠ
⌜ܕ⌝ܡܫܡܫܝܢ ⌜ܠ⌝ܐܒܐ ܒܒܢܝ
⌜ܐ⌝ܢܫܐ ܢܝܬܐ ܬܫܪܝܢ
ܡܘܪܐ ܘܫܒܫ ܕܫܡܫ
⌜ܡ⌝ܠܗ ܕܐܒܪܐ ܕܙܪܒ
ܒܡܘܢܗ ܕܓܠܒܒܐ
ܢܝܬܐ ܬܫܪܝܢ ܘܦܠܓܬܗ
ܒܗܡ ܕܐܬܐ ܓܠܠܐ
⌜ܘ⌝ܫܒ * ܠܐ ܡܢ ܥܒܕܐ

S. P. f. 156 a

ܐܪܒܥܐ ܘܒܡܥܪܒܗ̇
ܢܝܬܐ ܒܢܘ ܘܫܪ̈ܘܬܗ
ܒܗܡ ܒܢ̈ܟܠܐ ܘܟܪܘܒܐ
ܘܪܒܥܐ ܕܡܬܠܚܫ ܟܠ
* * ܐܦ ܒܝܪܬܐ ܀
ܢܝܬܐ ܒܢܘ ⌜ܘ⌝ܒܗܡ
ܬܠܓܐ ܘܐܓܠܝܕܐ
ܕܡܫܡܫܝܢ ܠܐܪܒܐ
⌜ܢ⌝ܝܬܐ ܥܓܠ ܒܪ̈ ܓܘܙܠܝܢ
ܟܠ ܒܬܦܬܗ ܓܒܬܐ
ܕܡܘܠܕܢ ܚܕܘܬܐ
ܢܝܬܐ ܐܪܙ ܒܪ̈ ܓܘܙܠܝܢ
ܐܘܩܪܐ ܠܡܪܝܐ ܐܡܪܐ
ܡܫܚܐ ܘܢܩ̈ܘܬܐ
⌜ܕ⌝ܗܒܝܢ ܬܫܒܚܘܬܐ.
ܗܢܝܐ ܓܠܘ ܫ̈ܠܝܚܐ
ܘܐܡܪܘ ܐܝܢ ܡܪܝܐ
⌜ܐ⌝ܠܗܐ ܕܫܪܪ ܠܒܪܗ
ܓܐܕܝܢ ܕܢܫܝܘܗ
⌜ܠ⌝ܥܠܡܐ ܡܢ ܓܠܠܘܬܗ
⌜ܬ⌝ܗܘܐ ܒܘܪܟܬܟ
ܥܡ ܐܪܒܥܐ ܘܒܡܥܪܒܗ̇
ܡܐ ܕܡܬܩܪܒ ܩܘܪ̈ܒܢܐ
⌜ܠ⌝ܡܪܬ̇ ܡܪܝܐ ܕܐܠܗܘܬܟ
⌜ܘ⌝ܬܗܘܐ ܓܒܘܬܟ

S. P. f. 151 b

ܕܝܥܩܘܒ. ܐܦܣܩܘܦܐ
ܐܚܝܢܢ ܕܟܬܒ. ܠܗ ܗܘ ܗܟܢܐ
ܕܗܠܝܢ ܦܘܩܕ̈ܢܐ
ܕܝܬܩܐ ܕܐܬܟܬܒܘ ܒܝ.
ܡܝܬܬ ܡܪܬܝ, ܡܪܝܡ
⌜ܢܘܚܝܢ ܘܒܘܪܐ⌝
ܦܟܝܢ ⌜ܘ⌝ܐܬܐ * * * *
* * * ܒܗ * * * * *
* * * * * * * * *
* * * * * * * * *
* * * ܫܠ ܫ * * *
* * * * * * * * *
* * * ܕܫܠܡ * * * *
* * * ܐܠܐ * * * *
ܕܐܝܬ ܐܟܡܢ ܕܫܒܬܘܒܘܢ ܠܗܘܢ
ܐܓܪܬܐ ܠܪܗܘܡܝܐ ܠܐܚܝ̈ܐ
ܕܬ * * * * * * * *
ܕܡܫܝܚܢ ܒܦܪܘܫ ܘܒܫܠܘܫ
ܡܫܬܒܚܝܢ ܗܠܝܢ ܫܒܩ̈ܐ
ܘܫܝܢܐ ܘܒܬܒܘ ܬܘܒ.
ܐܓܪ̈ܬܐ ܠܐܦܣܩܘܫ ܐܝܒܐ
ܕܐܝܬ ܡܪܝ, ܢܘܚܝܢ ⌜ܕܫܓܠ⌝
ܦܘܒܗ ܕܕܠܡܐ ܡܫܒܚ.
ܒܬܒܗ̇ ܕܝܠܕܬ ⌜ܐܠܗܐ⌝
ܬܡܢ ܘܐܦ ܡܫܒܚܝܢ
ܫܘܒܚܬܘܢ ܒܬܒܐ
ܐܘܕܒܘܢ ܠܝ ⌜ܒܐܓܪ̈ܬܐ⌝

ܐܝܕܝ̈ܗܘܢ ܐܝܬ ܒܫܦܪ̈ܐ cf. p. ܠ, col. a, l. 11
ܗܠܝܢ ܕܟܬܒܘ. ܘܢܝܚܘܬ̇ܗ
ܠܡܪܬܝ, ܡܪܝܡ ܕܐܡܬܝ,
ܢܗܘܐ ܠܗ ܕܘܒܪ̈ܢܐ
ܘܫܘܒ̈ܚܢܐ ܬܠܬ ܘܒܢܝܢ
ܒܫܢܬܐ ܘܫܘܠܫܘ ܘܦܪܘܫ
ܒܡ ܢܘܚܝܢ ܘܒܘܪܐ ܕܫܓܠ
ܦܘܒܗ. ܗܘܢ ܢܕܒܝܢ
ܕܐܒܐ ܐܬܗܘܢ ܗܠܝܢ ܫܦܪ̈ܐ
ܕܡܘܬ̇ܗ ܕܡܪܬܝ, ܡܪܝܡ
ܡܠܠ ܕܡܢ ܐܘܪܫܠܡ ܒܡܗܘܢ
ܐܬܘ ܘ ܗܘܐ
ܗܘܐ
ܐܦܣܩܘܦܐ ܘܠܝܪܘܫ
(sic) ܕܠܗ ܩܪܘ ܦܩܘܕܬܐ ܗܕܐ
ܘܒܬܒܘ ܐܓܪܬܐ ܠܦܘܪ
ܫܢܝ ܗܒܢܐ ܡܢ ܩܢܪܘ
ܐܦܣܩܘܦܐ ܕܐܘܪܫܠܡ
ܒܡ ܒܠ ܩܠܝܪܘܫ ܠܐܚܝܢ
ܒܗ̈ܢܐ ܘܐܟܗܝܢ ܕܐܝܬ
ܒܦܘܪ ܫܢܝ ܫܠܝܚܐ ܢܫܓܐ
ܐܓܪܬܐ ܕܢܘܒܒܘܢ
ܘܒܠܝܢ ܘܒܐܘܪܫܠܡ ܒܠܗ̇
ܫܐܠܝܢ ܡܦܠܠ ܡܦܘܩܗ̇
ܕܡܪܬܝ, ܡܪܝܡ ܘܠܐ
ܐܫܒܚܝܢ. ܘܒܬܪ ܐܬܗܘܢ,

# APPENDIX II.

The text of the *Transitus Mariae* in the Sinai Palimpsest No. 30.

S. P. f. 151 a

ܕܒܫܢܬ ܬܠܬܡܐܐ ܘܐܪܒܥܝܢ
ܘܫܒܥ ܫܢܝܢ ܕܢܦܩܬ ܡܪܬܢ،
ܡܪܝܡ ܡܢ ܥܠܡܐ ܗܢܐ
ܘܐܢܐ ܝܥܩܘܒ ܡܗܕܝܢܐ
ܕܐܬܘ ܫ̈ܠܝܚܐ ܕܡܫܝܚ
ܘܕܡܒܪܝܢ ܐܬܟܢܫܘ ܗܘܘ
ܘܐܬܘ ܘܒܪܝܬܐ ܒܠܝܬܐ
ܒܡ ܬܫ̈ܬܝܐ ܠܫܠܡܗ̇
ܕܛܘܒܢܝܬܐ ܘܡܢ ܢܦܩܬ
ܡܢ ܥܠܡܐ ܗܢܐ ܘܫܬܐ
ܣܦܪܝܢ ܐܬܟܬܒܘ ܒܠܝܗ̇
ܟܠ ܣܦܪܐ ܟܬܒܘܗ ܬܪܝܢ
ܥܠܝܗܝܢ. ܘܟܠ ܐܬܘܬܐ
ܘܬܕܡܪܬܐ ܘܥܒܕܢܝܬܐ
ܕܗܘܝ، ܘܡܕܒܪܢܗ̇ ܡܢ ܫܡܝܐ
ܘܡܢ ܐܪܥܐ ܘܝܗܒܬ
ܒܪܝܬܐ ܬܘܕܝܬܐ ܠܡܪܝܐ
ܘܠܗ ܕܐܡܐ ܕܝܠܕܬܗ
ܒܣܓܕܬܐ ܕܐܪ̈ܒܒܝܢܐ ܘܐܦ
ܒܝܘܒܒܐ ܕܡܪܝܬܐ ܕܣ̈ܦܪܐ
ܘܐܢܐ ܝܥܩܘܒ ܟܬܒܬ
ܒܫܢܬ ܐܝܪ̈، ܒܦܢܝܬܐ
ܗܕܐ ܕܗܠܝܢ ܣ̈ܦܪܐ
ܕܐܬܟܬܒܘ ܒܘܚܠܢ
ܙܟܘܪܐ ܕܫܛܓ ܛܘܒܗ
ܗܘ ܛܒܝܢ ܗܘܐ ܠ * * *

⌜ܐܝܠܝܕܐ⌝ ܡܢܗ̇. — cf. p. ܟܛ, col. a, l. 5
⌜ܕܐܘܪܫܠܡ⌝ ܘܒܒܕܢ ܫܒܥܐ
⌜ܝܥܩܘܒ⌝ ܐܦܣܩܘܦܐ ܕܗܘ
ܗܘ ܕܗܘܐ ܐܦܣܩܘܦܐ ܩܕܡܝܬ
ܒܐܘܪܫܠܡ ܒܗ ܒܝܘܡܝܢ
⌜ܗܘܘ⌝ ܫ̈ܠܝܚܐ. ܟܬܒܬ
* * * * ܦܢܝܬܐ ܗܕܐ
⌜ܒܫܢܬ⌝ ܐܝܪ̈، ܒܫܢܝܐ ܚܕܝܪ
⌜ܒܫܢܬ⌝ ܬܠܬܡܐܐ ܘܬܠܬܝܢ
⌜ܘܫܬ⌝ * * ܒܬܠܬܐ
⌜ܒܫܒܐ⌝ ܒܦܠܓܗ ܕܝܘܡܐ
⌜ܟܠ⌝ ܓܒܪܐ ܝܗܘܕܝܐ
ܕܐܬܘܗܝ، ܡܪܝܐ. ܘܡܫܝܚܐ
⌜ܠܝܥܩܘܒ⌝ ܐܦܣܩܘܦܐ ܘܡܫܬ
⌜ܡܛܠ⌝ ܕܢܦܠ ܫܒܝ ܗܘܘ ܠܗ
⌜ܝܗܘܕܝܐ⌝ ܠܝܥܩܘܒ.
⌜ܐܦܣܩܘܦܐ⌝ ܟܠ ܕܡܬܩܪܐ
⌜ܗܘܐ⌝ ܐܚܘܗܝ، ܕܡܪܢ
⌜ܘܫܐܠ⌝ ܐܦܣܩܘܦܐ
⌜ܘܩܠܝܪܘܣ⌝ ⌜ܕܝܠܗ⌝ ܡܛܠܠ
* * * ܛܘܒܢܐ ܘܠܐ
* * * ܐܫܬܒܚܘ ܠ * *
ܦܢܝܬܐ ܐܚܪܬܐ ܕܒܚܝܪܬ
ܐܚ̈ܘܗܝ، ܕܐܦܣܩܘܦܐ
ܟܬܝܒܐ ܗܘܬ
ܕܐܢܐ ܝܥܩܘܒ ܐܦܣܩܘܦܐ
ܟܬܒܬ ܗܟܢܐ ○ ○ ○ ○

· · · · · · ܐ
· · ܗ ⁚ ܐܢ · ܕܝ
· · · ܐܒܕܠܗ
ܒܝܫܬܗܘܢ : ܡܩܠܝܢ
ܐ · · · · · ·
· · · · ܝ ܠܗ.
ܒܗܪܢ ܡܢܪܒܐ ⁚
ܠܐ ܕܝܢ ܢܗܐ
ܡܩܕܡܝܢ
· · · · · ܐܠܐ
ܒܬܪܬܝܢ : ܐܘܦ
ܠܐ ܢܗܐ
ܡܬܚܫܒܝܢ
ܒܝܘܡ ܕܚܠܐ
ܘܐܡܪܝܢ · · ·
· · · · · · ·
· · · · · · ·
· · · · · · ·

· ܐ ܡܢ ܥܠܝܠܐ
ܢܦܫܗ ܘ · · ܪ · ⁚
ܐܘܦ ܠܐ ܗܠܘܦ
ܢܗܐ ܡܬܚܫܒܝܢ
ܕܟܠܗ ܗܠܝܢ
ܐܘܦ ܠܐ · · ܐ
ܡܝ · ܛ · ܦܝܢ
ܗܝܟ ܐ · · ܪܝܢ
ܡܬܚܫܒܠ ܕܝ
ܟܠ ܕܡܘܬܪ
ܘܠܬܚܫܕܐ ܗܝܟ
ܚܝܝܢ ܘܠܬܚܫܒ
ܒܝܘܡ · · · ܐ
· · · ܐܫܬܘ
· · · · · ·
ܘܡܟܛܠ · ·
ܘܠܗܐ ܬܐ · ·
ܘܡܢܬ · · ·

f. 2 is torn and much decayed. I have not been able to identify it; but it is probably part of the same text as its conjugate f. 1. The upper script has been recognized by Mr H. L. Pass as part of the Jerusalem Talmud. This Fragment therefore belongs to the same MS. as Fragments XXII. and XXIX.

ܐܬܡܠܠ
* ܦ * ܐܣܘܪ
ܕܦܪܘ ܟܪܣܝܗܘܢ
ܘܠܐ ܠܡܟܝܢ
ܢܗܘܢ ܠܐܦܝܢ
ܠ * ܘܒܟ * ܢ
* ܚܬܐ * ܐ *
ܠܚ * * * *
* * * * *
ܠܗ * * ܡܘܬܝܢ
* ܟܠ ܐܬܘ ܟܠܗܘܢ
ܕܡܘܩܦ ܠܐ
* * * * *
* * * ܗܕܐ
* * ܟܪܝܣܘܢܐ
* ܬ ܡܘܩܦ * *
* * * * *
* * * ܒܪܝ
ܐ * * * *

* * * * *
* * * * *
* * * * *
ܕܡܫܝܚܐ ܠܐ
* * ܡܫܘ * *
ܒܪ * ܐ ܕܐܬܐ
* * * ܒܘ *
ܠܘܬ ܦ *
ܐܢ ܐ * ܟܕܘ
ܦܪܝܐ * * *
* * * * *
ܡܟܠ * * * *
ܐܘܢ * * ܦ *
* * * ܦܪܝܢ
* ܗܬ * * *
* * * * *
* * * * *
* * * * *
* * * * *

ܐܡܪ̈ܝܢ ܐܬܐܝܢ
ܢܢܣܪ ܠܟ
ܐܠܦܘܢ. ܐܢܐ
* * * * *
ܘܗܘܢܬ * . ܐ:
* * ܦ * ܐ
ܗܘ ܗܕ * * *
ܕ * * * *
○ܡܢ * * ܬܪ
* ܦܪܝ * *
* * * * *
* * * * *
* * * * *
ܡܢ * * * *
ܐܢ * * * *
* * * * *
ܣ * * * *
ܣ * * * *
ܐܬ * * * *

ܐܢܐ ܗܘܝܬ
ܡܠ[ܟ]ܐ * * ܐ
ܡܢܕܝܢ ܡܢ
ܝ * * * * *
ܒܬ * * * * *
ܐܬ * * * * *
ܘܗܘܘ ܦ * *
* * * * *
ܘܡܢ * * ܬ
ܡܠܟܐ ܗ[ܘ]ܝܬ
ܡܫܝܢ * * *
* * * * *
* * * * *
* * * * *
* * * * *
* * * * *
* * * * *
* * * * *
* * * * *

ܘܟܘܠ ܐܢܬܬܗܘܢ
ܐ . . . . ܗܠܝܢ
ܬܘܒܢ ܐܢܐ
ܐܡܪ ܫܠܝ
ܕܒܢܝܢ ܗܘܘ
ܡܒܪܟܝܢ ܠܝ
ܘܐܢܐ ܗܘܝܬ
ܠܐܝܬ ܠܗܘܢ
ܒܢܝܡܗ ܕܡܪܐ
ܫܠܝ ܕܒܢܝܢ
ܗܘܘ ܐܡܪܝܢ
ܠ . . . . ܟܠ
. ܫ . . . . .
ܘܐܢܐ ܗ . .
. . . . . . .
. . . . . . .
. . . . . . .
. . . . . . .
. . . . . . .

Athanasii Vita S. Antonii (Coloniae 1686), vol. II. p. 474, l. 47 ܗܝܟ ܕܗܘܝܢ
ܒܢܝܢܗܘܢ :
ܘܟܠܗ ܒܢܝܬܐ
ܫܡܥܘܢ ܘܚܙܝܢ
ܘܪ̈ . . . : ܐܢܐ
ܕܝ ܗܘܝܬ . . .
Ps. xx. 7 . . . . ܗܠܝܢ
ܒܡܫܡܫܘܢ
ܘܗܠܝܢ ܕܡܪ̈ܟܒܝܢ
ܐܠܝܢ ܒܢܝܡܗ
ܕܡܪܐ ܐܠܗܢ
ܩܝܡ : ܒܝܠܬܐ
. . ܐ . . . ܦ . .
ܗܠܝܢ ܕܡ ܡܪܐ
ܘܐܬܘ ܬܘܒ
. . . ܪܘܢ
. . . . .
. ܗܢܗ . ܕܗܢܘ
. . . ܘܗܘܘ

αὐτά τις
ὡς Ἀντώνιον
ἐστι θεωρῶν·
[καὶ περιβαλλόμενος δὲ]
αὐτὰ, ὡς τὰς νουθεσίας
αὐτοῦ βαστάζων ἐστι
μετὰ χαρᾶς.
τοῦτο τῆς
ἐν σώματι ζῶης
Ἀντωνίου
τὸ τέλος,
κἀκείνη
τῆς ἀσκήσεως ἀρχή.
καὶ εἰ καὶ
μικρὰ ταῦτα
πρὸς τὴν
ἐκείνου ἀρετὴν,
ἀλλ' ἀπὸ
τούτων

[λογίζεσθε
καὶ ὑμεῖς
ὁποῖος ἦν]
ὁ τοῦ θεοῦ [ἄνθρωπος]
Ἀντώνιος·
ἐκ νεωτέρου
[μέχρι τῆς τοιαύτης ἡλικίας,
ἴσην τηρήσας
τὴν προθυμίαν
τῆς ἀσκήσεως·
καὶ μήτε διὰ]
τὸ γῆρας
ἡττηθεὶς πολυτελείᾳ
τροφῆς,
μήτε δι' ἀτονίαν
τοῦ ἑαυτοῦ σώματος
[ἀλλάξας]
τὸ σχῆμα
[τοῦ ἐνδύματος]

(*Reprinted*)

ܠܬܗ ܘܗܒܗܒܐ

ܕܠܐܠܦܘܒܝܢܐ

ܗܘܘ ܚܫ̈ܝܢ

ܘܒܕ * * ܘܬ

ܡܦܩ̈ܝܢ ܠܗ

ܒܚܕܘܐ ܗܘܘ

ܠܒܢܝܢ * * *

ܗܒܕ ܫܘ *

ܫܠܘܡܐ ܕܝܫܘܥ

ܕܐܠܦܘܒܝܢܐ

ܒܒܣܪܐ

ܘ * ܘ * * ܐ

ܫܠܘܡܐ * * *

ܕܠܗ: ܐ * *

ܐܝܬ * * *

ܘܒܘ̈ܪܐ ܠܗܘܒܠ

ܬܫܒܚܬܗ

ܕܗ̇ܘ: ܐܠܐ ܡܢ

ܗܠܝܢ ܐܘܦ

* * * * *

ܡ * * * *

* * * * *

ܕܐܠܗܐ

ܐܠܦܘܒܝܢܐ

ܕܡܢ ܦܠܠܝܘܬܗ

* * * * *

* * * * *

ܕܒܘ * * *

ܐܘܦ ܠܟܠܝܠ

ܣܝܒܘܬܐ

ܐܬܢܝܚ ܠܣܘܟܝܐ

ܕܩܘܝܡܐ

ܐܘܦ ܠܦܝܠܘܬ

ܬܫܒܘܚܬܐ

ܕܩܘܟܪܗ * * *

ܦܘܩܣܐ

ܕܬܒܣܝܬܐ

Athanasii Vita S. Antonii (Coloniae 1686, vol. II. p. 503, l. 38).

[μεθ' ὑμῶν ἐστι.
ταῦτα εἰπὼν,
καὶ ἀσπασαμένων
ἐκείνων αὐτόν.]
ἐξάρας
τοὺς πόδας
καὶ ὥσπερ φίλους
ὁρῶν τοὺς
ἐλθόντας ἐπ' αὐτὸν,
καὶ δι' αὐτοὺς
περιχαρὴς
γενόμενος
ἐφαίνετο γὰρ ἀνακείμενος
ἱλαρῷ τῷ προσώπῳ
ἐξέλιπε,
καὶ προσετέθη
πρὸς τοὺς πατέρας.
[κἀκεῖνοι] λοιπὸν
καθὰ δέδωκεν αὐτοῖς ἐντολὰς
[θάψαντες]

[καὶ εἰλίξαντας,] ἔκρυψαν
ὑπὸ γῆν [αὐτοῦ τὸ σῶμα,]
καὶ οὐδεὶς οἶδε τέως ποῦ
κέκρυπται πλὴν
μόνων αὐτῶν τῶν δύο ἱκετῶν.
λαβὼν δὲ
ἕκαστος
τὴν μηλωτὴν
τοῦ
μακαρίου
Αντωνίου,
καὶ τὸ τετριμμένον
[παρ' αὐτοῦ]

ἱμάτιον
[ὥς τι
μέγα
χρῆμα]
φυλάττει
καὶ γὰρ

καὶ βλέπων

(*Reprinted*)

* * * * * *

* * * * * *

ܘ * * * * *

ܠܟ̈ܘ * * * *

* * ܗ ܘܦܫܩܘ

* ܗܬ ܠܬ̈ܓܠܘܝ:

ܘܗܘܢ ܪ̈ܚܡܐ

ܚܡܐ ܠܗܠܝܢ

ܕܗ * * * * ܗ

ܘ * * ܠܒܙܠܗܘܢ

ܗܘܐ ܒܝܙܘܐ

ܗܘܐ ܪܒܝ ܢܒܪ

ܘܐܦ̈ܘܝ ܢܗܝܪܝܢ:

ܘ * ܣ * ܐܘܦ

ܘܗ ܘܐܬܘܣܦ

ܘܗ ܠܐܒܗܘܬܗ:

* * * * ܕܝܢ

* * * ܐܬܦ̈ܩܕܘ

* * * * * ܗܪ

* * * ܘܚܦܝܗ

ܒܐܪܥܐ ܘܐܝܟ

ܠܐ ܝܕܥ ܗܘ ܗܘ

ܡܢ ܠܒܪ ܡܕܝܪ

ܬܪ̈ܝܢܗܘܢ ܒ̈ܠܝܠܘܬ

ܘܗܠܝܢ ܕܢܫܒܘ

ܒܘܠ ܝܕ ܡܒܗܘܢ

ܠܒܘܙ ܡܝܬܝܢ

ܡܢ ܕܠܗ ܡܢ

ܕܡܒܪܒܝܢܐ

ܐܝܟ̣ܘܠ ܘܝܢܐ

ܘ * * ܡܐܝܢܐ

ܕܟܪ̈ܝܫܐ ܣ * *

ܗ * * * * ܐܢ

ܪ * * * ܐ ܒܘܠ

ܝܕ ܡܒܗܘܢ

ܡܒܝܦܪ ܠܗ

ܠܗܘܬܗ: ܡܢܟܪ

ܗܘܘ ܫܒ̈ܚܝܢ

## NOTES TO FRAGMENT XXXIV.

*v.* 9. Between ܠܒܕܘܠ and ܒܠܚܘܕ there is room for one word only.

*v.* 11. ⌜ܡܗܝܡܢܝܢ⌝ has disappeared in a rent.

ܠܒܕܘܠܗ is an improvement on the ܡܢ ܠܒܕܘܠܗ of the Vatican and Sinai Lectionaries. The punctuation of the verse is also better.

The ܕܐܦ in verse 9 seems like Edessene Syriac; but the ܠܒܕܘܠ in the same verse and the ܗܝܟ ܒܪܐ of *v.* 15 are Palestinian.

Verses 56, 57 of chapter XI. are not in the Palestinian Syriac Lectionary. The fact that they occur here immediately before chapter XII. confirms our belief that we have in these fragments the remains of a continuous text.

## NOTE TO FRAGMENT XIV.

I agree with Professor Ryssel that Fragment XXV. belongs to the same MS. as Fragment XIV. But it has been worn very thin by a long course of ill-usage, and I have therefore relinquished the attempt to coax anything further out of it.

* * * * * * 7b
* * * * * *
* * * * * *
* * * * * * 9
* * * * * *
* * * * * *
ܘܐܬܘ ܠܐ ܠܒܠܚܘܕ
* * * ܒܠܝܫܘܥ
ܐܠܐ ܕܐܦ ܠܠܥܙܪܘܣ
* * ܠܡܚܙܝ ܕܐܩܝܡ
ܡܢ ܒܝܢ ܡܝܬܝܐ
* * * * * * 10
ܒܡܝܢܝܐ ܕܐܘܦ
ܠܠܥܙܪܘܣ ܢܩܛܠܘܢ :·
11 ܕܣܓܝܐܝܢ ܡܢ ܝܗܘܕܝܝܢ
ܗܘܘ ܐܙܠܝܢ ܠܟܘܬܗ
ܘܗܘܘ ܡܗܝܡܢܝܢ
ܒܝܫܘܥ :·
12 ܠܝܘܡܐ * * *
ܐܟܠܘܣ * * *
ܐܬܟܢܝܫ * * *
* * * * * *
* * * * * *

ܐܬܐ ܠܝܪܘܫܠܡ
13 ܢܣܒܘ ܣܘܟܝܢ
* * * ܘܢܦܩܘ
* * * ܠܗ ܘܗܘܘ
ܡ * * * ܐܘܫܥܢܐ
ܡܒܪܟ ܗܘ ܗܕܝ
ܕܐܬܐ ܒܫܡܗ
ܕܡܪܝܐ ܡܠܟܐ
ܕܐܝܣܪܐܝܠ :·
14 ܒܟܐ ܕܝ ܕܐܫܟܚ
ܝܫܘܥ ܚܡܪ
ܪܟܒ ܥܠܘܝ :· ܗܝܟ
15 ܡܟܐ ܕܟܬܝܒ : ܠܐ
ܬܕܚܠܝܢ ܒܪܬܗ
ܕܨܝܘܢ ܗܐ ܡܠܟܟ
ܐܬܐ ܪܟܝܒ ܥܠ
ܥܝܠ ܒܪ ܐܬܢ :·
16 ܗܠܝܢ ܠܐ ܝܕܥܘ
ܬܠܡܝܕܘܗܝ ܡܢ
ܩܕܡ ܐܠܐ ܟܕ
ܐܫܬܒܚ ܝܫܘܥ
* * ܐܕܟܪܘ ܕܗܠܝܢ
* * ܟܬܝܒܢ ܥܠܘܝ

* * * ܐ * * * 56 b
ܠܪܒܢܐ * ܗ * 57
* * * * * *
ܦܩܘܕܝܢ * * *
ܐܢܫ * * * * *
* * * ܢܐܚܕܘܢ
ܝܬܗ : ܗܘ ܐܘܢ xii. 1
ܝܫܘܥ ܡܢ ܩܘܕܡ
ܫܬܐ ܝܘܡܝܢ
ܕܦܣܚܐ ܐܬܐ
ܠܒܝܬ ܥܢܝܐ ܗܢ
ܕܗܘܐ ܠܥܙܪܘܣ
ܗܕܢ ܕܐܩܡ
ܝܫܘܥ ܡܢ ܒܝܢ
ܡܫܬܝܐ : ܥܒܕܘ ܠܗ 2
ܬܡܢ * * ܗܘܢ
ܘܡܪܬܐ ܗܘܬ
ܡܫܡܫܐ ܠܗܘܢ
* * * * * *
* * * * * *
ܡܪܝܡ * * * * 3
ܠܝܛܪ ܕܡܫܚ ܢܪ
ܦܝܣܛܝܩܘܣ

* * * * * *
* * * * * *
* * * * * *
* * * * * *
* * * * * *
* * * * * * 4
* * * * * *
ܬܠܡܝܕܘܗܝ ܗܕܢ
ܕܗܘܐ ܥܬܝܕ
* * * * * *
* * * * * * 5
ܗܕܢ ܒܣܡܐ ܠܐ
ܐ * * * * *
ܕܝܢܪܝܢ ܘܐܬܝܗܒ
ܠܡܣܟܢܝܐ : ܗܕܐ ܕܝ 6
ܐܡܪ ܠܐ ܕܗܘܐ
ܚܫܒ ܠܡܣܟܢܝܢܐ
ܐܠܐ ܕܗܘܐ * *
ܘܓܠܘܣܩܘܡܐ * *
* * * * * ܒܗ
* * * ܗܘܐ ܫܩܝܠ
* * * * * * 7
* * * * * *

* * * * * * xiv. 25

ܕܪܘܒܥܡ ܡܠܟ
ܣܘܣܩܝܡ ܡܠܟܐ
ܕܡܨܪܝܢ ܥܠ ܐܘܪܫܠܡ
26 ܘܢܣܒ ܟܘܠܗܘܢ
ܣܝܡ̈ܝܐܘܐܬܐ
ܒܒܝܬܗ ܕܡܪܝܐ
ܘܣܝܡ̈ܝܐܘܐܬܐ
ܒܒܝܬܗ ܕܡܠܟܐ
ܘܪܘܡܚܝ̈ܐ
ܕܕܗܒܐ · · ܕܢܣܒ
ܕܘ * * * * *

* * * * * *
* * * * * *
* * * * * *
* * * * * *
* * * * * *
* * * * * *
* * * * * *
* * * * * *
* * * * * *
* * * * * *
* * * * * *
* * * * * *

## Fragment XXXII b] III (I) KINGS XIV. 28—XV. 4 a.

* * * * * *
* * * * * *
* * * * * *
* * * * * *
* * * * * *
* * * * * * xv. 3
* * * * ܩܘܕܡ
* * * * ܗܘܐ
* * * ܥܡ ܡܪܝܐ
* * * ܗܝܟ ܠ
4 ܐܒܘܗܝ ܠܒܕܝܠ

xiv. 28 ܘܗܘܐ ܟܕ ܗܘܐ
ܥܠܠ ܠܒܝܬܗ ܕܡܪܝܐ
ܘܐܪܝܡܘ ܝܬܗܘܢ
ܗܠܝܢ ܪܗܘ*ܛܝܐ
ܘܢܣܒܘ ܝܬܗܘܢ
ܠܒܝܬ ܪܗܘܛܝܐ:
29 ܘܫܪܝܟܬ ܡܠܘܗܝ
ܕܪܘܒܥܡ ܘܟܘܠ
ܡܐ ܕܥܒܕ ܠ*ܗܐ
ܗܘܢ ܡܬܟܬܒܝܢ
ܒܣܦܪܐ ܕܡܠܟܐ

A. S. L.

Fragmentum XXXIII. legi non potest.

* * * * * * John xv. 5 b
ܠܝܬ ܐܢ̈ܬܘܢ ܡܫܟܚܝܢ
ܕܬܥ̈ܒܕܘܢ ܟܠܘܡ :
ܐܢ ܠܝܬ ܐܢܫ ܡܩܘܝ ܒܝ 6
* * : ܡܬܪܡܐ ܗܘ ܠܒܪ
* * * ܕܟܘܡܬܐ ܘܝܒܫ
* * * ܡܟܢܫܝܢ ܠܗܘܢ ܘܠܢܘܪܐ
* * * ܡ ܠܗܘܢ ܘ * * ܝܢ
* * * : ܐܢ ܕܝ ܡܬܩܝܡܘܢ 7
* * * * ܡ̈ܠܝ ܒܟܘܢ
* * * ܪܢ ܡܐ ܕܬܐܒܘܢ
* * * ܝ ܫܐܠܘ ܘ * * *
* * * * ܒܗܕܐ ܡܫܬܒܚ 8
* * ܕܦܐܪ̈ܝܢ * * *
* * * * * *
* * * * * *
* * ܒ ܠܝ, ܐܒܐ ܐܦ 9
* * * * ܚܒܝܬ ܠܟܘܢ
* * * * * * ܚܒܝ, ܕܝܠܝ
* * * * * ܐܢ ܦܘ̈ܩܕܢܝ 10
* * * ܛܪܝܢ ܐܢܬܘܢ ܒ * * *
* * * ܕܐܦ ܐܢܐ * * ܛ * *
* * ܩܕܘ * ܕ * * : ܘ * *

ܘܢ * * * * *
12 ܗܕܐ ܗܝ ܕ * * * *
ܕܠܝ : * * * *
ܦܠܟܘܢ * * *
ܐܝܟ ܕ * * * *
13 ܪܚܡܘܢ : ܪܒ * * *
ܚܒܝܬܐ ܠܝܬ * *
ܕܢܣܝܡ * * ܢܦܫܗ
14 ܪ̈ܚܡܘܗܝ : ܐܢܬܘܢ
ܪ̈ܚܡܝ ܐܢ ܬ * *
* * ܦܩܕ * * *
* * ܒ * * * *
15 ܠܐ * * * * *
ܠܟܘܢ * * * * *
* * * * * * *
ܡܐ * * * * *
ܠܪ̈ܚܡܝ * * * ܢ :
ܕܫܡܥܬ * * * ܬ
ܡܢ ܐܒܝ * * * *
16 ܠܐ * * * * *
ܕ * * * * * ܬ
ܝܬܟܘܢ : * * *
* * * * * * *
* * * * * * *

M. D. G.

John xiv. 25 * * * * * * ܠܘܬܟܘܢ:
26 * * * * * * ܪܘܚܐ
* * * * * * ܕܐܒܐ
* * * * * * * ܗܘ
* * * * * * * ܘܠܐ
* * * * ܬܕܟܘܢ ܟܘܠ
ܡܐ ܕܐܡܪܬ ܠܟܘܢ:
27 ܫܠܡ ܐܢܐ ܫܒܩ ܠܟܘܢ
ܫܠܡܝ ܕܝܠܝ ܐܢܐ ܝܗܒ
ܠܟܘܢ: ܠܐ ܗܝܟ ܕܥܠܡܐ
ܝܗܒ ܐܢܐ ܠܟܘܢ: ܠܐ
ܬܬܪܥܒ ܠܒܟܘܢ ܘܠܐ
28 ܫܡܥܬܘܢ: ܫܡܥܬܘܢ
ܕܐܢܐ ܐܡܪܬ ܠܟܘܢ:
ܕܐܙܠ ܐܢܐ ܘܐܬܐ
ܠܘܬܟܘܢ: ܐܠܘ ܗܘܝܬܘܢ
ܪܚܡܝܢ ܠܝ: ܚܕܝܬܘܢ
ܚܕܝܬܘܢ ܕܐܢܐ ܐܙܠ
ܠܘܬ ܐܒܐ: ܕܐܒܐ
29 ܪܒ ܗܘ ܡܢܝ: ܐܦ ܟܕܘ
ܐܡܪܬ ܠܟܘܢ ܥܕܠܐ
ܝܗ̈ܘܢ: ܕܟܕ ܝܗ̈ܘܢ
30 ܬܗܝܡܢܘܢ: ܠܝܬܐ

* * * * * * * 31
ܕܐܢܐ ܪܚܡ ܠܐܒܐ
ܘܗܝܟ ܡܐ ܕܦܩܕ
ܠܝ ܐܒܐ ܐܢܐ ܥܒܕ
ܩܘܡܘ ܢܐܙܠ ܠܢ ܡܢ * *
XV. 1 ܐܢܐ ܗܘ ܓܘܦܢܐ
ܫܪܝܪܬܐ: ܘܐܒܐ ܗܘ
2 ܦܠܚܐ: ܟܘܠ ܫܒܘܩܐ
ܕܒܝ ܘܦܐܪܝܢ ܠܐ ܡܥܒܕܐ
ܦܐܪܝܢ ܗܘ ܫܩܠ ܠܗ: ܘܟܘܠ
ܗܘܝܐ ܕܝܗܒܬܐ
ܦܐܪܝܢ ܡܕܟܐ ܗܘ
* * * * * * ܕ
3 ܟܒܪ ܐܢܬܘܢ * * *
ܡܛܠ ܡܠܬܐ ܕ * *
4 ܠܟܘܢ: ܟܬܪܘ * *
ܘܐܢܐ ܒܟܘܢ * *
ܗܝܟ ܕܫܒ * * * *
ܠܐ ܡܫܟܚܐ ܕ * * *
ܡܢ ܢܦܫܗ * * *
ܒܓܘܦܬܐ
ܗܟܢ ܐܘܦ ܠܐ.
* * * * * * * 5

M. D. G.

Ecclus. xviii. 27

ܓܒܪܐ ܚܟܝܡܐ
ܒܟܠ ܙܒܢ ܗܘ
ܕܚܠ ܘܒܝܘܡܬܐ
ܕܚܛܝܬܐ ܗܘ
ܡܬܢܛܪ ܡܢ
ܒܫܝܫܘܬܐ ⁘
28 ܟܠ ܡܢ ܕܡܣܬܟܠ
ܝܕܥ ܚܟܡܬܐ ⁘
ܘܠܡܢ ܕܡܫܟܚ̈
ܠ · ܗ · ܡܫܒܚܐ
ܐܫܬܘܕܝܘ ⁘
29 ܗܠܝܢ ܕܡܣܬܟܠܝܢ
ܒܡ̈ܠܐ ܐܦ
ܗܢܘܢ ܐܬܚܟܡܘ
ܘܐܒܥܘ · ܘ ܡ̈ܬܠܝܢ
ܒܫܪܝܪܝܢ ⁘

30 ܠܐ ܬܗܘܐ ܐܙܠ
ܒܬܪ ܪܓܝܓܬܟ ⁘
ܘ * * * * ܬܟܠܐ
ܡ * * * * * *
31 ܐܢ * * ܫ * ܒ
* * * ܒܪܓܝܓܬܐ

ܕܬ * * * * * *
ܠܒ * * * * * *
ܠܟ ܠ * * * *
ܠܒ * * * * * *
ܠܐ ܫ * * ܫ *
ܒܠ ܫ * * ܒܘܣܡ ⁘
32 ܘܠܐ ܬܗܘܐ ܒܫܩܦ
ܒܠ ܗܟܢ ܒܘܣܡ ⁘
ܘܠܐ ܬܬܘܬܦܪ
ܠܒܝܫܘܬܗ ܕܒܘܣܡܐ ⁘
33 ܠܐ ܬܗܘܐ ܡܣܬܒܝܢ
ܒܗܒ ܚܠܘܦ
* * ܡܘܙܦܐ ܡܢ
* * * * ܘܟܠܘܣ
* * * * * * *
* * * * * * *
* * * * * * *
* * * * * * *
* * * * * * *
* * * * * * *
* * * * * * *
* * * * * * *
* * * * * * *
* * * * * * *
* * * * * * *

A. S. L.

(*Reprinted*)

Ecclus. xviii. 17 ܡܚܣܕ * * * *
18 * * * * * * *
* * * * * * ܐ
* * * * * ܐ:
19 ܩܕܡ * * * * ܦܐ
ܡܡܠܠ * * ܗܘܝ
ܐܠܦ: ܘܩܕܡ ܥܕ ܠܐ
ܒܘܫܐ ܗܘܝ
ܡܬܐܣܐ
20 ܩܕܡ ܥܕ ܠܐ ܕܝܢܐ
ܗܘܝ ܡܥܐܠ
ܒܢܦܫܟ. ܘܒܫܥܬܐ
ܕܦܘܩܕܢܐ ܐ * * *
ܬܫܟܚ ܚܢ * *
21 * * * ܥܕ ܠܐ * *
* * * * * * *
* * * * * * *
* * * * * * *
* * * * * * *
* * * * * * *
* * * * * * *
* * * * * * *

ܡܢܚܬ ܒ * * *
23 ܩܕܡ ܥܕ ܠܐ ܬܨܠܘܝ
ܥܬܕ * * * ܓܬܐ:
ܘܠܐ ܬܗܘܐ ܗܝܟ
ܒܪܢܫ ܕܡܢܣܐ
ܠܡܪܐ:
24 ܐܬܕܟܪ ܚܡܬܐ
ܒܝܘܡܐ ܕܫܘܢܝܐ:
ܘܦܘܪܥܢܐ ܕܢܘܡܐ[1]
ܒܡܗܦܟܐ ܕܐܦܝܐ
25 ܐܬܕܟܪ ܡܦܘܪܥܢܐ
ܕܟܦܢܐ ܒܡܦܘܪܥܢܐ
ܕܣܒܥܐ * * * ܐܬ
ܐܬ * * * * *
ܐ * * * * * *
ܒܥܘܬܪܐ ܕܥܘܬܪܐ:
26 ܩܕܡ ܨܦܪܐ ܥܕ
ܡܦܢܐ ܪܡܫܐ
* * * ܬ * * *
ܘܒܥܠܘܗ * * * *
ܗ * * * * * *
ܩܕܡ ܡܪܝܐ:

[1] Cod. ܕܢܡܘܡܐ

A. S. L.

ܠܦ

# APPENDIX I.

## FRAGMENTS FROM THE TAYLOR-SCHECHTER COLLECTION.

(*Reprinted*)

[Fragment XIV.

recto

ܢܘ[ܫ]ܝܢ
ܘܬܠܬܐ
ܠܝܠܘܢ ܕܪܒܝܢ
ܒܢܗܪܐ
ܕܐܬܓܝܕܘ
ܒܥܝܢܬܐ
ܟܘܠ ܗܠܝܢ
ܕܗܘܘ
ܒܐܠܦܐ.
ܘܡܝܩܪܝܢܝܐ
ܬܟܫ

ܐ[ܠܦ]ܐ
ܘܡܫܬ
ܒܐܬ[ܪ]ܐ
ܡܢ ܓܪܫܗ
ܐܚܝ ܕܝ ܡܢ
ܗܠܝܢ ܕܗܘܘ
ܒܐܠܦܐ ܠܐ
ܐܬܒܒܪ
ܗܘܬ ܕܝ
ܐܠܦܐ ܩ[ܫܡ]ܐ
ܘܠܐ * * *

verso

ܐܬܪܐ
ܕܗܠܘܦ
ܡ * ܦܝܢ
ܒܗ * * *
ܘܡܝܩ[ܪ]ܝ[ܢܝ]ܐ
* ܦ ܡܢ
* * * * *
[ܬ]ܡ[ܗܘܢ]
ܕܐܬ * * *
* * ܡܥܝܢ
* * * * *

ܡܕܝܢܬܐ
ܘܝܩܒܘ
ܒܥܝܢܐ
ܘܒܝܠܠܬܐ
ܘܡܝܒܠܘ
ܬ[ܗܘ]ܢ
ܒܐܬܪܐ
ܕܒܗ
ܡܫܡܥܝܢ
ܘܦܪܘܩܗܘܢ
ܕܡܪܝܬܪܐ

ܘܐܠܘ ܡܢ̈ܝܗܘܢ ܡܛܐ ܠܪ̈ܘܚܐ f. 145 b
ܟܕ ܬ̈ܠܘܕܐ ܗܘܘ. ܐܠܗܐ ܚܝܪ
ܒܝܘܡܝܗܘܢ ܠܐ ܡܨ̈ܒܘܗ ܐܠܗܗܘܢ.
ܘܐܢ ܕܪ̈ܘܡܐ ܠܡܛܥܡܗ ܠܚܫܐ
ܗܢܐ ܒܒܢܝ̈ܗܘܢ ܘܠܐ ܐܬܒܨܪ̈
ܒܗܝܡܢܘܬܗܘܢ. ܐܢܫܝܢ ܕܝܢ
ܬܪܬܐ ܢܬܘܕܘܢ ܠܢ ܕܢܣܡܣܢ
ܒܫܒܪ. ܘܠܐ ܢܬܐܟܠ ܟܠ
ܦܘܪܥܢܐ ܕܡܕܒܪܝܢ ܘܡܛܠ
ܕܬܪ̈ܬܝܗܘܢ ܢܦ̈ܠܘ ܠܡܕܡ
ܡܠܬܐ ܕܒܘܣܐܐ ܡܢ ܟܬ̈ܒܐ
ܩܕܝܫܐ. ܘܐܦ ܐܢܫܝܢ ܒܛܠܠܐ
ܠܡܫܡܫܬܒܘ ܡ * ܕ̈ܝܢ ܚܝܢ
ܬܘܕܝܬܐ ܡܢ ܟܬ̈ܒܐ ܩܕ̈ܝܫܐ
ܗܠܝܢ ܕܒܗܘܢ ܪ̈ܫܝܡܝܢ ܫܪ̈ܒܐ
ܕ * * * ܗܘܢ ܕܙܕܩܐ ܒܠܡ̈ܕܡ
ܗܘ ܕܒܐܬ̈ܪܘܗܝ, ܩܕ̈ܝܫܬܐ
ܕܐܠܗܐ ܐܬܛܒ * * ܠܡܛܥܡܗ
ܒܠܡܐ ܗܢܐ * * * * ܒܢ̈ܘܗ
ܫܘ̈ܪܝܐ ܢܦܫܗ ܒܫܒܪܐ ܠܡܛܐ
ܕܒܠ ܫܒܪܐ ܕܢܘܚܡܐ ܐܒܠܗ
ܐܒܒܕ ܘܬ * * * * ܠܗܠܝܢ ܒ * ܗ

# MISCELLANEA.

ܒܥܠܡܐ ܕܗܘ ܒܛܝܒܘܬܗ f. 145 a
ܐܝܟ ܒܐܪܥܐ ܐܠܗܘܬ * * * *
ܡܦܪܫ ܒܘܕܪܝܢܗ̇ * * * *
ܘܐܠܝܢ ܕܐܚܒܘ ܠܥܒܪܗ * * *
ܐܡܪܘ * * * ܕܚܙܐ ܒ * * ܗܘܢ
ܡܠܐ ܐ * * * ܕܡܪܝܐ * * * * *
ܘܡܪܝܐ ܢܣܒ ܢܗܘܐ ܙ * * ܒ
ܕܡ * * * * ܒܪܟ ܚܒܝܒ * ܐܢܬ
ܠܢ ܡܪܝܐ ܐ * ܕܒܐ ܐ * * * * ܐ
ܪܕܦ ܡܝܢ ܕܐܡܬ ܕܚܙܐ
ܘܡܛܐ ܩ̈ܒܒܪ ܘܒܚܒܒܝܢ ܢܡܛܐ
ܠܘܬ ܡܪܝ ܘܒܠܐ * * * ܒܕ * ܡ *
ܘܕܐܠܝܢ ܕܕܐܝܟ ܗܠܝܢ ܐܢܘܢ
ܛܠܝܐ ܕܝܠܗܘܢ ܗܝ ܡܠܟܘܬܐ
ܕܫܡܝܐ ܘܛܠܝܐ ܕܡܬܒܣܡܝܢ ܡܢ
ܒܥܠܡܐ ܗܢܐ ܒܫܝܢܐ ܘܒܪܘܚܬܐ
ܬܗܘܐ ܡܛܠ ܕܗܝ ܦܩܕ
ܐܠܗܐ * * * * * * ܟ ܐܠܐ
ܕܬܬܪܐܬ ܠܘܬ ܐܠܗܐ ܡܩܪ̈ܒܝܢ
ܒܗ ܕܡܩܕܫ ܘܒܒܪ ܠܗܘܢ
ܥܠܡܐ ܕܒܘܠܓܪܐ ܕܫܒܝܒܐ
ܡܫܬܒܪ̈ܝܢ. ܘܡܢ ܟܠܗ ܪܘܫܟܐ
ܕܒܥܠܡܐ ܗܢܐ ܡܫܬܡܫܝܢ

# MAR JACOB.

* * * * * * * * * * ܕܗ ܒܫܘܒܚܐ f. 140 b

ܠܐܒܐ ܘܠܒܪܗ ܘܪܘܚܗ ܡܫܒܚܬܐ

* * * * * ܒܥܠܡܐ ܘܠܥܠܡ ܥܠܡܝܢ

⁘ * * ܐܐ ܕܒ̈ܪܝ، ܢܡܘܣܐ ܕܡܠܐܟܐ ܕܕܡܐ

ܫܡܥܗ ܗܘ ܕܕܢܒ * * ܒܟܠ

* * * ܗܘ * * * ܕܒܢܝܢܘܬܐ

* * * * * * * * *

* * * * * * * * *

ܡܪ̈ܢܐ ܡܫܡܫܢܐ * * ܐ ܘܠܐ

ܗܠ ܠܐܘ * * * * * * * * *

ܗܕܢܐ ܘܠ * * ܐ ܬܘܩܦܐ. ܒ * * ܐܐ

ܫܬܝܬܐ ܬܚܬ * * * * * * * * *

ܕܢܬ * * ܗܡܢܐ ܓܢܝ ܕ * * ܐܬ

ܒܡܫܡܫܢܐ ܫܡܝܐ ܠܫܘ * ܐ

ܫܘܠܚܢܐ. ܗܕܢܐ * * * * * * *

ܕ * * * ܡܠܟ * * * ܠܘܒܒܐ

ܢܒܗ ܒܘܕܝܢܐ ܠܢܒܝܐ * * * ܗܘܬ

ܒܒܪܝܬܐ * * * * * * * * *

ܒ * * ܘܬܐ ܐܦ ܡܢܝܢ ܕܢܝܢ ܐܠܐܐ

ܒܘܕܝܢܐ ܕܒܗ ܗܦܟ. ܘܬ * ܢ

ܘܡܫܘܚܬܐ ܬܘܒ ܕܒ̈ܢܝ ܒܠܫܢܐ

ܗܢܐ ܐܦ ܢ * ܠܐ ܕܠܐ ܠܐܐ ܫܒܚܐ

ܕܒܗ ܥܠܝ * * * * * * * * ܘ ܢ

ܘܒܬܪܗ ܘܝܗܒ ܠܗ ܚܘܛܪܐ f. 140a
ܕܒ̈ܥܘܬܐ ܡܬܪ̈ܥܝܬܐ ܘܒܥܝܢܗ
ܒܥܡܪܐ ܡܝܬܪܐ ܘܥܘܕܪܢܐ
ܘܫܠܛܗ ܒܡܫ̈ܝܚܘܬܗ ܕܡܪܥܝܬܗ
ܗܘ ܕܒܪ ܟܠܬܗ ܡܪܥܝܬܐ.
ܬܕܒܪ * * * ܗ ܘܠܡܝܢܗ̇ ܗܘ
ܒ * * ܐ ܒܥܠܡܗ̇ ܘܠܡܢܕ ܘܠܡܒܪܝܢܗ̇
ܒܪܥܝܢܗܘܢ ܒܬܪܬܐ ܘܠܚܝܠܡ
ܒܪܗܡܝܢܗ̇. ܘܠܡܬܪ ܫܠܝܡܝܢܗ̇. ܚܝܘ
ܠܡܟܝܢܐ ܘܡ̈ܣܘܢܐ ܥܠ ܫ̈ܦܝܪܐ.
ܢܪܕܘܦ ܠܒܝܫܐ. ܘܢܬܦܠ ܠܬܠܠ ܠܐܦܠ
ܡܪܓܐ ܘܡܘܡ ܒܥܠܡܗ ܢ̈ܦܘܪܐ
ܠܒܢܗ ܘܠܒܢ̈ܘܢ ܕܚܝ̈ܠܢ ܘܫܒܚܝܢ.
ܕܐܬܬܝܢ ܘܠܘܬܝܢ ܠܢܦܫܐ
ܐܟܘܢ ܦܘܠܚܢܐ ܒܝܠܘܬܗ ܢܝܪ
ܬܦܠܘܢ ܦܘܪܩܢܐ ܥܒܝܕܐ ܗܘ
ܗܘܪ ܘܒܝܬܝ ܗܝ ܠܒܢ̈ܝܢ
ܘܠܒ̈ܢܬܗܘܢ ܘܠܟܠܗ ܥܒܕܐ
ܕܐܬ̈ܪܥܘܢ ܢܦܫܝ. ܘܟܠܗ ܒܚܝܕܐ
ܥܠܡܘܬܐ ܘܒܚܝܪ ܡܠܟܐ ܕ * * *
ܢܡܘܣ ܫܘܒܚܐ ܘܬܘܕܝܬܐ.
ܠܗܘ ܕܝܠܝܕܐ ܕܒܒܪܗ. ܘܒܝܢܝܗ
ܒܥܡܪܐ ܦܠܐ ܘܥܘܕܪܢܐ ܗܘ

ܦ ܦܘܠܝܛܐ ܚܒܝܒܬ ܠܟ ܒ * * * f. 122 b
ܒܕ ܠܟܝ: ܘܣܬܪ ܗܘܝܬ ܐܝܟ
ܡܐ ܕܡܣܡ ܪܒܐ ܐܘܚܪ
* * * * * * ܠܐ * * ܒ * * *
ܕܐܟܪܝ, ܠܦܘܠܝܛܝ ܠܐ ܐܝܬ ܠܗ
ܘܠܗ, ܕܝܢ ܐܝܟ ܕܠܐ ܐܟܪܐ ܐܦ
ܠܐ ܠܒܐܪܐ. ܦܘܠܝܛܐ ܕܟܝܢܬ:
ܐܟܪܐ ܐܒܐ ܠܟܢ ܠ * * * * ܡܐ
ܕܡܐܡ ܒܐܝܐ ܕܝܠܬ ܐܟܪܐ
ܠܩܠܝܡܘܗܝ, ܗܘ ܡܪܝ, ܕܒܝܢܐ cf. 1 Cor. ii. 9
ܠܐ ܚܙܬ ܘܐܕܢܐ ܠܐ ܫܡܥܬ
ܘܥܠ ܠܒܐ ܕܐܢܫܐ ܠܐ ܣܠܩ
ܡܕܡ ܕܛܝܒܬ ܝܗܒܐ ܗܘܝܬ
ܐܕܒ ܐܠܗܐ ܠܒܢܐ ܐܝܠ ܐܝܢܐ
ܐܝܬ ܗܘ ܕܡܒܝܢܐ ܘܐܦ ܠܗܘ
ܐܚܪܢܐ ܕܡܬܠܐ ܘܐܦ ܗܘ
ܕܒܡ ܐܡܪܐ ܐܘ ܒܡ ܡܢ ܠܒܪܢܐ
ܡܣܝܡ ܠܝ ܗܘ ܕܒܢܝܐ ܕܐܫܠܡ
ܢܦܫܗ ܕܦܪܩ ܡܪܒܝܬܐ * *
ܝ ܒܝܢܝܟ ܕܛܒܬܐ ܬܘܕܝܬܐ ܐܡܪܐ
ܬܡܒܝܢܐ ܘܡܪܢ ܡܣܝܡ ܠܝ
ܡܢܒܬ * * * ܕܐ ܡܪܒܝܬܟܘܢ
* * * * * * * * *
ܘܐܝܬܝܘ ܡܠܒܘܫܬܐ ܕܡܛܝܒܐ

# MISCELLANEA.

ܕܐܠܦܘܣ ܗ ܗܐ ܫܠܝ̈ܚܝܢ f. 117a
ܪܒܫ ܗܕܠܝܢ ܒܠܗܘ ܚܘ̈ܪܒܝܢ
ܕܠܦܠܓܗ * * * ܐ ܫܡܥܬ ܘܠܗ̇
ܘܐܬܒܠܗܬ ܕܒܓܠܐ ܐܬܦܪܥ.
ܠܐܬܪܐ ܕܚܝܠܐ ܐܬܚܝܒܬ: ܐܝ
ܘܗ ܕܦ * * ܬ * * * ܠܐ ܡܘܬܐ
ܠ ܚܝܬ ܒܢܘ̈ܗܝ ܗ ܗܐ
ܦܪ̈ܘܫܝܢ ܬܠܡܝ̈ܕܘܗܝ ܕܗܘ ܠܡܕܒܪܢܘܬܐ
* * ܕܝܬܗ ܘܠܝܕܐ ܕܬܘܒܠܗ.
ܘܕܐܡܪܐ ܠܗ̇ ܠܡܐܢܘܬܐ
ܐܬܐ ܠܗ̇ ܦܠ * ܒ * ܡܒܠ * ܗ
ܚܬ ܒܚܕܘܬܐ. ܕܗܝܢ ܦܐܪ̈ܐ
ܠܐܒܝܐ. ܦܠܚ ܒܗ ܒܒܪ̈ܝܒܝܢ
ܠܐ ܢܬܦܠܓ * * * * ܕܐܠ * *
ܢܗܘܐ ܦܠܝܓܘܬܝ̇ ܡܪܘܐܝܬ. ܒܕ
ܒܐܪܟܟܐ: ܕܒܠܒܐ ܗܢܐ
ܦܢܐ ܗܘܬ ܘܐܡܪ ܗܘܐ
ܪܒܝܢ ܒܢܘܒܐ[1] ܢܒܝܠܐ
ܦܠܓܘܬܐ ܘܠܐ * * ܬ ܕܚܝܠ ܗܘ
ܕܚܝܐ ܡܟܕܐܒܐ * * * ܠܐ * * * *
ܘ ܒܕܐ ܕܦܠܓܘܬܗ * * ܡ * *

[1] sic

ܕܒܟܝܢܘܬܐ ܐܫܪ ܠܒܢ̈ܘܗܝ ܒܫܠܡܗ f. 119b
ܛܘܒܘܗܝ ܠܐܝܢܐ ܕܝܗܒܐ ܠܗ ܠܗ
ܡܫܒܚܘܬܐ ܘܢܝܚ * * * * * *
ܛܘܒܘܗܝ ܠܐܝܢܐ ܕܒܣܝܡ ܦܐܝܕ
ܒܠܒܐ ܫܘܒܚܗ̇. ܛܘܒܘܗܝ
ܠܐܝܢܐ ܕܐܠܘܦܬܗ * * ܬ * *
ܢܗܝܪ ܒܗ. ܛܘܒܘܗܝ̈ ܠܐܝܢܐ
ܕܠ * * ܐ ܗܘ̈ܢܐ ܡܟܠ * * * * *
ܛܘܒܘܗܝ ܠܐܝܢܐ ܕܒܠܫܘ̈ܕܘܗܝ
ܫܘܒ ܒܠ ܡܒܪܟ ܠܗ ܫܘܒܚܗ.
ܛܘܒܘܗܝ ܠܐܝܢܐ ܕܐܒܝܬ * * * ܒܗ̇ܕܐ
ܠܢܘܬܐ ܒܡܪܗ * * * ܛܘܒܘܗܝ
ܠܐܝܢܐ ܕܫܒܩܗ̇ ܫܘܪ̈
ܒܡܪܘܗ̈ܐ ܒܫܠܡܐ ܛܘܒܘܗܝ
ܠܐܝܢܐ ܕܗܘ ܒܬܪܗ ܘܝܐ
ܠܗ ܒܬܪܐ ܕܠܫܠܡ ܛܘܒܘܗܝ
ܠܐܝܢܐ * * * * * * * ܠܦܘ
* * * * * * * * * ܛܘܒܘܗܝ
ܠܐܝܢܐ ܕܫܡܫܐ ܗܘ ܘ * * *
ܐ * * * * * * * *
* * * * * * * * *
* * * ܗ * * * ܐ ܕܫܡܫܬ ܘܒܢܢ

# MAR EPHRAIM.

ܒܥܡ ܕ* ܫܝܐ ܘܡܕܡܝܬܐ ܡܪܐ f. 116b
ܒܒ̈ܕ ܠܟܝ ܒܝܬܗ * * * *
ܟܠܗ ܒܗܠܟܝ ܘܗܡ * * * *
ܒܐܒܝܟܝ ܘܦܪܫ ܠ * * *
ܫܠܡܘ ܠܡܟܬܒ ܡܐܡܪ̈ܐ ܗܠܝܢ
ܕܡܬܐܡܪܝܢ ܒܠ ܝܘܡܗ

ܬܘܒ ܩ̈ܠܬܐ ܕܬܘܒ̈ܐ ܕܐܡܝܪܝܢ
ܠܡܪܝ ܐܦܪܝܡ ܡܠܦܢܐ ܒܠ
ܕܒܪܝܐ ܕܒܐܝܢܐ ܘܒܠ ܬܘܒ̈ܐ
ܕܐܝܬ ܠܗܘܢ ܠܘܬ ܐܠܗܐ
ܛܘܒܝܗܘܢ[1] ܠܟܝܢ ܕܗܘܐ ܒܢܪܐ ܒܒܠ ܒܪ:
ܛܘܒܝܗܘܢ ܠܟܝܢ * * * * * * *
ܛܘܒܝܗܘܢ ܠܟܝܢ ܕܗܘܐ ܡܠܝܟܐ * * *
ܛܘܒܝܗܘܢ ܠܟܝܢ ܕܗܘܐ ܫܠܝܐ ܘܫܬܝܩܐ
* * * * * * * * *
ܛܘܒܝܗܘܢ ܠܟܝܢ ܕܐܠܦ * * * ܒܒܕ
ܛܘܒܝܗܘܢ ܠܟܝܢ ܕܢܒܦ ܣܓܝܐ ܕܒ̈ܒܬܗ:
* * * * * * * * *
ܛܘܒܝܗܘܢ ܠܟܝܢ ܕܪܢܐ ܒܫܒܒ ܕܡܫܘܬܐ ܗܘ:
ܛܘܒܝܗܘܢ ܠܟܝܢ ܕܐܫܟܚ ܝܘܕܥܗ ܒܛܠܝܘܬܗ:
ܛܘܒܝܗܘܢ ܠܟܝܢ ܕܗܘܐ ܡܫܝܚܐ ܒܚܘܫܬܗ

[1] Cf. Lamy, *Sancti Ephraem Syri Hymni et Sermones*, tom. IV. pp. 783—786.

ܠܬܠܬܝܢ ܘܬܡܢܝܐ ܫܢܝܢ ܐܡܪ ܕܐܬܟܠܘܢ cf. John v. 5—10
ܒܪܘܫܝܢ ܘܗܠܝܢ ܒܢܘܡܣܐ ܕܡܫܒܚܬܐ * *
ܘܒܪܘܩ ܫܐܕܐ ܠܟܘܢܐ ܘܒܢܝܫܐ * * * cf. Mark iii. 11
ܕܦ * ܩ ܠܡܪܢܐ ܒܫܡܗ ܫܒܝܚܐ. ܐ * * *
ܕܕܡܐ ܠܡܪܢܐ ܒܒܢ ܡܠ̈ܐܟܐ. ܡܪܐ
ܐܝܬܘܗܝ، ܕܫ̈ܡܝܐ. ܘܕܠܐ ܫܢܐ ܕܝ * *
* * * * * * * * * *
ܐܡܬ ܕܟܢܫ ܠܗ̈ܘܢ ܠܡ̈ܝܐ ܕܢܬܟܢܫܘܢ f. 146 b cf. Ps. xxxiii. 7
ܠܒܘܫܝܐ ܚܕ. ܘܦܪܐ ܫܡܗܘܢ ܡܫ̈ܡܫܐ Ecclus. xxxix. 17
ܘܐܠܒܫܗ ܒܥܢܢܐ ܘܒܥܪܦܠܐ ܒܥܠܗ Job xxxviii. 9
ܣܡ ܠܗ ܡܠܝ̈ܢܐ ܘܬܪܥܐ ܘܐܡܪ
ܠܗ ܒܕܡܐ ܠܗܪܟܐ ܦܘܩ ܘܠܐ 11
ܬܥܒܪ. ܘܟܡܐ ܢܬܬܒ̈ܪܘܢ ܓܠܠܝ̈ܟܝ
ܘܣܡ ܠܗ ܬܚܘܡܐ ܣܠܐ. ܢܡܘܣܐ
ܕܟܠܗ ܒܠܡ̈ܝܢ. ܗܘܐ ܒܝܠ ܒܐܝܕܗ cf. Is. xl. 12
ܫ̈ܡܝܐ ܕܟܠܒ ܡܢ ܫܡܝܢܐ ܘܒܢܘܪܗ
ܐܚܝܕ ܠܟܘܠܗ ܐܪܒܥܐ. ܘܬܩܠ ܛܘܪ̈ܐ
ܒܡܬܩܠܗ. ܘܪ̈ܡܬܐ ܒܡܣܬܐ[1]
ܫܝܘܠ ܫܠܝܚܐ ܩܕܡܘܗܝ، ܘܠܝܬ Job xxvi. 6
ܠܒܘܫܐ ܠܐܒܕܢܐ. ܒܦܘܩܕܢܗ ܐܡܝܬ
ܠܓܢܝܢܐ. ܡܢܘ ܗܘܐ ܩܕܡܘܗܝ،
ܚܠܝܬܐ ܘܠܐ ܡܬܕܪܟܢܐ ܗܘ
ܕܡܫܢܐ ܠܦܘܪ̈ܐ ܘܠܐ ܢܕܒܚܝܢ ܘܗܦܟ

[1] sic, cf. Thes. Syr. p. 2498 ܣܐܬܐ

ܕܡܬܬܚ ܥܡܡܝܐ ܒܠܫܢܗܘܢ܆ ܘܡܗܠܟ ܥܠ
9 ܝܡܡܐ ܐܝܟ ܕܥܠ ܐܪܥܐ. ܗܘ ܕܒܪܐ
ܡܕܝܢܐ ܘܡܫܪܟܐ. ܒܪܝܬܐ ܘܬܡܝܡܬܐ
10 ܗܘ ܕܒܪܐ ܪܘܒܬܐ ܘܠܐ ܡܬܕܪܟܢܘܬܐ
ܥܒܝܕܬܐ܆ ܒܝܢ ܘܬܫܡܫܬܐ ܕܠܝܬ ܠܗܘܢ
ܡܢܝܢܐ. ܗܘ ܕܡܢܐ ܡܣܟܘܡܗܘܢ ܕܟܘܟܒܐ Ps. cxlvii. 4
ܘܠܟܘܠܗܘܢ ܩܪܐ ܫܡܗܐ. ܗܘ ܕܡܦܩ Ps. cxxxv. 7 (Peshitta cxxxiv)
ܥܢܢܐ ܡܢ ܣܘܦܗ ܕܐܪܥܐ ܘܒܪܩܐ
ܠܡܛܪܐ ܥܒܕ܆ ܡܦܩ ܪܘܚܐ ܡܢ ܐܘܨܪܐ
ܘܡܢܐ ܥܢܢܐ ܒܚܟܡܬܗ ܡܢܝܢ ܕܝܢ ܠܗ Job xxxviii. 37
ܐܦ ܛܘܦܐ ܕܡܛܪܐ. ܡܟܠ ܡܢܐ ܐܝܟ cf. Ecclus. i. 2
ܓܒܐ. ܗܘ ܒܪܝ ܒܠܫܢܗܘܢ܆ ܐܝܬ ܠܗ

* * * * * * * * * *

ܘܠܕܝܘܩܢܐ ܠܒܘܦܪܐ ܕܚܝܪܐ ܠܟܠܝܪܟܐ f. 146a
ܕܗܘܐ ܠܗ ܒܪܐ ܚܕܐ ܐܫܘܬܗ ܘܕܒܫܬܐ (cf. Matt. viii. 5 *Sinai Palimpsest*)
ܐܝܕܐ ܫܠܝܡܬܐ ܒܒܕ ܒܢܡܘܣܐ ܕܫܒܬܐ
ܘܟܐܐ ܒܐܫܬܐ ܕܚܡܬܗ ܕܦܛܪܘܣ cf. Luke iv. 38, 39
ܘܡܗܠܟ. ܗܘ ܕܗܠܟ ܥܠ ܓܠܠܐ ܐܝܟ ⌜ܥܠ⌝ cf. Matt. xiv. 25—31
ܝܒܝܫܬܐ. ܘܠܟܠܟܠܢ ܐܘܫܛ ܐܝܕܐ
ܕܠܐ ܢܛܒܥ ܘܒܝܡܐ ܒܕ ܫܓܝܫ
ܟܐܐ ܘܡܫܬܩܐ ܠܗ ܒܒܕ. ܘܐܫܬܒܩ cf. Mark iv. 39
ܒܬܫܒܘܚܬܗ ܒܛܘܪܐ ܩܕܝܫܐ ܕܬܒܘܪ cf. Matt. xvii. 1—3
ܘܐܫܬܠܚܠܒ ܩܕܝܡ[1] ܬܠܡܝܕܘܗܝ܆ ܘܐܬܐ
ܘܡܫܗ ܡܫܐ ܘܐܠܝܐ. ܘܠܗܘ ܡܫܪܝܐ

[1] sic

# HYMN.

* * * * * * ܘܫܒܚܐ * * * * * f. 45 a

ܒܒܝ ܡܢܗܪܬܐ ܘܗܦܟ ܦܠܓܐ ܒܐܝܕܘܗܝ

ܡܫܚܐ ܘ * * * * ܒܫܩܠܗ ܚܕ ܠܡܫܩܠܐ Wisdom xi. 21

ܪܘܪܒܬܐ ܡܢܗ ܗܘ. ܘܠܡܫܠܡ ܒܡܫܝܚܗ

ܕܕܪܫܗ ܡܢܗ ܢܗܘܐ. ܡܛܠ ܕܐܝܟ

ܪܡܫܬܐ ܒܦܠܐܬܐ ܕܒܣܘܟܬܐ ܒܥܠ

ܠܐܒܐ ܘܒܢܝܟ ܐܝܬܘܗܝ. ܡܢܗ ܘܒܗ ܐܝܬܘܗܝ

ܐܒܡܬܗ ܫܠܝܛܬܐ ܡܢ ܠܚܕܝܐ ܕܨܦܪܐ Amos v. 8

ܘܐܫܕ ܠܗܘܢ ܥܠ ܐܦܝ ܟܘܠܗ ܐܪܥܐ

ܡܪܝܐ ܐܠܗܐ ܫܠܝܛܐ * * * * *

ܐܫܕ ܒܘܠ ܫܡܝܗ. ܗܘ ܕܚܝܐ ܪܐܒܪܐ

ܘܪܝܒܐ ܘܡܚܒܐ[1] ܒܦܘܪܐ ܘܬܝܬܘܢ ܕܠܒܫ Ps. cxliv. 5 (cxliii)

ܘܗܪܐ ܐܝܟ ܡܪܛܘܛܐ ܘܡܬܚܫ ܫܡܝܐ Ps. civ. 2—4

ܐܝܟ ܝܪܝܥܬܐ. ܒܒܝ ܡܝܐ ܡܥܠܝܬܗ

ܘܣܡ ܥܠ ܥܢܢܐ ܡܪܟܒܬܗ. ܘܡܗܠܟ

ܥܠ ܟܢܦܝ ܪܘܚܐ ܒܒܝ ܡܠܐܟܘܗܝ Ps. civ. 4 Heb. i. 7

ܪܘܚ ܘܡܫܡܫܢܘܗܝ ܢܘܪ ܝܩܕܐ

* * ܒܪܘܓܙܗ ܗܘ ܕܡܙܝܥ ܐܪܥܐ f. 45 b Job ix. 6

ܡܢ ܫܬܐܣܝܗ. ܘܥܡܘܕܝܗ ܪܥܠܝܢ ܡܢ

7 ܡܕܡܘܗܝ. ܐܡܪ ܠܫܡܫܐ ܘܠܐ ܕܢܚ

8 ܘܟܘܟܒܐ ܒܚܬܡܬܗ ܐܝܬܘܗܝ ܗܘ

[1] sic

*Double Palimpsest.*

f. 80 a
(script. med.)

ܡܛܠ ܕܡܪܝܐ ܥܒܕ ܠܗܘܢ ܩܪܒܐ 25b
ܒܡܨܪܝܢ ܘܐܡܪ ܡܪܝܐ ܠܡܘܫܐ 26
ܐܪܝܡ ܐܝܕܟ ܥܠ ܝܡܐ ܘܝܗܦܟܘܢ
ܡ̈ܝܐ ܥܠ ܡܨܪ̈ܝܐ ܥܠ ܡܪ̈ܟܒܬܗܘܢ
ܘܥܠ ܦܪ̈ܫܝܗܘܢ ܘܐܪܝܡ ܡܘܫܐ ܐܝܕܗ 27
ܥܠ ܝܡܐ ܘܗܦܟ ܝܡܐ ܠܥܕܢ ܨܦܪܐ
ܠܕܘܟܬܗ ܘܡܨܪ̈ܝܐ ܥܪܩܝܢ ܠܩܘܒܠܗ
ܘܢܦܨ ܡܪܝܐ ܠܡܨܪ̈ܝܐ ܒܓܘ ܝܡܐ.
ܘܗܦܟܘ ܡ̈ܝܐ ܘܟܣܘ ܠܡܪ̈ܟܒܬܐ 28
ܘܠܦܪ̈ܫܐ. ܘܠܟܠܗ ܚܝܠܗ ܕܦܪܥܘܢ
ܕܥܠܘ ܒܬܪܗܘܢ ܠܝܡܐ ܘܠܐ
ܐܫܬܝܪ ܡܢܗܘܢ ܐܦܠܐ ܚܕ. ܘܒ̈ܢܝ 29
ܐܝܣܪܐܝܠ ܗܠܟܘ ܒܝܒܫܐ ܐܝܟ
ܕܒܝܒܫܐ. ܘܡ̈ܝܐ ܗ̈ܘܘ ܠܗܘܢ ܫܘܪܐ
ܡܢ ܝܡܝܢܗܘܢ ܘܡܢ ܣܡܠܗܘܢ. ܘܦܪܩ 30
ܡܪܝܐ ܒܝܘܡܐ ܗܘ ܠܐܝܣܪܐܝܠ
ܡܢ ܐܝܕܐ ܕܡܨܪ̈ܝܐ. ܘܚܙܐ ܐܝܣܪܐܝܠ
ܠܡܨܪ̈ܝܐ ܕܝ ܡܝܬܝܢ ܥܠ ܣܦܬܗ ܕܝܡܐ
ܘܚܙܐ ܐܝܣܪܐܝܠ ܐܝܕܐ ܪܒܬܐ 31
ܕܥܒܕ ܡܪܝܐ ܒܡܨܪ̈ܝܐ. ܘܕܚܠ ܥܡܐ
* * * * * ܗܝܡܢܘ ܒܡܪܝܐ ܘܒܡܘܫܐ

*Double Palimpsest.*

f. 80 b (script. med.)

ܘܐܝܩܪܗ ܥܠܝܟܝ ܢܬܚܙܐ ܘܢܐܬܘܢ 2b, 3
ܥܡ̈ܡܝܐ ܠܢܗܘܪܝܟܝ[1] ܘܡ̈ܠܟܝܐ ܠܢܗܘܪܐ
ܕܕܢܚܟܝ. ܐܪܝܡܘ[1] ܥܝܢ̈ܝܟܝ ܠܣܚܪ̈ܢܝܟܝ 4
ܘܚܙܝ، ܕܟܠܗܘܢ ܡܬܟܢܫܝܢ ܘܐܬܝܢ
ܠܟܝ ܒܢ̈ܝܟܝ ܡܢ ܪܘܚܩܐ ܝܬܘܢ[1] ܘܒܢܬܟܝ
ܥܠ ܦܪܘܬܐ ܝܬܛܥܢ ܗܝܕܝܢ ܬܚܙܝܢ ܘܬܬܢܗܪܝܢ 5
ܘܬܙܝܥܝܢ ܘܢܪܘܚ ܠܒܟܝ. ܡܛܠ ܕܗܦܟ
ܠܟܝ ܟܘܬܪܗ ܕܝܡܐ ܘܚܝܠܐ ܕܥܡ̈ܡܝܐ
ܝܐܬܘܢ ܠܟܝ. ܐܟܠܬܐ ܕܓܡ̈ܠܐ ܬܟܣܝܟܝ 6
ܒܟܪ̈ܝܐ ܕܡܕܝܢ ܘܕܐܝܦܐ ܟܠܗܘܢ ܡܢ
ܫܒܐ ܝܐܬܘܢ ܕܗܒܐ ܘܠܒܘܢܬܐ
ܝܥܠܘܢ. ܘܬܫ̈ܒܚܬܗ ܕܡܪܝܐ ܝܣܒܪܘܢ
ܟܠܗ̇ ܥܢܐ ܕܩܕܪ ܝܬܟܢܫܘܢ ܠܟܝ ܘܕܟܪ̈ܝܐ 7
ܕܢܒܐܘܬ ܝܬܡܫܡܫܘܢܟܝ ܘܝܣܩܘܢ ܠܪܥܘܢܐ
ܥܠ ܡܕܒܚܝ ܘܒܝܬܐ ܕܬܫܒܘܚܬܝ، ܐܫܒܚ

ܘܗܘܐ Exod. xiv. 24
ܒܡܛܪܬܐ ܕܨܦܪܐ ܘܐܬܚܙܝ، ܡܪܝܐ
ܠܡܫܪܝܬܐ ܕܡܨܪ̈ܝܐ ܒܥܡܘܕܐ ܕܢܘܪܐ
ܘܕܥܢܢܐ ܘܫܓܫ ܠܡܫܪܝܬܐ ܕܡܨܪ̈ܝܐ
ܘܩܛܥ ܓܝܓ̈ܠܐ ܕܡܪ̈ܟܒܬܗܘܢ ܘܗܘܢ 25
ܡܕܒܪܝܢ ܠܗܘܢ ܒܬܘܩܦܬܐ ܘܐܡܪܝܢ

* * * * * * * * * *

[1] sic

*Double Palimpsest.*

f. 134 a
(script. inf.)

⌜ ⌝ܠܢܟܣܐ ܒܒܘܨܪ ܘܩܛܠܐ ܪܒܐ
7 ܒܐܪܥܐ ܕܐܕܘܡ ܘܢܦܠܘܢ ܪ̈ܡܐ
ܥܡܗܘܢ ܘܬܘܪ̈ܐ ܥܡ ܐܝ̈ܠܘܢܐ
ܘܬܬܪܘܐ[1] ܐܪܥܐ ⌜ܡܢ⌝ ܕܡܗܘܢ
8 ܘܝܘܡܐ ܗܘ ܬܒܥܬܗܘܢ ܕܝܢܗ ܫܢܬ
ܕܢܘܩܡܐ ܕܬܒܥܬܐ ܠܨܝܘܢ. ܘܫܢܬܐ
ܕܦܘܪܥܢܢܐ ܠܕܝܢܐ ܕܨܗܝܘܢ
9 ܘܢܬܗܦܟܘܢ ܢܚܠܝܗ ܠܙܦܬܐ ܘܥܦܪܗ
ܠܟܒܪܝܬܐ. ܘܬܗܘܐ ܐܪܥܗ
10 ܙܦܬܐ ܕܝܩܕܐ. ܘܠܐ ܬܕܥܟ ܠܠܠܝܐ
ܘܐܝܡܡܐ ܘܠܥܠܡ ܝܣܩ ܬܢܢܗ
ܘܬܚܪܒ ܠܕܪ̈ܕܪܝܢ ܘܠܥܠܡ ܥܠܡܝܢ
11 ܐܝܟ ܠܐ ܢܥܒܪ ܒܗ ⌜ܘ⌝ܢܐܪܬܘܢܗ[1]
ܩܩ̈ܐ ܘܩܘ̈ܦܕܐ ܘܩܦܘ̈ܦܐ
ܘܢܥܒܐ ܢܫܪܘܢ ܒܗ ܘܢܬܡܬܚ
ܥܠܝܗ ܫܘܦܠܐ ܕܫܪܒܐ ܘܠܐ
12 ܬܗܘܐ ܬܡܢ ܫܕܘܬܐ ܘܐܦ
ܠܐ ܢܫܪܘܢ ܬܡܢ ܡܠܟܘܬܐ. ܘܡܠܟܝܗܘܢ
ܘܪ̈ܒܢܝܗ ܢ⌜ ⌝ܗܘܘܢ ܠܐܒܕܢܐ
13 ⌜ܘܢܐܟܠܘܢ⌝ ܟܘܒ̈ܐ ܒܡܫܝܢ̈ܬܗ
* * * * * * ܘܕܪ̈ܕܪܐ ܒܚܣܢܗ
ܘܬܗܘܐ ܕܝܪܐ ܕܬܢܝܢ̈ܐ ܘܒܝܬ

[1] sic

*Double Palimpsest.*

f. 134 b
(script. inf.)

1 ܩܪܘܒܘ ܥܡܡܐ ܠܡܫܡܥ
ܘܨܘܬܘܢ ܐܘܡܬܐ ܬܫܡܥ
ܐܪܥܐ ܒܡܠܐܗ̇. ܬܒܝܠ
2 ܘܥܠܡܗܘܢ ܒܥܡܘܪ̈ܝܗ̇. ܡܛܠ
ܕܪܘܓܙܗ ܕܡܪܝܐ ܥܠ ܟܠ ܟܠܗܘܢ
ܥܡܡܐ. ܘܚܡܬܗ ܥܠ ܟܠ ܟܠܗ
ܚܝܠܗܘܢ ܕܢܚܪܘܒ ܐܢܘܢ
3 ܘܢܩܠܦ ܐܢܘܢ ܠܩܛܝܠܐ. ܘܢܣܬܕܘܢ
ܘܦܓܪܝܗܘܢ ܘܢܣܝܩܐ ܪܝܚܐ
ܕܫܠܕܝܗܘܢ ܘܢܬܡܣܘܢ ܛܘܪ̈ܐ
4 ܡܢ ܕܡܗܘܢ ܘܢܬܡܣܘܢ ܟܠ
ܚܝܠܘܬܐ ܕܫܡܝܐ ܘܢܬܟܪܟܘܢ
ܫܡܝܐ ܐܝܟ ܡܓܠܬܐ ܘܟܠܗ
ܚܝܠܗܘܢ ܢܬܪ ܐܝܟ ܛܪܦܐ
ܕܢܬܪ ܡܢ ܓܦܬܐ ܘܐܝܟ
5 ܦ⌜ܩ⌝ܘܥܐ ܡܢ ܬܬܐ ܡܛܠ
ܕܬܬܪܘܐ ܚܪܒܝ ܒܫܡܝܐ. ܗܐ
ܥܠ ܐܕܘܡܝܐ ܬܚܘܬ ܥܠ
6 ܥܡܐ ܕܐ⌜ܬܬܚ⌝ܪܒ ܒܕܝܢܐ ⌜ܚܪ⌝ܒܗ
ܕܡܪܝܐ ܡܠܝܐ ܕܡܐ ܐܬܕܗܢܬ
ܡܢ ܕܡܐ ܘܡܢ ܬܪܒܐ ܕܡܦܠܦܐ
ܘܓܕܝܐ ܘܬܪܒܐ ܕܟܘܠܝܬܐ
ܕܕܟܪ̈ܐ. ⌜ܡ⌝ܛܠ ⌜ܕܕܒ⌝ܚܬܐ

*Double Palimpsest.*

f. 137 a (script. inf.)

ܠܫܛܝܐ ܫܠܝܛܐ ܐܦܠܐ ܠܡܫܪܝܘܐ
6 ܢܒܪܘܢ ܦܪܘܣܐ ܡܛܠܠ ܕܫܛܝܐ
ܫܛܝܘܬܐ ܡܡܠܠ ܘܠܒܗ ܚܫܠ
ܒܘܠܐ ܕܢܒܒܕ ܫܠܦܘܬܐ ܘܢܡܠܠ
ܒܠ ܛܥܝܘܬܐ ܘܢܣܪܘ ܢܦܫܐ
ܕܟܦܢܐ ܘܡܫܬܝܐ ܕܨܗܝܐ ܢܚܣܪ
7 ܒܝܫܝܢ ܐܢܘܢ ܡܐܢܘܗܝ ܕܡܪ̈ܝܦܐ
ܘܗܘ ܬܪܥܝܬܐ ܡܬܝܥܒ ܠܡܚܒܠܘ
ܠܡܣܟܝܢܐ ܒܡܐܡܪܐ ܕܫܩܘܪܐ
8 ܘܡܠܬܗ ܕܡܣܟܢܐ ܒܕܝܢܐ. ܘܪܒܐ
ܪܒܘܬܐ ܡܬܪܥܝܐ ܘܗܘ ܒܠ
ܪܒܘܬܐ ܢܩܘܡ ∘ ∘ ∘
9 ܢܫ̈ܐ ܥܬܝܪ̈ܬܐ ܩܘܡܝܢ ܫܡܥܝܢ ܩܠܝ
ܒܢ̈ܬܐ ܕܡܣܒܪܢ ܨܘܬܝܢ ܡ̈ܠܝ
10 ܘܡܢܬܐ ܕܫܢܬܐ ܢ̈ܓܙܢ ܐܠܝܢ
ܕܡܣܒܪܢ ܡܛܠ ⌈ܕܓܡܪ⌉ ܩܛܦܐ
11 ⌈ܘܐܬܥܢܒܠ⌉ ܘܠܐ ܐܬܐ ܘܕܥܝܢ
ܒܬܪ̈ܬܐ ܘܪܓܙܝܢ ܐܠܝܢ ܕܡܣܒܪܢ
* * * * * ܕܓܒܪܐ * * * ܒܪܛܠ
12 * * * * * * ܩܒܐ * * * ܬܕܝܢ
ܐܪܥܝܢ ܒܠ ⌈ܬܕܠܐ⌉ ܕܫܦܠܐ ܘܒܠ
13 ⌈ܓܦܢܬܐ⌉ ܘܦܐܪܝܗ ܘܒܠ ܐܪܥܗ
⌈ܕܥܡܝ⌉ ܟܘܒܐ ܘܚܪܐ ܢܐܒܘܢ
ܘܒܒܠܗܘܢ ܒܝܬܐ ܕܚܕܘܬܐ

*Double Palimpsest.*

f. 137 b (script. inf.)

6 ܬܘܒܘ ܟ̈ܠܗ ܐܝܣܪܐܝܠ ܕܐܥܡܩ⌜ܬܘ⌝ܢ
7 ܒܚܪܘܬܐ ܡܛܠ ܕܒܝܘܡܐ ܗܘ
ܢܣܠܩܘܢ ܐܢܫܐ ܦܬܟܪܐ ܕܣ⌜ܐ⌝ܡܐ
ܘܕܗܒܐ ܕܥܒܕ̈ܝ ܠܗܘܢ ܐܝܕܝܗܘܢ
8 ܬܦܠܬܐ ܘܢܦܠ ⌜ܐܬܘܪܝܐ⌝ ܒܚܪܒܐ
ܚܪܒܐ ܠܐ ܕܓܒܪܐ ܘܚܪܒܐ ܠܐ
ܕܓܒܪܐ ܬܐܟܠܝܘܗܝ ܘܢܥܪܘܩ ܠܗ
ܡܢ ܩܕܡ ⌜ܚܪܒܐ⌝ ܘܥܠܝܡܘܗܝ ܠܐܬܬܐ
9 ܢܗܘܘܢ ܘܒܟܐܦܐ ܕܡܬܟܪܟܝܢܗ
ܢܟܒܪ ܘܢܬܬܒܪܘܢ ܡܢ ܐܬܐ
ܘܪ̈ܒܢܘܗܝ ܐܡܪ ⌜ܡܪܝܐ⌝
ܕܢܘܪܗ ܒܨܗܝܘܢ ܘܬܢܘܪܗ
xxxii. 1 ܒܐܘܪܫܠܡ ܗܐ ܒܙܕܝܩܘܬܐ
ܡܠܟܐ ܘܪ̈ܘܪܒܢܐ ܒܕܝܢܐ ܢܫܠܛܘܢ
2 ܘܢܗܘܐ ܠܓܒܪܐ ܐܝܟ ܠܡܛܫܐ
ܠܪܘܚܐ ܘܐܝܟ ܡܫܘܪܐ ܠܡܫܪܝܬܐ
ܘܐܝܟ ܬܚܘܬ ܕܡܝܐ ܒܨܗܝܐ
ܘܐܝܟ ⌜ܛܠܠܐ⌝ ܕܟܐܦܐ ܒܥܢܝܬܐ
3 ܒܐܪܥܐ ܨܗܝܬܐ ܘܠܐ ܢܬܬܟܠܘܢ
ܒܒܢܝ̈ܗܘܢ ܕܐܠܗܝܢ ⌜ܕܫܡܥܝܢ⌝ ܘܐܕܢܝܗܘܢ
4 ܕܐܠܗܝܢ ⌜ܕܡܫܬܡܥܝܢ⌝ ⌜ܢܨ⌝ܘܬܘܢ ܘܠܒܐ
ܕܡܫܠ ܢܣܬܟܠ ܡܕܥܬܐ ܘܠܫܢܐ
ܕܠܓܓܐ ܢܝܠܦ⌜ܒ⌝ ܠܡܡܠܠܘ
5 ܫܠܡܐ. ܘܠܐ ⌜ܢܐܡܪܘܢ ܬܘܒ⌝

ܫܘܚܬ ܠܟܝ. ܘܐܦ ܟܠ ܙܒܢܐ ܕܒܢ̈ܝܐ ܕܐܬܝܢ ܠܥܠܡܐ
ܐܘܕܥܬܟܝ. ܘܟܠ ܡܕܡ ܕܐܡܪܬ ܠܟܝ ܢܗܘܐ. ܫܡܥܐ ܘܐܘܪܟܐ
ܢܣܒܪܘܢ ܘܢܬܠܘܢ ܠܗ ܢܚܙ̈ܘܢ. ܗܫܐ ܫܡܥܝ ܡܕܡ ܕܦܩܕ
ܐܒܝ ܠܟܝ ܡܪܝܡ ܡܕܡ ܕܒܥܬܝ. ܕܢܗܘܐ ܒܝܕܝܐ ܕܐܬܐ
ܐܒܝ ܒܗ. ܡܢ ܠܘܬ ܐܒܝ ܠܥܠܡܐ. ܐܡܪܬ ܡܪܝܡ ܫܪܝܪ̈ܢ
ܡ̈ܠܝܟ[1] ܕܟܠܗ ܡܬܠܠ ܕܡܢ ܩܕܡ ܐܒܘܟ ܐܬܦܣܡܬ.
ܘܟܠ ܡܕܡ ܕܐܡܪܬ ܠܝ ܒܗ ܟܠ ܐܪܥܐ ܗܘܪܬ ܐܬܪ̈ܬ
ܘܐܫܬܡܠܝ ܘܟܠܗܘܢ ܡ̈ܠܐ ܕܐܡܪܬ ܠܝ ܘܟܬܒܢܐ ܗܘ̈ܝ. ܘܟܠ
ܡܢ ܕܡܗܝܡܢ ܒܢ ܒܟܠ ܡܬܢܚܡ. ܘܢܪܬ ܫܘܒܚܐ ܕܠܥܠܡ
ܗܘ ܕܢܪܬܝܢ ܠܗ ܟܠܗ ܢܘܗܪܐ. ܘܡܗܝܡܢ ܠܗ ܙܕ̈ܝܩܐ ܕܟܠܗܘܢ.
ܡܛܠ ܕܠܟ ܙܕܩ ܘܡܬܬܚܝܒ ܫܘܒܚܐ ܥܡ ܐܒܘܟ ܘܪܘܚܟ
ܩܕܝܫܬܐ ܗܫܐ ܘܒܟܠ ܙܒܢ ܠܥܠܡ ܥܠܡܝܢ. ܢܗܘܘܢ ܫ̈ܡܝܢܘܗܝ،
ܕܐܠܗܐ ܐܒܐ [2]ܕܒܪܗ ܚܒܝܒܐ ܘܪܘܚܗ ܚܝܐ ܘܡܪܝܐ
ܥܠ ܐܡܗ̈ܬܐ ܘܥܠ ܩܕ̈ܘܫܐ ܘܥܠ ܫܡܘܥ̈ܐ ܘܥܠ ܩܪ̈ܝܐ
ܘܥܠ ܟܬܘܒܐ ܕܗܘܐ ܘܫܠܝܚܐ ܘܥܠ ܐܚ̈ܘܗܝ، ܡܘ̈ܬܝܢܐ
ܘܬ̈ܘܚܝܢܐ وعل كل الذى يشتوتاف به وامين كمل بعون الله تعالى
رب العالمين امين الحقير الدليل قسيس بلنعل اخو

## ܫܠܡܬ ܬܫܥܝܬܐ ܕܝܠܕܬ ܐܠܗܐ ܡܪܝܡ

ܡܬܫܬܐ ܥܘܡܝܢ ܒܕܘܟ ܐܝܪ، ܒܐܝܕܝ ܕܗܘܐ ܚܛܝܐ ܒܥܡ
ܡܫܡܫܐ ܐܚܐ ܒܟܒܕܘܗܝ، ܚܛܝܐ ܒܫܢܬ ܬܪ̈ܬܝܢ ܡ̈ܠܦܢܐ
ܘܡܟܐ ܐܫܬܝܢ ܘܬܡܢܝܐ ܕܝܘ̈ܢܝܐ ܢܩܒܠܐ امين

ܫܠܡ ܒܚܝܠ ܐܠܗܐ

| في سنة يونيا | في سنة مسحية |
|---|---|
| ٢١٦٨ | ١٨٥٧ |

[1] Cod. ܡ̈ܠܝܟ

[2] Cod. ܕܒܪܐܗ

ܣܓܝܐܐ ܘܢܗܘܐ ܐܒܕܢܗܘܢ ܒܚܪܒ ܕܡܫܝܚܝܐ ܚܕ ܡܢ ܚܕ.
ܘܐܫܬܪܪܬ ܗܝܡܢܘܬܐ ܒܟܠ ܐܬܪܐ ܘܐܬܪܐ ܡܫܝܚܝܐ ܒܪܝ.
ܘܠܐ ܡܫܟܚ ܗܘܐ ܡܫܡܫܢܘܬܐ ܒܟܠ ܐܬܪܐ. ܗܠܝܢ ܘܕܐܬܝܢ ܡܢ
ܗܠܝܢ. ܟܠܗ ܫܪܝ ܠܐܡܪܗ. ܘܗܝ ܟܠܗ ܐܬܝܢ ܠܗܘܢ. f. 232 b
ܘܡܪܢ ܐܡܪ ܠܗ ܠܡܠܟܐ ܡܪܝ ܡܐܢ ܫܡܥܐ ܗܘ ܒܫܢܝܐ ܘܡܟܢܐ
ܫܬܐܒ ܐܒܝܢܐ ܕܒܝܬܐ ܕܦܠܚܝܢ ܐܝܩܘܢܝܗܘܢ ܕܟܠܕܝܐ
ܢܗܘܘܢ ܦܪܝܩ ܠܗ. ܘܒܫܡܗ ܡܬܦܪܩܝܢ ܡܢ ܐܝܩܘܢܝܗܘܢ.
ܘܐܡܪܬ ܡܪܝ ܡܐܢ ܠܡܫܝܚܐ ܕܗܘܐ ܚܠܦ ܐܝܟ ܡܢܝ.
ܒܒܪ ܕܡܫܝܚܐ ܒܠ ܢܦܫܬܐ ܕܦܪܩ ܠܝ ܒܫܡܗ. ܘܐܡܪܬ
ܡܪܝ ܡܐܢ ܠܢܦܫܝ. ܐܢܬ ܢܦܫܝ ܡܫܒܚܬ ܗܘ ܡܫܝܚܐ ܐܝܬܝܟ. ܐܝܟ
ܕܐܡܪ ܠܝ ܪܒܝ ܡܪܢ ܕܐܡܪܐ ܐܝܟܐ ܠܝ ܥܒܕ ܘܒܪܐ.
ܒܬܒܐ ܕܡܫܡܫܢ ܕܡܢ ܚܠܡܐ ܗܢܐ. ܠܒܢܝܐ ܕܫܘܠܛܢܗ
ܕܚܠܡܐ ܕܢܦܩ ܠܒܪܝܬܐ. ܡܛܠ ܕܗܘܝܢ ܐܬܘܬܐ ܡܢܗ
ܡܐܬܝܬܗ ܕܪܒܝ. ܕܡܫܝܚ ܘܐܫܠܡ ܒܪܒܝܐ ܗܘ ܢܬܟܠܘܢ.
ܠܪܚܡܘܗܝ ܕܐܪܝܟܐ ܘܢܗܘܘܢ ܒܗ ܢܦܫܬܗܘܢ. ܘܗܘܒܢ
ܒܘܕܪܝܐ ܠܪܚܡܘܗܝ ܡܢ ܡܒܪܝܗܘܢ. ܘܡܒܪܟ ܫܘܒܚܐ
ܒܠ ܡܐܬܝܬܗ ܕܡܪܢܘܗܝ ܕܦܪܩܢܬ ܠܗ. ܒܪ ܡܫܬܠܚܝܢ f. 233 a
ܫܡܝܐ ܘܐܪܥܐ ܘܡܬܕܠܝܢ ܒܪܘܚܗ، ܕܟܠܡܐ ܦܪܩ ܕܢܐܬܐ
ܪܒܝ ܘܗܢܘܢ ܢܗܘܐ ܕܦܪܩܢܐ ܠܓܒܪܐ ܘܡܬܕܒܪܘܢ ܘܒܢܝܫܐ
ܒܡܘܪܒܢܐ ܘܒܬܠܬܐ. ܘܟܠ ܕܦܪܩܐ ܫܡܗ ܕܠܕܬ ܐܠܗܐ
ܢܬܦܪܩ ܡܢ ܐܘܠܨܢܗ. ܗܠܝܢ ܐܡܪܬ ܦܘܪܫܢܬܐ ܠܗܘܢ ܘܟܠܐ
ܢܦܫܗ ܘܫܒܩ ܠܐܠܗܐ. ܒܠ ܡܕܡ ܕܐܡܪܬ ܠܗ ܡܪܝ ܡܐܢ.
ܘܐܬܬܐ ܗܢܐ ܦܩܕܢܐ ܠܗܘܢ ܦܘܪܫܢܬܐ ܒܦܪܕܝܣܐ. ܘܫܒܩܘ
ܒܢܫܐ ܕܒܠܬܡܐ ܘܢܦܩܘ ܒܪܘܚܐ ܘܪܚܡܐ ܠܫܕܕܐ. ܐܚܪ
ܠܗ ܡܫܝܚܐ ܒܠ ܡܕܡ ܕܐܡܪܬ ܒܫܠܡܐ ܘܐܦ ܒܐܪܥܐ

ܩܕܡ ܬܪܘܢܘܣ ܕܒܪܗ. ܘܫܡܥܢ ܬܫܒܘܚܬܐ ܠܐܠܗܐ ܕܐܫܟܚ
ܠܢܛܪܬܗ ܘܫܘܝ ܠܗ ܫܒܝܚܐ· ܘܫܒܚ ܫܒܝܚܐ ܘܟܠ ܕܒܗܘܢ܀
ܘܡܠܟܘܬ ܕܟܠܗ ܐܬܐ ܐܙܕܘܝ. ܘܡܪܢ ܢܫܒܚ ܡܫܝܚܐ ܕܒܪܗ
ܠܐܡܗ ܘܐܬܝܐ ܠܦܪܕܝܣܐ ܕܥܕܢ. ܘܐܢܗܪ ܢܗܝܪܐ ܒܫܡܝܐ.
ܘܫܠܡ ܕܦܐܪܐ ܕܗܘܪܡܟܐ. ܠܟܠ ܡܢ ܟܠܗܘܢ܀ ܫܒܝܚܐ ܘܢܝܚܬܐ
ܕܝܢ̈ܐ ܘܡ̈ܠܐܟܐ ܒܗ ܕܠܒܝܢ ܠܡܫܐ̈ܪܝܗܘܢ܀. ܘܕܝܢ
ܫܒܚܘܗ ܕܡܪܢ܀ ܘܐܬܦܪܫܬ ܦܬܘܪܗ ܕܐܠܗܐ. ܘܢܝܚܬ
ܡܪܢ ܥܡ ܡܪܝܡ ܠܦܪܕܝܣܐ ܕܥܕܢ ܥܡ ܒ̈ܢܝܐ ܫܒܝ̈ܚܐ.
ܘܗܘܐ ܫܘܒܚܐ ܪܒܐ ܩܕܡ ܦܬܘܪܬܐ. ܕܢܚܬܘ ܠܥ̈ܠܡܝܗܘܢ܀.
ܕܕܝ̈ܢܐ ܕܟܠܗ ܐܪܥܐ ܡܣܦܩܝܢ ܗܘܘ ܘܫܒܩ ܪܚܡܐ ܒܫܡܝ̈ܐ
ܒܟܠܗܘܢ ܦܬܘ̈ܪܝܗܘܢ ܕܥܠܡܐ. ܘܕܒܪܬ ܡܪܝܡ ܠܢܦܫܗ ܘܫܘܝܬ
ܠܗ ܟܠܡܕܡ [1]ܕܫܘܝ ܠܗ ܡܫܝܚܐ. ܘܐܡܪܬ ܠܗ. ܐܘܕܝ
ܠܟ ܒܟܠܗ ܢܦܫܝ. ܕܫܘܝ ܠܟ ܪܒܝ. ܕܒܥܒܕܐ ܕܡܬܚܙܝܢܐ ܐܢܐ
ܠܝ ܐܡܪܐ ܐܢܐ ܠܝ. ܕܢܣܒܘܢ܀ ܢܦܫܢ [2]ܗܘܕ̈ܪܐ ܘܬܘܕܝܬܐ
ܕܢܫܬܠܡ ܕܒܗ ܢܗܘܘܢ ܠܝ ܕܟܢ̈ܫܐ ܘܡܘ̈ܥܕܢܐ ܠܙܟܝܐ ܕܐܬܝܐ
ܒܗ ܪܟܝ ܡܢ ܫܒܝܚܐ. ܡܛܠ ܕܫܒܝܚܐ ܟܗܢܬܗ ܕܒܪܝܬܐ.
ܘܐܘܠܝܢܐ ܡܫܒܚܐ ܕܫܒܚܘܗܝ ܠܗ ܠܐܠܗܐ. ܟܕ ܐܦ ܕܗܘܝܢ
ܐܬܬܐ ܕܫܒܠܬܐ [3]ܘܦܪܨܘܦܐ ܡܪ̈ܝܐ. ܘܗܘܐ ܒܟܢܫܐ ܘܢܝܚܐ
ܐܡܪܐ ܡܢ ܫܘܠܗ ܘܟܘܠܗ ܕܐܝܢܐ ܕܫܒܩܝܢ ܠܗ ܒܟܢܫܐ
ܕܘܬܟܐ. ܘܫܒܚܐ ܬܘܒ ܒܗܘ ܝܘܡܐ ܐܘܠܝܢܗ ܕܒܪܝܬܐ
ܗܘܐ ܫܘܒܚܐ ܒܐܪܥܐ ܕܫܒܝܚܐ. ܘܢܫ̈ܒܚܝܢ ܓܘܢܐ ܘܡܪܘܡܐ
ܘܬܘܕܝܬܐ ܙܕܝܩܐ. ܘܒܠܘܠܬܐ ܢܗܘܘܢ܀ ܒܫ̈ܢܝܐ ܒܗ ܢܫܘܢ܀

cf. J. S. L. p. ܢ f. 232 a

---

[1] Cod. ܫܘܐ   [2] Cod. ܗܕ̈ܪܐ   [3] Cod. ܘܦܫܐܟܝܢ

ܕܢܦܪܐ. ܘܩܠܝܢ ܕܐܦܣܩܝܢ ܡܬ̈ܒܥܒܬܐ ܕܠܒܘܗ̈ܝ ܘܟܠ ܒ̈ܪܘܟܐ
ܕܒ̈ܪܘܟܐ ܡܕܘܚ ܗܘܐ ܫܘܒܚܐ ܕܡܐܪܝܡ ܘܕܒܪܗ. ܘܠܒܠ
ܡܢ ܫܟܝܢܐ ܪܗܛܐ ܘܐܬܝܐ ܠܫܘܒܚܬܐ. ܘܫܡܥܘ ܡ̈ܠܐܟܐ
ܘܐܦ ܡܠ̈ܐܟܐ ܘܢܓܘ ܦܘܡܝܢܐ ܒܩܠܗܘܢ ܒܪ̈ܡܬܐ. ܕܫܘܒܚܐ
ܢܦܩܘ ܠܐܘܪܥܗ ܕܒܪ ܡܠܟܐ. ܕܐܬܐ ܕܢܣܒ ܐܦܐ ܠܐܡܗ
ܒܫܒ̈ܝܬܐ ܕܒܢܬ ܐܒܘܗ̈ܝ. ܘܢܦܩ ܚܙܘܝܢ ܘܐܬܐ ܐܠܝܐ.
ܘܡܫܚܝ ܘܦܪܢܣܗ ܘܫܢܝܘ ܡܢ ܡܥܒܝܢܐ ܘܡܢ ܐܡܗ.
ܘܐܟܡܝ ܡܘܬܐ ܕܫܟܝܢܐ. ܒܗ ܒܫܠܐ ܒܝܘܡܐ ܕܢܦܪܘܩ ܫܘܒܚܐ
ܠܡܠܟܐ ܡܫܝܚܐ. ܒܗܘ ܕܠܐ ܢܬܠ ܒܗ ܒܝܘܡܐ ܒܗ ܪ̈ܘܚܐ
ܐܚ̈ܪܢܝܢ ܠܫܪܪܐ ܕܢܛܪܘܗܝ ܘܫܪܪܬܐ ܠܡܪܢܘܗܝ. ܘܡܢ f. 231 a
ܒܪܢܫܐ ܡܢܝܢܐ ܘܡܠ̈ܐܟܐ. ܘܐܬܝܒܘ ܩܠܗܘܢ ܠܩܕܠܗ.
ܘܡܢ ܗܘܐ ܡܬܒܥܐ ܒܝܬ ܒܝܬܐ ܘܩܠܗܘܢ ܒܝܬܐ ܒܒܗ.
ܐܒܐ ܒܫܘܒܚܐ ܡܕܘܚ ܗܘܐ ܘܒܪܐ ܒܪܬܡܬܐ ܡܬܬܪܡܪܡ
ܗܘܐ. ܘܪܘܚܐ ܩܕܝܫ ܗܘܐ ܠܫܘܒܚܬܐ ܒܦܘܡ ܩܠܗܘܢ
ܫܠܝܬܐ. ܘܡܐܪܝܡ ܘܒܪܬܐ ܕܡܪܝܡ ܘܗܘܬ ܠܫܘܒܚܬܐ
ܒܫܟܝܢܐ. ܡܢ ܡܪܝܐ ܕܢܦܩܬ ܕܢܒܒܢ ܠܗ ܐܡܐ ܡܢ ܦܠܘܡܐ
ܕܒܝܬ ܡܪܘܬܐ. ܘܗܘܬ ܬܘܕܝܬܐ ܒܪܘܡܐ ܡܢ ܡܪܝܐ
ܕܪܘܡܐ. ܕܫܠܝܐ ܕܐܒܘܗ̈ܝ ܐܫܪܝܗ ܒܪܘܡܐ ܕܠܒܬܗ ܘܦܩܕܬ
ܠܫܘܒܚܬܐ ܕܩܠܗܘܢ ܫܡ̈ܝܢܐ ܕܬܫܥܝܬܐ ܡܪܝܡ ܠܬܫܥܝܬܗ.
ܘܐܦ ܪܘܡܪܡܗ ܕܗܘ ܕܐܬܝܠܕ ܡܢܗ ܡܢ ܬܪ̈ܬܝܢ ܬ̈ܚܡܝܢ
[1]ܒܝܫ ܒܫܒܚܐ ܒܕܡܝܐ ܠܬ̈ܠܬ ܬ̈ܚܡܝܢ. ܒܗ ܡܫܒܝܢ ܒܢ̈ܝܐ
ܘܡܠ̈ܐܟܐ. ܘܗܘܐ ܪܘܒܐ ܒܝܬ ܫܪ̈ܒܝܗܘܢ ܘܫܘܒܚܐ
ܘܐܦܪܐ ܕܡܘܪܡܐ ܦܫ ܡܢ ܒܢ̈ܝܗܘܢ ܕܪ̈ܘܚܢܐ. ܘܡܪܝܒܝܢ
ܗܘܘ ܒܢ̈ܝܗܘܢ ܢܦ̈ܪܐ ܘܩܪܝܢ ܠܐܡܗ ܕܡܪܝܡ ܠܪܘܡܗܘܢ ܕܡܢܪܡܐ f. 231 b

[1] Cod. ܘܫܒ

ܘܟܪܝܐ ܠܗܘܢ. ܟܕ ܡܢ ܦܪܘܣܐ ܦܢܝܢ. ܐܡܪܬ ܡܪܝܡ
ܠܡܫܝܚܐ ܪܒܘܠܝ ܚܙܝܐ ܐܢܘܢ ܗܠܝܢ. ܐܡܪ ܠܗ ܡܪܢ
ܗܕܐ ܕܢܗܘܐ ܘܕܚܝܠܐ. ܓܘܢܐ ܗܘ ܕܡܫܬܡܪܐ ܠܒܢܝ̈
ܒܢ̈ܝܬܐ. ܘܗܠܝܢ ܕܚܙܝܬܝ ܒܗ ܫܘܚܠܦܐ ܐܢܘܢ. ܕܡܢ ܦܪܘܣܐ
ܚܙܝܢ ܠܬܫܒܘܚܬܗܘܢ. ܘܢܩܒܠܘܢ ܚܢܢܐ ܢܗܘܪܐ ܠܗܘܢ ܒܥܘܗܕܢܐ
ܐܚܪܢܐ ܘܚܙܝܐ ܠܗܘܢ ܘܚܙܝܢ. ܠܐ ܓܝܪ ܡܛܠܬܐ ܗܘܬ ܘܗܘܐ
ܕܕܝܢܐ ܕܢܦܠܘܢ ܡܢܬܐ ܕܫܡܫܐ. ܘܐܦ ܒܥܘܕܢܐ ܐܚܪܢܐ f. 230a
ܒܗܕܐ ܓܒܘܠܬܐ ܡܫܬܡܗܝܢ. ܗܠܝܢ ܐܢܘܢ ܕܠܐ ܢܦܩܘ
ܦܓܪ̈ܝܗܘܢ، ܕܐܝܟ. ܒܗܕܐ ܢܘܪܐ ܡܫܬܘܕܝܢ. ܗܢܘܢ ܚܙܬ
ܠܦܘܪܥܢܘܬܐ ܒܗܘ ܐܬܪܐ ܕܕܝ̈ܢܐ ܕܒܗܝ̈ܐ ܥܬܝܕ ܒܪ ܡܬܕܡܪܐ.
ܘܒܗܘ ܕܚܘܠܐ ܕܒܗܝܐ ܣܓܝܐܐ ܘܕܚܝܠ. ܘܫܡܥܬ ܩܠܗܘܢ
ܕܕܝ̈ܢܐ ܒܪ ܐܢܫܐ. ܫܘܒܚܐ ܠܟ ܐܠܗܐ ܕܗܘܝܬ ܐܢܬ
ܦܪܘܩܐ ܠܕܝܢܐ ܒܝܘܡܐ ܐܚܪܝܐ. ܕܗܘ ܡܫܬܪܝܐ ܫܘܒܚܐ
ܘܐܪܒܐ. ܘܬܘܒ ܡܢܐ ܒܡܢܐ ܗܘ ܚܝ̈ܐ ܫܡܝܢܐ. ܐܬܚܙܝ
ܠܝܢ ܒܪܗ ܕܐܠܗܐ ܚܝܐ ܗܘܐ ܕܐܬܐ ܐܢܬ ܕܡܫܒܪܐ ܫܘܒܚܐ
ܘܐܪܒܐ. ܟܕ ܕܝܢ ܫܡܥܬ ܠܦܘܪܥܢܘܬܐ ܦܠܘܗܘܢ ܕܕܝ̈ܢܐ
ܚܙܝܬ. ܘܟܕ ܫܡܥܬ ܩܠܗܘܢ ܕܚܛܝ̈ܐ ܒܟܝܬ ܠܗ ܥܠܝܗܘܢ.
ܘܐܦܝܣܬ ܠܡܫܝܚܐ ܡܛܠܬܗܘܢ ܕܚܛܝ̈ܐ ܘܡܪܕܬ ܒܟܘܬܐ
ܫܠܝܚܐ. ܘܐܡܪܬ ܪܒܘܠܝ ܐܬܪܚܡ ܥܠ ܚܛܝ̈ܐ ܗܠܝܢ
ܡܢ ܕܕܐܢ̈. ܐܡܪ ܠܗܘܢ ܒܥܘܕܢܐ ܐܚܪܢܐ. ܡܛܠ ܕܫܡܥܬ f. 230b
ܦܠܘܗܘܢ ܘܒܟܝܬ ܠܝ ܥܠܝܗܘܢ. ܘܐܬܪܬ ܡܫܝܚܐ ܒܪ
ܐܚܪܢ. ܕܢܚܘܐ ܠܗ ܦܠܘܗܘܢ ܗܢܘܢ ܕܥܠ ܒܢ̈ܝܐ ܕܢܗܘܪܐ
ܢܬܚܪܪܘܢ. ܘܥܠ ܬܪܥܘܗܝ ܕܓܘܠܬܐ ܡܬܩܢ ܒܪܘܚܐ ܗܘ
ܕܬܫܡܫܬܐ. ܘܥܠ ܚܕܐ ܕܒܢܝܢܐ ܡܬܩܢ ܗܘ، ܒܚܕܐܠܐ

ܚܙܬ ܡܪܝܡ ܠܐܒܐ ܡܫܒܚܐ ܘܠܒܪܐ ܚܒܝܒܐ ܘܠܪܘܚܐ
ܦܐܪܩܠܝܛܐ ܟܕ ܡܫܬܒܚ ܐܒܐ ܥܡ ܡܠܟܗ ܘܒܪܐ ܥܡ f. 229 a
ܐܒܘܗܝ ܘܪܘܚܐ ܥܡ ܬܪܝܗܘܢ ܘܚܙܬ ܬܪܘܢܘܣ ܘܡܪܟܒܬܐ.
ܘܬܫܝܬ ܡܢ ܡܪܟܒܬܐ ܢܦܩ ܢܗܪܐ ܕܢܘܪܐ. ܘܐܬܐ ܘܫܪܐ
ܥܠ ܟܠܗܘܢ ܥܡܡܐ. ܟܕ ܡܕܡ ܠܐ ܡܗܡܝ. ܘܚܙܬ ܠܚܒܪܐ
ܕܠܚܒܝܫ ܡܪܟܒܬܐ ܥܡ ܠܬܚܬ. ܘܠܡܪܟܒܐ ܕܡܚܒܫܝܢ ܠܗ̇
ܡܢ ܠܥܠ ܘܠܟܪ̈ܘܒܐ ܕܦܪܝܣܝܢ ܓ̈ܐܦܝܗܘܢ ܘܡܚܒܫܝܢ ܠܗ̇
ܘܡܫܡܫܝܢ ܘܚܙܬ ܠܬܪܘܢܘܣ ܡܫܒܚܐ ܕܐܠܗܐ. ܟܕ ܢܦܩ
ܐܒܐ ܘܒܪܗ ܡܢ ܡܚܒܝܗ. ܘܪܘܚܐ ܕܦܐܡ ܘܡܪܝܡܐ. ܠܟܠ
ܡܠܘܗܝ. ܘܚܙܬ ܡܫܪܝܐ ܕܢܘܪܐ ܘܐܦ ܬܪܥܐ ܕܫܠܡܘܬܐ.
ܘܚܙܬ ܡܪܝܡ ܡܕܡ ܕܚܝܐ ܠܐ ܚܙܬ. ܘܐܕܢܐ ܠܐ ܫܡܥܬ.
ܘܥܠ ܠܒܐ ܕܒܢܝ̈ܢܫܐ ܠܐ ܣܠܩ. ܡܕܡ ܕܢܗܒ ܐܠܗܐ
ܠܪ̈ܚܡܘܗܝ ܒܗܘܢ ܢܗܝܪܐ. ܘܐܬܓܪܬ ܡܪܝܡ ܩܕܡ ܐܢܘܢ
ܩܠܝܢ. ܐܡܪ ܠܗ̇ ܡܫܝܚܐ ܩܠܝܢ ܐܬܝܢ ܡܠܠܝܗܘܢ[1]
ܕܪ̈ܘܚܐ. ܠܐ ܚܙܐ ܡܟܝܠ ܘܒܢܐ ܕܢܫܠܡܘܢ ܦܓܪ̈ܝܗܘܢ
ܐܠܐ ܥܡ ܢܦܫܐ ܚܕܝܢ ܠܗܘܢ ܘܚܕܝܢ. ܟܕ ܐܬܬ ܢܦܩ f. 229 b
ܢܦܫܐ ܕܢܫܠܡܘܢ (ܐܦܬܪ) ܐܓܢܘܣܝܗܘܢ. ܘܬܘܒ ܚܙܬ
ܡܪܝܡ ܐܬܪܐ ܕܢܫܒ ܒܗ̇. ܘܬܢܢܐ ܚܡܝܡܬܐ ܕܦܠܛ ܡܢܗ.
ܘܓܦܪܐ ܘܟܒܪܝܬܐ ܦܠܛ ܡܢܗܘܢ. ܘܢܘܪܐ ܡܫܝܬܐ
ܕܡܬܓܘܠܠܐ ܗܘܬ ܒܗ. ܘܐܬܬ ܗܘܐ ܦܠܛ ܕܗ̇ܝ ܢܘܪܐ.
ܐܝܟ ܓܠ ܕܟ̈ܘܒܐ ܩܫ̈ܝܐ ܟܕ ܡܫܬܓܪ ܗܘܐ ܒܫܠܝܬܐ. cf. J. S. L. p. ܟܛ
ܘܢܘܪܐ ܕܡܫܬܠܗܒܐ ܬܚܝܢ ܘܢܦܩܐ. ܘܐܙܠ ܗܘܐ ܦܠܛ
ܒܐܬܪܐ ܗܘ ܕܣܝܡܝܢ ܐܢ̈ܫܐ ܠܒܪ ܡܢܗ ܕܢܫܒܐ ܘܟܝܢ

[1] Cod. ܡܠܐܠܝܗܘܢ

ܘܣܒܪܬ ܕܐܢܫ ܠܗ ܬܪ̈ܥܝܗܝ ܬܪ̈ܥܝܢ ܒܥܡ ܬܪ̈ܥܝܗܝ ܩ̈ܠܝܕܐ.
ܘܟܠ ܚܕ ܬܪܥܐ ܩܠܝܕܐ ܦܬܚ. ܘܡ̈ܠܐܟܐ ܗܪ̈ܟܝ ܡ̈ܠܐܟܐ
ܕܡܫܒܚܝܢ ܘܡܩܕܫܝܢ ܘܒܗ ܒܬܪܥܐ ܠܓܘܐ ܬܪ̈ܥܝܗܘܢ ܒܬܪ
ܘܚܕ. [1]ܡܫܒܚܝܢ ܘܡܩܕܫܝܢ ܐܚܪ̈ܢܐ، ܒܬܪܥܐ ܐܚܪܢܐ ܡܢ
ܡܚܝܢܐ. ܘܗܦܟܬ ܩ̈ܠܝܕܐ ܗܕܐ ܒܗܠܝܢ ܬܪ̈ܥܐ. ܘܟܠ
ܘܗ̇ ܬܪܥܐ ܬܪܥܐ ܒܪܝܐ ܩܢܘܢ ܠܒܪ ܦܪ̈ܘܣܐ ܕܠܐ ܦܬܚܐ.
ܘܡܫܒܚܝܢ ܠܗ ܡܕܒܪܢܘܬܗ ܕܡܠܟܐ ܪܒܐ. ܘܢܦܩܝܢ ܟܠܗܘܢ
ܦܬܚܝܢ ܗܘܘ ܘܡܫܒܚܝܢ ܒܬܪ̈ܥܝܗܘܢ. ܐܒܪܗܡ ܘܐܝܣܚܩ
ܘܝܥܩܘܒ ܘܕܘܝܕ ܡܠܟܐ. ܘܫܐܠܬ ܐܢܘܢ ܠܡܠܟܐ ܡܫܝܚܐ
ܘܐܡܪ ܐܢܘܢ. ܗܢ ܐܬܪܐ ܕܬܫܐܠܝܢ ܒܐܘܪܫܠܡ ܕܫܡܝܐ.
ܘܥܠܬ ܒܬܪܥܐ ܩܕܡܝܐ ܘܣܓܕܘ ܠܗ̇ ܡ̈ܠܐܟܐ. ܘܥܠܬ
ܒܬܪܥܐ ܕܬܪ̈ܝܢ ܘܐܬܬܩܪܒܬ ܠܗ̇ ܣܓܕܬܐ ܕܪ̈ܘܚܐ. ܘܥܠܬ
ܒܬܪܥܐ ܕܬܠܬܐ. ܘܐܬܬܩܪܒܬ ܠܗ̇ ܣܓܕܬܐ ܕܫ̈ܪܦܐ. cf. J. S. L. p. ܟܒ
ܘܥܠܬ ܒܬܪܥܐ ܕܐܪܒܥܐ ܘܐܬܣܓܕܬ ܡܢ ܟܪ̈ܘܒܐ ܘܪ̈ܒܘ f. 228 b
ܐ̈ܠܦܐ. ܘܥܠܬ ܒܬܪܥܐ ܕܚܡܫܐ. ܘܫܡܥܬ ܩܕܡܝܗ̇ ܒܪ̈ܩܐ
ܘܪ̈ܥܡܐ. ܘܥܠܬ ܕܝܢ ܒܬܪܥܐ ܕܐܫܬ̈ܐ. ܘܫܡܥ ܩܕܡܝܗ̇
ܩܕܝܫ ܩܕܝܫ. ܘܥܠܬ ܒܬܪܥܐ ܕܫܒܥܐ ܘܣܓܕܘ ܩܕܡܝܗ̇
ܢܘܪܐ ܘܫܠܗܒܝܬܐ. ܘܥܠܬ ܒܬܪܥܐ ܕܬܡܢܝܐ ܘܣܓܕܘ ܠܗ̇
ܡܛܪܐ ܘܛܠܐ. ܘܥܠܬ ܒܬܪܥܐ ܕܬܫܥܐ ܘܣܓܕܘ ܠܗ̇
ܓܒܪܐܝܠ ܘܡܝܟܐܝܠ. ܘܥܠܬ ܒܬܪܥܐ ܕܥܣܪܐ ܘܣܓܕܘ ܠܗ̇
ܟܠܗܘܢ ܢܒ̈ܝܐ. ܘܥܠܬ ܒܬܪܥܐ ܕܚܕ ܥܣ̈ܪ ܘܣܓܕܘ ܠܗ̇
ܟܠܗܘܢ ܫ̈ܠܝܚܐ. ܘܥܠܬ ܒܬܪܥܐ ܕܬܪ̈ܥܣܪ. ܘܫܡܥܬ
ܘܒܪܟܬܗ ܠܒܪܐ ܕܒܗ̇ ܐܬܝܠܕ. ܘܗܘܝܢܐ ܟܠܗ ܠܗ̇ ܡܪܝܡ
ܠܐܘܪܫܠܡ ܕܫܡܝܐ ܘܚܙܬ ܡܢ ܬܡܢ ܐܡܐ. ܘܒܗ̇، ܥܒܕܬܐ

---

[1] Cod. ܘܡܫܒܚܝܢ

ܠܐܩܢܘܡܗܘܢ ܕܬܪ̈ܘܢܐ ܘܐܬܬܣܝܡܬ ܐܪܥܐ ܒܪܝܫܐ ܒܫܒܬܐ.
ܘܡܪܢ ܝܫܘܥ ܐܬܐ ܥܠ ܡܪܟܒܬܐ ܕܢܘܪܐ ܘܫܠܘܦ
ܘܐܠܝܐ ܠܦܢܝܬ ܐܢܘܢ ܒܥܓܠܐ ܕܢܘܪܐ. ܘܥܠܝܗ̇ ܕܗܕܐ
ܫܒܝܚܐ ܬܫܒܘܚܬܐ. ܘܝܗܒܬ ܛܒܘܬܗܘܢ ܐܝܩܪܗ ܕܐܠܗܐ.
ܘܐܦ ܟܕ ܐܬܬ ܠܐܬܪܐ ܘܠܒܝܬܐ ܘܡܦܪܣܐ. ܘܟܕ ܐܬܬ ܠܦܪܐ
ܘܦܐܠܐ ܘܟܕ ܐܬܬ ܪ̈ܘܚܐ ܘܟܪ̈ܘܒܐ ܘܟܕ ܐܬܬ ܒܪ̈ܦܠܐ ܘܡܠܠܬܐ.
ܘܡ̈ܠܐܟܐ ܕܡܫ̈ܡܫܘܗܝ، ܕܐܠܗܐ ܡܫ̈ܒܚܝܢ ܠܗ̇، ܘܝܗܒܬ ܬܘܒ
ܬܘܕܝܬܐ ܘܫܘܒܚܐ. ܕܗܟܢܐ ܕܐܬܦܢܝܡ ܢܦܫܐ ܠܡܪܝܬܐ ܘܝܗܒܬ
ܠܡܘܕܝܬܐ ܕܦܐܝܐ ܒܗ̇ ܐܠܗܐ ܘܡܚܠܐ. ܡܛܠ ܕܗܕܐ ܫܒܝܚܐ
ܬܫܒܘܚܬܐ ܐܝܬܝܗ̇. ܘܫܠܡܬ ܠܫܒܝ̈ܚܬܐ ܘܝܗܒܬ ܬܘ̈ܕܝܐ
ܕܪܘܚܐ. ܘܫܠܡܘܬܐ ܕܫܒ̈ܝܚܬܐ ܘܟܪ̈ܝܬܐ ܕܠܝܬ ܠܗܝܢ ܣܟܐ. f. 227 b
ܘܥܡܗ ܘܡܫܒܚܝܢ ܫܠܡܘܬܐ ܕܫܒ̈ܝܚܬܐ ܠܒܬܘܠܬܐ ܡܪܝܡ.
ܡܢܗ ܕܢܣܒܐ ܘܠܐ ܢܦܫܠ. ܟܕ ܩܝܡܝܢ ܟܠܗܘܢ ܘܡܩܪܒܝܢ
ܬܫܒܘܚܬܐ ܠܐܒܘܗ ܕܡܪܢ ܘܫܠܡܬ ܝܗܒܘܢ ܐܡܪܝܢ
ܟܠܢܐ ܩܕܝܫ ܩܕܝܫ ܒܪܗ ܕܐܠܗܐ ܚܝܐ. ܗܕܐ ܗ̇ܝ،
ܩܕܝܫܬܐ ܘܡܒܪܟܬܐ ܕܝܠܕܬܗ̇ ܕܠܐ ܫܘܚܬܐ. ܘܫܦܝܪܬ
ܠܦܩܕܢܬܐ ܕܡܢ ܐܒ̈ܗܝ ܘܝܗܒܬ ܫܘܒܚܐ ܠܐܠܗܐ ܕܐܘܪܒܗ̇ ܀
ܘܬܘܒ، ܫܠܡܬ ܠܟܠ ܡܢ ܫܒܝ̈ܚܬܐ. ܘܝܗܒܬ ܕܟܠ ܡܝܬܘܢ
ܕܚ̈ܝܠܐ ܦܩܕܝܢ ܗܘܘ ܗܕ̈ܪܐ ܕܡܠܟ̈ܘܬܐ. ܘܦܪܝܫܝܢ ܗܘܘ
ܠܐܦܝ̈ܗܘܢ ܘܚܕ̈ܝܗܘܢ ܫܒܩܘܢ ܠܟܠ ܚܕ ܡܢܗܘܢ. ܘܠܐ
ܡܟܝܠ ܗܘܘ ܕܢܬܬܠܘܢ ܡܢ ܦܠܚܐ ܕܦܠܚܝܢ ܘܐܡܪܝܢ. ܩܕܝܫ
ܩܕܝܫ ܩܕܝܫ ܡܪܝܐ ܚܝܠܬܢܐ ܘܐܠܗܐ ܕܟܠ ܟܠ. ܫܡܝܐ
ܡܠܝܢ ܠܟܠ ܡܢ ܫܘ̈ܒܚܐ ܘܫܘܒܚܐ ܠܗ̇ ܠܡܘܪܒܘܬܗ ܕܒܫ̈ܡܝܐ. cf. J. S. L. p. ܟܗ
ܕܒܗ̇ ܡܫܬܒܚ ܐܒܐ ܡܢ ܠܥܠ ܘܪܘܚܐ ܡܢ ܬܪ̈ܝܗܘܢ f. 228 a

ܠܒܢܝ̈ܢܫܐ. ܟܕ ܕܝܢ ܥܒܕܐ ܦܘܠܚܢܐ ܠܫܘܠܡܗ، ܕܦܘܪܫܢܐ
ܐܘܪܚ ܢܝܫܗ ܘܫܡܥ ܠܗ ܠܡܪܢܐ ܕܒܪ̈ܝܬܐ ܕܦܐܐ ܒܦܘܪܫܢܐ
ܘܫܡܥܗ ܠܫܘܬܦܗ. ܗܘ ܓܝܪ ܗ̇ܘܢܐ ܦܪܘܫܐ ܒܗܝ ܢܦܫܐ
ܐܝܬܘܗܝ، ܕܟܠܢܐ ܘܒܗܝ ܡܫܪܝܐ ܗܘ ܕܡܫܡ̈ܫܢܐ ܘܒܗܬ.
ܗܘܐ ܡܕܡ ܘܟܠ ܟ̈ܠܗܝܢ ܕܢܦܫܐ ܒܗܝ ܡܫܪܝܐ ܠܐܕܡ
ܢܝܫܐ ܕܦܘܠ̈ܚܢܐ ܘܕܝܪ̈ܬܐ. ܠܗ ܢܝܫ ܐܠܗܐ ܘܗܟܢ ܒܗܝ
ܐܝ̈ܠܢܐ ܟ̈ܠܝܠܐ ܕܦܘܪܫܢܐ. ܠܗܢܐ ܦܘܪܫܢܐ ܐܝܬܐ f. 226 b
ܦܠܚܗ ܕܡܫܝ̈ܚܬܐ ܝܠܕܬ ܐܠܗܐ ܡܪܝܡ. ܟܕ ܐܝܬܐ ܡܪܢ
ܠܘܬ ܐܒܘܗ ܘܐܡܪ ܠܗ. ܡܪܝܡ ܡܢܗܘܢ ܒܦܘܪܫܢܐ ܕܒܢ̈ܝܢ. cf. J. S. L. p. ܩܡ
ܘܐܬܚܫܒܬ ܘܗܒܬ ܘܡܫܒܬ ܥܠܡܐ ܠܡܪܢ ܝܫܘܥ ܡܫܝܚܐ.
ܐܡܪ ܠܗ ܡܪܢ ܕܐܝܬܐ ܠܟܝ ܫܘܒܚܐ ܕܒܗ ܐܒܝ ܐܬܝܬ
ܢܝܫܒܟ. ܘܐܝܬܐ ܠܦܘܪܫܢܐ ܚܠܦܝܟܝ ܘܐܠܗܐ ܘܡܫܒܚܢܐ.
ܘܦܪܘܫܘ ܘܫܠܡܘ ܠܡܫܝܚܐ ܘܠܝܠܕܬܗ. ܐܡܪ ܠܗ ܡܫܝܚܐ
ܠܡܪܝܡ ܐܡܗ ܐܬܟܦܝ ܗܘܝ، ܠܡܕܡ ܕܠܒܝ ܠܙ̈ܗܘܐ ܕܙ̈ܗܝܚܝܢ
ܠܝ. ܘܗܝܕܝܢ ܡܪܝܡ ܬܫܡ ܠܝܘܬܢܗܘܢ ܕܙ̈ܗܘܐ ܕܫܡܝܐ ܦܐܝܢ
ܘܫܦܝܪܝܢ. ܘܐܬܟܫܦܬ [1]ܒܡܚܠܠܘܬܗܘܢ ܕܟ̈ܠ ܢܘܗܪܐ. ܘܗܝܕܝܢ
[2]ܡܠܐܟ̈ܐ ܕܫܘܒܚܐ. ܘܗܝܕܝܢ ܟ̈ܐܢܐ ܕܦܪܨܘܦܝܢ ܒܗ. ܘܐܝܬܘ
ܡܥܒ̈ܕܢܗ ܩܠܝ̈ܠܗܘܢ ܕܫ̈ܡܝܐ ܟܕ ܓܠܝܢ. ܘܫܪܝܬܐ ܓܝܪ
ܕܙ̈ܗܘܐ ܟܕ ܡܦܠܚܝܢ ܠܗܘ ܗܘܝܐ ܕܢܘܗܪܐ. ܘܗܝܕܝܢ ܠܐܝ̈ܠܢܐ
ܕܦܘܪܫܢܐ. ܕܫܡܝܐ ܥܒܝܕܝܢ ܒܫܘܬܗܘܢ. ܘܡܫܒܚ ܢܘܗܪܐ f. 227 a
ܕܠܗܘܢ ܗܠܝܢ ܣܘܓ ܦܘܪܥܢܘܬܐ. ܒܦܘܪܫܢܐ. ܐܡܪ ܠܗ
ܡܪܢ ܬܘ ܗܘܝ ܚܙܝ ܠܫܡܝܐ. ܘܗܝ ܓܐܝܬܗ ܕܐܒܝ.
ܘܗܘܝܢ ܙܗܝ ܦܘܪܩܢܐ. ܘܦܫ، ܡܪܢܬܐ ܕܫܘܪܦܐ ܘܢܫܩܗ

---

[1] Cod. ܒܡܚܠܠܐܘܬܗܘܢ   [2] Cod. ܡܠܐܟܐ

ܘܕܠܒܪ ܕܡܗܝܡܢ ܒܐܠܗܐ ܘܒܒܪܗ ܘܒܪܘܚܐ ܩܕܝܫܐ ܘܒܝܠܕܬܗ̇
ܐܠܗܐ ܡܪܝܡ. ܘܒܒܬܘܠܘܬܐ ܘܕܝܠܕܬܐ ܘܒܡܫ̈ܡܫܢܐ ܕܩܘܕܫܐ ܕܟܠ
ܫܡܗ ܕܡܫܝܚܐ ܡܫܝܚܝܢ. ܢܫܒܘܚ ܒܬܫ̈ܒܚܬܐ ܚܕ ܐܠܗܐ f. 225 b
ܕܐܬܓܠܝ ܡܢ ܒܬܘܠܬܐ ܩܕܝܫܬܐ ܡܪܝܡ. ܘܥܠ ܕܥܒܕ ܠܗ̇
ܕܘܟܪܢܐ ܢܗܘܐ ܕܡܒܪܟܗ̇[1] ܠܟܠ ܒܫܡܝܐ ܘܠܬܚܬ ܒܐܪܥܐ.
ܘܥܠ ܟܠ ܕܟܬܒ ܠܗܘܢ ܠܫ̈ܦܝܪܐ ܟܠܗܝܢ ܘܩܪܐ ܒܗܘܢ.
ܢܥܒܕ ܡܪܝܐ ܪ̈ܚܡܐ ܥܠ ܢܦܫܗ ܘܥܠ ܦܓܪܗ ܒܬ̈ܪܝܗܘܢ
ܥ̈ܠܡܐ ܠܥܠܡ ܥ̈ܠܡܝܢ ܐܡܝܢ

ܡܢܗ ܕܝܢ ܡܢܗ ܕܫܘܦܪܐ ܕܐܝܬܐ ܥܠ ܫܘܒܚܗ̇ ܒܗ ܕܝܢ
ܐܬܬܣܝܡܬ ܛܘܒܢܝܬܐ ܡܪܝܡ ܒܥܘܗܕܢܐ ܕܒܗܝܢ ܘܐܬܬܠܠܬ
ܒܗ̇ ܒܥܘܗܕܢܐ ܗܢܐ. ܘܐܝܟ ܩ̈ܠܝܢܐ ܠܟܠܗܝܢ ܘܐܝܬܝܗ̇ ܡܢ
ܥܒ̈ܕܐ ܡܫܝܚܐ ܠܗܬ ܐܡܗ ܠܒܝܬܗ. ܘܢܝܚܬܗ̇ ܡܢܝܚܬܐ
ܕܪ̈ܘܚܐ ܡܢ ܥܡܠܐ. ܘܐܬܟܢܫ ܦܘܪܫܢܐ ܕܒܗܝܢ ܘܒܠܗܘܢ
ܫܦܝܪܐ ܕܥܒܕܬ ܠܗ. ܘܩܠܐ ܕܡܪܢ ܠܘܬ ܗܘܐ ܕܡܫܬܒܚ ܐܠܐ
ܕܒܢܝ̈ܢܐ ܕܦܠܚܝܢ ܘܡܠܐܟܐ ܕܡܫܬܥܝܢ ܒܝܕ ܢܦܫܗܐ. ܡܛܠ
ܕܦܘܪܫܢܐ ܕܒܗܝܢ ܒܐܪܥܐ ܐܝܬܘܗܝ، ܒܗ̇ ܗܘܦܟܐ ܒܪܝܐ f. 226 a
ܘܠܟܠ ܡܢ ܟܠܗܘܢ ܫܦܝܪܐ ܪ̈ܡܐ ܐܝܬܘܗܝ، ܘܡܬܐܡܪܢܘܬܗ،
ܒܐܪܥܐ ܫܒܝܚܝܢ ܘܢܦܩܝܢ ܡܢܗ ܐܪ̈ܒܥܐ ܢܗܪ̈ܘܬܐ
ܚܝ̈ܘܬܐ ܘܡܒ̈ܘܥܐ ܘܕܘ̈ܠܝܬܐ ܘܥܝܢܬܐ: ܘܟܕ ܗܘܐ ܦܪܕܝܣܐ
ܒܝܬܐ ܠܫܘ̈ܠܛܢܘܗܝ، ܕܦܘܪܫܢܐ ܗܢܐ ܡܢ ܒܝܢܐ ܐܬܚܫܒ ܒܝܕ
ܙܒܢܐ. ܠܐ ܒܝܬ ܐܡܝܢ ܗܘܐ ܕܠܟܠܗ ܦܘܪܫܢܐ ܩܕܝܫܐ
ܢܨܚܢ. ܡܪܝܡ ܒܝܬ ܕܦܘܪܫܢܐ ܗܘ ܢܦܩ ܫܘܒܚܐ ܬܡܢ ܘܒܗ
ܦܐܝܢ ܗܘܐ ܘܫܦܝܪ ܒܦܘܠܚܢܐ ܕܡܠܟܐ ܗܘܐ ܠܗܘܢ

[1] Cod. ܕܡܒܪܟܗ

ܡܢܗܘܢ̈ ܥܠܘ ܘܢܦܩܘ ܫܘܒܚܐ ܠܐܠܗܐ ܕܥܒܕܐ ܪܫܡ
ܐܢܘܢ̈. ܗܢܘܢ ܪܘܚܐ ܕܩܘܕܫܐ ܐܝܬܝܗ ܚܝܠܐ ܕܢܘܗܪܐ
ܘܟܠܗܝܢ ܡܢܗܘܢ̈. ܝܬܒ ܒܡܕܝܢܬܐ ܘܐܙܠ ܠܐܬܪܐ ܕܐܬܩܪܐ
ܡܢܗ. ܘܐܟܠܝܢ ܕܡܬܐܬܝܢ ܗܘܘ ܗܝܟܠ ܠܡܕܒܚܐ̈ ܘܢܦܩܘ
ܬܠܡܝܕܐ ܓܠܝܐ ܠܡܕܝܢܬܐ ܘܐܠܘ ܒܗ ܐܬܚܙܝܘ ܡܢܐ ܐܝܟܐ
ܕܝܗܒ ܚܕܝܐ· ܒܢܘܗܪܐ ܕܢܘܚܡܐ. ܘܒܟܠ ܬܠܡܝܕܐ ܡܢ
ܦܛܪܘܣ ܘܦܘܠܘܣ ܒܗ ܐܬܚܙܝܘ ܕܐܬܪܚܡ ܒܝܬܐ ܢܬܬܒܝܘܢ̈
ܡܢܗ ܕܒܬܐ ܗܢܐ ܘܟܠ ܚܕ ܦܬܚ ܢܐܙܠ ܒܒܝܬܐ ܒܒܗ.
ܘܒܝܬܐ ܦܛܪܘܣ ܘܐܡܪ ܠܗܘܢ̈ ܟܠܗܝܢ ܠܐܬܪܐ ܕܐܬܩܪܐ ܡܢܗ
ܢܬܬܒ ܐܦ ܢܗܘܐ ܠܒܠܥܕܐ ܗܘ ܡܢܡ ܕܡܠܟܐ ܪܘܚܐ
ܕܩܘܕܫܐ ܒܫܘܒܚܗ. ܗܒܝܐ ܠܟ ܠܒܥܕܐ ܕܐܙܠ ܢܦܫܘܗܝ
ܕܢܗܘܐ ܕܡܒܝܢܐ ܠܡܪܝܡ ܬܠܬ ܐܝܟ ܕܒܬܘܠܬܐ. ܘܐܡܪܬ
ܕܫܒܚ ܠܗ ܕܡܒܝܢܐ ܒܡܥܡܕܢܝܬܐ ܡܢܡ ܦܪܘܩܢ ܕܐܟܒܐ ܢܝܚ.
f. 225 a ܘܟܠ ܐܝܢܐ ܕܢܫܒܚ ܘܢܐܡܪ ܕܡܒܝܢܗ ܡܢܡ ܟܠܗܝܢ ܒܬܘܠܬܐ
ܢܬܒܝܟ ܡܢ ܐܠܗܐ. ܦܩܕܬܐ ܕܐܬܬܒܬܒ. ܫܠܡܗ ܡܢܝ
ܡܘܫܐ ܘܦܫܪ ܠܦܛܪܘܣ ܘܦܘܠܘܣ ܘܟܠܠ ܡܠܬܐ ܒܫܬܩܘܬܗܘܢ̈.
ܐܚܪܢܝܢ ܬܠܡܝܕܐ ܒܝܬ ܦܛܪܘܣ ܠܦܘܠܘܣ ܠܡܘܫܐ ܡܠܝܒܝܢ ܠܗ
ܠܦܘܩܕܢܐ ܗܕܐ. ܘܒܗ ܗܘܝܘܢ̈ ܡܠܝܒܝܢ ܕܢܒܝܐ̈ ܫܡܝܐ
cf. J. S. L. f. ܟܕ ܒܡ ܡܕܝܢܬܐ. ܘܦܠܓܐ ܐܝܟܐ ܡܢ ܫܡܝܐ ܘܟܠܠ ܒܒܗܘܢ̈
ܘܐܡܪ ܠܗܘܢ̈. ܘܠܐ ܒܫܠܡܗ ܠܦܘܩܕܢܐ ܘܗܘܝܬܘܢ̈
ܣܓܝܐܝܢ ܘܡܫܡܫܝܢ ܠܒܝܬܗ، ܕܡܢ ܫܡܝܐ. ܘܗܢܘܢ ܐܝܠܝܢ
ܬܠܡܝܕܐ ܘܐܚܪܢܐ ܘܐܠܗܐ ܠܡܫܡܫܐ ܕܐܝܠܝܢ ܠܗܘܬܗܘܢ̈ ܡܠܠ
ܐܡܗ ܕܡܫܝܚܐ ܕܐܝܬܝܗ ܢܦܩܬ ܡܢ ܟܠܗܝܢ ܗܢܐ. ܒܬܠܬܐ
ܕܢܒܝܐ ܘܕܬܠܡܝܕܐ ܘܕܫܡܗܪܐ ܘܕܡܥܡܕܢܐ ܘܕܟܐܢܐ ܘܕܡܗܝܡܢܐ

ܘܪܘܡܐܝܬ [1]ܘܡܫܡܥܗܝ، ܛ̈ܠܝܐ ܠܟܬܒܐ ܓܝܪ. ܘܡܒܠܝܢ ܪܘܫܡܗ
ܕܡܫܝܚܐ ܕܐܬܟܬܒ ܒܗ ܪܒܘܬܐ. ܘܗܘ ܠܚܝܢ ܗܘܐ ܠܗ. ܘܝܠܦܘ
ܛ̈ܠܝܐ ܘܩܪܘ ܠܡܪܢ ܝܫܘܥ ܡܫܝܚܐ ܕܢܐܬܐ ܘܢܒܪܟ
ܐܢܘܢ ܘܢܐܙܠ ܥܡ ܚܕ ܡܢܗܘܢ ܠܐܬܪܐ ܕܐܬܝܐ ܡܢܗ.
ܘܟܕ ܫܡܥܘܢ ܡܠܝܢ ܗܘܐ ܡܫܝܚܐ ܐܬܐ ܠܘܬܗܘܢ. ܘܐܬܐ
ܣܡܟ ܘܐܠܦܐ ܘܡܫܬܐ. ܘܝܠܦܘ ܒܪܝܐ ܦܬܟܪܐ ܘܢܫܒܬܗ
ܗܘ̈ܝ ܕܥ̈ܒܕܝܗܘܢ ܕܛ̈ܠܝܐ ܥܠ ܐܪܥܐ. ܒܥܕܢܐ ܕܝܢ ܕܐܬܦܬܠ
ܗܘܐ ܒܦܓܪܐ ܕܓܠܝܗ، ܡܢܚܬܝܢ ܗܘܘ. ܘܗܐ ܡܪܝܐ ܐܦܟ f. 224a
ܒܦܪܐ ܕܗܘܡܢܐ ܘܡܬܦܟܡܟܝܢ ܗܘܘ ܒܗ ܗܢܘܢ ܛ̈ܠܝܐ.
ܡܛܠ ܕܗܘܝܐ ܡܪܢܐ ܒܦܬܓܡܐ ܗܘܬ ܒܗܘܢ. ܘܡܫܒܠܗ
ܛ̈ܠܝܐ ܢܦ̈ܫܬܗܘܢ ܘܩܪܒ ܡܫܝܚܐ ܘܐܡܪ ܠܗܘܢ
ܠܦܘܩܕܢܗܘܢ ܒܟܝܢܐ ܕܒܒܝܢ ܠܗ ܠܐܒܐ ܘܠܒ. ܘܠܦܘܪܩܢܐ
ܡܪܢܐ ܪܒ ܗܘ ܫܘܒܚܐ ܕܡܠܦ ܠܗܘܢ. ܣܝܒܬܘܢ ܫܘܒܚܐ
ܕܢܦܩܬ ܡܢܗܘܢ ܐܡܪܐ ܡܢ ܟܠܡܐ ܩܕܡܐ. ܐܬܚܙܝ ܠܗ ܣܝܒܝܢ
ܘܐܡܪܝܢ ܕܐܝܬ ܗܘ ܡܫܝܚܐ ܒܪܗ ܕܐܠܗܐ ܚܝܐ. ܘܒܪܝܟ
ܗܘ ܐܒܘܟ ܕܫܡ̈ܝܐ ܕܫܕܪܟ ܠܥܠܡܐ. ܘܒܪܝܟܐ ܗܝ
ܡܪܝܡ ܕܝܠܕܬܟ. ܘܟ̈ܠ ܐܢܫܐ ܕܗܝܡܢܝܢ ܒܟ ܘܒܐܒܘܟ
ܘܒܪܘܚܟ ܡܢܝܢܐ ܢܫܒܚܘܢ ܒܟ ܫܘܒܚܐ ܕܠܥ̈ܠܡܐ ܕܥܠܡܝܢ
ܒܫܡܐ ܐܡܝܢ. ܗܢܘܢ ܡܢܗ ܡܫܒܚ ܡܫܝܚܐ ܦܫܛ
[2]ܡܫܝܚܝܢ ܥܠ ܛ̈ܠܝܘܬܗܘܢ ܘܐܡܪ ܠܗܘܢ [3]ܠܐ ܒܫܠܡܐ
ܠܐܬܪ̈ܘܬܐ ܕܐܬܝܬܘܢ ܡܢܗ. ܘܐܙܠܘ ܟܕ ܐܡܪܝܢ ܒܪܝܟܘܬܐ
ܒܟܠ ܝܘܡ ܕܢܦܩܘ ܐܢܘܢ. ܘܒܪܟ ܐܢܘܢ ܘܫܠܚ ܠܒܝܬܗܘܢ܀
ܘܛ̈ܠܝܐ ܡܢܚܝܢ ܗܘܘ ܘܫܒܚܝܢ ܠܗ. ܘܟܕ ܐܡܪܢ ܠܗ f. 224b

[1] Cod. ܘܡܫܡܥܗ

[2] Cod. ܡܫܝܚܗ

[3] Cod. ܠܐ

ܘܐܡܪ[1] ܠܗܘܢ܆ ܐܬܒܝܐܘ ܘܐܬܒܣܡܘ ܘܠܐ ܬܬܕܘܝܘܢ܆ ܡܛܠ
ܕܟܠ ܡܕܡ ܕܒܥܝܢ ܐܢܬܘܢ܆ ܡܬܝܗܒ ܠܟܘܢ܆ ܘܒܟܠܗܝܢ ܢܗܘܐ
ܨܒܝܢܝܟܘܢ܆ ܠܘܬ ܐܒܘܟܘܢ܆ ܕܒܫܡܝܐ. ܗܘܘ܆ ܕܝܢ ܫ̈ܠܝܚܐ
ܐܪܒܥܘ ܪ̈ܟܒܝܗܘܢ܆ ܘܐܬܒܪܟܘ ܡܢ ܡܪܢ܆ ܡܫܒܚ. ܘܡܚܕܐ f 223a
ܒܗ̇ ܒܗ̇, ܕܥܕܬܐ ܕܫܠܝܚܝܢ ܗܘܘ ܒܗ̇ ܘܐܡܪܘ ܬܘ ܢܣܒܬ
ܡܢ [2]ܛܘܪܐ ܕܙ̈ܝܬܐ[2] ܠܡܕܝܢܬܐ ܕܝܠܗ̇. ܘܢܬܩܒ ܕܐܝܢܐ
ܢܦܩܬ ܡܪܝܡ ܡܢ ܥܠܡܐ ܗܢܐ. ܘܐܬܚܫܠܦܬ ܒܒܝܬܐ
ܕܢܘܗܪܐ ܘܐܘܒܠܗ̇ ܡܫܝܚܐ ܠܦܪܕܝܣܐ ܕܥܕܢ. ܒܪ ܕܝܢ
ܫ̈ܠܝܚܐ ܢܦܩܘ ܡܢ ܛܘܪ ܙ̈ܝܬܐ ܠܐܘܪܫܠܡ ܠܡܕܝܢܬܐ ܕܝܠܗ̇.
ܘܡܚܕܐ ܦܪܥܐ ܕܟܦܪܐ ܘܢܓܠܘ ܘܐܡܪܘ ܗܟܢܐ. ܢܬܩܒ
ܟܬܒܐ ܗܢܐ ܦܘܫܩܘܢ ܟܠܗܘܢ ܫ̈ܠܝܚܐ ܡܕܡ ܐܠܗܐ. ܕܗܠܝܢ
ܚ̈ܝܠܐ ܘܐܬܘ̈ܬܐ ܣܓܝ̈ܐ ܡܪܢ ܝܫܘܥ ܡܫܝܚܐ ܥܒܕ
ܠܘܬܗ̇ ܒܬܪ ܢܦܩܬ ܡܢ ܥܠܡܐ ܗܢܐ. ܘܟܠ ܐܝܟ ܕܟܬܝܒܝܢ cf. J. S. L. p. ܟܛ
ܠܩ̈ܠܐ ܗܠܝܢ ܕܟܬܝܒܢ ܒܟܬܒܐ ܗܢܐ ܫܢܐ ܠܟܠܗ. ܘܐܢܫܐ
ܕܠܐ ܡܗܝܡܢ ܡܬܚܝܒ ܗܘܐ ܗ̇ܘ, ܐܝܟܢܐ ܕܐܬܚܝܒܬ ܡܢ
ܡܕܡ ܬܫܒܘܚܬܗ ܕܥܠܡܐ. ܕܒܬܪ ܗܟܢܐ ܐܠܗܐ ܕܝܗܒ ܒܗ̇.
ܘܬܘܕܝ ܠܗ ܡܫܝܚܐ ܕܗܘܐ ܒܪܗ ܕܐܠܗܐ. ܘܗܠܝܢ ܕܥܒܕܝܢ
ܕܥܒܕܝܢ ܠܗ̇ ܠܡܪܝܡ ܒܬܘܠܬܐ ܡܪܝܡܬܐ ܒܝܘܡܗ̇ f. 223b
ܘܒܩܘܠܬܐ ܘܒܩܘܪܒܢܐ ܘܒܥܘܬܪܐ ܘܬܫܒܘܚܬܐ ܘܒܡܕܒܚܢ̈ܝܬܐ
ܕܢܘܗܪܐ ܕܡܥܕܐ ܘܬܫܒܘܚܬܐ ܐܝܟ ܕܠܡܩܒܠܢܐ ܘܠܡܣܝܒܪܐ.
ܗܟܢܐ ܘܗܡ ܕܢܥܒܕܘܢ ܠܥܐܕܐ ܕܬܫܒܘܚܬܐ. ܒܪ ܦܐܝܢ ܪܚܡܐ
ܟܡܝܬܐ ܒܟܠܗܘܢ ܦܢ̈ܝܬܗ ܕܥܠܡܐ. ܘܗܘܝܢ ܒܢܘܗܪܗ ܒܟܠ
ܟܠܗܘܢ ܒܢ̈ܝܬܐ. ܐܬܟܬܒ ܟܬܒܐ ܗܢܐ ܒܫܪܪܐ. ܘܫܘܠܡܗ.

---

[1] Cod. ܘܐܡܪܘ

[2] Cod. ܛܘܪܐ ܙ̈ܝܬܐ

ܕܒܪܟ ܥܒ̈ܕܐ ܘܥ̈ܠܝܡܝܗܘܢ[1]. ܘܨܠܝܘ ܥ̈ܠܝܡܐ ܘܐܡܪܘ ܡܪܢ[2]
ܡܫܝܚ[2] ܡܚܝܢܐ ܥܡܟ ܒܟܠܗ ܕܬܠܡܝܕܘܬܢ ܘܒܪܟ ܥ̈ܠܝܡܝܗܘܢ.
ܕܬܪ̈ܬܥܣܪ ܫܠ̈ܝܚܐ. ܢܗܘܐ ܢܫܡ ܒܗ ܠܟܠܢ ܦܘܫܩܐ ܕܒܘܪ̈ܟܬܐ.
ܢܗܘܐ ܐܡܝܢ ܒܗ ܠܓܒܝܢ ܟܦܐ ܕܫܪ̈ܘܬܐ. ܢܗܘܐ ܫܡܥܢ
ܒܗ ܠܓܒܝܢ ܫܪ̈ܘܬܐ ܕܡܟܝܢܗ ܗܘܐ ܘܡܪ̈ܟܒܬܐ. ܢܗܘܐ ܬܫܒܘܚ
ܒܗ ܠܟܠܢ ܬܘܕܝܬܐ ܡܛܠ ܒܢܝ̈ܢܫܐ ܕܐܬܦܢܝܘ ܫܘܒܚܐ ܒܐܕܪ̈ܐ
ܕܟܠܗܝܢ ܫܪ̈ܘܬܐ. ܢܗܘܐ ܐܒ ܒܗ ܢܗܒ ܠܗ ܡܫܒ̈ܚܠܐ[3]
ܠܐܠܗܐ ܫܘܒܚܐ ܢܬܠܘܢ ܕܝܗܒ ܟܬ̈ܒܠܐ ܘܡܟ̈ܬܒܠܐ[4]. ܢܗܘܐ
ܐܝܬܘܠ ܒܗ ܡܘܕܐ ܘܡܫܒܚ. ܕܝܗܒ ܠܡܫܝܚܐ ܘܡܫܒ ܠܗ
ܕܡܒܪܟ ܥܒ̈ܕܐ ܘܫܡ̈ܫܐ. ܢܗܘܐ ܬܫܪܝܢ ܒܗ ܡܘܕܐ ܘܡܫܒܚ
ܕܝܗܒ ܠܗ ܕܐܒܪܗܡ ܕܘܝܕ ܒܟܘܠܗ ܕܨܠܝܒܐ. ܢܗܘܐ cf. J. S. L. p. ܡܡ
ܬܫܪܝܢ ܠܟ̈ܠܗܘܢ ܒܫܡܗ ܕܒܗ ܐܬܐ ܠܐܠܗܐ ܠܡ ܫܡܝܢܐ
ܘܡܫܪܘܗ ܐܪܥܐ ܘܡܫܒܚܘܪܬܗ ܀ ܢܗܘܐ ܗܘܢ ܘܫܪ̈ܘܬܗ f. 222 b
ܒܫܡܗ ܒܪ̈ܘܚܐ ܘܪ̈ܘܡܐ ܘܡܪ̈ܟܒܐ ܘܡܫܬܠܚܝܢ ܥܠ ܒܪ̈ܝܬܐ.
ܢܗܘܐ ܒܗܘܢ ܘܒܫܡܗ ܬܠܬܐ ܘܠܝܠܝܐ ܕܡܒܣܡ
ܠܐܪܥܐ. ܢܗܘܐ ܥܒܕ ܒܗ ܠܟܠܢ ܐܒܗܬܐ ܠܡܪܝܐ. ܢܗܘܐ
ܐܕܪ ܒܐܡܪ̈ܐ ܘܒܢܩܘܬܐ. ܫܒܚܐ ܨܠܘ ܥ̈ܠܝܡܐ ܘܐܡܪܘ
ܐܝܟ ܡܪܝܐ ܐܠܗܐ ܕܫܕܪ ܠܒܪܗ ܝܚܝܕܝ ܕܢܦܪܘܩܝܗ، ܠܥܠܡܐ
ܟܠ ܠܒܢܝܢ. ܬܗܘܐ ܒܦܘܪܩܢܟ ܡܪܝ، ܥܠ ܐܪܥܐ ܘܥܠ
ܫܡܝ̈ܘܗ ܡܢ ܕܓܠܝܬ ܦܘܪܩܢܐ ܠܥ̈ܠܡܝܢ. ܘܬܐܬܐ
ܠܫܒܝܢ ܠܘܬܝܢ ܘܬܬܚܙܐ ܠܝ ܒܥܕܢܐ ܗܢܐ. ܡܢܕܝܢ ܡܠܐ
ܕܬܠܡܝܕܘܗܝ ܕܥ̈ܠܝܡܐ ܗܝܡܢ ܠܥܠܡܐ. ܘܡܪܢ ܡܫܝܚ
ܡܚܝܢܐ ܐܬܐ ܠܘܬܗܘܢ ܒܥܢܢܐ ܕܢܘܗܪܐ. ܘܡܛܠ ܕܒܟܘܢ

---

[1] Cod. ܘܥ̈ܠܝܡܘܗܝ  [2] Cod. ܡܪܢܝܫܘܥ

[3] J. S. L. ܡܫܒܚܬܐ  [4] Cod. ܘܡܟ̈ܬܒܐ

ܢܐܬܘܢ ܥ̈ܢܢܐ ܕܢܘܗܪܐ ܒܗ ܠܟ̈ܢܫܝܢ ܩ̈ܐܦܐ ܕܐܘܪܚܐ
ܘܢܬܬܕܒܪܘܢ ܐܝܠܢ̈ܐ ܘܦܐܪ̈ܝܗܘܢ ܘܓܘܦܢ̈ܐ ܘܫܒ̈ܠܐ
ܕܠܗܘܢ ܘܐܝܠܝܢ ܕܐܟܠܝܢ ܡܢܗܘܢ[1] ܡܬܒܪܟܝܢ ܘܗܘܐ
ܦܘܪܩܢܐ ܕܚܝܠܐ ܥܠ ܥܠܡܐ. ܘܥܠ ܐܪܥܐ ܥܠ ܒ̈ܢܝܐ ܘܒ̈ܢܬܐ
ܥܠ ܐܟܘܬܗ. ܘܡܛܠ ܡܫܡܠܝܐ ܕܐܓܪܘܢܐ ܕܠܐ ܢܦܩ ܒܐܪ̈ܝܢܐ
ܘܢܦܠ ܦܐܪ̈ܝܗܘܢ. ܘܚܙܘ[2] ܫ̈ܠܝܚܐ ܕܢܦܩܐ ܠܗ ܕܗܘܕܢܐ
ܠܡܪܢ ܒܥܠܡ ܬܠܬ ܫ̈ܢܝܢ ܕܢܬܦܝܣܘܢ ܒܒ̈ܥܘܬܐ ܡܢ ܐܘܠܨܢܐ
ܡܪ̈ܝܪܐ. ܘܚܙܘ ܫ̈ܠܝܚܐ ܕܢܦܩܘܢ ܒܥܠܡܐ ܘܡܬܚ̈ܒܠܐ
ܡܫܬܥ̈ܢܐ ܒܥܠܡܐ ܕܕܘܒܪ̈ܐ ܒܥܕܬܐ ܠܡ̈ܠܟܝܢ ܥܡ̈ܝܢ. ܘܡܬܟ̈ܢܫ
ܥܡ̈ܡܝܢ ܢܗܘܘܢ ܠܗ ܡܘܕܝ̈ܢܐ. ܘܐܝܟܢܐ ܕܐܬܐ ܚܝܠܗ
ܕܡܠܟܐ ܘܡܫܪܐ ܒܗ. ܗܟܢ ܐܬܐ ܚܝܠܐ ܕܓܠܝܦܘܬܐ ܘܡܒܪܟ
ܠܐܪܥܐ ܕܡܬܦܪܢܣܝܢ ܒܗ ܡܘܪ̈ܒܢܐ. ܘܚܙܘ ܫ̈ܠܝܚܐ ܕܢܓ̈ܕܐ
ܘܡܘܪ̈ܒܢܐ. ܕܡܬܦܪܢܣܝܢ[3] ܠܡ̈ܕܝܢܬܐ ܒܥܠܡܐ ܕܠܗ ܢܬܢܦܪܘܢ
ܢܗܘܘܢ. ܘܟܠ ܐܢܫܐ ܕܡܬܦܪܢܣ ܡܢ ܡܘܪ̈ܒܢܘܗܝ ܐܝܠܢܐ ܡܬܬܚܝܢܐ
ܬܚܘܬ. ܟܠ ܐܢܫܐ ܕܐܝܬ ܕܢܦܩܘܢ ܒܗ ܒܒ̈ܥܘܬܐ ܬܐܙܠ[4]
ܘܬܬܚܢܐ ܬܚܘܬ ܘܬܬܕܒܪ[5] ܐܝܟ. ܘܬܬܦܢܐ ܦܩܕܘ ܫ̈ܠܝܚܐ
ܕܒܘܫܡܐ ܕܕܘܒܪܢܗ ܬܬܦܪܐ ܕܐܬܬܝܣܡ ܒܬܫܡܫܬܐ ܘܫܘܕܬܐ.
ܘܦܠܚܬܐ ܕܒܢܝܢܗ ܐܘܟܡܬ ܬܫܥܝܬܗ. ܘܗܝܕܝܢ ܢܬܦܪܐ
ܐܘܪ̈ܚܬܗ. ܘܟܠ ܚܪ ܕܐܙܠ ܘܢܦܩ ܡܢ ܡܘܪܒܢܗ ܢܦܩ
ܒܥܠܡܐ ܦܘܪ̈ܩܢܐ ܕܫܘܒܚܐ ܘܢܘܗܪ̈ܐ ܐܝܟ ܕܠܐܢܫܘܬܗ[6]. ܘܟܕ
ܡܢܢ ܘܒܢܝܐ ܕܐܬܐܗ ܢܗܘܘܢ ܘܒܢܝܢ ܘܐܦ ܫܒܩܝܢ ܒܥܠܡܗ
ܕܬܫܒܘܚܬܐ. ܘܡܛܝܒܝܢ ܐܝܟ ܢܗܘܐ ܠܟ̈ܢܫܐ ܕܡܫܝܚܝܢ ܠܐܠܗܐ
ܕܫܠܝܛ ܐܝܟ. ܠܡ̈ܫܩܝܐ ܒܥܠܡܐ ܕܢܘܗܪܐ. ܗܢܘܢ ܗܟܢܐ
ܫ̈ܠܝܚܐ ܦܪ̈ܩܝܐ ܕܒܫ̈ܡܝܐ ܘܡܪܘ ܠܡܪܢ ܢܫܒܚ ܡܫܒܚܢܐ

[1] Cod. + ܕܗܝ
[2] Cod. ܘܚܙܐ
[3] Cod. ܘܡܬܦܪܢܣܝܢ
[4] Cod. ܬܐܙܠ
[5] Cod. ܘܬܬܕܒܪܝ
[6] Cod. ܕܠܐܢܫܘܬܗ

## ܕܡܪܬܝ ܡܪܝܡ

ܕܒܟܘ ܐܪܒܥܐ ܡܒܝܢ f. 62 b col. a
ܒܕܡܐ ܕܡܬܦܩܕ ܠܗ cf. J. S. L. p. ܩܓ, l. 5
ܘܢܦܩ ܕܢܫܠܡ ܒܓܢܗ
ܕܡܪܗ ܘܡܪܐ
ܕܡܬܒܪܐ ܒܣܕܪܐ
ܫܒܐ ܡܬܒܪܐ ܘܐܒܘܐ
ܕܐܝܟ ܕܢܣܒܠ ܒܣܕܪܐ
ܫܒܐ ܡܣܒܠ ܘܡܣܪܒ
ܠܗ ܠܐܪܒܥܬܐ ܕܠܐ
ܢܗܘܐ ܡܣܟܢܐ
ܦܘܩܕܢܐ ܠܒܠܡܐ ◦ ◦
ܘܐܘܕܒܬ ܪܘܚܐ
ܕܡܘܕܝܢܐ ܠܫ̈ܠܝܚܐ
ܕܢܗܘܐ ܠܗ ܕܘܒܪܢܐ f. 67 a col. a
ܠܡܪܬܝ ܡܪܝܡ ܒܐܝܪ
ܝܪܚܐ ܡܛܠ ܕܝܠܕܗ
ܕܡܪܒܘ ܡܩܒܓܐ ܗܘ
ܘܡܠܐܟܐ ܕܪܘܓܙܐ
ܕܐܘܠܢ ܡܕܡܘܗܝ ܡܛܠ
ܫܛ̈ܦܐ ܡܫܟܐ ܕܡܣܝܢ
ܘܠܐ ܢܣܦܢ ܐܝܟܐ
ܕܡܫܬܕܪܝܢ ܗܘܘ
ܘܡܫܡܫܘܬܐ ܐܝܢ
ܕܢܦܩܘ ܘܡܫܡܫܝܢ ܠܟ̈ܘܠܐ

f. 62 b col. b ܕܐܪܒܥܐ ܕܡܬܚܫܒܬ
ܒܠܒܗ ܡܪܝܐ ܘܓܒܐ
ܕܐܬܬܩܢ ܚܕ ܡܢ
ܗܠܝܢ ܫܒܛܐ ܡܫܬܕܪ
ܒܠܒܗ ◦ ◦ ◦
ܘܦܩܕܘ ܫܠܝܚܐ
ܕܒܐܪܒܥܐ ܒܫܒܥܐ
ܘܒܪܘܒܬܐ ܘܫܕ ܒܫܒܥܐ
ܕܒܠܗܘܢ ܚ̈ܝܫ ܫܢܝܬܐ
cf. J. S. L. p. ܩܓ, l. 10 ܒܟܘܬܐ ܢܗܘܘܢ
ܘܢܬܠܛܪܘܢ ܗܠܝܢ
ܘܡܬܡܢܐ ܘܠܐ ܢܗܘܐ
ܒܗܘܢ ܡܕܡ ܐܠܐ
ܘܡܪܒܢܐ ܢܬܦܪܫܘܢ
f. 67 a col. b ܒܗܠܝܢ ܬܠܬܐ ܘܫܒ̈ܥܝܢ
ܒܫܒܥܬܐ ܒܠܒܗܘܢ
ܚ̈ܝܫ ܫܢܝܬܐ
ܘܦܩܕܘ ܫ̈ܠܝܚܐ
ܕܢܗܘܐ ܕܘܒܪ̈ܢܐ
ܠܛܘܒܢܝܬܐ ܒܐܒܝ
ܝܪܚܐ ܒܬܠܬ ܒܫܪ ܒܗ
ܡܛܠ ܒ̈ܢܝܐ ܕܛ̈ܠܝܢ
ܡܛܠ ܐܝܠܝܢ ܡܛܠ ܦܘܠܚܐ
cf. Cod. Harris f. 221 a l. 5 ܕܛܠܝܢ ܦܐܪ̈ܐ ܕܠܐ

ܡܠܟܗ̇ ܒܥܘܕ̈ܪܢܐ ܠܟ̈ܢܫܐ ܘܟܢܫ ܘܡܘܕܝܢܗ̇ ܘܒܢ̈ܝ ܠܘܬܗ̇ Codex Harris f. 220 a l. 3
ܠܬܕܒܘܪܗ̇ ܦܐܪܐ ܕܐܪܥܐ. ܘܫܠܡ ܪܘܚܐ ܒܫܒܝܚܐ
ܡܘܕܝܢܗ̇ ܘܒܫܡ ܠܡܫܝܚܐ. ܕܠܐ ܢܦ̈ܩܘܢ ܬܠܡܝܕܘܬܐ ܒܗ

ܫ̈ܕܕܐ ܕܠܬܐܝܢ ܕܗܟܐ f. 62 a col. a
ܕܐ̈ܝܢܐ ܗܝܟܠܐ ܟܠ
ܐܪܥܐ ܡܛܠ ܕܗܘܐ
ܐܡܬܝ ܕܗܘܝܢ ܡ̈ܕܒܪܐ
ܒܥܒܕܐ ܐܬܚܘܝܗ̇ cf. Cod. Harris f. 220 a l. 8
ܫܡܝܐ ܘܐܪܥܐ ܟܠ
ܩ̈ܠܝ ܐܒܗܐ ܕܡܛܠܬܗ
ܠܫ̈ܕܕܐ ܕܐܐܪ ܡܬܕܠܝܢ
ܘܡܬܚܠܦ ܪܘܚܐ ܕܐܐܪ
ܡܢ ܩ̈ܠܕܐ ܕܟ̈ܐܒܗܐ.
ܡܛܠ ܕܟܠܗ ܠܗܘܢ ܪܘܚܐ
ܕܗܘܕܝܐ ܕܡܟܐ ܕܒܗܘܢ
ܠܗܪܟܐ ܒܐܪܟܐ
ܕܒܥܠܡܐ ܐܪܟܬܐ f. 67 b col. a
ܕܚܕܕܐ ܒܫܘܬܐ
ܟܠܗ ܡܬܘܒܝܢ ܠܒܘܗܝ
ܘܡܢ ܢܫܡ ܪܘܚܐ
ܘܒܕܡܐ ܠܬܫܪܝ، ܡܕܡ
ܕܫܠܐ ܗܘ ܡܢ ܥܒܕܐ
ܐ ܒܝܠܬܐ ܘܒܡܘܕ̈ܝܢܐ
ܠܐ ܡܬܡܪܟܢ ܡܕܡ
ܐܠܗܐ. ܘܗܒܢܐ ܐܡܪܘ
ܩ̈ܠܝܚܐ ܕܢܗܘܐ
ܕܘܒܪܐ ܠܡܪܬܝ ܡܪܝܡ

f. 62 a col. b ܒ̈ܢܝܪܐ ܐܢܫ
cf. J. S. L. p. ܩ, l. 2 ܒܡܫܡܫܐܪܐ ܒܗ
ܡܛܠ ܙܪܥܐ ܕܙܪܝܥܝܢ
ܘܡܛܠ ܒܘܢܝܗ̇ ܕܢܛܪܬܐ
cf. J. S. L. p. ܩ, l. 3 ܕܢܗܘܐ ܕܗܘܒܪܢܐ
ܘܡܘܪܒܢܐ ܠܡܫܝܚܐ
ܘܠܡܪܬܝ ܡܪܝܡ.
ܘܦܘܩܕܐ ܩ̈ܠܝܚܐ ܕܟܠܗ
cf. Cod. Harris f. 220 b ܐܝܪ ܢܝܫܐ ܒܟ̈ܘܬܐ
ܘܡܠ̈ܘܬܐ ܢܦܪܘܗ̇ ܒܗ
ܡܘܪܒܢܐ ܒܬ̈ܝܢܝܐ
ܗܘܠܝܐܐ * * * * ܐܬ
ܡܕܡ ܐܠܗܐ ܡܛܠ
f. 67 b col. b ܗܘܠܠܐ ܕܙܒ̈ܢܐ ܕܠܐ
ܠܬܫܒܠ ܡܢ ܪܘܚܢܐ
ܘܡܛܠ ܡܡܪܐ ܦܢܝܐ
ܘܡܪܘ̈ܪܐ ܐܘܒܕܡܐ
ܘܫܒܩܐ ܘܫܘܪܐ
ܘܪܘܪܒܐ ܕܠܐ ܢܦܘܩ
ܢܫܒܠܝܗ̇ ܠܒܪܬܐ
ܘܢܗܘܐ ܒܥܒܢܐ
ܘܢܫܘܦ ܒܠܡܐ
ܘܐܡܪܬ ܪܘܚܐ
ܕܘܒܪܐ ܠܩ̈ܠܝܚܐ

ܒܫܘܒܚܐ ܘܒܪܘܪܒܐ f. 52 a col. a
ܕܟ̈ܠܝܠܐ ܘܕܬܫ̈ܒܚܬܐ cf. Cod. Harris
ܘܫܒܚܘܗ̇ ܒܒܢܝܢܐ f. 218 b, l. 13
ܢܗܪ̈ܬܐ ܘܫܘܒܚܗ̇
ܠܬܫܒܘܚܬܗ ܒܡܥܦܪܐ
ܕܢܘܪܐ ܒܝܢܬ ܐܝ̈ܠܢܐ
ܡܫܒܚܢܐ ܕܐܝܬ ܗܘܐ
ܒܦܪ̈ܕܝܣܐ ܕܥܕܢ.
ܕܡܫܝܚ ܪܫܝܐ ܫܬܪ
ܡܢ ܗܪ̈ܘܢܐ. ܘܡܫܒܚܝܢ
ܡܕܡܝܢܗ̇ ܚܝ̈ܐ ܘܡܠܐ̈ܟܐ
ܠܐܘܪܗ̇. ܘܡܫܒܚܝܢ
ܠܗ̇. ܘܡܫ⌜ܒ⌝ܚܝܢ ܠܗ̇
ܟܠܢܐ ⌜ܒ⌝ܬܫܒܚܬܐ f. 52 b col. a
ܡܛܠ ܐܠܗܐ ܒܫܡܝܐ
ܘܟܦܠܘ ܐܬܘ ⌜ܫ⌝ܠܝܚܐ
ܠܦܘܪ ܝܬ̈ܐ ܘܟܬܒܘ cf. Cod. Harris
ܕܢܗܘܐ ܠܗ̇ ܕܘܟܪܢܐ f. 219 a, l. 3
ܠܡܪܬܝ, ܡܪܝܡ ܬܠܬ cf. J. S. L. p. ܠܓ,
ܙܒ̈ܢܝܢ ܒܫܢܬܐ. ܡܛܠ l. 20
ܕܐܣܬܒܪܝܢ ܘܫܕܪܬ ܠܝ cf. Cod. Harris f. 219 b, l. 8
ܘܚܝܝܢ ܒܒ̈ܢܝܢ. ܕܡܢܐ
ܕܢܗܘܐ ܠܗ̇ ܕܘܟܪܢܐ
ܟܠܗܘܢ ܒܢ̈ܝܐ ܕܡܠ̈ܐܟܐ
ܚܘܪܐ ܠܒܫܝܢ ܡܛܠ
ܕܬܫܒܘܚܬܐ]¹ ܬܫܪܐܬ
ܡܛܠ ܐܠܗܐ ܗܘܐ.[

ܚܝܐ ܠܟܠܗܘܢ ܒܪ̈ܝܬܐ f. 52 a col. b
ܕܐܝܠܝܢ ܠܫܠܡܗ̇ ܕܥܠܬ
ܐܠܗܐ ܘܐܬܒܪܟ ܡܢܗ̇
ܟܠܢܫ ܘܦܢܘ. ܘܐܟܠܝܢ
ܕܡܐ̈ܬܝܢ ܗܘܘ
ܘܐܬܢܚܡܘ ܦܢܘ ܡܢ
ܡܒ̈ܪܢܗܘ ܘܕܚܝܝܢ
ܗܘܘ ܦܢܘ ܒܢ̈ܝܐ ܟܠ
ܐܢܫ ܠܐܬܪܐ ܕܐܬܐ
ܡܢܗ. ° ° °
ܫ̈ܠܝܚܐ ܕܝܢ ܬܪ̈ܥܣܪ
ܢܦܩܘ ܡܢ ܦܪ̈ܕܝܣܐ
ܘܡܢܐ ܕܡܩܘܪ̈ܒܝܢ
ܒܗ̈ܢܐ ܘܩܘܪ̈ܒܢܐ
[ܠܐ ܢܦܩ ܡܫܘܬܐ ܟܠ][1]
ܟܠܡܐ ܕܢܫܒܠܝܢܗ :· f. 52 b col. b
ܘܡܢܐ ܕܗܘܐ ܡܩܪܒܢܐ
ܠܦܘܠܚ⌜ܢ⌝ܬܐ ܐܚܪܬܐ
ܒܟܢܘ ܐܢܫ, ܒܒܢܬ
ܫܠܡܗ ܕܡܫܒܚܐ ⌜ܒ⌝ܬܒܝܢ
ܡܛܠ ⌜ܕܒܢܗ⌝ ܒܢܘܡܐ
ܕܫܠܕܗ ⌜ܢܦܩܬ⌝ ܡܢ
ܟܠܡܐ ܗܢܐ ܘܕܠܐ cf. J. S. L. p. ܠܓ, l. 21
ܡܢܝܢܐ ܕܢܗܘܐ
ܕܘܟܪܢܗ̇ ܒܒܢܬ ܫܠܕܐ cf. Cod. Harris f. 220 a
ܦܩܕܢ ܚܢܢ. ܕܒܬܪ ܬܪ̈ܝܢ
ܘܬܠܬ̈ܝܢ ܢܗܘܐ ܕܘܟܪܢܗ̇
ܕܦܘܠܚܢܬܐ ܕܢܗܘܐ

[1] Cod. Harris.

ܘܐܡܪܬ ܡܪܝܡ ܗܝ ܛܘܒܢܝܬܐ[1] ܦܩܘܕ ܒܫܠܡܐ ܕܡܪܢ.
ܘܗܘܐ ܫܢ̈ܝܐ ܐܝܟ ܠܡܐܬܬܝܢ ܡܢܝܢܐ. ܘܡܚܕܐ ܪܗܛܘ
ܦܪܩܘ ܘܢܫܩܘ ܘܨܠܘ ܘܐܬܒܣܡܘ. ܘܐܡܪܝܢ ܢܫܩܘ ܐܚ̈ܝܗܘܢ,
ܥܠ ܪ̈ܓܠܝܗ ܘܒܟܘ ܐܬܝܢ. ܘܦܪܩܘ ܘܨܠܘ ܘܫܒܩܘ ܠܗ
ܐܚ̈ܝܗ ܘܐܙܠܘ. ܘܒܬܪܗ ܠܐ ܫܒܩܘ ܡܢܗ ܐܠܐ ܒܗ
ܒܫܒܘܥܗ ܘܒܬܘܠܘܬܐ ܕܐܚܝܢ̈ܐ ܐܝܬܝܗ ܗܘܐ ܬܠܡܝܕܬܐ f. 218a
ܕܪܘܚܐ ܩܕܝܫܐ ܘܡܪܒܝܬܗ ܪܘܚܐ ܒܡܕܒܪܗ ܕܫܠܡܘܬܐ
ܘܦܠܚܬ ܣܓܝ̈ܐ ܒܨܘܡܐ ܕܚܙܝܬܐ. ܘܫܒܩܬ ܐܦܝ̈ܗ ܒܦܠܚܐ
ܕܗܝ̈ܡܢܐ. ܗ̇ܝܕܝܢ[2] ܣܝܡܝܢ ܗܘܘ ܦܘܡܗ ܥܠ ܚܕܝܗ ܘܒܟܝܐ
ܗܘܐ. ܘܦܪܩܘ ܘܨܠܘ ܘܢܫܩܘܗ̇ ܫܩܠܘܗܝ ܥܩܒܝܢ ܗܘܘ̈,
ܕܡܫܒܚܝܢ ܘܫܟܝܢ ܗܘܘ ܥܠ ܦܘܩܕܢܗ. ܒܝܘܡܐ ܪܒܐ
ܘܡܒܪܝܟܬܐ. ܘܫܠܡ ܕܝܢ ܐܡܪ ܗܘܐ ܡܫܬܡܥ ܠܗ ܡܪܝܡ
ܡܪܬܗ ܕܫܠܡܐ. ܗܝܕܝܢ ܡܪܝ ܢܫܩܗ ܡܪܝܡܐ ܦܘܡ
ܕܡܫܒܚܝܢ ܠܦܘܩܕܢܬܐ ܒܟܠ ܡܪܕܘܬܐ ܕܚܘܒܐ ܘܦܠܚܝܢ
ܗܘܐ ܠܗ ܬܘܕܝܬܐ ܫܠܝܚܐ. ܘܦܠܚܝܢ ܗܘܘ ܠܫܠܝܚܐ ܬܘܕܝܬܐ
ܡܪ̈ܒܝܬܐ ܘܡܠܟܐ ܕܡܪܝܐ ܕܡܫܝܚܐ ܐܝܟ ܗܘܐ ܗܘܐ ܡܪܡ
ܠܦܘܠܚܢܬܐ ܒܪ ܐܝܠܐ ܗܘܬ ܠܒܝܬ ܒܫܘܒܚܐ ܪܒܐ.
ܘܫܒܚܝܢ[3] ܗܘܘ̈ ܡܪܝܡܗ ܫܠܡܝܢ ܒܪܝܬܐ. ܘܐܙܠܝܢ ܗܘܘ̈ ܒܬܪܗ
ܒܪܬܐ ܐܝܠܐ ܗܘܬ ܐܡܝܗ ܕܡܪܬܝ ܡܪܝܡ ܘܢܦܩܐ ܐܡܢ
ܘܐܠܦܝܢ ܐܡܗ ܕܗܘܝܢ ܦܘܡܡܝܢܐ. ܘܫܠܡ ܬܠܬ ܒܬܫܥܝܬܐ f. 218b
ܕܡܫܬܒܚܝܢ ܗܘܘ ܠܗ ܘܡܪ̈ܒܝܬܐ ܕܚܘܒܐ ܐܙܠܝܢ ܗܘܘ̈,
ܡܕܡܪܝܢ ܕܦܘܠܚܢܬܐ. ܘܬܘܒ ܒܬܪ ܫܠܡ ܐܙܠܝܢ ܗܘܘ̈,
ܡܪ̈ܒܝܬܐ ܕܐܒܪܗܡ ܘܕܐܝܣܚܩ ܘܕܝܥܩܘܒ ܘܕܫܠܡܘ̈ܗܝ ܩܕܝܫܐ
ܘܢܒܝ̈ܐ ܘܐܒܗ̈ܬܐ ܘܫ̈ܠܝܚܐ ܘܡ̈ܪܝܐ. ܬܘܒ ܒܬܪ ܫܠܡ
ܡܪ̈ܒܝܬܐ. ܐܙܠܝܢ ܗܘܘ ܬܘܕܝܬܐ ܫ̈ܠܝܚܐ ܘܦ̈ܫܝܛܝܢ ܗܘܘ̈,
ܐܝ̈ܕܝܗܘܢ ܠܫܡܝܐ ܡܢ ܟܢܫܐ ܕܢܘܗܪܝܢ ܗܘܐ ܒܗܝܢ. ܘܦܠܚܝܢ
ܠܡܪܒܝܬܐ ܕܡܪܬܝ ܡܪܝܡ: ܘܪܘܚܐ ܕܩܘܕܫܐ ܪܐܙ ܗܘܐ
ܦܪܝܫܐ ܥܠ ܐܩܢܗ ܫܠܡܐ ܘܥܡܪܐ ܐܬܝܢ ܗܘܘ ܘܡܫܒܚܝܢ
ܡܕܡܝܢ ܦܫܩܐ ܕܟܠ ܘܕܬܒܝܬ ܘܡܘܬܒ ܫܘܒܚܐ ܘܬܘܕܝܬܐ
ܘܦܐܝܫ ܗܘܐ ܪܒܝܐ ܒܡܫܒܚܐ ܒܟܠܗܝܢ ܦܪ̈ܬܝܗ ܕܫܠܡܐ.
ܘܡܢ ܕܒܠܬ ܠܦܪܕܝܣܐ

[1] + ܐܡܢ in margine  [2] Cod. ܗ̇ܝ ܕܝܢ  [3] Cod. ܘܫܒܚܝܢ

ܘܢܦܪܘܢ ܒܥܕܢ ܢܐܬܘܢ ܒܥܠܡܐ ܠܬܚܬܝܗܘܢ ܘܫܩܠܬܐ Codex Harris f. 216 b l. 8
ܕܢܗܘܢ ܡܘܪܒܝܢܐ ܠܐܝܡܪ̈ ܕܢܬܒܪܟܘܢ[1] ܘܢܘܠܕܘܢ ܦܐܪܐ.
ܘܠܓܦܢܐ ܢܬܠܝܢ ܣܓܘܠܐ ܕܒܘܪܟܬܐ. ܘܢܬܒܪܟܘܢ ܒܢ̈ܝܢܫܐ
ܕܡܩܪܒܝܢ ܠܝ ܩܘܪܒܢܐ ܘܢܫܘܘܢ ܠܒܘܪܟܬܐ ܘܠܚܡܝܪܐ
ܕܙܕܝܩܘܬܐ. ܘܥܠ ܒܢܘ̈ܗܪܐ ܕܚܫܘ̈ܟܬܐ ܘܥܛ̈ܠܐ ܕܢܘܟܪܝܐ
ܢܒܪܘܢ ܡܢܗܘܢ. ܘܢܗܘܐ ܫܝܢܐ ܘܫܠܡܐ ܥܠ ܟܠܗܘܢ
ܒܢ̈ܝܬܐ ܕܡܪܝܡ [2]ܒܫܡܟܝ ܡܢܫܝܐ ܘܢܗܘܐ ܥܠܝܠܐ ܕܫܢܝܬܐ
ܘܕܫܢܝܐ ܡܒܢ̈ܝܟܝ ܘܡܕܡܟܝ. ܘܒܫܡܐ ܕܡܩܪܒܝܢ ⌜ܩܘܪܒܢܐ⌝ f. 217 a cf. J. S. L. p. ܠܛ
ܘܒܫܡܗܪܐ ܡܕܡܟܝ ⁖ ܘܥܠ ܡܪܝ, ܘܩܘܪܒܢܝܗܘܢ. ܘܒܫܡܟܝ
ܡܫܡܫܝܗܘܢ. ܘܐܡܪܬ ܗܝܠܝܢ ܒܬܫܒܚܬܐ. ܘܒܫܡܗ
[3]ܬܘܒܪ̈ ܙܘܗܪ̈ܢܐ. ܘܒܢܬ ܬܠܡܝܕܐ ܚܝܢܐ ܢܗܘܐ ܘܒܢܬ
ܕܒܢܐ ܥܠܡܐ. ܘܒܘܪܟܬܐ ܘܫܪܘܬܐ ܥܠ ܐܦܝܗ̇ ܕܟܠܡܐ
ܠܥܠܡ ܥܠܡܝܢ ܐܡܝܢ. ܫܠܡ ܓܠܘܬܐ ܕܒܘܪܟܬܐ ܐܡܪܬ
ܡܪܝܡ ܟܕ ܡܫܒܚܐ ܐܝܬ ܠܗܘܗ ܘܐܡܪܬ ܠܗ̇. ܟܕ ܐܢܐ
ܠܟ ܡܨܠܝܐ ܘܐܝܠܝܢ ܕܦܬܚ ܠܝ ܥܝܢ̈ܝ ܐܚܙܐ ܥܠܝܗܘܢ
ܪ̈ܚܡܐ. ܘܬܘܒ ܐܝܠܝܢ ܕܢܚܙܘܢ ܠܟ ܕܦܬܚܝܢ ܐܦ
ܩܘܪܒܢܐ. ܘܡܬܟܪܟܝܢ ܠܟ ܕܢܦܩܬ, ܡܢ ܥܠܡܐ ܗܢܐ
ܘܒܙܒܢܐ ܕܐܘܠܨܢܐ ܢܩܪܒܘܢ ܠܘܬܟ ܩܘܪܒܢܐ ܐܚܪܢ
ܥܠܝܗܘܢ ܪ̈ܚܡܐ. ܘܐܝܠܝܢ ܕܢܚܙܘܢ ܠܟ ܒܥܘܗܕܢܐ ܐܢܫܐ
ܐܢܘܢ ܘܐܢܫ ܥܠܝܗܘܢ. ܘܐܬܠ ܢܘܬܪܢܐ ܠܟܢܐ
ܒܒܝܬܗܘܢ. ܘܐܦ ܒܦܪ̈ܨܘܦܝܗܘܢ ܐܬܒܘܢ. ܘܬܫܪܐ ܒܒܪܬܗ
ܕܐܒܝ ܕܒܫܡܝܐ ܥܠ ܟܠ ܩܘܪܒܢܐ ܕܒܫܡܝ ܘܡܛܠ ܡܘܬܒ f. 217 b
ܡܬܡܪܢ ܠܥܠܡ ܥܠܡܝܢ ܐܡܝܢ. ܗܢܝܢ ܡ̈ܠܝ ܒܪ̈ܬܐ ܘܫܡܥܝܢ
ܠܡܫܝܚܐ. ܘܡܪܐ ܡܫܝܚܐ ܠܗܝ, ܢܦܩܬ ܘܐܡܪܬ ܠܗ ܠܐ
ܬܕܚܠܝ ܠܟܝ ܡܛܠ ܡܪܝܡ. ܐܡܪ ܡܪܝ, ܢܦܩܬ ܙܒܢ ܡܪܝܡ
ܠܐ ܡܬܒܥܬܐ: ܘܬܘܒ ܡܪܐ ܠܫܠܝܚܘܗܝ ܘܐܡܪ ܠܗ.
ܡܚܝܠ ܒܢܝܐ ܕܒܘܪܐ ܐܡܪܐ ܕܒܡܕܒܪܐ· ܕܠܟܝ ܘܒܢ̈ܝܢ
ܟܠܗܘܢ ܒܢ̈ܬܐ ܗܠܠܘܝܐ. ܘܟܕ ܟܠܢ ܒܚܠܝ ܬܫܒܚܬܐ
ܘܐܠܝܢ ܡܪܝ ܢܫܒܚ ܡܫܒܚܐ. ܘܢܗܘܐ ܬܫܒܘܚܬܐ
ܩܠܐܡܐ. ܘܡܫܒܚܐ ܫܢܬ ܡܪܝܡ ܠܬܘܬ ܐܘܢܝܐ ܕܒܝܬ ܐܒܐ.

[1] Cod. ܘܢܘܠܕܘܢ [2] Cod. ܫܡܟܝ [3] Cod. ܬܘܒܕܢ

ܘܡܥܒܕܝܢ ܠܗ̇ ܕܘܒܪܢܐ f. 51 b col. a
ܘܡܬܩܪܒܝܢ ܠܗ̇ ܩܘܪ̈ܒܢܐ
ܘܡܫܒܚܝܢ ܕܘܒܪܢܗ̇
ܕܡܪܬܝ ܡܪܝܡ ܝܠܕܬ
ܠܡܫܝܚܐ. ܡܛܠ ܡܪܝ
ܡܢܗܘܢ ܘܩܘܪ̈ܒܢܝܗܘܢ.
ܘܡܛܠ ܨܠܘܬܐ ܕܥܠܡܐ
ܡܩܪܒܝܢ. ܘܡܛܠ ܒܥܘܬܐ
ܕܒ̈ܢܝ ܐܢܫܐ ܘܕܡܟܐ
ܕܡܬܐܫܫܢ ܡܢ ܒܢ̈ܝܗܘܢ
ܘܐܒܒܪ ܡܢ ܐܪܒܥܐ
ܗܝ ܕܡܬܦܪܢܣܝܢ ܒܗ̇
ܩܘܪ̈ܒܢܝ ܚܪܒܐ
ܘܫܒܝܐ ܘܟܦܢܐ ܘܡܘܬܢܐ f. 47 a col. a
ܘܡܚܘ̈ܬܐ ܒܝ̈ܫܬܐ
ܘܡܛܠ ܐܘܠܨܢ ܕܓܕܫܝܢ
ܠܒܢ̈ܝ ܐܢܫܐ ܒܓܠܠ ܡܢ
ܚܛܗܐ ܕܡܣܪܒܝܢ
ܩܘܪ̈ܒܢܐ ܡܩܪܒܝܢ ܀
ܘܬܘܒ ܓܠܝܬ ܘܐܡܪܬ
ܪܘܒܠ ܡܫܝܚܐ ܕܐܝܬ
ܠܗ ܒܫܡܝܐ ܐܪܒܥܐ
ܕܡܬܦܪܢܣ ܒܗ̇
ܩܘܪܒܢ ܒܪܟܗ̇ ܡܪܝ
ܠܟܠܠ ܫܢܬܐ ܒܩܘܪܒܬܐ

f. 51 b col. b ܕܢܬܝܗܒ ܠܒܣܘܪ̈ܝܗ
ܕܢܬܦܩܝܢ ܐܪ̈ܒܥܬܐ ܗܠܝܢ
ܒܩܘܪ̈ܒܢܐ ܗܠܝܢ
ܕܡܬܦܪܢܣܝܢ ܠܗ ܡܢ
ܡܡܓܐ ܕܠܐ ܢܣܒܠ.
ܘܡܢ ܫܘܒܐ ܕܠܐ ܢܒܫ.
cf. Cod. Harris f. 216 b ܘܡܢ ܝܪܘܩܐ ܕܠܐ ܢܒܠܐ
ܟܠܝܗܝܢ. ܘܡܢ ܟܦ̈ܢܐ
ܕܒܪܢܫܐ ܕܠܐ ܢܫܬ
ܟܠܝܗܝܢ ܡܢ ܫܒܝܐ.
ܘܟܠ ܡܢ ܕܟܪܝܗ
ܢܬܐܣܐ. ܘܡ̇ܢ ܕܐܠܝܨ
ܢܬܪܘܚ. ܘܕܒܥܐ ܢܫܟܚ.
f. 47 a col. b ܘܕܡܫܡܫܝܢ ܠܫܬܪܬܚ[1]
ܘܕܡܫܬܢܩܝܢ[2] ܡܢ ܪܘܚܐ
ܕܣܛܢܐ ܘܡܪܐ ܒܫܡܝ
ܬܫܬܪܪ ܠܗ ܐܣܝܘܬܐ.
ܘܕܐܣܝܪ ܒܟܘܠܐ ܡܢ
ܒܢ̈ܝ ܐܢܫܐ ܢܫܬܪܐ
ܐܣܘܪ̈ܘܗܝ. ܘܐܝܠܝܢ
ܕܒܝܡܐ ܪܕܝܢ ܘܡܫܬܡܫܝܢ
ܟܠܝܗܘܢ ܒܐܘܪ̈ܚܐ
ܘܢܦܩܘ ܒܫܡܗ ܕܡܪܝܐ
ܘܢܬܦܨܘܢ ܡܢ ܒܝ̈ܫܬܐ.
ܘܐܝܠܝܢ ܕܒܐܬܪ̈ܘܬܐ
ܪ̈ܚܝܩܐ ܐܝܬܝܗܘܢ

[1] sic, see p. ܟܓ col. b, l. 4.

[2] Cod. ܘܕܡܫܬܢܩ

ܕܡܒܪܢܐ ܘܡܗܝܡܢܝܢ f. 51 a col. a
ܒܐܠܗܐ. ܕܗܘ ܫܕܪ cf. Cod. Harris f. 215 b l. 4
ܠܒܪܗ ܘܫܪܐ ܒܢܝ.
ܡܘܕܝܢ ܕܒܪܗ ܗܘ
ܕܐܠܗܐ ܗܘ ܕܐܬܝܠܕ
ܡܢܢ. ܘܡܫܒܚܝܢ
ܠܪܘܚܐ ܕܩܘܕܫܐ
ܗܝ ܕܡܕܝܚܐ ܠܢ.
ܘܢܒܥܘܕ ܕܡܒܪܢܐ cf. J. S. L. p. ܠܕ, l. 21
ܬܘܕܝܘ ܡܢ ܐܘ̈ܠܝܢܐ
ܡܫܝܚܐ ° ° °
ܗܕܝܢ ܝܠܕܬ ܦܬܓܡܬܐ
ܘܗܟܢܐ ܐܡܪܬ ܒܝܠܬܗ̇. f. 47 b col. a
ܐܠܗܐ ܕܝܗܒ ܒܝܡܝܢܗ
ܘܐܬܪܟܒ ܒܣܘܟܗ
ܘܫܪܪ ܠܒܪܗ ܡܢ ܫܡܝܐ.
ܘܫܪܐ ܒܒܝܬ ܗ̈ܕܡܝܗ cf. J. S. L. p. ܠܗ
ܗܘ ܕܐܬܪܚܡ ܥܠ
ܥܠܡܐ ܕܡܪܐ ܠܗ.
ܘܬܘܒ ܝܠܕܬ ܘܐܡܪܬ
ܡܫܝܚܐ ܒܪ ܡܠܟܐ
ܕܫܡܝܐ ܒܪܗ ܕܐܠܗܐ
ܕܠܐ ܟܒܪ. ܘܟܠ
ܝܠܘ̈ܬܗ ܕܟܠ ܐܢܫܐ

ܕܡܪܝܡ ܘܡܕܒܪܢܝܢ ܫܡܥ̈ܘܗܝ f. 51 a col. b
ܕܠܝܠܬܟ ܡܕܒܚܝܢܟ.
ܘܐܡܒܪܟ ܡܫܒܚܘ ܒܫܘ̈ܒܚܐ
ܘܟܠܠ ܡܢ ܐܪܒܥܐ ܙ̈ܢܝܐ
ܡܫܝܚܐ. ܘܬܘܒ ܝܠܕܬ cf. Cod. Harris f. 216 a
ܘܐܡܪܬ. ܡܪܝ ܝܫܘܥ
ܡܫܝܚܐ ܗܒ ܟܠܠܐ
ܠܡܫܒܘܚܬܐ ܘܪܘܒܢܐ
ܠܬܠܝܠܘܬܐ ܘܟܒܪ
ܠܢܘ̈ܦܬܐ ܕܡܪܝܡ ܠܟ.
ܘܠܗܡ ܕܟܒܪ ܕܡܒܪܢܐ
ܠܪܘܚ ܘܠܦܓܪ. ܕܢܫܘ
ܡܢ ܒܠܒܐ ܗܢܐ ܘܫܠܡܬ f. 47 b col. b
ܐܝܕ̈ܘܗܝ ܕܡܪܝ ܝܫܘܥ
ܡܫܝܚܐ ܘܫܡܥܬ ܐܢܝܢ
ܟܠ ܢ̈ܫܘܗ. ܘܡܫܝܚܘܬܐ
ܗܘܬ ܠܗܘܢ ܘܐܡܪܬ
ܒܟܢܫܐ ܐܢܐ ܡܫܒܚܟ
ܡܪܝ ܝܫܘܥ ܡܫܝܚܐ
ܕܡܢ ܕܟܒܝܫ ܒܒܝܬ
ܒܫܒܝܐ ܘܒܐܪܒܥܐ
ܗܕܐ ܡܪܝ ܡܫܝܚܐ
ܐܢܐ ܠܟ ܕܟܠܘ ܐܡܒܪܐ
ܕܡܬܒܥܝܢ ܩܕܡ ܐܢܫܐ

f. 61 b col. a
ܘܐܬܐ ܐܠܐ ܒܗ̇
ܠܒܪܬܐ. ܐܡܪܐ ܠܗ
ܡܪܝܡ ܪܒܘܠ ܦܫܘܛ (cf. J. S. L. p. ܠܒ, l. 15)
ܐܝ̈ܕܝܟܝ ܘܣܝܡ ܐ̈ܝܕܝܢ
ܥܠ ܒ̈ܢܝܟܝ ܘܒܪܟܝ.
ܘܦܫܛ ܡܫܝܚܐ
ܐܝ̈ܕܘܗܝ، ܘܣܡ ܐ̈ܝܕܝܢ
ܥܠ ܒ̈ܢܝܗ̇ ܕܐܡܗ.
ܗܝ، ܕܝܢ ܛܘܒܢܝܬܐ
ܡܪܬܝ، ܡܪܝܡ ܠܒܟܬ
ܐܝܠ̈ܘܗܝ، ܘܡܒܣܡܢܐ
ܗܘܬ ܠܗܘܢ. ܘܒܟܝܬ
ܘܐܡܪܐ ܦܓܪܐ ܐܝܟܐ
ܠܗܠܝܢ ܐ̈ܝܕܝܐ ܡܒܪ̈ܟܬܐ (f. 68 a col. a)
ܕܗܠܝܢ ܒܒܪ ܫܡܝܐ
ܘܐܪܥܐ ܕܠܐ ܒܥܠܐ
ܡܘܕܐ ܐܝܟܐ ܘܦܓܪܐ
ܐܝܟܐ ܘܡܪܡܪܢܐ ܐܝܟܐ
ܠܗ̇، ܫܒܬܐ ܕܫܝܪܝܟ
ܐܒܘܟ ܐܕܡ، ܡܢ
ܫܡܝܐ ܕܐܝܩܪܗ.
ܢܚܬܐ ܗܘܬ ܥܢܪ ܒܕ
ܒܪܘܫ ܐܝܬܝܟ ܗܘܬ
ܕܢܣܒܝܢ ܡܠ̈ܟܘܗܝ،

f. 61 b col. b
ܕܐܒܘܟ ܘܣܓܕܘ
ܘܕܡܫܝܟ ܘܫܪܝܐ ܗܘܬ
ܒܐܬܪܐ ܕܢܘܗܪܐ
ܘܡܙܝܚܝܢ ܠܗ ܡܠ̈ܐܟܐ
ܕܬܫܒܘܚܬܐ. ܘܬܘܒ
ܐܘܕܝܬ ܘܐܡܪܬ
ܒܪܗ ܕܐܠܗܐ ܡܫܝܚܐ
ܐܢܬ ܗܘ ܡܪܝ، ܫܢܝܗ
ܕܒܠܚܕܐ ܘܡܢ ܫܬܒܪܘܢ
ܒܠܠܝܗܘܢ ܕܒܗ̈ܘܢܐ
ܕܐܘܕܝܘ ܒܢ ° ° °
ܘܒܕ ܗܠܝܢ ܐܡܪܬ
ܗܘܬ ܦܘܠܚܢܬܐ ܢܗܒܝܢ
ܗܘܘ ܫܘܒܚܐ ܒܠܒܗ̇ (f. 68 a col. b)
ܚ̈ܠܠܝܐ ܘܬܫ̈ܬܝܐ
ܠܡܫܝܚܐ ܕܢܚܬ ܡܢ
ܫܡܝܐ ܕܢܚܝܗ ܠܐܡܗ
ܒܬܘܠܬܐ ܡܕܝܫܬܐ
ܕܝܠܕܬܗ. ܘܡܢ ܢܦܩܐ
ܡܢ ܒܠܡܐ ܗܢܐ. [1]ܗܝ، (cf. Cod. Harris f. 215 b)
ܕܝܢ[1] ܡܪܒܘ ܫ̈ܠܝܚܐ
ܘܐܡܪܝܢ ܠܡܪܬܝ، ܡܪܝܡ
ܫܒܘܩܝ ܒܘܪܟܬܐ (cf. J. S. L. p. ܠܒ, l. 20)
ܠܥܠܡܐ ܕܢܦܩܬ، ܡܢܗ
ܕܐܠܝܢ ܕܒܒܢܝܢ ܠܒ

---

[1] ܗܘܝܢ

## ܘ ܘ ܡܟܘܢܗ ܕܡܪܬܝ ܡܪܝܡ ܘ ܘ

ܕܠܒܫܝܢ ܠܗ ܒܗ ܡܬܠܒܫܝܢ
ܫܘܒܚܝܐ ܘܐܬܐ
ܘܠܒܝܢ ܚܝܫܐ ܕܓܠܝܒܐ
ܘܐܬܐ ܕܢܚܘܬ ܓܒܪ
ܡܪܬܝ ܡܪܝܡ ܘܢܚܬ
ܓܐܕܗ̇. ܘܒܪܟ ܒܠܗܝܢ
ܒܪ̈ܝܬܐ ܘܫܠܡ ܠܗ̇.
ܘܦܪܐ ܡܪܝ ܢܫܘܒ
ܡܫܝܚܐ ܠܐܡܗ
ܘܐܡܪ ܠܗ̇. ܡܪܝܡ. ܗܘܝ
ܐܡܪܬ ܠܗ ܗܐ ܐܢܐ
ܪܒܘܠ ܕܡܬܐܡܪ
[ܡܠܘܢܐ. ܐܡܪ ܠܗ̇]
ܡܪܝ ܠܐ ܬܒܪܐ ܠܒ
ܦܘܡܟ ܘܚܙܝ ܫܘܒܚܝܐ
ܕܝܗܒ ܠܝ ܐܒܝ.
ܘܐܬܬ ܕܐܫܝܒܝ.
ܘܢܚܬܬ[1] ܗܘ ܒܬܘܠܬܐ
ܦܪܫܬܐ. ܘܚܙܬ
ܬܫܒܘܚܬܐ ܕܠܐ
ܡܝܐ ܦܘܡܐ ܕܒ̈ܢܝܢܫܐ
ܕܢܡܠܠܗ̇. ܐܡܪ ܠܗ̇
ܡܫܝܚܐ ܠܐܡܗ ܫܪ
ܒܠܡܕܡ ܕܐܡܪܬ ܠܒ

ܡܪܝܡ. ܗܘܝ ܐܡܪܬ
ܠܗ ܐܝܟ ܒܦܫܬܐ
ܪܒܘܠ ܫܪ ܒܠ ܕܐܡܪܬ
ܠܝ. ܐܡܪ ܠܗ̇ ܡܒܝܠ
ܠܦܪܕܝܣܐ ܕܒܙ̈. ܡܒܠ
ܐܢܐ ܫܠܒܝ ܘܬܡܢ
ܗܘܝܐ ܒܕܡܐ ܠܢܘܚܡܐ
ܐܦ ܡܠܐܟܐ ܝܗܒܝܢܐ
ܠܐܝܩܪܝ ܕܩܘܡܒܘ
ܘܡܡܚܒ[2] ܒܗ ܠܒܢܝܢ
ܢܗܪ̈ܐ ܘܠܦ̈ܠܓܘܬܐ
ܒܙ ܐܬܐ ܐܢܐ ܐܫܪܐ
ܫܡܝܐ ܘܐܪܥܐ ܘܐܬܠ
ܦܬܟܐ ܠܕ̈ܡܘܬܐ ܘܫܘܩܢܐ
ܘܫܘܒܚܐ ܠܒܠ̈ܐ. ܗܢܐ
ܠܒܪ ܡܕܡ ܕܚܙܝܬ ܗܫܐ
ܡܪܝܡ ܡܠܝܠ ܗܘ ܡܢ
ܫܘܒܚܝܐ ܕܐܒܝ. ܐܬܐ
ܒܒܝ ܕܬܚܙܝܢ ܘܬܚܙܝܢ.
ܠܗܘ ܠܒܪ ܡܢܟܐ ܐܢܫܪܐ
ܕܐܬܠܝܐ ܒܫܘܒܚܝܐ
ܪܒܐ ܕܚܘܫܐ ܠܒܠܒܐ
ܡܕܡ ܕܠܐ ܡܚܝܢܐ
ܒܢܝܢܐ ܕܩ̈ܠܝ ܐܢܫܐ
ܠܡܦܪܩܘ ܠܗ̇ ܬܫܒܘܚܬܐ

1 Cod. ܘܢܚܬ

2 Cod. ܡܡܚܒ

ܠܐܝܩܪܗ. ܕܗܢܝܢ ܒܗ f. 125 b col. a
ܐܬܓܠܝܬ܆ ܒܒܪܗ cf. Cod. Harris f. 212 a l. 5
ܕܡܟܐ ܗܘܬ ܕܐܠܗܐ
ܕܡܫܝܚܐ ܐܬܐ ܘܫܪܐ
ܒܗ. ܘܐܬܐ ܐܒܘܢ
ܐܝܟ ܘܫܪܬ ܒܪܗ
ܘܣܡܟ ܘܢܘܚ ܕܗܘܐ cf. Cod. Harris f. 212 b
ܫܢܝܪܐ ܠܒܠܥܐ. ܘܣܠܩܘ
ܡܕܡܝܢ ܘܐܡܪܘ
ܡܘܕܝܢܐ ܠܟ ܐܠܗܐ
ܕܐܬܬ ܡܢ ܫܡܝܐ
ܘܫܪܬ ܒܒܪܬ܆ ܘܫܡܫܬ
ܡܠܟ ܟܠܗ ܫܘܠ
ܘܚܕܬܢܝ ܕܠܒܫܬ ܦܓܪ f. 130 a col. a
ܘܐܣܩܬܢܝ ܠܫܡܝܐ
ܐܝܟܢܐ ܕܐܡܪ ܠܢ
ܦܘܡܟ ܡܩܕܫܐ
ܒܦܪ̈ܕܝܣܐ. ܘܐܬܚܝܢ
ܡܪ̈ܟܒܬܐ ܐܚܪ̈ܢܝܬܐ
ܕܐܬܚܝ: ܕܐܒܪܗܡ
ܘܕܐܝܣܚܩ ܘܕܝܥܩܘܒ.
ܘܡܪܝ܆ ܕܘܝܕ ܡܕܒܪܢܐ
ܕܒܝܬܐ ܒܡܗܘܢ. ܘܫܠܡܘ
ܡܕܡܝܢ ܕܦܘܪܩܢܘܬܐ

f. 125 b col. b ܡܪܝܡ ܘܐܬܚܙܝܢ
ܡܪ̈ܟܒܬܐ ܕܢܒ̈ܝܐ
ܕܐܬܚܙܝܢ ܘܦܪܨܘܦܗܘܢ
ܒܐܪ̈ܙܝܗܘܢ ܘܡܫܠܡܘ
ܡܕܡܝܢ ܕܦܘܪܩܢܘܬܐ.
ܘܐܬܚܙܝܢ ܡܪ̈ܟܒܬܐ
ܕܫܡܗ̈ܪܐ ܕܐܬܚܝܢ
ܘܢܗܝܪ̈ܐ ܒܐܪ̈ܙܝܗܘܢ
ܕܫܠܡܘ ܡܕܡܝܢ
ܕܒܬܘܠܘܬܐ ܡܕܡܝܬܐ.
ܘܐܬܚܙܝܢ ܡܪ̈ܟܒܬܐ
ܕܫܒܥܝܢ ܘܬܪ̈ܝܢ ܥ̈ܠܝܢ
ܕܐܬܚܝ ܘܫܠܡܘ ܡܕܡܝܢ
f. 130 a col. b ܕܦܘܪܩܢܘܬܐ. ܘܒܬܪ ܗܠܝܢ
ܐܬܚܙܝܢ ܡܪ̈ܟܒܬܐ
ܕܡܠ̈ܐܟܐ ܘܕܒܢ̈ܝ܆
ܥܠܡܐ ܘܕܪ̈ܘܒܐ
ܘܕܣܦ̈ܪܐ ܕܠܒܝܒܝܢ
ܥܦܘܪ̈ܐ ܘܡܒܝܢ
ܥܘܒܕܢܐ ܡܕܡ ܡܪܗܘܢ
ܕܐܬܐ ܘܢܚܬ ܠܝܕ
cf. J. S L. p. ܠܓ, l. 10 ܐܡܗ ° ܗܕܝܢ
ܐܬܚܝܝ܆ ܦܪܘܩܗ
ܕܡܠܟܐ ܡܫܝܚܐ ܒܠ
ܡܪ̈ܟܒܬܐ ܕܫ̈ܦܝܪܐ

M. D. G.

ܒܗܘ ܒܝܘܡܐ ܕܐܬܝܠܕܬܗ f. 125 a col. a
ܒܗ ܢܦܩܬ ܡܢ ܥܠܡܐ
ܗܢܐ. ܐܡܪܝܢ ܫ̈ܠܝܚܐ
ܠܪܘܚܐ ܕܩܘܕܫܐ
ܘܠܡܫܝܚ ܒܐܝܕܐ ܫܒܬܐ
ܐܬܐ ܡܪܢ ܡܢ ⌜ܫܡܝܐ⌝
ܓܐܕܝܢ. ܘܐܡܪܬ ܠܗܘܢ
ܪܘܚܐ ܕܩܘܕܫܐ.
ܕܠܡܫܝܚ ܒܬܫܥ ܫܥܝܢ
ܐܬܐ ܓܐܕܒܘܢ ܡܢ
ܫܡܝܐ. ܘܬܘܒ cf. J. S. L. p. ܠܗ, l. 4
ܐܡܪܬ ܠܗܘܢ ܪܘܚܐ
ܕܩܘܕܫܐ ܠܫ̈ܠܝܚܐ.
ܕܗܟܢܐ ܗܝܡܢܘ f. 130 b col. a
ܘܗܟܢܐ ܐܘܕܘ. ܕܒܚܕ
ܒܫܒܐ ܐܣܬܒܪ ܕܐܬܐ cf. Cod. Harris f. 210 a
ܠܥܠܡܐ. ܘܒܚܕ ܒܫܒܐ
ܒܚܕܘ ܐܚܪܝ, ⌜ܒܫܒܬܐ⌝
ܒܗ ܐܬܐ ܠܥܠܡܐ
ܘܐܬܬܠܕ ⌜ܒ⌝ܒܝܬ ܠܚܡ.
ܘܒܚܕ ܒܫܒܐ ܢܦܩܘ
ܒ̈ܢܝ ܐܘܪܫܠܡ ܟܕ ܠܐ
ܓܕܝܢ ܘܫܒܚܘܗܝ ܗܘܘ
ܒܐܘܫܥܢܐ ܫܒܝܚܐ

f. 125 a col. b ܘܐܪܒܥܝܢܐ. ܘܒܚܕ ⌜ܒ⌝ܫܒܐ
ܩܡ ܡܢ ܩܒܪܐ
ܘܐܚܘܝܬ ܐܦ ܠܟܠܗܘܢ
ܬ̈ܠܡܝܕܘܗܝ ∘ ∘
⌜ܬ⌝ܘܒ ܒܬܪ ܐܪܒܥܝܢ
ܝܘܡܝܢ ܕܩܝܡܬܗ
ܒܝܘܡܐ ܕܚܡܫܐ ܒܫܒܐ
ܣܠܩ ܠܫܡܝܐ. ܘܒܚܕ
ܒܫܒܐ ܐܬܐ ܒܝܘܡܐ
ܐܚܪܝܐ ܐܠܐ ܦܝܫ
ܦܘܪܩܢܐ ܕܠܡܫܝܚ ܐܬܐ
ܓܒܕ ܐܡܪܗ. ܘܐܬܬ
cf. Cod. Harris f. 211 b l. 13 ܚܘܐ ܐܡܐ ܕܟܠܗܘܢ
ܒ̈ܢܝܬܐ ܘܐܡܪܗ̇ ⌜ܕܡܪܬܝ⌝,
f. 130 b col. b ܡܪܝܡ. ܘܟܠܗܝܢ ܕܝܢ
ܒܬܘ̈ܠܬܐ ܕܡܫܡܫܢ
cf. Cod. Harris f. 212 a ܗܘ̈ܝ ܠܗ̇ ܠܡܪܬܝ, ܡܪܝܡ
ܓܐܕܝܗ̇ ܗ̈ܘ, ܘܟܠܗܘܢ
ܗܠܝܢ ܫܘܒܚܪܐ ∘ ∘ ∘
ܘܦܪܒܬ ܐܡܗ̇ ܕܡܪܬܝ,
ܡܪܝܡ ܘܣܡܟܬ ܦܘܡܗ̇
ܥܠ ܚܕܝܗ̇ ܘܢܫܩܬܗ̇.
ܘܐܡܪܬ ܠܗ̇ ܒܪܬܝ
ܗܘ ܐܠܗܐ ܕܝܗܒ ܠܗ
ܕܬܗܘܝܢ ⌜ܒ⌝ܥܝܬ ⌜ܡ⌝ܫܒܪܐ

M. D. G.

f. 8 b col. a

ܘܢܣܒܐ ܫܠܡܐ ܡܩܕܡ
ܡܪܗ ܒܐ̈ܕܢܝܗ̇
ܕܛܘܒܢܝܬܐ ܕܫܪܐ ܒܗ̇.
ܐܬܐ ܓܒܪܐܝܠ ܕܢܩܪܐ
ܫܠܡܐ ܠܛܘܒܢܝܬܐ.
ܕܗܐ ܡܪܝ، ܥܡܟܝ
ܕܐܠܗܐ ܐܝܬܘܗܝ،
ܗܘ ܕܫܪܐ ܒܟܝ. ܘܟܕ
ܗܘ ܠܐ ܫܠܡ ܗܘܐ
ܫܠܡܗ ܡܩܕܡ ܡܪܗ
ܘܟܠ ܘܫܪܐ ܒܟܪܣܗ̇
ܕܛܘܒܢܝܬܐ. ܟܕ ܕܝܢ
ܦܓܥ ܓܒܪܐܝܠ ܡܩܕܡ
ܡܪܝܡ. ܠܐ ܗܘܐ

f. 5 a col. a

ܠܡܪܝܡ ܦܓܥ ܒܠܚܘܕ
ܐܠܐ ܐܦ ܠܡܪܗ. ܐܦ
ܗܘ ܡܚܝܠ ܓܒܪܐܝܠ
ܒܪܗܒܘܬܐ ܗܘܐ
ܟܕ ܢܣܒ ܕܢܬܠ ܫܠܡܐ
ܠܡܪܗ ܡܩܕܡܗ ܡܪܗܘ
ܕܒ̈ܢܝܐ ܠܐ ܢܓܪܗ. ܘܟܠ
ܕܢܫܪܐ ܒܟܒܘܠܬܐ
ܡܩܕܫܬܐ. ܘܟܡܗ ܟܕܢܐ
ܐܡܪ ܠܗ̇ ܫܠܡ ܠܟܝ

f. 8 b col. b

ܒܪܝܟܬ ܒܢ̈ܫܐ ܗܐ
⌜ܐ⌝ܠܗܐ ܥܡܟܝ ܐܝܟ ܐܢܫ
ܢܐܡܪ ܕܗܐ ܡܩܕܡܟܝ
ܘܟܠ ܘܫܪܐ ܒܟܒܝܪܬ
ܗܕܡܝܟܝ ○ ܟ̈ܠܝܐ ܓܒܪ
ܫܪ⌜ܘ⌝ ܟܕ ܐܫܬܠܚ
ܡܫܝܚܐ ܠܒܪܣܗ̇
ܕܒܬܘܠܬܐ ܡܪܝܡ.
ܘܫܘܒܚܐ ܝܗܒܘ ܗܘܘ
ܠܐܠܗܐ ܕܓܒܐ ܒܚܘܒܗ
ܕܢܣܘܬ ܢܠܒܫ ܦܓܪܐ
ܕܐܕܡ ܡܣܟܢܘܬܐ.

f. 5 a col. b

ܗܠܝܢ ܐܡܪܬ ܠܗܘܢ
ܪܘܚܐ ܕܩܘܕܫܐ
ܠܫ̈ܠܝܚܐ ܕܟܢܫ ܒܢܝܫܝܢ
ܐܣܬܒܪܬ ܒܬܘܠܬܐ
ܡܩܕܫܬܐ ܕܡܩܒܠܐ
ܠܡܪܒܘ. ܘܗܘܐ

cf. Cod. Harris f. 209 b

ܒܪܘܚܗ̇ ܟܕܡܐ ܠܟܠܘ
[1]ܐܚܪ⌜ܝ⌝، ⌜ܘ⌝ܒܟܠܗ ܒܟܠܘ
[2]ܐܚܪܝ، ܒܥܬܐ ܒܗ
ܒܫܕ ܒܥܒܐ ܘܡܩܐ
ܡܩܥܐ ܒܒܬܘܠܘܬܗ̇
ܒܟܢܝܐ ܕܬܥܒܕ ⌜ܡܫ̈⌝ܝܚܝܢ

---

[1] Cod. Harris ܒܡܣܪܐ

[2] Cod. Harris ܡܩܒܐ

ܗܘܬ ܠܒܢܝܢܘܬܐ ܕܚܝܐ f. 8a col. a cf. Cod. Harris f. 208 a l. 4
ܒ̈ܢܝ ܐܢܫܐ ܕܐܒܝܕܝܢ
ܗܘܘ ܚܝܐ ܡܫܘ̈ܕܥܐ.
ܪܗܛܝܢ ܗܘܘ ܘܡܬܦܪ̈ܫܝܢ
ܠܗܘܢ ܕܐܢ ܟܠܝܢ ܐܢܬܘܢ
ܕܡܪܝܡ ܐܫܠܡܬܘܢ
ܗܪܟܐ ܡܬܝܢ ܐܢܬܘܢ.
ܡܛܠ ܕܣܟܠ ܚܘܢ ܗܘܘ
ܠܗ̇ ܡܫܘ̈ܕܥܐ ܠܡܪܬܝ,
ܡܪܝܡ ○ ○ ○
ܟܘܠ ܐܢܫܐ ܒܪ ܕܡܢܟ. cf. J. S. L. p. ܠܗ, l. 12
ܠܐܠܗܐ ܘܠܡܪܬܝ, ܡܪܝܡ
ܕܐܝܠܕܬܗ. ܢܒܪܐ
ܘܪܚܡܐ ܠܝܡܘ̈ܕܝܐ ܠܐ f. 5 b col. a
ܢܗܘܐ. ܕܐܦ ܗܘܐ.
ܦܪܝܩ ܗܘ ܚܘܒܗ
ܕܡܫܝܚܐ ܡܢܗ ○ ○
ܫܠܡ ܫܦܝܪܐ ܕܝܠܕܬܐ
○ ○ ○ ○ ○
ܫܦܝܪܐ ܕܐܪܒܥܐ
ܘܒܪ ܬ̈ܠܝܬܐ ܡܫܡܫܝܢ
ܚܠܦܝܗ̇ ܕܦܠܚܢܘܬܐ ܒܟܘ
ܡܪܬܐ ܐܘܕܥܬ ܐܢܘܢ

f. 8 a col. b ܪܘܚܐ ܕܩܘܕܫܐ
ܕܒ̈ܢܝܢܫܐ ܕܐܫܬܐ
ܐܫܬܠܚ ܗܘܐ ܠܒܪܢܫܐ
ܡܠܐܟܐ ܠܘܬ ܐܡܗ
ܕܪܒܘܢ ܡܪܬܝ, ܡܪܝܡ.
ܘܣܒ ܠܗ̇ ܫܠܡܐ
cf. J. S. L. v. 7, p. ܠܗ ܘܡܒܪܗ̇ ܡܛܠ ܗܘ
ܠܒܪܐ ܘܩܕܝܫܐ ܕܐܬܝܠܕ
ܡܢܗ̇ ܠܦܘܪܩܢܗ ܕܥܠܡܐ.
ܘܪܘܚܐ ܕܫܬܐ ܢܦܫܢ
ܐܬܘܗܝ, ܒܢܝܫ ܒܢܝܫܢ
ܒܢܘܡܐ ܕܢܫܝ ܒܫܒܐ
ܕܝ ܠܬܒܐ ܡܪܬܝ, ܡܪܝܡ
ܘܫܢܝܡܝܢ ܘܕܡܝܢܗ̇
ܢܘ̈ܒܢܐ ܕܐ̈ܦܝ ܬܪܒܐ
f. 5 b col. b ܕܒܒܕܐ ܗܘܬ ܠܒܢܬܗ
ܕܡܪܝܐ. ܘܠܒ̈ܢܝܐ ܗܘܬ
ܘܕܝܫܐ ܗܕܐ ܒܐܝܕܗ̇
ܘܬܒܐ ܒܒܢܬܗ̇. ܗܘܐ
ܪܡܝܐ ܒܢܬ ܐܒܐ
ܠܝܠܕܗ. ܘܫܠܝܚ ܠܒܪܗ̇
ܡܢ ܒܘܒܗ̇ ܕܢܐܬܐ
cf. Cod. Harris f. 209 a ܢܦܪܘܩ ܒܪ̈ܢܬܐ ܘܫܕܪ
ܐܠܗܐ ܠܓܒܪܐܝܠ
ܕܢܐܬܐ ܘܫܡ ܒܪ ܡܠܟܐ

ܘܕܫ̈ܠܝܚܐ ܬܠܬܐ ܐܢܫ̈ܝܢ ܘܬܠܬܐ ܢ̈ܫܐ. ܘܟܕ ܗܘܝܢ ܡܨ̈ܕܝܐ
ܡܫܒܚܝܢ ܠܡܪܢ ܘܠܐ ܐܫܟܚܘ ܐܢܘܢ. ܙܘܥܐ ܕܡܘܕܥܢܐ
ܚܙܘ ܒܢܝ̈ܢܫܐ ܕܠܐ ܢܣܒܘܢ ܠܬܠܡܝ̈ܕܐ ܘܠܡܪܝܡ ܘܐܬܘ
ܢܘܗܪܐ ܘܐܬܘ ܥܠ ܬܪܥܐ ܕܡܥܪܬܐ ܗܝ، ܟܕ ܠܐ ܢܕܥܝܢ.
ܗܘܘ ܡܫܬܐܠܝܢ ܚܕ ܥܡ ܚܕ. ܙܒܢܐ ܟܢ ܕܢܘܗܪܐ ܡܒܗܐ
ܐܢܘܢ. ܘܬܪܥܐ ܕܡܥܪܬܐ ܐܬܦܬܚ ܡܢ ܩܕܡܝܗܘܢ. ܘܥܠܘ
ܟܗܢܐ ܕܗܝܟܠܐ ܘܡ̈ܠܐܟܐ ܘܫ̈ܠܝܚܐ ܕܡܢܗܝܢ ܟܕ ܡܫܡܫܝܢ.
ܘܢܫ̈ܝܐ ܩ̈ܕܝܫܬܐ ܐܝܟ ܗܘܐ ܬܡܢ. ܘܐܡܪܝܢ ܬܠܬܐ
ܡܢܗܘܢ ܘܩܠܘ ܠܗܘܢ ܫ̈ܠܝܚܐ ܠܟܘ ܡܪܬܐ. ܘܟܕ ܟܠܗ
ܐܬܟܢܫܘ ܢܘܗܪܐ ܕܢܦܩܐ ܗܘܬ ܬܡܢ ܘܐܬܩܪܒܘܢ. ܘܐܬܪܟܢ f. 207 b
ܒܠܚܘܕ ܠܫ̈ܠܝܚܐ. ܘܐܡܪܘ ܣܓܕܘܗܝ ܕܬܠܝܢ ܕܡܛܐ ܢܚܙܘܢ
ܡܠܐ. ܥܠ ܕܐܝܟܘ ܡܢܢ ܕܗܘܐ. ܘܐܡܪ ܠܗ. ܘܫܢܝܢ ܗܘܘ
ܘܫܡ ܠܡܪܝܡ. ܠܡ̈ܠܐܟܐ ܘܠܫ̈ܠܝܚܐ ܕܡܫܡܫܝܢ ܗܘܘ ܩܕܡܝܗ.
ܘܡܢ ܕܐܡܪܘ ܒܢ̈ܬܐ ܬܠܬܐ ܗܠܝܢ. ܐܬܪܐ ܩܕܝܫܐ ܗܘܐ ܗܘ̈ܢܐ
ܕܡܪܝܡ ܘܒܢ̈ܬܐ ܕܟܠܗܝܢ. ܘܡܛܘ ܒܗܘܢܐ ܥܘܗܕܢܐ ܩܕܝܫܐ
ܠܒܢ̈ܬܐ ܕܐܘܠܝܐ ܠܗܟܝܢ ܕܠܐ ܢܚܠܘܢ ܠܒܝܬ ܐܒܐ ܕܡܪܢܝܬ
ܡܢܗܘܢ ܐܒܐ ܗܟܝܢ. ܘܐܢ ܢܚܠܘܢ ܒܠܗ ܚܡܫܐ ܝܘܡܐ
ܠܗ ܒܬܪ ܡܪܝܡ ܘܒܢܬܗ. ܘܟܕ ܫܡܥܘܢ ܕܡܪܝܡ ܗܝ، ܙܟܝܐ
ܡܪܝܡ ܠܗܘܢ ܐܠܗܐ ܐܠܐ ܐܡܪܘ ܕܠܐ ܢܚܝܢ ܗܠܝܢ ܒܢ̈ܬܐ
ܠܐܢܫܐ ܐܘܠܝܐ ܡܢ ܚܫܝܢ. ܐܡܪܘ ܗܠܝܢ ܒܢ̈ܬܐ ܗܟܢܐ.
ܐܝܟ ܕܐܡܪ ܠܗܘܢ ܬܪܝ ܒܗ̈ܢܐ. ܐܝܟ ܗܘܐ ܠܗܘܢ ܒܪܬܐ ܕܟܠ
ܐܡܬ، ܒܪ ܕܐܙܠ ܗܘܐ ܚܕ ܡܢ ܩܕ̈ܝܫܐ ܠܘܬ ܢܦܫܬ ܐܠܗܐ.
ܘܡܬܒܝܠ ܗܘܐ ܢܗܝܪ ܗܘܘ ܠܗ ܡܘܫܒܐ ܘܐܬܩܢܝܢ ܠܗ. f. 208 a
ܕܠܐ ܬܐܡܪ ܕܡܪܝܡ ܐܚܠܬܗ. ܐܠܐ ܐܡܪ ܕܒܗ̈ܢܐ
ܗܢܘ ܒܠܗ ܐܘܪܚܬܐ ܘܐܬܢܚܬܗ. ܘܟܠ ܐܫܘܬܐ ܕܗܟܢܐ

ܠܬܪܥܐ ܕܐܘܪܫܠܡ. ܘܟܢܫܗ ܠܗܘ ܚܘܛܪܐ ܢܦܫܐ.
ܠܐܣܟܘܦܬܐ ܕܬܪܥܐ ܕܡܕܢܚܐ. ܘܟܕ ܥܒܕܬܗ ܐܦܘܕ
ܦܛ̈ܪܐ. ܘܥܒܕܐ ܗܘܐ ܡܦܝܣܢܐ ܘܐܡܪ ܒܪܝܟ ܗܘ ܡܫܝܚܐ
ܕܐܬܬܠܝ ܡܢ ܒܬܘܠܬܐ ܡܪܝܡ. ܐܬܚܙܝ ܠܗ ܡܘ̈ܪܝܐ ܡܢܝܐ
ܒܚܙܘܢ. ܐܡܪ ܠܗܘܢ ܡܦܝܣܢܐ ܐܢܐ ܐܬܬܠܡܕܬ ܠܡܫܘܒ
ܡܥܒܝܢܐ ܒܪܗ ܕܐܠܗܐ ܡܫܒܚܐ. ܘܠܡܪܝܡ ܐܡܗ ܕܝܠܕܬܗ
ܕܐܬܦܫܩܘ ܕܪ̈ܒܐ ܬܪܥܘܗܝ ܘܐܬܬܠܝܘ ܒܒܪܫܐ
ܐܝܟ ܢܩܠܐ ܘܟܬܢܬ ܐܝܟ ܡܢ ܡܪܝܡ. ܘܫܒܩܬ ܐܝܟ ܠܝ. f. 206 b
ܘܡܙܝܢܐ ܕܫܬܒܩܬ. ܐܬܬܦܝܘ ܕܪ̈ܒܐ ܘܐܬܬܩܠܬ. ܘܫܒܩܬ
ܠܝ ܚܘܛܪܐ ܡܢ ܝܕܝܐ ܘܗܘܐ ܢܘܚ ܐܝܬܘܗܝ ܠܗ ܕܐܦܘܕ
ܦܛ̈ܪܐ. ܘܐܢܐ ܡܫܬܝܫܢ ܐܢܐ ܒܗ. ܕܗܘ ܝܠܕܬ ܐܠܗܐ.
ܐܬܚܙܝ ܠܗ ܡܘ̈ܪܝܐ ܡܕܝܢܐ ܥܢܝܬ ܐܢ ܡܦܝܣܢܐ. ܐܡܪ ܠܗܘܢ cf. Wright,
ܐ ܡܕܝܢܐ ܥܢܝܬ ܘܐܦ ܠܐ. ܬܘ ܚܙܘ ܡܢܐ ܒܟܕ ܚܘܛܪܐ p. ܡܛ
ܡܕܝܢܐ ܗܘ ܕܐܦܘܕ. ܐܬܚܙܝ ܠܗ ܡܘ̈ܪܝܐ ܡܢܐ ܟܕ.
ܐܡܪ ܠܗܘܢ ܦܛܪܘܣ ܐܚܪ ܠܝ ܒܪ ܣܘܟ ܠܝ ܚܘܛܪܐ
ܗܢܐ. ܕܟܠ ܐܢܫܐ ܒܪܝܫܐ ܕܡܣܒ ܐܝܬ ܠܗ ܘܩܐܡ ܐܢܬ
ܓܠܗ، ܠܚܘܛܪܐ ܗܢܐ ܡܬܝܠܡ. ܘܓܠ ܠܘܬ ܦܘܩܕܢܐ ܕܓܒ
ܒܪܝܟ ܐܡܪܗ. ܘܫܡܥܘ ܠܗܘ ܚܘܛܪܐ ܟܠ ܚܝ̈ܠܘܗܝ، ܕܗܘ
ܦܘܩܕܢܐ ܘܡܚܘܝܐ ܐܬܦܩܚܘ ܘܐܘܪ، ܗܘܐ ܒܡܥܒܝܢܐ. ܘܟܠ
ܕܒܪܗ ܗܘܐ ܘܫܐܡ ܗܘܐ ܓܠܗ، ܐܝܕܐ ܡܚܘܝܐ ܡܬܝܠܡ
ܗܘܐ. ܘܡܬܦܫܪ ܗܘܐ ܕܫܝܢܐ ܗܘܐ ܕܟܐܒܐ ܠܗܘܢ ܕܢܫܒܘܢ.
ܒܪܝܟܐ ܗܘ، ܡܪܝܡ ܘܒܪܝܟ ܗܘ ܡܥܒܝܢܐ ܕܐܬܬܠܝ ܡܢܗ. f. 207 a
ܘܡܬܐܡܪ ܗܘܐ ܡܦܝܣܢܐ. ܘܡܬܬܒܪܝܟ ܗܘܐ ܒܠ ܦܠܓܘܢ
ܕܪ̈ܒܗܐ. ܘܐܠܗܐ ܒܐܝܕܗ ܡܒܕܪ ܗܘܐ ܠܗܘܢ. ܘܟܕ ܡܓܠܝ
ܥܠܝܡܐ ܠܦܘܠܝܢ ܡܬܕܪܐ ܕܗܘܐ ܦܪܫ ܢܫܬܐ. ܒܡܫ ܡܕܢܝܚܬܐ
ܦܫܝܩܘܬܗ ܠܬܠܬ ܐܠܗܐ. ܘܦܪܨܘܦ ܒܠܘܬ ܬܫܡܫܬ ܕܩܠܝܠܐ

ܠܡܪܝܡ ܘܐܙܠܬ. ܗܝ، ܠܦܓܥܬܐ ܫܪܝܪܐ ܗܘܬ ܘܪܚܡܬܗ ܡܥܝ̈ܪܐ Codex Harris f. 205 a l. 12
ܠܫܡܝ̈ܐ ܘܐܡܪܝܢ ܗܘܘ. ܗܘܐ ܡܒܪܟܬ ܠܗ ܡܪܝܡ ܕܒܬܘܠܬܐ
ܘܐܙܠܬ ܡܢ ܐܘܪܫܠܡ: ܘܐܝܟ ܗܘܐ ܬܠܬܝܢ ܚܕ ܠܒܪܐ
ܕܛܘܪܐ ܗܘܐ ܡܘܫܐ ܠܒܪܐ ܘܪܡ ܗܘܐ ܘܫܒܝܚ
ܒܫܡܫܬܗ ܐܡܪ ܠܗ ܡܠܐܟܐ ܕܐܫܬܐܠ ܘܢܦܩ. ܝܘܣܦ ܢܓܪܐ f. 205 b
⌜ܘܦܓܥ⌝ ܒܡܪܝܡ ܘܫܐܠ ܠܗ̇ ܡܢ ܒܥܘܬܐ. ܕܗܐ ܒܪ ܫܒܥܬ
ܠܗ̇ ܘܠܬܠܡܝܕܘܗܝ، ܕܗܘ ܡܠܦܢܐ ܕܒܐܘܘܗ̇ ܠܐܘܪܫܠܡ.
ܘܐܡܪ ܝܘܣܦ ܚܙܐ ܕܐ̈ܒܗܘܗܝ، ܬܐܪܝܘ̈ܗܝ ܟܠ ܒܥܘܬܗ̇ ܕܡܪܝܡ
ܘܡܠܐܟܐ ܕܓܒܪܐ ܡܫܝܚܐ، ܟܦܢܐ ܕܠܘܬܐ ܘܐܬܦܫܛܘ
ܕܐ̈ܒܗܘܗܝ، ܬܐܪܝܘ̈ܗܝ ܡܢ ܥܢܘܬܗ̇. ܘܦܫܛ ܕܐ̈ܒܗܘܗܝ، ܒܒܥܘܬܐ
ܐܝܟ ܚܢ̈ܢܐ ܘܚܒܐ ܗܘܐ ܘܡܠܠ ܘܐܬܐ ܟܬܒ ܫܠ̈ܝܚܐ
ܘܦܬܚܐ ܘܐܡܪ ܫܠ̈ܝܚܐ ܕܝܫܘܥ. ܡܫܝܚܐ ܐܬܪܚܡ ܥܠܝ.
ܐܡܪܝܢ ܠܗ ܫܠ̈ܝܚܐ ܠܝܘܚܢܢ. ܠܡܪܝܐ ܦܪܐ ܐܢܬ ܓܝܪ. ܘܐܙܠ
ܠܡܪܝܡ ܐܡܗ ܕܡܫܝܚܐ. ܗܝ ܕܓܒܝܬ ܕܬܬܟܪܙ ܒܥܘܗ̇.
ܐܡܪ ܝܘܚܢܢ ܠܐܬܬ ܐܠܗܐ ܐܬܪܘܡܝ[1] ܥܠܝ. ܗܝܕܝܢ ܐܓܪܬ cf. Wright, p. ܚܝ
ܡܪܝܡ ܠܦܛܪܘܣ. ܘܒܝ ܠܗ ܕܐ̈ܒܗܘܗܝ، ܠܝܘܚܢܢ ܡܢ ܓܘܫܐ.
ܘܡܢܐ ܕܕܒܪ ܠܝ ܡܫܝܚܘ. ܐܡܪ ܗܘܐ ܕܒܫܡܗ ܕܡܪܝ، ܘܐܦ
ܕܡܪܝܡ ܝܠܕܬ ܐܠܗܐ ܕܒܪ ܠܝܘܚܢܢ. ܘܡܢ ܟܬܒ ܕܕܒܪ cf. J. S. L. p. ܠܗ
ܐܝܟ ܕ̈ܐܒܐ ܠܝܘܚܢܢܬܗܘܢ. ܫܦܠ ܦܛܪܘܣ ܚܒܪܐ ܡܫܒܚܐ f. 206 a
ܘܝܗܒܗ ܠܗ ܠܝܘܚܢܢ ܘܐܡܪ ܠܗ. ܐܦ ܝܗܘܐ ܚܝܠܗ ܕܐܠܗܐ
ܠܟܠܗܘܢ ܡܫܝܚܐ ܒܪܐ ܒܫܡܝܢ. ܐܡܪܝܐ ܠܗ ܡܪܝܡ ܠܡܪܝܐ
ܒܕܒܪܬ ܗ̇ܕܐ. ܘܒܥܐ ܠܗ ܝܘܚܢܢ ܕܫܠ ܒܠ ܒܥܘܬܗ̇ ܘܐܦ
ܡܫܝܚܐ ܠܗ̇ ܘܐܡܪ ܟܠܐ ܐܝܟܐ ܡܢܟܝ ܝܠܕܬ ܐܠܗܐ ܒܠܝ.
ܟܠ ܘܐܙܠ ܐܟܘ ܢܬܝܚܝܢ ܒܫܡܝܐ ܕܝܘܕܝܐ. ܘܐܬܦܢܝ ܒܐܘܠܦ
ܕܟܦܢܝܢ ܒܢܠܐܟ ܩܕܝܫܐ ܝܠܕܬ ܐܠܗܐ. ܘܐܙܠ ܝܘܚܢܢ ܘܫܠܚܐ

[1] Cod. ܐܬܪܘܡܝ

ܘܢܦܠ ܡܢܗ ܒܢܫܐ f. 7 b col. a
ܗܘ ܘܐܒܕ. ܘܡܢ ܕܐܙܠ
ܦܪܘܩܐ ܫܟܝܢܐ ܢܬܒ
ܕܢܠܒܫ ܠܚܘܒܐ. ܘܗܦܟ
ܗܘܐ ܡܫܘܗ̈ܝ، ܘܒܢܘܗܝ،
ܗܘܐ ܠܒܢܫܐ ܗ̇ܘ
ܘܠܐ ܐܫܬܡܗ. ܘܒܒܐ
ܗܘܐ ܘܡܝܠܠ ܘܐܬܐ
ܒܐܘܪܚܐ ܘܡܢܓܠܐ
ܘܐܡܪ. ܡܪܬܝ، ܡܪܝܡ
ܐܬܪܚܡܝ[1] ܥܠܝ. ܗܝܕܝܢ
ܡܪܬܝ، ܡܪܝܡ ܐܬܪܚܡܬ
ܥܠܘܗܝ، ܘܕܒܪܬܗ
ܘܐܘܒܠܬܗ ܥܠ ܒܢܫܐ f. 6 a col. a
ܗܘ ܕܕܢܝܪ̈ܐ ܘܫܘܠ
ܕܠܗ ܘܠܐ ܐܘܒܕ ܡܢܗ
ܡܕܡ. ܘܒܕ ܗܠܝܢ ܚܝ̈ܠܐ
ܥܒܪܬ ܡܪܬܝ، ܡܪܝܡ
ܒܪܘܡܐ ܘܒܐܬܘ̈ܬܐ
ܠܗܘܢ ܥ̈ܠܝܡܐ ܕܐܝܟ ܗ̇ܝ
ܗܘܘ ܒܐܘܪܫܠܡ ○ ○ ○
ܘܒܕ ܥ̈ܠܝܡܐ ܘܡܪܬܝ،
ܡܪܝܡ ܐܬܚܙܝܘܢ ܗܘܘ
ܒܐܘܪܫܠܡ ܘܢܓܗܐ
ܗܘܬ ܒܪܘܒܬܐ ܐܡܪܬ cf. Cod. Harris f. 205 a

f. 7 b col. b ܠܗܘܢ ܪܘܚܐ ܕܩܘܕܫܐ
ܕܡܢܗ ܒܝܩܪܐ ܠܦܘܢܝܗ̇
ܠܡܪܬܝ، ܡܪܝܡ ܘܩܦܘ
ܡܢ ܐܘܪܫܠܡ ܒܐܘܪܚܐ
ܕܩܦܐ ܠܓܘ ܢܫܠܐ.
ܕܠܒܐ ܡܢ ܦܘܪ ܙܢ̈ܬܐ
ܗܐ ܐܝܬ ܒܗ ܬܠܬ
ܡܕ̈ܝܢ. ܡܕܝܢܬܐ ܪܒܬܐ
ܒܪܬܐ ܘܡܕܝܢܬܐ
ܐܚܪܬܐ ܠܓܘ ܡܢܗ̇.
ܘܡܕܝܢܬܐ ܕܒܘܪܬܐ
ܓܘܢܬܐ. ܘܡܬܦܦܬܐ
ܕܦܝܠܐ ܡܢ ܡܕܝܢܐ
f. 6 a col. b ܘܐܬܠܘ ܫܝܒܘܗ̇
ܠܦܘܢܝܬܐ ܥܠ ܗ̇ܝ،
ܡܬܦܦܬܐ[2] ܘܫܡܫܘ
ܥܠܝܗ̇ ܒܥܡܐ ܕܐܡܪ
ܠܗܘܢ. ܘܥܕܡܘ ܒܝܩܪܐ
cf. J. S. L. p. ܠܗ ܘܡܫܘ ܥ̈ܠܝܡܐ ܘܫܦܠܘ[3]
ܠܦܘܢܝܬܐ ܘܢܦܩܘ
ܡܢ ܐܘܪܫܠܡ. ܘܫܗ̈ܕܝܐ
ܢܣܒܝܢ ܗܘܘ ܘܡܫܒܚܝܢ
ܘܐܡܪܝܢ ܠܫܕ̈ܐ. ܗܐ
ܬܠܡܝ̈ܕܘܗܝ، ܕܗ̇ܘ
ܡܦܝܣܐ ܠܦܢܝܢ ܠܗ̇

[1] Cod. ܐܬܪܚܡ [2] Cod. ܡܬܦܦܬܐ [3] Cod. ܘܫܦܠ

ܘܐܬܬܢܝܚܬ ܗܪܟܐ f. 7a col. a
ܒܪܗܘܡܐ ܠܓܒܪܐ
ܚܕ ܕܒܪܝܗ ܗܘܐ
ܐܬܬܟܣܪܐ ܫܪܝܢ ܘܠܐ
ܐܬܥܒܝܘ ܐܣܘܬܐ
ܕܠܒܪܘܢܝܗ ܡܕܡ
ܒܗܢܐ ܟܠܗ ܢܘܓܪܐ
ܕܫ̈ܢܝܐ ܀ ܗܝܕܝܢ ܐܝܬܝ
ܦܪܝܫܐ ܘܐܡܪܬ ܒܗ
ܒܩ̈ܠܐ ܘܐܬܕܒܪܬ݀
ܠܦܘܠܚܢܬܐ ܘܐܡܪܬ.
ܡܪܬܝ ܡܪܝܡ ܠܝܬ
ܐܠܗܐ ⌜ܐܣܝܢ⌝ܝ.

f. 7a col. b ܛܠ̈ܠܐ ܕܢܗܪܐ ܘܦܠܚܝܢܐ
ܗܘܬ ܢܦܫܬܐ ܕܒܢܝܢܫܐ
ܕܢܦ⌜̈⌝ܠܐ ܠܢܫܐ ܘܠܫܓܝܐܐ
ܦܓܝܬ ܘܠܐ ܚܣܪܘ ܀
cf. J. S. L. p. ܠܚ, l. 11 ܘܬܘܒ ܐܬܚܙܝܬ
ܠܬܪ̇ܬܝܢ ܢܫ̈ܝܢ ܒܐܪܒܥܐ
ܕܡܓܪܝܢ ܒܗ ܐܘܠܝܢ ܗܘܝ
cf. Cod. Harris f. 204 b ܒܐܘܪܚܐ ܘܢܦܩ ܚܘܝܐ
ܚܕ ܪܒܐ ܠܡܘܠܟܗܘܢ
ܘܪܗܛ ܒܬܪܗܘܢ ܕܢܒܠܥ
ܐܢܝܢ. ܘܩܪܝ ܒܫܡܗ̇
ܕܦܘܠܚܢܬܐ ܡܪܬܝ
ܡܪܝܡ. ⌜ܗܝܕܝܢ⌝ ⌜ܐܬܚܝ⌝ܢܬ

ܘܡܚܝܢܐ ܐܬܬ f. 6b col. a
ܠܐܕܘܗܝ ܘܐܣܝܬܗ
ܘܫܕܪܬܗ ܠܒܝܬܐ
ܕܪܗܘܡܐ ܦܓܪ ܟܠܗ
ܒܫܡܐ ܀ ܘܬܘܒ
ܐܬܚܙܝܬ ܕܐܬܬܒܪܬ
ܐܠܦܐ ܘܢܦܠܘ ܐܢܫܐ
ܫܓܝܐܐ ܕܐܝܬ ⌜⌝ ܗܘܐ
ܒܗ ܒܓܘ ܝܡܐ.
ܘܐܬܚܙܝܬ ܡܪܬܝ
ܡܪܝܡ ܕܗܪܟܐ ܟܠ

f. 6b col. b ܠܗܘܢ ܡܪܬܝ ܡܪܝܡ
ܘܡܚ⌜̈⌝ܝܬܗ ܠܚܘܒܐ ܗܘ
ܟܠ ܦܘܡܗ ⌜⌝ܘܐܓܪܬܝ
ܠܬܪ̈ܝܢ ܘܐܬܦܨܝ ܢܫ̈ܐ
ܗܠܝܢ ܘܠܐ ܐܒܕܝ܀
ܘܬܘܒ ܐܬܚܙܝܬ
cf. J. S. L. p. ܠܚ, l. 2 ܗܪܟܐ ܠܓܒܪܐ ܚܕ
ܬܓܪܐ ܕܐܒܝܕ ܐܠܦ
ܕܡܠܝ̈ܢ ܘܐܙܠ ܕܢܬܬܓܪ
ܒܗܘ ܒܐܬܪܐ ⌜ܚܪ⌝ܢܐ.
ܘܗܘ ܐܙܠ ܒܐܘܪܚܐ

ܕ⸢ܐܝܟܢܐ⸣ ܡܒܕܪܐ f. 124 b col. a
ܠܒܘܫ̈ܬܐ ܕܦܪܝܫ ܠܗ̇
ܘܡܫܡܫܝܢ ܩܘܪܒܐ
ܒܗ̈ܘܡܐ ܦܫܝܛ
ܡܬܚܢܢܐ ܠܒܪܝ̈ܬܐ
ܕܡܘܕܝܢ ܒܫܠܘܬܗ̇
ܐܬܚܢܢܬ ܠܒܪ ܩܘܪܒܐ
ܒܫܒܝܐ ܕܐܫܬܠܛ ܘܒܙ. cf. Wright p. ܟܗ
ܘܐܙܠ ܕܢܣܒܠ ܐ̱ܠܦܐ
ܕܪ̈ܕܝܢ ܒܗ̇. ܘܦܪܘ
ܐܠܦ̈ܝܐ ܒܫܡܗ̇ ܕܡܪܬܝ,
ܡܪܝܡ. ܘܐܡܪܘ ܡܪܬܝ,
ܡܪܝܡ ܝܠܕܬ ܐܠܗܐ
ܐܬܪܚܡܝ¹ ܥܠܝܢ. ܘܒܪ f. 131 a col. a
ܫܥܬܗ ܕܢܫܬ ܥܠܝܗܘܢ
ܐܝܟ ܫܡܫܐ ܘܦܓܪܬ
ܐܝܢ ܠܐܠܦܐ ܗܠܝܢ
ܕܗܘܝܢ ܗܘ̇ ܬܫܥܝܢ
ܘܬܪܬܝܢ ܐܠܦܝܢ. ܘܦܪܩܬ
ܐܢܝܢ ܡܢ ܫܒܝܐ. ܘܠܐ
ܐܚܕ ܡܢܗܝܢ ܡܕܡ.
ܘܬܘܒ ܐܬܚܙܝܬ
ܒܐܣܟܡܐ ܒܦܘܪܐ
ܕܢܦܠܘ ܟܘܡܐ ܥܠ ܐܢܫܝܢ.

f. 124 b col. b ܘܥܒܕ ܕܢܦܠܘܢ ܐܝܟܢ.
ܘܩܒܠܘ ܗܠܝܢ ܐܢܫܐ
ܘܐܡܪܝܢ. ܡܪܬܝ, ܡܪܝܡ
ܝܠܕܬ ܐܠܗܐ ܐܬܪܚܡܝ¹
ܥܠܝܢ. ܘܐܬܚܙܝܬ
ܥܠܝܗܘܢ ܐܝܟ ܒܪܩܐ
ܕܢܘܗܪܐ ܘܥܒܪܬ
ܒܝܢܬܗܘܢ ܕܟܘܡܐ. ܘܠܐ
ܐܬܚܙܝ ܠܗܘܢ. ܘܠܐ
ܗܘܐ ܠܗܘܢ ܚܒܠܐ.
ܘܐܬܚܙܝܬ ܗܪܟܐ
ܠܐܢܬܬܐ ܐܪܡܠܬܐ
ܕܐܙܠ ܒܪܗ ܐܣܝܪ
⸢ܠܒܐܪܐ ܕܡܝܐ⸣ ܘܢܦܠ
f. 131 a col. b ܒܗ ܘܠܝܬ ܗܘܐ ܐܢܫܐ
cf. Cod. Harris f. 204 a ܠܡܦܩܘܬܗ ܕܢܣܩܘܢܝܗܝ,
ܘܐܝܠܠܬ ܐܡܗ ܗ̇ܝ,
ܥܠ ܦܘܡܗ ܕܒܐܪܐ.
ܘܐܡܪܬ ܡܪܬܝ, ܡܪܝܡ
ܝܠܕܬ ܐܠܗܐ ܐܬܪܚܡܝ¹
ܥܠܝ. ܘܒܗ̇ ܒܫܥܬܐ
ܐܬܚܙܝܬ ܠܗ̇ ܡܪܬܝ,
ܡܪܝܡ ܘܢܦܩܬܗ ܠܛܠܝܐ
ܘܗܘ ܕܠܐ ܐܬܚܙܝ
ܘܝܗܒܬܗ ܠܐܡܗ

○ ○ ○ ○ ○

¹ Cod. ܐܬܪܚܡ

M. D. G.

f. 124a col. a

ܒܡܠܟܐ. ܗܘܐ ܓܒܝܢ
ܠܒܪܝܬܐ ° ° ° °
ܒ.. ܗܘ ܫܡܥ ܡܪܬܝ،
ܡܪܝܡ. ܘܟܠ ܡܕܡ
ܦܝܫ ܠܗ ܐܝܟ ܠܒܪܗ.
ܡܫܡܘܢܐ ܕܝܢ ܐܫܬܪܝ،
ܘܠܘܩ ܡܢ ܐܘܪܫܠܡ
ܘܐܙܠ ܠܒܝܬܗ ܠܪܘܗܡܐ
ܡܕܝܢܬܐ ܡܓܠܠ ܕܡܢ
ܬܡܢ ܗܘܐ. ܘܟܕ ܐܙܠ
ܠܪܘܗܡܐ ܟܠ ܦܩܕ
ܡܠܟܐ ܘܦܩܕ ܙܘܪ̈ܒܢܐ
ܕܪܘܗܡܐ. ܘܐܫܬܡܥ
ܠܗܘܢ ܫ̈ܠܝܐ ܒܥܠܘܗܝ f. 131b col. a
ܘܬܕܡܪ̈ܬܐ ܕܥܒܕܬ
ܗܘܬ ܡܪܬܝ، ܡܪܝܡ
ܒܐܘܪܫܠܡ. ܘܫܡܥܬ ܠܗܡ.
ܘܐܝܟ ܐܦ ܬܠܡ̈ܝܕܘܗܝ
ܕܦܪܘܗ ܘܕܦܠܚܘܗ
ܕܐܝܬ ܗܘܘ ܠܗܘܢ
ܒܪܘܗܡܐ ܡܕܝܢܬܐ.
ܘܟܬܒܘ ܡܠܝܢ ܡ̈ܠܐ
ܘܕܝ̈ܢܬܐ ܕܫܡܥܘ ܡܢ
ܡܫܡܘܢܐ. ܘܟܬܒܘ

f. 124a col. b

ܠܗܘܢ ܬܠܡ̈ܝܕܘܗܝ
ܠܫ̈ܠܝܚܐ ܕܦܘܩܕܢܝܬܐ
ܡܢ ܦܘܡܗ ܕܗܘ
ܡܫܡܘܢܐ. ܘܟܬܒܘ
ܐܓܪܬܐ ܠܟܠܗ ܥܕܬܐ
ܠܦܘܪ ܣܢܝ ܘܠܐܓܒܦܘܣ
ܘܠܬܒܐܣ ܘܠܐܣܝܐ
ܘܠܥܦܘܣ. ܘܟܬܒܘ ܗܟܢܐ.
ܕܪܒ ܗܘ ܫܘܒܚܐ
ܕܝܗܒܬ ܒܗ ܡܪܬܝ، ܡܪܝܡ
ܡܢ ܟܠܡܐ ܗܢܐ ° °
ܘܟܬܒܘ ܠܗܘܢ ܬܠܡ̈ܝܕܘܗܝ
ܠܫ̈ܠܝܚܐ ܕܥܡܐ ܕܒܦܘܬܘܗ̇
ܠܦܘܩܕܢܝܬܐ ܕܟܬܒܐ
f. 131b col. b ܕܒܘܢܕܢܗ̇ ܕܐܝܟܢܐ
ܢܦܩܬ ܒܗ̇ ܡܢ ܟܠܡܐ
ܐܝܬܘܗ̇، ܒܡܫܟܘܢ.
ܡܛܠ ܕܗܘܐ ܡܠܝܢ ܟܠܗܝܢ
ܐܬܘ̈ܬܐ ܡܢ ܬܫܒܘܚܬܗ̇
ܕܦܘܩܕܢܝܬܐ. ܘܗܟܢ ܒܪ̈ܝܬܐ
cf. Cod. Harris f. 203 b ܕܟܝ̈ܢܐ ܘܕܢ̈ܘܚܐ ܕܠܝܬ
ܠܗܘܢ ܡܢܝܢܐ ܗܫܟܢܘ
ܒܗ̇ ܡܢ ܕܥܠ ܡܫܡܘܢܐ
ܕܐܝܬ ܗܘܐ ܒܐܘܪܫܠܡ
ܘܐܫܬܥܝ ܠܢ ܗܪܟܐ

ܡܢ ܥܠܡܐ ܗܘܐ ܗܘ f. 115 b col. a
ܘܒܢ̈ܝܐ ܕܡܠܐ̈ܟܐ
ܐܬܐ ܓܐܕܝ ܐܝܟ
ܕܒܢܫ ܠܬܠܡ̈ܝܕܘܗܝ
ܘܐܬܐ ܓܐܕܝ ܡܢ
ܐܬܪ̈ܘܬܗܘܢ ܡܢ
ܐܪܒܥ ܦܢ̈ܝܬܗ ܕܥܠܡܐ.
ܗܟܢ ܚܙܪܐ ܐܢܐ ܠܗ
ܕܐܬܐ ܓܐܕܝ ܡܢ
ܡܥܪܒܐ. ܘܚܙܝܐ ܐܢܐ
ܠܗ ܘܫܐܠ ܐܢ̈ܕܘܗܝ
ܥܠ ܚܢ̈ܢܝ ܘܡܦܩ ܠܗ
ܡܢ ܥܠܡܐ ܗܘܐ ܒܥܝܐ.
ܘܡܫܬܪ ܠܗ ܠܦܓܪ̈ܝ f. 1 a col. a
ܘܡܥܒܘܒ. ܠܪܘܚܝ ܐܝܟ
ܕܐܝܬ ܠܗ ܓܒܢ̈ܝܐ.
ܗܠܝܢ ܡ̈ܠܐ ܒܫܝ̈ܚܬܐ
ܐܡܪܬ ܡܪܬܝ ܡܪܝܡ
ܡܪܝܡ ܝ̈ܠܝܕܬܐ ܘܡܪܝܡ
ܗܓܡܘܢܐ ܕܐܬܬ
ܠܒܝܬܗ. ܘܩܡܬ ܠܗ
ܘܗܝܡܢ ܗܓܡܘܢܐ ܩܡܬ
ܒܡܪܬܝ ܡܪܝܡ. ܘܡܪܢ.
ܒܪܗ ܘܡܕ̈ܒܪܗ ܥܠ
ܐܦ̈ܘܗܝ ܥܠ ܐܪܥܐ
ܘܡܕܡ̈ܢ ܕܐܝܬ ܗܘܐ

ܠܗ ܒܟܐܒܐ ܡܪܝܪܐ f. 115 b col. b
ܘܐܘܡܝܗ̇ ܒܝܡܝܢܐ cf. Cod. Harris f. 203 a
ܘܐܡܪ ܠܗ̇ ܒܥܐ ܐܢܐ cf. Wright, p. ܡܗ, l. 1
ܡܢܟܝ ܕܠܝܬ ܐܠܗܐ
ܐܦܝ ܠܝ ܠܗܢܐ
ܫܝܢܝܕܐ ܕܝܗܒ. ܠܝ
ܐܠܗܐ. ܘܦܫܩܬ
ܐܝܕܝܗ̇ ܠܩܘܒܠܝܢܬܐ
ܘܚܡܬܗ ܠܩܠܝܠܐ
ܘܗ̇ ܗܘܒܢܐ ܐܡܪܬ
ܠܗ. ܒܫܡܗ ܕܪܒܘܠܝ
ܡܫܝܚܐ ܕܐܝܬ ܠܝ
ܒܫܡܝܐ ܐܬܐܣܐ.
ܘܡܚܝܕܐ ܐܬܚܠܡ f. 1 a col. b
ܩܠܝܠܐ ܗ̇ܘ ܒܫ̈ܠܘܬܗ̇
ܕܡܪܬܝ, ܡܪܝܡ. ܘܐܙܠ
ܗܓܡܘܢܐ ܠܒܝܬܗ
ܘܒܬܒ ܟܘܠ ܡܕܡ.
ܬܕܡܪ̈ܬܐ ܘܚܝ̈ܠܐ
ܘܐܫܘ̈ܬܐ ܕܥܒܕܐ
ܗܘܬ ܠܩܘܒܠܝܢܬܐ
ܒܥܠܡܐ. ܡܛܠ ܕܠܐ
ܒܥܬ ܡܕܡ ܠܡܚܝܢܐ
ܕܠܐ ܝܗܒ ܠܗ̇. ܡܛܠ
ܕܐܡܪܗ ܗ̇ܝ ܕܗܘܐ ܚܝ

ܡܛܠܠܐ ܕܗ̈ܝܡܢܘܬܐ ܡܦܩܢ f. 115 a col. a
ܗ̈ܘܝ، ܠܟܠܗ ܒܢܝܬܐ
ܕܝܬܒܐ ܗܘܬ ܒܗ.
ܘܡܢ ܒܬܪ ܫܠܡܐ
ܘܣܒܪܝܢ ܫܢܝ ܠܗ cf. Wright, p. ܟܒ
ܡܠܐܟܐ ܡܢ ܠܥܠ،
ܘܩܡܬ ܘܣܡܬ ܦܝܪܡܐ
ܕܒܣ̈ܡܐ ܠܐܠܗܐ.
ܘܨܠܝܬ ܥܠ ܐ̈ܦܝ
ܘܫܒܚܬ. ܫܡܐ ܕܦܪܘܩܘܬܗ
ܕܡܪܝܐ. ܕܢܚܬܬ
ܬܕܡܘܪܬܐ ܗܕܐ.
ܘܡܢ ܕܗܘܬ ܒܥܕܢܐ ܠܐ
ܫܒܩܝܢ. ܘܐܬܝܠܕ
ܡܢܝ ܐܝܟ ܕܟܬܝܒܐ ܐܝܟ f. 1 b col. a
ܒܪ ܐܢܫܐ. ܘܐܬܪܒܝ
ܐܝܟ ܟ̈ܠܗܝܢ ܐܢܫ
ܘܐܝܟ ܝܠܘܕܐ ܒܝܬ
ܫܘܒܐ ܘܐܝܟ ܫܒܪܐ
ܒܝܬ ܫܒܪ̈ܐ ܗܒܝܢܐ
ܐܬܪܒܝ ܘܚܝܐ،
ܐܬܬ̈ܐ ܘܡܒܒܝ
ܬܕܡܪ̈ܬܐ ܘܣܒܒܪ
ܚܝ̈ܠܐ. ܘܗܠܝܢ ܒܟܠܡܐ
ܐܝܟ ܐܠܗܐ. ܘܟܠܡܕܡ
ܕܐܡܪ ܠܝ ܥܪ ܘܫܠܡ.

f. 115 a col. b ܘܚܝܝܬ ܕܒܢ̈ܝܢܫܐ
cf. Wright, p. ܟܒ, l. 9 ܠܐ ܐܫܟܚܘ ܕܢܒܥܘܢ
ܬܡܝ̈ܗܬܐ ܕܥܒܕ.
ܘܐܚܕܘܗܝ، ܝ̈ܗܘܕܝܐ
ܘܨܠܒܘܗܝ، ܘܐܬܬܣܝܡ
ܒܩܒܪܐ ܬܠܬܐ ܝܘ̈ܡܝܢ.
ܘܢܚܡ ܗܘ ܠܢܦܫܗ.
cf. Cod. Harris f. 202 b ܘܩܡ ܘܐܬܚܙܝ،
ܠܟܠܗܘܢ ܬܠܡ̈ܝܕܘܗܝ،
ܒܪ ܣܒܪ ܬܕܡܪ̈ܬܐ
ܘܫ̈ܒܝܠܐ ܕܐܒܘܗܝ،
ܡܫܒܚܐ. ܘܣܠܩ
ܒܫܘܒܚܐ ܠܘܬ ܐܒܘܗܝ،
ܕܫܕܪܗ ܠܥܠ، ܘܐܦ
f. 1 b col. b ܝܗܘܕܝܐ ܠܐ ܡܗܝܡܢܝܢ
cf. Wright, p. ܟܒ, l. 14 ܒܗ ܐܝܟܐ ܘܕܝܘܩܐ
ܢܛܪܐ ܘܬܠܡ̈ܝܕܘܗܝ،
ܡܗܝܡܢܝܢ ܚܝܢ ܕܗܘܝܘ
ܝܫܘܥ ܡܪܢ ܡܫܝܚܐ
ܒܪܗ ܕܐܠܗܐ. ܘܐܫܪܬ
ܘܗܝܡܢܬ ܕܗܘܝܘ ܗܘ
ܕܐܬܐ ܘܬܒܥ ܠܕܡܗ
ܡܢ ܝܠܘܕܘܗܝ،. ܘܠܐ
ܐܡܪ ܠܝ ܘܦܩܕ. ܐܡܪܐ
ܦܘܩܝܢܬܐ ܕܡܪܐ ܕܦܓܪ،

f. 4 b col. a

ܥܠ ܪ̈ܓܠܝܗܘܢ ܕܥ̈ܠܝܡܐ.
ܘܐܡܪ ܠܗܘܢ. ܫܠܡܐ
ܒܟܒܘܢ ܒܬ̈ܝܐ ܕܒܝܢ
ܠܐܠܗܐ ܡܢ ܩܕܡ
ܒܚܠܡܐ. ܘܫܠܡܐ
ܠܡܫܝܚܐ ܕܟܒܒܘܢ
ܕܬܗܘܘܢ ܠܗ ܒ̈ܢܘܐ.
ܒܫܠܡܐ. ܐܡܪܝܢ ܠܗ
ܥ̈ܠܝܡܐ ܫܡܥܢ ܡܕܡ
ܕܒܒܕܬ ܠܛ̈ܠܘܒܐ ܘܫܠܛ
ܓܠܝܢ ܐܢܫܝܢ ܒܠܝܟ.
ܐܡܪ ܠܗܘܢ ܡܓܘܫܐ
ܫܒܩ ܠܗܘܢ ܒܗܬܬܐ
ܕܗܘܘ ܩܕܡ ܐܠܗܐ f. 9 a col. a
ܘܩܕܡ ܒ̈ܢܝ ܐܢܫܐ.
ܐܡܪܝܢ ܠܗ ܥ̈ܠܝܡܐ. cf. Cod. Harris f. 199 b, l. 14
ܘܡܪܢܐ ܒܒܪܘ ܕܠܐ
ܒܗܬܬܐ ܗܘܬ ܠܗܘܢ. cf. Wright, p. [illegible], l. 22
ܗܠܝܢ ܐܡܪܘ ܥ̈ܠܝܡܐ cf. Cod. Harris f. 201 b, l. 7
ܠܡܓܘܫܐ ܟܕ ܐܬܠ
ܫܠܡ ܠܗܘܢ ܘܠܡܪܬܝ cf. Wright, p. [illegible], l. 13
ܡܪܝܡ ܘܐܡܪ ܠܗ̇. cf. J. S. L. p. [illegible], l 13
ܒܒܢܐ ܡܕܒܪ ܡܪܬܝ
ܡܪܬܗ ܕܥܠܡܐ ܐܠܦ

f. 4 b col. b

ܡܢ ܒܬܘܠܘܬܟܝ ܘܒܬܘܠܘܬܟܝ
ܕܐܝܟܢܐ ܫܪܐ ܒܟܝ
ܐܠܗܐ. ܐܡܪܐ ܠܗ
ܡܪܝܡ ܠܡܓܘܫܐ.
ܫܡܥܘ ܘܩܒܠܘ ܡ̈ܠܝ
ܘܗܒܘ ܫܘܒܚܐ ܠܗܘ
ܕܝܠܕ ܠܝܫܘܥ ܡܢ
ܫܡܝܐ ܕܐܝܩܪܗ ܘܠܐ
ܡܕܡ ܡܢ ܐܝܟܐ ܥܠ
ܠܒܝܪܬ ܡ̈ܕܒܪ ܐܠܐ
ܟܕ ܡܬܟܐ ܐܢܐ ܒܒܝܬܝ
ܘܟܒܕܐ ܐܢܐ ܗ̈ܘܝ
ܬܪܒܐ ܕܡܘܠܐ ܕܐܠܗܐ
f. 9 a col. b cf. Cod. Harris f. 202 a ܒܝܕ ܒܥܒܕܐ ܒܬܒܝ
ܫܒܚܝܢ. ܦܪܚ ܡܠܐܟܐ
ܕܡܪܝܐ ܘܐܬܐ ܠܘܬܝ.
ܘܕܝܢ ܢܘܗܪܐ ܒܥܠܡܐ
ܒܢܬܐ ܕܢܛܒܬܐ ܗܘܬ
ܒܗ. ܘܗܟܢ ܐܡܪ ܠܝ.
ܫܠܡ ܠܟܝ ܡܒܪܟܬܐ ܒܢ̈ܫܐ.
ܡܪܝ، ܒܚܒܝ ܘܡܒܪܟܝ
ܕܢܝܫ ܘܡܫܝܚܐ ܪܝܫܐ
ܒܫܡܝܐ ܒܠܒܗ ܒܢܝܬܐ
ܕܐܢܬܐ ܗܘܬ ܒܗ.
ܘܗܟܝܢ ܐܫܘܝ ܕܒܝܬܐ

ܠܛܠܝܬܗ̇ ܒܒܝܬܗ ܐܡ̇ܪ f. 4 a col. a
ܠܗ̇ ܗܝܡܢܘܬܐ ܒܟܠ
ܐܡ̇ܪܝ، ܠܗ̇ ܠܡܪܬܝ،
ܡܪܝܡ ܕܗܝܡܢܘܬܐ
ܕܡܕܝܢܬܐ ܐܘܪܫܠܡ
ܟܕܐ ܕܢܫܟܚ ܠܗ. ܦܩܕܬ
ܕܝܢ ܡܪܬܝ، ܡܪܝܡ
ܕܢܦܬܚ ܠܗ ܬܪܥܐ.
ܘܟܠ ܘܒܪܢ ܫܟܪ ܠܗ̇
ܘܢܫܩ ܬ̈ܠܝܗ̇ ܘܩܒܐ
ܘܐܡܪ ܠܗ̇. ܫܠܡ ܠܟܝ
ܝܠܕܬ ܐܠܗܐ. ܘܫܠܡ ܠܗ
ܠܦܐܪܐ ܕܐܬܝܠܕ ܡܢܟܝ.
ܕܫܠܡ ܠܗܘܢ ܠܫܡܝܢܐ f. 9 b col. a
ܗܠܝܢ ܕܠܒܝܫܝܢ ܒܘܪܣܝܢܐ
ܕܐܠܗܘܬܗ ܕܒܪܟܝ
ܡܪܐ ܡܫܝܚܐ. ܕܡܢܟܝ
ܕܢܚ. ܘܚܘܪ ܗܘ ܦܘܡܐ
ܘܠܫܢܐ ܕܢܬܢܐ ܬܫܒܘܚܬܐ cf. Wright,
ܕܝܠܟܝ ܘܕܒܪܟܝ ܝܠܕܐ p. ܟܡ
ܩܕܝܫܐ. ○ ܐܪܒܐ
ܕܡܗܠܟܬܝ[1]، ܒܠܝܗ̇ ܫܡܝܐ
ܬܗܘܐ. ܫܡܝܐ ܕܚܝܐ
ܠܟܝ ܒܘܪܟܬܐ ܬܬܠܠ
ܠܒܪ̈ܬܐ ܕܡܗ̈ܝܡܢܝܢ ܒܟܝ.
ܘܠܝ̈ܕܐ ܕܚܝܝܢ ܠܟܝ

f. 4 a col. b ܢܣܒܘܢ ܚܕܘܬܐ. ܒܪ̈ܝܬܐ
ܕܐܬܝܢ ܠܐܝܕܟ ܬܬܠܝܢ
ܠܗܘܢ ܚܘܠܡܢܐ. ܫܟܪ
ܐܢܐ ܠܟܝ ܡܪܬܝ، ܡܪܝܡ.
ܦܫܘܩ ܡܚܢܟܝ ܘܒܪܟܝܢ
ܠܝ. ܘܠܗܢܐ ܚܫܝܕܐ ܕܐܝܬ
cf. Cod. Harris f. 199 b ܠܝ ܘܝܠܝ ܟܠ ܢܦ̈ܫܬܐ
ܕܐܝܬ ܠܝ ܒ̈ܪܗܘܡܐ
ܡܕܝܢܬܐ ܕܐܙܠ ܐܚܪܐ
ܐܢܝܢ ܒܫܠ̈ܡܐ ܘܐܦܠܝܢ
ܐܝܩܪܐ ܘܩܘܪ̈ܒܢܐ
ܘܐܬܐ ܐܫܟܘܕ ܠܟܝ.
ܡܪܬܝ، ܡܪܝܡ ܕܝܢ ܦܢܬܐ
ܗܘܬ ܘܡܣܝܒܐ ܘܫܝܡ
f. 9 b col. b ܦܬܓܡܐ ܕܒܫܡܝܐ ܒܐܝܕܗ.
ܘܟܕ ܫܡܥܬ ܡ̈ܠܘܗܝ،
cf. J. S. L. p. ܟܠ, l. 1 ܕܗܝܡܢܘܬܐ ܐܬܦܢܝܬ
ܘܩܡܬ ܘܦܫܛܬ ܐܝ̈ܕܝܗ̇
ܘܒܪܟܬܗ ܠܗ ܘܠܒܝܬܗ
ܘܐܡܪܬ ܠܗ ܕܬܬܒ ܠܟ
ܫܠܝܡܘܬ، ܕܝܢ ܕܡܪܝ
ܬܡܢ ܗܘܘ ܠܘܬܗ̇
ܕܦܘܩܕܢܐ ܒܗ ܒܒܝܬܐ.
ܘܒܕ ܐܡܪܬ ܠܗ ܠܗܝܡܢܘܬܐ
ܕܬܒ ܠܟ ܠܐ ܒܟܐ ܕܢܬܒ.
ܐܠܐ ܪܗܛ ܢܦܠ ܡܚܕܐ

[1] Wright ܕܡܗ̇ܠܟܐ ܐܢܬܝ

ܕܬܪܝܢ ܓܢ̈ܣܐ ܢܐܡܪܘܢ f. 39 b col. a
ܒܢܘܪܐ. ܘܠܒܢܝܗ ܕܝܫܘܥ
ܢܬܬܚܙܘܢ ܒܗܝܟܠܐ
ܕܐܘܪܫܠܡ. ܘܢܫܬܒܚ:
ܡܢ ܟܠܗܘܢ ܒܪ̈ܝܬܐ.
ܐܡܪ ܠܗܘܢ ܡܫܝܚܐ
ܠܐ ⌜ܦܫܛ⌝ ܐܢܐ ܡܢ
ܡܠܟܐ ܕ⌜ܗ⌝ܘܐ ܐܒܘܟ.
ܐܠܐ ܒܥܐ ܐܢܐ ܠܟܘܢ
ܒܗܘܬܐ ܪܒܬܐ ܘܢܦܫ
ܟܠܗ ܒܪ̈ܝܬܐ. ܠܒܢܝܗ
ܒܪ ܕܡܫܝܚܐ ܐܢܐ
ܠܐ ܦܪܥ ܐܢܐ ܠܗ.
⌜ܗܘ⌝ ܒܪ ⌜ܡܫܝܚܐ⌝ f. 42 a col. a
ܕܐܬܓܠܝ ܠܟܘܢ، ܗܘܝܘ cf. Cod. Harris f. 198 b
ܡܫܬܐ ܠܗ ܡܢ ܐܪܟܐ
ܕܦܬܪܝܢ ܒܗ̇. ܦܘܫ ܒܪ
ܡܫܝܚܐ ܡܚܝܕܐ
ܘܐܬܬܘ ܡܚܝܕܐ
ܕܒܐܦܐ ܪܘܪܒܬܐ
ܘܒܥܘ ܟܠ ܕܘܒܬܐ
ܕܦܬܪܝܢ ܒܗ̇ ܦܘܫܩܐ
ܗܠܝܢ ܘܗ̈ܠܝܢ ܒ⌜ܫ⌝ܪܐ.
ܐܡܪ ܠܗܘܢ ܡܫܝܚܐ
⌜ܠܗܕܐ⌝ ܕܘܒܬܐ ⌜ܐܬܝܢ⌝

f. 39 b col. b ܗܘܬܘܢ ܘܫܠܝܢ ܡܢܗ̇
ܒܕܪܝܐ ܗܘܐ ܒܫܢܬ
ܟܠܗ ܡܕܪܐ ܘܫ̈ܒܐ
ܐܝܟ ܕܠܐ ܢܦܘܩ
ܒܕܪܝܐ ܡܢ ܐܘܦܗ
ܕܡܫܝܚܐ ܠܒ̈ܢܝ ܐܝܣܪܝܠ.
ܗܕܝܢ ܐܡܪܘ ܠܗ ܗܠܝܢ
ܕܡܗܝܡܢܝܢ ܒܡܫܝܚܐ
ܠܗ̇ܝ ܡܫܝܚܐ ܐܢܬ ⌜ܒ⌝ܥܝ
cf. J. S. L. p. ܠ ⌜ܒܪ⌝ ܬܠܬܝܢ ܫܢ̈ܝܢ ܡܢ
ܝ̈ܠܕܗ ܕܐܘܪܫܠܡ ܘܟܕ
ܐܢܘܢ ܡܟܝܠ ܫܢܝܗ
ܕܡܫܝܚܐ ܘܡܟܝܠ
f. 42 a col. b ܕܫܬܩܘܗ ܠܡܪܬܝ، ܡܪܝܡ
ܒܚܐܪܬ. ܘܒܥܕ ܢܦܩܐ
ܘܒܬ ܗܘܐ ܡܫܝܚܐ
ܒܪ ܡܫܝܚܬ ܒܦܪܕܝܣ
ܕܠܗ. ܘܒܪ ܦܪܐ ܬܪܓܠܐ
ܢܦܩ ܗܘܐ ܡܫܝܚܐ
ܗܘ ܘܬ̈ܪܝܢ ܬܠܡܝ̈ܕܘܗܝ،
cf. J. S. L. p. ܠ, l. 4 ܘܟܕ ܒܪܗ ܒܥܡܗ. ܕܐܝܬ
ܗܘܐ ܠܗ ܠܒܪܗ ܒܐܒ
ܡܥܝܢܐ ܘܒܐܒܐ ܕܢܚܪܐ
cf. Cod. Harris f. 199 a ܘܢܦܫ ܗܘܐ ܒܬܪܥܗ̇
ܕܦܘܒܝܢܬܐ ܘܢܦܫܬ

ܘܫܒܩܗ ܕܐܗܪܘܢ ܘܗܦܢ f. 39 a col. a
ܗܒܝܢ ܚܘܠܡܢܐ ܠܟܠ
ܐܝܠܝܢ ܕܐܙܠܝܢ ܠܬܡܢ.
ܘܗܫܐ ܡܫܡܘܢܐ ܢܝܫܐ
ܐܬܐ ܠܗܘܢܒ ܘܢܓܕܘܗܝ،
ܡܛܠ ܕܚܕ ܙܟܐ ܐܝܬ
ܒܒܝܬܗ ܡܢ ܗܠܝܢ
ܕܡܬܐܣܝܢ ܗܘܘ
ܒܐܝ̈ܕܘܗܝ ܕܡܫܝܚܐ.
ܚܡܫܡܐܐ ܢܦ̈ܫܬܐ
ܦܪܩ ܡܢ ܡܘܬܐ ܘܚܝܬ
ܠܗ ܘܠܐ ܡܕܡ ܕܡܚܒܐ
ܦܫܐ ܐܘ ܐܢܫܐ ܡܢ
ܢܫ̈ܐ ܐܘ ܡܢ ܐܒܗ̈ܬܐ f. 42 b col. a
ܕܒܒܕܘ ܚ̈ܝܠܐ ܘܐܘܣܦ
ܒܢ̈ܝܗܐ ܘܦܪܩ ܐܢܫܐ
ܡܢ ܡܘܬܐ ܐܝܟ
ܝܠܕܬܐ ܕܒܪ ܡܪܝܡ.
ܘܐܝܟ ܚܕ ܡܢ ܙ̈ܟܐ
ܕܐܬܐܣܝܘ ܒܐܝ̈ܕܘܗܝ.
ܚܝ، ܒܡܫܚܐ ܗܘ ܚܝܠܗ
ܕܡܫܝܚܐ ܕܐܝܓܠܒ
ܠܟܘܠܗܝ، ܕܢܬܠ ܒܡܘܕܝܢܐ
ܠܒܪ̈ܝܬܐ ܕܡܘܕܝܢ ܒܗ.
ܘܢܫܒܚܘܢܗܝ، ܠܝܠܘܕܗ

f. 39 a col. b cf. Cod. Harris f. 198 a ܡܢ ܒܦܘܪܐ ܕܡܛܒܝܪ ܒܗ
ܘܡܢ ܣܘܦܐ ܠܣܘܦܐ
ܕܐܪܒܥܐ ܢܐܬܘܢ ܒܥܢ̈ܢܐ
ܘܠܥܡ̈ܡܐ ܘܢܣܓܕܘܢ ܠܝܠܘܕܗ
ܕܒܪܗ ܕܐܠܗܐ. ܕܝܗܒ
ܚ̈ܝܐ ܠܟܠܗ̇ ܒܪܝܬܐ.
ܐܡܪ ܗܓܡܘܢܐ ܪܒ
ܗܘ ܡܕܡ ܕܡܫܡܥ ܗܘܐ
ܒܒܝܬܗܘܢ. ܘܗܫܐ
ܕܫܡܥܬ ܠܗܘܢ ܟܠ
ܚܙܝܐ ܒܠܬܘܢܘܗܝ، ܐܢ
ܫܡܥ ܡܠܟܐ ܡܪܩܦܬܐ
ܕܟܠܟܘܢ ܫܡܠ. ܗܠܟܘ
f. 42 b col. b ܬܘ ܚܘܐܘܢܝ ܐܝܟܐ
ܛܡܝ̈ܪܝܢ ܗܠܝܢ ܝܠܝ̈ܕܐ
ܘܐܝܟܐ ܒܒܝܬܐ ܠܟܘܢ
ܗܝ، ܒܟܘܬܐ ܟܠ ܪܝܫ
ܝܠܝܕܐ ܕܡܫܝܚܐ.
ܕܫܟܠܝܢ ܐܝܬܘܢ ܡܢܗ
ܒܡܕܝܢܐ. ܘܐܙܠܘ
ܘܫܐܠܘܗܝ، ܐܡܪ ܠܗܘܢ
ܡܢܐ ܐܥܒܕ ܠܟܘܢ ܗܫܐ.
cf. Wright, p. ܩ ܐܡܪܝܢ ܠܗ. ܦܩܘܕ ܡܪܝ،
ܕܢܣܩܘܢ ܗܘ ܡܣܩܐ
ܕܐܝܓܠܒ ܟܠܗܝ، ܡܪܢ
ܘܗܠܝܢ ܬܪ̈ܝܢ ܝܠܝܕܝܢ

f. 40 b col. a

ܒܥܘܬܐ ܫܠܝܢܝܬܐ ܒܟܠܗ
ܐܪܥܐ. ܐܝܟ ܕܬܗܘܐ
ܡܦܝܣܐ ܐܝܕܗ ܕܐܢܫ
ܟܝܬ ܙܘܒܢܗ ܕܡܪܢ.
ܕܡܢܐ ܕܗܘܐ ܐܘܠܨܢܐ
ܠܒܢܝ ܡܢܢ. ܐܝܠ ܡܢܫܦ

cf. Cod. Harris f. 197 a

ܐܝܕܗ ܟܝܬ ܪܫܐ ܘܡܫܟܐ
ܕܢܠܒܫܗ ܕܡܪܢ ܘܡܫܝܚܐ
ܥܠ ܒܘܕܪܢܐ ܘܡܬܚܫܠܢ
ܗܘ ܕܒܪܝܗ. ܘܒܫܢ̈ܝܢ
ܡܚܝܢ ܡܪܝ، ܗܓܡܘܢܐ
ܢܓܫܐ ܘܠܐ ܡܕܓܠܝܢ ܫܠܢ
ܕܝܬܝܪ ܚܣܝܪ ܚܫܒܐ

f. 41 a col. a

ܙ̈ܠܝܩܝܢ ܘܚܫܫܒܐܐ
ܢܘ̈ܗܬܐ ܕܒܬܘܒܝܢ
ܫܒܗ̈ܘ ܕܐܣܝ
ܘܝܦܗ ܕܢܫܘܒ ܕܓܒܪ̈ܐ
ܘܕܢܚ̈ܐ ܘܕܪ̈ܓܠܝܐ ܘܦܪܚ
ܐܠܝܢ ܡܢ ܚܒܠܐ.
ܘܐܬܝܗܝܢ[1] ܡܢ
ܐܘܪܫܠܡ ܘܡܢ ܒܘܪܐ
ܕܠܗ̇. ܘܡܢܐ ܕܚܙܝܢ ܫܠܢ
ܠܐܢܫ ܕܒܪܝܗ ܕܒܪܢܫܗ،
ܐܝܠܝܢ ܐܘܣܦ ܐܝܕܗ

f. 40 b col. b

ܒܗ، ܒܥܘܬܐ ܐܬܚܫܠܢ
ܡܢ ܒܘܪܗܢܗ. ܘܠܐ
ܒܠܫܘܢ ܗܘ ܡܬܚܫܠܢ
ܗܘܐ. ܐܠܐ ܐܦ ܐܝܬ
ܗܘܐ ܠܗ ܒܪ̈ܝܗܐ
ܒܒܢܝܬܗ. ܫܘܠ ܗܘܐ

cf. Wright, p. ܠܦ

ܡܢ ܡܕܪܗ ܕܗ̇، ܒܥܘܬܐ
ܒܓܒܒܗ ܘܐܝܠ ܘܫܐܦ
ܒܠ ܗܕ̈ܡܘܗܝ، ܕܗ̇ܘ
ܕܒܪܗ ܘܡܫܝܚܐ ܡܬܚܫܠܢ
ܗܘܐ. ܘܡܢ ܐܝܟܐ
ܕܡܬܚܫܠܢ ܗܘܐ ܥܘܠܢ
ܗܘܝܢ ܡܢܗ ܐܓܪ̈ܐ
ܘܡܦܩܢ ܗܘܐ ܠܢ ܒܢܝܬ.

f. 41 a col. b

ܕܓܒܪ̈ܐ ܕܝܠܘܗܝ، ܠܐܪ̈ܝܐ
ܗܢܐ ܢܗܘܐ ܡܬܦܠܠ.
ܗ̇ܘ ܘܐܢܬܬܗ ܘܡ̇ܢ
ܕܦܐܫ ܡܢ ܫܪܒܬܗ
ܡܬܦܪܕ ܡܢ ܟܠܗ ܒܡܐ.
ܘܐܡܪܝܢ ܒܢܝܬ ܕܐ
ܡܫܐܠ ܠܢ ܐܢܫ ܕܡܢܢܐ
ܐܝܬ ܒܗ̇، ܒܥܘܬܐ
ܕܡܬܐܣܝܐ ܡܢܝܢܗ̇
ܒܠܡܐ. ܢܐܡܪ ܠܗ.

cf. Cod. Harris f. 197 b

ܘܫܘܬܐ ܕܡܢܝܢܐ ܐܝܬ
ܬܡܢ ܘܡ̇ܢܝܢܐ ܕܒܫܪܝܢܐ

[1] sic

ܐܝܟܢܐ ܡܠܦܝܢ. ܐܡܪ f. 40 a col. a
ܗܝܡܢܘܬܐ ܠܟܦܘܪ̈ܐ.
ܐܡܪܘ ܘܟܠܗ ܟܠܡܕܡ
ܕܐܡܪܝܢ ܠܟܘܢ ○ ○
ܐܡܪܝܢ ܒܟܦܘܪ̈ܐ ܘܗܢܘܢ
ܕܒܢܝܢ ܐܢܘܢ ܡܕܡ ܕܢܫܝܢ
ܕܒܢܝܢ ܐܢܫܝܢ ○ ○
ܗܝܡܢܘܬܐ ܕܝܢ ܒܪ ܢܫܐ
ܡܢ ܟܠ ܒܢܝܢ ܕܠܠܗ.
ܘܐܡܪܝܢ ܐܢܘܢ ܠܗܘܢ
ܐܢܫܐ ܕܐܘܕܝܘ ܗܘܘ
ܒܡܫܝܚܐ. ܘܐܡܪ[1]
ܠܗܘܢ ܒܗ̇ܘ ܡܫܝܚܐ
ܕܐܬܬܠܝ ܡܢ ܒܬܘܠܬܐ
ܘܝܕܥܬܐ ܕܐܘܕܝܬܘܢ f. 41 b col. a
ܒܗ. ܐܦ ܐܢܐ ܡܗܝܡܢ
ܐܢܐ ܒܗ. ܟܠܗ ܘܐܡܪܘ
ܠܟܘܡܪܐ ܕܒܢܝܢ ܐܢܬܘܢ cf. Wright, p. ܠܫ
ܡܛܠ ܡܫܝܚܐ ○ ○ ○
ܗܝܕܝܢ ܘܒܗ ܪ̈ܚܡܝܢ
ܠܡܫܝܚܐ ܒܚܕ ܘܠܐ
ܘܐܡܪܝܢ. ܕܐܢܐ ܫܒܩܐ
ܘ, ܠܐ ܡܢ ܕܐܢܗ ܕܡܫܝܚܐ
ܒܢܘܡܐ ܐܚܪܢܐ. ܘ,
ܠܐ ܡܢ ܕܐܝܟ ܒܪ ܡܪܝܡ

f. 40 a col. b ܕܡܠܦܝܢ. ܘ, ܠܐ ܒܡܪܐ
ܠܡܠܦܝܢ. ܘܟܠ ܠܝ ܠܡܠܦܝܢ
ܒܠܫܢܗ. ܐܠܐ ܐܦ ܠܐܒܐ
ܕܒܪܝܢ ܠܒܥܠܕܒܒܐ ○ ○
ܐܡܪ ܠܗܘܢ ܗܝܡܢܘܬܐ
ܟܠܗ ܠܝ ܐܝܟܘ ܢܦܫܐ
ܗܘ ܕܐܬܓܠܝ ܒܟܠܗܘܢ.
ܘܒܠܝܠܝܐ ܕܒ̈ܫܒܐ
ܘܠܒܫܬܐ ܗ̇ܝ ܕܒܠܒ ܒܗ̇
cf. Cod. Harris f. 196 b ܘܫ̈ܒܬܐ ܕܒܝܫܐ ܗܠܝܢ
ܕܐܠܒܫܬܘܢܗܝ ○ ○
ܐܡܪܝܢ ܗܘܘ ܗܟܢܐ
ܕܒܫܡܝܢ ܘܡܠܘ ܠܫܪ ܡܢܝܢ.
ܘܫܒܩܝܢ ܐܢܘܢ ܘܠܘܬ
f. 41 b col. b ܢܚܒܫܘܢܗ ܐܬܬܣܝܡܘ.
ܘܫܦܪܝܢ ܐܪܟܐ ܘܒܡܫܡܫܝܢ
ܐܝܟ ܬܠܬܝܢ ܐܡ̈ܗܝܢ
ܘܟܬܒܝܢ ܟܠ ܢܦܫܗ
ܕܡܫܝܚܐ ܘܦܪܘܩܢܗ,
ܫܠܝܠ ܡܢ ܗܠܝܢ ܬ̈ܪܝܢ
ܘܡ̈ܦܐ ܕܟ̈ܫܐ. ܘܫܡܥܝܢ
ܒܡ̈ܦܐ ܘܒܡܘ̈ܬܐ ܒܥܠܡܗܘܢ
ܕܘܡ̈ܦܐ. ܘܐܬܦܠܡܪܘ
ܦܠܓܐܬ ܘܠܘܩܒܠ ܪܫܐ
ܘܡ̈ܦܐ ܕܡܫܝܚܐ ܒܒܢܝܢ

[1] Cod. ܘܐܡܪܘ

ܕܢܐܬܐ ܘܐܬܐ. ܘܐܬܐ ܡܛܠ f. 3 b col. a
ܕܠܗ ܡܫܡܫܝܢ ܗܘܝ ܟܠܗܘܢ
ܒܪ̈ܘܚܬܐ ܕܒܗ ܢܕܢܚ
ܠܗܘܢ ܢܘܗܪܐ. ܘܡܫܝܚܐ
ܕܐܬܝܠܕ ܡܢ ܡܪܝܡ
ܒܛܠ ܫܘܠܛܢܗ ܕܚܛܝܬܐ.
ܘܠܐ ܐܝܟ ܫܡ̈ܝܢܐ ܘܠܐ
ܐܝܟ ܡ̈ܠܐܟܐ ܘܠܐ
ܐܝܟ ܬܫܒ̈ܚܬܐ ܘܠܐ
ܐܝܟ ܐܣܘ̈ܬܐ ܘܠܐ
ܐܝܟ ܫܘܠܛܢܐ ܘܠܐ
ܐܝܟ ܐܬܘ̈ܬܐ. ܠܐ
ܡܫܡܫܝܢ ܦܘܡܐ ܕܢܡܠܠ cf. Cod. Harris
ܐܦܠܐ ܠܫܢܐ ܕܢܦܪܘܫ f. 195 b
ܠܐ ܕܟܠܢܐ ܘܠܐ ܕܬܫ̈ܬܐ f. 10 a col. a
ܡܕܡ ܕܒܟܒ ܡܫܝܚܐ
ܒܪܗ ܕܐܠܗܐ ܒܟܠܡܐ.
ܗܕܝܢ ܦܘܕ ܡܓܕܠܢܝܐ
ܘܐܬܠܟܕܘ ܐܢܫܐ ܡܢ cf. J. S. L.
ܒܦܘܪ̈ܐ ܡܢ ܐܢܫܬܐ p. ܠ, l. 1
ܐܢܫܬܐ ܠܒܢ̈ܝܢ ܠܟ̈ܕܐ
ܡܥ̈ܝܢܐ. ܘܡܢ ܒܬܪ
ܕܐܬܠܟܕܘ ܐܡܪܝܢ
ܢ̈ܫܡܬܐ ܡܫܝܚܐ ܠܦܘܪܐ
ܡܟܝܠ ܕܫܒܩܝܢ ܐܢܬܘܢ

f. 3 b col. b ܕܙܟܝܢ ܐܢܬܘܢ ܠܗ ܐܝܟ ܕܟܝܢ
ܐܢܬܘܢ ܡܫܘܚܝܢ ܠܟܘܢ
ܡܢܐ ܒܒܕܝܢ ܡܢܟܘܢ.
ܘܓܠܝܢ ܟܠܗܘܢ ܕܓ̈ܠܬܐ
ܕܗܘܝ ܒܐܘܪܫܠܡ ܡܕܡ
ܗܢܐ ܗܓܡܘܢܐ ܕܙܝܦܐ
ܕܐܠܗܐ ܫܕܪܗ ܕܢܬܒܥ
ܒܐܝܕܝܟܘܢ ܢܓܒܪܗ
ܕܡܫܝܚܐ ܕܩܛܠܬܘܢ ܀
ܐܡܪ ܗܓܡܘܢܐ ܠܪ̈ܘܫܡ
ܡܫܝܚܐ ܐܡܪܘ ܟܠܡܕܡ
ܕܥܒܕܬܘܢ ܘܠܐ ܬܕܚܠܘܢ.
ܐܡܪܝܢ ܡܫܝܚܐ. ܐܝܟܐ
ܡܦܩܝܢ ܢܦܫܐ ܗ̇ܘ
f. 10 a col. b ܕܐܬܓܠܠ ܟܠܗܘܢ ܡܫܝܚܐ.
ܘܐܝܟܐ ܐܒ̈ܝܢ ܫܡ̈ܝܐ
ܗܠܝܢ ܕܐܬܥܒܕ ܒܐܝ̈ܕܘܗܝ
ܘܒܪ̈ܓܠܘܗܝ. ܘܐܝܟܐ
ܫܝܡ ܗܘ ܐܣܦܘܓܐ
ܕܡܪܒܝܢ ܠܗ ܚܠܐ ܒܗ̇
ܘܐܝܟܐ ܗܝ ܗ̇ ܠܘܟܝܬܐ
ܕܒܠܒ ܒܗ̇. ܘܐܝܟܐ ܗܘ
ܟܠܝܠܐ ܕܟ̈ܘܒܐ ܕܣܡܝܢ
ܠܗ ܒܪܫܗ. ܘܐܝܟܐ
cf. Cod. Harris f. 196 a, l. 6 ܐܢܘܢ ܡ̈ܣܡܪܐ ܕܒܐܝܕܝܐ
ܕܐܠܒܫܝܢܗܝ. ܐܡܪܘ

ܒܐܐ ܒܫ̈ܢܝܐ ܘܐܬܒܕܪ f. 3a col. a
ܡܢ ܦܪܨܘܦܗܘܢ، ܘܠܫܡܥܘܢ
ܒܪ ܒܒܐ ܝܡܐ ܕܢܒܠܥܗ
ܦܩܕ ܠܗ ܐܝܕܗ ܘܐܦܣܗ
ܕܠܐ ܢܓܒ. ܘܐܠܘ ܟܠ
ܝܡܐ ܘܝܒܫܐ ܘܟܠܗܘܢ
ܒܪ̈ܝܬܐ ܠܐ ܫܠܛܬ ܗܘܐ
ܡܫܝܚܐ ܡܢ ܐܝܟܢܐ
ܡܫܬܡܥܝܢ ܗ̈ܘܝ ܠܗ
ܗܠܝܢ ܒܪ̈ܝܬܐ ܡܢܐ
ܕܦܩܕ ܗܘܐ ܠܗܝܢ.
ܐܡܪܝܢ ܒܥܘܪ̈ܐ ܠܝ̈ܗܘܕ cf. Wright,
ܠܡܫܝܚܐ ܠܐ ܡܫܒܚܝܢ p. ܠܗ, l. 14
ܕܢܕܪܘܫ ܒܡܒܥܘܢ. f. 10b col. a
ܡܦܠܠ ܕܡܫܝܚܗ ܕܗܘ
ܝܘܠܦܢܐ ܕܒܪ ܡܪܝܡ
ܦܠܚܘܢ. ܘܐܬܠܦܘܢ.
ܦܪܘܬܐ. ܘܡܢ ܣܦܪ̈ܐ
ܐܢ ܕܪܫܝܬܘܢ ܡܦܠܚܝܢ
ܐܝܬܘܢ ܠܗ. ܐܡܪܝܢ
ܝ̈ܗܘܕ ܠܡܫܝܚܐ. ܘܠܐ
ܚܙܐ ܡܠܬܐ ܕܐܝܬ
ܒܗ ܢܝܫܐ ܠܐܠܗܐ
ܐܡܪܝܢ ܐܝܬܘܢ. ܐܦܠܐ cf. Cod. Harris f. 195a
ܘܒܘܬܐ ܥܡܠܝܢ ܐܝܬܘܢ.

* * * * * *

ܐܡܪܝܢ ܒܥܘܪ̈ܐ ܠܝ̈ܗܘܕ f. 3a col. b
ܠܡܫܝܚܐ ܘܠܐ ܕܘ̈ܝܕ
ܡܬܩܪܝܢܐ ܕܪܘܚܐ
ܕܩܘܕܫܐ. ܘܠܐ ܐܠܝܫܥ
ܒܪ ܫܦܛ ܕܐܚܝ ܡܝܬܐ
ܘܠܐ ܚܝܘܩ ܗܘ
ܕܫܝܢܗ ܐܠܗܐ ܘܠܐ
ܢܕܥ ܒܪܝܬܐ ܐܝܟܢܐ
ܡܠܐ ܠܝܬ ܕܡܬܝܪ ܒܗܘܢ
ܦܩܕ ܐܠܗܐ ܐܝܟ
ܡܫܝܚܐ ܗܢܐ ܕܐܬܝܠܕ
ܡܢ ܡܪܝܡ ܕܡܬܩܪܐ
ܒܪ ܢܟܪܝܐ. ܐܡܪܝܢ
ܝ̈ܗܘܕ ܠܡܫܝܚܐ ܠܐ
ܒܫܡܝܐ ܘܠܐ ܒܐܪܥܐ f. 10b col. b
ܠܝܬ ܕܡܬܝܪ ܡܢ ܒܪܐ
ܕܐܠܗܐ ܕܐܬܝܠܕ ܡܢ
ܒܬܘܠܬܐ ܩܕܝܫܬܐ
ܐܠܐ ܐܒܘܗܝ ܗܘ
ܕܫܠܚܗ ܠܐܕܡ. ܘܗܒܢܐ cf. Wright,
ܩ̈ܝܢ ܚܠܝܢ ܘܡܗܘܕܝܢ ܚܠܝܢ p. ܠܕ, l. 1
ܘܒܢܝܕܐ ܡܢ ܩܒܪܐ
ܦܗܕܝܢ ܒܫܒܬܐ ܗܕܐ.
ܕܗܢܐ ܡܫܝܚܐ
ܕܐܬܝܠܕ ܡܢ ܡܪܝܡ
ܒܬܘܠܬܐ ܗܘ̈ܝܘ ܗܘ
ܡܫܝܚܐ ܕܒܝܬ ܗܘܐ

f. 114 b col. a

ܐܡܪܝܢ ܒܩܘܪ̈ܝ ܕܠܡܐ
ܡܢܬܪ ܗܘ ܡܫܝܚܐ
ܕܡܬܢܪܝܢ ܐܢܫܘ ܒܗ
ܡܢ ܐܝܣܝܦܘܣ ܕܗܘܐ
ܘܩܘܪܒܢܐ ܘܣܠܩ ܪܝܫܐ (cf. Cod. Harris f. 193 b)
ܕܩܘܪܒܢܗ ܠܟܠ ܘܟܣܦ
ܒܗ ܫܡܝܐ ܘܐܪܥܐ.
ܐܡܪܝܢ ܢܫ̈ܐ ܠܡܫܝܚܐ
ܠܩܘܪ̈ܐ. ܒܩܠܗ ܕܠܐ
ܐܬܦܬܠ ܐܝܣܝܦܘܣ
ܒܟܠܬܐ ܕܒ ܦܪܟܗ
ܐܒܪܗܡ ܡܛܠ ܕܒܬܗ
ܗܘܐ ܡܫܝܚܐ ܕܢܬܝܠܕ
ܡܢ ⌈ܡܪܝܡ⌉ ܒܬܘܠܬܐ. (f. 2 a col. a)
ܘܗܘ ܢܡܘܬ ܚܠܦ
ܟܠܗܝܢ ܒܢ̈ܬܐ ܘܒܡܘܬܗ
ܢܦܪܘܩ ܟܠܡܐ ⌈ܟܠܗ⌉ ܡܢ
ܦܘܫܬܐ. ܐܝܣܝܦܘܣ ܠܢܪ
ܐܠܘ ܡܢܬ ܚܕ ܩܘܪܒܢܐ
ܡܬܩܪܒ. ܗܘܐ. ܡܫܝܚܐ
ܕܡܢ ܕܡܢܬ ܩܘܪܒܢܐ
ܕܟܠܗܝܢ ܒܢ̈ܬܐ ܒܗ
ܐܬܩܪܒ ܠܐܠܗܐ.
ܐܡܪܝܢ ܒܩܘܪ̈ܐ ܕܠܡܐ
ܡܢܬܪ ܗܘ ܡܫܝܚܐ

f. 114 b col. b

ܡܢ ܝܥܩܘܒ. ܕܐܝܟ
ܚܙܘܐ ܕܚܙܐ ܠܐ ܚܙܘ
ܒܢ̈ܝ ܐܢܫܐ. ܕܣܠܩ ܕܡܟ
ܒܓܠܝܕ ܛܘܪܐ. ܘܦܬܚ
ܐܠܗܐ ܫܡܝܐ ܘܡܠܠ
ܥܡܗ ܘܡܬܚ ܗܘܐ
ܣܒܠܬܐ ܕܢܘܪܐ ܡܢ
ܐܪܥܐ ܠܫܡܝܐ ܘܢܚܬܘ
ܐܦ ܡܠܐ̈ܟܐ ܠܥܠܡܗ.
ܐܡܪܝܢ ܢܫ̈ܐ ܠܡܫܝܚܐ (cf. J. S. L. p. ܟܛ, l. 1)
ܝܥܩܘܒ ܘܡܠܐ̈ܟܐ
ܘܣܒܠܬܐ ܕܚܙܐ ܒܗ
ܡܐܬܝܬܗ ܕܡܫܝܚܐ
ܘܒܗ ܪܘܐ ܕܡܘܬܗ ⌈ܗܘܐ⌉. (f. 2 a col. b)
ܐܡܪܝܢ ܒܩܘܪ̈ܐ ܢܒܝܬܐ (cf. J. S. L. p. ܟܛ, l. 12)
ܡܘܫܐ ܘܐܬܘ̈ܬܗ ܕܢܓܕ
ܒܗܘܢ ܠܡܨܪ̈ܝܐ ܘܦܪܩ (cf. Cod. Harris f. 194 b)
ܠܐܝܣܪܝܠ. ܘܟܠ ܕܒܥܐ
ܦܪܥܘ ܕܢܒܠܐ ܠܗ ܡܢ
ܕܡܛܠܝܢ ܠܝܡܐ. ܐܦ
ܡܘܫܐ ܚܘܛܪܐ ܕܒܢܝܐ
ܕܐܝܕܗ ܘܒܥܐ ܐܢܘ
ܠܓܠܠܘ̈ܗܝ ܕܡܝܐ ܬ̈ܠܠܝܢ
ܬ̈ܠܠܝܢ. ܐܡܪܝܢ ܢܫ̈ܐ
ܠܡܫܝܚܐ. ܐܦ ܝܥܩܘܒ
ܕܐܬܝܠܕ ܡܢ ܡܪܝܡ

ܕܝܗܘܕܐ ܘܦܠܓܕܝܢ f. 114 a col. a
ܠܡܫܝܚܐ ܕܡ⌈ܬ⌉ܝܠܕ
⌈ܬ⌉ܡܢ ܡܢ ܒܬܘܠܬܐ
ܡܕܝܢܬܐ. ܘܗܟܢܐ
ܗܘܬ. ܘܐܬܘ ܡܓܘ̈ܫܐ
ܘܐܝܬܝܘ ܩܘ̈ܪܒܢܐ
ܘܐ⌈ܬ⌉ܝܘ ܕܝܬܒܐ
ܕܐܕܡ ܒܗܘܢ ܘܡܢ
ܕܝܬܒܐ ܕܐܕܡ ܐܝܠܦ
ܟܠܗܝܢ ܒܪܝܬܐ ܕܒܒܕܢ
ܕܢܬܦܣ ܘܡܢ cf. Cod. Harris f. 193 a
ܡܫܝܚܐ ܕܐܬܝܠܕ ܡܢ
⌈ܡܪܝܡ ܢܗܪ̈⌉ ܒܟܠܗܝܢ f. 2 b col. a
ܒܢ̈ܬܐ ܕܚܘܒܝܢ ܗ̈ܘܝ.
ܘܡܢ ܐܕܡ ܠܥܢܬ ܗܒܝܢܐ
ܐܬܟܬ⌈ܒ⌉. ܘܡܢ ܥܢܬ
ܐܬܟܬܒ ܒܬܝܒܬܐ
ܠܐܒܗܐ ܘܠܟܠܗ⌈ܝ⌉ܢ ܒܢ̈ܬܐ
ܘܐܡ̈ܗܐ ⌈ܢ⌉ܗܒܘ ܠܒܢ̈ܝܐ
ܘܒܢ̈ܝܐ ܢܗܒܘ ܠܒܢ̈ܝ
ܒܢ̈ܝܐ ܘܐܡܪܘ ܕܐܬܐ
⌈ܡܫܝܚܐ⌉ ܘܡܬܝܠܕ ܡܢ
ܡܪܝܡ ܒܬܘܠܬܐ ܒܪܬ
⌈ܠܘܝ⌉. ܘܐܝܟܢ ܠܐ

ܒܗܬܢ ܚܝܢ ܒܡܕܡ f. 114 a col. b
ܕܐܡܪܝܢ ܚܝܢ. ܐܢܬܘܢ
ܡܢܐ ܐܡܪܝܢ ܐܢܬܘܢ. cf. J. S. L. p. ܩܚ, l. 1
ܐܡܪܝܢ ܒܦܘܪ̈ܐ ܕ⌈ܕܠܡ⌉ܐ
ܠܒ ܗܘ ܒܪ ܡܪܝܡ ⌈ܡܢ⌉ cf. Wright, p. ܠܕ, l. 19
ܐܒܪܗܡ ⌈ܕܩܪܐ⌉ ܠܐܠܗܐ
ܕܦܬܚ ܫܡܝܐ ܘܡܠܠ
ܥܡܗ ܐܝܟ ܕܡܠܠܝܢ
ܚܝܢ ܥܡ ܚܕ̈ܕܐ.
ܐܡܪܝܢ ܪ̈ܚܡܗ
ܠܡܫܝܚܐ ܠܟܦܘܪ̈ܐ.
ܚܙܝܬܘܢ ܕܠܐ ⌈ܡܕܒܝܢ⌉
ܐܢܬܘܢ ⌈ܡܕܡ⌉. ܕܚܝܢ
ܕܪ̈ܚܡܘܗܝ, ܐܚܝܢ
ܕܡܫܝܚܐ ܡܕܝܢ ܕܒܪܗ̇ f. 2 b col. b
ܕܡܪܝܡ ܗܘ ܒܪ⌈ܘ⌉ܗܝ,
ܠܐܒܪܗܡ ܒܒܪܟܐ
ܕܐܡܗ. ܡܫܝܚܐ
ܐܝܬܘܗܝ, ܗܘܐ ܡܢ
ܩܕܡ ܟܠܗܝܢ ܒܪ̈ܝܬܐ.
ܘܗܝ, ܕܐܡܪܬܘܢ ܕܡܠܠ
ܐܠܗܐ ܥܡ ܐܒܪܗܡ
ܡܢ ܫܡܝܐ. ܗܘܝܘ
ܡܫܝܚܐ ܕܡܠܠ ܗܘܐ
ܥܡ ܐܒܪܗܡ.

ܐܬܘܗܝ ܘܩ⌜ܪ⌝ܐ f. 26 b col. a
⌜ܠ⌝ܦܫܗ ܡܫܝܚܐ. cf. J. S. L.
ܐܡܪܝܢ ܚ̈ܝܠܐ p. ܟܒ, l. 4
⌜ܠ⌝ܡܫܝܚܐ ܠܒܘܪܐ
ܫܘܘ ܐܢܬܘܢ ܐܬܘ̈ܬܐ
ܘܕܒܒܕ ܡܕܒ̈ܪܢܐ
ܘܡ̈ܦܪܫܢܐ ܘܐܚܪ̈ܢܐ
ܘܐܠܝܨܝܢ ܡܫܘܕܝܢ ܚܝܠ
ܐܬܘ̈ܬܐ ܕܒܒܕ.
ܡܫܝܚܐ ܕܫ̈ܦܝܪܢ ܬ̈ܚܝܢ
ܡܢ ܟܠܗܘܢ ܒ̈ܪܝܬܐ.
ܐܡܪܝܢ ܒܦܘܪܐ
ܠ̈ܚܡܐ ܡܫܝܚܐ ܡܢ
ܐܒܐ ܡܫܘܢ ܐܢܬܘܢ f. 23 a col. a
ܠܝ ܕܒܪ ܡܪܝܡ ܐܢܬܘܢ
ܡܫܝܚܐ. ܐܡܪܝܢ
ܚ̈ܝܠܝ ܠܡܫܝܚܐ
ܡܫܘܢ ܚܝܠ. cf. Cod. Harris
ܐܡܪ ܠܗܘܢ ܗܝܡܢܘܬܐ f. 192 b
ܠܐ ܒܟܒܬܐ ܐܦܠܐ
ܒܛܝܒܘܬܐ ܬܐܡܪܘܢ
⌜ܡ̈ܠܝܟܘܢ⌝ ܫܕ. ܠܗܘܒܠ
⌜ܫ⌝ܕ. ܐܠܐ ܒܟܠܐ ܡܟܝܟܐ
⌜ܡ⌝ܠܠܘ ܥܡ ܫ̈ܕܪܐ ܡܢ

f. 26 b col. b ܦܩܘ̈ܕܝܗܘܢ ܐܚܝܢܐ
ܘܐܙܕܒ ܒܒܢܝܐ ܕܐܢܝܐ
ܐܬܚܙܝܢ ܫܒܩܬܘܢ.
ܐܡܪܝܢ ܚ̈ܝܠܐ
ܠܡܫܝܚܐ. ܐܒܘܢ ܐܕܡ
ܒܕ ܡܐܬ ܦܘܕ ܠܚܢܬ
ܒܪܗ ܘܐܡܪ ܠܗ ܒܪܝ
ܚܢܬ ܗܐ ܒܦܪܕܝܣܐ
ܦܬܝܢ ܠܝ ܒܡܪܬ ܓܢܐ.
ܕܗܒܐ ܘܡܪܘܪܐ ܘܠܒܘܢܬܐ.
ܡܛܠ ܕܟܬܝܒ ܗܘ ܐܠܗܐ
ܕܝܐܬܐ ܠܒܠܡܐ
ܘܢܬܠܒܝܢ ܡܢ ܐܝܢܐ
f. 23 a col. b ܒܠ̈ܝܐ. ܘܝܡܬܘܢ ܘܢܒܒܕ
ܠܘܚܡܐ ܒܡܘܬܗ
ܠܒܠܗܘܢ ܒܡ̈ܡܐ.
ܘܠܝܘܡܐ ܕܬܠܬܐ
ܢܩܘܡ ܘܢܣܩ ܠܦܓܪܗ
ܕܐܕܡ ܒܡܗ ܠܚܒܝܢܐ
ܘܢܬܒܢܘܗܝ܆ ܡܢ ܡܚܒܢܐ.
ܘܗܐ ܐܬܝܢ ܡܓܘܫ̈ܐ
ܡܢ ܦܪܣ. ܘܡܠܝܢ ܠܗܘܢ
ܠܩܘܪ̈ܒܢܐ ܗܠܝܢ ܕܫܡܬ
ܘܐܙܠܝܢ ܠܒܢܬ ܠܚܡ

ܘܚܙܝܬܘܢ ܘܐܡܪܬܘܢ f. 26 a col. a
ܕܒܪܗ ܗܘ ܕܐܠܗܐ.
ܚܙܝܬܘܢ ܕܫܪܝܪܐ
ܐܡܪܬܘܢ. ܐܡܪܝܢ ܠܗ
ܗ̇ܢܘܢ ܕܥܘܪ̈ܐ ܠܡܠܟܘܬܐ.
ܡܪܝ، ܡܢ ܦܬ̈ܚܝܢ ܕܝܠܝ
ܠܐ ܒܥܡܠ ܐܬܐ
ܡܫܝܚܐ. ܐܡܪ ܠܗܘܢ
ܡܠܟܘܬܐ. ܘܡܢܐ ܫܟܚܝܢ
ܐܢܬܘܢ ܠܗ ܠܗܢܐ
ܕܐܬܐ. ܐܡܪܝܢ ܠܗ cf. J. S. L. p. ܠܒ
ܫܒ̈ܝܠܝܢ ܠܗ ܕܐܬܘܗܝ،
ܡܟܪܙܢܐ. ܕܐܦܠܐ ܐܝܟ
ܚܕ ܡܢ ܢܒܝ̈ܐ ܩܕܡ.
ܡܠܟܘܬܐ ܕܝܢ ܡܫܝܚܐ f. 23 b col. a
ܗܘܐ ܠܐܠܗܐ ܒܪܢܫܐ.
ܕܗ̇ܢܘܢ ܕܐܘܕܝܘ
ܒܡܫܝܚܐ ܢܗܘܘܢ ܘܢܬܐ.
ܡܛܠ ܕܗܘܝܢ ܗܘܐ
ܠܗ ܐܦ ܗܘ ܡܠܟܘܬܐ
ܒܓܘܒܝܢܘܬܐ ܡܪܝܡ
ܘܒܠܕܐ ܕܐܬܝܠܕ ܡܢܗ.
ܘܐܡܪ ܡܠܟܘܬܐ ܠܗܘܢ
ܕܐܘܕܝܘ ܒܗ ܒܡܫܝܚܐ.
ܡܢܐ ܐܡܪܝܢ ܐܢܬܘܢ؛

f. 26 a col. b ܒܫܘ̈ܪܬܐ ܕܐܝܬ ܒܝܢܬܟܘܢ
ܒܒܢܐ ܕܐܬܓܠܝ. ܒܪܡܐ
cf. Cod. Harris f. 192 a ܒܪ ܠܗܢܐ ܒܡ ܝܠܘ̈ܕܐ
ܗܢܘܢ ܕܝܠܕܘ ܠܒܪܗ
ܕܐܠܗܐ ܫܟܚܝܢ ܗܘܝܬܘܢ
ܠܝ ܡܢ ܩܕܡ ܒܪ ܘܠܗܠ
ܘܕܡ ܕܬܬܦܪܫܘܢ ܐܝܟ
ܐܢܫܐ ܕܐܘܕܝܘ ܒܒܪܗ
ܕܐܠܗܐ. ܘܒܡܢܗ ܬܬܦܠܓ
ܠܝ ܡܢܬܐ ܠܝ ܘܠܟܘܢ
ܒܝܘܡܐ ܐܚܪܝܐ ܡܢ
ܕܐܬܐ ܥܠ ܒܢ̈ܝܢ
ܥܡܐ ܒܥܘܒܕܗ ܒܡ
ܡܠܟ̈ܐܘܗܝ، ܘܒܢ̈ܝܐ.
f. 23 b col. b ܐܠܐ ܐܝܟ ܐܢܫܐ
ܕܐܘܕܝܘ ܒܗ. ܟܠܗ ܠܝ
ܐܬܬ̈ܬܐ ܘܬܕܡܪܬܐ
ܕܒܒܢ ܒܐܘܪܫܠܡ ܐܡܪܝܢ
ܒܦ̈ܘܪܐ. ܐܚܝܢ ܐܡܪܝܢ
ܚܝܢ ܘܡܕܡܐܬ °
ܐܡܪ ܠܗܘܢ ܡܠܟܘܬܐ
ܐܡܪܘ. ܐܡܪܝܢ
ܒܦ̈ܘܪܐ. ܐܬܚܬܒ ܠܝ
ܒܡܦܪܝܢ ܕܐܬܐ ܡܫܝܚܐ
ܘܒܥܡܠ ܠܐ ܐܬܐ
ܘܗܢܐ ܒܪ ܡܪܝܡ

f. 49b col. a

ܦܘܩܕܢܗ ܕܡܠܟܘܬܐ.
ܐܬܐ ܘܩܡ ܥܠ ܒܝܡ
ܕܠܗ ܘܐܘܡܝ ܐܢܘܢ
ܐܝܟ ܕܐܠܦܗ ܠܠܒ
ܒܐܠܗܗ ܕܐܝܣܪܝܠ
ܘܒܫܦܪܐ ܡܪ̈ܝܐ
ܘܐܘܪܝܬܐ. ܒܟܠ ܕܝܢ
ܕܡܗܝܡܢ ܒܡܪܬܝ ܡܪܝܡ
ܘܒܝܠܕܐ ܕܐܬܝܠܕ ܡܢܗ̇
ܕܡܫܝܚܐ ܗܘ ܒܪܗ
ܕܐܠܗܐ. ܢܦܪܘܩ ܢܦܫܗ.
ܘܢܩܘܡ ܡܢܗ ܘܠܗ
ܘܡܢ ܕܠܐ ܡܗܝܡܢ
ܢܫܘܐ ܢܦܫܗ ܕܠܐ
ܡܗܝܡܢ. ܗܝܕܝܢ
ܐܬܦܠܓ ܥܡܐ ܠܬܪ̈ܬܝܢ f. 46 b col. a
ܦܠܓܝܢ. ܘܐܝܠܝܢ ܕܡܗܝܡܢܝܢ
ܗܘܘ ܦܪܫܘ ܢܦܫܗܘܢ
ܠܚܕ ܓܒܐ. ܐܡܪ ܠܗܘܢ
ܡܠܟܘܬܐ ܠܗܠܝܢ
ܕܡܗܝܡܢܝܢ ܗܘܘ
ܒܡܫܝܚܐ. ܡܢܝܐ
ܐܡܪܝܢ ܐܢܬܘܢ
ܡܗܝܡܢܝܢ ܐܢܬܘܢ
ܒܗ. ܒܗܢܐ ܠܒܪܐ ܕܐܬܝܠܕ
ܡܢ ܡܪܝܡ. ܐܡܪܝܢ

f. 49 b col. b

ܡܗܝܡܢܝܢ ܕܡܫܝܚܐ
ܐܝܬܘܗܝ. ܐܡܪ ܠܗܘܢ
ܡܠܟܘܬܐ ܘܗܝܡܢܘܬܟܘܢ
ܕܡܫܝܚܐ ܐܝܬܘܗܝ
ܒܪܗ ܕܐܠܗܐ ܚܝܐ ○
ܗܝܕܝܢ ܩܡܘ ܒܠܗܘܢ
ܘܐܡܪܝܢ ܕܫܪܝܪܐܝܬ
ܐܢܚܢܢ ܡܗܝܡܢܝܢ ܕܗܢܐ
ܝܠܕܐ ܕܐܬܝܠܕ ܡܢ
ܠܒܝܬܘܠܬܐ ܡܪܝܡ ܒܪܐ
ܕܐܠܗܐ ܐܝܬܘܗܝ.
ܕܒܦܘܩܕܢܗ ܡܕܒܪ
ܥܠܡܐ ܘܐܪܥܐ ○
ܒܗܝ ܡܠܟܘܬܐ ܘܐܡܪ
cf. Cod. Harris f. 191 b ܠܗܘܢ ܐܢܐ ܠܟܘܢ
f. 46 b col. b ܡܗܝܡܢ ܐܢܐ. ܐܦ ܡܢ
ܒܬܚ̈ܡܐ ܒܪܝܐ.
ܕܐܢܬܘܢ ܕܠܝܕܝܢ ܐܢܬܘܢ
ܘܡܪ̈ܒܝܢ ܐܢܬܘܢ
ܒܐܘܪܫܠܡ. ܕܗܐ ܡܢܟܘܢ
ܐܫܬܒܚܘ ܫܘܠܛ̈ܢܐ.
ܘܡܢܟܘܢ ܒܦܘܪ̈ܐ ܠܘ
ܡܠܝܪܐ ܕܝܢ ܡܢ ܡ̈ܠܟܐ
ܐܬܐ ܠܟܘܢ ܕܢܐܠܨܘܢܟܘܢ.
ܘܕܠܐ ܒܝܕܝܟܘܢ ܬܗܘܘܢ
ܒܡܫܝܚܐ. ܐܠܐ ܐܢܬܘܢ

ܗܢܐ ܗܘܐ ܦܘܠܓܐ f. 49 a col. a
ܡܢ ܡܠܟܐ ܕܠܐ ܢܗܘܐ
ܠܟܘܢ ܡܠܟܘܬܐ ܡܢ
ܐܬܪܟܘܢ. ܡܛܠ ܕܟܝܢܐ
ܐܢܬܘܢ ܘܒܢܝܐ ܠܡܠܟܐ.
ܐܢܬܘܢ ܕܝܢ ܒܬܒܬܘܢ
ܠܗ ܠܗܪܘܕܣ ܡܛܠ
ܡܫܝܚܐ ܗܘ̇ ܕܐܬܝܠܕ.
ܡܢ ܗܕܐ ܒܬܘܠܬܐ.
ܘܕܝܢܬܐ. ܘܡܫܝܚܘܬܗ
ܠܗ ܕܟܝܢܐ ܗܘ. ܘܗܟܢܐ
ܒܗܝܢ ܐܢܬܘܢ ܒܦܠܚܘܬܟܘܢ
ܕܬܘܒܘܢܗ̇ ܠܐܡܗ
ܕܡܫܝܚܐ. ܡܢܐ ܦܪܟܝܢ
ܐܢܬܘܢ ܠܐܢܬܬܐ ܗܕܐ. f. 46 a col. a
ܠܐ ܒܗܬܝܢ ܐܢܬܘܢ
ܒܒܪܐ ܐܬ̈ܘܬܐ ܘܫܠܝܐ
ܦܪܝ ܐܠܗܐ ܒܐܝܕܗ̇.
ܐܢܐ ܓܝܪ ܠܐ ܦܪܫ ܐܢܐ cf. Cod. Harris f. 190 a
ܠܗܢܐ ܫܘܦܠܗܐ ○ ○
ܗܝܕܝܢ ܦܩܕ ܡܠܟܐ ܘܕܘܩܝܐ
ܕܡܗܝܡܢ ܗܘܐ ܒܗ cf. Cod. Harris f. 190 b
ܒܡܫܝܚܐ ܘܒܦܘܠܚܢܬܐ
ܡܪܝܡ. ܘܕܚܠ ܗܘܐ
ܕܢܘܕܥ ܢܦܫܗ ܡܢ ܩ̈ܠܝ

f. 49 a col. b ܒܒܗ. ܘܠܘܬ ܠܗ
ܠܗܓܡܘܢܐ ܘܐܡܪ ܠܗ.
cf. J. S. L. p. ܟܗ ܕܗܟܢܐ ܐܝܟܢܐ ܐܢܘܢ
ܒܗܕܐ ܡܘܡܬܐ ܕܐܡܪ
ܐܢܐ ܠܟ ܕܒܐܠܗܐ
ܕܐܝܣܪܐܝܠ. ܕܐܣܘܦܗ
ܡܢ ܡܨܪ̈ܝܢ ܘܒܣܦܪ̈ܐ
ܩ̈ܕܝܫܐ ܕܐܘܪܝܬܐ ܗܠܝܢ
ܕܐܬܟܬܒܘ ܒܐܝ̈ܕܘܗܝ
ܕܐܠܗܐ. ܘܐܬܓܗܝܬ
ܠܡܘܫܐ ܕܢܬܠܝܗ̇
ܠܐܝܣܪܐܝܠ. ܐܠܐ
ܬܐܡܪܘܢ ܠܝ ܕܐܝܟ
ܫܒܩܝܢ ܐܢܬܘܢ ܠܗ
f. 46 a col. b ܠܒܪܗ ܕܡܪܝܡ ܢܒܝܐ
ܩܪܝܡ ܐܢܬܘܢ ܠܗ. ܘܕܝܘܐ
ܫܒܩܝܢ ܐܢܬܘܢ ܠܗ
ܡܫܝܚܐ ܒܪܗ ܕܐܠܗܐ.
ܒܪ ܐܢܫܐ ܐܘܕܥܘܢ
ܐܝܟܢܐ ܕܝܕܥ ܐܢܐ
ܕܦܪܫܝܢ ܢܡܘܣܐ ܐܢܬܘܢ.
ܗܟܢܐ ܐܠܦܗ ܟܠܒ
ܘܕܘܩܝܐ ○ ○
cf. Cod. Harris f. 191 a, l. 2 ܗܝܕܝܢ ܦܩܕ ܕܢܝܐ
ܕܢܬܬܟܢܫ ܟܠܗ̇ ܐܘܪܫܠܡ.
ܘܟܕ ܐܬܟܢܫܬ ܐܝܟ

f. 22 b col. a

ܒܗ̇ ܦܠܓܘܬܐ. ܗܝܟܠܐ
ܕܝܢ ܩܐܡ ܗܘܐ ܡܢ
ܪ̇ܘܚܡܐ ܘܚܙܐ. ܘܗܘܢ
ܒܗ̇ ܡܦܠܝܢ ܕܪܬܐ.
ܐܫܟܚܘ ܐܢܘܢ ܠܬܪ̈ܥܐ
ܒܗ̇ ܐܚܝܕܝܢ. ܘܐܬܪܡܝܘ — cf. J. S. L. p. ܡܗ
ܐܬ̈ܪܘܗܝ ܕܒܡܪܘܢ ܐܢܘܢ܆
ܒܪ ܫܒܥܬܗ ܡܠܐܟܘܗܝ
ܕܡܪܝܐ ܦܬܪ ܒܪ̈ܓܠܘܗܝ
ܒܠ ܐܫ̈ܟܚܘܢ. ܘܦܬܚܝܬ
ܢܘܪܐ ܡܢ ܬܪܥܐ
ܘܡܬܟܠܘܠܐ ܗܘܬ
ܫܠܗܒܝܬܐ. ܒܪ ܐܢܫ
ܠܐ ܡܕܝܢ̇. ܘܡܡܕ ܗ̇ܘ̇,
ܐܩ̈ܝܡܘܢ ܘܣܒܪܐ — f. 27 a col. a
ܕܪ̈ܝܫܗܘܢ ܕܐܢܫܐ ܗܠܝܢ
ܕܐܝܠܘ ܗܦܟܘ ܠܬܪܥܐ
ܕܕܪܬܗ̇ ܕܦܠܓܘܬܐ.
ܘܗܦܬܘ ܡܒܝܢܘܢ ܐܢܫܐ
ܗܘܝܢܐ. ܘܗܘܬ ܕܚܠܬܐ
ܪܒܬܐ ܒܟܠܗ̇ ܐܘܪܫܠܡ.
ܗܝܟܠܐ ܕܝܢ ܒܪ ܚܢܐ
ܚܘܐ ܗܢܐ ܕܕܠܩܬ ܢܘܪܐ
ܡܢ ܬܪܥܐ ܕܕܪ̈ܬܐ ܒܪ
ܐܢܫ ܠܐ ܐܬܠܡܗ. ܘܒܢ̈ܝ
ܐܢܫܐ ܗ̈ܦܟܐ ܕܐܘܡܕܘ

f. 22 b col. b

ܦܫܛ ܐܝ̈ܕܘܗܝ ܠܘܬ
ܫܡܝܐ. ܘܗܟܢܐ ܐܡܪ
ܫܪܝܪܐܝܬ ܕܗܢܐ
ܣܒܪܢܐ ܕܚܝܘܬ ܕܒܪܗ
ܗܘ ܕܐܠܗܐ ܚܝܐ. ܗܘ
ܕܐܬܓܠܝ ܠܢ ܒܬܘܠܬܐ
ܩܕܝܫܬܐ. ܘܐܣܬܠܩ̇
ܘܐܫܬܒܚ. ܘܦܩܕ
ܗܝܟܠܐ ܡܢ ܒܬܪ
ܝܘܡܐ ܘܫܕܪ ܐܝܬܝ, — cf. Cod. Harris f. 189 b
ܐܢܘܢ ܠܒܢ̈ܝ ܐܘܪܫܠܡ
ܠܟܗ̈ܢܐ ܘܠܩܫ̈ܝܫܐ
ܘܠܝܗܘ̈ܕܝܐ. ܘܐܡܪ ܠܗܘܢ܆
ܒܗܢܐ ܡܫܝܚܐ ܘܒܗܢܐ — f. 27 a col. b
ܕܝܼܠܕ ܠܐܠܗܐ ܕܐܬܐ
ܨܐܕܘܗܝ. ܐܢܫܐ ܐܢܬܘܢ
ܡܢܝܢ, ܢܦܫܐ ܘܡܫ̈ܝܢ
ܩܕܠܐ ܘܒܢ̈ܝ̈ܕ, ܨܒܝܢܐ
ܕܢܦ̈ܫܗܘܢ܆ ܘܐܢܫܐ ܡܘܕܐ
ܐܢܫ ܠܐܠܗܐ ܕܠܘ ܡܢ
ܐܬܪܒܘܢ ܐܢܬܘܢ, ܐܠܐ
ܦܪ̈ܝܣܘ ܡܠܟܐ ܒܒܢܝ
ܗܝܟܠܐ. ܘܫܕܪܝܢ
ܟܠܗܘܢ. ܘܗܠܝܢ ܕܒܗܐ
ܐܢܬܘܢ ܗܦܟܝܢܐ ܗܠܝܢ

f. 22 a col. a ܐܡܪ ܗܓܡܘܢܐ ܠܒܢܝ̈
ܥܡܗ ܠܘܬ. ܕܐܢ ܗܘ
ܕܐܫܬܡܥܬܘܢ[1] ܠܦܘܡܗܘܢ
ܒܢܘܟ. ܠܟܘܢ ܐܢܘܢ
ܘܐܢܬܘܢ ܐܢܘܢ ܠܝ ○ ○ ○
ܘܗܝ ܒܬܪ ܫܡܥܐ ܗܠܝܢ
ܐܬܡܠܟܘ ܠܗܘܢ
ܡܠܐܟܘܗܝ, ܕܡܕܝܢܬܐ
ܕܥܐܠܝܢ ܘܢܦܩܝܢ ܠܒܝܬܗ
ܕܡܪܬܝ, ܡܪܝܡ ܒܐܘܪܫܠܡ.
ܘܐܬܚܙܝܘ ܠܗܘܢ ܦܪ̈ܫܐ
ܟܕ ܢܦܩܝܢ ܠܒܪ ܡܢ ܒܝܬܗ
ܘܡܬܪܡܪܡܝܢ. ܘܐܬܒܥܝܘ
f. 27 b col. a ܗܘܘ ܐܢܫܐ ܦܠܓ̈ܐܐ
ܡܢ ܟܠ ܕܘܟ ܘܦܢܝܢ
ܗܘܘ ܠܚܘ̈ܕܝܢ ܠܚܘ̈ܕܝܢ
ܘܡܫܒܚܝܢ ܘܡܒܟܝܢ
ܘܐܡܪܝܢ ܛܘܒܝܟܝ ܡܪܝܡ
ܠܘܬ ܐܠܗܐ ܘܕܚܠܘ
ܟܕ ܐܘܪܫܠܡ ܕܚܠܬܐ
cf. Cod. Harris f. 188 b, l. 5 ܪܒܬܐ. ܘܫܕܪܘ ܟܗ̈ܢܐ
ܟܦܪܐ ܘܐܡܪܝܢ. ܘܠܐ
ܫܐܠܘ ܡܢܗ ܫܪܐ
ܒܫܒܒܘܬܐ ܗ̇ܝ. ܘܐܬܘ
ܟܗ̈ܢܐ ܘܫܐܠܘ ܘܐܡܪܝܢ

f. 22 a col. b ܠܗܘܢ ܟܕ ܫܒܒܘܬܐ ܗܝ
ܡܪܬܝ, ܡܪܝܡ ܠܒܪܬ
ܐܠܗܐ ܐܬܬ ܠܒܝܬܗ
ܘܐܬܬ, ܗܠܝܢ ܬܫܒ̈ܚܬܐ
ܡܙܡܪܝܢ. ܘܝܗܒܝܢ ܫ̈ܠܘܬܐ
ܕܫܡܝܐ ܘܣܓܕܝܢ ܡܙܡܪܝܢ.
ܘܐܬܘ ܐܠܝܢ ܕܐܫܬܪܝܘ
ܘܐܡܪܘ ܠܟܗ̈ܢܐ ܟܠܡܕܡ
ܕܫܡܥܘ. ܘܫܕܪܘ ܟܗ̈ܢܐ
ܘܪܘ̈ܡܢܝܐ ܘܫܡܥܘ
ܒܐܦܝܪܘܢ. ܘܐܡܪܝܢ
ܠܗܓܡܘܢܐ ܫܓܝܐ ܪܒܬܐ
ܗܘܬ ܒܡܕܝܢܬܐ ܗܕܐ
f. 27 b col. b ܐܘܪܫܠܡ. ܡܛܠ ܐܢܬܬܐ
ܗܕܐ. ܐܡܪ ܠܗܘܢ
ܗܓܡܘܢܐ. ܘܡܢܐ ܐܥܒܕ
ܠܗܘܢ. ܐܡܪܝܢ ܠܗ ܒܢܝ̈
ܐܘܪܫܠܡ. ܢܦܩ ܢܘܪܐ
ܘܢܘܩܕܐ ܘܢܐܪܥ ܢܘܩܕ.
ܕܪܬܐ ܕܝܬܒܐ ܒܗ.
ܐܡܪ ܠܗܘܢ ܗܓܡܘܢܐ
ܡܢܡ ܕܟܕܝܢ ܐܬܝܬܘܢ ܘܠܐ
cf. Cod. Harris f. 189 a ܒܒܢܝ. ܗܢܝܢ ܐܬܒܢܝܘ
ܟܕ ܐܘܪܫܠܡ. ܘܢܦܩܘ
ܢܘܪܐ ܘܢܘܩܕܐ ܘܐܙܠܘ
ܠܬܪܥܐ ܕܒܝܬܐ ܗܘܬ

[1] Cod. ܕܡܫܬܡܥܬܘܢ

ܕܛܘܒܝܢܘܬܐ. ܪܘܚܐ f. 21 b col. a
ܕܩܘܕܫܐ ܛܥܝܢܐ ܗܘܬ
ܠܫ̈ܠܝܚܐ ܘܠܛܘܒܢܝܬܐ
ܘܡܕܒܪܐ ܗܘܬ ܠܗܘܢ
ܠܟܠ ܡܢ ܓܒܪ̈ܐ ܕܐܬܝܢ cf. Cod. Harris f. 187 a
ܗܘܘ ܟܠܗܘܢ ܘܠܐ
ܚܙܘ ܐܢܘܢ. ܘܟܕ ܓܒܪ̈ܐ
ܗܠܝܢ ܟܕ ܒܠܝܠܝܐ
ܐܬܝܢ ܗܘܘ ܠܒܝܬ ܠܚܡ.
ܫܡܥܘ ܩܠܐ ܕܪܘܒܐ
ܕܥܒܪ ܠܟܠ ܡܢܝܗܘܢ
ܘܫܡܥܘ ܚܙ̈ܝܢ ܘܐܡܪܝܢ
ܠܚܕ̈ܕܐ. ܕܫܡܥܘ ܩܠܐ f. 28 a col. a
ܗܢܐ. ܫܡܥܘ ܗܘܘ ܓܝܪ
ܩܠ ܓܦ̈ܐ ܕܣܪ̈ܦܐ
ܕܢܩܫܝܢ ܘܟܦܪܐ ܒܫܡܝܐ
ܕܦܐܫ ܒܟܠܗ ܐܬܪܐ
ܗ̇ܘ. ܘܥܠ ܟܢ̈ܫܐ
ܕܡܠܐܟܐ ○ ○ ○ ○
ܘܟܠܗ ܫ̈ܠܝܚܐ ܠܒܝܬܗ̇
ܕܡܪܬܝ، ܡܪܝܡ ܐܝܟܢܐ
ܕܐܝܬ ܗܘܐ ܠܗ̇
ܒܐܘܪܫܠܡ. ܘܡܠܐ̈ܟܐ
ܘܪܘܚܐ ܕܩܘܕܫܐ ܟܕ
ܡܫܡܫܝܢ ܠܗ̇. ܘܩܡܬ

f. 21 b col. b ܟܠܗ̇ ܬܫܡܫܬܐ ܚܡܫܐ
ܐܠ̈ܦܝܢ ܘܚܡܫܐ
cf. J. S. L. p. ܟܒ ܠܝܠ̈ܘܢ. ܘܟܕ ܡܠܦܘ ܓܒܪ̈ܐ
ܗܠܝܢ ܕܐܫܬܕܪܘ ܠܒܝܬ
ܠܚܡ ܥܠܝܐܝܬ ܡܬܚܫܒܝܢ
ܗܘܘ ܕܢܦܬܚܘܢܗ
ܠܬܪܥܐ ܕܒܝܬܐ ܕܠܐ
ܠܡ ܢܦܠܛ ܡܢ ܐ̈ܢܫܝܢ
ܚܕ ܡܢ ܬܠܡ̈ܝܕܘܗܝ
ܕܡܪܢ. ܘܟܕ ܦܬܚܘ ܬܪܥܐ
ܕܒܝܬܐ. ܟܠܘ ܠܗ ܘܡܕܡ
ܠܐ ܐܫܟܚܘ ܒܗ̇ ܠܐ
f. 28 a col. b ܠܬܠܡ̈ܝܕܐ ܐܦ ܠܐ
cf. Cod. Harris f. 187 b ܠܛܘܒܢܝܬܐ ܡܪܝܡ.
ܗܝܕܝܢ ܟܠܗ ܒܢ̈ܝ ܒܝܬ
ܠܚܡ ܠܐܘܪܫܠܡ ܘܗܠܝܢ
ܓܒܪ̈ܐ ܒܡܡܘܗܝ. ܘܐܡܪܘ
ܩܕܡ ܗܓܡܘܢܐ ܘܩܕܡ
ܟܘܡܪ̈ܐ ܕܡܕܡ ܠܐ
ܐܫܟܚܢ ܒܒܝܬܐ ܕܡܪܝܡ.
ܒܥܘ ܟܘܡܪ̈ܐ ܘܐܡܪܝܢ
ܠܗܘܢ ܕܗܠܝܢ ܬܠܡ̈ܝܕܘܗܝ
cf. Cod. Harris f. 188 a ܕܗ̇ܘ ܡܛܥܝܢܐ ܥܒܕܘ
ܠܗܘܢ ܚ̈ܪܫܐ ܘܥܒܘܪܘ
ܒܝ̈ܢܬܗܘܢ ܘܠܐ ܚܙܝܬܘܢ ܐܢܘܢ.

ܗܝܕܝܢ ܒܫܝܢܐ ܫܠܡܘ f. 21 a col. a
ܠܗܓܡܘܢܐ ܘܐܡܪܝܢ
ܠܗ. ܗܓܡܘܢܐ ܢܝܫܐ
ܦܩܘܕ ܡܟܝܠ ܗܕܐ
ܐܢܬ̈ܬܐ. ܕܠܐ ܬܩܘܐ
ܠܐ ܒܝܬ ܠܚܡ ܘܠܐ
ܟܠܗ ܫܘܠܛܢܗ ܕܐܪܫܠܡ.[1]
ܐܡܪ ܠܗܘܢ ܗܓܡܘܢܐ.
ܠܐ ܐܠܐ ܩܪܒ ܐܢܐ
ܐܫܕܪ ܐܓܪܘܪ ܐܢܬܬܐ
ܡܢ ܒܝܬܗ. ܐܡܪܝܢ ܠܗ
ܘܐܠܐ ܐܢܫܝܢ ܒܒܕܝܢ.
ܐܡܪܘ ܠܗ ܘܐܠܐ
ܫܕܪ ܠܒܪܐ. ܒܚܘܦܪܐ f. 28 b col. a
ܘܢܬܘܢ ܐܢܘܢ ܠܬܠܡ̈ܝܕܘܗܝ،
ܕܗܘ ܡܓܒܝܢܐ ܘܠܗ
ܢܬܘܢܗ ܒܝܒܪܐ ܗܓܝܐܐ.
ܘܡܢ ܒܬܪ ܕܫܠܡܘ ܗܠܝܢ
ܐܡܪܝܢ ܠܗ ܚ̈ܝܘܗܝ،
ܕܓܒܝܪܘܗܝ ܕܐܢ ܠܐ ܬܥܒܕ
ܢܒܝܢ ܠܗ ܡܘܕܒܝܢ ܢܣܝܢ
ܘܒܕ ܫܢܐ ܠܗ ܗܓܡܘܢܐ
ܕܩܡܘ ܠܗܘܢ ܒܠܘܗܝ،
ܒܠܗܘܢ ܐܒܫܕܐ ܦܩܕ
ܗܘܐ ܠܟܠܝܪܒܐ ܕܢܐܙܠ cf. Cod. Harris f. 186 b

f. 21 a col. b ܗܘ ܘܬܠܬܝܢ ܠܒ̈ܢܝܢ
ܒܫܡܗ ܠܒܝܬ ܠܚܡ.
ܘܢܬܘܢܝܗ̇ ܠܡܪܝܡ
ܘܠܬܠܡ̈ܝܕܐ ܥܡܗ̇.
ܘܗܢܘܢ ܢܦܩܘ ܘܐܙܠܘ.
ܘܪܘܚܐ ܕܩܘܕܫܐ
ܐܡܪܬ ܠܫܠ̈ܝܚܐ. ܕܗܐ
ܟܒܪ̈ܐ ܐܬܝܢ ܟܠܗܘܢ
ܡܢ ܐܘܪܫܠܡ. ܘܩܘܡܘ
ܦܘܩܘ ܠܟܘܢ ܡܟܐ ܘܠܐ
ܬܕܚܠܘܢ. ܐܢܐ ܓܒܝܪܐ
ܐܢܐ ܘܡܥܒܪܢܐ ܐܢܐ ܠܟܘܢ
ܒܐܐܪ ܕܫܡܝܐ ܘܠܟܠ
ܡܢ ܒܢ̈ܝܐ ܕܐܬܝܢ ܥܠܝܟܘܢ
f. 28 b col. b ܒܥܝܢ ܐܢܬܘܢ ܘܠܐ ܚܙܝܢ
ܠܟܘܢ. ܫܠܗ ܓܒܪ ܕܒܪܐ
ܦܓܕܪܐ ܗܘ ܢܠܘܐ ܠܟܘܢ.
ܘܡܚܘ ܫܠ̈ܝܚܐ ܘܢܦܩܘ
ܡܢ ܒܝܬܐ ܘܦܓܥ ܦܘܠܘܣ
ܘܦܛܪܘܣ ܘܬܐܘܡܐ
ܘܝܘܚܢܢ ܒܪܙܒܕܝ
ܕܦܓܥܢܬܐ. ܘܫܪܒܐ
ܕܫܠ̈ܝܚܐ ܘܕܡܠܐܟ̈ܐ
ܡܫܒܚܝܢ ܗܘܘ ܘܐܙܠܝܢ
ܩܕܡܝܗ̇. ܘܒܕ ܫܠ̈ܝܚܐ
ܓܒܝܢ ܗܘܘ ܠܒܪܝܗ̇

[1] sic

f. 48 b col. a

ܘܩܪܒ ܒܗ̈ܢܐ ܠܓܒܪ̈ܐ
ܕܐܬܘ ܡܢ ܒܝܬ ܠܚܡ
ܘܐܡܪܝܢ ܠܗܘܢ ܕܐܙܠܘ
ܐܦܘܩܘܗ̇ ܡܢ ܬܡܢ. ܘܟܕ
ܐܬܘ ܥ̈ܕ ܒܝܬ ܠܚܡ
ܘܫܪܘ ܙܪܐ ܒܝܬܗܘܢ
ܕܢܐܙܠܘܢ ܘܢܝܬܘܢ ܠܗ̇
ܫܠܝ̈ܡܐ. ܘܒܗܘ ܠܠܝܐ
ܕܢܓܗ ܬܠܬܐ ܒܫܒܐ
ܒܬܫܪܝ, ܐܚܪܝ, ܒܚܕ.
ܘܡܫܪܝܢ ܒܗ ܒܢܝܢܐ
ܡܢ ܕܒܥܕ ܗܘܒܐ ܘܕܡܟ
¹ܒܠܒܐ ܒܘܠܗ ܗܘܬ
ܬܫܒܘܚܬܐ ܕܐܠܗܐ

f. 50 a col. a — cf. Cod. Harris f. 185 b

ܡܛܘ ܡܪܬܝ, ܡܪܝܡ ܘܟܕ
ܡܠܟܐ ܗܘܬ ܒܠܒܬܗ̇
ܡܛܘ ܥ̈ܕ ܒܝܬ ܠܚܡ
ܒܠܠܝܐ ܘܚܙܝܢ ܗܘܘ
ܕܢܦܠܘ ܒܠ ܬܠ̈ܝܚܐ
ܘܡܬܚܐ ܬܪ̈ܥܐ ܕܒܝܬܐ
ܐܬܦܬܚܘ ܘܚܙܘ̈ܪܐ
ܡܠܐܟܐ ܕܢܚܬ ܠܗܘܢ
ܡܢܝܐ ܐܬܚܝܘ ܘܒܦܪ̈ܐ
ܕܗܪ̈ܘܡܐ ܦܐܝ ܗܘܐ
ܒܠ ܒܠܗ ܒܝܬ ܠܚܡ
ܘܚܙܝܢ ܗܘܘ ܡܢ ܫܡܝܐ¹

f. 48 b col. b

ܡܠܐܟܐ ܕܢܘܪܐ
ܘܡܫܬܦܝܢ ܗܘܘ ܚܝܬܐ
ܕܫܠܗܒܝܬܐ. ܘܦܬܚ
ܢܘܚܝܢ ܬܪܥܐ ܕܒܠܝܬܐ
ܘܢܦܩ ܘܚܙܪ ܒܫܡܝܐ
ܘܚܙܐ ܠܣܝܒܬܗܘܢ
ܕܒܪܘܟܐ ܘܕܒܝܒܪ̈ܐ
ܘܕܪ̈ܘܚܢܐ ܕܦܣ̈ܩܝܢ
ܘܠܚܬܝܢ ܡܢ ܫܡܝܐ.
ܘܟܠ ܢܘܚܝܢ ܘܐܡܪ ܠܗ
ܠܦܪܘܩ ܕܗܐ ܒܢ̈ܝܐ
ܫܡܝܢܐ ܐܬܝܢ ܕܐܝܢ.
ܘܡܪܫܬܗ ܐܬܦܬܚܘ

f. 50 a col. b

ܬܪ̈ܥܐ ܕܒܠܝܬܐ ܘܢܦܩܘ
ܡܠ̈ܐܟܐ ܘܬ̈ܠܝܚܐ ܗܠܝܢ
ܕܐܝܬ ܗܘܘ ܒܒܠܝܬܐ.
ܘܡܒܠܘ ܠܗܠܝܢ ܕܐܬܘ
ܡܢ ܐܘܪܫܠܡ ܘܡܫܟܚܝܢ[2]
ܗܘܘ ܘܗܒܢܐ ܐܡܪܝܢ
ܗܘܘ ܒܪܝܟ ܐܢܬ ܡܪܝܐ
ܡܪ̈ܝܐ ܒܪܗ ܕܐܠܗܐ̇

cf. Cod. Harris f. 186 a, l. 3

ܘܟܠܗ ܘܣܘܣܘ ܟܠܗܘܢ
ܐܬ̈ܘܬܐ ܘܬܕܡܪ̈ܬܐ
ܕܐܬܥܒܪ ܗ̈ܘܝ, ܟܕ
ܡܪܬܝ, ܡܪܝܡ ○ ○

[1–1] This portion is not palimpsest.   [2] sic

f. 48 a col. a ܘܐܠܝܨܝܢ ܒܥܒܕܬܐ ܕܟܠܗ
ܠܒܝܬܗ̇ ܘܐܚܝܕܘ ܒܗ̇
ܠܓܘܫܐ ܒܪܒܝܢܬܐ
ܘܗܘܕܥܬܐ ܕܡܪܬܝ ܡܪܝܡ
ܒܗ̇ ܒܥܒܕܬܐ ܐܬܚܠܡܘ
ܗܘܘ ܡܢ ܐܘܠܨܢܗܘܢ܀
ܘܗܘܐ ܒܐܕܐ ܒܐܘܪܫܠܡ cf. J. S. L. v. 6, p. ܟܚ, l. 17
ܘܐܬܟܢܫܘ ܠܗ̇ ܚܒ̈ܪܝܐ
ܫܠ̈ܝܚܐ. ܘܐܬܘ ܒܥܢ̈ܢܐ
ܘܐ̈ܠܝܨܐ ܕܐܬܘ ܠܐܘܪܫܠܡ.
ܕܐܝܟܐ ܐܝܬܝܗ̇ ܡܪܬܝ
ܡܪܝܡ ܐܡܗ ܕܡܪܢ.
ܘܐܡܪܝܢ ܠܗܘܢ ܒܝܬܠܚܡ
ܐܝܬܝܗ̇. ܘܢܦܩܘ ܒܪ̈ܝܬܐ f. 50 b col. a
ܕܠܝܬ ܠܗܝܢ ܡܢܝܢܐ
ܘܐܙܠ ܠܒܝܬ ܠܚܡ ܘܢܦܩܘ
ܒܬܪܥܐ ܕܒܝܬܗ̇
ܕܦܓܘܪܬܐ. ܘܠܐ ܫܒܩܘ
ܠܗܘܢ ܫ̈ܠܝܚܐ ܬܪܥܐ.
ܘܟܕ ܠܐ ܫܒܩܘ ܠܗܘܢ
ܬܪܥܐ ܒܒܝܢ ܗܘܘ
ܘܐܡܪܝܢ ܕܡܪܬܝ ܡܪܝܡ
ܠܟܠ ܐܢܫܐ ܐܬܪܚܡܝ[1]
ܥܠܝܢ. ܘܫܡܥܬ ܡܪܬܝ
ܡܪܝܡ ܩܠܐ ܕܒܪ̈ܬܐ cf. J. S. L. p. ܟܛ

f. 48 a col. b ܕܢܦܩܐ ܠܗ̇. ܘܨܠܝܬ
ܘܐܡܪܬ ܪܒܘܢ ܡܫܝܚܐ
ܕܐܫܬ ܠܝ ܒܥܡܕܐ. ܫܡܥ
ܒܩܠܐ ܕܒܥ̈ܘܬܐ ܗܢܝܢ
cf. Cod. Harris f. 185 a ܐܠܝܨܬܐ. ܘܒܪ ܫܥܬܐ
ܢܦܩ ܩܠܐ ܪܒܐ
ܘܒܥܕܪܢܐ ܡܢ ܦܓܘܪܬܐ
ܠܪ̈ܝܫܗܐ ܟܠܗܘܢ ܘܐܬܦܫܛܘ
ܗܘܝܢ. ܗܘܘ ܕܝܢ ܗܢܘܢ
ܕܐܬܐܣܝܘ ܬܪ̈ܝܢ ܐܠ̈ܦܝܢ
ܘܬܡܢ̈ܝܢܐ ܢܦ̈ܫܬܐ.
ܓܒܪ̈ܐ ܘܢܫ̈ܐ ܘܛ̈ܠܝܐ
ܘܗܘܬ ܬܫܒܘܚܬܐ
f. 50 b col. b ܒܝܘܡܐ ܗ̇ܘ ܠܐܠܗܐ
ܘܗܠܝܢ ܕܐܬܚܠܡܘ[2] ܡܚܝܕܐ
ܐܝܟ ܠܦܓܪܗܘܢ ܘܥܕܡ
ܗܠܡܢܐ ܘܡܗ̈ܝܢܐ
ܐܡܪܘ ܒܥܠܡܐ ܕܫܡܥܬ
ܠܗܘܢ ܡܪܬܝ ܡܪܝܡ
ܒܝܠܘܬܗ̇ ܘܐܬܡܫܚܘ
ܬܪ̈ܝܢ ܐܠܦܝܢ ܘܬܡܢܝܢܐ
ܢܦ̈ܫܬܐ ܘܫ̈ܒܥܝܢ ܒܢܝ̈ܗܘܢ
ܕܝܗ̈ܘܕܐ ܘܟܠܗܘܢ ܟܗ̈ܢܐ
ܘܐܬܪܗܒܘ ܕܕ̈ܩܝܢܐ
ܘܐܡܪܘ ܕܢܦܫܐ ܗܘܐ
ܒܐܘܪܫܠܡ.

[1] Cod. ܐܬܪܚܡܝ

[2] Cod. ܕܐܬܚܠܡ

f. 25 b col. a

ܬܣܠܘܢܝܩܝܐ. ܕܫܪܝܢ
ܗܘܐ ܣܦܝܢܐ ܒܝܢܝܗ̇
ܕܡܫܝܢܐ ܘܒܪ ܫܒܬܗ
ܕܐܘܫܦܬ ܐܝܕܗ̇ ܡܪܝܡ
ܘܢܦܩܬ ܠܗ̇ ܐܬܚܠܡܬ.
ܘܐܬܬ ܬܘܒ ܐܟܝܕܗ̇
ܡܠܟܘ ܒܪܬܗ ܕܫܒܝܢܐ
ܐܦܪܘܟܐ ܕܐܝܬ ܗܘܐ
ܒܗ̇ ܫܢ̈ܕܐ ܬܪܝܢ ܫܢ̇
ܕܡܫܝܢ ܗܘܐ ܠܗ̇ ܒܠܠܝܐ
ܘܫܪܝܐ ܕܐܬܐ ܗܘܐ
ܥܠܝܗ̇ ܒܐܝܡܡܐ ܘܡܦܪܫ
ܗܘܐ ܠܗ̇ ܘܐܦܝܣܬ
ܠܡܪܬܝ، ܡܪܝܡ. ܘܡܫܚܐ
ܕܨܠܘܬ ܥܠܝܗ̇ ܘܫܡܫܬ

f. 24 a col. a

ܥܠܝܗ̇ ܐܝܕܗ̇ ܘܐܬܡܪܬ
ܗܘܬ. ܒܫܡܗ ܕܒܪܗ̇
ܕܐܝܬ ܠܗ̇ ܒܫܡܝܐ
ܡܫܡܫܢܐ ܐܝܟ ܒܕܒܪܐ
ܗܢܐ ܥܠ ܢܦܫܐ ܗܕܐ
ܕܬܬܐܣܐ. ܘܡܫܚܕܐ
ܢܦܩܘ ܡܢܝܗ̇ ܗܠܝܢ
ܫ̈ܐܕܐ ܘܡܫܠܠܝܢ ܗܘܘ
ܘܡܒܟܝܢ ܘܐܡܪܝܢ. ܡܢܐ
ܠܢ ܘܠܟܝ ܐܡܬܗ ܐܠܗܐ

f. 25 b col. b

ܘܡܛܘ ܫ̈ܐܕܐ ܗܠܝܢ
ܒܡ̈ܪܥܝܬܗ ܕܫܘܥܐ
ܠܒܐ ܡܢ ܬܪܥܐ ܕܒܠܬܗ̇
ܕܡܪܬܝ، ܡܪܝܡ. ܘܐܡܪܝܢ
ܗܘܘ ܠܟܢ ܒܠܥܕ ܕܐܢܬܝ،
ܘܠܝܕܐ ܕܐܬܝܠܕ ܡܢܟܝ
ܐܘܟܠܘܣܗ، ܠܠܓܝܘܢ
ܕܡ ܩ̈ܛܠܘܬܗ. ܗܘܝܢ
ܠܒܪܬ ܒܘܗܢ ܡܪܬܝ،
ܡܪܝܡ ܒܫܡܗ ܕܡܪܢ
ܝܫܘܥ ܡܫܝܚܐ. ܘܒܪ
ܫܒܬܗ ܫܢܝܘ ܠܘܬ ܝܡܐ
ܘܢܦܠܘ ܒܗ ܘܐܬܚܢܩܘ.
ܘܐܬܬ ܬܘܒ ܠܘܬܗ̇

f. 24 a col. b cf. Cod. Harris f. 184 b

ܕܡܪܬܝ، ܡܪܝܡ ܦܠܢܝܐ
ܚܕ ܡܢ ܡܕܝܢܝ ܒܪ ܚܝܬܗ
ܕܫܘܦܪܘ ܡܠܟܐ ܕܡܕܝܢ
ܕܐܝܬ ܗܘܐ ܠܗ ܐܢܬܐ
ܒܪܫܡܗ. ܘܒܥܒܐ ܗܘܐ
ܡܕܡܫܢܗ̇. ܘܒܪ ܫܒܬܗ
ܕܐܘܫܦܬ ܐܝܕܗ̇
ܘܠܒܒܬܗ ܒܪܫܡܗ
ܐܬܚܠܡ ܡܢ ܒܐܟܒܗ.
ܘܐܫܠܝܡ ܬܘܒ ܕܐܬܘ
ܒܚܡܗ ܕܒܪܫܡܗ ܗܘܘ

ܘܒܢ̈ܬ ܙܘ̈ܒܢܝܐ ܕܒܥ̈ܡܡܐ. f. 25 a col. a
ܘܒ̈ܢܬ ܐܦܪ̈ܟܝܐ ܘܫ̈ܠܝܛܢܐ cf. Cod. Harris f. 183 b
ܘܠܟܠܗܝܢ ܗ̈ܘܝ, ܐܝܩܪܐ
ܘܦܘܪ̈ܥܢܐ ܘܐܬܝܢ ܗ̈ܘܝ,
ܘܣܓܕ ܠܗ ܠܡܪܬܝ, ܡܪܝܡ. cf. J. S. L. p. ܟܒ
ܘܡܫܡܫܝܢ ܒܡܫܝܚܐ
ܕܐܬܝܠܕ ܡܢܗ ܘܡܫ̈ܐܠܝܢ
ܗ̈ܘܝ, ܠܗ ܘܡܦܝܣܝܢ ܠܗ
ܕܐܡܪ ܠܢ ܡܪܬܝ, ܡܪܬܗ
ܕܥܠܡܐ ܐܝܟܢܐ ܐܬܝܠܕ
ܡܢܟ ܡܪܢ ܝܫܘܥ ܡܫܝܚܐ
ܕܠܐ ܫܘܬܦܘܬܐ ܕܓܒܪܐ.
ܘܗ̣ܝ, ܡܪܬܝ, ܡܪܝܡ
ܐܡܪܐ ܗܘܬ ܠܗܝܢ
ܒܠܡܕܡ ܕܒܥܝܢ ܗ̈ܘܝ, ܠܗ. f. 24 b col. a
ܘܐܝܟܐ ܕܐܝܬ ܠܗ ܒܐܒܐ
ܡܐܣܝܐ ܗܘܬ ܠܗ ܘܡܐ
ܕܐܙܠ ܗ̈ܘܝ, ܠܐܬܪ̈ܘܬܗܘܢ
ܘܠܟ̈ܬܗܘܢ. ܡܒܪܟܐ ܗܘܬ
ܠܗܘܢ ܘܡܣܝܥܐ ܗܘܬ
ܒܠܗܘܢ. ܘܡܗܒܐ ܗܘܬ
ܠܗܘܢ ܒܡܬ̈ܒܥܬܐ ܕܒܐܝܠܢ
ܒܡܗܝܢ ܠܒܝܬ ܐܢܫܗܝܢ
ܕܐܝܟܢܐ ܢܗܝܡܢܘܢ. ܘܡܢ
ܫܘܐ ܠܫܘܐ ܐܬܝܢ ܗ̈ܘܝ,
ܐܢ̈ܫܝܢ ܒܢ̈ܬ ܡ̈ܠܟܐ ܘܒܢ̈ܬ
ܪ̈ܘܪܒܢܐ ܘܡܢ ܗܘ, ܕܗܘܢܝܢ.

f. 25 a col. b ܕܡܪܢ ܝܫܘܥ ܡܫܝܚܐ
ܘܐܬܬ ܐܢ̈ܬܬܐ ܚܕܐ
ܓܝܕ ܡܪܬܝ, ܡܪܝܡ ܡܢ
ܒܪܘܦ̈ܛܘܣ ܕܐܝܬ ܗܘܐ
ܠܗ ܫܐܕܐ ܘܟܠ ܒܪ
ܚܒܫ ܗܘܐ ܠܗ. ܘܐܬܬ
ܬܘܒ ܓܕܝܪܗ ܘܒܥ̈ܒܪ
ܡܢ ܐܠܟܣܢܕܪ̈ܝܐ ܒܪܬܗ
ܕܢܘܢܐ ܗܘܦܪܟܐ ܕܒܠܝܗ
ܡܠܝܐ ܗܘܬ ܟܪ̈ܝܗܐ
ܘܐ̈ܬܬ, ܘܣܓܕܬ, ܩܕܡ
ܡܪܬܝ, ܡܪܝܡ ܘܡܫܝܕܐ
ܫܐܠܬ ܗ̈ܢܝܐ ܘܫܡܫܬ
ܐܘܟ. ܒܫܡ ܐܒܐ
f. 24 b col. b ܘܒܪܐ ܘܪܘܚܐ ܕܩܘܕܫܐ
ܘܪܦܬ ܟܠ ܟܐܒ̈ܝܗ
ܘܒܪܫܬܗ ܐܫܬܠܡܝܢ.
cf. Cod. Harris f. 184 a ܘܐܬܬ ܠܘܬܗ ܐܟܣܢܝܐ
ܡܓܪܬܐ ܒܪܬܗ ܕܓܝܣܘ
ܒܬܪܐ ܘܚܬܗ ܗܘܬ
ܕܡܠܟܐ ܕܡܓܪܡ ܘܐܝܬ ܗܘܐ
ܠܗ ܒܐܒܐ ܕܓܡܪܐ
ܘܐܦܝܣܬ ܡܪܬܝ, ܡܪܝܡ
ܘܡܫܝܢܐ ܕܓܠܝܬ ܒܠܝܠܗ
ܐܬܚܠܡܬ. ܘܐܬܬ
ܠܘܬܗ ܦܠܘܓܐ ܡܢ

ܘܢܣܬܡ ܠܡܫܝܚܐ. ܘܟܕ ܚܙܐ f. 113 b. col. a
ܪܘܒܐ ܪܒܐ ܒܢܝܬ cf. Cod. Harris f. 182 a
ܟܢܘ⌈ܫ⌉ܝܗܘܢ ܕܟ̈ܠܝܐ ܘܠܐ
ܐܝܟ ܒܢܝܢܫܐ ܡܟܠܠ.
ܗܘܐ ܟܠܗ ܡܬܕܡܪܬܐ
ܕܒܪܘܒܐ ܕܗܡܝܢ ܠܟܠ
ܡܢ ܟܠܝܠܬܐ ܕܡܠܟܘܬܐ
ܗܘܬ ܒܗ̇ ܠܦܘܢܝܬܐ
ܡܪܝܡ. ܘܟܠܗ ܒܢ̈ܝ ܒܝܬ
ܠܚܡ ܘܐܡ⌈ܪ⌉ܘ ܠܗ̇ ܡܠܟܘܬܐ
ܘܠܟܗܢܐ ܕܐܘܪܫܠܡ
ܡܪܝܡ ܕܢܣܒ ܘܩܒܪܗ.
⌈ܫ⌉ܠܡ⌈ ⌉ ܣܦܪܐ ܕܬܪ̈ܝܢ f. 110 a col. a

ܣܦܪܐ ܕܬܠܬܐ.

ܘܐܬܐ ܠܒܪ̈ܐ ܡܢ ܒܝܬ
ܠܚܡ ܘܟܕ ܫܡܥ ܬܡܢ
ܐܬܘ̈ܬܐ ܕܡܫܬܪܪ
ܗ̇ܘ, ܡܫܡܫ ܡܪܬܝ,
ܡܪܝܡ ܒܪ ܡܠܝܩܐ
ܟܠܝܠܬܐ ܕ⌈ܒ⌉ܝܬ[1] ܠܚܡ ܒܪ
ܐܬܘ ܫ̈ܠܝܚܐ ܘܡܫܡܫܢܝܢ
ܗܘܘ ܠܘܬܗ̇ ܒܟܠܝܠܬܐ.
ܘܣܝܘ ܒܪ ܐܬܦܢܝܘ
ܥܡܝܐ ܘܢܣܒܘ ܫ̈ܘܠܡܬܐ

f. 113 b col. b ܕܡܠܟ̈ܘܬܗܘܢ, ܕܡܕܝܢܬܐ
ܘܡܕܡܪܝܢ ܗܘܘ ⌈ܟܠ⌉
ܟܠܝܠܬܐ ܗ̇ܝ. ܘܣܝܘ ܒܪܘܚܐ
ܘܥܒܕܘ ܥܠ ܪ⌈ܟ⌉ܒܐ
ܘܣܝܘ ܒܒܢܝܐ ܕܐܬܝܢ
ܠܘܬ ܟܠܝܠܬܗ̇ ܕܦܘܪܫܢܝܬܐ
ܗܠܝܢ ܐܬܘ̈ܬܐ
ܘܬܕܡܪ̈ܬܐ. ܘܕܦܓܪܐ
ܘܕܬܘܣܦܬ ܡܢ ܗܠܝܢ
ܣܝܡ ܗܘܘ ܒܢ̈ܝ ܒܝܬ
ܠܚܡ. ܘܡܗܝܡܢܝܢ ܗܘܘ
cf. Cod. Harris f. 183 a, l. 10 ܫܘܒܚܐ ܠܐܠܗܐ ܒܪ
ܠܐ ܢܓܝܢ. ܘܡܫܠܠ ܕܠܘ
f. 110 a col. b ܡܓܢ̈ܝܢܗܘܢ ܡܦܪܟܝܢ
ܗܘܘ ܦܓܪܬܐ ܠܗܘ
ܠܒܪܐ ܡܕܝܢܐ ܕܐܬܠܕ.
ܡܢ ܒܬܘܠܬܐ ܡܕܝܢܬܐ.
ܘ⌈ܟ⌉ܠܗܝܢ ܗܘܘ ܡܢ
ܬܕܡܪ̈ܬܐ ܕܡܫܬܟܚܢ ܒܪ
ܗ̈ܘ. ܐܬܝܢ ܗ̈ܘ ܢܫ̈ܐ
ܡܢ ܡܕܝܢ̈ܬܐ ܘܡܢ
ܐܬܪ̈ܘܬܐ ܪ̈ܚܝܩܐ
ܘܡܢ ܪܘܡܝܐ ܘܡܢ
ܐܠܟܣܢܕܪܝܐ ܘܡܢ ܡܨܪܝܢ
ܘܡܢ ܐܬ⌈ܢ⌉ܘܣ ܒܢ̈ܬ ܡ̈ܠܟܐ

[1] Cod. ܒܝܬ

ܐܓܪܗ ܘܟܕ ܫܡܫܬ f. 113 a col. a
ܡܪܬܝ ܡܪܝܡ ܗܠܝܢ ܡܢ
ܥܠܝܡܐ. ܒܓܠܝܬ ܐܘܪܚܗ
ܠܘܬ ܫܡܫܐ ܘܓܠܝܬ
ܘܐܡܪܬ ܗܟܢܐ ܐܢܐ
ܘܡܫܒܚܐ ܐܢܐ
ܘܡܪܡܪܐ ܐܢܐ
ܘܡܗܠܠܐ ܐܢܐ ܕܠܐ
ܗܘܝܬ ܡܫܒܚܐ ܠܫܪܒܬܐ
ܕܡܫܝܚܐ. ܘܠܐ ܢܫܪܝܢ
ܡܠܝ̈ܗܘܢ ܕܝܗܘܕܝܐ.
ܕܐܡܪܘ ܕܒܢܘܪܐ
ܡ̈ܘܩܕܝܢ ܠ[ܗ] ܡܢܗ
ܕܡܝܬܬ. ܐܠܐ ܗܝܡܢܬ f. 110 b col. a
ܘܐܫܪܬ ܕܗܘ ܕܐܬܝܠܕ cf. Cod. Harris f. 181 b
ܡܢܝ ܗܘܐ ܡܕܒܪ ܫܡܝܐ
ܘܐܪܥܐ ܕܡܫܒܚܢܐ ܐܢܐ
ܠܫܡܐ ܕܝܠܕܘܬܗ. ܠܥܠܡ
ܥܠܡܝܢ. ܘܠܐ ܫܦܘܐ
ܐܢܐ ܕܐܬܠ ܫܘܒܚܐ
ܠܝܠܕܘܬܗ. ܕܠܬܠܡ̈ܝܕܘܗܝ,
ܘܒܝ̈ܕܝܐ ܫܕܪ ܐܓܪ̈ܬܐ
ܘܡܢ ܕܝܠܕܬ ܡܪܝܡ ܫܡܥܘ cf. J. S. L. p. ܟܐ
ܥ̈ܠܝܡܐ ܦܪܝܫܐ ܕܒܩ̈ܘܡܐ

f. 113 a col. b ܘܟܪܙܘ ܥܠ ܐܦ̈ܝܗܘܢ
ܘܓܠܝܘ. ܘܒܗ ܒܫܥܬܐ
ܪܡܫܐ ܪܒܡ ܒܫܡܝܐ.
ܘܠܐ ܐܫܬܡܥ ܐܝܟ
ܡܠܐ ܕ̈ܓܠܐ ܪܗܝܒܘܬܐ
ܕܢܡܫܡ ܥܠ ܐܦ̈ܝܗ
ܕܐܐܪ. ܘܡܫܝܚܐ ܪܘܚܐ
ܒܫܡܝܐ ܠܫ̈ܠܝܚܐ ܡܢ
ܫܡܝܐ. ܘܢܚܬܘ ܡܠ̈ܐܟܐ
ܘܪ̈ܒܘܐ ܣܘܓܐܐ ܕܡܠܐܟܐ
ܠܝܬ ܗܘܐ ܠܓܘܕ̈ܝܗܘܢ
ܘܠܐ ܠܡܢ̈ܝܢܗܘܢ
ܘܫܒܚܘܗ̇ ܗܘܘ ܠܒܬܘܠܬܐ
f. 110 b col. b ܗܝ, ܕܡܫܟܚܐ ܗܘܬ ܒܗ̇
ܡܪܬܝ, ܡܪܝܡ ܒܟܦ̈ܝܗܘܢ
ܘܠܐ ܐܚܪܢܐ ܕܡܕܡ
ܠܐ ܡܫܬܡܥ ܗܘܐ.
ܐܠܐ ܗܢܐ ܡܠܐ ܕܐܡܪܝܢ

* * * * * * *

ܡܪܝܐ ܐܠܗܐ ܕܠܗ ܗܘ
ܫܒܝܚ ܫܡܝܐ ܘܐܪܥܐ.
ܘܗܘܬ ܕܚܠܬܐ ܪܒܬܐ
ܒܟܠܗ ܒܝܬ ܠܚܡ ܘܗܘܘ
ܐܬܘ̈ܬܐ ܕܚܝ̈ܠܬܐ
ܘܠܐ ܟܠܝܢ ܗܘܘ ܫ̈ܠܡܘܬܗ
ܕܡܪܝܐ ܡܢ ܕܥܠܡܝܢ

ܒܝ. ܘܐܘܠܦܬܢܝ ܡܢ f. 64 b col. a
ܒܝܬ ⌜ܡܪ̈ܬܐ⌝ ܕܡܛܠܗ
ܗܘܝܬ ⌜ܓܕܥܘܢ⌝ cf. J. S. L. p. ܡ
ܘܩܡܬ ⌜ܡܢ⌝ ⌜ܩܒܪܐ⌝
ܘܪܘܚܐ ܕܩܘܕܫܐ
ܫܡܬܢܝ ܒܒܢܝܢܐ
ܕܢܘܗܪܐ ܘܓܕܥܘܢ
ܐܬܝܬܝܢ ܥܢܐ
ܠܘܩܐ ܘܐܡܪ ܐܢܐ
ܡܢ ܩܒܪܐ ܩܡܬ ܘܩܘܫ
ܒܐܕ̈ܢܝ ܐܝܟ ܩܠܐ ܕܪܥܡܐ
ܕܫܦ̈ܐ. ܘܕܢܚ ܢܘܗܪܐ
ܒܩܒܪܐ ܕܡܛܠܗ ܗܘܝܬ
ܒܗ. ܘܫܡܥܬ ܠܝ ܕܢܩܫܐ
ܕܢܘܚܡܐ ܡܛܠ. ܪܘܚܐ f. 65 a col. a
ܕܩܘܕܫܐ ܫܡܬܢܝ
ܒܒܢܝܢܐ ܕܢܘܗܪܐ
ܘܓܕܥܘܢ ܐܬܝܬܝܢ.
ܥܢܐ ܐܢܕܪܐܘܣ ܘܐܡܪ
ܐܦ ܐܢܐ ܡܢ ܩܒܪܐ cf. Cod. Harris f. 181 a
ܩܡܬ. ܘܩܠܐ ܕܟܢܪܗ
ܕܐܠܗܐ ܢܫܒ ܒܐܕ̈ܢܝ
ܘܐܡܪ ܠܝ ܐܢܕܪܐܘܣ
ܩܘܡ ܐܠ ܒܪ ܚܕ̈ܝܝ
ܠܒܝܬ ܠܚܡ. ܘܐܢܐ

f. 64 b col. b ܘܒܫܢܐ ܕܡܠܟ̈ܐ. ܐܢܐ
ܐܬܐ ܓܕܥܘܢ ܡܛܠܠ
ܕܡܛܠܐ ܠܗ ܘܒܢܐ
ܕܐܬܛܠܠ ܒܗ ܛܘܒܢܝܬܐ
ܡܪܝܡ. ܘܬܦܘܫ ܡܢ
ܒܠܥܕ ܗܢܐ. ܘܒܪ ܫܒܬܗ
ܪܘܚܐ ܕܩܘܕܫܐ ܫܡܬܢܝ
ܒܒܢܝܢܐ ܕܢܘܗܪܐ
ܘܓܕܥܘܢ ܐܬܝܬܝܢ.
ܥܢܐ ⌜ܒܪ⌝ ܬܘܠܡܝ ܘܐܡܪ
ܐܦ ܐܢܐ ܒܬܒܐܝܫ
ܐܝܬܝ ܗܘܝܬ ܘܟܠ
ܛܝܒܘܬܗ ܘܫܠܡܗ
f. 65 a col. b ܕܡܪܢ ܝܫܘܥ ܡܫܝܚܐ
ܡܟܪܝ ܗܘܝܬ. ܘܚܙܝܬ
ܪܘܚܐ ܕܩܘܕܫܐ ܕܒ
ܐܬܝܐ ܐܝܟ ܒܪܩܐ
ܡܢ ܫܡܝܐ. ܘܟܕ ܫܒܬܗ
ܛܘܒܢܝܬ⌜⌝ ܘܒܒܢܝܢܐ ܕܢܘܗܪܐ
ܫܡܬܢܝ. ܘܓܕܥܘܢ
ܐܬܝܬܝܢ ° ° ° °
ܗܠܝܢ ܡܠܠܘ ܫ̈ܠܝܚܐ
ܥܠ ܡܪܬܝ ܡܪܝܡ.
ܘܗܝ ܒܟܠ ܚܕ ⌜ܚܕ⌝
ܡܫܡܫܢ ܕܐܒܢܐ ܐܬܐ

f. 64 a col. a

ܒܐܘܪܫܠܡ ܐܚܬܝ,
ܗܘܬ. ܘܒܥܕܬܐ ܕܝܗܘܕܝܐ
ܠܬܡܢ ܗܘܬ. ܘܡܛ̈ܐܢܐ
ܕܬܫܡܫܬܗ ܕܡܪܝܐ
ܒܟܢ ܗܘܘ. ܘܗܟܢ ܒܕܟ
ܘܟܢܐ ܢܦܩܬ ܡܢ
ܐܘܪܫܠܡ ܠܒܝܬ ܠܚܡ
ܘܡܨܠܝܬܗ̇ ܗܘܬ
ܠܦܘܠܚܢܬܐ ܡܪܝܡ ܒܕ
ܒܪܗܐ. ܡܛܠ ܕܝܗ̈ܘܕܝܐ
ܡܛܘ ܠܡܘܒܠܗ̇ ܘܠܐ
ܫܒܩܝܢ ܗܘܘ ܠܗ̇ ܕܬܐܙܠ
ܬܬܦܠܐ ܚܕ ܡܒܪܐ f. 65 b col. a
ܘܟܠܘܬܐ ܕܡܫܝܚܐ.
ܘܢܦܩܬ ܡܢ ܬܡܢ
ܘܐܬܬ ܠܒܝܬ ܠܚܡ
ܘܐܝܟ ܠܐ ܚܕ ܗܘܬ
ܕܗ̈ܘܝܐ ܒܠܗ ܫܘܒܚܐ
ܢܦܩܬ ܡܢ ܗܘܢ ܒܠܚܕܐ
ܘܡܠܠܬ ܐܝܟ ܕܢܘܚܐ
ܕܡܘܫܐ ܘܐܡܪܬ ܠܗ
ܕܐܡܪܗ ܕܪܒܒܘܢ ܡܪܢ
ܠܗ ܘܒܢܐ ܕܬܦܠܐ ܡܢ

f. 64 a col. b

ܒܠܒܐ ܗܢܐ. ܘܒܕ ܐܢܐ
ܐܦܘܩ ܡܐܪܗ̇ ܢܘܪܢܐ
ܕܡܘܫܐ ܣܦܩܬܢܝ.
ܘܡܐܪܒܘܢ ܐܫܬܝܬܢܝ.
Tisch. 102, l. 9 ܐܡܪܬ ܡܢܗ, ܐܢܐ ܕܗܒܬ
ܘܗܒ ܐܢܐ ܫܘܒܚܐ
ܠܐܠܗܐ ܕܒܕ ܒܐܠܦܐ
ܢܦܩ ܗܘܬ ܘܗܦܘ
ܒܐܘ̈ܢܐ ܕܢܒܫܘܬܗ̇
cf. Cod. Harris f. 180 b ܘܒܕ ܕܕܚܡ ܠܗ̇ ܒܫ̈ܘܒܚܐ
ܠܐܠܦܐ ܗܐ ܓܘܪܢܐ
ܕܡܘܫܐ ܐܡܪܬ ܒܠܝ
ܘܒܢܝܢܐ ܕܢܘܪܐ
f. 65 b col. b ܣܦܩܬܢܝ ܘܡܐܪܒܘܢ
ܐܫܬܝܬܢܝ. ܘܒܢܝܐ
ܒܠܦܘܗ ܐܡܪ ܐܢܐ
ܒܢܝܬ ܗܘܬ ܘܒܫܒܚܬ
ܒܠܐ ܕܡܢܝܢ ܒܠܦܘܗ
ܘܗܡ. ܘܐܦܩܬܢܝ ܓܘܪܢܐ
ܕܡܘܫܐ ܠܒܪ ܡܢ ܡܒܪܐ.
ܘܒܢܝܢܐ ܕܢܘܪܐ ܗܘܒܬܢܝ
ܘܡܐܪܒܘܢ ܐܫܬܝܬܢܝ.
ܐܡܪܬ ܫܡܥܘܢ ܡܢܢܐ
ܘܐܢܐ ܡܢ ܡܒܪܐ ܡܦܬܚ
ܘܢܦܩܬ ܡܚܢܐ ܕܐܬܬܠܬ

f. 127 b col. a

ܫܒܚܬܗ ܕܡܪܬܢ ܘܡܪܒܝܢܐ
ܪܘܚܐ ܕܩܘܕܫܐ
ܣܠܩܬܢ ܒܒܢܝܐ ܕܢܘܗܪܐ
ܘܒܢܝܬ ܫܡܝܐ ܠܐܪܥܐ
ܡܐܢ ܗܘܝܬ ܘܚܙܝܬ
ܡܪ̈ܟܒܬܐ ܕܟܠܗܘܢ ܫ̈ܠܝܚܐ
ܕܦ̈ܪܚܝܢ ܘܐܬܝܢ ܠܐܕܪ
ܒܢܝܐ ⌜ܦܘܠܘܣ⌝ ܘܐܡܪ
ܘܐܦ ܐܢܐ ܒܡܕܝܢܬܐ
ܪܘܡܝܐ ܡܢ ܪܗܘܡܐ
ܕܬܡܘܪܬܐ ܠܟܢܫܘܬܗ
ܐܝܬ, ܗܘܝܬ. ܘܝܗ̈ܘܕܝܐ
ܕܝ̈ܢܝܢ ܗܘܘ ܥܡܝ ܬܡܢ
ܘܪܘܚܐ ܕܩܘܕܫܐ f. 128 a col. a
ܐܘܒܠܬ ܘܐܡܪܬ ܠܝ.
ܕܐܡܗ ܕܪ̈ܒܟܘܢ ܩܪܒ
ܠܗ ܝܘܡܐ ܕܬܦܢܐ ܡܢ
ܥܠܡܐ ܗܢܐ. ܠܐ ܢܐܕܥܘܗ̇
ܠܒܝܬ ܠܚܡ. ܘܒܪ ܫܒܬܗ
ܚܢܢܗ ܕܡܪܝܐ ܣܠܩܬܢ
ܘܐ̈ܝܬܝܬܘܢ ܐܝܬܝܬܢ.
ܒܢܝܐ ܬܐܘܡܐ ܘܐܡܪ
ܠܝ ܒܗܢܐ ܐܘܕܒܩܬܢ
ܪܘܚܐ ܕܩܘܕܫܐ ܒܪ
ܟܠܬ ܐܣܝܬܘܢ ܠܚܝܬܗ cf. J. S. L. p. ܛܘ

f. 127 b col. b

ܕܠܘܬ ܦ̇ܠܚܐ ܕܗ̈ܝܡܢܘܬܐ.
cf. J. S. L. v. 6, p. ܛܘ ܘܪܘܚܐ ܐܡܪܬ ܠܝ ܕܠܐ
ܠܒܝܬ ܠܚܡ ܡܛܠ ܕܐܡܗ
ܕܪ̈ܒܟܘܢ ܩܪܒ ܠܗ ܝܘܡܐ
ܕܬܦܢܐ ܡܢ ܥܠܡܐ ܗܢܐ.
ܘܒܪ ܐܢܐ ܡܬܕܒܪܢܐ
ܒܗܢܐ ܡܕܡ ܕܐܬܡܠܠ
ܥܡܟ. ܪܘܚܐ ܕܩܘܕܫܐ
ܣܠܩܬܢ ܘܐ̈ܝܬܝܬܘܢ
ܐܝܬܝܬܢ ܐܡܪ
ܡܪܘܡܐ ܐܢܐ
ܬܫܡܫܬܐ ܕܬܠܬ ܫ̈ܢܝܢ
cf. Cod. Harris f. 180 a ܡܫܡܫ ܗܘܝܬ. ܘܒܪ
f. 128 a col. b ܐܢܐ ܡܢ̈ܠܢܐ. ܪܘܚܐ
ܕܩܘܕܫܐ ܐܡܪܬ ܠܝ
ܒܪ ܡܫܡܐ ܗܘܝܬ ܡܕܡ
ܕܐܡܗ ܕܪ̈ܒܟܘܢ ܩܪܒ ܠܗ
ܝܘܡܐ ܕܬܦܢܐ ܡܢ ܥܠܡܐ
ܗܢܐ. ܐܠܐ ܩܘܡ ܙܠ
⌜ܠ⌝ܒܝܬ ܠܚܡ. ܘܒܪ ܐܢܐ
ܬܗܝܪ ܐܢܐ ܪܘܚܐ
ܕܩܘܕܫܐ ܣܠܩܬ⌜ܢ⌝ ܒܒܢܝܐ
ܕܢܘܗܪܐ ܘܐ̈ܝܬܝܬܘܢ
ܐܝܬܝܬܢ ⌜ܐܡܪ⌝
ܒܡܡܘܕ. ܐܢܐ

M. D. G.

ܘܗܫܐ ܒܒܥܝܐ ܐܢܐ f. 127 a col. a
ܕܬܬܐܡܪܘܢ ܠܝ ܕܡܒܥܘ
ܚܘܣܝܢ ܕܡܚܝܠܬܐ ܐܢܐ
ܠܝ. ܘܗܢ ܐܝܠܝܢ ܐܬܘ̈ܬܐ
ܐܬܬܘܢ ܠܘܬܝ، ܘܐܠܝܢ
ܕ̈ܒܘܟܐ ܪܒܒܬܘܢ ܕܗܫܐ
ܡܠܠ ܡܟܬ̈ܒܬܘܢ ܟܠܗ
ܠܝ. ܘܫܐܘܠܝܢ ܡܟܠܠ
ܕܢܒܝܐ ܐܢܐ ܕܫܪܝܪܐܝܬ cf. J. S. L. p. ܣ
ܕܗ̇ܘ ܕܐܬܝܠܕ ܡܢܝ
ܒܪܗ ܗܘ ܕܐܠܗܐ.
ܡܫܒܚܐ ܐܢܐ ܘܡܘܕܝܐ
ܐܢܐ ܘܣܓܕܐ ܐܢܐ ܠܗ cf. Cod. Harris f. 179a
ܕܐܝܟ ܡܫܒܚܬܐ f. 128 b col. a
ܕܐܡܬܗ ܗܘܝܬ ܣܒܪ
ܐܝܟ.. ܐܡܪ ܒܦܛܪܘܣ.
ܠܟܠܗܘܢ ܚ̈ܠܝܫܐ ܒܟܠ
ܫ. ܫ. ܡܢܝ ܐܝܟ
ܕܡܠܠܬ ܒܡܗ ܪܘܚܐ
ܕܩܘܕܫܐ ܒܢܒܝ̈ܘܗܝ
ܠܬܫܒܘܚܬܐ ܡܪܝܡ. ܘܗܢ
ܐܝܟܐ ܐܬܝܢ. ܐܡܪܝܢ
ܚ̈ܠܝܫܐ ܘܡܣܝܢ ܕܗܦܟ
ܠܦܘܡܗ ܗܘ ܕܐܬܐ

f. 127 a col. b ܘܕܡܐܝܬ. ܗܘ ܢܦܫܗ̇
ܕܐܝܟܢܐ ܐܬܐ
ܒܢܐ ܢܘܣܝܢ ܘܐܡܪ
ܒܐܦܣܘܣ ܦܓܪܬܝ
ܪܘܚܐ ܕܩܘܕܫܐ ܒܝ
ܒܐܠ ܐܢܐ ܒܬܪܒܐ
ܕܗܝܟܠܐ ܘܩܪܒܬ ܝܕ̈ܝ
ܡܕܒܚܐ ܘܠܫܒܬ ⸢ܠܝ⸣
ܕܐܡܗ ܕܪܒܒܘܢ ⸢ܘܪܒ⸣
ܠܗ ܘܒܢܐ ܕܬܦܠܪ ܡܢ
ܚܠܡܐ ܗܢܐ. ܘܠ ܝܕܐܘܗ̇
ܠܒܢܬ ܠܚܡ. ܘܪܘܚܐ
ܕܩܘܕܫܐ ܫܦܠܬܝ
f. 128 b col. b ܒܒܢܐ ܕܢܘܗܪܐ ܫܡܬܝ
ܘܠܬܪܒܐ ܕܒܠܬܐ ܡܦܠܬܝ.
ܒܢܐ ܦܛܪܘܣ ܘܐܡܪ
ܘܐܦ ܠܝ ܒܪܘܗܡܐ
ܦܓܪܬܝ ܪܘܚܐ ܕܩܘܕܫܐ
ܒܕܢܐ ܕܝܦܪܐ ܒܐܪܒܥܐ
ܒܣܒܐ. ܘܐܡܪܬ ܠܝ
ܕܡܣܢܐ ܕܡܘܪܒ ܐܢܬ
ܘܡܪܒܢܐ ܘܠ ܠܒܢܬ ܠܚܡ
ܝܕ̈ ܐܡܗ ܕܪܒܒܘܢ ܘ
cf. Cod. Harris f. 179 b ܕܪܒ ܠܗ ܘܒܢܐ ܕܬܦܠܪ
ܡܢ ܚܠܡܐ ܗܢܐ. ܘܒܪ

M. D. G.

f. 126 b col. a

ܐܝܟ ܡܙܡܪܝܢ
ܘܡܙܡܪ ܗܘܐ ܘܐܡܪ
ܗܟܢܐ. ܫܘܒܚܐ ܠܐܠܗܐ
ܘܒܪܐ ܘܪܘܚܐ ܕܩܘܕܫܐ
ܗܠܠܘܝܐ. ܘܟܕ ܡܦܝܣ
ܛ̈ܠܝܐ ܠܒܝܬ ܠܚܡ. ܡܢ
ܡܙܡܪܝܢ ܕܛ̈ܠܝܐ
ܓܒܪܐܝܠ ܘܡܝܟܐܝܠ
ܡܠܐ̈ܟܐ ܕܫܠܡܐ. ܘܟܠܗ
ܘܐܡܪܝܢ ܛ̈ܠܝܐ. ܫܠܡܐ
ܟܠܟܘܢ ܬܫ̈ܒܚܬܗ,
ܕܡܠܟܐ ܡܫܝܚܐ. ܟܕܘ
ܛ̈ܠܝܐ ܘܐܡܪܝܢ ܠܗܘܢ
ܠܡܠܐ̈ܟܐ. ܫܠܡܐ ܒܟܘܢ (f. 129 a col. a)
ܡܠܐ̈ܟܘܗܝ ܕܡܪܝܐ.
ܘܪܘܚܐ ܕܩܘܕܫܐ (cf. J. S. L. v. 6, p. ܒ, l. 8)
ܐܘܕܥܬ ܠܝܘܣܦ ܒܒܝܬ
ܠܚܡ. ܕܩܘܡ ܫܩܠ ܐܢܘܢ
ܠܛ̈ܠܝܐ ܚܒܝ̈ܒܝܢ ܘܥܪܘܩ
ܥܡ ܐܡܗܘܢ ܘܗܦܘܟ ܠܗܘܢ
ܘܕܒܪ ܐܢܘܢ ܘܥܠܘ ܠܘܬܗ̇
ܕܦܘܪܩܢܘܬܐ ܘܟܠܗ ܛ̈ܠܝܐ (cf. Cod. Harris f. 178 b)
ܘܡܠܐ̈ܟܐ ܐܟܚܕܐ
ܠܟܠܝܬܐ ܕܦܘܪܩܢܘܬܐ

f. 126 b col. b

ܘܫܒܘܚܗ̇ ܛ̈ܠܝܐ ܟܠ
ܚܕܝܗ̇ ܘܟܠ ܒܘܪ̈ܟܝܗ̇
ܘܣܓܕܘ ܠܗ̇ ܘܡܠܐ̈ܟܐ
ܡܢ ܪܘܚܐ ܩܪܒܘ ܠܗ̇
ܣܓܕܬܐ ܘܫܠܝܘ ܛ̈ܠܝܐ
ܘܗܘܘ ܡܙܡܪܝܗ̇ ܕܦܘܪܩܢܘܬܐ
ܘܟܝܢܘ ܘܐܡܪܝܢ ܠܗ̇. ܠܐ
ܬܕܚܠܝܢ ܒܪܬܟ ܒܢܝ̈ܐ
ܘܠܐ ܬܒܪܐ ܠܟܝ. ܡܪܝܐ
ܐܠܗܐ ܗܘ ܕܐܬܝܠܕ
ܡܢܟܝ. ܗܘ ܡܟܣܐ ܠܟܝ
ܡܢ ܟܠܡܐ ܗ̇ܢܐ
ܒܫܘܒܚܐ. ܘܡܫܪܐ ܠܟܝ

f. 129 a col. b

ܒܐܘ̈ܢܐ ܡܫ̈ܒܚܐ ܕܐܠܗܐ.
ܡܒܪܟܐ. ܗܠܝܢ ܕܒܪܝ
ܥܠܝܟ ܟܠܗܘܢ ܘܒܗܘܢ
ܡܒܣܡ ܠܡܙܝܐ ܕܪܚܡܘܗܝ.
ܘܬܠܬ ܢܦܫܗ̇ ܡܪܬܝ
ܡܪܝܡ ܘܬܒܬ ܒܒܪܗܐ.
ܘܐܡܪܬ ܠܗܘܢ ܠܛ̈ܠܝܐ.
ܗܢܐ ܗܘ ܒܪܬ ܠܝ
ܕܐܬܐ ܪܒܘܠ ܡܢ ܫܡܝܐ.
ܘܚܝܐ ܐܢܐ ܠܗ ܘܡܢ
ܡܢܬܐ ܐܢܐ. ܐܡܒܢܐ
ܕܐܬܬܘܢ ܐܬܝܘܢ ܘܫܪܝܬܘܢ

M. D. G.

f. 126a col. a ܘܒܢܝܐ ܕܬܫܦܪ ܡܢ ܥܠܡܐ
ܗܢܐ. ܘܪܘܚܐ ܕܩܘܕܫܐ cf. J. S. L. v. 6, p. ܩ, l. 14
ܐܘܕܥܬ ܠܡܟܝܪܘܣ
ܘܐܡܪܬ ܠܗ. ܕܐܡܪܗ
ܕܢܒܥܘܢ ܡܢܗ ܠܗ ܘܒܢܝܐ
ܕܬܫܦܪ ܡܢ ܥܠܡܐ ܗܢܐ.
ܘܠ ܠܫܠܡܗ̇ ܠܒܝܬ ܠܚܡ.
ܗܠܝܢ ܐܘܕܥܬ ܪܘܚܐ
ܕܩܘܕܫܐ ܠܫ̈ܠܝܚܐ
ܩܕ̈ܝܫܐ. ܘܥܡ ܬܠܡܝ̈ܕܝܗܘܢ
ܫ̈ܠܝܚܐ ܒܐܬ̈ܪܘܬܐ
ܗܠܝܢ ܕܐܬܝܗܘܢ ܒܗܘܢ ܀
ܕܐܡܝܢܐ ܢܐܬܘܢ ܥܕܡܐ ܕܐܡܝܢ
ܕܬܫܒܘܚܬܐ ܡܪܬܝ ܡܪܝܡ ܠܒܝܬ f. 129b col. a
ܠܚܡ. ܘܐܡܪܝ ܟܠ ܚܕ ܚܕ
ܡܢܗܘܢ ܒܠܫܢܗ ܕܐܬܝܠܕ ܒܗ
ܐܝܟ ܕܢܒܥܐ ܦܘܠܘܣ ܫܠܝܚܐ cf. Cod. Harris f. 177b
ܕܐܙܠ ܠܒܝܬ ܠܚܡ ܘܒܗ
ܒܡܪܝܚܘܬܐ ܘܒܫܘܒܚܐ
ܐܬܟܢܫܘ ܗܘܘ ܒܗܠ
ܚܕ ܚܕ ܡܢܗܘܢ ܕܫ̈ܠܝܚܐ.
ܡܪܗܘܢ ܫܕܪ ܠܗܘܢ
ܪܘܟܒܐ ܡܢ ܫܡܝܐ.
ܘܡܪܟܒܬܐ ܘܢܘ̈ܪܐ

f. 126a col. b ܕܢܘܗܪܐ ܕܢܦܩ ܐܝܟܢ
ܘܢܣܒܬ ܒܢܝܐ ܕܢܘܗܪܐ
ܘܣܦܩܬܗ ܗܘܬ ܠܦܝܠܛܘܣ
ܘܒܢܬ ܫܡܝܐ ܠܐܪܥܐ
ܩܐܡ ܗܘܐ ܘܡܫܡܫܐ
ܠܫ̈ܠܝܚܐ ܚܒܪ̈ܘܗܝ
cf. J. S. L. p. ܒ ܕܢܐܬܘܢ ܐܝܟ ܕܗܝ
ܘܒܗ̇ ܒܫܥܬܐ ܣܦܩܬ
ܐܝܟ ܪܘܚܐ ܕܩܘܕܫܐ
ܠܟܠܗܘܢ ܫ̈ܠܝܚܐ
ܒܡܪܟܒܬܐ ܕܢܘܗܪܐ
ܘܐܬܘ ܠܘܬ ܦܝܠܛܘܣ.
ܘܫܒܚܘ ܪܘܚܐ ܕܫ̈ܠܝܚܬܐ
f. 129b col. b ܘܢܗܪܬ ܫܡܝܐ ܘܐܪܥܐ
ܡܢ ܒ̈ܢܝܐ ܕܡܒܪܟܝܢ
ܗܘܘ ܀ ܒܝܦܪܐ ܕܝܢ
ܒܡܫܟܐ ܐܪܟܒܐ ܒܫܒܐ
ܐܬܦܪܫܘ[1] ܫ̈ܠܝܚܐ ܡܢ
ܪܘܚܐ ܕܩܘܕܫܐ ܘܒܗ
ܦܠܛ ܡܫܟܐ ܕܐܪܟܒܐ
ܒܫܒܐ ܐܬܒܫܘ ܢ̈ܝܫ
ܬܫܒܘܚܬܐ ܡܪܬܝ ܡܪܝܡ ܠܒܝܬ
ܠܚܡ. ܘܗܘܬ ܕܫܠܡܬܐ
ܪܒܬܐ ܒܒܢ̈ܝܐ ܗ̇ܘ.
cf. Cod. Harris f. 178a, l. 5 ܘܐܬܐ ܗܘܐ ܕܢܘܚ ܒܪ

M. D. G.

[1] Cod. ܐܬܦܪܣܘ

f. 63b col. a

ܕܡܬܝܠܕܐ ܗܘܐ ܝܬܒ
ܝܡܝܢ ܒܪܘܚܗ̇ ܘܡܫܠܠ
ܒܟܡܗ̇. ܘܪܘܚܐ ܕܩܘܕܫܐ
ܕܢܚܬ ܒܠܘܗ, ܐܝܟ
ܢܘܗܪܐ. ܘܠܒܫܬ ܠܗ
ܘܐܡܪܐ ܠܗ ܕܐܡܗ
ܕܪܒܒܘܢ ܩܪܒ ܠܗ ܘܒܢܝܐ
ܕܬܫܦܪ ܡܢ ܟܠܡܟܐ
ܗܢܝܐ. ܐܠܐ ܐܠ ܠܒܢܬ
ܠܚܝܢ ܠܫܠܡܗ̇. ܘܟܕ
ܫܡܥ ܬܐܘܡܐ (cf. J. S. L. p. ܡܘ, l. 15)
ܐܬܪܗܒ. ܘܒܪ ܫܒܬܗ
ܐܝܠ ܠܒܪܬܐ ܘܣܡ
ܦܝܪܡܐ ܘܒܣ̈ܡܐ (f. 66a col. a)
ܘܒܪܝܟ ܘܝܠܕ. ܘܪܘܚܐ
ܕܩܘܕܫܐ ܐܘܕܒܬ ܠܒܢܬ,
ܘܐܡܪܐ ܠܗ ܕܐܡܗ
ܕܪܒܒܘܢ ܩܪܒ ܠܗ ܘܒܢܝܐ
ܕܬܫܦܪ ܡܢ ܟܠܡܟܐ ܗܢܝܐ.
ܘܪܘܚܐ ܐܘܕܒܬ (cf. J. S. L. p. ܡܘ, l. 2)
ܠܒܢܝܢ ܕܒܐܘܪܫܠܡ
ܘܐܡܪܐ ܠܗ ܕܐܡܗ
ܕܪܒܒܘܢ ܩܪܒ ܠܗ ܘܒܢܝܐ
ܕܬܫܦܪ ܡܢ ܟܠܡܟܐ ܗܢܝܐ.

f. 63b col. b

ܐܠܐ ܦܘܡ ܠܫܠܡܗ̇ ܠܒܢܬ
ܠܚܝܢ ܘܪܘܚܐ ܕܩܘܕܫܐ
ܐܘܕܒܬ ܠܬܠܡܝܕܝܗ
ܘܐܡܪܐ ܠܗ ܕܐܡܗ
ܕܪܒܒܘܢ ܩܪܒ ܠܗ ܘܒܢܝܐ
ܕܬܫܦܪ ܡܢ ܟܠܡܟܐ ܗܢܝܐ
ܐܠܐ ܐܠ ܠܫܠܡܗ̇ ܠܒܢܬ
ܠܚܝܢ. ܐܝܟ ܕܝܡ ܡܢ
ܥ̈ܠܝܡܐ ܠܐ ܡܢܝܬ ܗܘܐ
ܐܠܐ ܐܢ ܐܝܕܪܐܘܣ
ܐܝܣܗ ܕܫܡܥܘܢ ܟܐܦܐ
ܘܦܝܠܝܦܘܣ ܘܠܘܩܐ ܘܫܡܥܘܢ
ܡܢܝܢܐ. ܗܠܝܢ ܡܢܬܘ ܗܘܘ.
(f. 66a col. b) ܘܒܬܪ ܢܘܡܐ ܐܘܕܒܬ
ܐܢܘܢ ܪܘܚܐ ܕܩܘܕܫܐ
ܟܠܘ ܡܩܒܪ̈ܝܗܘܢ ܘܡܫܬܘ
ܡܢ ܠܘ ܥܒܘܠ. ܘܐܡܪܬ
ܠܗܘܢ ܪܘܚܐ ܕܩܘܕܫܐ.
ܠܐ ܬܣܒܪܘܢ ܠܒܘܢ
ܕܢܘܚܡܐ ܡܛܠ. ܐܠܐ
(cf. J. S. L. p. ܡܘ, l. 13) ܟܠܗ ܕܐܬܢܚܡܬܘܢ ܢܩܘܡ
ܡܢ ܡܩܒܪ̈ܝܗܘܢ. ܡܛܠ
ܕܐܬܐܠܘܢ ܠܫܠܡܗ̇ ܕܐܡܗ
ܕܪܒܒܘܢ ܡܛܠ ܕܩܪܒ ܠܗ

f. 63 a col. a
ܕܢܘܗܪܐ ܕܢܐܬܘܢ
ܠܘܬ ܦܘܒܝܢܬܐ ܡܪܝܡ
ܠܒܝܬ ܠܚܡ ◦◦
ܠܫܡܥܘܢ ܟܐܦܐ — cf. J. S. L. p. ܡܘ
ܐܘܕܥܬܗ ܒܪܗܘܡܐ
ܟܕ ܥܐܠ ܕܢܩܪܒ
ܘܩܪܒܢܐ ܒܥܕܬܐ
ܒܐܪܒܥܐ ܒܫܒܐ ܕܐܝܬ
ܗܘܐ ܬܡܢ ܩܘܪܒܢܐ
⌈ܕܐ⌉ܒܗ̈ܬܢܐ. ܘܗܘܐ ܓܗܝܢ
ܘܓܝܠܐ ܡܢ ܡܕܒܚܐ.
ܘܪܘܚܐ ܕܩܘܕܫܐ
ܠܫܬ ܠܗ ܕܡܫܝܚܐ
⌈ܐܬ⌉ܩܪܒܬ ܩܘܪܒܢܐ

f. 63 a col. b
ܠܦܘܠܘܣ ܟܕ ܐܝܬ ܠܗ
ܡܓܘܬܐ ܥܡ ܝܗ̈ܘܕܝܐ
ܕܕܝܢܝܢ ܗܘܘ ܥܡܗ
ܘܡܓܕܦܝܢ ܠܗ. ܘܐܡܪܝܢ
ܠܗ ܕܡܠܝܟ ܕܠܝܟ ܠܐ
ܡܬܘܒܠܝܢ ܕܡܕܒܪ ܐܢܬ
ܥܠ ܡܫܝܚܐ ܡܛܠ ܕܡܢ
ܦܪܘܣܘܣ ܐܢܬ. ܘܒܪ
ܠܘܠܝܐ ܐܢܬ. ܘܡܛܠܠ
ܕܒܪ ܡܫܒܚܢܐ ܐܢܬ
ܗܐ ܠܒܝܟ ܐܢܬ ܥܡܗ
ܕܡܫܝܚܐ ⌈ܘܫܐ⌉ܪ ܐܢܬ
ܒܗ. ܘܡܩܪܒܬ ܪܘܚܐ
ܕܩܘܕܫܐ ܐܘܕܥܬ

f. 66 b col. a — cf. Cod. Harris f. 176 b
ܐܠ ܠܒܝܬ ܠܚܡ ܠܘܬ
ܐܡܗ ܕܡܪܢ ܡܛܠ
ܕܡܠܐ ܠܗ ܙܒܢܐ ܕܬܦܩ
ܡܢ ܥܠܡܐ ܗܢܐ. ܘܠܦܘܠܘܣ
ܬܘܒ ܐܘܕܥܬܗ. ܠܓܘ
ܡܢ ܪܗܘܡܐ ܒ⌈ܡ⌉ܕܝܢܬܐ
ܫܪܐ ܕܫܡܗ ܛܒܪܝܘܣ
ܘܪܚܝܩܐ ܗܘܬ ܡܢ
ܪܗܘܡܐ ܫܬܝܢ
ܡܝ̈ܠܝܢ ܘܐܫܬܕܪܬܗ

f. 66 b col. b
ܕܐܡܗ ܕܡܪܢ ܩܪܒ
ܠܗ ܙܒܢܐ ܕܬܦܩ ܡܢ
ܥܠܡܐ ܗܢܐ. ܘܬܡܗ
ܦܘܠܘܣ. ܘܟܕ ܫܡܥܗ
ܣܡ ܦܘܪܣܐ ܘܒܩ̈ܝܡܐ
ܘܒܪܝܟ ⌈ܘܓܠܐ⌉. ܘܐܘܕܥܬ
ܬܘܒ ܪܘܚܐ ܕܩܘܕܫܐ
cf. Cod. Harris f. 177 a — ܠܬܐܘܡܐ ܒܗܢܕܘ
ܕܒܠܠ ܗܘܐ ܕܢܫܒܘܪ
cf. J. S. L. p. ܡܘ, l. 17 — ܠܫܬܗ ܕܠܘܝ ܡܠܟܐ

f. 112 b col. a

ܕܢܦܩܬ ܡܢ ܥܠܡܐ ܗܢܐ.
ܡܢܐ ܢܥܒܕܘܢ ܒܐܢܐ
ܘܪ̈ܚܡܐ ܡܢܐ ܕܢܦܫܢ
ܡܢ ܐ * ܪ ܗܕܐ
ܒܡܘܪܬܐ ܠܥܠܡܐ ܕܠܐ
ܥܒܪ. ܘܒܢ̈ܝܗ ܗܘ ܗܟܢ
ܩ̈ܠܠܐ ܒܪ̈ܝܫܗܘܢ. ܗܟܢܐ
ܟܕ ܐܘܕܥܬܢ ܪܘܚܐ
ܕܩܘܕܫܐ ܒܡܕܒܚܐ
ܕܐܦܣܘܣ ܘܐܡܪܬ ܠܢ.
ܕܢܦܘܩ ܘܠ ܝܐܕܢܗ ܒܕ
ܐܬܝܢ ܫ̈ܠܝܚܐ ܚܒܪ̈ܝܗ
ܠܘܝܕܥܬܗ. ܐܡܪܐ ܠܗ
ܓܠܐ ܘܦܫܛ ܦܢܝܡܐ. (f. 111 a col. a)
ܗܕܝܢ ܒܪܝܟ ܛܘܒܢܐ
ܟܠ ܒܘܪ̈ܟܘܗܝ, ܘܓܠܐ
ܘܗܟܢܐ ܐܡܪ[1] * *
ܡܪܝ ܫܘܒ ܡܫܝܚܐ
ܫܡܥ ܒܩܠܐ ܕܓܠܘܬܗ
ܕܫܠܡܬܝ. ܘܬܐ ܓܐܕܢܗ
ܘܬܚܝܢ ܘܒܕ ܬܦܘܣ
ܡܢ ܥܠܡܐ ܗܢܐ ܐܝܟ
ܕܐܡܪܬ ܠܗ ܦܘܡܝ
ܘܫܡܥܐ ܕܐܬܬ ܓܐܕܢܗ (cf. Cod. Harris f. 176 a)
ܘܢܗܘܐ ܢܝܫܢ ܕܝܠܝ

f. 112 b col. b

ܘܕܐܒܘܟܝ ܘܕܐܘܚܝܟܝ
ܕܩܘܕܫܐ. ܘܬܐ ܓܢܕ
ܐܡܟܝ ܘܬܚܝܢܝܟܝ ܒܡ
ܒܪ̈ܝܟܝ ܡܫܒ̈ܚܐ. ܘܢܚܬܘܢ
ܠܟܝ ܫܡܝܐ ܘܐܪܥܐ
ܬܫܒܘܚܬܐ. ܘܟܕ
ܢܘܚܢ ܡܠܐܟܐ ܗܘܐ
ܘܡܕܒܪ ܠܐ ܥܠܡ ܗܘܐ
ܓܠܘܬܗ. ܘܠܐ ܐܫܬܡܥ
ܡܢ ܫܡܝܐ ܕܐܡܪ ܠܗ
ܐܡܝܢ ܐܬܒܫܪܘ ܟܠܟܘܢ
ܘܬܘ. ܘܓܬ ܢܘܚܢ ܘܫܡܥ
ܠܩܠܐ ܗܢܐ. ܘܐܬܬ
f. 111 a col. b ܪܘܚܐ ܕܩܘܕܫܐ ܠܘܬ
ܢܘܚܢ ܘܐܡܪܐ ܠܗ.
ܫܡܥܬܗ, ܠܩܠܐ ܗܢܐ
ܕܐܒܘܟ ܒܫܡܝܐ. ܐܡܪ
ܢܘܚܢ ܫܡܥܬ. ܐܡܪܐ
ܠܗ ܪܘܚܐ ܕܩܘܕܫܐ
ܗܢܐ ܩܠܐ ܐܝܠܕܐ
ܐܬܘܗܝ, ܩܕܡ ܫ̈ܠܝܚܐ
ܚܒܪ̈ܝܟ ܕܐܬܝܢ ܠܫܠܡܗ
ܕܐܡܗ ܕܡܪܢ. ܘܟܕ
ܢܘܚܢ ܡܠܐܟܐ: ܪܘܚܐ
ܕܩܘܕܫܐ ܐܘܕܥܬ ܐܢܘܢ
ܠܫ̈ܠܝܚܐ ܐܝܟܢܐ

[1] a hole

ܒܦܘܪ̈ܐ ܕܠܐ ܗܝܡܢܘ f. 112a col. a
ܕܒܪܗ ܐܢܬ ܕܐܠܗܐ.
ܡܛܠ ܕܫܡܝܢܐ ܘܐܪܥܢܐ
ܦܘܪܩܢ ܕܗܘܐ ܗܘ,
ܒܬܘܠܬܐ ܘܝܠܝܕܬܐ
ܕܝܠܕܬܟ. ܘܐܢܬ ܗܘ ܒܪܗ
ܕܐܠܗܐ ܡܫܒܚܐ. ܘܟܠ
ܕܡܘܕܐ ܒܟ ܚܝܐ ܠܥܠܡ.
ܘܟܕ ܫܠܡ ܠܡܬܠܘܗܝ ܐܡܪܬ
ܡܪܬܝ, ܡܪܝܡ ܠܡܪܝ ܝܘܚܢܢ.
ܩܪܘܒ ܓܐܕܝ, ܐܡܪ ܠܟ
ܘܩܪܒ ܠܘܬܗ̇ ܝܘܚܢܢ
ܘܫܐܠܬ ܠܗ ܘܐܡܪܬ f. 111b col. a
ܕܒܠܡܕܡ ܕܐܡܪ ܠܝ ܪܒܢ
ܫܪ. ܘܟܘܠ ܐܬܘ̈ܬܐ
ܘܬܕܡܪ̈ܬܐ ܕܐܡܪ ܠܝ
ܗ̈ܘ. ܘܗܒܢܐ ܐܡܪ ܠܝ
ܒܪ ܠܐ ܢܣܒ ܠܫܡܫܢܐ
ܓܕ ܐܒܘܗ, ܕܡܪܐ ܕܢܦܩ
ܡܢ ܒܠܡܐ ܗܢܐ ܗܘ
ܘܒܫܡܐ ܕܡܠ̈ܟܐ ܐܬܐ
ܓܐܕܝ. ܐܡܪ ܠܗ̇ ܝܘܚܢܢ
ܐܬܐ ܗܘ ܡܪܢ ܢܫܘܒ
ܡܫܝܚܐ ܘܢܚܝܬ ܠܗ

f. 112a col. b ܐܝܟܢܐ ܕܐܡܪ ܠܟܝ.
ܐܡܪܐ ܠܗ ܝܘܚܢܢ
cf. Wright, p. ܠܒ, l. 5 ܕܡܝܢܐ ܠܗܘܢ ܡ⌜ܗܝܡ⌝ܢܘܬܐ
ܘܡܥܡܕ ܠܗܘܢ ܒܡܝܐ.
ܕܡܐ ܕܡܢܬܐ ܐܢܐ
ܢܦܩܘܢܗ̇ ܠܥܠܡ, ܒܢܘܪܐ.
ܐܡܪ ܠܗ̇ ܝܫܘܥ. ܘܐܡܪ
ܗܘ ܠܝ ܡܪܝ ܝܫܘܥ.
ܡܫܝܚܐ. ܐܡܪܐ ܡܪܬܝ,
ܡܪܝܡ. ܘܐܦ ܡܠܬܐ ܐܢܐ
ܐܝܟܢܐ ܡܒ⌜ܪ⌝ܐ ⌜ܐܢܬ⌝ ܠܝ.
ܐܡܪ ܠܗ̇ ܐܝܟܢܐ ܕܦܩܕ
cf. Cod. Harris f. 175b ܠܝ ܐܒܝ ܘܫܦܝܪ ܗ̈ܘ,
f. 111b col. b ܕܟ̈ܒܝܢܗ̇ ܕܦܓܪܢܝܬܐ.
ܘܝܫܘܥ ܡܟܦܪ ܗܘܐ
ܠܗܘܢ. ܒܐ[1].. ܪ̈ܙܐ ܘܒܟܐ
ܗܘܐ ܝܫܘܥ ܘܫܦܝܪ.
⌜ܗܘܐ⌝ ܕܡܟ̈ܘܢܗ, ܘܕܗܠܝܢ
ܒܬܘܠܬܐ ܒܡܪܗ. ܡܛܠ
ܕܒܪܝܐ ܗܘܬ ܠܗܘܢ ܫܦܝܪ
ܡܛܠ ܡܪܬܝ, ܡܪܝܡ.
ܘܩܪܒ ܝܫܘܥ ܘܐܡܪ
ܠܗ̇ ܠܡܪܬܝ, ܡܪܝܡ. ܐܢ
ܐܢܬ, ܕܐܝܬܝܟܝ ܥܠܕܬ
ܐܠܗܐ. ܗܟܢܐ ܒܪܝܐ ܠܟܝ

[1] a hole.

ܠܡܪܝܐ ܒܟܒܝܗ̇. ܕܐܫܬܪܪܬ ܕܐܙܠ ܡܢ ܡܪܝܐ ܘܫܡܥܬ
ܒܡܪܟܐ ܘܪܚܡܬ ܡ̈ܪܝ ܢܫܘܥ ܡܫܝܚܐ ܒܪܗ ܕܐܠܗܐ ܚܝܐ.
ܗ̇ܝ ܚܝ ܒܡ̈ܟܠ ܘܐܙܠ ܐܝܟܐ ܘܠܐܬܪܗ̇ ܠܒܝܬ ܠܚܡ ܡܛܠ
ܡܕܡ [1]ܕܦܩܕ ܠܝ ܪܘܚܐ ܩܕܝܫܬܐ. ܩܕܡ ܡܕܒܚܢܐ. ܐܙܠ
ܐܚܪܐ ܠܐܡܝܢ ܒܪ ܢܦܫܐ ܡܢ ܥܠܡܐ ܒܕܠܐ [2]ܬܡܘܬ.
ܗ̇ܢ ܐܡܪ ܢܘܚܡ ܠܐ ܢܦܠ ܗܘܐ ܕܪܘܚܐ ܩܕܝܫܬܐ ܫܠܦܐ f. 174b
ܠܗ ܒܟܝܢܐ ܕܢܘܗܪܐ. ܐܠܐ ܗ̣ܘ ܫܒܩ ܗܘܐ ܕܒܬ̈ܓܠܗܘܢ
ܐܙܠ ܠܒܝܬ ܠܚܡ. ܘܒܕܠܐ ܬ̣ܠܡ ܢܛܘܬܗ ܪܘܚܐ ܩܕܝܫܬܐ
ܪܦ̇ܬ ܒܠܗܘܢ.. ܘܒܒܝܬܐ ܕܡܫܡܫܢܘܬܗ ܘܠܬܪܬܐ ܕܒܠܝܬܐ
ܐܡܛܠܬܗ. ܗ̇ܝ ܕܡܢܬܐܢܐ ܗܘ̣ܬ ܒܗ ܠܦ̈ܪܘܣܝܬܐ ܘܦܬܚ
ܢܘܚܡ ܬܪܥܗ̇ ܕܒܠܝܬܐ. ܘܥܠ ܘܐܫܟܚܗ̇ ܕܝܢ ܠܦܘ̈ܪܣܝܬܐ ܒܕ
ܡܨܠܝܐ ܒܡܪܝܐ. ܘܩܪܒ ܢܫܩܗ̇ ܠܗ̇ ܚܕܝܗ̇ ܘܟܠ ܒܦܘܪ̈ܝܗ̇
ܘܐܡܪ ܠܗ̇ ܫܠܡ ܠܟܝ ܡܠܕܬ ܐܠܗܐ ܘܫܠܡ ܠܗ ܠܡܫܝܚܐ
ܕܐܬܝܠܕ ܡܢܟܝ. ܠܐ ܬܕܚܠܝܢ ܠܟܝ ܡܪܬܝ. ܕܒܫܘܒܚܐ ܪܒܐ
ܢܦܩܐ ܐܢܬܝ ܡܢ ܥܠܡܐ ܗ̇ܢܐ. ܘܗܕܝܢ ܝܠܕܬ ܐܠܗܐ ܚܕܝܬ
ܗܟܝܢ ܕܐܡܪܐ ܡܪܝ. ܢܘܚܡ ܡ̈ܝܬܐ. ܘܫܒܚ ܗ̇ܠܝܢ ܒܬܘ̈ܠܬܐ
ܗܟܢܐ. ܠܗ̇ ܘܠܐ ܒܬܪܗ ܡܠܟܗ̇. ܐܡܪܐ ܠܗ ܕܝܢ ܡܪܝܡ
ܠܢܘܚܡ ܫܒܩ ܦܓܪܗ ܘܒܥܘܬܐ ܘܫܡ ܘܐܡܪ ܗ̇ܒܝܐ. ܡܪܝ
ܢܫܘܥ ܡܫܝܚܐ ܒܒܪܐ ܬܫܒܘܚܬܐ ܘܕܡ ܐܡܝܢ. ܒܪ ܢܦܫܬ f. 175a
ܡܢ ܥܠܡܐ ܗ̇ܢܐ. ܕܒܫܡܗ ܘܬܘܒ

[1] sic [2] Cod. ܬܡܘܬܝ

ܘܝܠܕܬ ܗܒܢܐ ܘܐܡܪܬ. ܪܒܘܠܝ ܡܫܒܚܐ ܫܒܚ ܦܠܐ Codex Harris f. 173 b, l. 3
ܕܝܠܕܬܟ. ܘܫܕܪ ܠܝ ܡܪܝ، ܡܦܫܚ. ܕܐܫܬܘܕܝܗ، ܘܐܘܕܐ ܠܟ
ܥܠ ܛܝܒܘܬܟ. ܢܕܒܪܐ ܐܢܐ ܕܢܥܒܕ ܐܢܬ ܠܝ ܒܥܒܕܝܟ
ܕܬܒܥܐ ܐܢܐ ܡܢܟ. ܘܗܘܐ ܝܠܕܬ ܦܘܒܢܝܬܐ. ܘܐܬܝܗ،
ܗܘܐ ܡܦܫܚ ܫܠܝܚܐ ܒܐܦܣܩܘ ܡܕܝܢܬܐ. ܘܚܙ ܗܘܐ.
ܘܪܘܚܐ ܕܩܘܕܫܐ ܐܘܕܥܬܗ ܘܐܡܪܬ ܠܗ. ܕܐܡܪܗ ܕܪܒܟ
ܡܢܐ ܠܗ ܘܒܥܐ ܕܬܦܘܩ[1] ܡܢ ܥܠܡܐ. ܘܗܘ ܐܙܠ ܠܘܬܗ
ܠܘܬ ܠܣܡ. ܘܬܒܥ ܫܒܩ ܕܬܪܒܝܬܐ ܢܦܩ ܡܦܫܚ ܕܝܠܗ
ܒܒܝܬܐ ܕܐܦܣܩܘ. ܒܪ ܡܠܟܐ ܠܬܪܒܐ ܕܗܝܟܠܐ. ܘܪܘܚܐ
ܕܩܘܕܫܐ ܐܘܕܥܬܗ ܒܪ ܐܒܪܡ ܥܠܘܗ، ܐܝܟ ܒܪܘܚܐ ܕܢܒܪܐ
ܘܐܡܪ ܠܗ ܒܟܠ ܠܗܝܟܠܐ. ܘܥܠ ܘܐܬܟܢܫܘ ܕܝܠܗ ܡܢ
ܡܕܒܚܐ. ܘܪܘܚܐ ܕܩܘܕܫܐ ܐܡܪܬ ܠܗ ܕܐܡܪܗ ܕܪܒܟ f. 174 a
ܡܢܐ ܠܗ ܘܒܥܐ ܕܬܦܘܩ[2] ܡܢ ܥܠܡܐ. ܘܗܘ ܐܙܠ ܝܠܕܬܗ
ܠܘܬ ܠܣܡ ܕܦܠܚ ܙܒܢܐ ܠܣܝܡܟ. ܘܗܘܐ ܡܕܒܪܢܐ ܐܢܐ
ܠܫܠܝܚܐ ܚܒܪܝܟ ܕܬܠܡܝܕܘܗܝ ܥܠܡܐ ܠܘܬ ܠܣܡ. ܡܢ
ܐܬܪܘܬܐ ܕܐܬܟܢܫܘ ܒܗܘܢ. ܗܢܘܢ ܕܝܐܡܝܢ ܘܗܢܘܢ
ܕܡܐܬܝܢ. ܗܠܝܢ ܐܡܪܬ ܪܘܚܐ ܕܩܘܕܫܐ ܠܡܦܫܚ ܘܫܒܩܬ
ܡܢ ܝܠܕܗ، ܘܬܡܢܥ ܡܦܫܚ ܘܒܪܟܬ ܠܗ ܫܠܡ. ܘܠܘܬܗ
ܕܚܡܝܐ ܡܢ ܕܢܐܙܠ. ܘܦܩܕ ܐܢܘܢ ܠܬܠܡܝܕܘܗܝ، ܥܠ
ܬܫܡܫܬܐ ܕܒܝܬܐ ܕܐܪܥܬ ܒܐܦܣܩܘ. ܬܗܘܐ ܝܠܕܬܐ

[1] Cod. ܕܬܦܘܩ [2] Cod. ܕܬܦܘܩ

ܘܐܚܪܬܐ ܐܝܬܝܗ̇ ܫܡܫܗ̇ f. 31 b col. a
ܢܗܪܐ ܒܪܬܗ ܕܥܡܢܘܐܝܠ
ܪܫ ܒܟܢܘܫܬܐ ܕܝܗ̈ܘܕܝܐ.
ܕܒܕܡܘܬܗ̇ ܕܢܫܪܐ
ܡܬܠ ܡܠܟܐ ܡܫܝܚܐ.
ܕܥܠ ܓܦ̈ܘܗܝ ܕܡܬܦܫܛܝܢ
ܫ̈ܕܘܗܝ، ܦܓܡ ܘܣܚܝܗ̇
ܠܒܪܬܐ ܩܕܝܫܬܐ ܕܡܒܣܪܐ
ܠܗ ܡܢ ܩܕܡ ܡܬܝ̈ܠܕܘܬܗ
ܕܒܠܒܐ. ܘܗܝ ܕܫܡܫܗ̇
ܦܓܬܐ ܐܝܬܝܗ̇ ܒܪܬܗ
ܕܦܘܒܢܐ ܘܡܘܦܠܢܐ.
ܕܐܝܬܘܗܝ، ܗܘܐ ܘܗ
ܗܢܐ ܡܢ ܓܢܣܐ ܕܒܝܬ f. 34 a col. a
ܐܪܟܠܐܘܣ ܡܠܟܐ. ܘܗܘ
ܐܪܟܠܐܘܣ ܐܝܬܘܗܝ، cf. J. S. L. p. ܠ
ܗܘܐ ܡܢ ܫܪܒܬܐ
ܕܒܐܪܘ ܡܠܟܐ ܗܘ
ܕܐܘܦܗ ܠܫܡܥܘ ܪܫ
ܬܠܡ̈ܝܕܐ. ܐܝܬܘܗܝ، ܕܝܢ
ܦܘܫܩܐ ܕܗܠܝܢ ܫ̈ܡܗܐ
ܗܟܢܐ. ܒܠܬܐ ܒܪܬܐ
ܘܬܘܠܕܬܐ ܗܝ ܕܐܝܬܝܗ̇
ܐܘܪܫܠܡ ܕܒܫܡܝܐ

f. 31 b col. b ܘܗܕܐ ܒܥܕܬܐ ܕܐܝܬ
ܠܟ ܒܐܪܥܐ ܕܡܫܘܬܗ̇ ܗܝ
ܕܗܝ، ܕܐܝܬ ܠܟ ܒܫܡܝܐ
ܘܒܗ ܡܬܠܡ ܒܦܘܪܩܢܗ
ܕܐܠܗܐ ܡܫܝܚܐ. ܘܢܗܪܐ
ܐܝܬܘܗܝ، ܡܫܝܚܐ
ܕܡܢ ܢܡܢ ܐܒܘܗܝ، ܝܬܒ
ܥܠ ܡܪܟܒܬܐ ܕܣܪ̈ܦܐ.
ܘܦܠܓܬܐ ܐܝܬܝܗ̇ ܙܘܓܐ
ܕܩܘܕܫܐ. ܕܡܢܗ̇ ܡܬܗܡܢܝܢ
ܚܝ̈ܐ ܠܟܠܗܘܢ ܒܢ̈ܝܢܫܐ.
ܗܠܝܢ ܫܡ̈ܗܐ ܐܝܬ
ܗܘܐ ܠܗܠܝܢ ܒܬܘܠܬܐ
ܕܡܫܡܫܝܢ ܗ̇ܘ، ܠܗ̇
f. 34 a col. b ܠܡܪܬܝ، ܡܪܝܡ. ܘܩܡ
ܒܬܘܠܬܐ ܗܠܝܢ ܒܡ
ܦܘܩܕܢܬܐ ܘܢܦܩ ܠܒܝܬ
cf. Cod. Harris f. 173 b ܠܚܡ ܒܫܡܫܐ. ܒܫܒܐ
ܘܒܬ، ܬܡܢ. ܘܒܟܪܘܒܬܐ
ܐܬܐܠܝܨܬ ܠܗ̇ ܦܘܩܕܢܬܐ.
ܘܐܡܪܬ ܠܗܘܢ ܡܪܝܡ
ܠܟ ܦܬ̈ܓܡܐ ܕܒܣܡܐ ܕܒܢܝܐ
ܐܢܐ ܐܡܠܐ ܠܢܒܘܠ.
ܡܫܝܚܐ ܕܐܝܬ ܠܟ
ܒܫܡܝܐ. ܘܩܪܒ ܠܗ̇
ܗܠܝܢ ܒܬܘܠܬܐ ܦܬ̈ܓܡܐ.

ܐܝܕܝܗ̇ ܕܛܘܒܢܝܬܐ f. 31 a col. a
ܘܡܕܡ ܒܢܦܫܗ̇ ܡܫܘܚܢ
ܗܘ، ܠܗܝܢ ܘܡܚܫܒܢ. ܘܒܕܚܠܐ
ܪܒܐ ܡܫܡܫܝܢ ܗ̈ܘܘ ܠܗ̇
ܗܠܝܢ ܒܬ̈ܘܠܬܐ ܠܒܬܘܠܬܐ
ܡܕܝܢܬܐ. ܘܟܕ ܨܦܪܐ cf. Cod. Harris f. 172 b, l. 4
ܐܬܘ ܐܢܫܐ ܘܢܫܐ
ܘܣܓܕܘ ܠܛܘܒܢܝܬܐ
ܘܐܬܒܪܟܘ ܡܢܗ̇. ܘܦܫܛܬ
ܐܝܕܝܗ̇ ܡܪܬܝ، ܡܪܝܡ
ܘܒܪܟܬ ܐܢܝܢ ܠܟ̈ܢܘܫܬܐ
ܗܠܝܢ ܘܐܡܪܬ ܠܗܝܢ. cf. Wright, p. ܟܠ, l. 6
ܬܬܘܟܠ ܠܒܘ̈ܬܟܝܢ ܒܫܡܝܐ
ܡܕܡ ܕܒܥܠ ܕܐܬܐ ܠܝ ܬܬܡܝ.
ܕܡܢ ܒܗܠܝܢ ܫܒ̈ܬܐ f. 34 b col. a
ܕܐܣܦܪܠ ܠܐ ܐܢܫ ܠܘܬ
ܡܢܗܝܢ ܐܠܐ ܐ̄ ܐܢܬܝܢ.
ܘܒܥܕ ܝܘܡܐ ܘܒܬܬ ܡܪܬܝ،
ܡܪܝܡ ܒܐܘܪܫܠܡ. ܘܒܠܠܝܐ
ܐܬܐ ܓܒܪܝܐܝܠ ܪܝܫ
ܡܠܐ̈ܟܐ ܘܐܬܚܘܝ، ܠܗ̇.
ܘܐܡܪ ܠܗ̇ ܠܛܘܒܢܝܬܐ.
ܘܗܫܐ ܦܘܩ، ܠܒܝܬ ܠܚܡ
ܘܬܗܘܝܢ ܗܘ، ܒܕܡܐ
ܕܢܚܝܬ ܠܩ̈ܕܝܫܐ
ܕܡܠܐ̈ܟܐ ܘܕܪ̈ܘܚܢܐ

f. 31 a col. b ܘܟܠܗܝܢ ܒܢ̈ܬܐ ܕܐܬܝܢ
ܠܫܠܡܗ̇. ܘܚܙܝ، ܬ̈ܠܬܐ
ܗܠܝܢ ܠܡܠܐܟܐ ܕܐܠܗܐ
ܕܐܬܐ ܐܝܕܝܗ̇ ܘܕܗܠܝܢ
ܐܡܪ ܠܗ̇. ܘܕܚܠ ܕܚܠܬܐ
cf. Cod. Harris f. 173 a ܪܒܬܐ. ܘܟܕ ܗܘ ܐܝܕܝܗ̇
ܡܠܐܟܐ. ܘܗܘܐ ܨܦܪܐ.
ܘܩܪܬ ܡܪܬܝ، ܡܪܝܡ
ܠܒܬ̈ܘܠܬܐ ܗܠܝܢ ܘܐܡܪܬ
ܠܗܝܢ ܒܠܚܘܕ ܘܦܬܚܬ
ܦܪܕܝܣܘܣܐ ܘܐܦܩܬ
ܡܟ̈ܬܒܢܗ̇ ܘܦܬܓܡܐ ܘܐܬܡܠܝ
ܥܠ ܡܕܡ ܕܐܙܠ ܒܥܡܗ̇
cf. J. S. L. p. ܢܒ, l. 10 ܠܒܝܬ ܠܚܡ. ܘܗܢܝܢ ܗܠܝܢ
f. 34 b col. b ܒܬ̈ܘܠܬܐ ܐܝܬܝܗܝܢ
ܗ̈ܘܘ، ܒܢ̈ܬ ܐܢܫܐ ܥܬܝܪ̈ܬܐ
cf. Wright, p. ܠ, l. 13 ܘܡܕܒܪ̈ܢܝܗ̇ ܕܐܘܪܫܠܡ.
ܗܠܝܢ ܕܫܡܫ̈ܗܝܢ
ܐܢܬܬܗܘܢ ܗܠܝܢ. ܟܠܬܐ
ܘܢܫܪܐ ܘܦܬܟܬܐ. ܟܠܬܐ
ܐܬܝܗ̇ ܗܘܬ ܒܪܬܗ
ܕܢܝܩܘܕܡܘܣ ܪܫܢܗ
ܕܡܫܝܚܐ. ܕܒܫܡܗ̇
ܕܟܠܬܐ ܪܫܢܝܐ ܒܕܬܐ
ܡܫܝܚܬܐ ܟܠܬܐ
ܡܟܝܪܬܗ ܕܒܪܗ ܕܐܠܗܐ.

ܡܫܒܠܐ ܒܐܘܪܚܬܐ ܡܢ f. 71 b col. a
ܐܠܗܐ. ܐܝܟ ܓܝܪ ܬܒܝܠܐ cf. J. S. L.
ܐܝܟ ܟܠ ܪܒܘܬ ܕܐܝܬ p. ܠܕ
ܠܟ ܒܫܡܝܐ. ܕܠܡܫܡܫ
ܕܒܢܝܐ ܐܝܟ ܠܗ ܒܥܕ ܠܟ
ܒ̈ܢܝܢܐ. ܘܒܕ ܐܡܪܬ
ܡܪܬܝ, ܡܪܝܡ ܠܒ̈ܢܬ
ܐܘܪܫܠܡ. ܕܐܝܕܐ ܕܒܢܝܐ cf. Cod. Harris
ܕܬܐܙܠ ܒܥܡܗ ܠܒܝܬ ܠܚܡ. f. 171 b
ܦܪܟܐ ܗܠܝܢ ܒܬܘܠܬܐ
ܕܡܫܡܫܢ ܗܘ̈ܝ, ܠܗ. ܘܐܡܪܝ̱
ܠܗ. ܕܐܝܕܐ ܕܒܢܝܐ
ܕܒܢܝܐ[1] ܕܬܐܙܠ ܠܒܡܥܝ
ܡܪܬܝ, ܡܪܝܡ ܡܫܒܠܐ
ܒܐܘܪܚܬܐ ܡܢ ܐܠܗܐ. f. 74 a col. a
ܐܢܫܝܢ ܓܝܪ ܠܐ ܫܒܩܝܢ[1]
ܫܠܡ ܠܟܝ ܘܡܫܒܚܝܢ[1] ܫܠܡ
ܕܡܥܠܬܟܝ ܫܒܩܝܢ ܫܠܡ
ܐܒܗܝܢ ܘܐܚ̈ܝܢ ܘܟܘܠ
ܕܐܝܬ ܠܝ. ܘܐܠܗܝܢ[1] ܫܠܡ
ܒܦܟܝ ܕܢܦܫܟܝ ܘܒܦܟܝ
ܒܟܝܢ ܫܠܡ ܕܢܦܫܬ ܘܒܦܟܝ
ܒܟܝܢ ܫܠܡ ܕܢܦܫܐ. ܗܢܝܢ
ܕܝܢ ܗܠܝܢ ܒܬܘ̈ܠܬܐ ܒܥܡܗ̇
ܗܘ̈ܝ, ܕܡܪܬܝ, ܡܪܝܡ
ܐܝܡܡܐ ܘܠܠܝܐ. ܕܡܫܡܫܢ

f. 71 b col. b ܗܘ̈ܝ, ܠܗ. ܘܡܫܒܚܢ ܗܘ̈ܝ,
ܠܗ ܦܪܝܫܐ ܕܒܫܡܝܐ.
ܘܟܠܢܫ ܐܦܝܣ ܗܘ̈ܝ, ܠܗ
ܕܐܡܪ ܠܟܝ ܡܪܬܝ, ܡܪܬܗ
ܕܟܠܡܐ ܘܐܠܦܝ ܠܟܝ ܐܝܟܢܐ
ܐܬܟܠ̈ܝ ܡܢܟܝ ܡܪܝ̱ ܫܘܒ
ܡܫܝܚܐ ܕܠܐ ܫܘܬܦܘܬܐ
ܕܓܒܪܐ. ܘܗܘ, ܡܪܬܝ, ܡܪܝܡ
ܐܡܪܐ ܗܘܬ ܠܗܝܢ ܟܠ
cf. Cod. Harris ܡܕܡ ܘܗܢܝܢ ܡܫܘܝܢ ܗܘ̈ܝ,
f. 172 a ܒܪܘܚܗ ܘܡܫܠܡܢ ܗܘ̈ܝ, ܓ̈ܒܠܝܗ.
ܘܟܠܢ ܡܐ̈ܢܝܗ ܘܦܩܕܝܢ
ܒܦܘܡܐ. ܘܟܘܠ ܡܕܡ
ܕܡܫܬܡܫܐ ܗܘܬ ܒܗ̇
f. 74 a col. b ܡܪܬܝ, ܡܪܝܡ ܡܢܗ̇ ܘܠܗ̇
ܒܒܢܝܢ ܗܘܐ ܠܗܝܢ
ܠܒܬܘ̈ܠܬܐ ܗܠܝܢ. ܘܠܐ
ܡܡܪܚܐ ܗܘܬ ܚܕܐ
ܡܢܗܝܢ ܕܬܦܫ ܡܢ ܡܕܡ
ܕܡܫܬܡܫܐ ܗܘܬ ܒܗ̇
ܡܪܬܝ, ܡܪܝܡ ܘܬܦܠܚܡ
ܒܗ ܡܕܡ. ܡܛܠ ܕܫܦܝܪ
ܕܚܠܝܡ ܗܘ̈ܝ, ܡܢܝܢܗ̇
ܕܦܘܠܚܢܐ ܡܛܠ ܐܬ̈ܘܬܐ
ܕܚ̈ܝܠܬܐ ܕܚܙܝܢ ܗܘ̈ܝ,
ܒܐܝܡܡܐ ܘܒܠܠܝܐ

[1] sic

ܗܘ̈ܦܟܝܗܘܢ. ܐܢܬܘܢ ܓܝܪ܆ f. 71 a col. a
ܠܐ ܐܬܝܬܘܢ. ܘܗܫܐ
ܕܐܬܝܬܘܢ ܓܒܝ̈ܢܝܗܘܢ
ܡܪܝܡ ܠܐ ܒܒܕܐ.
ܗܕܝܢ ܗܦܟܘ ܫܠܝ̈ܚܐ
ܒܫܒܚܬܐ ܡܢ ܓܢܕ
ܦܪܕܝܣܐ. ܘܠܓܦܪܐ ܬܘܒ
ܐܬܘ ܫܠܝ̈ܚܐ ܠܘܬܗ̇.
ܘܐܡܪܝܢ ܠܗ̇ ܡܪܝܡ
ܒܪܝܟܐ ܐܦܝܣܩܘܦܝ ܘܠܐ
ܡܠܟܬܝ, ܦܘܩܝ. ܗܦܟܬ ܗܘ cf. Cod. Harris f. 170 b
ܒܪ ܥܢܢܐ ܕܐܬܠܕ ܡܢܟܝ.
ܕܐܢܬܝ, ܡܪܬܝ, ܠܗ ܒܪܗ
ܕܐܠܗܐ. ܘܐܢܫܝܢ ܡܪܝܡ f. 74 b col. a
ܠܗ ܒܪ ܐܢܫܐ. ܒܕ ܡܕܒܝܢ
ܕܒܪ ܡܠܘ ܘܐܝܟ ܐܬܠܕ.
ܘܒܬܪ ܐܬܪܒܝ. ܘܐܢܫܝܢ
ܠܚܫܘܗܝ, ܘܨܠܝܒܗܝ, ܘܡܠܝܠܐ
ܕܒܗ̈ܒܐ ܗܦܟܝܢ ܒܪܝܫܗ.
ܘܕܩܝܪܝܢܗ, ܒܠܘܒܢܬܐ.
ܘܦܪܝܩܬ ܘܐܬܩܒܪ. ܬܘܒ
ܕܦܓܥܘܬܐ ܡܢ ܟܠ ܕܠܐ
ܐܬܚܒܫܬ ܠܒܝ ܒܬܘܠܬܐ
ܕܬܫܒܝܢ ܟܠ ܥܠܡܗ ܒܕ.
ܡܫܬ. ܘܐܠܘ ܢܗܘܐ ܒܠܘܦܬܐ

f. 71 a col. b ܠܐ ܥܒܕ ܒ⌜ܗ̇⌝ ܦܩܘܕܬܐ
ܘܐܦ ܠܗ ܫܢܝܐ ⌜ܘ⌝ܡܬܢܐ
ܘܡܒܪܗ ܘܡܫܝܚܢ ܓܐܕܝܢ
⌜ܘ⌝ܐܠܐ ܕܒܒܕ ܗܒܢܐ. ܫܡܥܬ
ܗܘܐ ܠܗ ܠܫܢ⌜ܘ⌝ܠ. ܗܠܝܢ
ܐܡܪܘ ܫܠܝ̈ܚܐ ܠܡܪܬܝ,
ܡܪܝܡ. ܘܠܐ ܡܠܟܬ ܐܢܘܢ.
ܗܕܝܢ ܕܐܬܐ ܕܦܓܣܐ
ܗܘܬ ܒܗ̇ ܦܩܘܕܝܬܐ
ܒܐܘܪܫܠܡ. ܠܝܘܣܦ ܓܒܪܐ
ܕܒܝܬܐ ܗܘܬ ܡܢ ܕܒܝܬ
ܕܠܒܐ ܕܕܘܝܕ ⌜ܘ⌝ܡܪܒܝܐ
cf. Cod. Harris f. 171 a ܗܘܬ ܠܕܪܬܗ ܕܝܘܚܢܢ.
f. 74 b col. b ܘܡܢ ܒܬܪܟܢ ܐܬܒܪܗܬ
ܡܪܬܝ, ܡܪܝܡ. ܘܫܕܪܬ
ܩܪܬ ܠܫܠܝܚܐ ܕܫܢ̈ܐ
ܕܒܒܥܘܬܐ ܕܡܬܒܐ
ܗܘܬ ܒܗ̇ ܘܐܡܪܬ
ܠܗܝܢ. ܦܘܩܘ ܒܫܠܡܐ
ܐܢܐ ܐܙܠܐ ܐܢܐ ܠܝ
ܠܒܝܬ ܠܚܡ. ܠܒܝܬܐ ܕܐܝܬ
ܠܝ ܬܡܢ. ܡܒܝܢ ܕܠܐ
ܢܗܒܝܢ ܠܝ ܫܘ̈ܕܥܐ ܐܙܠ
ܐܝܠܐ ܓܝܪ ܠܦܠܘܛܗ
ܕܡܫܝܚܐ. ܐܠܐ ܐܝܕܐ
ܕܒܒܝܐ ܕܐܬܬܐ ܒܡܢ

f. 72 b col. a
cf. J. S. L. p. ܟܐ, l. 4

ܘܓܠܝܘܬܐ ○ ○ ܐܡܪ
ܗܟܢܐ ܠܫ̈ܠܝܚܐ ܕܢܐܙܠܘ
ܐܢܬܘܢ ܦܘܩܕܗ̇ ܕܡܪܢ
ܕܒܒܝܢ ܐܢܬܘܢ ܘܐܬܘ
ܒܫܝܢܐ ܠܘܬ ܡܪܬܝ
ܡܪܝܡ ܘܐܡܪܝܢ ܠܗ̇.
ܗܟܢܐ ܦܩܕ ܕܠܐ
ܬܐܙܠܝܢ ܬܛܠܝܢ ܟܕ ܡܒܪܐ
ܘܓܠܝܘܬܐ. ܘܗܫܐ ܡܪܝܡ
ܐܡܪܝܢ ܣܝܡ ܠܟܝ. ܐܬܕܟܪܝ
ܫܠ̈ܡܐ ܕܒܒܝܕܝܢ ܠܟܝ
ܡܕܡ ܐܠܗܐ. ܘܠܐ ܬܬܠܒܝܢ
ܠܒܪ̈ܝܬܐ ܘܬܬܐܡܪܝܢ ܕܗ̇ܘ
ܕܐܬܬܠܕ ܡܢܟܝ ܡܫܝܚܐ
ܗܘ. ܫܡܥܝܢ ܐܢܘܢ ܫܡܝܐ
ܘܐܪܥܐ ܕܒܪܗ ܗܘ
ܕܡܘܫܐ ܢܒܝܐ. ܐ˙ ܐܢ ܕܝܢ
ܟܕܢܐ ܐܢܬܝ ܕܬܛܠܝܢ ܟܘܠ
ܠܟܝ ܠܟܠܗ̇ ܥܒܕܬܐ ܘܫܡܥܝ
ܢܡܘ̈ܣܘܗܝ ܕܡܘܫܐ.
ܘܐܢ ܫܠ̈ܡܐ ܕܒܒܝܢ ܠܟܝ
ܡܫܚܫܝܢ ܣܝܡ ܥܠܝܟܝ ܘܩܪܝܢ
ܣܝܡ ܠܐܠܗܐ ܘܡܪܝܡ
ܥܠܝܟܝ. ܘܟܘܠ ܘܦܘܩ ܠܒܝܬ
ܓܠܘܬܐ ܥܡ ܣܒܪ̈ܬܟܝ

f. 72 b col. b

ܫܡܥܝܢ ܣܝܡ ܥܠܝܟܝ
ܐܘܪܝܬܐ ܘܡܬܚܫܚܝܢ
ܣܘܟܠܟܝ ܟܒܪ ܡܢ ܪܒܝܟܝ
ܡܫܐ: ܡܪܝܡ ܠܐ ܡܪܦܝܢ
ܣܝܡ ܟܕ ܐܝ̈ܕܝܐ ܘܕܚܝܠܟܝ
ܕܟܝܪܗܬܝ, ܡܢܝܢ ܐܢܚܝܢ
ܒܫܒܘܪܐ ܒܐܕ̈ܢܝܟܝ

cf. Cod. Harris f. 170 a
cf. J. S. L. p. ܟܐ, l. 14

ܘܡܣܝܕܐ [1]ܡܬܐܣܝܬܝ.
ܘܐܦ ܠܗܠܝܢ ܡ̈ܠܐ ܠܐ
[1]ܡܟܝܠܬܝ, ܦܘܩ ܠܟܝ ܡܢ
ܐܘܪܫܠܡ. ܘܟܘܠ ܠܟܝ
ܠܒܝܬܟܝ ܠܒܝܬ ܠܚܡ. ܓܝܪ
ܡܒܪܐ ܒܪ ܘܓܠܝܘܬܐ ܠܐ

f. 73 a col. b

ܢܗܘܝܢ ܣܝܡ ܠܟܝ ܕܬܬܠܝܢ.
ܡܢܐ ܐܡܪܬܝ, ܡܪܝܡ.
ܒܝܬ ܦܘܠܒܢܝܬܐ ܘܐܡܪܬ.
ܠܐ ܘܠܐ ܗܘܐ ܠܟܘܢ
ܕܬܐܬܘܢ ܠܘܬܝ, ܟܡܠܝܢ
ܡ̈ܠܐ. ܐܢܐ ܓܝܪ ܦܘܩܕܢܟܘܢ
ܠܐ ܟܒܪܐ ܐܢܐ. ܘܠܡ̈ܠܝܟܘܢ
ܠܐ ܫܡܥܐ ܐܢܐ. ܘܠܐ
ܟܒܪܐ ܐܢܐ ܓܒܝܟܘܢ.
ܘܐܠܘ ܒܒܝܬܘܢ ܕܬܬܦܪܘܢ
ܚܐܪܘܬܐ ܡܢ ܒܪ
ܐܫܡܥܬܘܢܝ ܡ̈ܠܝܐ
ܕܟܘܣܪܢܐ. ܐܒܝܬ ܠܟܠܗܘܢ

f. 73 a col. a

[1] sic

f. 72 a col. a
cf. J. S. L. p. ܒ, l. 8

ܘܒܪ ܐܬܐ ܐܒܓܪ ܡܠܟܐ
ܠܢܗܪܐ ܦܪܬ. ܡܬܚܫܒ
ܗܘܐ ܒܪܥܝܢܗ ܕܐܝܟ ܒܒܪ
ܗܘܝܐ ܠܗ̇ ܒܡܠܕܒܒܘܬܐ
ܒܬ ܠܝ ܠܦܓܪܝܗܘܢ ܘܥܕܪ
ܘܒܬܪ ܗܘܐ ܐܒܓܪ
ܐܓܪܬܐ ܘܫܕܪ ܗܘܐ
ܠܡܒܥܝܘ ܐܦܘܪܘܣܐ ܘܗܘ
ܦܒܝܢܐ ܫܕܪ ܐܢܝܢ
ܠܦܓܪܝܘܣ ܡܠܟܐ. ܒܬܒ
ܠܗ ܓܝܪ ܗܟܢܐ. ܡܢ ܐܒܓܪ
ܡܠܟܐ ܒܪܡܥܢܘ ܕܐܘܪܗܝ،
ܡܕܝܢܬܐ ܕܒܝܬ ܢܗܪܝܢ.
ܫܠܡܐ ܣܓܝܐܐ ܠܡܠܟܘܬܟ
ܡܪܝ ܦܓܪܝܘܣ. ܡܛܠ ܕܠܐ
ܬܫܬܘܕܥ ܡܠܟܘܬܟ
ܐܝܕܐ. ܠܐ ܒܒܪܬ ܢܗܪܐ
ܦܪܬ. ܕܒܟܐ ܗܘܬ[1] ܕܐܣܒ
ܠܐܘܪܫܠܡ ܘܐܣܪܒܝܗ̇.
ܡܛܠ ܕܦܠܛܬ ܠܡܫܝܚܐ
ܐܣܝܐ ܚܝܒܐ. ܐܠܐ
ܐܢܬ ܐܝܟ ܡܠܟܐ ܪܒܐ
ܕܫܠܝܛ ܐܢܬ ܒܠܗ. ܫܕܪ
ܒܒܪ ܠܝ ܕܝܢܐ ܡܢ ܬ̈ܢܝܢ
ܐܘܪܫܠܡ ܕܦܠܛܬ ܠܡܫܝܚܐ
ܕܢܣܒ ܠܐ ܐܫܟܚ ܒܗܘ
ܕܐܠܘ ܝܒܐ ܒܪ ܚܝ ܫܕܪܬ

cf. Cod. Harris f. 169 a
f. 73 b col. a

f. 72 a col. b

ܗܘܬ ܐܦܝܣܬܗ ܕܐܬܐ
ܠܗ ܓܝܪ، ܠܐܘܪܗܝ، ܗܘ
ܒܪ ܡܪܝܡ ܕܒܥܐ ܠܐ ܒܒܪ
ܡܦܠܛܗ، ܒܕܝܢܐ ܡܫܝܚܐ
ܬ̈ܢܝܢ ܐܘܪܫܠܡ. ܬܗܘܐ ܕܝܢ
ܕܒܟܐ ܡܠܟܘܬܟ ܕܕܝܢܐ
ܒܒܐ ܕܬܬܒܥ ܠܝ ܡܫܝܚܘ
ܘܢܩ̈ܦܐ. ܗܕܐ ܐܓܪܬܐ
ܐܫܬܕܪܬ ܡܢ ܐܒܓܪ
ܡܠܟܐ ܠܡܒܝܢܐ ܐܦܘܪܘܣܐ
ܘܡܢ ܦܒܝܢܐ ܐܦܘܪܘܣܐ
ܐܙܠܬ ܠܦܓܪܝܘܣ ܡܠܟܐ.
ܘܒܪ ܐܬܩܪܝܬ ܒܕܡܘܗܝ،
ܐܬܒܥܝ ܦܓܒ ܦܓܪܝܘܣ
ܡܠܟܐ. ܘܒܟܐ ܗܘܐ ܕܢܘܒ
ܘܢܦܠܛ ܠܒܠܗܘܢ ܝ̈ܗܘܕܝܐ.
ܘܒܪ ܫܡܥܘ ܬ̈ܢܝܢ ܐܘܪܫܠܡ
ܐܬܬܙܝܥܘ. ܐܡܪܝܢ
ܠܗ ܝ̈ܗܘܕܝܐ ܠܗܓܡܘܢܐ.
ܡܛܠ ܡܪܬ، ܡܪܝܡ ܗܦܟ
ܠܗ̇ ܕܒܝܠܕܐ ܕܠܝܠܬ
ܐܬܝܠܕ ܒܠܗ ܐܘܪܫܠܡ.
ܘܟܠ ܕܗܘܪܐ ܢܦܫܗ ܒܒܪܐ
ܕܐܠܗܐ ܘܦܝܣܗ ܘܦܠܛܝܗ.
ܘܗܫܐ ܦܩܕܗ̇. ܕܠܐ
ܬܐܙܠ ܬܓܠܐ ܓܝܪ ܡܒܪܐ

f. 73 b col. b

cf. Cod. Harris f. 169 b

[1] sic

f. 32 b col. a

ܠܗ ܐܦ ܒܐܪܥܐ ܐܦ
ܒܫܡܝܐ. ܘܗܘܐ ܢܒܝܐ.
ܗܠܝܢ ܡܠܐ ܡܠܠ ܥܡܗ̇
ܓܒܪܝܐܝܠ. ܘܬܘܒ ܒܪܬ
ܡܪܬܝ, ܡܪܝܡ ܘܝܠܕܬ
ܕܢܚܬ ܕܐܬܐ ܡܠܐܟܐ
ܢܐܕܝܗ̇ ܘܐܘܕܥܗ̇ ܒܟܠܡܕܡ.
ܗܝܕܝܢ ܢܛܘܪ̈ܐ ܐܡܪܘ
ܠܫܠܝ̈ܚܐ ܕܐܬܬ ܡܪܝܡ
ܘܗܐ ܡܬܝܠܐ ܥܕ ܡܒܪܐ.
ܘܩܪܒܬ ܣܓܕܬ ܘܐܬܬ
ܠܒܝܬܗ̇ ܠܐܘܪܫܠܡ. ܘܗܘܐ
ܫܘܒܚܐ ܒܐܘܪܫܠܡ ܥܠ
ܡܪܬܝ, ܡܪܝܡ. ܐܡܪܝܢ
ܠܗ ܒܢ̈ܝܐ ܠܡܥܡܘܕܝܐ. (f. 33 a col. a)
ܫܕܪ ܦܘܕܝܗ̇ ܠܡܪܝܡ ܕܠܐ (cf. J. S. L. p. ܟ, l. 3)
ܬܐܙܠ ܬܬܝܠܐ ܥܕ ܡܒܪܐ
ܘܦܩܕܬܐ. ܘܟܕ ܗܘܐ (cf. J. S. L. p. ܛ, l. 17)
ܡܬܚܙܝܢ ܗܠܝܢ. ܐܓܪ̈ܬܐ
ܐܬܝ, ܡܢ ܐܒܓܪ ܡܠܟܐ
ܐܘܟܡܐ ܕܐܘܪܗܝ,
ܡܕܝܢܬܐ ܠܛܒܪܝܢܐ
ܐܦܛܪܘܦܐ ܕܒܒܠ ܗܘܐ
ܠܣܒܝܢܘܣ ܒܥܙܪ ܘܒܕܡܐ
ܠܦܪܬ ܢܗܪܐ ܐܝܬܘܗܝ,
ܗܘܐ ܫܘܠܛܢܗ ܕܣܒܝܢܘܣ
ܐܦܛܪܘܦܐ ܡܛܠ ܕܢܚܬ
ܗܘܐ ܐܕܝ, ܫܠܝܚܐ ܚܕ

f. 32 b col. b

ܡܢ ܫܒܥܝܢ ܘܬܪܝܢ ܘܒܢܝܐ
ܕܐܬܐ ܒܐܘܪܗܝ, ܘܐܣܝ
ܟܐܒܐ ܕܐܝܬ ܗܘܐ ܠܗ
ܠܐܒܓܪ ܡܠܟܐ. ܡܚܕܐ ܗܘܐ (cf. Cod. Harris f. 168 b)
ܠܗ ܓܒܪ ܐܒܓܪ ܡܠܟܐ
ܕܐܘܪܗܝ, ܠܝܫܘܥ ܡܫܝܚܐ
ܘܡܫܐܠ ܗܘܐ ܒܠܒܗ
ܡܛܠܬܗ. ܘܟܕ ܡܫܠܡ
ܗܘܐ ܡܫܝܚܐ ܒܓܠܝܠܐ
ܕܝܠܐ ܢܪܕܦܘܗܝ, ܝܗܘ̈ܕܝܐ
ܫܠܚ ܗܘܐ ܠܗ ܐܒܓܪ
ܕܬܐ ܠܝ ܢܐܕܝ, ܡܛܠ
ܕܫܡܥܬ ܕܝܗܘ̈ܕܝܐ ܒܥܝܢ
ܕܢܩܛܠܘܢܝ. ܘܟܕ ܡܝܬ
ܡܫܝܚܐ ܘܫܡܥ ܐܒܓܪ (f. 33 a col. b)
ܡܠܟܐ ܕܒܙܩܝܦܐ ܩܛܠܘܗܝ,
ܝܗܘ̈ܕܝܐ. ܐܡܪ, ܗܘܐ ܐܒܓܪ
ܬܐܪܬܝ ܥܠ ܕܫܕܪ ܗܘܐ
ܡܪܝ ܢܐܕܘܗܝ, ܠܐܕܝ, ܡܢ
ܫܒܥܝܢ ܘܬܪܝܢ ܘܐܣܝܗ
ܡܢ ܟܐܒܐ ܕܐܝܬ ܗܘܐ
ܠܗ. ܘܡܢ ܐܒܓܪ ܘܪܒܐ
ܗ̇ܘ ܘܟܠܗ ܚܝܠܗ ܘܐܬܬܐ
ܒܕܡܐ ܠܦܪܬ ܢܗܪܐ.
ܘܟܠܐ ܗܘܐ ܕܢܣܒ ܥܠ
ܐܘܪܫܠܡ ܘܕܢܚܪܒܝܗ̇ ܥܠ
ܕܩܛܠܬ ܡܫܝܚܐ ܡܪܗ

○ ○ ○ ○ ○ ○ ○

ܘܠܐ ܝܕܥܝܢ ܡܢܐ ܐܡܪܝܢ. f. 32 a col. a
ܡܫܕܐ ܠܒܪ ܕܐܫܡܥܘܗ̇
ܗܘܘ ܡ̈ܢܝܐ ܕܒܘܣܪܢܐ
ܠܒܢܘ ܢܦܫܗܘܢ ܡܢܗ̇
ܘܟܕ ܫܐܠܘܗ̇ ܕܐܝܟܢܐܝܬ
ܐܬܬܐ ܘܡܠܝܠܐ ܝܗܒ
ܠܫܠܡܘܬܐ ܘܡܒܪܐ ܠܒܪܗ
ܒܡܢܗ̇ ܡܝܘܬܐ. ܐܝܟ
ܕܢܗܘܪܘܢ ܒܡܢܗ̇. ܘܟܢܘ
ܢܘܪܐ ܘܐܡܪܘ ܠܡܠܟܐ.
ܐܢܐ ܝܗܒ ܡܒܪܐ ܠܐ ܫܡܥ cf. Cod. Harris f. 167 b
ܫܡܥ. ܐܠܐ ܐܢ ܡܪܝܡ
ܕܨܦܪܐ ܘܪܡܫܐ ܐܬܝܐ
ܘܡܨܠܝܐ ܬܡܢ. ܐܡܪܝܢ
ܠܗܘܢ ܟܗ̈ܢܐ ܘܠܡܢܐ ܝܗܒܝܢ
ܐܬܝܢ ܠܗ̇ ܕܐܬܝܠ ܘܬܨܠܐ f. 33 b col. a
ܬܡܢ. ܐܡܪ̈ܝܢ ܢܘܪ̈ܐ
ܘܨܠܝܢ ܐܬܝܢ ܕܢܠܠܗ̇.
ܐܡܪ̈ܝܢ ܠܗܘܢ ܟܗ̈ܢܐ.
ܐ[ܢ] ܗܘܬ ܐܬܝܐ ܠܬܡܢ
ܒܨ̈ܦܪܐ ܪܘܓܙܘܗ̇ ܠܗ̇,
ܡܒܝܫܘܬܗ ܕܐܝܣܪܐܝܠ. cf. Wright, p. ܟܘ, l. 11
ܐܡܪܝܢ ܢܘ̈ܪܐ ܚܢܢ ܠܐ
ܐܡܪܝܢ ܚܢܢ ܠܗ̇ ܡܕܡ ܐܠܐ
ܡܢ ܕܐܬܝܐ ܕܬܨܠܐ
ܬܡܢ ܐܬܝܢ ܘܡܘܕܥܝܢ ܚܢܢ
ܠܟܘܢ. ܘܟܠ ܡܕܡ ܕܨܒܝܢ
ܐܢܬܘܢ ܥܒܕܘ ܠܗ̇:

f. 32 a col. b ܘܒܒܪܘܟܬܐ ܐܬܦܢܝܬ
ܡܪܝܡ ܕܐܬܝܠ ܝܗܒ ܘܡܒܪܗ
ܕܡܪܢ ܘܦܢܝܐ ܗܘܬ ܒܫܡܝܐ
ܘܢܘܪܐ. ܘܟܕ ܗ̇ܘ ܡܠܝܠܐ
ܘܐܪܡܝܬ ܒܢ̈ܝܢܗ̇ ܘܫܪܬ
ܒܫܡܝܐ. ܘܟܪ ܫܡܥܬܗ
ܬܪ̈ܥܐ ܕܫܡܝܐ ܐܬܦܬܚܘ
ܘܦ̈ܠܘ ܠܦܪܐ ܕܗܪܘܡܐ
ܕܐܪܡܝܬ ܡܪܬܝ ܡܪܝܡ
ܒܦܪܕܝܣܐ ܘܦܬܚ ܪܘܚܗ
ܒܟܠܗܘܢ ܐܬܪ̈ܘܬܐ
ܕܫܡܝܐ. ܘܟܕ ܒܫܒܬܐ
ܐܬܐ ܠܦܪܕܝܣܐ ܡܠܐܟܐ
ܡܢ ܫܡܝܐ ܠܘܬܗ̇ ܘܒܪܟ
ܥܠܝ ܠܗ̇ ܘܐܡܪ ܠܗ̇. ܫܠܡ
f. 33 b col. b ܠܟܝ ܡܠܬ ܐܠܗܐ. ܛܘܒܝܟܝ
ܐܬܩܒܠܬ ܒܫܡܝܐ ܩܕܡ
ܒܪܟ ܡܪܝ ܢܫܘܒ ܡܫܝܚܐ.
ܘܡܟܝܠ ܢܦܫܬܝ, ܠܒܝ ܡܢ
ܚܠܡܐ ܗܢܐ ܠܫܢܐ ܕܠܟܠܡ
cf. Cod. Harris f. 168 a ܚܠܡܝܢ. ܗܟܢܐ ܠܒܪ
ܐܫܬܪܪܬ ܕܐܡܪ ܠܟܝ
ܘܐܘܕܥܝ ܕܒܥܕܢܐ ܕܡܝܠܬ
ܒܐܪܥܐ ܒܪ ܫܡܥܬܗ
ܡܬܒܥܝܬ ܒܫܡܝܐ ܘܟܠ
ܡܕܡ ܕܒܥܝܬ ܡܢ ܡܫܝܚܐ
ܒܪܐ ܕܐܝܬ ܠܟܝ ܒܫܡܝܐ
ܡܢ ܡܫܝܚܐ ܕܐܠܗܐ ܢܗܘܐ

ܘܢܝܚܐ ܓܝܪ ܡܪܢܐ ܘܦܪܩ ܫܘܠܡܗ ܒܪ ܫܒܬܗ ܠܡܝܬܘܬ.
ܘܡܚܒܪܐ ܫܩܠܘ ܗܘܘ ܡܘ̈ܬܐ ܠܝܒܗܘܢ ܕܥ̈ܝܢܐ ܘܬ̈ܠܝܒܐ
ܐܚܪ̈ܢܐ. ܘܗܝ ܠܡܫܝܚܘܬܐ ܕܒܠܒ ܗܘܐ ܒܗ ܦܪܘܩܢ.
ܘܐܣܬܟܠܐ ܕܦܪܘܩܗ ܠܗ ܒܗ ܢܚܐ. ܘܗܠܝܢ ܢܫ̈ܘܬܐ ܒܢܝܐ
ܕܐܠܗܝܢܘܗܝ. ܘܗܘ ܚܠܝܠܐ ܕܒܗ̈ܢܐ ܕܣܒܩܘ ܠܗ ܒܪܝܫܗ.
ܘܗܢܘܢ ܥܡܪ̈ܐ ܕܫܒܩܘ ܠܗ ܒܐܪ̈ܥܬܗܘܢ. ܘܐܦ ܒܬ̈ܓܠܘܬܗܘܢ.
[1]ܘܫܩܠܘ ܘܦܠܛܘ ܐܢܘܢ. ܡܛܠ ܕܥܒܘ ܘܕܝܠܘ. ܕܕܠܡܐ ܚܕ
ܡܢ ܡܬ̈ܠܡܐ. ܐܘ ܡܢ ܙ̈ܒܢܐ ܐܬܝܢ ܘܡܫܐܠܝܢ ܡܛܠ ܡܛܠܬܗ
ܕܡܪܢ ܘܟܠ ܢܗܘܐ ܚܝܢ ܗܘܘ ܠܗ ܠܡܪܝܡ ܕܐܬܝܐ ܗܘܬ f. 167 a
ܓܒܗ ܡܪܢܐ. ܒܗ ܠܓܒܝܐ ܒܫܡ̈ܝܐ ܘܡܪ̈ܘܡܐ ܘܢܘܪܐ ܘܥ̈ܡܐ
ܕܐܬܝܐ ܗܘܬ ܒܪܘܚܐ ܗܘܬ ܥܠ ܐܦ̈ܝܗ ܥܠ ܐܪܥܐ.
ܘܡܓܠܝܐ ܘܐܡ̈ܪܐ ܒܓܠܝܘܬܗ ܒܗ ܚܝܐ. ܕܡܠܟ. ܫܕܪ
ܕܒܪܘܚܐ ܡܢ ܗܢܐ ܚܠܡܐ. ܘܫܡܥ ܕܢܠܐ ܗܘܬ ܡܢ ܒܒܐ
ܕܡܪ̈ܝܐ ܒܗ ܕܒܢ̈ܝܢ ܗܒ̈ܝܠܐ ܚܒܝܢ ܗܘܘ ܕܢܬܠܒܘܢܗ.
[2]ܕܠܐ ܚܝܠܗ ܕܐܠܗܐ ܕܐܬܝܠܕ ܡܢܗ ܘܗܒܪ ܗܘܐ ܒܗ.
ܐܠܐ ܡܢ ܡܘ̈ܕܝܐ ܦܠܓܐ ܗܘܬ ܘܡܢܐ ܕܒܗ ܟ̈ܠܝ ܐܢܫܐܝܬ
ܕܢܬܠܒܘܢܗ. ܡܚܝܐ ܐܢܘܢ ܪܝܫܐ ܕܡܫܝܚܘܬܐ ܕܢܦܩ ܗܘܐ
ܡܢ ܠܘܒܝܬܐ. ܘܐܬܕܘܕ ܪ̈ܚܝܡܘܗܝ.

---

[1] Cod. ܘܫܩܠ [2] Cod. ܐܠܐ

ܠܟܠ ܐܬܪܐ[1] ܒܡܕܝܢܬܐ ܪܗܘܡܝܬ ܗܝ܇ ܬ. ܘܠܐ ܠܒܪ ܡܢܗ̇ܐ Cod. Harris f. 165 b, l. 15
ܐܝܟ ܕܢܬܒܥܐ ܠܗ ܥܠ ܥܘܡܪܐ ܪܒܐ ܕܒܗ ܗ̈ܘ ܢܚܦܬ ܠܘܬܗ̇ f. 166 a
ܐܠܗܐ ܡܪܝܡ ܡܢ ܟܠܗܝܢ ܗܢܝܐ. ܘܠܐ ܐܬܪܐ ܠܡܫܒܚܘ[2]
ܘܐܦܠܐ ܒܢ̈ܝܐ ܕܢܫܝܢ. ܒܪ ܡܬ̈ܒܥܬܐ ܕܟܠܝܐ ܘܬܫ̈ܬܝܐ
ܐܝܠܝܢ ܗ̈ܘܝ، ܡܕܡܝܢ ܠܦܪܘܫܐ ܡܬܕܒܢܐ ܕܒܕܡ. ܘܢܦܩܬ
ܦܩܝܕܬܐ ܗܕܐ ܡܢ ܠܥܠܐ ܫܘܝܐ ܠܩܦܪܝܢܐ ܘܐܬܬܟܒܬ
ܘܐܬܠܬ ܠܗܘܢ ܫܢܝܢ. ܘܐܬܬ ܠܐܘܪܫܠܡ. ܘܟܠܗ ܒܒܪܢܐ ܗܢܐ
ܢܗܪܐ ܠܐܠܗܐ ܕܒܢܘܒܗ ܚܠܡ. ܠܒܪܗ ܘܐܬܚܐ ܠܒܠܝܬܐ
ܕܢܫܘܒ ܠܗ ܡܢ ܓܗܢܐ. ܕܒܝܕ ܬ̈ܠܘܬܗ ܕܠܒܪܬ ܐܠܗܐ
ܡܪܝܡ ܘܐܦ ܕܟܠܗܘܢ ܡܕ̈ܝܢܐ ܢܒܒܪ ܐܠܗܐ ܡܢ ܐܪܒܐ
ܘܡܢ ܐܬܪܐ ܗܢܐ ܕܐܝܬܝ ܒܗ ܦܠܩܝܬܐ ܗܕܐ. ܫܪܒܐ
ܘܡܒܝܐ ܘܟܒܝܐ ܘܡܗܘܬܐ ܘܟܠܗܘܢ ܡܬܝܘܬܐ ܘܡ̈ܟܠܬܐ ܕܪܘܓܙܐ
ܐܚܪܢ.. ܒܡܢܬ ܬܬܠܬ̈ܥܐ ܘܐܪ̈ܒܥܝܢ ܘܐܪ̈ܒܥ. ܒܐܝܪܚ. ܬܫܪܝܢ
ܐܚܪ، ܒܬܠܬܐ ܝܘܡܝܢ ܒܗ ܐܬܝܬܘܗܝ، ܝܘܡ ܬܠܬܐ ܒܫܒܐ ܒܬܠܬ f. 166 b
ܫ̈ܥܝܢ ܢܦܩܬ ܡܪܝܡ ܡܢ ܒܝܬܗ̇ ܘܐܙܠܬ ܠܘܬ ܩܒܪܗ ܕܡܫܝܚܐ.
[ܗܦܟܬ[3] ܕܝܢ ܒܒܥܘܬܐ] ܡܛܠ ܕܟܠ ܝܘܡ ܐܙܠܐ ܗܘܬ ܠܘܬ ܩܒܪܗ ܕܡܪܢܐ.
ܝܗ̈ܘܕܝܐ ܕܝܢ ܡܫܝܕܐ ܕܡܚܝܕ ܡܫܝܚܐ ܐܚܕܘܗ̇، ܠܩܒܪܐ
ܘܒܢܫܘ ܥܠܝܗ̇، ܒܐܒ̈ܢܐ ܪܘܒܪܬܐ ܘܐܩܝܡܘ ܥܠܝܗ̇، ܘܥܠ
ܟܠܗܠܬܐ ܢܛܘܪܐ. ܘܡܢܘ ܐܢܫܝܢ ܕܝܢ ܐܝܟ ܒܐܬܐ

[1] Cod. ܐܬܠܐ [2] Cod. ܠܡܫ̈ܒܚܘ [3] in margin

ܕܢܗܘܐ ܕܘܒܪܟܐ ܕܡܪܬܝ، f. 87 b col. a
ܡܪܝܡ ܝܠܕܬ ܐܠܗܐ
ܬܠܬ ܙܒܢܝܢ ܒܫܢܬܐ
ܘܐܡܪܘ ܠܗܘܢ ܠܫܠܝܚܝܢ
ܠܐ ܬܫܒܩܘܢ ܠܗܘܢ ܕܡܝܬܪ
ܐܠܐ ܗܘ ܐܡܪܐ ܒܟܠܗ
ܐܪܒܥܐ ܩܐܡ ܐܢܐ ܘܫܐܪ
ܐܢܐ ܠܟܘܢ ܕܐܬܐ ܡܢ
ܫܡܝܐ ܘܐܡܪ ܠܗ ܕܗܐ

* * * * * * * * * cf. J. S. L. p. ܣ

ܗܕܐ ܐܬܐ ܫܝܡ ܫܠܡ
ܘܐܟܝܢ ܘܐܬܗܦܟܝܢ.
ܘܒܕܫܠܐ ܐܒܪ ܗܘܫܠܡ
ܘܫܒ ܠܦܘܒܢܐ ܡܢ ܨܐܕ f. 94 a col. a
ܘܐܢܫܝܢ ܠܡܗܝܢܝܢ ܫܝܢ
ܘܗܘ ܦܝܪܘܡܪܝܐ ܦܬܫ
ܬܪܒܐ ܘܒܠ ܐܡܒܐ ܕܪܕܐ
ܫܢܝܗ ܕܡܪܝ، ܡܘܫܝܢ.
ܘܐܫܒܥ ܬܡܢ ܦܘܡܝܬܐ
ܒܬܝܒܐ ܘܦܝܡܒܐ ܒܠ
ܦܘܡܗ̇ ܕܗܝ ܡܒܪܬܐ.
ܕܪܕܐ ܫܢܢܝܐ ܡܢܝܗ̇
ܫܘܠܗ̇ ܩܕܡ ܒܠܗ
ܒܡܐ ܘܦܬܫܗ̇ ܘܐܫܒܫ.
ܕܒܬܒ ܒܒܪܝܬ

f. 87 b col. b ܘܦܢܝܐܬ ܘܪܗܒܐܬ
ܘܐܬܬ ܒܗ̇ ܪܡܝ ܐܬܕܐ
ܕܫܒ̈ܚܝܢ ܘܬ̈ܘܬܝܢ[1] ܬ̈ܠܝܫܝܢ.
cf. Cod. Harris f. 165 b ܘܒܬܝܒ ܒܗ̇ ܗܒܢܐ.
ܕܗܢܐ ܫܘܒܚ ܡܫܝܚܐ
ܕܐܬܝܠܕ ܡܢ ܡܪܝܡ
ܒܬܘܠܬܐ ܗܘܘ ܐܠܗܐ
ܒܫܡܝܐ ܘܒܐܪܥܐ. ܘܒܠ
ܡܢ ܕܡܗܝܡܢ ܒܗ ܫܢܐ
ܘܡܪܬܝ، ܡܪܝܡ ܕܝܠܕܬܗ
ܒܫܒܘܚܐ ܪܒܐ ܢܦܘܩܬ
ܡܢ ܥܠܡܐ ܗܢܐ
ܘܡܗܕܝܢ ܬ̈ܫܒܚܪ ܬ̈ܠܝܫܝܐ
ܘ̈ܬܠܝܫܝܐ ܫܒܚܝܢ ܘܬ̈ܘܬܝܢ
f. 94 a col. b ܒܠ ܬܕܡ̈ܪܬܐ ܕܒܒܕ
ܡܫܝܚܐ ܩܕܡ ܐܡܗ
ܒܕ ܢܦܩܬ ܡܢ ܥܠܡܐ
ܗܢܐ. ܫܠܡܗ، ܬ̈ܠܝܫܝܐ
ܠܬܒܬܐ ܘܡܗܒܘ ܠܡܪܝ،
ܘܫܢܝܢ ܕܗܘ ܢܣܗܕ ܒܗ
ܡܠܠ ܕܠܗ ܪܫܡ ܗܘܐ
ܡܫܝܚܐ ܘܬܫܪ ܡܢ
ܫܒ̈ܪܘܗܝ. ܘܐܬܒܒܕܬ
ܗܕܐ ܦܘܡܝܬܐ ܩܕܡ
ܒܠܗ̇ ܐܦܣܘܣ. ܘܒܗ، ܫܒܬܐ
ܕܐܬܦܬܫܬ ܦܘܡܝܬܐ ܗܕܐ
ܒܐܦܣܘܣ ܫܒܝܢܐ ܡܢ

[1] Cod. Harris ܡܫܒ̈ܚܢܐ

f. 87 a col. a
ܐܝܠܝܢ ܕܣܓܝ ܦܘܪܥܢܐ
ܕܠܗܘܢܐ ܡܫܬܒܚ ܬܡܢ
ܒܬܒܗ̇ ܕܡܪܬܝ، ܡܪܝܡ
ܠܡܬܠ ܐܠܗܐ. ܘܐܦ ܗܘ
ܕܡܫܒܚܐ ܒܕܘܟܪܢܗ̇
ܒܬܒܐ ܐܘܕܒܘ ⌜ܠܝ⌝
ܒܐܓܪܬܐ ܕܐܦ ܒܐܘܪܫܠܡ
ܬܬܟܬܒ ܦܢܩܝܬܐ
ܕܒܗܘܕܢܗ ܕܦܘܩܕܢܝܬܐ
ܕܢܒܣܘܪ ܒܗ̇ ܠܥܡܐ
ܕܗܘܕܝܐ ܘܫܠܘ ⌜ܠܡܪܝܐ⌝
ܒܫ̈ܘܢܗܝ ܕܡܫܝܚܐ ܚܠܝܢ
ܘܐܝܠܬ ܐܝܩܪܬܐ ܡܢ f. 94 b col. a
⌜ܐܘܪܫܠܡ⌝ * * ܣ * *
ܘܡܢ * * * * * *
* * * * * * * *
ܐܝܩܪܬܐ * * * * *
⌜ܘܠܐܠܟܣܢܕܪܝܐ ܘܠܡܨܪܝܢ⌝
ܘܠܬܒܐܣ. ܘܐܝܟ ܐܢ̈ܫܐ (cf. Cod. Harris f. 164 b)
ܘܫܐܠܘ ܠܐ * * ܐ
ܒܗܠܝܢ ܐܬܘ̈ܬܐ ܘܠܐ
ܐܫܬܒܚܘ. ܘܐܬܘ
ܠܐܦܣܘܣ ⌜ܘܒܬܘ⌝ ܬܡܢ
⌜ܒܒܝܬܗ ܕܡܪܝ، ܝܘܚܢܢ⌝

f. 87 a col. b
ܘܓܠܘ ܒܟܠܠܝܐ ܘܩܪܘ ܒܩܪܝܐ
ܐܡܪܝܢ ܡܪܢ ܢܫܘܥ
ܡܫܝܚܐ ܕܐܬܚܒܬܗܝ،
ܠܡܪܝ، ܘܟܘܠܢ ܫܠܝܚܐ ⌜ܒܬܪ⌝
ܡܢ ܚܒܪ̈ܘܗܝ، ܐܝܟ ܐܝܬ
⌜ܢܝܫܐ⌝ ܠܐܠܗܘܬܟ ܕܬ * *
ܒܡ ܬܫܒܘܚܬܟ ܗܠܝܢ
ܕܣܒܪܬ ܒܪܡ ܡܪܬܝ،
ܡܪܝܡ ܐܠܗܘܬܟ ܕܢܬܟܠܝܢ
ܠܥܠܡܐ ܬܫܬܐ * * *
ܘܫܝܡ ܫܠܝܚܐ ܕܒܟܠܠ
ܒܗܢ ܟܠܠܝܐ ܗܢܐ ⌜ܘܢ⌝ܦܠܘ
ܐܦ̈ܝܐ ⌜ܥܠ⌝ ⌜ܐܦ̈ܝ⌝ܗܘܢ
f. 94 b col. b [ܘܒܙ ܗܢܘܢ ܕܡܒܘ ܠܗܘܢ]
ܘܗܐ ܡܪܝ، ܘܟܘܠܢ ܫܠܝܚܐ
ܥܡ ܐܕܪ̈ܗܘܢ ܘܐܡܪ
ܠܗܘܢ. ܠܐ ܬܒܪܐ ܠܒܘܢ
ܦܘܪ̈ܥܢܐ. ܕܡܫܝܚܐ ܫܡܗ
ܐܝܩܪܐ ܒ⌜ܪ̈⌝ܝܠܟܘܢ ܕܗܠܟܬܘܢ
ܒܐܬܘ̈ܬܐ. ܘܡܢܘ ܫܒܘ
ܒܬܒܐ ܕܡܦܢܩܗ̇ ܕܐܡܪܗ
ܕܒܪܝ ܡܦܠܠ ܕܗܘܐ ܓܐܕ،
ܐܝܬܘܗܝ،. ܘܢܠܘ ܠܦܘܪ ܫܢܐ
ܘܫܐܠܘ ܒܫܠܡܐ ܕܐܚܝܢ
cf. Cod. Harris f. 165 a ܘܐܡܪܘ ܠܗܘܢ ܕܡܘܚܝܢ
ܫܪܪ[1] ܠܒܘܢ ܒܬܒܐ ܗܢܐ

[1] Cod. ܫܪܪܘ

f. 43 b col. a

ܠܐܠܗܐ ܕܝܠܕܬܗ ܒܡܫܪܬܐ
ܕܐܪ̈ܒܥܝܐ ܘܒܥܘܒܐ — cf. Cod. Harris f. 163 b
ܕܡܪ̈ܢܬܐ ܕܫܪ̈ܦܐ. ܘܐܢܐ
ܒܥܘܒܝ ܐܦܣܩܘܦܐ
ܕܐܘܪܫܠܡ ܟܬܒܬ ܒܒܝܪܬ
ܐܢ̈ܝ ܒܦܩܝܕܬܐ ܗܕܐ
ܘܗܠܝܢ ܫܦܝܪ̈ܐ ܕܐܬܟܬܒܘ
ܢܗܘܢ ܕܒܘܪܐ ܕܫܠܝܚ̈ܐ
ܦܬܓܡܗ ܗܘ ܦܬܓܡܝܢ ܗܘܐ
ܠܗܘܢ ܘܕܠܡܘܢ ܫ̈ܠܝܚܐ
ܒܢܝܬ ܐܬܕ̈ܗܘܢ ܐܝܬ
ܒܫܦܪܐ ܗܠܝܢ ܕܟܬܒܘ.
ܘܢܣܚܘܢ ܠܡܪܬܝ، ܡܪܝܡ
ܕܐܡܬܝ، ܢܗܘܘܢ ܠܗ̇
ܡܘܕ̈ܥܢܐ ܘܕܟܘܪ̈ܢܐ — f. 38 a col. a
ܠܦܘܠܚܢܬܐ ܬܠܬ ܙܒܢܝܢ
ܒܫܢܬܐ ܘܦܘܠܘܣ ܘܦܛܪܘܣ
ܘܢܗܘܢ ܕܒܘܪܐ ܕܫܠܝܚ̈ܐ
ܦܬܓܡܗ. ܗܘ ܢܕܟܪܝܢ — cf. J. S. L. p. 1, l. 5
ܕܐܢܒܐ ܐܬܢܒܝܘܢ ܗܠܝܢ
ܫܦܝܪ̈ܐ ܕܡܘܬܗ̇ ܕܡܪܬܝ،
ܡܪܝܡ. ܡܛܠ ܕܡܢ
ܐܘܪܫܠܡ ܒܫܡܗܘܢ
ܐܬܘ ܘܐܡܪܝܢ ܫܠܝܚܝܢ
ܘܡܕܫܘܬܦܘܢ ܐܟܡܢ
ܕܡܬܒܥܝܢ ܒܦܘܪ ܫܢܝܢ

f. 43 b col. b

ܘܫܕܪܘ ܐܓܪܬܐ
cf. J. S. L. p. ܘ, l. 19 — ܐܦܣܩܘܦܐ ܕܐܘܪܫܠܡ
ܘܠܝܪܘܣ ܕܠܗ ܡܢ ܩܘܪܐ
ܐܦܣܩܘܦܐ ܕܐܘܪܫܠܡ
ܘܟܠܗ ܠܝܪܘܣ ܩܕܝܫܐ
ܠܐܢܫܝܢ ܒܗܢܐ. ܘܐܟܗ̈ܢ
ܕܡܬܒܥܝܢ ܒܦܘܪ ܫܢܝ. ܫܠܡܐ
ܫܠܝܐܐ. ܐܓܪܬܐ ܕܐܬܬ
ܡܢ ܐܕܝܒܘܢ ܡܒܠܝܢ
ܘܒܐܘܪܫܠܡ ܥܠܗ̇ ܫܐܠܝܢ.
ܡܛܠ ܬܦܩܝܢܗ̇ ܕܡܪܬܝ،
ܡܪܝܡ. ܘܠܐ ܐܫܟܚܝܢ.
ܘܒܬܪ ܐܢ̈ܕܘܗ، ܕܝܥܩܘܒ
cf. Cod. Harris f. 164 a — ܐܦܣܩܘܦܐ ܐܫܟܚܝܢ.
f. 38 a col. b — ܕܟܬܒ ܠܗ ܗܟܢܐ ܕܗܠܝܢ
ܫܦܝܪ̈ܐ ܫܬܐ ܕܐܬܟܬܒܘ
ܟܕ ܡܝܬܬ ܡܪܬܝ، ܡܪܝܡ.
cf. J. S. L. p. 1, l. 4 — ܢܗܘܢ ܕܒܘܪܐ ܦܬܓܡܝܢ ܗܘܐ
ܠܗܘܢ ܘܐܘܕܥܝܢ ܐܢܫܝܢ
ܠܡܕܝܢܬܐ ܘܟܠܗܘܢ ܐܟܗ̈ܢܝܢ
ܕܡܬܒܥܝܢ ܒܦܘܪ ܫܢܝ ܕܫܕܪܘ
ܐܓܪܬܐ ܠܪܗܘܡܐ ܠܐܢ̈ܫܐ
ܕܡܕܝܢ ܦܛܪܘܣ ܘܦܘܠܘܣ
ܟܕ ܡܫܬܟܚܝܢ ܗܠܝܢ
ܫܦܝܪ̈ܐ ܩܕܝܫܐ ܬܡܢ
ܘܟܬܒܘ ܬܘܒ ܐܓܪ̈ܬܐ
ܠܐܦܣܩܘܦܐ ܐܟܢܐ ܕܐܝܬ

f. 43 a col. a
ܡܝܬܬ. ܘܠܐ ܐܫܟܚܘ
cf. Cod. Harris f. 163 a
ܘܐܫܟܚܘ ܠܬܠܬܐ ܝܘ̇
ܕܬܒܬ ܗܟܢܐ. ܕܐܟܢܐ
ܕܢܦܩ[1] ܡܫܒܚܝܢܐ ܕܐܝܬܝ,
ܐܠܗܝܐ ܡܢ ܐܘܪܫܠܡ.
ܘܒܒܕܢ ܡܫܡܫܢܐ
ܢܗܘܘܢ ܐܦܣܩܘܦܐ
ܘܗܿ ܕܗܘܐ ܡܕܒܪܢܝܬ
ܐܦܣܩܘܦܐ ܒܐܘܪܫܠܡ
ܟܕ ܡܩܝܡܝܢ ܗܘܘ ܩ̈ܠܝܢܐ.
ܒܬܒܬ ܗܟܢܐ ܒܟܢܘܫܬ
ܫ̈ܢܝ, ܒܐܝܪܚ[2] ܚܝܪܢ ܢ̇
ܒܫܢܬ ܬܠܬܡܐܐ ܘܬܠܬܝܢ
ܘܫܬ ܫ̈ܢܝܢ ܒܬܠܬܐ ܒܫܒܐ
ܒܠܠܝܗ ܕܘܡܟܐ ܠܐ ܨܦܪܐ f. 38 b col. a
ܝܗܘܕܝܐ ܕܐܝܬܘܗܝ,
ܦܢܐ. ܘܡܫܝܚܗ, ܠܝܫܘܥ
ܐܦܣܩܘܦܐ ܘܡܕܝܢܬ. ܡܛܠ
ܕܦܠܓ ܦܢܝܢ ܗܘܘ ܠܗ
ܝܗܘܕܝܐ ܠܝܫܘܥ ܥܠ
ܕܡܬܘܪܐ ܗܘܐ ܐܚܘܗܝ,
ܕܡܪܝ ܘܫܐܠ ܐܦܣܩܘܦܐ
ܕܐܘܪܫܠܡ ܘܠܝܥܩܘܒ
ܕܠܗ ܡܛܠ ܕܒܬܒܐ
ܕܡܦܩܢܗ̇ ܕܦܓܪܢܝܬܐ
ܡܪܝܡ. ܘܠܐ ܐܫܟܚܘ.

f. 43 a col. b
ܐܫܟܚܘ ܕܝܢ ܦܠܘܣܬܐ
ܐܚܪܬܐ ܕܒܬܒ ܒܗ
cf. J. S. L. p. ܘ, l. 8
ܒܒܝܪܬ ܐܚ̈ܝܗܘܢ, ܕܢܗܘܘܢ
ܐܦܣܩܘܦܐ ܕܐܟܢܐ
ܢܗܘܘܢ ܒܬܒܬ ܗܟܢܐ.
cf. Cod. Harris f. 163 a l. 5
ܕܒܫܢܬ ܬܠܬܡܐܐ ܘܐܪ̈ܒܥܝܢ
ܘܫܒܥ ܫ̈ܢܝܢ ܡܝܬܬ
ܡܪܬܝ, ܡܪܝܡ ܡܢ ܥܠܡܐ
ܗܢܐ. ܒܒܢܘ ܐܚܪ, ܒܗ
ܢܗܘܡܐ ܕܝܠܕܬ ܒܗ
ܠܡܫܝܚܐ ܒܗ ܒܝܘܡܐ
ܗܘ ܢܦܩܬ ܡܢ ܥܠܡܐ
ܗܢܐ. ܘܐܢܐ ܢܗܘܘܢ ܦܘܩ̈ܕ
ܐܢܐ. ܕܐܬܘ ܩ̈ܠܝܢܐ ܕܝܘܡ.
f. 38 b col. b
ܘܕܒܝ̈ܢܝܢ ܐܬܠܝܚܡܘ
ܘܒܪ̈ܝܬܐ ܥܠ̈ܝܬܐ ܡܢ
ܬܫ̈ܒܘܚܬܐ ܐܬ, ܠܥܠܡܗ̇
ܕܦܘܩܕܢܝܬܐ ܘܒܗ ܢܦܩܬ
ܡܢ ܥܠܡܐ ܗܢܐ. ·ܘ·
ܘܐܬܟܬܒܘ ܐܫܬܐ ܣܦܪ̈ܐ
ܟܘܠ ܣܦܪܐ ܬܪ̈ܝܢ ܫ̈ܠܝܚܝܢ
ܟܬܒܘܗܝ, ܥܠ ܐܬ̈ܘܬܐ
ܘܬܕܡܪ̈ܬܐ ܘܬܕܡܪ̈ܬܗ
ܕܗܘ̇, ܡܕܡܝܢ̇ ܡܢ ܥܡܢܐ.
ܘܡܢ ܐܪܒܐ. ܘܡܢܗܘܢ ܚܕ
ܬܘܕܝܬܐ ܠܡܪܝܐ ܕܗܦܟ

[1] Cod. Harris ܐܦܩܘ [2] sic

ܘܐܒܝܫܝܢ ܐܠܝܢ ܣܓܝܢ f. 75 b col. a
ܕܡܬܚܘܐ ܥܠ ܡܪܝ
ܗܘܝܢ ܥܠܝܡܬܐ ܠܒܘܪܐ
ܕܩܛܠ ܡܪܝܡܗ ܡܪܗ.
ܡܫܝܚܐ ܘܐܬܓܠܝܬ
ܠܗ ܒܬܘܠܬܐ ܕܝܠܕ ܗܘܐ cf. J. S. L. p. ܐ, l. 10
ܠܗ ܡܪܝ ܠܡܪܝ ܗܘܝܢ
ܠܬܪ ܡܢ ܫܒ̈ܝܪܘܗܝ
ܘܐܬܒܢܐ ܕܝܠܕ ܗܘܐ
ܠܗ ܡܫܝܚܐ ܗܘܒܢܐ
ܪܘܚܬܗ ܐܦ ܡܪܬܝ
ܡܪܝܡ ܗܘܐ ܡܪܝ ܗܘܝܢ
* ܠ * ܐܪܥܐ * * ܒܕ f. 70 a col. a
ܣܝ ܗܘܐ ܒܫ̈ܒܘܚܘܗܝ
ܗܒ ܠܗ ܠܗܘ ܣܓܕܐ
ܕܠܒܫܐ ܘܢܦܩ ܡܢ ܐܪܒܥܐ
ܘܗܘܐ ܡܠܟܗ ܒܘܕܪܢܐ
ܠܒܢܝ ܐܢܫܐ ∘ ∘ ∘
ܒܫܢܬ ܬܡܢܡܐܐ ܘܬܫܥ
* * * * * * ܩܕܡ
ܒܝܘܡܐ ܕܒܝܬ ܝܠܕܗ
ܕܡܫܝܚܐ ܒܪ ܩܝܡܝܢ
ܒܠ̈ܝܐ ܒܡ ܬܫ̈ܬܐ
ܘܡܫܒܚܝܢ ܒܝܬ ܝܠܕܗ
ܕܡܫܝܚܐ ܐܬܝܠܝܕܬ

f. 75 b col. b ܡܪܬܝ ܡܪܝܡ ܠܡܪܝ،
ܗܘܝܢ ܠܐܦܣܩܘܦ ܘܐܡܪܬ
ܠܗ ܒܬܒܐ ܕܐܝܬ ܓܐܕܝܢ
ܕܡܦܩܝ ܕܡܢ ܒܠܒܐ
ܗܢܐ ܗܒ ܠܓܒܪܐ
ܕܐܬܝܢ ܓܐܕܝܢ ܡܢ ܛܘܪ
ܦܢܝ ܡܛܠ ܕܡܛܝܐ ܠܗ
ܘܡܒܐ ܕܐܬܐ ܒܗ
ܪܒܢ ܡܢ ܥܡܝܢܐ ܢܦܩ
ܒܬܒܐ ܕܡܦܩ ܕܢܗܘܘܢ
ܠܗ̇ ܕܡܒܪܢܐ ܘܩܘܪܒܢܐ
ܐܢܬ ܠܝ ܗܘܝܢ ܘܩ̈ܠܝܫܐ
ܣܒ̈ܪܝܢ ܐܬܬܘ ܓܐܕܝܗ̇
f. 70 a col. b ܠܒܝܬ ܠܚܡ * * ܬ *
ܘܐܢܐ ܗܐ ܐܘܕܒܬܢ
ܕܡܛܬ ܠܗ ܫܒܬܐ
ܕܐܬܐ ܡܢ * * * *
* * ܠܒܠܗܘܢ ܒܪ̈ܝܬܐ
ܘܐܬܚܘܐ ܥܠ ܫܘܒܚܝ
ܕܐܝܒܢܐ ܢܦܩܬ ܡܢ
ܒܠܒܐ. ܘܒܕ ܐܬܒܬܒܬ
ܐܓܪܬܐ ܡܢ ܛܘܪ ܦܢܝ
ܘܐܬܘ * * * ܐܝܟܐ
ܘܐܬܚܘܗ ܠܐܘܪܫܠܡ
cf. J. S. L. p. ܘ, l. 7 ܘܐܬܩܪܬ ܩܕܡ ܒܠܗ
ܐܘܪܫܠܡ. ܘܒܟܘ ܒܬܒܗ̇
ܕܡܪܬܝ ܡܪܝܡ ܐܡܒܢܐ

f. 75 a col. a
ܠܒܪܬܐ ܢܒܥܘܪ ܒܩܒܐ
ܘܢܘܩܕ ܐܪ̈ܙܐ ܘܢܫܡܫ
ܩܕܡܝ ܘܢܩܒܠ ܘܢܙܕܗܦ
ܩܘܪܒܢܐ. ܘܢܫܠܡܝܗ ܫܠܡܐ.
ܘܢܪܘܒ ܫܝܢܐ ܟܠ
ܟܠܗܝܢ ܒܪ̈ܬܗ ܕܫܠܡܐ.
ܐܝܟ ܘܐܢ̈ܘܢ ܟܠܗܘܢ
ܫ̈ܒܘܥܐ ܡܫܡ̈ܗܝܢܐ:
ܐܝܟ ܐܢܫܐ ܕܙ̈ܗܝܡܝܢ
ܠܡܫܝܚܐ ܡܒܣܡܝܢ
ܠܗܘܢ ܡܛܠ ܕܬܒܐ ܗܢܐ
ܕܡܪܬܝ ܡܪܝܡ ܕܐܝܟܢܐ
f. 70 b col. a
ܐܬܟܠܠ ܒܗܢܐ ܙܒܢܐ.
ܫܘܠ ܠܒܢܐ ܗܟܝܠ
ܦܝܐܐ ܗܘܐ ܠܐܢܫܐ
ܛܘܒܢܐ ܒܛܘܪ ܣܝܢܝ.
ܡܪܝ ܕܘܝܕ ܡܫܝܚܐ
ܘܡܪܝ ܝܘܚܢܢ ܡܥܡܕܢܐ.
ܘܡܪܝ ܦܘܠܘܣ ܡܫܡܫܢܐ.
ܡܛܠ ܕܬܠܬܝܗܘܢ ܗܠܝܢ
cf. Cod. Harris f. 162 b
ܛܘܒܢܐ ܒܗܘ ܡܫܒܚܐ
ܕܗܝܡ ܒܪܝ ܛܘܪܐ
ܕܛܘܪ ܚܘܪܒ. ܐܝܟܢܐ ܕܐܝܬ
ܗܘ ܚܘܒܐ ܕܡܠܠ ܡܪܝܐ

f. 75 a col. b
ܥܡ ܡܘܫܐ. ܬܡܢ ܒܗܘ
ܡܠܠܐ ܐܬܚܙܝܘ ܗܠܝܢ
ܛܘ̈ܒܢܐ. ܘܒܢܝܢ ܡܩܕ̈ܫܐ
cf. J. S. L. p. ܘ
ܕܗܘ ܒܝܬ ܩܘܕ̈ܫܐ ܕܒܢܐ
ܒܪܝܫ ܛܘܪܐ ܕܛܘܪ ⌜ܣܝܢܝ⌝.
ܘܗܢܘܢ ܗܠܝܢ ܛܘ̈ܒܢܐ
ܫܠܝܛܝܢ ܥܠ ⌜ܬܠܬܡܐܐ⌝
ܘܒܫ̈ܢܝܢ ܕܫܢܬܐ ܕܐܝܬ
ܒܛܘܪ ⌜ܣܝܢܝ⌝ ܡܛܠ ܟܠܗ
ܛܘܪ ܣܝܢܝ ܒܗܝܟܠܘܗܝ,
ܕܡܪܝܐ ܡܠܟܬ. ܘܒܬܒܘ
ܗܠܝܢ ܛܘ̈ܒܢܐ ܐܚܪ̈ܢܝܬܐ
f. 70 b col. b
ܡܢ ܛܘܪ ܣܝܢܝ ܠܐܘܪܫܠܡ
ܠܘܬ ܒܘܪܐ ܐܦܣܩܘܦܐ
ܕܐܘܪܫܠܡ. ܕܝܗܘܐ
ܫܘܠܛܢܐ ܠܒܝܫܘܬܗ.
ܘܫܐܠܘ ⌜ܡܛܠ⌝ ܟܬܒܐ
ܕܡܦܩܢܗ ܕܡܪܬܝ ܡܪܝܡ.
ܕܐܝܟܢܐ ܢܦܩܬ ܡܢ
ܥܠܡܐ ܗܢܐ ܡܛܠ ܕܗܟܢ
ܪܓܐ ܠܝ ܕܢܕܥ ܕܐܝܟܢܐ
ܫܘܒܚܐ ܐܬܟܠܠܬ.
⌜ܫܐܠܝܢ⌝ ܚܢܢ ⌜ܡܛܠܬܗ
ܕ⌜ܟܬܒܐ⌝ ܗܢܐ.⌝[1] ܘ⌜ܠܐ
ܐܬܐ ܠܐܕܪ̈ܝܢ ܡܕܡ.⌝[1]

[1] From Cod. Harris.

## ܡܦܩܢܘܗ̇ ܕܠܦܘܒܢܢܬܐ

f. 76 b col. a

ܒܬܪ ܐܢܫܐ ܐܙܕܩܦ ܗܘ̇
ܦܓܪܐ ܩܕܝܫܐ ܕܠܘܬܗ
ܒܬܘܠܬܐ ܩܕܝܫܬܐ.
ܠܒܬܐ ܗܘܬ ܠܒܪ
ܕܚܕܘܬܐ ܕܠܒܢܝܐ ܗܘܬ
ܠܐܠܗܐ ܡܢ ܩܕܡ ܟܠܗܝܢ
ܒܪ̈ܝܬܐ ܘܫܕܪ ܐܠܗܐ cf. Cod. Harris f. 162 a
ܠܒܪܗ ܘܫܪܐ ܒܗ̇ ܘܐܬܠܕ
ܡܢܗ̇ ܕܠܐ ܫܘܚܠܦܬܐ
ܕܠܒܢܝܐ ܐܝܟ ܕܐܡܪ cf. J. S. L. p. ܗ
ܐܫܥܝܐ ܡܫܡܫܢܐ ܕܢܒܝܐ.
ܗܠܝܢ ܐܝܟ ܠܡܘܕܐ
ܡܕܡܘܗܝ. ܘܐܝܟ ܒܡܪܐ
[ܡܢ ܐܪܒܐ ܕܝܗܒܬܐ.]
ܘܬܘܒ ܗܘ ܒܪ ܗܘ̇. f. 69 a col. a
ܢܒܝܐ ܐܡܪ. ܕܗܐ
ܒܬܘܠܬܐ ܒܦܓܪܐ ܘܝܠܕܐ
ܒܪܐ. ܘܢܬܩܪܐ ܫܡܗ
ܥܡܢܘܐܝܠ ܕܡܬܪܓܡ
ܐܠܗܢ ܥܡܢ. ܐܦ ܗܝ
ܡܪܬܝ ܡܪܝܡ ܩܕܝܫܐ
ܗܘܬ ܘܠܒܢܝܐ ܠܐܠܗܐ
ܡܢ ܩܕܡ ܕܬܬܠܕ ܘܢܠܠܬ
ܢܦܫܗ̇ ܡܢ ܒܠܗܘܢ
ܚܘ̈ܒܐ ܦ̈ܢܝܐ
ܕܬܘܒܠ ܗܝ ܠܡܫܝܚܐ

f. 76 b col. b

ܕܐܬܐ ܝܐܕܝܗ̇. ܘܒܬܪ
ܡܠܦܢܐ ܗܒܝܠ ܘܒܢܝܐ
ܕܢܫܬܒܚ ܗܘ̇ ܡܪܢ
ܕܐܒܢܝ ܗܘܐ ܘܢܬܦܢܐ
ܗܘ̇ ܕܡܠܦܢܐ ܗܘܐ.
ܘܢܬܒܢܐ ܗܘ ܕܡܒܢܐ
ܗܘܐ. ܘܢܬܦܪܥ ܗܘ
ܕܫܒܩܐ ܗܘܐ. ܠܟܠܗ
ܢ̈ܣܡܘܗܝ ܕܐܠܗܐ ܒܠ
ܒܪܢܐ ܕܡܠܦܢܐ ܗܘܐ.
ܗܘܠ ܕܝܢ ܒܠ ܠܒܝܫܐ
ܕܒܢܝܬ ܐܕܡ. ܘܫܕܪ
ܠܒܪܗ ܘܢܒܝܒܗ ܡܢ
ܫܡܝܐ ܘܐܬܐ ܘܫܪܐ
ܒܒܬܘܠܬܐ ܩܕܝܫܬܐ f. 69 a col. b
ܕܒܝܠܝܕܘܬܗ ܕܡܢܗ̇
ܢܦܘܗܝ ܠܒܠܡܐ ܕܒܠܐ
ܒܢܦܫܗ̈ܘܗܝ. ܗܕܐ ܗܝ
ܐܢܬܬܐ ܩܕܝܫܬܐ
ܕܗ̇ܠܐ ܠܝ ܕܢܒܒܕ ܕܘܒܪܢܗ̇.
ܗܕܐ ܗܝ ܒܪܬܗ ܒܢ̈ܫܐ
ܕܡܢܗ̇ ܐܬܝܠܕ ܦܪܘܩܐ
ܕܒܠܡܐ. ܗܕܐ ܗܝ
ܐܪܒܐ ܕܒܘ̈ܒܬܐ
ܕܡܢܗ̇ ܐܬܝܠܕ ܐܒܪܐ
ܕܫܘܒܬܐ. ܕܒܦܘܩܕܢܗ̇

f. 76a col. a

ܘܫ̈ܠܝܚܐ ܡܬܟ̈ܢܫܝܢ
ܘܫ̈ܠܝܚܐ[1] ܫܡܥܝܢ ܘܐܬ̈ܝܢ
ܘܙܘ̈ܥܐ ܘܫܘ̈ܒܗܪܐ
ܘܒܐ̈ܢܐ ܘܡܫܡ̈ܫܢܐ
ܘܡܙ̈ܡܪܐ ܘܩܘ̈ܠܣܐ
ܘܚܢܘܟ ܘܡܘܫܐ
ܘܐܠܝܐ ܥܡ ܣܕܪ̈ܐ
ܕܡܠܐ̈ܟܐ. ܘܟܢܫܝܗܘܢ
ܕܐܒܗ̈ܬܐ ܟܠܗܘܢ
ܘܐܒܪܗܡ ܘܐܝܣܚܩ.
ܘܝܥܩܘܒ ܘܕܘܝܕ ܡܙܡܪܢܐ
ܕܟܢܘ̈ܬܐ. ܗܠܝܢ ܟܠܗܘܢ
ܟܬ̈ܝܒܬܐ ܕܡܠܟܝܢ ܥܡ
ܕܢܚܬ ܐܬܘ، ܠܫܘܠܡܗ̇
ܘܠܡܩܒܪܬܗ̇. ܘܐܬܐ ܡܪܢ
ܝܫܘܥ ܡܫܝܚܐ ܘܟܢܘܪܐ
ܕܣܪ̈ܘܦܐ ܩܕܡܘܗܝ، ܥܕ
ܠܒܢܝܢ ܫܘܒ̈ܚܐ ܘܡܙܡܪܝܢ

f. 69b col. a

ܘܥܕܪܐ ܕܡܠܐ̈ܟܐ ܕܒ
ܠܚܝܠ ܡ̈ܢܘܬܐ ܘܡܥܒܕܝܢ
ܘܐܬܐ، ܫ̈ܡܥܬܐ ܕܟܪ̈ܘܒܐ
ܟܕ ܠܩܒܠܝܢ ܢܘܗ̈ܪܐ
ܕܫܡܫܐ ܘܐܬܝܢ ܒܗ̇
ܩ̈ܠܐ ܕܥܝ̈ܪܐ ܘܦܪ̈ܫܝܢ
ܘܗܘ ܠܦܘܬܗ̇ ܘܐܬܟܢܫܘ

cf. Cod. Harris f. 161 b

f. 76a col. b

ܒܢ̈ܝܢ ܫܡܝܐ. ܘܐܬܬ
ܡܪܢ ܝܫܘܥ ܡܫܝܚܐ
ܘܚܙܗ̇ ܠܦܘܠܚܢܬܐ ܘܟܡ
ܡܢܬܬ. ܘܐܡܪ ܐܢܬܘܢ
ܫܡܥܘܢܐ ܡܬܗ̈ܡܢܢܐ
ܚܦܝܛܐܝܬ ܘܦܪ̈ܝܫܐܝܬ
ܫܡܥܘ ܒܟܠܗ̇ ܕܦܘܠܚܢܬܐ
ܕܐܢܫܐ ܕܡܗܝܡܢ ܒܐܒܐ
ܕܠܐ ܦܠܓܐ ܢܫܪ ܒܗ
ܡܗܕܪܐ ܕܫܕܪ ܐܠܗܐ
ܒܪܗ ܘܐܬܓܠܝ ܡܢ
ܐܢܬܬܐ ܘܐܢܫܐ ܕܢܚܡ
ܠܫܡܥ ܡܫܝܚܐ. ܢܘܚܡ
ܕܐܬܝܠܕ ܒܪܐ ܕܐܠܗܐ

f. 69b col. b

ܡܢ ܡܪܝܡ ܕܠܐ ܙܘܘܓܐ
ܘܟܘܠ ܕܟܒܐ ܕܢܘܟܠ
ܦܘܪܢܣܐ ܠܓܒܐ ܢܘܕܐ
ܘܢܣܓܘܕ ܠܪܘܚܐ ܕܩܘܕܫܐ
ܬܠܬܐ ܩܢܘܡܝܢ ܘܬܠܝܬܝܘܬܐ
ܫܒ̈ܚܗܘܢ ܚܕ ܐܕܪܐ
ܐܠܗܐ ܡܫܒܚܐ ܠܥܠܡ
ܥܠܡܝܢ. ܕܠܗ ܗܘ ܫܘܠܛܢܐ
ܫܘܒܚܐ ܘܐܝܩܪܐ. ܘܗܘ
ܐܠܗܐ ܕܙܪ̈ܥܐ ܕܐܬܝܠܕ
ܡܢ ܡܪܝܡ ܒܬܘܠܬܐ ܕܠܐ
ܡܢ ܡܠܐ̈ܟܐ ܘܠܐ ܡܢ

[1] Cod. Harris ܘܡܫܡܫܢ̈ܐ

f. 44 b col. a

ܢܐܡܪܘܢ ܒܕܝܢ ܗܘ

ܐܠܗܐ ܕܕܪܕܪ ܠܒܪܗ

ܘܫܪܐ ܒܡܪܝܡ ܘܒܪܢ

ܗܘ ܡܫܝܚܐ ܕܐܘܪܒ

ܠܝܠܕܬܗ ܒܢܘܡܐ

ܕܡܦܩܢܗ̇ ܕܡܢ ܥܠܡܐ

ܗܢܐ. ܕܠܗ ܫܘܒܚܐ

ܘܠܗ̇ ܕܘܒܪܢܐ ܠܦܒܐ

ܒܕܡܐ ܠܥܠܡ. ܘܢܗܘܐ

ܡܪ . . . ܐ ܘܫܠܡܐ ܥܠ ܠ

ܥܠܡܐ ܟܘܠܗ ܠܥܠܡ

ܠܥܠܡܝܢ ܐܡܝܢ ° °

ܒܪܝܟܐ ܦܪܘܩܢ ܐܠܗܐ

ܕܡܝܬܬ ܕܬܚܘܝ * ܒܪ

f. 44 b col. b

ܘܡܢ ܩܒܪܐ ܠܢܘܚܡܐ.

ܘܡܢ ܢܘܚܡܐ ܠܫܡܝܐ.

ܘܗܐ ܝܬܒ ܐܢܬ ܡܢ

ܝܡܝܢܐ ܕܫܘܒܚܐ. ܘܥܬܝܕ

ܡܪܝ، ܡܫܝܚܢ ܡܢ

ܬܪܥܘܗ̇ ܡܫܒܚܐ

ܕܐܘܪܝܢ. ܒܒܪܝܐ ܗܢܐ.

ܘܒܪܝܢ ܠܒܢܝܡ ܕܡܫܒܚ

ܠܕܘܒܪܢܗ̇ ܕܐܡܪܢ ܒܪܝܟܬ

ܒܢ̈ܝܐ ܘܡܦܩܬܗ̇ ܕܡܢ

ܥܠܡܐ ܗܢܐ ܒܪܢ ܡܪܝ

ܝܫܘܥ ܡܫܝܚܐ ܠܥܠܡ

* * * * * * * * *

cf. Cod. Harris f. 161 a

f. 37 a col. a

ܡܠܟܐ ܕܐܬܬܚܝܬ، ܠܐ

ܡܐܬ ܕܝܒܐ ܘܡܝܬܬ.

ܕܢܚ ܡܢ ܐܒܐ ܠܡܪܝܡ

ܘܡܢ ܡܪܝܡ ܠܐܘܪܝܐ.

ܘܡܢ ܐܘܪܝܐ ܠܢܘܪܬܐ.

ܘܡܢ ܢܘܪܬܐ ܠܥܘܒܕܐ.

ܘܡܢ ܥܘܒܕܐ ܠܢܓܪܐ.

ܘܡܢ ܢܓܪܐ ܠܡܘܦܫܐ.

ܘܡܢ ܡܘܦܫܐ ܠܝܘܣܦܐ.

ܘܡܢ ܝܘܣܦܐ ܠܡܘܬܐ.

ܘܡܢ ܡܘܬܐ ܠܩܒܪܐ.

f. 37 a col. b

ܐܢܫ̈ ܫܡܥܘܢܐ ܘܥܠܗܘܢ

ܡܗ̈ܝܡܢܐ ܠܦܘܪܥܢܐ

ܕܥܠܡܐ. ܚܕܬܐ ܓܠܘ

ܐܪ̈ܙܝܗܘܢ ܘܦܬܟܘ ܪ̈ܚܡܝܗܘܢ

ܘܫܡܫܘ. ܒ̈ܬܒܗ̇.

ܕܦܘܠܚܢܬܐ ܡܪܬܝ

ܡܪܝܡ ܝܠܕܬ ܐܠܗܐ

ܐܝܟܢܐ ܢܦܩܬ ܡܢ

ܥܠܡܐ. ܘܐܬܝ، ܒ̈ܢܝܬܐ

ܕܠܥܠ ܥܡ ܕܠܬܚܬ

ܠܦ̈ܩܐ ܘܫ̈ܒܠܬܐ

ܕܥ̈ܠܝܢܐ ܥܡ ܢܥܝܐ

f. 44 a col. a
ܒܫܡܝܐ ܘܪܡ ܡܠܟܐ
ܡܫܝܚܐ. ܘܗܘ ܟܠܗܘܢ
ܐܘܪܚܐ ܕܒܝܬ ܐܒܐ.
ܢܛܪܘܢ ܦܘܩܕܢܘܗܝ ܕܒܪܐ.
ܘܢܫܡܫܘܢ ܬܫܒܘܚܬܐ
ܠܡܠܟ ܬܫܒܘܚܬܐ ܘܬܘܕܝܬܐ
ܡܢ ܬܘܕܝܬܐ ܘܡܘܕܝܢܘܬܐ
ܠܡܠܟ ܡܫܝܚܘܬܐ.
ܘܬܫܒܘܚܬܐ ܘܬܘܕܝܬܐ
ܒܫܡܝܐ ܠܐܠܗܐ.
ܘܬܘܕܝܬܐ ܘܫܘܒܚܬܐ cf. J. S. L. p. ܗ
ܠܡܫܝܚܐ. ܘܡܘܠܟܢܐ
ܡܢ ܗܘܠܠܐ ܠܦܪܘܩܐ
ܕܡܘܕܝܢܐ . ○ .
ܡܦܩܢܗ̇ ܕܬܫܒܘܚܬܐ f. 37 b col. a
ܡܪܬܝ، ܡܪܝܡ ܕܡܢ
ܒܠܗܐ ܗܘܐ. ܐܡܝܢ
ܘܕܡܫܝܚܘܢ ܡܟܗܢܝܢ ܚܠܡ
ܦܘܩܕ ܡܪܝ، ܒܘܪܟܬܐ
ܠܟܠܗ ܒܢܝܢ ܕܡܥܡܕܝܢ cf. Cod. Harris f. 160 b
ܠܬܫܡܫܝܟ ܕܢܕܝܫܘܢ ܚܠܡ.
ܦܝܡ[1] ܠܚܣܝܐ ܕܡܕܒܚܝܢ
ܒܠܝܠ ܡܠܟܐ ܡܫܝܚܐ
ܕܒܗܐ ܐܝܟ ܠܐܝܣܚܩ.
ܦܘܩܕ ܡܪܝ، ܒܘܪܟܬܐ

f. 44 a col. b
ܘܐܝܩܪܐ ܠܒܢܐ ܠܒ̈ܢܝ
ܬܫܡܫܬܐ ܕܢܫܡܫܘܢ.
ܠܒܬܘܠܐ ܕܢܗܠܠܘܢ.
ܠܡ̈ܦܩܢܐ ܕܢܫܬܒܚܘܢ.
ܠܥܡܐ ܕܢܠܒܫܘܢ ܠܒܠܘܫ̈ܐ
ܕܢܚܪܒܘܢ. ܘܠܥܒ̈ܕܐ ܕܢܫܒܚܘܢ.
ܘܠܢܫ̈ܐ ܒܢ̈ܝܗ ܕܚܘܐ
ܒܢܝ ܛܘܒܝܢ ܡܪܝ، ܡܠܟܘܬܐ.
ܡܐ ܕܩܪܝܢ ܠܟ ܕܡܒܗܝܢ
ܐܬܝܠܝܕܬ ܐܢܬܬܐ
ܒܬܘܠܬܐ ܘܩܕܝܫܬܐ
ܕܓܒܗ̇ ܐܠܗܐ ܡܢ ܩܕܡ
ܟܠܗܘܢ ܥܠܡܐ ܘܐܬܝܠܕ
ܡܢܗ̇ ܡܪܗ̇ ܕܬܫܒܘܚܬܐ
ܒܪܗ ܕܐܠܗܐ ܡܫܒܚܐ.
f. 37 b col. b ܒܗܪܐ ܗܒܝܠ ܒܕܝܢܐ
ܠܐܬܘܢ ܕܕܝܢ̈ܐ
ܘܦܠܚ̈ܝܗܘܢ ܘܠܒ̈ܢܝܐ
ܘܫܒܘܩ̈ܝܗܘܢ ܘܠܪ̈ܝܫܢܐ
ܘܒܪ̈ܘܪܬܗܘܢ ܘܫ̈ܦܪܐ
ܡܢ ܟ̈ܠܠܝܗܘܢ ܘܢܩܘܫܘܢ
ܐܪ̈ܒܥܝܢ ܒܕ ܚܢܝܢ
ܒܟ̈ܢܘܫܝܐ ܘܢܫܬܡܗܘܢ
ܕܡܝܬܐ ܕܒܠܝ̈ܠܐ ܡܢ
ܕܬܫ̈ܬܐ ܘܗܡܢܝܢܐ

[1] Cod. Harris ܦܐܡ

ܠܡܪܝܐ ܡܫܝܚܐ ܒܦܓܪ. f. 88 b col. a
ܐܢܐ [1]ܕܝܢ ܝܥܩܘܒ ܟܬܒܬ cf. Tisch. xxv
[2]ܗܢܐ ܬܫܥܬܐ[2] ܟܕ ܗܘܐ
ܫܓܘܫܝܐ ܒܐܘܪܫܠܡ. ܟܕ
ܡܝܬ ܗܪܘܕܣ ܡܘܬܐ
ܡܪܝܐ. ܘ[3]ܥܪܩܬ ܠܡܕܒܪ
ܠܐܬܪܐ ܚܘܪܒܐ ܕܒܝܫܐ
ܕܫܠܐ ܫܓܘܫܝܐ ܡܢ
[4]ܐܘܪܫܠܡ.
ܡܫܒܚ ܐܢܐ ܕܝܢ
[5]ܠܡܪܝܐ ܗܘ[5] ܕܝܗܒ ܠܝ
ܚܟܡܬܐ ܕܐܟܬܘܒ
ܒܬܫܥܬܐ ܗܢܐ ∴ f. 93 a col. a

f. 88 b col. b ܕܡܪܝ ܘܦܪܘܩܬܐ ܕܡܫܝܚ
ܫܠܡܗ ܕܗܘ ܡܪܐ
ܒܪܬܐ ܕܠܐ ܡܫܒܚܝܢ
ܒܪܬܐ ܕܢܫܝܢ ܫܒܘܚܐ
ܕܐܠܗܘܬܗ ܘܫܒܚܘ
ܡܪܟܒܬܐ ܕܡܝܒܬܐ
ܒܡܪܘܡܐ ܟ̈ܠܝܐ
ܘܐܬܐ ܫܪܐ ܒܟܪܣܗ
ܕܡܪܝܡ ܒܬܘܠܬܐ.
ܢܗܘܐ ܒܢܝ ܘܒܢ ܥܠܗ
ܒܢܝܢ ܕܢܒܪܟ ܥܠܝܗܘܢ
ܕܗ̈ܢܝܐ ܐܟ̈ܠܝܢ ܕܝܬܒܝܢ
f. 93 a col. b ܒܪܫܝܐ ܕܡܪܕܝܬܗܘܢ
ܠܥܠܡܝܢ ܐܡܝܢ ∴ ∴
ܦܬܚ ܡܪܝ ܬܪܥܐ
ܕܫܡܝܐ ܠܨܠܘܬܢ ܒܕܢܐ
ܗܢܐ ܘܢܣܒ ܩܘܪܒܐ
ܒܫܡܝܐ ܡܢ ܒܢܝܢ
ܠܫܘܕܪܗܘܢ ܕܟܠܝܐ
ܘܢܡܚܝܢ ܡ̈ܛܠܬܐ ܕܪܒ
ܡܠܐ̈ܟܐ ܒܫܡܝܐ
ܘܢܩܘܡܘܢ ܠܩܘܕܡܘܗܝ
ܕܟ̈ܠܝܐ ܠܥܠܡܝܢ ܠܥܠܡܝܢ
ܘܬܗܘܐ ܬܫܒܘܚܬܐ

Rubrics illegible

ܫܠܡܗ ܕܐܠܗܐ ܕܫܪܝܪ cf. J. S. L. page 𐋇
ܠܡܪܝܗ ܘܐܬܐ ܠܥܠܡܐ. cf. Cod. Harris
ܘܫܠܡܗ ܠܡܪܝܐ ܕܢܚ f. 160 a
ܡܢ ܫܡܝܐ ܘܫܪܐ
ܒܡܪܝܡ. ܘܫܠܡܗ ܕܪܘܚܐ
ܕܩܘܕܫܐ ܦܪܩܠܛܐ

---

[1] ܗܟܠ [2] ܬܫܥܬܐ ܗܢܐ [3] ܥܪܩܬ
[4] ܐܘܪܫܠܡ. [5] ܠܐܠܗܐ

ܘܒܢܝܐ ܘܠܐ [1]ܡܕܡ[1] ܗܘܘ[1] f. 88a col. a
ܒܢ̈ܝ ܐܣܦܪܠ [2]ܕܐܝܟܢܐ cf. Tisch. xxiv
ܐܬܦܠܠ. ܐܠܐ ܒܟܕܢܐ
ܕܫܠܡܐ ܐܪ̈ܟܘ[3] [4]ܒܫ̈ܢܝܐ
ܘܠܐ ܐܪܒܬܐ ܐܘܟ ܐܝܟ[5]
ܕܝܢܐ[5] ܒܐܪܒܬܗ ܕܒܢܝܐ.
[6]ܘܡܫܟܚܝܢ ܗܘܘ[7] ܒܫ̈ܢܝܐ
ܘܡܫܡܫܝܢ ܠܗ ܠܒܢܝܐ
[4]ܐܝܟ ܕܢܫܐܠܘܢ[8] ܒܫܠܡܗ
ܒܨܠܘܬܐ. ܘܢܫܒܚܘܢ
[9]ܠܡܪܝܡܐ. ܘܟܕ [10]ܐܫܬܘܕܥ
ܠܗ. ܕܝܠܗ ܒܠܗܘܢ
ܘܐܡܪܝܢ [4]ܗܘܐ ܚܕ f. 93b col. a
ܡܢܗܘܢ ܘܟܠ ܠܟܢܫܬ
ܡܘܕܝܢܐ ܘܫܢܝܐ ܟܠ
ܚܕ ܡܕܒܪܢܗ ܕܡܪܝܐ
ܕܡܪܐ ܕܐܝܟܢܐ ܘܡܟܝܠ.[11]
ܘܠܐ [12]ܐܫܬܡܥ. ܕܐܡܪ.
ܒܢܝܐ ܐܬܦܠܠ. ܘܠܐ
ܢܬܫܦܟ ܕܡܗ ܕܒܢܝܐ
ܕܢܐܬܐ ܬܟܘܒܐ [5]ܘܟܕ
ܫܡܥ ܗܠܝܢ ܡ̈ܠܐ ܕܝܠ
ܘܢܦܩ ܘܐܘܕܥ ܠܒ̈ܢܝܐ[5]

f. 88a col. b [13]ܡܕܡ ܕܝܢܐ ܘܫܡܥܘܢ
ܘܐܡܪܝܢ ܗܘܘ
ܘܫܢܘ ܡܕܡ ܕܗܘܐ * *
ܥܠ ܒ̈ܢܝ ܡܣܦܪܘܡܐ
ܕܗܝܟܠܐ. ܘܐܝܠܠܘ ܒܠܗܘܢ
ܘܪ̈ܓܘ ܠܒܘܫܝܗܘܢ ܡܢ
ܠܟܠ ܒܕܡܐ ܠܬܝܬ
cf. Cod. Harris f. 113b ܘܦܓܪܗ ܠܐ ܐܫܟܚܘ
ܐܠܐ ܕܡܗ ܐܫܟܚܘ
ܟܕ ܡܟܝܟ ܐܝܟ ܟܐܦܐ
ܘܕܚܠܘ[13]. ܘܢܦܩܘ ܐܘܕܥܘ
ܕܒܢܝܐ ܐܬܦܠܠ. ܘܟܕ
[14]ܫܡܥ [4]ܒܠܗܘܢ ܫܪ̈ܒܬܐ
f. 93b col. b ܕܥܡܐ ܐܬܐܟܠܘ ܘܒܟܘ
[4]... ܬܠܬܐ ܝܘ̈ܡܝܢ
[13]ܘܬܠܬܐ ܠܠ̈ܝܘܢ[13] ܘܒܬܪ
[15]ܬܠܬܐ ܝܘ̈ܡܝܢ[15] [13]ܘܬܠܬܐ
ܠܠ̈ܝܘܢ[13]. ܐܬܡܢܝܘ ܒܫ̈ܢܝܐ
ܕܠܡܢܘ ܢܩܝܡܘܢ [16]ܒܗܢܐ
ܒܕܘܟܬܗ ܕܒܢܝܐ.
ܘܢܦܠܬ ܦܣܬܐ [17]ܕܫܡܥܘܢ.
[18]ܗܢܐ [13]ܗܘܐ ܒܪ ܗܘ[13]
ܕܐܬܟܠܠ ܠܗ ܡܢ ܪܘܚܐ
ܕܩܘܕܫܐ ܕܠܐ ܢܛܥܡ
ܡܘܬܐ ܒܕܡܐ [19]ܕܡܫܝܚܐ

---

1 ܡܕܡ 2 ܐܝܟܢ 3 + ܐܝܟ ܚܙܝܐ. 4 om. 5—5 om.
6 ܡܫܟܚܝܢ 7 + ܗܡ 8 + ܗܘܘ 9 ܠܐܠܗܐ. 10 ܐܘܕܥ
11 + ܐܝܟ ܟܐܦܐ. 12 ܗܘܐ 13—13 om. 14 ܫܡܥܘ
15 ܬܠܬܐ ܝܘ̈ܡܝܢ ܬܠܬܐ 16 ܒܫ̈ܢܝܐ 17 ܠܫܡܥܘܢ 18 ܗܘ
19 ܕܢܝܚܐ

f. 91 b col. a

ܘܫܩܠܬܗ ܠ[1]ܛܠܝܐ
ܘܟܪܟܬܗ ܒܥܙܘܪ̈ܐ
ܘܐܪܡܝܬܗ ܒܐܘܪܝܐ
ܕܬܘܪ̈ܐ. ܐܦ
ܐܠܝܫܒܥ ܟܕ ܫܡܥܬ
ܕܡܬܒܥܐ ܝܘܚܢܢ ܫܩܠܬܗ
ܘܣܠܩܬ [2]ܒܗ ܠܛܘܪܐ.
ܘܚܙܝܐ ܗܘܬ ܕܐܝܟܐ
ܬܛܫܝܘܗܝ.[3] ܗܝ ܕܝܢ
ܐܬܬܢܚܬ ܐܠܝܫܒܥ
ܘܐܡܪܐ ܠܛܘܪܐ. ܛܘܪܐ
ܕܐܠܗܐ ܩܒܠ ܠܐܡܐ
ܥܡ ܒܪܗ̇. ܘܠܐ[4]

f. 90 a col. a

ܡܫܟܚܐ ܗܘܬ ܐܠܝܫܒܥ
ܕܬܣܩ.[4] ܘܡܚܝ [5]ܫܠܝܐ
ܐܬܦܬܚ ܛܘܪܐ[6]
ܘܩܒܠܗ̇. ܘܢܘܗܪܐ ܪܒܐ

cf. Cod. Harris f. 112 b

ܡܢܗܪ ܗܘܐ ܠܗܘܢ
ܛܘܪܐ.[6] ܡܛܠ ܕܡܠܐܟܗ
ܕܡܪܝܐ ܐܝܬ ܗܘܐ
ܥܡܗܘܢ[7] ܘܡܢܛܪ[8] ܠܗܘܢ.

cf. Tisch. xxiii

ܗܪܘܕܣ ܕܝܢ ܒܥܐ
ܗܘܐ ܠܝܘܚܢܢ. ܘܫܕܪ
ܕܫ̈ܡܫܐ ܠܘܬ ܙܟܪܝܐ
ܠܗܝܟܠܐ ܘܐܡܪ ܠܗ.

f. 91 b col. b

ܐܝܟܐ ܛܫܝܬܘܗܝ ܠܒܪܟ.
ܘܥܢܐ[9] ܙܟܪܝܐ ܘܐܡܪ
ܠܗܘܢ. ܐܢܐ ܡܫܡܫܢܐ
ܐܝܬܝ ܕܐܠܗܐ [10]ܘܩܐܡ
ܐܢܐ[10] [11]ܒܗܝܟܠܗ ܕܡܪܝܐ.[12]
ܠܐ[13] ܝܕܥ ܐܢܐ ܕܐܝܟܘ
ܒܪܝ. ܘܐܙܠܘ ܕܫ̈ܡܫܐ
ܘܐܡܪܘ ܠܗ. [10]ܗܠܝܢ
ܟܠܗܝܢ.[10] [14]ܘܪܓܙ ܗܪܘܕܣ
ܘܐܡܪ ܗܘܐ.[14] ܒܪܗ
[15]ܥܬܝܕ ܕܢܡܠܟ ܥܠ
ܐܝܣܪܐܝܠ. ܘܫܕܪ ܕܫ̈ܡܫܐ

f. 90 a col. b

[16]ܘܐܡܪ ܠܗ ܐܡܪ [2]ܠܝ
ܫܪܝܪܐܝܬ ܐܝܟܐ ܒܪܟ.
ܐܘ ܠܐ [17]ܝܕܥܬ ܕܕܡܟ
ܬܚܝܬ ܐܝܕܝ ܗܘ ܕܝܠܝ.
ܘܐܙܠܘ ܕܫ̈ܡܫܐ ܘܐܡܪܘ
ܠܗ [10]ܗܠܝܢ ܟܠܗܝܢ.[10] ܘܐܡܪ[18]
ܢܣܗܕ [19]ܐܠܗܐ ܕܐܫܕܕܬ
ܕܡܝ. ܪܘܚܝ ܕܝܢ ܡܪܝܐ
ܡܩܒܠ ܠܗ̇. ܕܕܡܟܐ ܘܥܢܐ
[20]ܐܫܕܬ. ܕܠܐ ܫܘܠܡܬܐ.
[21]ܒܫܦܪ ܬܪ̈ܥܐ ܕܗܝܟܠܗ
ܕܡܪܝܐ. ܐܦܠܐ ܝܕܥ
ܐܢܫ. [21]ܐܝܟܢܐ ܐܬܩܛܠ

cf. Cod. Harris f. 113 a

---

[1] ܠܥܘܫܒ [2] om. [3] + ܘܠܝܬ ܗܘܐ ܐܬܪܐ. [4–4] om. [5] ܒܥܠ
[6] + ܗܘ̇ [7] ܘܗܘܐ ܡܢܛܪ [8] + ܗܘܐ [9] ܥܢܐ [10–10] om.
[11] ܘܒܗܝܟܠܗ [12] + ܐܡܝܢ ܐܢܐ. [13] ܘܠܐ [14] ܘܐܡܪ ܗܪܘܕܣ.
[15] + ܗܘܐ [16] ܘܐܡܪܘ [17] ܝܕܥ ܐܢܬ

Wright, p. 1

[18] + ܙܟܪܝܐ. [19] ܡܪܝܐ [20] ܐܫܕ ܐܢܬ [21] ܒܒܝܬܐ ܕܡܢ ܠܓܘ ܡܕܒܚܐ

f. 91 a col. a

ܕܝܗܘܕܝܐ [1]ܡܬܝܠܕ. ܗܘܝܐ
ܚܙܝ ܒܬܘܒ[1] ܘܫܐܠ ܐܢܘܢ
ܠܡܓܘ̈ܫܐ ܘܐܡܪ ܠܗܘܢ.
ܡܢܐ ܐܬܐ ܚܙܝܬܘܢ.
[2]ܒܫܡܝܐ [3]ܟܠ ܡ̈ܠܟܐ
ܗܢܐ[3] ܕܐܬܝܠܕ. ܐܡܪܝܢ
[2]ܠܗ ܡܓܘ̈ܫܐ ܚܙܝܢ
ܒܟܘܟܒܐ ܕܡܕܢܚܪ[4]
ܒܪܘܬܗ [5]ܕܐܢܫܪ ܒܢܝܬ
ܗܠܝܢ ܒܟ̈ܘܟܒܐ[6]. [7 8]ܘܡܢ
ܢܘܗܪܗ ܒܢܗܪܐ ܕܐܦ
ܠܐ [2]ܡܬܚܙܝܘ ܡܬܚܙܝܢ
ܗܘܘ. ܘܢܨܒܝܢ ܕܡ̈ܠܟܐ

f. 90 b col. a

ܐܬܬܠܕ ܠܐܝܣܪܐܝܠ.
ܘܐܬܝܢ ܠܡܣܓܕ ܠܗ.
ܘܐܡܪ ܠܗܘܢ ܗܪܘܕܣ.
[2]ܡܠܟܐ. ܙܠܘ ܒܥܩܒܗ [9]ܟܠܗܘܢ،
ܘܐܢ [9]ܐܫܟܚܬܘܢܝܗܝ، ܬܘ
[10]ܐܡܪܘ ܠܝ[10]. [11]ܕܐܬܐ ܐܦ
ܐܢܐ[11] ܘܐܣܓܘܕ ܠܗ. cf. Cod. Harris f. 109 a
[12]ܘܢܦܩܘ ܡܓܘ̈ܫܐ ܘܗܐ
ܒܟܘܟܒܐ ܗܘ ܕܚܙܘ
[2]ܗܘܘ ܒܡܕܢܚܐ [1]ܐܬܚܙܝ،
ܠܗܘܢ[1] ܐܙܠ ܗܘܐ
ܩܕܡܝܗܘܢ ܒܕܡܐ
ܕܐܬܘ [2]ܠܡܕܝܢܬܐ. [13]ܘܩܡ

f. 91 a col. b

ܠܥܠ ܡܢ [14]ܪܝܫܗ ܕܛܠܝܐ[14]
ܘܒܕ ܚܙܐܘܗܝ، [2]ܡܓܘ̈ܫܐ
ܠܛܠܝܐ ܥܡ ܡܪܝܡ
ܐܡܗ. ܢܦܠܘ [15]ܘܣܓܕܘ
ܠܗ. [16]ܘܦܬܚܘ ܘܐܡܪܘ
ܫܘܒܚܐ ܠܐܠܗܐ
ܒܡܪܘܡܐ ܘܫܠܡܐ
ܥܠ ܐܪܥܐ ܘܣܒܪܐ
ܛܒܐ ܠܒܢ̈ܝܢܫܐ. ܘܦܬܚܘ
ܣܝ̈ܡܬܗܘܢ[16] ܘܩܪܒܘ ܠܗ
ܩܘܪ̈ܒܢܐ ܕܗܒܐ
[17]ܘܠܒܘܢܬܐ ܘܡܘܪܐ[17]
ܘܐܬܟܠܝ ܠܗܘܢ[18] ܡܠܐܟܐ

f. 90 b col. b

[16]ܘܐܡܪ ܠܗܘܢ[16] ܕܠܐ
[19]ܢܗܦܟܘܢ ܠܗܪܘܕܣ. [20]ܗܢܘܢ ܕܝܢ[20]
ܒܐܘܪܚܐ ܐܚܪܢܬܐ
cf. Tisch. xxii [21]ܐܙܠܘ. [22]ܘܟܕ ܢܦܩ[22]
ܗܪܘܕܣ ܕܟܢܫܘ ܒܗ
ܡܓܘ̈ܫܐ ܙܟܝ. ܘܫܕܪ
[23]ܩܛܘܠܐ ܘܩܛܠ ܠܗܘܢ
ܠܡܩܛܠܘ [2]ܠܟܠܗܘܢ ܛܠ̈ܝܐ
ܡܢ ܒܪ ܬܪ̈ܬܝܢ ܫܢܝܢ
ܘܠܬܚܬ. [24]ܠܡܕܝܢܬܐ ܕܒܢܐ[24]
[25]ܕܐܡܪܘ ܠܗ[25] ܡܓܘ̈ܫܐ.
[26]ܘܟܕ ܫܡܥܬ ܡܪܝܡ
ܕܛܠ̈ܝܐ ܡܬܩܛܠܝܢ ܕܚܠܬ.

---

[1—1] om. [2] om. [3] ܡܛܠ ܗܢܐ ܡ̈ܠܟܐ [4] + ܛܒ
[5] ܕܢܘܗܪ [6] + ܐܚܪ̈ܢܐ [7] + ܘܐܬܬܚܒܠܘ ܟܘ̈ܟܒܐ [8] ܡܢ
[9] ܥܠ ܛܠܝܐ. ܘܡܐ ܕ [10] ܚܘܐܘܢܝ [11] ܕܐܦ ܐܢܐ ܐܙܠ
Wright, p. ܘ [12] ܘܟܕ ܢܦܩܘ [13] ܘܩܡܘ [14] ܛܠܝܐ [15] ܘܣܓܕܘ [16—16] om.
[17] ܘܡܘܪܐ ܘܠܒܘܢܬܐ [18] + ܡܢ [19] sic ܢܗܦܘܢ [20] ܘܗܢܘܢ
[21] ܐܙܠܘ ܠܐܬܪܗܘܢ ܀ [22] ܟܕ ܕܝܢ ܚܙܐ ܗܘܐ [23] ܠܩܛܘܠܐ
[24] ܐܝܟ ܕܒܢܐ [25] ܕܐܡܪܝܢ ܡܢ [26] ܟܕ

f. 138 b col. a

cf. Cod. Harris f. 108 a

ܘܕܢܒܡܒ ܘܠܐ
ܬܦܪܘܫܝܢ ܡܕܡ ܒܢ̈ܝ
¹ܐܝܣܪܐܝܠ. ²ܐܠܐ ⌜ܚܕܪ⌝
ܠܐܠܗܝܢ ܕܠܘܩܒܠܗ² ܡܪܝܐ
ܐܝܟ ³ܕܢܒܥܐ ܕܒܫܡܝܢ
⁴ܒܥܕܐ ܗܘܝܬ ܐܣܘܬܐ⁴
ܘܐܦܪܝܐ ܡܠܝܢ ⁵ܗܘ
ܢܦܫܐ ܗܘܝܬ ⁶ܘܗܘܐ
ܡܠܐܟܐ ܚܢܐ⁶ ܘܐܡܪ
⁵ܠܫܠܘܡ ܫܠܘܡ ܥܡܟ
ܡܪܝܐ ܒܒܘܬܟ. ܐܠܐ
ܡܢܟ ܐܬ̈ܕܒܝ ܠܛܠܠܐ.
⁵ܘܫܒܘܩܠܘܗܝ, ܘܬܗܘܐ
⌜ܠܟ⌝ ܐܣܝܘܬܐ. ⁵ܘܦܘܪܩܢܐ

f. 133 a col. a

ܘܐܬܡܠܟܬ ⁷ܫܠܘܡ
ܚܕܘܬܐ ⁸ܘܐܬܦܪܩܬ
ܠܘܬ ܛܠܠܐ ⁹ܘܦܪܥܬ ܠܗ
ܘܐܡܪܐ ܡܪܝܐ ܐܝܟ
¹⁰ܗܕܐ ܚܙܝ ܐܣܬܟܠܬ¹⁰
ܟܠܗ ܕܐܣܟܘܕ ⁵ܠܗ
ܛܠܠܐ. ܘܐܡܪܬ ¹¹ܕܡ̈ܠܟܐ
ܐܬܠܝܕ ⁵ܗܢܐ ܠܐܝܣܪܐܝܠ.
ܘܐܬܡܣܝܬ ⁵ܫܠܘܡ
ܘܢܦܩܬ ܡܢ ܡܕܝܢܬܐ
ܒܕ ܡܚܒܘܩܐ. ⁵ܘܗܘܐ

f. 138 b col. b

¹²ܘܡܠܐ ܐܫܬܡܥ ܠܗ.
ܘܐܡܪ ܠܗ ܫܠܡ¹². ܠܐ
ܬܕܚܠܝܢ ¹³ܗܠܝܢ ܬܕܡܘܪ̈ܬܐ
ܦܪܥܘܬܐ ܕܚܣܝܬ ¹³ܒܕܡܐ
¹⁴ܕܢܒܥܠ ܛܠܠܐ ܠܐܘܪܫܠܡ.

cf. Tisch. xxi

ܘܗܘܐ ܢܘܦܐ ܐܬܛܠܒܢ
⁵ܘܗܘܐ ¹⁵ܠܡܠܟܐ ܠܢܘܗܕ.
ܘܗܘܐ ¹⁶ܪܘܒܐ ܒܢܝܬ
ܠܝܡ ܕܢܗܘܕܐ.¹⁶ ܐܬܘ
ܒܝܪ ܡܓܘ̈ܫܐ ⌜⌝ ܘܐܡܪܝܢ
¹⁷ܐܝܟܐ ܗܘ¹⁷ ܡ̇ܠܟܐ

cf. Cod. Harris f. 108 b

⁵ܕܝܗܘܕܝܐ ܕܐܬܝܠܕ.¹⁸
ܟܘܟܒܗ ܚܙܝܢ ܣܝܡ

f. 133 a col. b

ܒܡܕܢܚܐ ܘܐܬܝܢ
ܠܡܣܓܕ ܠܗ. ܘܟܕ ܫܡܥ
ܗܪܘܕܣ ܐܬܕܠܚ ⁵ܣܓܝ.
ܘܫܕܪ ܕܢ̈ܚܐ ܒܬܪ
ܡܓܘ̈ܫܐ ¹⁹ܘܫܕܪ ܬܘܒ¹⁹
²⁰ܡܪܐ ܠܝ̈ܠܝ ܒܗ̈ܢܐ.
ܘܫܐܠ ܐܢܘܢ ⁵ܒܦܪܘܫܝܢ.
ܘܐܡܪ ܠܗܘܢ. ܐܝܟܐ
ܒܬܒ ⁵ܠܗܘܢ ܕܡܠܟܐ.
²¹ܡܫܝܚܐ. ²²ܘܐܝܟܢܐ
⌜ܫܟܝܚ⌝ ܠܗܘܢ ܠܘܬܗ.
ܐܡܪܝܢ ܠܗ. ܒܒܝܬ ܠܚܡ

M. D. G.

---

¹ ܐܢܫܐ. ²⁻² om. ³ ܢܥܒܕ ܐܝܟ. ⁴ ܐܣܝܘܬܐ ܚܕܒܐ ܗܘܝܬ
⁵ om. ⁶ ܐܡܠܐܟܐ ܚܢܐ ⁷ ܫܠܡ sic ⁸ ܘܦܪܥܬ
Wright, p. ܗ ⁹ ܦܪܥܬ ¹⁰ ܗܠܝܢ ܕܡܣܬܟܠܬܐ ܗܘܝܬ ܠܝ ¹¹ ܡ̈ܠܟܐ
¹² ܘܐܫܬܡܥ ܩܠܐ ܕܐܡܪ ܠܫܠܡ ¹³ ܬܕܡܘܪ̈ܬܐ ܗܠܝܢ ¹⁴ ܕܢܒܥܠ
¹⁵ ܠܢܘܗ ¹⁶ ܫܡܥܢܐ ܪܒܐ ܒܐܘܪܫܠܡ ܕܢܗܘܐ. ¹⁷ ܐܝܟܐ
¹⁸ + ܒܢܘܗܕ. ¹⁹⁻¹⁹ om. ²⁰ ܘܦܪܥܐ. ²¹ ܡ̈ܠܟܐ. ²² ܘܐܝܟܢܐ

f. 138 a col. a

ܘܡܫܝܚܐ[1] ܠܡܕܝܢܬܐ ܕܢܝܚܝܢ
ܒܢ̈ܝ ܘܡܫܝܚܐ ܬܕܡܪ̈ܬܐ
ܪ̈ܘܪܒܬܐ ܘܡܫܒ̈ܚܬܐ.
ܕܦܪܘܩܐ ܐܬܓܠܝ.
ܠܐܘܪܫܠܡ ܡܢ ܫܠܝܐ
ܡܬܓܠܝܐ ܗܘܬ ܗ̇ܝ,
ܒܒܢܐ ܡܢ ܡܒܪܬܐ
ܘܐܬܚܙܝ, ܒܗ̇ ܒܡܒܪܬܐ
ܢܘܗܪܐ ܪܒܐ ܐܡܒܘܒܐ
ܕܒܢ̈ܝܢ ܠܐ ܐܫܟܚ
ܠܡܫܒܪܘܬܗ. ܘܟܠܠ
ܘܠܝܠ ܡܬܒܥܐ ܗܘܐ
ܗ̇ܘ ܢܘܗܪܐ[1] ܒܕܡܐ
ܕܐܬܚܙܝ, ܒܥܠܡܐ ܘܐܬܐ
ܗܘܐ[2] ܘܢܦܩ[3] ܬܕܐ ܡܢ
ܡܪܝܡ ܐܡܗ. ܘܩܒܠܬ
ܐܘܟܝܬܐ ܘܐܡܪܬ
ܕܡܫܝܚܐ[4] ܗܘ ܠܝ ܪܒܐ
ܘܡܫܝܚܐ[2] ܕܢܘܚܬ ܗܢܐ[5]
ܫܘܝܐ ܪܒܐ[5] ܘܡܫܝܚܐ[2].
ܘܒܕ ܢܦܩܬ ܐܘܟܝܬܐ[2]
ܡܢ ܡܒܪܬܐ ܐܙܒܪܬܗ̇
ܫܠܘܡ ܘܐܡܪܐ ܠܗ̇[2]:
ܫܠܘܡ[6]. ܐܠܗܐ[1] ܒܒܢܝ[1]
ܫܘܝܐ ܫܒܬܐ ܐܝܬ ܠܝ

f. 133 b col. a; cf. Cod. Harris f. 107 b

f. 138 a col. b

ܕܐܫܬܒܚܐ ܠܒܝ[7] ܒܬܘܠܬܐ
ܠܕܬ ܡܪܝܡ ܕܗܢܐ ܒܢܝܐ
ܠܐ ܦܫܛ ܠܗ. ܘܐܡܪܬ[8]
ܫܠܘܡ ܚܝ ܗܘ ܡܪܝܐ
ܐܠܗܝ,[9] ܕܐܠܐ[10] ܚܝܐ
ܐܢܐ ܒܒܢܝ ܠܐ ܡܫܝܚܐ[a]
ܐܢܐ ܕܐ ܒܬܘܠܬܐ
ܝܠܕܬ.[10] ܘܟܠܠܬ ܐܣܝܬܐ
ܠܡܒܪܬܐ ܘܐܡܪܬ ܠܗ̇[11]
ܠܡܪܝܡ[11]. ܡܪܝܡ ܡܪܝܡ
ܚܘܝ, ܢܦܫܟܝ. ܠܐ ܗܘܐ
ܓܒܪ ܓܒܪ ܐܠܝܢܐ ܕܐܝܬ
ܚܠܝܒ ܐܠܐ ܚܘܝ, ܢܦܫܟܝ.
ܕܐ ܒܬܘܠܬܐ ܐܢܬ,

cf. Tisch. xx

f. 133 b col. b

ܘܒܠܬ[11] ܫܠܘܡ[11] ܘܩܪܒܬ.
ܘܚܙܬ ܕܒܬܘܠܬܐ ܗܝ:
ܘܐܝܠܠܬ[2] ܫܠܘܡ[12] ܘܐܡܪܬ
ܘ, ܠܒܠܘܬ, ܘܠܡܫܪܘܬ
ܡܥܡܪܢܘܬ, ܕܢܦܫܬ
ܠܐܠܗܐ ܚܝܐ. ܘܗܐ
ܐܝܕܝ, ܝܩܕܐ ܘܢܦܠܐ ܡܢܝ.
ܘܦܫܛܬ ܫܠܘܡ ܒܪܘܚܐ
ܦܩܕ ܡܪܝܐ ܘܐܡܪܐ.
ܐܠܗܐ ܕܐܒܗ̈ܝ,[13]
ܐܬܕܟܪܢܝ ܡܛܠ ܕܙܪܥܐ
ܐܢܐ ܕܐܒܪܗܡ[14] ܘܐܝܣܚܩ

M. D. G.

[1–1] om. [2] om. [3] ܢܦܩ [4] ܡܫܝܚܐ
[5] ܫܘܝܐ ܗܘܐ ܢܘܗܪܐ. [6] ܫܠܡ ܠܟܝ. [7] ܒܒܘܢܝ. [8] ܐܡܪܬ
[9] ܐܠܗܐ [10] ܕܠܐ ܡܫܝܚܐ ܐܢܐ. ܐܠܐ ܢܦܫ ܕܒܬܘܠܬܐ ܗܝ.
[11–11] om. [12] ܘܐܡܪܬ. [13] ܐܒܝ. [14] ܘܕܐܝܣܚܩ [a] Cod. ܡܫܝܚܐ

f. 35 b col. a

¹ܠܐ ܠܒܫܝܢ ܘܡܫܡܫܝܢ
ܒܗ ܠܐ ܡܫܡܫܝܢ ܘܒܗ
ܡܩܪܒܝܢ ܗܘܘ
ܐܝܕܝܗܘܢ ܠܦܘܠܚܢܗܘܢ
ܠܐ ܡܩܪܒܝܢ ܐܠܐ
ܦܪܨܘܦܗܘܢ ܒܠ ܠܒܠ
ܫܒܪܝܢ ܗܘܘ ܘܫܝܚܬ ܒܗ
ܡ̈ܪܝܢ ܗܘܘ ܠܓܪܒܝܗܘܢ
ܕܓܪܒܝܗܘܢ ܕܝܢ ܡܟܣܝܢ
ܗܘܘ ܠܗܘܢ ܘܐܪܝܟ
ܐܝܕܗ ܪ̈ܓܠܐ ܕܕܒܝܫܐ
ܐܝܟ ܘܐܝܕܗ ܘܩܡܬ
ܘܫܠܡܬ ܠܟܠ ܘܫܝܚܬ ܟܪ̈ܘܒܐ
ܒܗ ܩ̈ܕܡܝܢ ܠܗ̇ ܢܗܪܐ
ܘܫܝܚܬ ܠܓܕܐ ܒܗ ܦܬܓܡܝܢ
ܦܘܩܕ̈ܢܝܗܘܢ ܒܡܠܬܐ
ܠܡܫܬܐ ܘܠܐ ܫܬܩܝܢ

f. 30 a col. a

ܗܘܘ.¹ ܘܡܢ ܫܠܝܐ²
ܐܫܬܪܝ ܘܪܗܛ ܒܠܘ³
ܡܛܠ ܕܠܒܫܗ ○ ○

cf. Cod. Harris f. 107 a

ܗܝܕܝܢ ܢܚܬܬ ܐܢܬܬܐ
⁴ܒܗ ܢܚܬܐ⁴ ܡܢ ܛܘܪܐ.
ܘܐܡܪܐ ܠܗ ܠܒܒܪܐ⁵
ܠܐܒܐ ܐܙܠ ܐܢܬ.⁶
ܘܐܡܪܬ ܠܗ̇ ܐܡܬܐ
ܒܒܪܝܬܐ ܒ̇ܒܐ ܐܒܐ.

f. 35 b col. b

ܘܐܡܪܬ ܠܝ. ܡܢ
ܐܝܣܪܝܠ ܐܢܬ. ܘܐܡܪܬ
ܠܗ̇. ܐܝܢ. ⁷ܘܐܡܪܐ ܠܝ.
⁸ܘܡܢ ܗܝ ܗܕܐ ܕܠܥܠܐ
ܒܗܕܐ ܡܕܒܪܬܐ.
ܘܐܡܪܬ ܠܗ̇ ܡܕܒܪܬܝ
ܗܝ. ⁷ܘܐܡܪܐ ܠܝ. ܠܐ
ܗܘܬ ܐܢܬܬܝ.⁹ ܘܐܡܪܬ
⁵ܐܢܐ ܠܗ̇. ܡܪܝܡ ܗܝ
ܗܝ ܕܐܬܪܒܝܬ ¹⁰ܒܗܝܟܠܗ
ܕܡܪܝܐ¹⁰ ܘܡܛܠܬ ܓܒܪ¹¹
ܒܦܓܬܐ ܕܬܗܘܐ ¹¹ܠܝ
ܐܢܬܬܐ. ܘܠܐ ܗܘܬ
ܐܢܬܬܝ. ܐܠܐ ܡܢ

f. 30 a col. b

ܪܘܚܐ ܕܩܘܕܫܐ ܒܦܓܪܐ.
⁷ܘܐܡܪܐ ܐܡܣܝܬܐ
ܗܕܐ ܥܪܝܪܬܐ ܗܝ.
ܐܡܪ ܠܗ̇ ܢܘܦܫ
⁵ܠܐܡܣܝܬܐ. ܬܝ ܘܬܚܙܝܢ.
ܘܐܙܠܬ ܒܡܗ ܘܦܡ¹²
¹³ܒܕܘܒܬܐ ܗܕܐ ܕܐܝܬ
ܗܘܬ ܒܗ ܒܡܕܒܪܬܐ.¹³
ܒܒܢܝܐ ܕܝܢ ܕܢܘܗܪܐ
¹⁴ܡܛܠܠܐ ܗܘܬ ¹⁵ܒܠܝܗ̇ ܒܠ
ܡܕܒܪܬܐ.¹⁵ ¹⁶ܘܐܡܪܬ
ܐܢܬܬܐ ܡܕܘܝܐ ܢܦܫܝ¹⁶

---

¹⁻¹ om. ² ܒܠ ³ ܟܠ ⁴ ܕܢܚܬܐ ⁵ om. ⁶ + ܒܒܪܐ.
⁷ ܘܐܡܪܬ ⁸ ܡܢ ⁹ + ܗܕܐ.

Wright, p. ܗ

¹⁰ ܒܝܬ ܡܩܕܫܐ. ¹¹ ܗܠ ܕܬܗܘܐ ¹² ܘܡܦܩܬ ¹³ ܒܗ ܒܡܕܒܪܬܐ.
¹⁴ ܡܛܠܠܐ ¹⁵ ܒܡܕܒܪܬܐ ¹⁶⁻¹⁶ om.

f. 35 a col. a

ܩ̈ܠܝ ܐܣܛܪܛܝܠ ܬܘܒ.
ܕܒܝܢ ܕܠܐ ܗܘܬ ܒܪܬ.
ܒܪܡ ܕܝܢ [1]ܗܘ ܝܗܒܗ
ܕܡܪܝܐ ܠܥܒܕ ܐܝܟ
ܕܢܒܥܐ ܘܨܒܘ، ܥܠ ܫܡܪܗ
ܘܐܘܬܒܗ̇ ܘܢܓܕ ܒܪܗ.
[2]ܐܬܐ ܗܘܐ ܢܘܗܪ
ܘܒܢ̈ܘܗܝ،[2] ܘܒܪ ܡܠܟܘ
ܡܠܟܐ ܕܬܠܬܐ ܫܡܗ̇ (cf. Cod. Harris f. 106 a)
ܢܘܗܪ [3]ܒܪ ܒܡܒܪܝܐ[3]
ܘܐܡܪ ܢܘܗܪ. ܒܒܪ
ܗܘ ܕܐܝܬ ܒܗ [4]ܡܘܒܥܐ
ܘܡܫܝܢ ܠܗ̇. ܗܝܕܝܢ
ܬܘܒ ܐܬܦܢܝ ܢܘܗܪ (f. 30 b col. a)
ܘܫܝܗ̇[4] ܒܪ ܠܥܒܕܐ
ܘܐܡܪ ܠܗ̇. ܡܪܝܡ. [5]ܡܢܐ
[5]ܗܘ ܗܢܐ [6]ܕܒܝܡ ܚܙܐ
ܐܢܐ ܦܪ̈ܘܦܒܝ ܒܪ
[7]ܚܝܝܢ. ܘܒܝܡ [1]ܒܪ ܒܡܪܝ.
[8]ܘܐܡܪܬ [1]ܠܗ ܠܢܘܗܪ:
ܬ̈ܪܝܢ ܒܢ̈ܡܝܢ ܚܙܝܐ
ܐܢܐ ܒܒܝܬ. ܚܕ ܒܡܪܐ
ܒܪ ܒܒܐ ܘܡܪܘܪ ܘܚܙܝܐ
[1]ܒܡܪܐ [9]ܒܪ ܚܕܐ[9] ܘܪܘܪ.

f. 35 a col. b

ܘܒܪ ܡܠܟܘ ܦܠܓ̇ܗ̇
ܕܐܘܪܚܐ. ܐܡܪܐ ܠܗ
[1]ܡܪܝܡ ܠܢܘܗܪ [10]ܐܚܝܬܝ
ܡܢ ܫܡܪܐ ܡܠܠ ܕܗܢܐ
ܕܐܝܬ ܒܝ ܒܡܘܪܗܒ [1]ܠܝ
ܕܢܦܩ. [11]ܘܐܚܝܬܗ̇ ܢܘܗܪ
ܘܐܡܪ ܠܗ̇ ܠܐܝܢܐ
ܐܘܒܠܝ ܐܘ ܐܝܢܐ
ܐܒܫܐ ܢܒܦܘܬܝ ܗܐ
ܒܒܪ ܒܐܬܪܐ ܐܚܝܢ
ܚܘܪܒܐ[11] ܘܐܒܫܝ [1]ܬܡܢ
ܡܒܪܬܐ[12] ܘܐܒܠܗ̇ ܠܬܡܢ.
(f. 30 b col. b) ܘܐܡܝܢ ܥܠ ܒܒܗ̇
(cf. Cod. Harris f. 106 b) ܠܒܢ̈ܘܗܝ، ܘܢܦܩ [13]ܕܢܒܥܐ
ܐܫܝܬܐ [14]ܒܒܪܝܬܐ
ܒܐܬܪܐ[14] [15]ܕܒܝܬ ܠܫܡ.
ܐܢܐ ܕܝܢ ܢܘܗܪ ܡܗܠܟ
ܗܘܝܬ. ܘܚܝܬ [16]*ܒܡܘܦܟܐ
ܕܫܒܝܢܐ ܒܪ ܢܝܡ ܘܚܙܝܬ
ܒܐܬܪ ܘܚܙܝܬܗ[16] ܒܪ
ܬܡܢܗ [17]ܘܦܪܚܬܐ ܒܪ
ܥܠܝܐ. ܘܚܪܬ ܒܐܪܒܐ
ܘܚܝܬ ܚܪܒܐ ܒܪ ܫܡܝܐ
ܘܦ̈ܠܐ ܒܪ ܫ̈ܡܝܢܡ
ܘܐܬܚܙܝܡ ܗܘ، ܐܝܕܝܗܘ
ܒܗ ܒܒܪܟܐ ܘܠܒܫܝܢ ܒܪ[17]

---

Wright, p. ܠ

[1] om. [2–2] om. [3] ܠܒܪܝܡ ܕܒܡܒܝܪܐ. [4] ܒܒܐ ܕܢܦܩܘ. ܘܬܘܒ ܫܐܠܗ̇ [5] ܡܢܘ [6] ܕܗܢܐ ܒܝܬ [7] ܫܢܐ. [8] ܐܡܪܬ [9] ܕܫܢܐ [10] ܐܚܝܬܝ [11–11] om. [12] + ܫܢܐ. [13] ܒܒܒܐ [14–14] om. [15] ܒܒܝܬ [16] ܥܠ ܡܒܪ * Cod. ܒܡܘܬܒܐ [17–17] om.

ܠܐ ܬܫܡܥܘܢ ܕܟܠܬܐ f. 36 b col. a
ܐܠܐ ܐܡܪ ܫܪܝܪܐܝܬ
ܐܢܬ ܟܢܫܬ ܡܫܬܥܝܬܢ
ܘܠܐ ܐܘܕܥܬ ܠܒܢ̈ܝ
ܐܝܣܪܝܠ. ܘܠܐ ܐܪ̈ܒܥܬ
ܪ̈ܫܥܢ ܬܫܥܝܬ ܐܝܕܝܗ
ܫܠܝܚܘܬܐ ܕܡܪܝܐ
ܕܐܝܟܢܐ ܢܗܘܐ ܡܟܪܢ
ܙܪܟܢ. ܝܘܣܦ ܕܝܢ ܫܬܩ
ܠܗ. ܘܐܡܪ ܠܗ ܟܗܢܐ cf. Tisch. xvi
ܦܢܐ ܟܬܘܠܬܐ ܗܝ
ܕܕܒܪܬ ܡܢ ܗܝܟܠܗ
ܕܡܪܝܐ. ܝܘܣܦ ܕܝܢ
ܩܐܡ ܗܘܐ ܘܡܬܕܡܪ f. 29 a col. a
ܘܐܘܣܦ ܬܘܒ ܟܗܢܐ
ܘܐܡܪ ܠܗ ܡܫܡܫܐ
ܐܢܐ ܠܟܘܢ ܡ̈ܢܝܐ
ܕܡܟܣܢܘܬܐ ܕܡܪܝܐ
ܘܗܢܘܢ ܢܟܠܘܢ ܢܫܡܥܘܢ
ܡܕܡ ܒܢ̈ܝܟܘܢ ܘܫܒܘܩ
ܟܗܢܐ ܘܐܫܟܚܗ ܠܡܫܒ
ܘܫܪܝܗ ܠܦܘܪܐ ܘܡܠܐ
ܘܢܫܩܬ ܒܝ ܫܠܝܡ
ܘܐܫܟܚ ܬܘܒ ܐܦ

f. 36 b col. b ܠܦܠܠܬܐ ܘܫܪܝܗ ܠܦܘܪܐ
ܘܢܫܬܬ ܐܦ ܗܝ، ܟܝ
ܫܠܝܡܐ ܘܐܬܕܡܪ
ܟܠܗ ܥܡܐ ܕܝܣܦܗܐ
cf. Cod. Harris f. 105 b ܠܐ ܐܫܬܟܚ ܟܗܢܘܢ
ܘܐܡܪ ܠܗܘܢ ܟܗܢܐ
ܐܢ ܡܪܝܐ ܐܠܗܐ ܠܐ
ܓܠܐ ܚܛܗܝܟܘܢ ܐܦܠܐ
ܐܢܐ ܕܐܢ ܐܢܐ ܠܟܘܢ
ܘܫܪܐ ܐܢܘܢ ܠܡܐܙܠ
ܘܕܒܪܗ̇ ܝܘܣܦ ܡܪܝܡ
ܘܐܘܒܠܗ̇ ܠܒܝܬܗ. ܟܕ
ܚܕܝܐ ܘܡܫܒܚ
f. 29 a col. b ܠܐܠܗܐ ܕܐܝܣܪܝܠ.
ܗܘܐ ܗܘܐ ܕܝܢ
ܦܘܩܕܢܐ ܕܡܠܟܐ
ܕܢܬܟܬܒܘܢ ܐܢܫܐ
ܕܐܝܬ ܒܝܬ ܠܚܡ
ܕܝܗܘܕܐ. ܘܐܡܪ ܝܘܣܦ
ܐܢܐ ܡܟܬܒ. ܐܢܐ
ܠܒܢܝ. ܠܗܕܐ ܕܝܢ ܛܠܝܬܐ
ܡܢܐ ܐܟܬܒ ܠܗ̇
ܕܐܟܬܒܝܗ̇ ܐܢܬܬܝ،
ܒܗܬ ܐܢܐ ܘܕܐܟܬܒܝܗ̇
ܒܪܬܝ، ܡܕܚܠ ܐܢܐ ܘܗܐ

ܘܢܦܩ ܡܢܗ ܠܐ f. 36 a col. a
ܐܬܚܙܝܬ ܒܒܪܢܫܘܬܐ.
ܘܐܡܪ ܠܗ ܝܘܣܦ
ܡܛܠ ܕܠܐܝܐ ܗܘܝܬ
ܡܢ ܐܘܪܚܐ ܘܐܬܠܚܝܬ
ܘܡܢܐ ܡܕܡܝܐ ܘܐܬܗܦܟܬ
ܫܡ ܘܫܡܗ ܠܡܪܝܡ ܒܪ
ܝܒܐ ܒܪܘܫܗ. ܘܐܙܠ ܠܘܬ
ܪܒ ܒܗܢܝܐ ܘܐܡܪ ܠܗ
ܝܘܣܦ ܗܘ ܕܐܝܬ
ܦܩܕܬ ܒܠܒܗ، ܒܒܪ
ܒܠܘܐ ܪܒܐ. ܘܐܡܪ
ܒܗܢܐ ܡܢܘ ܗܢܐ
ܘܐܡܪ ܫܡ ܦܚܪܐ f. 29 b col. a
ܝܘܣܦ ܒܬܘܠܬܐ ܗܝ،
ܕܕܒܪ ܡܢ ܗܝܟܠܗ ܕܡܪܝܐ
ܦܓܪܗ ܘܢܒܛ ܡܫܬܘܬܗ
ܘܠܐ ܐܘܕܥ ܠܟܗ̈ܢܐ
ܐܝܣܪܝܠ. ܘܐܡܪ ܠܗ
ܫܡ ܦܚܪܐ ܥܕܪ ܕܢܫ̈ܐ
ܘܡܫܒܚ ܐܢܬ ܠܗ̇
ܠܒܬܘܠܬܐ ܕܫܒܝܠܐ
ܒܪܫܗ ° ° °
ܘܐܙܠܘ ܕܢܫ̈ܐ ܘܐܫܟܚܘ
ܐܢܫ ܕܐܡܪ ܫܡ

f. 36 a col. b ܘܐܘܒܠܘ ܐܢܘܢ ܠܗܝܟܠܐ
ܘܐܘܩܡܘ ܐܢܘܢ ܒܕܝ̈ܢܐ
ܘܐܡܪ ܠܗ̇ ܟܗܢܐ
ܠܡܪܝܡ. ܡܪܝܡ ܡܢܘ
ܗܢܐ ܕܒܛܢܬܝ، ܘܡܢܐ
ܡܒܝܢܐ ܒܛܢܬܝ، ܢܦܫܟܝ
ܘܛܢܦܬܝ، ܠܡܪܝܐ ܐܠܗܟܝ
ܐܢܬܝ ܕܐܬܪܒܝܬܝ، ܒܝܬ
ܩܘܕܫ ܩܘܕܫܝ̈ܢ ܘܩܒܠܬܝ
cf. Cod. Harris f. 104 a ܡܝܒܪܬܐ ܡܢ ܐܝܕܐ
ܕܡܠܐܟܐ ܘܫܡܥܬܝ،
ܬܫܒܚܬܗܘܢ ܬܪܬܝܢ
f. 29 b col. b ܕܝܟܝ، ܡܕܡܝܢܘܗܝ ܡܢܐ
ܗܘܐ ܟܠ ܗܢܐ ܕܒܛܢܬܝ.
ܗܝ، ܕܝܢ ܒܟܬ ܡܪܝܪܐܝܬ
ܘܐܡܪܐ. ܚܝ ܗܘ ܡܪܝܐ
ܐܠܗܝ، ܕܐܢܐ ܕܟܝܐ
ܐܢܐ ܡܕܡܘܗܝ، ܘܓܒܪܐ
ܠܐ ܚܟܝܡ ܠܝ. ܘܐܡܪ
ܟܗܢܐ ܠܝܘܣܦ ܡܢܘ
ܗܢܐ ܕܒܛܢܬ. ܐܡܪ
ܝܘܣܦ ܚܝ ܗܘ ܡܪܝܐ
cf. Cod. Harris f. 105 a ܐܠܗܝ، ܕܐܢܐ ܕܟܝܐ ܐܢܐ
ܡܢܗ̇. ܘܐܡܪ ܠܗ ܟܗܢܐ

ܗܟܢܐ ܘܦܩܕܬܝ ܠܡܪܝܐ. f. 139 b col. a
ܠܡܠܠܐ ܗܢܐ ܟܘܠܗ
ܐܬܡܟܟܬܝ ܢܦܫܟܝ
ܐܢܬܝ ܕܐܬܪܒܝܬܝ ܒܝܬ
ܩܕܘܫ ܩܘܕܫܐ. ܗܝ
ܕܝܢ ܒܟܬ ܡܪܝܪܐܝܬ
ܘܐܡܪܐ ܚܝ ܗܘ ܡܪܝܐ
ܐܠܗܝ. ܕܐܢܐ ܕܟܝܐ
ܐܢܐ ܘܓܒܪܐ ܠܐ ܚܟܝܡ
ܠܝ ܐܡܪ ܠܗ̇ ܝܘܣܦ
ܡܢ ܐܝܟܘ ܗܟܝܠ
ܗܢܐ ܕܐܝܬ ܒܟܪܣܟܝ
ܐܡܪܐ ܡܪܝܡ ܚܝ ܗܘ
ܐܠܗܐ ⌜ܕܐܝܣܪܐܝܠ⌝ ܠܐ
ܝܕܥܐ ܐܢܐ ܡܢ ܐܝܡܟܐ f. 132 a col. a
ܗܘ ܗܢܐ ܕܐܝܬ ܒܝ
ܘܕܚܝܠ ܝܘܣܦ ܛܒ cf. Tisch. xiv
ܘܒܪܝܬ ܠܗ ܒܠܒܗ̇
ܘܐܫܠܗ̇ ܕܗܟܢܐ ܢܥܒܕ
ܠܗ̇. ܘܐܡܪ ܒܢܦܫܗ ܐܢ cf. Cod. Harris f. 103 a
ܐܟܣܐ ܟܠܝܗ̇ ܗܢܐ
ܚܛܗܐ ܗܘ. ܘܡܬܚܫܒ
ܐܢܐ ܕܐܬܟܬܫ ܐܢܐ
ܠܘܩܒܠ ܢܡܘܣܗ ⌜ܕܡܪܝܐ⌝.
ܘܐܢ ܐܓܠܐ ܟܠܝܗ̇ ⌜ܠܟܠܢ⌝

f. 139 b col. b ܐܝܣܪܐܝܠ ܕܚܝܠ ܐܢܐ
ܕܠܡܐ ܪܘܚܐ ܕܡܠܐܟܐ
ܐܝܬ ܒܗ̇ ܘܡܬܚܫܒ
ܐܢܐ ܕܕܡܐ ܘܚܝܒܐ
ܡܫܠܡ ܐܢܐ ܠܕܝܢܐ
ܕܡܘܬܐ. ܡܢܐ ܗܟܝܠ
ܐܥܒܕ ܠܗ̇ ܒܟܣܝܐ
ܐܫܪܝܗ̇ ܡܢ ܓܒܝ. .
ܗܝܕܝܢ ܐܕܪܟܗ ܗܘܐ
ܠܠܝܐ ܘܗܐ ܡܠܐܟܗ
ܕܡܪܝܐ ܐܬܚܙܝ ܠܗ
ܒܚܠܡܐ. ܘܐܡܪ ܠܗ
ܝܘܣܦ ܠܐ ܬܕܚܠ ܡܢ
⌜ܦܠܠܝܬܐ⌝. ܡܛܠ ܕܗܘ
f. 132 a col. b ܕܐܝܬ ܒܗ̇ ܡܢ ܪܘܚܐ
ܗܘ ܕܩܘܕܫܐ. ܘܬܐܠܕ
ܠܟ ܒܪܐ ܘܬܩܪܐ
ܫܡܗ ܝܫܘܥ ܡܛܠ
ܕܗܘ ܢܦܪܘܩܝܗ̇ ܠܥܡܗ
ܡܢ ܚܛܗ̈ܘܗܝ. ܘܩܡ
ܝܘܣܦ ܡܢ ܫܢܬܗ
ܘܥܒܕ ܠܐܠܗܐ ⌜ܕܐܝܣܪܐܝܠ⌝
ܗܘ ܕܝܗܒ ⌜ܦܘܩܕܢܗ⌝
cf. Tisch. xv ⌜ܘ⌝ܢܛܪܗ̇. ܘܐܬܐ ܠܘܬܗ̇
cf. Cod. Harris f. 103 b ⌜ܚܢܢܝܐ⌝ ܣܦܪܐ ⌜ܘܐܡܪ⌝ ܠܗ

M. D. G.

ܡܢ ܐܝܟ ܕܗܘܐ ܒܠܗܘܢ f. 139 a col. a
ܫܒܝܬܐ ܗܘܒ ܠܝ ܦܘܠܚܢܐ
ܘܗܘܬ ܠܘܬ ܐܠܝܫܒܥ cf. Cod. Harris
ܝܪ̈ܚܐ ܬܠܬܐ ܘܝܘܡܐ f. 102 a
ܡܢ ܝܘܡܐ ܕܒܪܫܗ
ܪܒܐ ܗܘܬ. ܘܕ⌜ܚ⌝ܠܬ
ܡܪܝܡ ܘܐܬܬ ܠܒܝܬܗ̇.
ܘܡܦܩܢܐ ܗܘܬ ܢܦܫܗ̇
ܡܢ ܒܢܝ ܐܝܣܪܐܝܠ
ܐܝܬܝܗ̇ ܗܘܬ ܕܝܢ ܒܪܬ
ܬܠܬܥܣܪܐ ܫܢܝܢ ܟܕ
ܗܘܘ ܗܠܝܢ ܐܪ̈ܙܐ.
ܘܟܕ ܗܘܐ ܠܗ̇ ܝܪܚܐ cf. Tisch. xiii
ܕܫܬܐ. ܘܐܬܐ ܝܘܣܦ f. 132 b col. a
ܡܢ ܒܢܝܢܐ ܕܒܢܐ ܗܘܐ
ܘܥܠ ܘܐܫܟܚܗ̇ ܠܡܪܝܡ
ܕܒ ܥܘܒܠܐ ܒܟܪܣܗ̇
ܘܦܪܥ ܐܝ̈ܕܘܗܝ ܥܠ
ܐܦ̈ܘܗܝ ܘܫܕܐ ܢܦܫܗ
ܥܠ ܐܪܥܐ ܘܒܟܐ
ܡܪܝܪܐܝܬ ܘܐܡܪ
ܒܐܝ̈ܠܝܢ ܐܦ̈ܐ ܐܚܘܪ
ܠܘܬ ܡܪܝܐ ܐܠܗܐ
ܡܢܐ ܐܓܠܐ ܥܠ ܗܕܐ

f. 139 a col. b ܕܒܪ ܦܠܠܝܬܐ ܡܦܘܠ
ܒܬܘܠܬܐ ܗܝ ܕܒܪܬܗ̇
ܡܢ ܗܝܟܠܗ ܕܡܪܝܐ
ܐܠܗܐ ܘܠܐ ܢܛܪܬܗ̇.
ܡܢܘ ܒܝ ܢ⌜ܟ⌝ܠ ܐܘ ܡܢܘ
ܒܒܕ ܗܕܐ ܒܝܫܬܐ
ܒܒܝܬܝ. ܡܢܘ ܫܒܐ ܡܢܝ
ܗܕܐ: ܒܬܘܠܬܐ
cf. Cod. Harris ܬܡܝܗܬܐ ܘܦܠܫܗ̇.
f. 102 b ܕܠܡܐ ܠܝ ܒܝ ܓܒܪ. ܡܢ
ܕܪܫ ܗܘ ܡܕܡ ܕܠܐܕܡ
ܓܒܪ ܒܒܕܢܐ ܓܢܝܪ
ܕܡܫܒܚ ܗ̇ܘܐ ܐܕܡ.
f. 132 b col. b ⌜ܠܐܠܗܐ ܘܐ⌝ܫܒܚܗ̇
ܠܚܘܐ ܒܠܚܘܕܝܗ̇
ܘ⌜ܐ⌝ܦܠܚܗ̇ ܘܦܠܚܐܗ̇
ܗܟܢܐ ܓܒܪ ܐܦ ܠܝ
ܘܦܩ ܢܣܒ ܡܢ ܣܘܣܐ.
ܘܩܪܗ̇ ܠܡܪܝܡ ܘܐܡܪ
ܠܗ̇. ܐܢܬܐ ܕܒܦܠܝܚܘܬܐ
ܕܐܠܗܐ ܐܝܬ ܗܘܬ
ܒܠܒܗ̇ ܗܢܐ ܡܢܐ ܗܘ
ܕܥܒܕܬܝ ܦܓܥܬܝ ܠܡܪܝܐ
ܐܠܗܐ ܡܢܐ ܥܒܕ⌜ܬ⌝ܝ

M. D. G.

ܠܗ̇. ܠܐ ܬܕܚܠܝܢ ܡܪܝܡ f. 92 b col. a
ܗܐ ܓܒܪ ܢܒܥܬܝ،
ܠܦܝܒܘܬܐ ܘܕܡ ܡܪܐ
ܒܘܠ ܘܬܦܠܓܝܢ ܡܢ
ܡܠܬܗ. ܗܝ ܕܝܢ ܒܕ.
ܫܡܥܬ ܡܬܚܫܒܐ
ܗܘܬ ܒܢܦܫܗ̇ ܐܡܪܐ
ܐܝ ܐܦܢ ܐܢܐ ܘܐܠܕ.
ܡܢ ܡܪܝܐ ܐܝܟ ܠܕ.
ܒܘܠܗܘܢ ܢܫ̈ܐ ܘܗܐ
ܡܠܐܟܗ ܕܡܪܝܐ
ܐܫܬܠܚ ܘܐܡܪ ܠܗ̇
ܠܐ ܗܟܢܐ. ܡܪܝܡ
ܐܠܐ ܚܝܠܗ ܕܡܪܝܐ f. 89 a col. a
ܢܓܢ ܥܠܝܟܝ. ܡܛܠ ܕܗ̇ܘ
ܕܡܬܝܠܕ ܡܢܟܝ ܩܕܝܫܐ
ܗܘ ܘܒܪܗ ܕܥܠܝܐ cf. Cod. Harris f. 101 b
ܬܘܪܐ ܘܬܘܪܝܢ
ܫܡܗ ܝܫܘܥ ܗܘ ܓܒܪ
ܢܦܪܘܩܘܗܝ ܠܥܡܗ
ܡܢ ܚܛܗ̈ܐ. ܘܐܡܪܬ
ܡܪܝܡ. ܗܐ ܐܢܐ
ܐܡܬܗ ܐܢܐ ܕܐܠܗܐ
ܗܘܐ ܠܝ ܡܢ
ܦܬܓܡܘܗܝ، ܐܝܟܢܐ

f. 92 b col. b cf. Tisch. xii ܕܐܡܪܬ. ܘܒܥܕܬ ܡܪܝܡ
ܐܪܓܘܢܐ ܘܐܘܒܠܬܗ
ܠܟܗܢܐ ܘܒܪܟܬܗ̇ ܟܗܢܐ
ܘܐܡܪ ܡܪܝܡ ܐܘܪܒ.
ܡܪܝܐ ܐܠܗܐ ܫܡܒܫ
ܘܬܗܘܝܢ ܡܒܪܟܐ
ܒܟܠܗܘܢ ܫܪܒܬܗ
ܕܐܪܥܐ. ܘܐܬܡܠܝܬ
ܡܪܝܡ ܚܕܘܬܐ
ܘܐܙܠܬ ܠܘܬ ܐܠܝܫܒܥ
ܐܚܬܢܝܬܗ. ܘܢܩܫܬ
ܒܬܪܥܐ ܘܟܕ ܫܡܥܬ
ܐܠܝܫܒܥ ܫܕܬ ܪܒܠܐ
f. 89 a col. b ܕܐܝܕܐ ܗܘܬ ܘܐܬܬ
ܠܘܬ ܬܪܥܐ ܘܦܬܚܬ
ܠܗ̇ ܘܒܪܟܬܗ̇ ܐܠܝܫܒܥ
ܘܐܡܪܐ ܡܢܘ ܒܕܝ ܠܝ
ܗܕܐ ܕܐܡܗ ܕܡܪܝ،
ܬܐܬܐ ܠܘܬܝ.. ܗܐ ܓܒܪ
ܡܢ ܕܡܠܠܬܝ، ܕܝ ܗܘ
ܕܐܝܬ ܒܝ ܘܒܪܟܟܝ ◦◦⁘◦◦
ܡܪܝܡ ܕܝܢ ܦܠܓܬ ܬ̈ܠܬܝܢ
ܠܚ̈ܠܐ ܗܠܝܢ ܕܡܠܠ
ܒܡܗ̇ ܓܒܪܐܝܠ ܘܢܛܪܬ
ܒܟܡܢܐ ܘܐܡܪܐ ܡܪܝܐ

ܡܪܝܐ ܗܘ ܢܗܘܐ f. 92 a col. a
ܠܗ ܡܦܪܢܣܢܐ ○ ○ ○
ܗܘܐ ܗܘܐ ܕܝܢ ܡܠܟܐ cf. Tisch. x
ܠܟܗܢܐ ܘܐܡܪܝܢ
ܢܥܒܕ ܐ̈ܦܝ ܬܪܥܐ
ܠܗܝܟܠܗ ܕܡܪܝܐ
ܘܐܡܪ ܟܗܢܐ ܪܒܐ
ܠ ܬܩܪܝܐ ܒܬܘܠܬ ⌜ܡܢ⌝
⌜ܫ⌝ܒܛܐ ܕܡܠܟܐ ܕܘܝܕ
⌜ܕ⌝ܕܟܝܢ ܘܩܕܝܫܢ
ܘܐܙܠܘ ܕܚܫܐ ܘܒܥ⌜ܘ⌝
ܘܐܫܟܚܘ ܫܒܥ ܘܐܝܬܝܘܢ
ܒܗܝܢ ܠܡܪܝܡ ܒܬܘܠܬܐ f. 89 b col. a
ܐܦ ܗܝ ܐܝܬܝܗ̇ ܡܢ
ܫܒܛܐ ܕܒܝܬ ܕܘܝܕ
ܘܕܟܝܬܐ ܗܝ ܠܐܠܗܐ
ܘܐܙܠܘ ܕܚܫܐ ܘܐܝܬܝܘܗ̇
ܠܗܝܟܠܐ ܘܐܡܪ ܟܗܢܐ
ܪܡܘ ܦܣܐ ܕܐܝܕܐ ܡܢܟܝ̈ܢ
ܠܗ̇ ܕܬܓܕܘܠ ܕܗܒܐ
ܘܐܝܕܐ ܐܡܝܢܛܘܣ ܘܐܝܕܐ
ܒܘܨܐ ܘܐܝܕܐ ܫܝܪܐ
ܘܐܝܕܐ ܬܟܠܬܐ
ܘܐܝܕܐ ܙܚܘܪܬܐ
ܘܐܝܕܐ ܐܪܓܘܢܐ

f. 92 a col. b ܘܡܛܠܐ ⌜ܠܡܪܝ⌝ܡ ܐܪܓܘܢܐ
ܘܙܚܘܪܬܐ ܘܢܣܒܬ
ܘܐܙܠܬ ܠܒܝܬܗ̇. ܒܗܘ
ܕܝܢ ܙܒܢܐ ܐܫܬܬܩ
ܗܘܐ ܙܟܪܝܐ ⌜ܘܒܗ⌝
ܗܘܐ ܚܠܦܗ ⌜ܫ⌝ܡܘܝܠ
ܒܕܡܐ ܕܡܠܠ ܘܒܪܝܐ.
ܡܪܝܡ ܕܝܢ ܐܘܒܠܬ
ܙܚܘܪܬܐ ܘܥܙܠܐ
cf. Cod. Harris f. 101 a ܗܘܬ ܘܢܣܒܬ ܩܘܠܬܐ
Tisch. xi ܘܐܙܠܬ ܠܡܡܠܐ ܡܝ̈ܐ
ܘܗܐ ܩܠܐ ܐܫܬܡܥ
ܕܐܡܪ ܠܗ̇ ܫܠܡ ܠܟܝ
f. 89 b col. b ܦܐܝܬܐ· ܡܪܝܐ ܥܡܟܝ
ܒܪܝܟܬ ܒܢܫ̈ܐ ܘܚܝܪܐ
ܗܘܬ ܡܪܝܡ ܠܝܡܝܢܐ
ܘܠܣܡܠܐ ܕܬܚܙܐ ܡܢ
ܐܝܟܢܐ ܐܫܬܡܥ ܠܗ̇
ܗܢܐ ܩܠܐ ܘܟܕ ܕܚܠܐ
⌜ܐܝܬܝ⌝ܗ̇· ܥܠܬ ܠܒܝܬܗ̇
ܘܐܢܝܚܬ ܩܘܠܬܗ̇
ܘܢܣܒܬ ܐܪܓܘܢܐ
ܘܝܬܒܬ ܘܦܣܩܐ ܗܘܬ
ܠܗ ܠܐܪܓܘܢܐ
ܘܗܐ ܡܠܐܟܐ ܕܡܪܝܐ
ܩܡ ܩܕܡܝܗ̇ ܘܐܡܪ

ܐܝܬܘܗܝ، ܗܘܐ ܠܫܒܚܗ ܘܠܡܩܒܠܬ ܡܘܢܐ ܡܢ ܥܠܡܐ ܘܡܫܒܚܬ f. 100a
ܥܠ ܪܝܫܗ ܕܝܘܣܦ ܘܐܡܪܘ ܠܗ ܟܗ̈ܢܐ ܝܘܣܦ ܠܟ ܡܛܬ
ܒܬܘܠܬܐ ܡܢ ܡܪܝܐ ܒܦܣܬܐ ܕܠܟ ܕܬܕܒܪܝܗ̇ ܘܬܛܪܝܗ̇.
ܟܕܢܐ ܝܘܣܦ ܘܐܡܪ ܒܢ̈ܝܐ ܐܝܬ ܠܝ. ܘܣܒܐ ܐܢܐ ܘܗܕܐ
ܥܠܝܡܬܐ ܗܝ. ܕܠܡܐ ܢܓܚܟ ܒܢܝܢܫܐ ܡܕܡ ܘܐܗܘܐ ܫܥܕܐ
ܒܝܬ ܐܝܣܪܐܝܠ ܘܐܡܪܘ ܠܗ ܟܗ̈ܢܐ ܝܘܣܦ. ܕܚܠ ܡܢ ܐܠܗܐ.
ܘܐܬܕܟܪ ܡܢܐ ܥܒܕ ܠܕܬܢ ܘܩܘܪܚ ܘܕܐܬܐ ܘܐܒܝܪܡ ܐܝܟܢܐ
ܐܬܦܬܚܬ ܐܪܥܐ ܘܒܠܥܬ ܐܢܘܢ ܥܠ ܕܐܩܒܘ ܒܚܪܝܢܐ.
ܘܗܫܐ ܕܚܠ ܘܕܒܪܗ̇ ܐܝܟ ܕܢܛܪܝܗ̇. ܘܕܚܠ ܝܘܣܦ. ܐܡܪ
ܠܡܪܝܡ ܗ̇ܐ ܕܒܪܬܟ ܡܢ ܗܫܐ ܕܡܪܝܐ ܘܗܫܐ ܗܘܐ ܢܛܪ
ܐܒܢܐ ܠܟ ܒܒܝܬܝ، ܘܐܙܠ ܐܢܐ [1]ܐܒܢܐ ܒܢ̈ܝܢܐ[1] ܕܐܝܬ ܠܝ.
ܘܡܢܕܡ ܐܬܐ ܐܢܐ ܠܘܬܟܝ. ܡܟܝܠ ܡܪܝܐ ܢܛܘܪܐ ܠܟ f. 100b
ܡܦܓܥܢܐ.

[1] Cod. ܐܒܢܐ ܒܢܝܢܐ

ܒܫ̈ܢܐ ܘܫܡܥܘܗ̇ ܘܐܡܪܘ ܠܗ̇ ܢܘܗܪ ܡܪܢܐ ܫܡܫ ܒܚܠܡܗܘܢ̇
ܪ̈ܙܐ. ܡܛܠ ܕܫܡܫ ܓܠܐ ܡܪܢ̱ ܦܘܪܫܢܐ ܠܒܢܝ̈ܢܫܐ. ܘܐܘܬܒܗ̇
ܠܛܠܝܬܐ ܗ̇ܘ ܒܗܘܢܐ ܥܠ ܕܪ̈ܓܐ ܕܬܠܬܐ ܕܗܝܟܠܐ ܘܫܪܝܐ
ܥܠܝܗ̇ ܐܠܗܐ ܠܡܦܩܬܐ. ܘܦܫܛܐ ܗܘܬ̇ ܒܪ̈ܓܠܝܗ̇ ܘܪܗܛܗ̇
cf. Tisch. viii ܥܠܡ ܒܗܟܢܐ ܕܒ̈ܢܝ ܐܝܣܪܐܝܠ. ܘܩܪܘ ܫܡܗ̇ ܕܡܪܝܡ. ܘܢܫܩܘܗ̇
ܐܒܗ̈ܝܗ̇ ܡܢ ܬܡ̇ܢ ܟܕ ܡܘܕܝܢ ܠܡܪܝܐ ܕܠܐ ܐܬܦܢܝܬ ܠܘܬܗܘܢ̇
ܐܝܬܝܗ̇ ܗܘܬ̇ ܒܗܝܟܠܗ ܕܡܪܝܐ ܐܝܟ ܝܘܢܐ ܕܪܒܝܐ ܘܡܣܬܒܪܐ
ܗܘܬ̇ ܠܗ̇ ܡܫܡܫܢܝܬܐ ܡܢ ܐܝܕܝ̈ܐ ܕܡܠܐܟܐ ܘܟܕ ܙܒܢܝܬ
ܘܐܬܡܠܟܘ ܒܫ̈ܢܐ ܘܐܡ̈ܪܝܢ ܗܐ ܡܪܝܡ ܗܘܬ̇ ܒܪܬ ܬ̈ܪܬܝܢ
ܬܬܪܒܝܐ ܒܗܝܟܠܐ ܕܡܪܝܐ. ܟ̈ܗܢܐ ܢܟܣܘ ܠܗ̇ ܕܠܐ
ܠܡܐ ܬܬܛܘܫ[1] ܗܝܟܠܗ ܕܡܪܝܐ ܐܠܗܐ. ܘܐܡ̈ܪܘ ܒܫ̈ܢܐ ܠܪ̈ܒ[2]
ܒܫ̈ܢܐ ܐܝܬ ܚܘܠ ܠܒܝܬ ܡܩܕܫܐ ܘܨܠܝ̈ܐ ܥܠܝܗ̇ ܘܗ̇ܘ ܡܪܝܡ f. 99b
[3]ܕܓܠܐ ܠܟ ܐܠܗܐ ܗ̇ܘ ܢܥܒܕ ܘܠܒܝܬ ܡܩܘܕܫܝܢ ܟܕ
ܐܝܬ ܥܠܘܗܝ. ܬܬܪ̈ܒܝܐ ܕܓܒܝܢ. ܘܨܠܝ ܥܠܝܗ̇ ܘܒܥܐ ܡܢ
ܐܠܗܐ ܘܐܠܗܗ ܕܡܪܝܐ ܓܒܐ ܘܐܡܪ ܠܗ ܕܡܪܝܐ ܡܪܝܐ
ܒܥܝ ܚܠܦܝܗܘܢ̇ ܓܒܪ̈ܐ ܐܪ̈ܡܠܬܐ ܕܒܝܬܐ ܘܢܣܒܘܢ̇ ܠܟ ܚܠܝܕ
ܡܢܗܘܢ̇ ܥܒܕܐ. ܘܟܐܢܐ ܥܒܕܐ ܕܡܬܚܘܐ ܠܟ ܡܪܝܐ
ܐܬܐ ܕܒܠܗ ܬܗܘܐ ܡܪܝܡ ܐܢܬܬܐ. ܘܗܝܕܝܢ ܢܦܩܘ ܟܪ̈ܘܙܐ
ܒܟܠܗ̇ ܐܬܪܐ ܕܝܗܘܕ. ܘܩܪܬ ܩܪܢܐ ܕܡܪܝܐ ܘܟܢܫܐ ܐܬܟܢܫܘ
cf. Tisch. ix ܘܐܬܘ ܠܘܬ ܪ̈ܒ ܟܗ̈ܢܐ ܘܝܗܒܘ ܫ̈ܒܛܝܗܘܢ̇ ܘܟܕ ܩܒܠ ܐܢܘܢ̇
ܒܗܘܢܐ ܥܠ ܠܗܝܟܠܐ ܘܨܠܝ. ܟܕ ܕܝܢ ܫܠܡ ܨܠܘܬܗ ܫܩܠ
ܐܢܘܢ̇ ܠܫ̈ܒܛܐ ܘܢܦܩ. ܘܝܗܒ ܠܗܘܢ̇ ܫ̈ܒܛܝܗܘܢ̇
ܘܐܬܐ ܡܕܡ ܠܐ ܐܬܚܙܝܬ. ܫܒܛܐ ܕܝܢ ܐܚܪܝܐ ܕܝܘܣܦ

[1] sic   [2] Cod. ܠܪ̈ܒܢ   [3] Cod. ܕܕܓܠܐ

ܒܗ ܕܝܢ ܗܘܬ ܛܠܝܬܐ ܒܪܬ ܫܢܬܐ ܚܕܐ. ܒܥܒܕ ܡܢܗܪܢ
ܡܠܟܐ ܪܒܐ.. ܘܩܪܐ ܠܟܗܢܐ ܘܠܣ̈ܒܐ ܟܗܢܐ ܘܠܥܡܐ
ܘܠܡܦܪܢܣܐ ܕܒܝܬܐ. ܘܒܪܟܘܗ̇ ܘܐܡܪܘ ܐܠܗܐ ܕܐܒܗ̈ܬܐ f. 98 a
ܢܒܪܟܝܗ̇ ܠܛܠܝܬܐ ܗܕܐ ܘܢܬܠ ܠܗ̇ ܫܡܐ ܡܫܡܗܐ ܒܟܠܗܘܢ
ܕܪ̈ܐ ܘܒܟܠܗܘܢ ܒܪ̈ܝܬܐ. ܘܐܡܪܘ ܟܠܗ ܥܡܐ ܐܡܝܢ.
ܘܒܗ ܩܪܒܗ̇ ܬܘܒ ܠܟܗܢ̈ܐ ܘܒܪܟܘܗ̇ ܘܐܡܪܘ ܐܠܗܐ
ܕܐܒܗ̈ܬܐ ܕܪܘܡܐ ܒܪܟܝܗ̇ ܠܛܠܝܬܐ ܗܕܐ ܒܘܪܟܬܐ
ܫܪܝܬܐ ܗܝ، ܕܠܐ ܚܪܬܐ ܘܠܐ ܡܫܬܪܝܐ. ܘܢܛܠܬܗ̇ ܐܡܗ̇
ܘܐܣܩܬܗ̇ ܠܒܝܬ ܡܩܕܫܐ ܕܩܘܕܫ ܠܗ̇ ܒܡܛܠܬܗ̇. ܘܥܒܕܬ
ܬܫܒܘܚܬܐ ܘܪܫܬܐ ܘܐܡܪܬ ܕܫܒܚܬ ܡܪܝܐ ܘܐܡܪܬ ܫܒܚܐ
ܕܒܠܫܢܗ ܦܫܝ. ܘܫܒܚ ܠܝ ܡܪܝܐ ܐܠܗܝ ܦܪܘܩܐ ܕܕܡܘܬܐ..
ܘܒܝܘ ܢܦܩܬ ܠܒܪ ܙܘܦܠ ܕܝܘܡܐ ܗܘ ܡܛܠܬܐ. ܥ̈ܡܪܝܢ
ܬܪܬܝܢ ܫܢܝܢ ܕܒܬܪ ܐܣܬܪܩܠ ܕܝܘܡܐ ܗܘ ܡܛܠܬܐ ܘܫܡܥܬܗ̇
ܠܛܠܝܬܐ ܒܗܝܟܠܗ ܘܢܦܩܬ ܘܡܫܡܫܐ ܗܘܬ ܠܩܕ̈ܝܫܐ. ܘܒܗ f. 98 b
cf. Tisch. vii ܫܠܡܬ ܫܡܫܘܬܐ ܢܦܩܘ ܒܗ ܣܝ̈ܡܝ ܘܡܫܡܫܝܢ ܠܐܠܗܐ. ܠܛܠܝܬܐ
ܕܝܢ ܡܬܬܘܣܦܝܢ ܗܘܘ ܝ̈ܘܡܐ. ܕܟܕ ܕܝܢ ܗܘܬ ܒܪܬ ܬܪ̈ܬܝܢ ܫ̈ܢܝܢ
ܐܡܪ ܝܘܚܢܢ ܠܚܢܐ ܐܢܬܬܗ. ܢܬܠܝܗ̇ ܠܛܠܝܬܐ ܗܕܐ
ܠܗܝܟܠܗ ܕܡܪܝܐ. ܐܝܟ ܡܕܡ ܕܐܫܬܘܕܝܢ ܕܠܐ ܢܦܘܩ
ܐܒܘܗ̇ ܒܝܢ ܗܘ ܡܪܝܐ. ܘܠܐ ܢܣܒܠ ܡܢܗܪܝܢ. ܘܐܡܪܬ
ܚܢܐ ܢܗܘܐ ܠܚܢܬܐ ܕܬܠܬ ܕܠܐ ܬܗܘܦܐ ܒܚܢܐ ܠܐܒܘܗ̇
ܘܠܐܡܗ̇. ܘܐܡܪ ܝܘܚܢܢ ܫܦܝܪ ܐܡܪܬ،. ܘܒܗ ܗܘܬ ܛܠܝܬܐ
ܒܪܬ ܬܠܬ ܫܢܝܢ ܐܡܪ ܝܘܚܢܢ ܡܢ ܒܬ ܒܪ̈ܬܐ ܒܬܘܠܬܐ ܕܠܐ
ܐܬܛܢܦ ܘܢܫܩܢ ܠܡܪ̈ܝܬܐ ܡܪܝܡ ܒܗ ܕܠܝܡܝ. ܕܠܐ ܬܬܗܦܟ
ܠܒܣܬܪܗ ܘܢܬܒܝܐ ܠܒܗ̇ ܡܢ ܒܝܬܗ ܕܡܪܝܐ. ܘܥܒܕܘ ܗܟܢܐ
ܒܕܡܐ ܕܫܠܡܘ ܠܗܝܟܠܗ ܕܡܪܝܐ. ܘܒܗ ܡܛܠܬ ܠܗܝܟܠܗ ܘܥܠܘܗ̇ f. 99 a

ܚܙܐ ܟܠ ܚܕ ܐܦܝܘܣܐ. ܘܫܠܚܬ ܠܝܘܚܢܢ ܘܐܬܬܠܝܬ ܒܐܦ̈ܘܗܝ
ܘܐܡܪܬ ܠܗ ܗܫܐ ܝܕܥܬ ܕܪ̈ܚܡܝ ܡܪܝܐ ܐܠܗܝ ܠܟ. ܗܐ ܒܪܝ
ܐܢܐ ܐܪܡܠܬܐ ܗܘܝܬ ܡܛܠ ܠܐ ܗܘܝܬ ܐܪܡܠܬܐ ܕܡܟܝܟܐ f. 97a
ܗܘܝܬ ܘܠܝܬ ܗܘܐ ܠܝ ܒ̈ܢܝܐ ܗܐ ܐܠܐ ܐܝܟܐ. ܘܟܕ ܐܬܬܢܝܚ
cf. Tisch. v ܝܘܚܢܢ ܗܘܐ ܡܫܡܫܢܐ ܒܟܠܗܘܢ. ܡܢ ܗܪܟܐ ܒܥܘܡܪܗ
ܘܐܡܪ. ܕܐܝܟ ܐܬܪܒܝ ܠܝ ܡܪܝܐ ܐܠܗܝ، ܢܬܒܪܟ ܒܠܒܘܫܐ
ܕܒܠܬ ܚ̈ܝܘܗܝ، ܕܒܘܣܝܐ. ܒܝܘܡܐ ܕܫܠܡ ܠܡܕܒܪܢܘܬܗ ܕܡܪܝܐ
ܘܠܐ ܚܙܐ ܒܗ ܣܘܦܐ. ܘܐܡܪ ܝܘܚܢܢ ܗܫܐ ܝܕܥܬ ܕܐܬܪܒ
ܠܝ ܡܪܝܐ ܐܠܗܝ. ܘܥܒܕ ܠܝ ܚܠܘܦܝ ܣܘܦܗ. ܘܫܠܚܬ ܝܘܚܢܢ
ܡܢ ܒܝܬܗ ܕܡܪܝܐ ܒܪ ܡܪܝܡ ܘܐܙܠ ܠܒܝܬܗ. ܘܟܕ ܐܬܡܠܝܘ
ܝܘ̈ܡܬܐ ܕܚܝܐ ܕܒܝܘܡܐ ܬܫܥܐ ܢܠܕܬ. ܘܐܡܪܬ ܚܙܐ
ܡܪܝܡܐ ܢܦܫ ܠܡܪܢܐ ܒܝܘܡܐ ܗܢܐ ܘܐܬܟܢܫܬ ܒܒܝܬܐ.
ܘܟܕ ܫܠܡܘ ܝܘ̈ܡܬܐ ܫܒܥܐ ܚܙܐ ܐܝܟ ܕܠܬܕܝܢܬܐ ܘܝܒܫܬ
cf. Tisch. vi ܬܕܐ ܠܒܪܬܗ. ܘܫܡܗܐ ܡܢ ܚܕܘܬܗ ܡܬܚܫܒܐ ܗܘܬ ܠܠܒܬܐ. f. 97b
ܘܟܕ ܗܘܬ ܒܪܬ ܬܠܬܐ ܫܢܝܐ. ܐܫܟܚܬܗ ܐܡܗ ܥܠ ܐܪܒܐ
ܕܬܚܝܐ ܕܐܝܟ ܡܟܢܫܝܐ ܕܬܫܒܘܚܐ ܘܐܪܗܛܬ ܪܓܠܝܗ ܥܒܕ
ܕܟ̈ܝܢ ܘܐܬܝܬ ܠܘܬ ܐܡܗ. ܘܗܝܕܝܢ ܐܡܗ ܣܠܩܬܗ̇[1] ܘܐܡܪܬ
ܚܝ ܗܘ ܠܝ ܡܪܝܐ ܐܠܗܝ، ܕܠܐ ܬܗܠܟܝܢ ܥܠ ܗܕܐ. ܒܕܡܐ
ܕܬܦܠܚܝ ܠܒܝܬܗ ܕܡܪܝܐ. ܘܒܕܘ ܠܗ ܐܒܗ̈ܝܗ [2]ܡܠܘܫܗ
ܒܝܬ ܡܩܕܫܐ. ܘܠܐ ܫܒܩܝܢ ܗܘܘ ܕܬܬܪܒܐ ܠܬܡܢ ܡܕܡ
ܕܡܣܐܒ ܐܘ ܕܠܐ ܕܟܐ. ܘܐܡܪܬ ܐܡܗ ܠܐ ܬܬܪܒܐ ܠܬܡܢ
ܐܝܟ ܕܠܐ ܕܟܐ ܒܪܡ ܢܐܬܐ ܒܥܠܬܐ ܐܢܬܝ ܕܠܐ ܐܬܦܩܕܬ
ܒܝܬ ܩܘܕܫܐ. ܘܢܣܒܘܗ̇ ܠܘܬܗ̇ ܘܐܬܝܢ ܘܡܩܪ̈ܒܢ ܗ̈ܘܘ ܠܗ̇.

---

[1] Cod. ܣܠܩܬܗ [2] Cod. ܡܠܠܘܫܗ

ܐܢܬܬܐ ܕܒܪܟܬ ܠܐܠܗܐ ܗܢܐ ܘܫܒܚܬ ܠܗ ܒܪܐ ܐܝܟܢܐ.
cf. Tisch. iii ܘܟܕ ܐܡܪܬ ܗܠܝܢ ܐܪܝܡܬ ܥܝܢܝܗ ܠܐܦ̈ܝ ܫܡܝܐ ܘܚܙܬ ܩܢܐ
ܕܨܦܪܐ ܒܐܝܠܢܐ ܕܕܦܢܝܢ. ܘܐܬܬܢܚܬ ܒܢܦܫܗ ܘܐܡܪܬ.
ܡܢܘ ܕܠܐ ܝܠܕܢܝ. ܐܘ̄ ܐܡܬܐ ܘܐܝܢܐ ܡܕܡܐ ܐܬܕܡܝܬ ܠܝ f. 96 a
ܕܗܐ ܐܢܐ ܠܚܘܕܝ ܗܘܝܬ ܠܡܠܬܐ ܠܒܢ̈ܝ ܐܝܣܪܝܠ. ܘܒܙܚܘ
ܘܡܝܩܘ ܒܝ. ܘܫܕܐܘܢܝ ܡܢ ܗܝܟܠܗ ܕܡܪܝܐ. ܐܠܗܐ. ܐܘ̄
ܠܡܢܐ ܠܐ ܐܬܕܡܝܬ ܘܠܐ ܠܚܝܘܬܐ ܚܪ̈ܫܬܐ. ܕܐܦ ܗ̈ܢܝܢ
ܡܦܪ̈ܝܢ ܩܕܡܝܟ ܡܪܝܐ. ܘܠܡܢܐ ܠܐ ܐܬܕܡܝܬ ܠܐܪܥܐ
ܗܕܐ ܕܐܦ ܗܝ ܝܗܒܐ ܦܐܪ̈ܐ ܒܙܒܢ̈ܝܗܘܢ ܘܡܒܪܟܐ ܠܟ
cf. Tisch. iv ܡܪܝܐ. ܘܟܕ ܐܡܪܬ ܗܠܝܢ ܚܙܬ. ܡܠܐܟܐ ܕܡܪܝܐ ܡܢ
ܫܡܝܐ ܘܐܡܪ ܠܗ̇ ܚܢܐ ܚܢܐ ܫܡܥ ܡܪܝܐ ܨܠܘܬܟܝ ܬܒܛܢܝܢ
ܘܬܐܠܕܝܢ ܘܢܬܡܠܠ ܙܪܥܟܝ ܒܟܠܗ ܬܐܒܝܠ. ܘܐܡܪܬ ܚܢܐ
ܚܝ ܗܘ ܡܪܝܐ ܐܠܗܝ ܕܐܢ ܝܠܕܐ ܢܩܒܬܐ ܐܢ ܕܟܪܐ ܘܐܢ
ܢܩܒܬܐ. ܠܡܪܝܐ ܐܠܗܐ ܐܬܠܝܘܗܝ. ܘܢܗܘܐ ܡܫܡܫ ܩܕܡܘܗܝ
ܟܠܗܘܢ ܝܘ̈ܡܬܐ ܕܚܝ̈ܘܗܝ. ܘܗܐ ܒܫܥܬܐ ܐܬܘ ܬܪܝܢ ܡܠܐܟ̈ܐ f. 96 b
ܘܐܡܪܝܢ [1]ܠܗ̇ ܕܗܐ ܝܘܝܩܝܡ ܐܬܐ ܥܡ ܡܪ̈ܥܝܬܗ ܡܛܠ
ܕܡܠܐܟܗ ܕܡܪܝܐ ܐܡܪ ܠܗ. ܝܘܝܩܝܡ ܫܡܥ ܡܪܝܐ ܨܠܘܬܟ
ܙܠ ܢܚܘܬ ܠܟ ܡܢ ܗܪܟܐ. ܗܐ ܓܝܪ ܚܢܐ ܐܢܬܬܟ ܒܛܢܐ.
ܘܢܚܬ ܝܘܝܩܝܡ ܘܩܪܐ ܠܪ̈ܥܘܬܐ ܕܝܠܗ ܟܠܗܘܢ ܘܐܡܪ ܠܗܘܢ.
ܐܝܬܘ ܠܝ ܠܗܪܟܐ ܥܣܪ ܦܐܪ̈ܐ ܕܟܝܢܐ ܕܠܝܬ ܒܗܘܢ ܡܘܡܐ
ܘܢܗܘܘܢ [2]ܒܫܪ̈ܬܗܘܢ ܦܐܪ̈ܬܐ [3]ܕܫܡܝܢ ܠܡܪܝܐ ܐܠܗܐ. ܘܐܝܬܘ
ܠܝ ܬܪܥܣܪ ܦܐܪ̈ܝܢ ܕܫܡܝܢ ܘܡܒܚܪܐ ܠܟܗܢ̈ܐ ܕܢܗܘܘܢ
ܠܟܗ̈ܢܐ ܘܠܩܫܝ̈ܫܐ ܕܥܡܐ ܘܡܐܐ ܓܕܝ̈ܐ ܕܥܙܐ ܕܢܗܘܘܢ
ܠܟܠܗ ܥܡܐ. ܘܟܕ [ܐܬܐ] ܝܘܝܩܝܡ ܥܡ ܡܪ̈ܥܝܬܗ. ܩܝܡܐ ܗܘܬ

[1] Cod. ܠܗ [2] Cod. ܒܫܪ̈ܬܝܢ [3] Cod. ܕܫܡܝܢ

ܠܐܢܬܬܗ[1] ܘܠܐ ܐܙܠ ܠܒܝܬܗ. ܐܠܐ ܢܦܩ. ܢܦܫܗ ܠܐܬܪܐ
ܚܘܪܒܐ ܘܝܬܒ ܬܡܢ ܡܫܬܒܚ. ܘܥܒܕ ܬܡܢ ܐܪܒܥܝܢ ܐܝܡܡܝܢ
ܘܐܪܒܥܝܢ ܠܠܝܢ. ܘܐܡܪ ܒܠܒܗ ܕܠܐ ܐܟܘܠ ܘܠܐ ܐܫܬܐ
ܥܕܡܐ ܕܢܬܚܢܢ ܡܪܝܐ ܐܠܗܐ. ܐܠܐ ܨܠܘܬܐ ܗܝ ܬܫܒܘܚܬܐ f. 95 a
cf. Tisch. ii ܠܝ ܕܗܘܬ ܡܐܟܘܠܬܐ ܘܡܫܬܝܐ. ܚܢܐ ܕܝܢ ܐܢܬܬܗ ܡܬܒܟܝܐ
ܗܘܬ ܒܬܪܝܢ ܐܒܠܐ. ܘܬܪܬܝܢ ܐܘ̈ܠܝܬܐ ܡܬܘܕܝܐ ܗܘܬ ܘܐܡܪܐ.
ܐܡܪܐ[1]، ܥܠ ܐܪܡܠܘܬܝ، ܠܘܩܒܠ.. ܘܬܪ̈ܬܝܢ ܡܛܠ ܕܐܬܟܠܝܬ ܡܢ
ܝܠܕܐ. ܟܕ ܕܝܢ ܩܪܒ ܡܘܥܕܐ ܗܘ ܕܡܪܝܐ. ܐܡܪܬ ܠܗ̇ ܝܘܕܝܬ
ܠܡܛܠܬܗ̇ ܥܕܡܐ ܠܐܡܬܝ، ܡܬܟܪܝܐ ܐܢܬܝ، ܢܦܫܟܝ. ܕܗܐ
ܡܛܐ ܠܗ ܡܘܥܕܐ ܪܒܐ ܕܡܪܝܐ ܘܠܐ ܫܠܝܛ ܠܡܬܐܒܠܘ.
ܐܠܐ ܣܒܝ ܠܟܝ ܐܣܘܪܐ ܕܪܫܐ ܕܝܗܒܬ ܠܝ ܡܪܬܝ، ܐܝܟܢܐ
ܕܠܐ ܘܐܣܘܪܝܗ، ܐܢܬܝ. ܠܝ ܠܐ ܫܠܝܛ ܠܝ ܕܐܣܘܪܝܗ، ܡܛܠ
ܕܐܡܬܐ ܐܢܐ ܘܪܘܫܡܐ ܕܡܠܟܘܬܐ ܐܝܬ ܒܠܗ،.. ܐܡܪܬ
ܠܗ̇ ܚܢܐ ܠܡ ܡܢܐ ܘܡܢ ܫܘܠܡܐ ܗ̇ܠܝܢ ܠܟܝ ܒܥܒܕܬ ܗ̇ܝ ܡܚܒܠ
ܡܪܝܐ ܠܟܝ. ܘܟܒܪ ܗܢܐ ܒܢܟܠܐ. ܐܬܝܗܒ ܠܟܝ ܘܐܬܟܬܫܬܝܗ، f. 95 b
ܕܬܫܬܘܬܦܝܢ ܠܝ ܒܣܘܪܚܢܗ[2]. ܐܬܟܪܝܬ ܠܗ̇ ܝܘܕܝܬ ܫܦܝܪܐ
ܐܡܪܐ [3]ܠܡ ܐܠܝ ܠܟܝ[3] ܕܗܐ ܐܚܕ ܐܠܗܐ ܪ̈ܚܡܗ̇، ܡܟܝܠ
ܕܠܐ ܬܬܠܝܢ ܦܐܪܐ ܒܐܝܣܪܐܝܠ. ܘܟܕ ܫܡܥܬ ܚܢܐ ܗܠܝܢ
ܒܟܬ ܠܗ̇ ܠܟܝ. ܘܫܠܚܬ ܡܢܗ̇ ܡ̈ܐܢܐ ܕܐܒܠܐ ܘܐܬܥܛܦܬ
ܪܝܫܗ̇ ܘܠܒܫܬ ܡ̈ܐܢܐ ܕܟܠܠܘܬܐ. ܘܒܥܕܢܐ ܕܬܫܥ
ܫ̈ܥܝܢ ܢܚܬܬ ܠܡܗܠܟܘ ܒܦܪܕܝܣܐ ܘܝܬܒܬ ܬܚܝܬ ܐܝܠܢܐ
ܕܕܦܢܕܝܢ. ܘܨܠܝܐ ܗܘܬ ܘܡܬܟܫܦܐ ܘܐܡܪܐ ܠܡܪܝܐ
ܘܐܡܪܬ ܐܠܗܐ ܕܐܒܗ̈ܬܝ ܒܪܟܝܢܝ. ܘܫܡܥ ܨܠܘܬܝ، ܘܒܥܘܬܝ،

---

[1] sic [2] Cod. + ܠܡ ܐܠܝ ܠܟܝ [3] Cod. om.

ܒܚܝܠ ܣܒܪܐ ܕܬܠܝܬܝܘܬܐ ܡܫܒܚܬܐ ܘܫܒܝܚܘܬ ܒܐܘܦܝܢܐ Cod. Harris
ܡܫܪܝܢܢ ܕܢܟܬܘܒ ܟܬܒܐ ܕܬܫܥܝܬܗ ܕܝܠܕܬ ܐܠܗܐ ܡܪܝܡ 73 f. 94 a
ܡܢ ܝܘܡܐ ܕܡܘܠܕܗ̇ ܘܥܕܡܐ ܠܝܘܡܐ ܕܡܫܘܢܝܗ̇ ܕܡܢ ܗܢܐ
ܥܠܡܐ [1] ܨܠܘܬܗ̇ ܥܡܢ ܐܡܝܢ امين ܣܦܪܐ ܩܕܡܝܐ ܥܠ
ܐܒܗ̈ܝܗ̇ ܘܐܦ ܥܠ ܣܘܒܪܗ̇ ܕܡܢ ܡܠܐܟܐ ܐܝܟ ܗܘܐ
cf. Tischendorf Protevangelium Jacobi cap. i ܓܒܪܐ ܚܕ ܕܫܡܗ ܝܘܢܚܝܪ ܕܥܬܝܪ ܗܘܐ ܦܠܚ ܒܕܚܠܬ
ܐܠܗܐ. ܘܡܩܪܒ ܗܘܐ ܩܘܪ̈ܒܢܘܗܝ، ܠܡܪܝܐ ܒܐܝܩܪܐ. ܘܐܡܪ
ܗܘܐ ܒܢܦܫܗ ܕܗܢܐ ܝܬܝܪܐ ܕܡܦܩ ܐܢܐ ܢܗܘܐ ܚܠܦ ܟܠܗ
ܥܡܐ. ܘܗ̇ܝ، ܡܢܬܐ ܕܚܛܝ ܐܝܬܐ ܡܢ ܢܟܣܝܐ ܐܦܪܫ ܠܡܪܝܐ
ܕܗ̇ܘܝܐ ܠܝ ܠܚܘܣܝܐ. ܘܟܕ ܡܛܐ ܝܘܡܐ ܪܒܐ ܕܡܪܝܐ
ܕܢܩܪܒܘܢ ܗܘܘ ܒܢ̈ܝ ܐܝܣܪܐܝܠ ܩܘܪ̈ܒܢܝܗܘܢ. ܩܡ ܠܘܩܒܠܗ
ܕܝܘܢܚܝܪ ܪܘܒܝܠ ܘܐܡܪ ܠܗ ܠܐ ܫܠܝܛ ܠܟ ܕܬܩܪܒ ܡܩܕܡ f. 94 b
ܩܘܪܒܢܐ. ܡܛܠ ܕܠܐ ܥܒܕܬ ܙܪܥܐ ܠܐܝܣܪܐܝܠ. ܘܟܪܝܬ
ܠܗ ܠܝܘܢܚܝܪ ܛܒ ܦܠܚ. ܘܐܙܠ ܠܒܝܬܗ ܟܕ ܟܪܝܐ ܠܗ.
ܘܠܬܪ̈ܥܣܪ ܫܒ̈ܛܐ ܕܐܝܣܪܐܝܠ ܐܚܪ ܗܘܐ ܐ ܐܝܟ
ܕܠܫܘܪܝ، ܠܐ ܥܒܕܬ ܙܪܥܐ ܒܐܝܣܪܐܝܠ. ܘܟܕ ܚܙܐ ܘܒܥܐ
ܘܐܫܟܚ. ܒܕ̈ܪܐ ܕܒܢܘ ܐܫܟܚ ܕܟܠܗܘܢ ܙܕ̈ܝܩܐ ܦܐܫ
ܒܗܘܢ ܙܪܥܐ ܒܐܝܣܪܐܝܠ. ܘܐܬܕܟܪ ܠܪܫ ܐܒܗ̈ܬܐ
ܐܒܪܗܡ ܘܣܒܪܐ ܐܝܬܝܬܗ ܕܒܝܘ̈ܡܬܐ ܐܚܪ̈ܝܐ [2] ܗܘܐ ܠܗܘܢ
ܠܐܝܣܚܩ ܒܪܐ. ܘܟܪܝܬ ܠܗ ܠܝܘܢܚܝܪ ܛܒ. ܘܠܐ ܐܬܚܙܝ

[1] Cod. ܨܠܘܬܗ [2] Cod. ܚܪ̈ܝܐ

ܬܫܒܘܚܬܐ ܕܡܪܬܝ ܡܪܝܡ